DATE DUE

APR 2 1 2015

BRODART, CO.   Cat. No. 23-221

Small-Town America

Small-Town America

Finding Community, Shaping the Future

Robert Wuthnow

PRINCETON UNIVERSITY PRESS

PRINCETON AND OXFORD

Copyright © 2013 by Princeton University Press
Published by Princeton University Press, 41 William Street, Princeton, New Jersey 08540
In the United Kingdom: Princeton University Press, 6 Oxford Street,
Woodstock, Oxfordshire OX20 1TW

press.princeton.edu

Library of Congress Cataloging-in-Publication Data

Wuthnow, Robert.
Small-town America : finding community, shaping the future / Robert Wuthnow.
pages cm
Includes bibliographical references and index.
ISBN 978-0-691-15720-7 (hbk. : alk. paper) 1. Cities and towns—United States.
2. Communities—United States. I. Title.
HT123.W88 2013
307.760973—dc23
2012042793

British Library Cataloging-in-Publication Data is available

This book has been composed in Sabon with Erazure for display

Printed on acid-free paper. ∞

Printed in the United States of America

1 3 5 7 9 10 8 6 4 2

CONTENTS

LIST OF FIGURES

LIST OF PROFILES

PREFACE

I LIVE IN A SMALL TOWN. The population of my community is approximately 4,200, just slightly more than it was twenty-five years ago. The three-block expanse that passes for Main Street is home to a post office, bagel shop, pizza parlor, pet grooming salon, and a couple other vital establishments, all neatly sandwiched between branch office banks at either end, and facing an old Presbyterian church and a private school with its own golf course on the opposite side. At the end of my block, there is a five-acre field that the farmer double crops year after year while the depleted soil waits to become a housing development. Across the road is an old farmstead that has been there for more than a century, and is now accompanied by a large machine shed and three shiny grain storage tanks. Around the corner is a farm with a big green barn that a Polish family used for three generations to feed cows and chickens. One cold rainy day, I stood ankle deep in mud while an auctioneer sold off the remaining machinery. Now the farm is an upscale organic food cooperative.

While most of us who live here would call our community a small town, in reality it is not. In every direction its edges blend imperceptibly with adjacent municipalities that are larger. More than 35,000 people live in the township and nearly 370,000 live in the county—which has grown by about 10 percent per decade for the past century. More than 1 million people live in a twenty-mile radius, and more than 10 million live within fifty miles. On Election Day, I usually see a neighbor or two as we stand in line at the fire station, but otherwise it is rare to identify a familiar face. Although a serious effort has been made to preserve an occasional farm and keep some space open for parks, nearly everything in sight has been turned into housing developments and highways. For two hours every morning and evening, these arteries are clogged with cars and trucks.

My community is not the kind of small town this book is about. Lots of people like me live in communities that we may think of as small towns, but these are in reality municipal subdivisions of large metropolitan areas. They are not the kind of small towns that have retained autonomy from larger places and have a distinctive identity. A better example of these communities is the town in which I was raised. Thirty-five hundred people live in the community, about a thousand fewer than when I grew up there in the 1950s. As the county seat, it is the largest town in the county, which totals just over 10,000 residents. The nearest city of any size is sixty-five miles away. Nearly everyone works locally, tending the forty-odd small shops that huddle around the town square, working at one of the town's two small manufacturing firms, or farming the open land that surrounds the town on all sides. Settled a century and a half ago, it is still a part of rural America, but it has adapted as well. A large consolidated high school sits on one edge of town, and a new hospital has recently been constructed a few blocks away. There is a new ethanol plant several miles in one direction from town, and a large wind energy farm in another.

Living as I currently do in a large metropolitan area, I find that the fellow residents I talk to and newspapers that land in my driveway offer ill-informed opinions about the lifestyles and attitudes of people who live in small towns. Without too much simplification, these perceptions can be placed into one of two categories. The first consists of "ah, wouldn't it be nice" perceptions—as in, wouldn't it be nice to get up in the morning and sit lazily on the veranda listening to the birds singing, and then wander a few blocks down to the post office, chatting with some neighbors along the way. Or, wouldn't it be nice to live like people used to when nobody locked their doors, the air was fresh, morals were pure, and life was uncomplicated. These are the sentiments that easily spring unbidden to mind after commuting through rush-hour traffic from a harried day at the office. They spark the imagination as we read of rustic weekend getaways and contemplate the possibility of escaping there permanently. The other category takes nearly the opposite stance. Small towns, in this view, are the sorry remnant of an America that has been left behind, passed over by the inevitable march of urban progress. The enterprising populace lives in cities and suburbs. Small towns are the refuge of hapless, poorly educated Americans who have little better to do than watch the grass grow.

It is difficult to write about small towns without falling victim to such expressions of nostalgia or mild disdain. Pundits visit small towns looking for homespun wisdom and old-fashioned values. These are the places, they believe, to find colorful old-timers who chew on a cornstalk and tell tales of the good old days. Others imagine dull communities devoid of entertainment and lacking in cultural sophistication. Surely this is where ignorance and bigotry reside.

Another view of small towns recently seems to have become even more common. This is the notion, to put it bluntly, that information about small towns should serve chiefly for the entertainment of people who live in cities and suburbs. From this perspective, a memoir written by someone in a small town should be rich with humorous anecdotes. A reader should expect to chuckle at events that could happen only among folks in some remote setting. A novel set in a small town should titillate readers with a

murder or two, sexual escapades, dark secrets, and revelations of hypoc-
risy. A mental escape to a small town should thus be the twenty-first-
century equivalent of an earlier urban bourgeoisie attending a minstrel
show or amusing themselves with an occasional visit to the slums. It would
be a shock to learn that people in small towns are pretty much like other
Americans, or that residents are complicated, reflective persons who spend
time making sense of their lives and relate to their communities in complex ways.

This book provides an account of how the residents of America's small
towns find community, what it means to them, and why it is important.
The evidence comes from hundreds of in-depth qualitative interviews
with residents in dozens of small towns across the country. We hear from
people like Bud Janssen, a resident of a small town on the high plains
who spends his days farming more than fifteen-square miles of rich cropland, and Larry Yeager, a crew chief who, like a surprising number of
small-town residents, earns a comfortable living for his young family at
a small manufacturing plant. We meet Dorothy Martin, a widow who
supplements her monthly Social Security checks running a five-and-dime
store in a riverfront town of nine hundred, and Maria Sanchez, a daughter of migrant farm laborers who tutors children of recent immigrants.
The diversity that characterizes small-town America comes into focus as
Mato Tanka describes his Lakota heritage, Mary Remmert discusses the
effects of mining closures on her community, and Clarence Brown recalls
the struggles in his town to combat racial discrimination.

From time to time, the US Census Bureau tries to track the demographic changes taking place in small-town America, but the statisticians
have seldom settled on whether the relevant topics should be farmers,
the rural population, rural counties, incorporated places, or people living
outside metropolitan areas. The data has gotten better, yet it paints with
only the broadest brushstrokes what small-town America is like. A few
surveys have asked questions as well, hoping to discover if Americans
think they live in small towns or would like to reside in one. I have made
use of these statistical sources, but have tried to use them judiciously and
as context for the qualitative information.

The central question I address in this book is what it means to the residents of America's small towns to live there. How do they regard their
communities? What exactly is it about a town that makes it seem like a
community? How do people in small towns explain their decision to live
there? What place do neighbors, friends, and community organizations
have in their lives? What are the moral and political issues that concern
them? Why are these issues particularly troubling?

These are questions that can only be addressed by talking to people,
and asking them to speak about their lives and communities. With the

help of several research assistants, I was able to do this over a five-year period. In all, we interviewed more than seven hundred people, asking them to talk in their own words about their experiences living in small towns. We employed a design that provided for regional diversity along with the nearly equal representation of men and women, old and young, and members of racial and ethnic minorities as well as the white Anglo majority. The design included wide variation in occupations and levels of education, and involved interviews with community leaders and ordinary residents.

The academic discipline in which I was trained is sociology. It is a discipline rich in methodological techniques that produce solid quantitative and qualitative research, and is replete with concepts that pose interesting questions about society. But the discipline has also entertained pretensions about discovering scientific generalizations. Until a few decades ago, a favorite conceit was telling almost any population under investigation that it did not understand itself as well as sociologists did. That was because folks themselves were likely suffering from false consciousness or could not perceive the social structures that only enlightened social scientists could see. If it seemed that people were in medical school to become doctors, for example, the truth was that they were really there to gain social status, or if they appeared to be a poor community with fragile social ties, they were actually getting along quite well because of strong but invisible social bonds. In my view, it is good that those pretensions have become less common than they used to be. In learning about the lives of people in small towns, I do not claim to have found some deep insight that they themselves would not have recognized. I have tried instead to discover the grassroots meanings of community that people themselves acknowledge and understand in these out-of-the-way places.

My argument is not only *that* people in small towns find community there—we could have figured they did—but that they do so in subtle and highly varied ways, and yet in ways that are profoundly influenced by the scale in which their daily social interaction takes place. The fact that most Americans no longer live in small towns shapes the perceptions of those who do. People account for their choice of residence by explaining how living in a small community fulfills their aspirations and why they are content with the decisions they have made. The meaning of small-town life is thus an implicit dialogue that emerges in conversation with broader perceptions of the United States and the world.

To understand how residents of small towns find community, it is imperative that we listen closely to the language they use to describe their day-to-day lives. As is always the case with language, familiar phrases are employed, drawn from a kind of repertoire, and these phrases become familiar precisely because they are frequently used. People who live in small towns commonly describe them as places in which everybody knows everybody else, for instance, or as locations in which a slow-paced life can be found. Yet these phrases have distinct meanings that depend on the interaction that happens within local contexts. It is not that everyone literally knows everyone else but rather that enough interaction does occur over sufficiently extended periods that people gain familiarity with one another, become visible in the community, and share background information about one another. Feelings of camaraderie and loyalty to a particular locale emerge through seemingly trivial instances of sidewalk behavior, acts of neighborly kindness, town festivals, homecoming celebrations, and athletic competitions. In addition, expectations are shared about people in leadership roles, and narratives emerge that communicate common information about such important topics as neighborliness, personal responsibility, faith, moral issues, and politics. None of this suggests that a strong sense of community cannot be found in urban and suburban neighborhoods. Nevertheless, it is found differently in small towns. *How* it is found and what it *means* are the questions that interest me.

The answers I hope to persuade readers of include the following. First, small-town America is not so different in many respects from urban and suburban America. The residents of small communities lead busy and productive lives, care for their families, and grapple with difficult social and moral issues in ways that are complex and diverse. This is not because all of America is fundamentally a small-town culture, as observers sometimes argued in the past, but because all of us, no matter where we live, are part of the same society, share in its laws and institutions, and participate in a media-driven culture. Second, though, the scale in which social relations in these communities take place is of immense importance. Understandings of time and space, the activities that symbolize community identity, the norms that govern casual encounters, and the lens through which social issues are interpreted are all inflected by living in a community that includes a relatively small population, and by being aware of that fact.

These observations should serve to further undermine the lingering impression in some quarters that America could save itself from impending doom by somehow reinstituting the values and lifestyles of the small town. That notion was implicit in many of the discussions about modernism and modernity that emerged in the nineteenth century, and that warned of the problems associated with industrialization and urbanization. It has continued in versions of social commentary that decry the growth of large-scale institutions as well as call for a return to the commonsense values of neighborliness and civic responsibility that presumably exist in small towns more than in other parts of the nation. The problem with this argument is that the distinctive social relationships and meanings of community that exist in small towns are truly shaped by the fact that these communities are small. Efforts to strengthen civic values in larger places have to be different. They have to take into account the wider scale in which social interaction takes place, greater diversity of needs and interests, and more open-ended meanings of community. It makes sense to understand small-town life for what it is, with all its attractions and limitations, but not to imagine that it is the solution to the problems of the larger society.

That point may be disappointing to readers who hope for unusually practical insights about the dilemmas of modern society to come from an examination of small towns. It is a hope that is symptomatic of the penchant for generalizations that I mentioned before. In busy times, we aspire to quick answers that can be gleaned from books turned into sound bites. The message from listening to hundreds of people who live in small towns talking about their lives is different. Listen closely to why we feel neighborly with our neighbors. Consider what it means when a school closes or family moves away. Understand how an annual festival unites and divides. Then draw the lessons that may apply to other situations.

The message for my fellow social scientists is equally about the need to move beyond the search for broad generalizations. The tool kits that social scientists use to think about communities are useful—ideas about group size, closed networks, the symbolic boundaries separating and connecting people of different social strata, collective representations, deference and demeanor, norms of responsibility, and narratives of place and time. But these elements combine in manifestly different ways in different places. It is the local work of cultural construction that builds and maintains townspeople's sense of community. We can investigate the various ways in which people understand their towns, and identify some issues and themes that emerge repeatedly, but that does not imply that small towns are the same or that they are all notably different from large metropolitan areas. People who live in small-town America share many of the habits and values of people who live in larger places. And yet the fact of living in a small town becomes part of how they make sense of their lives. They form accounts of why it is good or bad to live in a small community, how that has shaped their careers and values, and what it means for their faith, understandings of morality, and politics.

My indebtedness is greatest to the hundreds of people in small towns who gave up an hour or two of their time to talk about their lives and communities, and thus to help a researcher they knew little about write a book in which they would not even be mentioned by their real names. Such are the oddities of social research, governing boards that dictate what can and cannot be asked, and requirements that must be followed to elicit candid and honest assessments from residents about the strengths as well as weaknesses of their communities. I benefited from the able assistance of Aislinn Addington, Sarah Brayne, Bruce Carruthers, Phillip Connor, Janice Derstine, Emily Dumler, Justin Farrell, Julia Gelatt, Brittany Hanstad, Sylvia Kundrats, Carol Ann MacGregor, Christi Martone, Karen Myers, Steve Myers, Cynthia Reynolds, Charles Varner, Erik Vickstrom, Melissa Virts, and Lori Wiebold-Lippisch, and the students in my graduate seminars who patiently interacted with me as I discussed the substantive and methodological issues that arose. Funding for the project was provided by several units of Princeton University, including the University Center for Human Values, Woodrow Wilson School of Public and International Affairs, and Offices of the Dean of Faculty and Provost. The questions that have guided my research owe much to the fact that I grew up in a small town and perhaps all too often still imagine the metropolitan area in which I now live to be one.

Small-Town America

- 1 -

Introduction

IMAGINE LIVING IN A COMMUNITY WITH NO TRAIN, no light-rail service, no buses, and in fact no public transportation of any kind. Not even a taxi. The nearest airport is two hundred miles away. Imagine living in a town with only one small grocery store where prices are high and fresh produce is seldom fresh. The selection of items there is small. The best local alternative to home cooking is a high-calorie meal at a fast-food franchise. A nice sit-down restaurant is forty miles away. That is also the distance to the nearest Walmart and shopping mall. If you are a woman with a college degree, your best options for employment are the public school, the bank, a government office, or the nursing home. Whether you are a woman or man, your salary is 30 to 40 percent lower than if you lived in a city. Your children are likely to do reasonably well in high school, play sports, perhaps graduate with honors, and go to college, but they will not have had advanced placement classes and will find adjusting to a large state college campus as confusing as it may be exhilarating. They are unlikely ever to return as permanent residents of your community. As you grow older, they will come to visit you once or twice a year. You are happy to have a doctor and the nursing home nearby. The doctor is a general practitioner. The nearest specialists are an hour's drive. If you suffer a heart attack and call 911, the county dispatcher will phone a volunteer, who will then drive to the fire station where the emergency vehicle is parked. If you survive, a helicopter will fly in and take you to a hospital a hundred miles away.

Put this way, it is hard to imagine why anyone would want to live in a small town. Yet at least thirty million Americans do reside in these small, out-of-the-way places. Many of them could have chosen to live elsewhere. They could have joined the vast majority of Americans who live in cities and suburbs. They could perhaps be closer to better-paying jobs, convenient shopping, a wider range of educational opportunities, and specialized health care. Rich or poor, they would then be within minutes of shopping malls, restaurants, and hospitals. They could decide to live as anonymously as they might want to, pick and choose among a wide variety of friends, and enjoy mingling with people of vastly diverse backgrounds. There would be chances to explore specialized employment, entertainment, and leisure interests. But they have opted to live differently.

Why? Is it only because of where they were raised? Did they originate in small places and simply find themselves left behind as others moved on? Are their options limited because of family obligations? By the kind of work they do? Are they stuck in rural America because they lack education? Or have they made a considered decision to reject what they regard as distasteful about cities and suburbs? Have they found local amenities that make up for the lack of better jobs as well as more convenient access to goods and services?

The standard answer to these questions is that people live in small towns because they value community and cherish the support it provides. They might well have chosen to live elsewhere—indeed, many of them have—but they prefer living in a small town because the community gives them a sense of belonging. They know everyone. They see their neighbors at backyard barbeques, school functions, and church. The community is familiar, and a place they know and cherish as their home. Its inhabitants share similar values and lifestyles—ones that probably were more common in the past than they are today.[1]

But these easy assertions about community need to be interrogated. Most of what is known about community in small towns is from brief journalistic accounts that focus on newsworthy events, such as a mining accident or shooting spree, or that provide quotes from the hinterland as background coverage of a political campaign. Or it comes from polls in which questions about small-town life are posed in broad terms that give only a general impression of how Americans feel about their places of residence.[2] Hardly anyone bothers to find out how townspeople actually think and talk about community.

Nearly a century ago, sociologist H. Paul Douglass wrote that small towns—of which there were about twelve thousand scattered across the United States—were popularly regarded as "a sort of unsexed creature" that carried neither the romance of the countryside nor intrigue of the city. This was the sentiment expressed in the saying that God made the country, humans made the city, but small towns were made by the Devil. That view was mistaken, Douglass contended. The hope of America, he believed, lay in the strength of its small towns.[3]

The questions animating Douglass's interest in small towns were quite different than the ones that arouse my interest now. He was especially intrigued by the tensions between townspeople and farmers, and the differences between Americans who strolled on sidewalks and those who walked on dirt. It struck him, however, that there was something perennially distinctive about these small communities. It mattered that they were incorporated, and were places in which people worked and lived, not apart from one another as they did in the countryside, but together on a small scale. It was the togetherness that mattered. "There's a town under every town," he wrote. To find it was the difficult task.[4]

In the recent social science literature, a great deal of attention has been devoted to the role that social capital plays in communities. There is no question that social capital is important. People who are connected with one another, the research suggests, tend more often to work on community projects, serve as volunteers in their community, vote, pay attention to political issues, and for that matter feel better about themselves. Networking has come to be of increasing interest as data are collected in surveys about friendship patterns and memberships in organizations, and as email and online social networking sites have increased in popularity. Still, social capital and networking are by no means all that matters in understanding community.[5]

Small towns can only be understood by paying attention to the cultural constructions that give them meaning. They exist as ideas or concepts that provide the people who live in them an identity and way of talking about themselves. Only by understanding this cultural aspect of community can we make sense of the deep role that it plays in the lives of small-town residents. Their sense of community is reinforced by social interaction, but is less dependent on social networks than we might imagine. Community is maintained as an identity by symbols and rituals such as town festivals that actually do not take up much of residents' time. Social network studies would suggest that community is important because people spend a lot of time making friends and visiting with one another. But social network theory does not explain why people behave as if they know one another even when they do not or why a brief exchange at the post office can communicate more about community than a long conversation might in some other setting.

To be sure, friends and neighbors are crucial to people who live in small towns. But so is the fact that they live in a community. The town has an identity as a community. Its meanings are inscribed in particular places and the tangible aspects of these places—the park, school building, and stores on Main Street. The town's identity is reinforced in festivals and ball games, small acts of kindness, recovering from a disaster, and the stories that are repeated about these events, and by the local cultural leaders who keep the stories alive. Towns are defined as well by that which they are not—cities, unfamiliar places, and big government. The stories and symbolic markers of difference define a place as a community.

Questions about the real or imagined decline of communities also need to be addressed by examining the ways in which community is culturally constructed. Too often the decline of community has been studied by looking at particular questions in surveys because those data happened to be available. Data on memberships in voluntary associations, voting, and spending evenings with neighbors are examples. It is interesting, though, that in talking with hundreds of people, many of whom did in fact think their community was declining or that communities like theirs were disappearing, not a single person mentioned these standard indicators. Membership in voluntary associations, voting, and spending evenings with neighbors simply did not come up. What did matter were the changes that served as public symbols of community. Decline is symbolized by the hardware store on Main Street that now stands empty or vacant lot where the drugstore used to be. Decline is evident in the fact that the school has closed, or if it remains open, is now a consolidated district that goes by a numbered designation and includes children from someplace else. If anything about social networking comes up at all, it is not that volunteer organizations and dinner parties are lacking but rather that there is no longer a crowd on the street on Saturday evenings.

When residents of small towns describe their communities, a rich tapestry of meanings, narratives, family histories, and personal experiences emerges. People tell of moving to a small community to raise their children without the hassles of city life. They confess to having lost their job in a larger place and seeking refuge where housing was cheap. For some, the hope of taking over the family farm when a father or uncle retired kept them tethered to a small rural community. For others, it was a decision to marry—perhaps fraught with ambivalence about giving up an ambitious career—or live near an ailing relative.

Viewed from the inside, community ceases to be a bland abstraction. Townspeople do talk about knowing everyone, but we learn what that means, who is excluded, and how that is reinforced in the small details of sidewalk behavior and expectations about participation in community events. We gain an understanding of how it is possible to say that everyone in town is the same when there is actually almost as much inequality in small towns as in larger places. We see the enormous diversity of lifestyles, occupations, family arrangements, hobbies, and personal stories.

Townspeople are close observers of their communities. An outsider may gain the impression that small towns embrace a slower pace of life than in cities, but it is from townspeople themselves that we learn what a slower pace of life means and why it is valued. A public opinion poll may find that many Americans believe small towns are good places in which to raise children, but what that actually means to people living in small towns requires listening to parents' accounts of their own experiences.[6]

How community is found in small towns requires paying attention as well to what it lacks. Rosy scenarios entertained by Americans who have never lived in small towns become more nuanced when townspeople themselves describe their communities. Residents are well aware of the challenges they face. When a store closes, the gap on Main Street leaves a psychological scar. Physical damage from a tornado or flood takes a long time to heal. Newcomers find it difficult to assimilate. The difficulties they experience have more to do with learning the subtle expectations of community life than with actually meeting people or making friends.

The hope that somehow America could regain a stronger sense of community if only it could revive small-town values diminishes when townspeople themselves share their insights. They are the first to argue that what happens in small towns is largely a function of size. Knowing one's neighbors and being known in the community is limited by the size of a town's population. It also matters that people work in town, share similar occupations and backgrounds, and above all stay for a while. These qualities are not easily reproduced in cities and suburbs.

Small towns are themselves undergoing change. Many are slowly losing population. Some are being absorbed into sprawling metropolitan zones. Others are adapting to immigration along with changing relationships among racial and ethnic groups. Better roads and easier transportation are turning some small towns into bedroom communities. The Internet and shifts in agriculture are reshaping their economic base. In out-of-the-way places one finds novel experiments with sustainable energy and new technology. Small towns are surprisingly resilient. While they preserve the past, they forge new connections with the future. Many of the residents who grow up in small towns choose to stay. Others choose to relocate from cities and suburbs in hopes of finding something lacking in those larger places.[7]

Asking why people live in small towns—and what it means to do so— is a bit like probing the reasons people become fundamentalist Protestants or orthodox Jews. These are the paths not taken by most Americans, especially by ones who consider themselves progressive, enlightened, and successful by worldly standards. The fact that millions of Americans do embrace conservative religious practices poses interesting questions about America as a society.[8] Are there aspects of American culture that are truly not shared, or indeed that are rejected by a sizable minority? Or is conservative religion little more than an alternative lifestyle grounded in the same essential values shared by nearly everyone? Does it nevertheless matter what religion people choose? Are their chances of attaining education, working as productive citizens, and providing for their families impaired? Do they hold different political opinions and vote in ways that could affect the nation's policies?

The decision to live in a small town evokes similar questions for our understanding of American society. The fact that most Americans live in cities and suburbs cannot go unnoticed by those who live in small towns.

How does that knowledge of being in the minority shape their outlooks? Do they feel as if they are embattled, left behind, or ignored? Are they glad to be in the minority, and if so, what value do they place on having made this choice? Does it influence their politics, religion, or sense of what it means to be a good American?

There are ample reasons to think that residence is associated with distinct attitudes and beliefs. Political candidates say they represent the particular values of small-town America. Pundits sometimes argue that small communities are the guardians of homespun virtue. Maps of red and blue differences in electoral outcomes suggest that states dominated by small towns vote differently from areas populated by large cities. Small towns are stereotypically associated with conservative moral and political outlooks. They differ from cities in factors that further shape beliefs and attitudes, such as racial and ethnic diversity.[9]

Social scientists have been particularly interested in the historic differences between small towns and metropolitan areas. Max Weber, Emile Durkheim, Karl Marx, Alexis de Tocqueville, and Ferdinand Tönnies were among the influential nineteenth-century social scientists exploring these differences. Small towns emerged in these inquiries as places of traditional family values and strong social solidarity, but also as backwaters in the march of modern history compared with the advances of industry and population growth that were shaping cities and suburbs.[10] American scholars in the twentieth century examined the decline of small towns along with the corresponding development of industry, business, ethnic enclaves, slums, the middle class, science, and education in cities. By the 1950s, attention had shifted increasingly toward questions about community life in suburbs.[11]

But relatively little research has been devoted to small towns since the 1950s. One reason is that cities and suburbs continued to grow and absorb most of the population growth from both natural increase and immigration. Questions of poverty, social welfare, racial discrimination, crowding, urban planning, housing renewal, and transportation all focused attention on urban areas. What had once been considered small-town virtues, such as warm community relationships, were found increasingly in suburbs, as were conservative political and religious values, which shifted the attention of political analysts to those locations. To the extent that they were lumped under the heading of rural America, small towns were viewed as part of a declining sector populated by fewer people, and of interest more as the location of food production and tourism than as places where people still lived. As a result, data have been available from census reports about the number, size, demographic composition, and economic characteristics of small towns, but little effort has been made to learn what residents of small towns think and believe.[12]

The fact that little research has been done does not mean that small towns have ceased to be of interest. Novels, movies, and television programs continue to present fictional accounts of small-town life. Journalists visit small towns in hopes of capturing a piece of Americana. Writers carry on the tradition of looking for down-home wisdom by talking to small-town sages and reporting on insights gleaned from living in remote communities. Increasingly the blogosphere has become a location of lively postings about the glories and deficiencies of small-town life.

From these various sources, two contradictory images of small-town America emerge. One is a nostalgic, almost-bucolic view in which towns and villages are dominated by warm neighborly relationships. The proverbial stranger who comes to town finds the townspeople at first a bit parochial, but then discovers them to be thoroughly good-hearted. The other view presents the small town as a place to leave as quickly as possible. The townspeople are unhappy, inbred, and reluctant to let go of the heroine who knows she must exit. The stranger who arrives is caught in a spiral of deceit and intimidation that cannot be escaped soon enough. In either case, the town serves as a convenient setting in which to tell of drama and intrigue, but there is little information about what the inhabitants of small towns are actually like.[13]

The research I present here was conducted principally through in-depth semistructured qualitative interviews with people currently living in small towns. More than seven hundred people were interviewed in three hundred towns scattered among forty-three states. The people we talked to included community leaders, such as mayors, town administrators, school superintendents, business owners, and clergy, who were knowledgeable about community issues, trends, and challenges, and could give us a bird's-eye view of local events in addition to describing their own experiences. We also spoke with ordinary residents—farmers, factory workers, teachers, office managers, homemakers, and retirees, among others—who ranged from lifelong members of their communities to recent (or not-so-recent) newcomers. These townspeople supplied us with an exceptionally rich sense of what it is like to live in a small town and the various ways in which residents find community in these places. For comparative purposes, we also conducted interviews with people living in selected cities and suburbs. Additional information came from national surveys that measured attitudes about social, moral, religious, and political issues. Statistical evidence offers some indications about numbers of towns, changes in population size, and variations in occupations, incomes, education levels, racial composition, and age.[14]

The US Census Bureau estimates that there are approximately 19,000 incorporated places in the United States—a number that has edged up modestly over the past half century. Of this total, more than 18,000—or

93 percent of all incorporated places—have populations of fewer than 25,000. By that standard, almost 53 million Americans might be classified as living in a small town. Approximately 20 percent of these incorporated places, however, are located within an "urban fringe," which the US Census Bureau defines as a contiguous, closely settled area with a combined population of 50,000 or more. Omitting those places leaves approximately 14,000 towns of under 25,000 people that are not part of an urbanized area. Almost 30 million Americans live in these communities.[15]

Besides towns that are officially classified as incorporated places, towns in New England and New York that are classified as "minor civil divisions" have functioned as local municipalities, usually with an incorporated name, town hall, governing board, and business district that give residents a distinct sense of their locale as a community. Examples include Canaan, Connecticut, a town of 1,200 some forty miles northwest of Hartford; Willsboro, New York, a town of 2,000 thirty miles south of Plattsburgh; Merrimac, Massachusetts, a town of 6,300 near the New Hampshire line above Boston; and Litchfield, Maine, a town of 3,600 located fifty miles north of Portland.[16] In 2010, there were 1,723 of these towns with populations of fewer than 25,000 located in nonurban areas. Approximately 4.5 million people lived in these communities. When these towns are included, the total number of small towns in the United States with populations of less than 25,000 and located outside urban-fringe areas rises to 16,307, and the number of people living in these communities totals 33.7 million.[17]

Of the nonurban places and minor civil divisions that might by this definition be classified as small towns, the majority of them are quite small. More than 9,000 or 56 percent have populations of under 1,000 people (figure 1.1). Another 16 percent have populations between 1,000 and 2,000, and an additional 16 percent have populations between 2,000 and 5,000. Only 7 percent have populations between 5,000 and 10,000, and only 4 percent have populations between 10,000 and 25,000.[18]

Most Americans who live in small towns, though, live in the larger of these communities. Twenty-nine percent live in towns of 10,000 to 25,000 residents. Twenty-three percent live in towns of 5,000 to 10,000 residents. Another 24 percent live in communities of 2,000 to 5,000 residents. Twelve percent live in towns with populations between 1,000 and 2,000. And only 11 percent live in towns with populations under 1,000.[19]

In sheer numbers, small nonurban towns of no more than 25,000 residents comprise 75 percent of all towns and cities nationally. That proportion is highest (exceeding 90 percent) in Alaska, Arkansas, Iowa, Kansas, Maine, Mississippi, Montana, Nebraska, North and South Dakota, Oklahoma, Vermont, and Wyoming, and lowest in California, Connecticut, Massachusetts, and Rhode Island. The proportion of people who live in

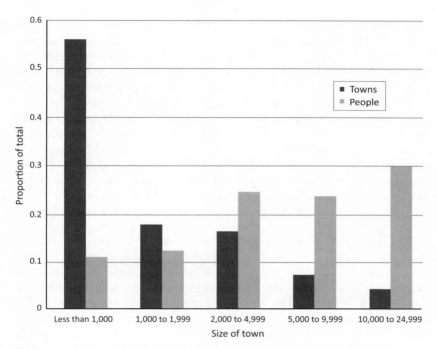

Figure 1.1 Distribution of nonurban towns and people

these small nonurban towns (out of all those who live in any town or city) is highest in Alabama, Arkansas, Iowa, Kansas, Kentucky, Louisiana, Maine, Mississippi, Nebraska, New Hampshire, North and South Dakota, Vermont, West Virginia, and Wyoming, and lowest in Arizona, California, Connecticut, Florida, Massachusetts, New Jersey, Nevada, and Rhode Island.

When asked if they consider their community a small town, the residents we interviewed in nonurbanized towns of up to 25,000 mostly indicated that they did. Naturally, they drew distinctions between towns near the upper range and ones closer to the lower range. But the relevant comparisons that made them regard their communities as small towns were cities. The contrast in their minds was a place of several hundred thousand or larger. By that standard, their community was compact, self-contained, and more easily identified as a distinct place.[20]

Although the residents who live in small towns are well aware that their communities are indeed small, it is less apparent whether people who live in cities have a clear impression of small-town America. One impression is that small-town America exists geographically as well as culturally at a great distance from metropolitan centers. Perhaps it is located far away in a remote corner of the prairie or isolated section of hill country. It is true that an urban resident probably has to travel some distance before the city is left behind. But once out of the city, it is abundantly clear that small towns are still an important feature of the nation's landscape. On average, there is a town of no more than 25,000 people every twelve miles nationally. States as different as Florida, Mississippi, Texas, and Virginia resemble the national average in this respect. In a number of other states, including Illinois, Indiana, Iowa, Ohio, and Pennsylvania, there is a town on average every seven or eight miles. Only in sparsely populated western states, such as Montana, Nevada, New Mexico, and Wyoming, are towns on average more than thirty miles apart.[21]

The interviewees who participated in the research were selected to represent small towns of varying size. Nearly one-third lived in towns of fewer than 1,000 people. Another third lived in communities of more than 1,000, but fewer than 10,000 residents. Approximately 10 percent lived in towns of 10,000 to 25,000. And for comparison's sake, approximately one-fifth lived in larger communities, of whom about half lived in towns of 25,000 to 50,000, and the remainder lived in larger places. The interviewees who lived in towns of under 25,000 residents were further selected by choosing towns that were located in nonurbanized areas. The mean distance from an urban area of more than 50,000 was sixty-seven miles and the median distance was fifty-four miles.

The interviews invited townspeople to talk at length as well as in their own words about how and why they had come to live in their current community, what their daily life was like, what they did for a living, their hopes and aspirations, and how they thought about the trajectory of their lives. Residents described their communities and the local ambience, discussed what they did and did not like about their towns, and told how they and their neighbors were faring financially. People talked about local politics, challenges and innovations in their community, and larger social and moral issues. The interviews with town leaders, clergy, heads of voluntary organizations, and local officials provided additional information about the beliefs, values, and meanings associated with living in small towns.[22]

The next chapter offers an initial view of the people who live in small towns, emphasizing the diversity of social strata of which small communities are composed. At the top are a small group of gentry, who in most towns consist of wealthy landowners, owners of successful businesses, and select members of the professions, such as doctors and lawyers. Next is a large service class that is generally college trained, and has increased in size as a result of the continuing need for schools in most towns and an increasing need for medical services as well as other services provided by businesses, and services offered through government agencies. The other large stratum consists of wageworkers who generally do not have college training, and are employed in manufacturing and construction jobs, or as office assistants and agricultural laborers. Small towns also include a sizable stratum of pensioners who are retired or semiretired, and are supported by Social Security, retirement plans, and part-time employment. With differences among social strata nearly as great in small towns as in cities, the question is why residents of small towns so often insist that everyone is the same. Chapter 2 examines the marks of distinction that residents use to describe social strata in their communities and discusses the local expectations that blur these distinctions.

The following two chapters take up the central question of how residents of small towns construct the meaning of their community in ways that reinforce loyalty to it and one another. Although the attractions of knowing neighbors and living in familiar places reflect common views about small towns, the evidence from residents themselves points to the need to pay closer attention to what these attractions actually mean. Chapter 3 looks at what people mean when they say a small town offers a slower-paced life or more authentic place in which to raise children. That chapter demonstrates that residents are fully aware of the disadvantages of living in a small town, and shows how residents compensate by, for example, organizing local cultural events and traveling more frequently to cities. It concludes by considering the challenges residents talk about as they see their communities changing. In many towns, immigration and new ethnic diversity are the principal changes on residents' minds. In many others declining population, diminishing services, and lower standards of living are the major concerns. Understanding what leads people to say that their communities are dying or were better in the past than now, or deny that these changes are taking place, requires going beyond population statistics. The chapter shows the particular events that residents associate with decline, and how they make sense of departures and loss.

Chapter 4 explores in further detail what residents understand as the most important sources of community spirit in their towns. Although it is widely believed that small towns do encourage community participation, scarcely anything has been studied about the meanings of community spirit or its sources in towns' activities, such as homecoming weekends, athletic events, and community festivals. The chapter examines how narratives about the goodness and decency of a community are formulated, and how they reflect special occasions in which personal or collective tragedy is overcome. A key part of community spirit is the perception that acquaintances in town are in fact good neighbors. How neighborliness is demonstrated even through small greetings and sidewalk behavior is the secret behind these perceptions. The extent to which these expectations are taken for granted nevertheless poses difficulties for newcomers, and these inhabitants are a critical source of insight about what they have learned in attempting to adjust to local norms.[23] The chapter ends with a discussion of the stories that townspeople tell to combat negative stereotypes imposed on them by city people along with tales that emphasize the relative freedom, openness, and closeness to nature that small-town life provides.

Chapter 5 moves from a consideration of the perceptions residents have of their communities to a look at the ways in which residents in small towns make sense of their own lives. The chapter contends that small communities create a frog-pond identity that residents draw on to formulate narratives about why they chose to live in a small town, how that choice has limited or enriched their career opportunities, and whether they feel regret or are satisfied. Residents do describe a number of ways in which being raised in a small town or choosing to live in one has restricted their chances of getting better jobs and higher pay. Equally important are the justifications residents provide to explain these limitations. Personal networks, family loyalties, and a lack of guidance about higher education decisions are commonly mentioned. In addition, narratives sometimes emphasize the desire for a balanced life that includes time for family and friends, or a sense that a more authentic life can be found for oneself and one's children in a small town. Although townspeople generally include choice in these narratives about where to live, a significant number of them acknowledge that they live where they do because of unforeseen circumstances and events over which they have little control. These choices and circumstances are often portrayed differently by women than by men, leading the former especially to underscore being good wives and mothers as substitute gratification in view of opportunities foregone. The legacy of farming also has a considerable impact on the lives of small-town residents. Although the farm population itself has declined considerably over the past two generations, the impact of having been raised on farms or expecting at some point to take over farming from parents and grandparents remains crucial.

The next two chapters focus on the town leaders and associations that play key roles in small communities' efforts to adapt to changing social and economic conditions. Chapter 6 examines formal and informal leaders, including local public officials and heads of voluntary organizations. It shows how residents confer respect on leaders and how leaders draw on this respect in performing their roles. Leaders discuss why they take on civic responsibilities, the gratifications and frustrations involved, and how these activities serve as stepping-stones for public office in larger venues. Although small towns are sometimes considered to lack interesting cultural amenities, local cultural leadership is particularly important, and figures prominently in communities' understanding of their distinctive history and identity. Small communities have high expectations about the need to attract new residents and jobs, and hold on to local schools and businesses. But leaders with experience in meeting these expectations note resistance to change, and argue that smaller-scale and more realistic programs are better suited to their communities. Small towns nevertheless are laboratories for social innovation, judging from leaders' descriptions of new technologies, electronic communications, sustainable energy projects, and efforts to rebuild following natural disasters.

Chapter 7 considers the roles played in small towns by religious organizations. Although it is the case that religious participation is somewhat higher in small towns than in larger communities, the differences are relatively small. The perception among residents that religion is important has more to do with the presence of religious buildings along with the public activities of religious organizations than with statistical measures of belief and practice. Religious organizations also serve significantly as carriers of collective narratives about caring behavior in the community, and these organizations increasingly provide links between small towns and the wider world through mission trips as well as humanitarian and relief efforts. In small communities with declining populations, religious organizations are adapting in creative ways to meet the needs and interests of their constituents. The clustering of congregations, shared pastorates, mergers, and church closings are among the solutions that are being attempted.

The following two chapters examine how social and political issues are framed in small towns. Chapter 8 shows how perceptions of moral decline intersect with the reality of living in towns with declining populations and diminishing job opportunities. The specific moral issues of concern that residents of small towns most frequently mention are abortion, homosexuality, and schooling issues, such as teaching the Ten Commandments and the biblical creation story alongside evolution. Although residents take different perspectives on these issues, the conservative side is more commonly featured in public discourse and includes a rhetorical style that makes it easier for this to happen than for a discourse to be emphasized that focuses on personal choice.

Chapter 9 demonstrates that antipathy toward big government is inflected in several ways among residents of small towns. These ways include concerns about the scale of big bureaucracy, its inability to adapt to the particular norms and practices of small towns in which people know one another, and government's unresponsiveness to the needs of small communities in comparison with its attentiveness to problems in cities. Antipathy toward government is further reinforced by negative opinions about people on welfare. Compared with perceptions of state and federal government, attitudes toward local government are typically more charitable, but register conflicts as well. With residents of small towns on average being only slightly more favorably inclined toward Republican candidates than Democratic ones, Republicans nevertheless seem to be better represented in many small towns. The chapter discusses the reasons for Republican popularity and concludes by considering the possibilities present in small towns for grassroots populist activism.

Chapter 10 delves into an aspect of small-town life that generated almost more anxiety than any other in our interviews: the future these communities may—or may not—hold for the next generation. As residents nearly always see it, young people who grow up in small towns should go to college in order to be well prepared for whatever the future may hold. Once again, though, the reasons given along with the concerns underlying these reasons are more complex than broad-stroked surveys and census data reveal. Although they consider higher education critical, residents—parents and educators alike—acknowledge that there are aspects of small-town culture that make it difficult for young people to plan appropriately in order to make the most of college or university training. Some worry about pressures to marry young, while others identify a lack of self-confidence as the most serious disadvantage. Variation is also present in the goals that residents consider important in advising young people about the future. One of the most interesting narratives that surfaces in these interviews emphasizes the need to take one's community values along, no matter where one lives—and for those who remain in a small town to keep their options open.

In the final chapter, I offer reflections that pull together my observations about the various factors that contribute to residents' sense of community in small towns. I draw from Suzanne Keller's ethnographic study of community life in which she identifies ten key building blocks of community. These include tangible aspects of social relationships that have been of interest to students of social capital, especially social networks, sharing, and cooperation, but also stress territory, governance, leadership, rituals, and the beliefs, values, and norms that guide behavior.

Running through all these topics is a larger observation to which I repeatedly return. The meaning of community in small towns is a bit like common sense, which as Clifford Geertz once noted, "lies so artlessly before our eyes it is almost impossible to see."[24] I had that sense more than once while doing the research and was reminded of it especially when a scholar known for a career of studying community asked why I thought it should be studied in small towns at all. "Everyone knows there's community in small towns," he said. True enough, but shouldn't that make it all the more important to find out what community means?[25]

And the answer to that question is not to carve up meanings into large digestible chunks—not to create boxes of typologies in which to categorize the complexities of small-town culture. It is rather to analyze how the reflexive self-awareness of living in a small community figures into the language in which residents characterize their lives. Viewed in this way, community is not only a place of residence or set of social networks but also a component of a person's worldview. Being part of a community—living in a small town—commands a place as part of a person's self-identity, just as a person's race, gender, occupation, national origin, or citizenship does.

From examining the taken-for-granted self-perceptions of people who live in small towns, we see that their awareness of this fact shapes how they understand the distinctions that define and separate social strata. Being fellow members of a community offers a way to see the relationships among strata and level the differences. Community mindedness further inflects the meaning of disparate experiences and values, such that the pace of life, distances, entertainment, authenticity, children, and neighborliness are all perceived through the lens of living in a small place. This is also the case with understandings of the frog pond in which career choices and the meaning of money are interpreted. It infuses particular valences into moral, religious, and political sentiments.

None of these observations is meant to imply that outlooks in small towns are fundamentally different from attitudes in cities and suburbs. There is good reason to believe, as scholars have argued, that television, advertising, ease of travel and communication, geographic mobility, and even standardized food processing—McDonaldization—have all contributed to a common culture that includes small towns and rural areas as well as cities and suburbs.[26] The point is rather that community has specific meanings in different places, and some of what makes these meanings special is the size as well as location of the place in which a person lives. Understanding community requires paying special attention to what it means to the people who live there. The task is like understanding motherhood. It may be universal, but its meaning varies from person to person, and has value precisely because of those variations. In real life, people define themselves by weaving narratives that give coherence to their day-to-day experience. Community is significantly—and for most residents of small towns, *deeply*—woven into these narratives.[27] In small communities, the intuitions and emotions, personal accounts and town legends, routine sidewalk behavior and annual festivals, interweaving of family history and neighborly relations among the people who live there all converge to forge an almost inexplicably powerful attachment.

- 2 -

You Have to Deal with Everybody
The Inhabitants of Small Towns

BRIAN PARKER LIVES IN A rambling two-story house built in the 1920s. Out back there is a badly weathered garage that doubles as a storage shed, and to the south of that is a large garden with rows of overripe tomatoes and zucchini. Mr. Parker farms several acres of rented land a few miles from town, and he and his wife, Laverne, operate a small hardware store that serves the local population of four hundred. They are plainspoken people who have a lot to say about living in a small place, if one is willing to listen.

When the Parkers moved here twenty-five years ago, the community was almost 50 percent larger than it is today. Farms in the area have become larger in acreage and fewer in number. Young people have moved away. Besides the hardware store, Main Street now serves as host only to a farm supply store that sells tractors and fertilizer, the post office, a senior citizens' center, the branch office of a state bank, a coffee shop, and five vacant buildings. To see the doctor or purchase groceries (other than a few essentials), the Parkers drive fifteen miles to the county seat of fifty-five hundred residents. The county seat's population has also dropped by nearly 50 percent since the 1970s.

Unlike most of their neighbors, the Parkers did not grow up here. They were raised in different suburbs of a large city two hundred miles away. After high school, each of the Parkers went away to college, graduated, and took jobs in another state. But Mrs. Parker's grandparents lived in a small town and as a girl she reveled in visiting them. She especially enjoyed breathing the fresh air and seeing the nearby farms. When the Parkers' first child was born, they decided they wanted to raise their family in a small town. They took the risk of leaving their jobs in the city, lived on as little as possible, and somehow made it work. Having lived in cities, the Parkers are keenly aware of how small towns differ. "We've reflected a lot on the differences between rural and urban life," Mr. Parker says. "In the city, you tend to hang out with people who are of the same socioeconomic class that you are. Your friends and your relationships are, well, as they say, birds of a feather that flock together. In a rural community, you can't do that. You have to deal with everybody. Rich people, poor people, farmers, veterinarians, accountants. You can't retreat into a world of your own making."

To understand how people in small towns view their communities, and how their communities shape their behaviors and attitudes, we must begin with the people themselves—people like the Parkers who have left the city to live in small towns and their neighbors who have lived in small towns for generations. In so doing, we confront an interesting irony. The millions of people in the United States who live in small towns are quite diverse. They vary in national background, race, age, family style, sexual orientation, education level, occupation, and income. At the same time, townspeople argue that they are not so different from one another. They see their fellow residents as similar to themselves: profoundly democratic, neighborly, and basically equal.

In It Together

The truth is that life in small towns is stratified, just as it is elsewhere in the United States. In their research on rural and small-town America in the 1970s, demographers Glenn V. Fuguitt, David L. Brown, and Calvin L. Beale found considerable variation in individual incomes, for example, with as many as two-thirds of white males in some towns enjoying standards of living above the national mean, while 12 to 16 percent of the population in nonmetropolitan towns were living in poverty.[1] More recent data show that 1.1 percent of households in nonurbanized towns of fewer than twenty-five thousand people earn incomes at least five times the median amount. At the lower end of the spectrum, among residents in these towns, approximately 25 percent of households have incomes less than half the median amount.[2]

It is nevertheless the case that economic diversity is slightly lower on average in small towns than in larger places. As shown in figure 2.1, an index of diversity in which a larger value indicates a lower probability that any two households will fall into the same income category increases as towns become larger. Income diversity is especially low in the smallest towns, and diversity scores are approximately the same when all small towns are considered or only those in nonmetropolitan areas. Among the smallest towns, income diversity does vary considerably, though. For instance, the lowest income diversity occurs in towns such as Corral City, Texas; Hamer, Idaho; Kief, North Dakota; and Mildred, Kansas (all with populations under a hundred). In contrast, several small towns with larger

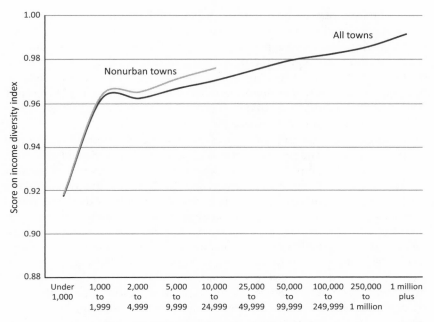

Figure 2.1 Income diversity by size of place

populations—such as Kuttawa, Kentucky; Middleburg, Virginia; and Oxford, Maryland (with populations of more than six hundred)—have as
much income diversity as many small cities.[3]

Ethnographic studies conducted in small towns between the 1920s and
1960s nearly always described status differences between the rich and
poor, the powerful, and those lacking in power. The authors of these
studies, however, were similarly struck by the frequency with which the
inhabitants they talked to insisted that everyone was the same. For example, anthropologist Carl Withers, who wrote under the pseudonym
James West, observed in the early 1940s that the residents of Plainville,
a town of 275 people in southwestern Missouri, "completely deny the
existence of class in their community." They spoke openly of differences
they had witnessed between rich and poor in other places, but declared
with pride, "This is *one* place where ever'body is equal." Similarly, when
sociologists Arthur J. Vidich and Joseph Bensman studied Springdale, a
rural New England community of 1,000 residents in the 1950s, they concluded that "we're all equal" was one of the townspeople's most important ways of characterizing themselves.[4]

It was common in community studies of that era to pass off residents'
perception of their basic equality as a kind of false consciousness. This

understanding of their communities was rooted, scholars argued, in residents' naive unwillingness to acknowledge local differences in social class, as the Plainville study suggested, or was masked by meaningful but superficial norms of local etiquette, such as exchanging greetings with passersby, as Vidich and Bensman observed. The task of social science, as practitioners in those decades understood it, was to bring to light the cold facts of social stratification that residents themselves may have been oblivious of or reluctant to acknowledge.[5]

A different perspective, though, is more useful for understanding the status differences and self-perceptions of contemporary residents in small towns. This view emphasizes that status differences do exist and are understood to exist by residents themselves, but that there are also expectations associated with these differences that contribute to the community well-being, and thus reinforce the sense of everyone being in it together. In other words, social norms exist in small towns that encourage feelings of solidarity despite differences in income and occupational prestige. How this works cannot be understood without paying close attention to what actually constitutes these status distinctions. While they are rooted in differences of income, education, occupation, and lifestyle, just as they are in cities and suburbs, they also reflect the different functional roles that people play in their communities—that is, roles such as doctor, teacher, banker, homemaker, wage laborer, or retiree. The result is a division of labor, as it were, that begins to tell us something about how small communities sustain themselves and why residents find these communities attractive. At least some of these status distinctions further reflect changes that have taken place in small towns in the decades since many of the earlier ethnographic studies were conducted.

One version of the division of labor present in small towns is evident even in fictional accounts, such as in novels and films. Depictions of small towns in these sources typically highlight stark status distinctions. Characters include town patriarchs who lord it over the rest of the community, families who live on the right or wrong side of the tracks, and individuals who are considered by the townspeople as outsiders or outcasts. Many of these contrasts are overdrawn, serving better for narrative purposes than as accurate descriptions of status differences. Yet they capture an important aspect of small-town life. In real life, residents do draw contrasts among themselves and place fellow residents in categories that mark status differences.

In *Distinction*, Pierre Bourdieu argued that social status cannot be reduced to simple measures of wealth or power but instead has to be understood in terms of the cultural dynamics that prevail in particular locations. These dynamics involve the deployment of symbolic boundaries that separate groups from one another both in self-perception and how they are perceived by other groups. The distinctions so drawn become part of the habitus—the taken-for-granted habits of life—that shapes individual behavior and social relations. As people carry out the daily tasks of ordinary life, they reinforce these distinctions. Some lines of demarcation, such as race under apartheid, are hard distinctions perpetuated through force as well as by custom, while others involve soft lines that are easily crossed and blurred. Status markers, in Bourdieu's account, not only separate people but also reveal underlying social relationships that constitute the social order and bases of solidarity within communities.[6]

The marks of distinction in small towns in the twenty-first century reflect the familiar ladders of stratification that involve differences in income, educational attainment, and occupation. In addition, the major categories of distinction reveal important understandings about the expected relationships of individuals and families to their communities. At the top are the gentry who occupy positions of formal and informal power. The gentry play an important role in the economic and civic life of small communities. They are followed by two other groups, which make up the largest share of the population in most small towns: the service class and wageworkers. Pensioners, who include residents who are retired or semiretired, make up a fourth category, and there are always a few residents who cannot be classified in any of these categories.

The gentry seldom make up more than 2 to 5 percent of the overall population of small towns, which means that their numbers range from only a handful in the smallest towns to a few hundred in larger towns. They are distinguished by wealth, but also by reputation as prominent landowners, inheritors of old money, and people of influence.[7] Beneath them, members of the service class have less wealth and influence than the gentry, but nowadays in even the most rural communities have often been to college, and are employed in white-collar and other middle-class occupations. They work at jobs that are popularly understood as valued services to the community and its residents, such as teaching, health care, government services, or in many cases, operators of retail stores and farms. Whereas the service class is salaried or depends on business income and investments, wageworkers typically are employed in hourly jobs, and usually have only a high school education or some vocational or technical training beyond high school. They work in small manufacturing plants, as office staff, as aides for teachers and nurses, in construction, and as farm laborers. Pensioners are retired and semiretired residents who depend on pensions, private savings, and Social Security for support. Interviews with individuals who occupy these statuses in small towns show what sets them apart from one another, but also reveal the bonds that link them together.

THE GENTRY

The landed gentry are well illustrated by Bud Janssen, a farmer who lives in a town of approximately forty-five hundred people populated by farmers and farm laborers, construction workers, and an ample supply of government employees, teachers, store clerks, and retirees. A row of cedars and tamarack separates the Janssens' spacious ranch-style home from a county road that marks the edge of town. Beyond the road, huge fields of soybeans and corn stretch across the high plains for miles. The town was 20 percent larger in 1980 than it is today, having lost population as a result of farms in the area becoming larger. But there is an interstate highway nearby, and the town is a county seat, has a technical school, a radio station, and a hospital—all of which make it an important regional hub and mean that the community is in no danger of dying.

Today Mr. Janssen has just returned from clearing the remains of an abandoned farmstead on land he purchased several years ago. He used his own bulldozer, which he keeps with his fleet of tractors, combines, and cultivating equipment at a farm fifteen miles from town. On his way home, he detoured past another field, where he intends to plant millet in the fall. "I had to see what kind of weeds was growing and how soon they needed to be sprayed," he says. Unless it rains tonight, he will be tilling a field twenty-five miles away tomorrow.

Mr. Janssen is a third-generation farmer, but unlike many of his neighbors whose grandfathers homesteaded land in the nineteenth century, he has owned land in the county only since the 1960s. He grew up on a small farm in another part of the state, helping his dad raise cattle, and expected to do the same when he finished high school. Money was always tight, but the cattle market was steady, and by working as a day laborer he was able to make his first down payment on a piece of ground of his own. Over the decades he and his wife have lived frugally, worked hard, and gradually expanded their holdings.

He currently farms more than nine thousand acres or about six times as much as the average farmer in his community. That acreage includes land he owns or rents, and is spread across two counties and spans an eighty-mile radius. His largest field encompasses two-square miles or more than twelve hundred acres. At age seventy, he shares the farming with his son, but still does much of the tractor work himself. With a 550-horsepower tractor that costs more than $150,000 and pulls a sixty-foot cultivator, he can till forty acres an hour on a good day. "I'm old enough to retire," he says, "but that word isn't in my vocabulary. I'm just going to keep going as long as I can."

The Janssens are by no means the richest family in town. Several other farmers own more land than they do. But big farmers are clearly the local elite. The Janssens live in a new section at the edge of town. Their house is worth twice as much as the average home. Their annual income puts them in the top 1 to 1.5 percent in the community. From year to year their cash flow varies, depending on rainfall and grain prices. But crop insurance and government subsidies even out those fluctuations, and over the decades land values have steadily risen.

The Janssens' lifestyle is an indication of their position in the upper stratum of the community. They are regulars at the Presbyterian Church, the most upscale congregation in town, and have enough money to travel. Like others of the town's elite, the Janssens are expected to take leadership roles in the community and do so largely through their volunteer activities. Mr. Janssen has served for years on the church board and belongs to the Elks club, which until a few years ago operated the town's finest dining facility. His wife volunteers at the hospital, and he chairs a community-wide committee for the Lions club.

The landed gentry are often wealthy enough to own a vacation home in another state or private airplane. It is hard for them not to stand out in a small community. They usually live in a house that is newer or larger than average, have enough money to pay for hired help, and are able to spend weekends away going to ball games or shopping. How they are viewed in the community depends on how they attained their wealth and what they have done to care for their land. "Oh yes, those are the farmer gods, the rancher gods," a shopkeeper in a town surrounded by large farms and ranches observes, registering the ambivalence that people of lesser means frequently feel toward the wealthy.

In Mr. Janssen's case, he sometimes feels like a newcomer, compared with neighbors whose grandfathers came as pioneers, but the fact that he was once poor and has accumulated land by working hard is a source of respect in the community. The landed gentry who are definitely not respected are the ones who are known to have attained wealth and purchased land because of having squeezed out poor farmers during the Great Depression, or because of oil or natural gas being found on their property. The ones who are respected are usually people like Mr. Janssen who are seen working in the fields themselves and serving on civic boards in their communities.

Although physical labor comes with the territory, daily life for the landed gentry is currently dominated by office work and managerial tasks. "I spend an awful lot of time behind the computer," a rancher who manages a large spread of irrigated cropland in another high plains community remarks. His day begins with checking the overseas financial markets, and determining whether or not to sell some of his grain. With forty to fifty thousand bushels on hand, fluctuations of ten or twenty cents make a significant difference. Other days he studies online crop reports, learns about new varieties of genetically modified seed, and makes decisions about farm loans and new equipment. Lately, for example, he has been figuring the relative costs of purchasing new engines for his irrigation wells to take advantage of alternative fuels. He still spends long days in the fields during planting season and harvest, but says his work is increasingly done indoors.

For people who live in cities and know little about farming except what they read in urban newspapers, it is important to understand that many of the people who live in or near small towns and farm are not truly part of the landed gentry. This is because someone else owns most of the land they farm, and much of the machinery they use is heavily mortgaged to the bank. An instance would be a couple in their early forties we met in a town of about thirteen thousand. They farmed fifteen hundred acres, which was well above average for the county in which they lived. But they owned only eighty acres. The woman's mother along with several aunts and uncles who had retired, or who had inherited land from the previous generation and kept it because it had been in the family, owned the rest of the land. This couple might eventually join the landed gentry if they do well and inherit the land they now rent. Yet they are currently heavily in debt because of the machinery they had to purchase and expect that will continue to be their financial situation. By the time the loans on the machinery are repaid, the machinery is worn out and needs to be replaced with even more expensive equipment. At present, they feel more like wageworkers than gentry. The woman has taught school and worked for an insurance company in lean years to make ends meet.

In most towns, fewer of the elite are involved in agriculture nowadays than have attained status in other ways. Over the decades, one of the surest ways of attaining elite status in small towns, apart from farming and ranching, has been serving as the community's doctor or lawyer. The stereotypical country doctor or lawyer was a well-educated person who had probably grown up somewhere else, lived in a city while attending medical or law school, cultivated a taste for the arts and literature, and then moved to a small town because of its simple amenities and opportunities for community leadership.[8] In recent decades, small rural communities with declining populations have struggled to attract as well as retain doctors (lawyers have not been as scarce) who otherwise would choose to practice in cities and suburbs where hospitals were better and the opportunities for specialization were greater. Towns of five to twenty-five thousand residents have nevertheless been able to secure enough revenue from government programs and through patients' health insurance plans to maintain decent clinics and small hospitals. For doctors at these clinics and hospitals, opportunities to be among the local gentry have continued.

Merely the fact of having an advanced professional degree places them in the upper echelon of their community.[9]

Dr. Richard Schnell lives in a spacious brick house on a corner lot three miles from the center of this Sunbelt town of twelve thousand. The neighborhood is one of the town's newer and most expensive subdivisions. If his home were on the market, it would sell for approximately four times the median price here and would be among the top fifty in terms of value. Last year when he retired, his income was in the top 1.5 percent among families in the community, and he earned enough from selling his practice that he and his wife are living comfortably from the interest on their investments.

Life has never been better for Dr. Schnell. As a boy, he lived in utter poverty, helping his dad—who worked as a coal miner—farm a few acres of cotton and peanuts with a team of mules. Most of his high school classmates followed their fathers into the coal mines, he recalls, but he decided early to lead a different life if he possibly could. He joined the army, spent four years in the military, saved enough money to attend junior college, landed a job teaching school, got married, and then with his wife's help worked his way through college and medical school. His decision to locate in a small town was dictated by an opening that simply became available at the right time. Over the decades the town's population grew by a third, and his practice expanded.

Dr. Schnell could have devoted his working hours to his patients, and then spent the rest of the time on the golf course or taking vacations. But in a small town it proved impossible to escape becoming involved in the community. He remembers an evening more than two decades ago when some friends invited him and his wife to their house for a Christmas party. These friends lived in the same neighborhood, and knew each other from church and civic clubs. One was a banker; another held investments in oil and gas. The conversation turned to politics. "We were looking for somebody to run for city commission," he says. "We went to George and asked him to run." George did run and won.

That would have been the end of the story. But Dr. Schnell's wife, Elizabeth, picks up the narrative and finishes it. She explains that because of their friend George, her husband was also drawn into community service. Too modest to mention it himself, he served for twenty-two years on the city commission, including a term as mayor, and received a citizen of the year award.

Besides the opportunities afforded for doctors themselves, the health and related social services industry has become prominent enough in many of America's smaller towns to provide well-paying jobs for the executives who own or manage clinics, hospitals, rehabilitation centers, and assisted living programs. In towns of fewer than ten thousand residents, these health-related businesses sometimes have staffs of a hundred, while in larger towns the number of employees is often considerably more. Other residents can easily regard a top executive of one of these large, prominent local businesses as a member of the gentry.

Joseph Grimshaw is an example of a small-town resident who has achieved a position among the gentry by virtue of success in leading a health-related business. Mr. Grimshaw lives in a town of just under twenty thousand people that has grown in recent years as a regional hub for natural gas production, trucking, and agribusiness. He grew up here, the son of a car dealer who made a decent living but was by no means rich. After high school, Mr. Grimshaw joined the army, gained the maturity and direction he figured he lacked, got married, and went to college in his hometown, majoring in business. He planned to relocate to a large city where jobs were said to be plentiful, but a family acquaintance asked him to apply for a managerial position at the local hospital. He did, and within a few years was the CEO of a rapidly expanding regional medical facility with three hundred employees.

With skill and some luck, Mr. Grimshaw turned his investments into a sizable enough portfolio to step down from his CEO position before his fiftieth birthday. Now in his late fifties, he runs a private investment banking firm in the mornings, and spends his afternoons overseeing the thousand acres of farmland he owns, playing golf, and doing volunteer work. He has been president of the Kiwanis club and active in the chamber of commerce. Currently he divides his time among the local historical society, activities at the Catholic Church, and serving as an appointed member of a state health commission. He says the dream he is most pleased about is being "totally financially independent." Like Mr. Janssen and Dr. Schnell, his hard work, bootstrap upward mobility, and leadership in voluntary service activities make him a respected member of the local gentry.

How the gentry are changing even in small, traditional rural communities is nicely illustrated by another successful businessperson, Raymond Breyer, a commodities broker who lives with his wife in a rural town of just over twenty thousand. His community has also grown in recent years as a result of light manufacturing and a fledgling alternative energy facility. Until recently, it would have been unheard of for anyone to earn a handsome living in a small town as a commodities broker, but the Internet, changes in banking regulations, and greater interest in commodities trading and the derivatives market among residents of small towns have made this occupation a possibility. Mr. Breyer enjoys the good life by virtue of two things. First, he inherited modest wealth, and second, he cultivated networks well beyond the town that have allowed him to earn considerable wealth without having to leave. As a teenager he worked in the family business, and after college thought seriously about going to law school, but always knew he wanted to stay in his hometown, so decided to return and build up the business.

By the time he was forty, Mr. Breyer was supplying fuel and other petroleum products to most of the county. That was good because the population was growing and fuel prices were high. It also put him in contact with a large number of people locally and throughout the region. "Go out and meet as many people as you can" was his motto. One of the people he met told him about a franchise through which he could become a commodities broker. With electronic communication and satellite connections, businesspeople even in small towns were purchasing hedge funds and trading commodities futures. He added that to his repertoire, and was soon doing well for himself and his family.

The Breyers live in a new golf course community where houses come with three-car garages and cost three times as much as homes in average neighborhoods. "This is the place to live," he says, pointing out the window to the green grass and trees surrounding the golf course. The Breyers do not particularly like the harsh weather where they live, so they travel a lot, often to foreign countries with cooler climates in the summer and warm sunshine in the winter. They are firmly anchored in the community, but it is as much a place to get away from as to be.

The gentry are usually not called that, of course. Townspeople refer to them as rich farmers, big landowners, the elite, the moneyed people, sometimes pejoratively as the snobs, and frequently as the country-club set. Country clubs became popular in small towns during the 1950s, having spread widely in larger communities earlier in the century, and soon were one of the clearest status markers in small communities.[10] There was usually a golf course along with an exclusive restaurant and sometimes tennis courts. Membership and annual fees were high enough that all but the wealthy few were excluded. In racially and ethnically mixed communities, membership was also reserved for the white majority. The exclusive restaurant provided better food and a more attractive ambience than any other eating spot in town. It generally served drinks as well, and frequently was the only place in town that, as a private club, was able to escape restrictive or prohibitive liquor laws pertaining to public establishments. Knowing how to play golf was a sign of refinement; it was also a form of conspicuous consumption that implied having enough free time to have learned it, and enough money to have paid for lessons and purchased equipment. "Oh, what sold us" on coming here, says a doctor's wife in a town of thirteen hundred, "was the golf course. We live on the back of number nine green. It's a real treasure."

For many of the people we talked to, it was taken for granted that playing golf as a member of the country club or living in a neighborhood with a private golf course was a mark of status. In one community, though, the extent to which this was the case became even more apparent when the town decided that if it was to compete successfully with other towns, it needed to expand the nine-hole golf course to an eighteen-hole one. The cost of membership in the country club was already quite high, so members decided they could not afford to expand the facility. The town council and chamber of commerce stepped in, proposing to underwrite the expansion in return for opening the course to the public and renaming it. As soon as the name was changed from Country Club to Mountain Lakes, business on the course doubled. Yet that was a mixed blessing. It kept fees low, but it increased waiting times on weekends. Mostly what people noticed was that the clientele changed. Rather than the few wealthy residents mingling only with their own kind, a broader set of the population was now present. The gentry wished for the old days when just their friends belonged and a person seldom had to wait to tee off. If nothing else, the controversy showed how important the country club had been in separating the gentry from the rest of the community.

The Service Class

Below the gentry is the service class, which consists of salaried workers who generally have at least some college education, plus business owners and farm operators who are not salaried, but whose educational backgrounds and incomes are sufficient to give them a similar lifestyle in terms of housing, vacations, leisure time, and expectations about children's educations. Examples of occupations that fall into this category include accountants, bank managers, teachers, registered nurses, and government officials. The largest number of people, who comprise approximately 20 percent of the civilian labor force in small nonurban towns, are employed as teachers, school administrators, and the various health professions. Another 15 percent of the civilian labor force in small towns is employed in public administration, financial administration, insurance, and miscellaneous services.[11] Unlike the gentry who have large landholdings or other investments that solidify their ties to a particular place, the service class includes people who could have and perhaps did live elsewhere, but have chosen to live in their particular town. Being there by choice, they value family origins that may link them to the town, an affinity for the region, or job opportunities and ambience. Although they are not as wealthy as the gentry, they are usually well respected in the community, involved in its civic activities and social life, and regard themselves as the providers of valuable local services. Being of service to the community is especially important, both to their own sense of self-worth and how they are viewed by fellow residents.

An example is Greg Parsons, a congenial man who grew up on a small farm in corn country where dairy cows and hogs were the farmers' mainstay. In the 1970s, he married a farm girl in the community and began renting some land from her dad. With borrowed money, Mr. and Mrs. Parsons invested in hogs and were earning a decent living until the year disease wiped out most of their animals. The Parsons were struggling. "We sat down," he recalls, "and decided that if we could sell and liquidate what we had, we could pay off our debt." That plan was successful, and with help from his family and wife's job, Mr. Parsons earned enough credits at a local community college to receive an associate degree in accounting. As he was nearing graduation, the instructor mentioned hearing about a job opening at a bank in a small town about an hour away. Mr. Parsons applied and got the job. The town covered less than a half-square mile and had fewer than seven hundred residents, but that was OK with Mr. and Mrs. Parsons. It was similar to the farming community in which they had been raised, was less than two hours' drive from their parents and siblings, and Mr. Parsons could make use of his farm background in dealing with the bank's farm loans. He eventually became a vice president at the bank, and Mrs. Parsons got a job as a teacher in a neighboring community's elementary school. Both are proud that their jobs are of service to the community and give them ample opportunities to know their neighbors. The Parsons are happy to have raised their children here. One of their children still lives about an hour away. He and his dad have a few acres outside town. Mr. Parsons calls it hobby farming. He has fixed up an old tractor like the one his dad used decades ago. It keeps him in touch with his roots.

Besides schools and banks, the most common businesses in small towns are often the ones that are connected to the health industry. They are seldom as large as the regional health system Mr. Grimshaw headed as a CEO. Usually they serve a smaller area and operate with a staff of no more than five to ten employees. These small businesses include doctors' offices, noncritical care hospitals, nursing homes, rehabilitation centers, assisted living facilities, and medical clinics. Health workers, such as registered nurses and office managers, thus make up an important segment of the service class in small towns.

As a case in point, it was during his junior year in college that Alex Keller, now in his early forties, came to the realization that he would soon have to earn his own way in the world. Up to that point he had been content to work at odd jobs during the summer, take required courses, study a little, make passing grades, drink beer with his buddies, and play golf or softball on weekends. He knew it was unlikely that he would ever return to the remote town of twelve hundred where he had grown up. He rather liked the town of fifty thousand where he went to college. In fact, he enjoyed going to the large city nearby and fully anticipated that he would live in one when he graduated. But somehow he also wanted to keep open the option of living in a small town where people knew one another. An anonymous suburb was where he knew he did not want to live. Thinking health administration was one career that might have openings both in cities and small towns, he enrolled in a course on health policy.

Two decades and two master's degrees later, Mr. Keller is the director of a small family practice medical clinic in a county seat town of five thousand that prides itself on having a stable population and new municipal swimming pool. He and his wife along with their daughter live in a comfortable house in a newer section of town. His job is challenging. Most days there is some crisis on the horizon demanding his attention. Much of the health industry in his state, like in all states, is regulated by a state board, which in turn governs according to legislative mandates. These regulations pertain to everything from safety standards to billing. Then there are constant issues with the insurance companies that want to sock patients with as hefty premiums as the law allows, he says, and find ways to pay as little and as late as they can get away with. It falls on him to keep the clinic's doctors and nursing staff happy as well as recruit new personnel when someone leaves. He is also the clinic's main liaison with the community. That means keeping abreast of major community events, organizing public health fairs, handling public relations with the local newspaper, and dealing with disgruntled patients.

From someone in Mr. Keller's position, a small town can seem like Peyton Place at times. The sordid loosely guarded secrets and other sources of controversy in his town include a doctor whose license was suspended because of a sexual harassment complaint, a woman who rescinded a sexual harassment complaint after it was determined that the complaint was likely to be proven bogus, a newspaper editor who hobnobbed with a doctor at Alcoholics Anonymous meetings and learned things that should not have been disclosed, news that should have been published that was not, and nasty rivalries among doctors and between clinics. For Mr. Keller, it is all in a day's work to deal with these issues. In fact, he felt that his service to the community consisted of not only doing his job well at the clinic but also smoothing over local conflicts.

Despite all the unpleasantness, life in a small town can be quite accommodating to someone in a management position like Mr. Keller. He could lose his job if some scandal turned on him. But he is good with people, enjoys the local give-and-take, and knows how to keep his head down when necessary. He says he might consider running for the county commission someday because it seldom deals with anything controversial. He would not run for the school board because it is always embroiled in controversy. He knows his views would be liberal enough to get him into hot water with conservatives. If he wants to let his hair down, eat a nice steak, and drink a few more beers than he should, he goes to another town to do it. Meanwhile, he figures a nine- or ten-hour day at the clinic is not a bad way to earn a good living. Housing is cheap. He has a five-minute commute. He still has plenty of time for golf and softball.

The service class in small towns is increasingly supported through government programs, subsidies, and transfer payments. This is certainly true for health workers, who depend heavily on patients who receive government-subsidized retirement and welfare benefits. Transfer payments that contribute to the life of small towns include everything from farm subsidies to Social Security and Medicare to park services and pollution management. County seat towns have been the main beneficiaries of these programs. County offices typically include a register of deeds, a county clerk, and often a county supervisor or manager as well as an elected council. Many counties include an economic development specialist and most include a county superintendent of schools. In farming districts, counties usually include a county extension agent who works with farmers on soil conservation programs and supervises federal farm-subsidy payments.[12] These agents are an important part of the service class.

Megan Clarke is the county extension agent in a rural county of eight thousand people, and nearly as many cows and pigs. Agriculture is as key as it ever was, but the work of an extension agent now includes advising nonfarm residents about lawns, gardens, bushes, shrubs, and potted plants, and providing information about nutrition, organic foods, pollution, and pesticides. Ms. Clarke lives in the county seat, a town of thirty-three hundred. She earned an undergraduate degree from the state's agricultural college, majoring in agricultural education, and a master's degree in agronomy. She taught high school biology and general science for two years, and now, at age thirty, has been at the extension job for five years. She is the main conduit through which the latest developments in scientific agriculture flow to and from the local community. She handles everything from financial questions about lease agreements to technical questions about planting dates, pesticides, fertilizers, seed varieties, and expected crop yields.

Ms. Clarke says a typical day begins with opening the mail, checking email, and reading the local newspaper in print or online to get a quick overview of any developments in the community she should know about. Those might range from weather forecasts to reports of storm damage to announcements of a farm sale or civic event. Much of her day is then spent answering questions from walk-ins or by telephone, and making two or three site visits to farms where her expertise about weed control, erosion, crops, or livestock is needed. She conducts her own research as well, usually in the late afternoons. Lately she has been working on a potassium deficiency problem in no-till soybeans comparing results in three test plots. Because of the wide range of scientific issues that come up, she consults frequently by email and in person with experts at the agricultural college as well as test stations around the state.

Besides providing her technical expertise, Ms. Clarke also plays a crucial public relations role in the community. Much of the work of planning the annual county fair falls on her shoulders. She has one or two evening meetings a week, which range from speaking at a 4-H club event to appearing at a county commissioners hearing to hosting a demonstration about homegrown food. Although her primary constituents are farmers, she works closely with many townspeople in her area. Many residents have gardens or want advice about their lawns and shrubs, some have children in the 4-H, and all—she hopes—are interested in healthy food.

"I really get a big boost from working with homeowners and farmers," she comments. "I like to be able to take a situation where they are kind of at their wits end and don't know what to do next, and help them reason it through using the research-based information that's available." She says many times there are no easy or straightforward solutions. But usually some next steps that can be implemented come out of the conversations. "If I have shared with them something that they hadn't thought about before and are willing to try, even if it doesn't always work the first time around, then that makes me feel like I'm having a success in my community."

Those within the service class vary in the degree to which they can be said to have chosen to live where they do. On the one hand, a person like Mr. Parsons was not making it in farming and wound up in a small town partly because he preferred that size community, but mainly because the job was available and housing was affordable. Ms. Clarke, in contrast, could have majored in anything in college and likely have opted for a career best pursued in a city. But she is an example of someone whose love for the land was so strong that it guided her into a career in which she could do a lot of what farming involves without actually having to farm. She grew up on a cattle ranch twenty miles from the nearest town. She loved living in the country and following her dad around as he worked with the livestock. Her parents were college educated, and she expected to go to college as well. In high school, however, she planned to study in college to become a teacher. She dreamed of marrying a farmer and living on a farm. She knew she did not have the capital to become a farmer herself. So being a farmer's wife and having teacher training that she could use in any rural community was her goal. She even bet one of her high school teachers that she would be living on a farm in a few years. As her thinking matured, she realized she could combine her interests in teaching and agriculture, and in so doing, would be more in command of her own destiny rather than needing to marry Mr. Right. When she did find Mr. Right, he was not a farmer or even from a farm background. Yet her plan to do something in agriculture has been realized. "Ultimately, things aren't that much different from what I expected," she notes.

The service class also typically includes some of the established business owners who operate stores on Main Street that have been there for years. Other than the bankers, though, these merchants in many of the smaller towns have seen their ranks seriously diminished in recent decades. For food, clothing, furniture, appliances, and most durable consumer goods, townspeople are willing to travel thirty or fifty miles to a larger area where shopping is more abundant and prices are lower. That leaves Main Street to the businesses that can stay afloat through consumer loyalty and the attraction of being local, and thus more convenient. At the high end, a few insurance agents, realtors, accountants and appraisers, pharmacists, and attorneys can find a local clientele. At the lower end, Main Street is most likely to include a hairdresser, coffee shop, and tavern, and be supplemented on the outskirts by fast-food franchises, pizza parlors, gas stations, and automobile repair shops.

Some of the farmers we met could reasonably be considered part of the service class as well. This was especially true of younger farmers with specialized college degrees in agriculture, agronomy, social science, economics, or business who rented enough land to have state-of-the-art equipment on loan from the bank, or who operated feedlots or poultry farms. They were among the few with farm backgrounds whose fathers or uncles had done well enough to pass a farm along to the next generation. Although their income depended on crops and livestock rather than a regular salary, they could almost be thought of as service professionals engaged in tending land, caring for animals, and producing food. Like many others in the service class, government programs, including government-subsidized crop insurance as well as government-mandated soil conservation and food safety standards, heavily influenced these farmers' work. The young farmers hedged against fluctuations in grain and livestock markets by trading in commodities futures. They timed the sale of commodities to produce a regular income. A typical day focused on monitoring carefully blended feed mixtures, inspecting sick cattle or hogs, checking soil samples for fertilizer and pesticide levels, reading the latest science reports and business forecasts, and supervising low-skilled workers who performed most of the manual tasks. One farmer we talked to had a global positioning system that guided his tractor through the field and automatically adjusted cultivation depths while he made business calls on his cell phone from the air-conditioned cab and did computer work on his laptop.

WAGEWORKERS

Small towns seldom have the large manufacturing plants found in most cities, but it is rare to find a small community devoid of workers employed at low to moderate hourly wages. Except in the smallest towns, it is possible to find small firms that manufacture such items as pallets, mops, brooms, wiring for computers, aircraft navigation components, or recreational vehicles. Other examples among the towns we studied include bank supply companies that print checks, telemarketing companies, insurance-claims-processing firms, biodiesel facilities, and metal-fabricating plants for steel and aluminum roofs. In towns of fifteen hundred to three thousand residents, a typical plant of this kind might employ between twenty-five and a hundred workers. In addition, wageworkers include residents employed in meat-processing plants, oil refineries, mines, and pipeline stations, at feedlots or on truck farms, in construction, and working as waitresses, cooks, school bus drivers, and janitors. On average, approximately 15 percent of the civilian labor force in small nonurban towns of twenty-five thousand people or less work in manufacturing, 8 percent work in construction, and 6 percent are employed in transportation occupations such as trucking and delivery services. Wageworkers in small towns also include many of the clerks and office assistants who work in retail stores and administrative agencies.[13]

Mr. Yeager and his wife, Brenda, live with their three children in a town of about twelve thousand people that became the location of a small oil refinery in the 1930s, and more recently has attracted several manufacturing firms because of its cheap labor supply and proximity to an interstate highway. The Yeagers' home is a comfortable three-bedroom, two-car garage house in a quiet section of town that was added in the early 1970s. It is heavily mortgaged, but if they were to sell it, the price would be slightly above the median value of housing in the community. He is a crew chief at a factory that manufactures machinery and light equipment. She has worked until recently as a dental assistant. After high school, Mr. Yeager took classes at a technical school, where he specialized in automobile collision repair. He did body repair and painting for eight years before switching to his present job, which he has held for nine years. He commutes twenty-five miles each way to work. Mrs. Yeager was commuting thirty, but has recently quit because gas, automobile maintenance, and child care are costing more than she was earning.

The Yeagers are typical of small-town wageworkers in some respects and atypical in others. The factory where he works is one of the few left in their area and was purchased a few years ago by a company in Finland that also has plants in Brazil. It is a nonunion plant and wages are low, but several new product lines in recent years have resulted in steady employment. Mr. Yeager gets up at 3:30 or 4:00 every morning, starts his shift at 5:00 a.m., and works until 3:30 p.m. It is a good schedule because he can be home during the late afternoon and evening hours when his children are at home too. He feels fortunate because manufacturing jobs in the area are rare. One plant recently closed. He says he could earn more if he worked a swing shift, rotating days and nights, but he considers being with his family more important.

The Yeagers' commute is increasingly typical of wageworkers in small towns. They live in one community because they like the schools or because it is central to both spouses' jobs, but they are not well integrated into the town. In the Yeagers' case, they appreciate being able to send their children to a good Catholic school, but Mr. and Mrs. Yeager are too busy commuting to know many of their neighbors or be involved in community organizations. What they like best about their town is that it is quiet. What they do not like is that housing prices are about 50 percent higher than in some of the smaller towns nearby. In these ways, the Yeagers differ from small-town residents who live there because they have close friends and enjoy being well integrated into the community. They are also atypical in having relatively well-paying jobs. He says he wishes he had gone to college, but was not able to afford it and figures it would not have helped him improve his finances anyway.

Down the scale a notch and more typical of modest-income wageworkers in small towns is Gail Saunders, a thirty-year-old mother of two whose husband, Don, works in construction. They live in a town of fifteen hundred people that has declined by about a third since 1980. She finished a year of junior college before they got married. Her husband began working full-time right after high school. For several years, they lived in another state where he was able to find employment as a roustabout for an oil-drilling company, and she worked at whatever she could find. That included jobs at casinos, hotels, and restaurants as well as in telemarketing.

For a while the Saunders lived in a town of fifty thousand near a city. Construction was booming, but housing was expensive. During an economic downturn, they found themselves falling behind on bills, and so decided to move back to the small town where Mrs. Saunders had been raised and near where her parents owned a farm. Her husband drives thirty to fifty miles each way to and from construction jobs in the area. She worked briefly as a waitress, then as a clerk in one of the county offices, and most recently as a teacher's aide at the school.

Mrs. Saunders says that while growing up, she always imagined she would live in a city. She never thought she would return to her hometown. But it has been nice to be near her parents. Her mother helps with the children. Finances are tight. Mrs. Saunders says a lot of their bills are on payment plans because her husband's income varies from week to week and month to month. Their biggest expense is the payments on her husband's truck along with the gas and maintenance it requires for his daily commute. Still, housing is cheap and life is simple. She enjoys the children she works with at the school and has time to help with the annual 4-H club's fair.

Then there are the wageworkers who have chosen to stay in their hometowns for one reason or another, even though they might be better off financially in a larger place. Unlike the Saunders, they have not tried living in a city, and have not been forced to live in a small town because of job loss or financial difficulties. They are perhaps uncertain about what they want in life, lack ambition, or want to be helpful to their parents.

Sam Ferguson was twenty-seven when we met him at his home in a town of three thousand. The town has a Main Street with an antique store, a pizza parlor, a post office, and a few other stores. At one edge of town is a recently added modern gas station with a convenience store, a repair shop, and the trucking company where Mr. Ferguson works. He drives eighteen-wheelers delivering and picking up goods in thirty different states.

The reason he lives here is that this is where he grew up. His father farms some land in the area, and Mr. Ferguson helps with the farming when he is not on the road. As a boy he imagined himself becoming a fighter pilot, but as an adult he would prefer to farm instead of driving a truck. The reason, he says, is that he would like to be his own boss— which is part of what he likes about being on the road most of the time as well. Maybe someday when his father retires, he will get a chance to farm. Meanwhile he lives here in this small town, and other than the church he was raised in, he belongs to no community organizations and is away too much of the year to feel part of the activities that make up the town. Asked what he likes best about the community, he replies, "It is just my home."

Although manufacturing is not as common in small towns as it used to be, communities of no more than two thousand residents may have as many as a hundred workers in manufacturing jobs, while larger communities have considerably more.[14] Because of that history, residents frequently argue that the future of their town rests on being able to attract a new manufacturing plant of some kind. But the chances of that happening are not good. If it does, it may not spell success either. Chances are, the firm will be a nonunion plant and will hire only a small number of employees. In one of the communities we studied, for example, there had been a cigarette lighter plant for some years. The pay was $6.50 an hour at a time when jobs in construction were paying twice that much. "Do you think we can compete with China?" a community development specialist asked. "Manufacturing is not the answer. It's not going to be the union manufacturing jobs that our grandparents knew about." And yet when he was pressed to say what might take the place of these jobs, he was at a loss. Perhaps the community could attract low-income retirees. Or revitalize the dairy business. Those too, however, would provide only a few low-paying jobs.

In other towns, community leaders described a class of people they called the working poor. Not all of the working poor were wageworkers. Some were small farmers and business owners whose incomes had never been high, and were now depressed because of weak crop and livestock markets, lost jobs in mining and manufacturing, and declining populations. The working poor included men and women earning low hourly wages in fast-food businesses, as farm and construction laborers, and doing office assistant work. In many cases, they did not have health insurance or retirement plans. Some were living in homes that were in bad repair or had been condemned. Others were living in aging mobile homes or flood zones.[15]

PENSIONERS

Pensioners are another identifiable category of residents in small towns. They are usually older and are retired or semiretired, and for this reason exhibit a different lifestyle and have different needs from those who work full-time. In many small towns, older residents make up a larger share of the population than would be true in most cities and suburbs (as shown in figure 2.2).[16] There are of course exceptions. In fact, the percentage of residents age sixty-five and older in more than three thousand small non-urban towns—approximately 20 percent of all such communities—is actually the same or lower than in large cities. But with these exceptions, older residents generally constitute a distinct and important group in small towns. They may have lived in their town all their lives, be intensely loyal to it, have children or grandchildren in the area, and expect to stay until they die. The relatively slow pace and inexpensive housing in small towns suit them. In other cases, they may have moved to a smaller community after having lived in a city or suburb in order to experience these benefits. They vary considerably in their standard of living, ranging from those who live comfortably because of retirement savings and investment incomes, to those who exist on meager Social Security checks.

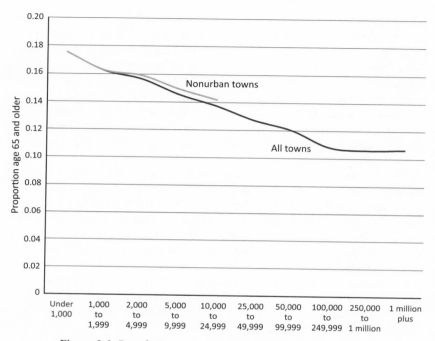

Figure 2.2 Population age sixty-five and older by town size

George Ainsley and his wife, Mary, live in a town of sixty-five hundred that derives most of its income from farming and the petroleum industry. The population is about 10 percent smaller than it was in 1970, but about the same as it was in 1940. Mr. Ainsley is seventy-five, retired, and suffers from Parkinson's disease. He is the fourth generation of his family to make his home here. One of his uncles still farms in the area.

When Mr. Ainsley was growing up he worked on his uncle's farm, played basketball, and imagined himself becoming a coach someday. After high school, he took some bookkeeping courses at the local junior college and decided he was good enough at it to think about accounting as a career. He went off to a college, which was in a city about eighty miles away, and majored in accounting. His farmwork in high school helped him land a job in the finance department of a government farm credit office in that city. But Mr. Ainsley's dream was to live in a smaller town. He earned a license as a certified public accountant and returned to his home community. Eventually the work became too demanding and began to destroy his personal life. He quit doing public accounting, worked for a while at the junior college, and then found an administrative job for a government bureau that had an office in his town.

With Social Security and the savings he put away while he was employed, Mr. Ainsley says he and his wife are able to live pretty comfortably. It helps that his wife owns some land. They live about a mile from the center of town near a golf course. Mr. Ainsley enjoys eating breakfast at McDonald's, runs a few errands in the mornings downtown, and when the weather cooperates, plays golf in the afternoon. His skills in accounting keep him busy the rest of the time. He keeps the books for one of the community's volunteer organizations and serves as treasurer at his church.

"We have a pretty unique community," Mr. Ainsley says. "It's a division point for the railroad. We have a junior college. We have a great hospital and some good doctors. We have a nice downtown area, and it's easy to get around, and you know most of the people. We don't have a lot of crime or traffic." For him and his wife, the town is just the right size. It has the services they need, including doctors who come out once a week from the city. And as much as Mr. Ainsley likes having people around, it is the fact that there are not more of them that matters just as much. "In the cities," he remarks, "you have to fight for a tee time at the golf course. Maybe get up at four o'clock in the morning. Here, you jump on the course and play nine holes, and probably do not see anybody."

Older couples like the Ainsleys live where they do because they know people, do not mind eating at McDonald's, and enjoy amenities that they could just as well find in a city or suburb, but can participate in less expensively and more easily in a small place. Other pensioners are oriented more toward the land, even though they may live in or near a small town. They may appreciate having friends and family in the community, but it is the chance to do some hobby farming and have a garden or backyard workshop that is most appealing. An example is John and Katherine Bradford, a couple in their late sixties. They live just outside a town of six hundred populated mostly by other retirees. This is Mrs. Bradford's hometown. She says her family has lived here for seven generations. Mr. Bradford is a newcomer. He has lived here only for forty years. He grew up in a larger community 125 miles away, moving here to take a job as a high school teacher.

The Bradfords are not rich, but they live comfortably. During the summers when he was not teaching, Mr. Bradford built houses and saved enough money to purchase the small farm they live on now. He grew up on a farm, hating every minute of it. The old tractor his father owned never ran well, and his parents made him do chores before school and every evening. He envied schoolmates who lived in town. But after going away to college and working for several years as a teacher, he missed the farm. He would rather have turned full-time to farming instead of teaching, yet there was no way he could afford the land and equipment he would have needed. So he settled for a few acres with a barn where he could raise a few cows and have a garden. Mrs. Bradford had a little store in town. Her dad was a cowboy. Eventually she inherited some land, when her father died. One of their sons farms the land. Between Mr. Bradford's pension from teaching and some income she receives from the land she inherited, they pay their bills and have enough money to pursue their hobbies.

People like the Bradfords would never leave the small community they call home. Being a teacher in a small town, Mr. Bradford knows everyone. He was also a county commissioner for nearly a decade. Having run a store, Mrs. Bradford knows everyone as well. They mostly enjoy having a barn with a few cows and lots of cats. Mr. Bradford has nearly lost the use of one of his legs. So he has difficulty getting around. Driving is hard and he doesn't like to travel. Mrs. Bradford does. She drives several hundred miles to visit children and grandchildren. Her hobby is gardening and painting china. She goes to conventions in big cities around the country where hand-painted china is displayed and classes are given. As small as their town is, they feel closely connected to the rest of the world. That sense of connection has increased in recent years. Every evening they read and send emails. They have family and friends all over the world.

Although the Ainsleys and Bradfords lived in their towns before they retired, they are similar to a small but growing number of people who have lived elsewhere, usually in cities or suburbs, and then move to a smaller community to retire because housing is cheaper and life is simpler. A community leader we talked to in a town of only a thousand that was two hours from a metropolitan area said this was increasingly true in his town. "We have a number of retirees who have come from larger communities and are financially comfortable, or at least aren't hurting for money," he said. "You can buy a fixer-upper in this town for under twenty thousand dollars, a decent house for fifty thousand, and a really nice house for under a hundred thousand." Those people sometimes sold their home in the city for three hundred thousand dollars and invested the difference. But there were retired people in that community and many others like it who were struggling. For them, staying in a small town was what made it possible to meet their expenses at all.

Mr. and Mrs. Ted Dallek are an example of an elderly couple that can barely survive on their subsistence income. They live in an unincorporated town that consists only of a paved highway, railroad crossing, and several old buildings that once served as the town's stores, but long ago were turned into garages and storage sheds for the few people who remain here. Grass grows between the railroad ties because the train no longer comes. A few rusted farm implements lie in the weeds behind one of the storage sheds.

The Dalleks lived in a different state for more than half a century. He served in the Korean War right out of high school and then worked as a farm laborer for several years. After that he purchased a small hardware store, got married, and raised two children. Mrs. Dallek helped in the store, mothered the children, and eventually got a part-time job caring for the elderly at a nursing home. By the early 1970s, competition from chain discount stores had become intense and the Dalleks had lost most of the money they had invested in the hardware store.

Their daughter lived near their present location, so the Dalleks decided to move closer to her. Mr. Dallek took an hourly job at a small sheet-metal-fabricating plant eleven miles away. They put a down payment on the house in this unincorporated town because it was all they could afford and because it had a big backyard. With his income and her work at a retirement home, they were able to pay off the mortgage. He has a woodworking shop, and they enjoy growing apples and pears in their backyard. They have few expenses, do not travel, and still own the small black-and-white television set they purchased decades ago. There is a town of seventeen thousand six miles away that has all the medical services and stores they need. Their daughter looks after them when they need help. At eighty-seven, Mr. Dallek says the past decade has been the best time of his life. He explains that they will be OK until one of them goes to a nursing home. At that point, they will have nothing.

Like the Dalleks, many of the older people who live in small towns are not dependent solely on Social Security or pensions from previous employment. They have children who send them money, or help in small ways with transportation and home repair. Sometimes they continue to work at part-time jobs or operate small businesses well past the normal age of retirement. They hang on to the business as long as their health permits. It supplements their income and gives them something to do.

Dorothy Martin is a seventy-year-old widow who lives in a riverfront town of nine hundred. Her husband died eight years ago. She received Social Security as his survivor and now that she is seventy draws her own Social Security. She grew up in this town, raised by grandparents who owned a farm in the area. After high school she took a short business course and moved away to a large city, where she got an office job working for an insurance company. It was there that she met her husband, who worked in retail sales.

In their early forties, the Martins decided they wanted a slower pace of life where the cost of living was less expensive. They had tried running a lamp store for about a year and were having financial difficulties, but they both enjoyed having a business of their own. Mrs. Martin had never thought about returning to her hometown, but she had a brother there and through him had kept up on news from the community. She learned that a five-and-dime store had closed recently, and the townspeople were hoping someone would come and reopen it. She and her husband decided to try it. The town's population was declining and other stores went out of business, yet they managed to keep afloat. At seventy, she still has the store. She has tried to sell it, but nobody wants it. It gives her something to do and helps with her bills. She figures as long as her health permits, she will keep running the business.

Pensioners also include the elderly poor who are nearly destitute, such as widows, widowers, or couples who have never owned enough land to break even or a business that earned enough to set aside money for retirement. They have worked for an hourly wage most of their lives and now are faced with medical bills. If they are a couple, and one is younger or healthier than the other, the younger or healthier person may continue to work at odd jobs or part-time. They cannot afford to move because their home, if they own it, is worth little or because they could not afford an assisted living facility in a larger place. They get by on Social Security and Medicaid along with help from their neighbors. If they are fortunate, some of their family still live in the area, and can help with transportation and home repairs. Others are less fortunate. Their savings have dwindled dramatically because of reverses in the economy. Perhaps they expected to work longer, but lost their jobs as they neared retirement, or lost their pensions or health care. If they have lived long enough, they might have depleted their savings.

Mr. Ainsley says there are a lot of people like this in his community of sixty-five hundred, where there have never been many high-paying jobs. People work at a low hourly rate and often have a pretty hard time of it, he says. He mentions an elderly couple he sees when he eats breakfast at McDonald's. "He's up in the nineties, and she's in her late eighties. I know they have a difficult time. They drive an old beat-up car and they've rented their house all their lives. They were never able to accumulate much. Somebody said that their kids send them some money every month to where they can go out and eat."

Another couple we talked to, Myron and Frieda Epworth, live in a town of nine hundred people. He is sixty-nine, and she is sixty-five. They live in a small farmhouse on the edge of town. Their oldest son and his wife live across the road. Mr. Epworth's father died when Mr. Epworth was seventeen. Mr. Epworth quit school and took over the farming as best he could at that point with help from an uncle who lived nearby. Only fifty acres of the land could be tilled for crops, so the farm income came mostly from hogs and cows. It was never enough to cover the mortgage, and thus Mr. Epworth worked during the week at whatever hourly jobs he could find. He worked as a day laborer at the grain elevator, ran a truck at the quarry, and for many years worked as a janitor at the local nursing home. Mrs. Epworth, whose education also stopped with high school, worked as a nurse's aide and filled in for a few years as the local social services director before her lack of training disqualified her from retaining the job. She took several different part-time jobs doing office work and as a private-duty nurse's aide, and for the past decade has been the dispatcher at the sheriff's office.

By almost any standard, the Epworth's are among the elderly poor. Mr. Epworth's income is seven hundred dollars a month from Social Security. He is no longer able to work as a janitor, so spends his time puttering in the yard and is essentially retired. Mrs. Epworth earns eight dollars an hour from her job. She works twelve-hour shifts. She enjoys the work, but finds it increasingly difficult at her age and only keeps at it because they need the money. She drives a car they bought used for two hundred dollars fifteen years ago. He drives a thirty-five-year-old pickup. "If you sit on the passenger side," she says, "you have to be careful where you put your feet because you might be acting as a brake."

Marks of Distinction

Much of what people say about their towns, as we will see in the next chapter, suggests that people get along well with one another, and indeed, there is plenty of reason to believe that many aspects of small-town life do serve well to strengthen communities. Because neighborliness and community service are such vital elements of town life, we need to pause briefly at this point to note that social distinctions not only exist but also that these distinctions are sources of misgiving. This is especially true of attitudes among middle- and working-class townspeople toward the very rich and very poor. In a hill town of thirty-six hundred where the median household income was only fifteen thousand dollars, for example, a life-long resident who worked at the bank told us that two local families seemed to own most of the rental properties in the area and had enough money to go on vacation whenever they felt like it. Residents criticized these families, she said, with remarks such as "Their money is just because of their parents" and "They think they're big stuff." A county supervisor in a small rural town on the West Coast summarized a similarly negative attitude toward rich families in her community by describing them as people with "toys"—"nice toys, airplanes, boats, race cars, summer homes." We heard complaints in small towns with declining populations that it was the landed gentry who were responsible for the community's downfall. "All we have left here are the rich," a man in a town of little over a hundred griped, referring to "massive landowners." He said "they won't tell you they are rich" but they are. In another small community, a longtime resident complained that "the have's pretty much do what they want, whether it is for the good or not."

Not surprisingly, the gentry in small towns are sensitive to these criticisms, and sometimes try to hide their wealth by living below their means or at least refraining from ostentatious conspicuous consumption. Mr. Janssen, for example, drives a weathered pickup truck instead of purchasing a new one. The Janssens could easily afford a more luxurious home. A large landowner in another community says, "A BMW out here sticks out like a sore thumb. If somebody is driving a Cadillac, well, Jimminy Christmas, they've got their nose in the air! I drive a Chevrolet." The doctor's wife I mentioned who lives near the ninth green of the local golf course says they never owned a boat or purchased anything very expensive, but she knows there have been criticisms. "If we got something new, it might be because [my husband] had to admit a patient and charge. That's where we got our money. But he never overcharged. Those stories aren't true."

Generational misgivings are evident, too. Usually the elderly are objects of veneration, as demonstrated in comments about how self-sufficient they are and how they may have endured hardship as children of early settlers. Less favorable sentiments emerge, though, in remarks like this one from a thirty-year-old: "Seventy percent of the people in our town are elderly. They like it here. They can be eighty years old and unable to see, but they still drive their cars. The rest of us have to swerve out of their way." There are equally negative comments from elderly people about the younger generation. Typical complaints focus on young people not having good morals as well as being too busy or materialistic to help with community projects. The reason the community is not prospering, elderly residents sometimes say, is that younger people are no longer willing to work hard. "They just want everything to fall into their lap."

As between the service class and wageworkers, the distinction rests principally with having or not having been to college. Longtime residents suggest that this distinction is growing wider. "I had a lot of friends who chose not to go to college when they got out of high school," a man in his sixties says. "They went to work in manufacturing or something like that. They have done OK." But now, he explains, things are different. "That person is going to be lucky if he works for a nine or ten dollar an hour job. And ten years from now, he'll be getting only twelve or thirteen dollars an hour. He has nothing to look forward to." In contrast, someone with a college education has a more promising future. "There's a pretty big divide there," the man notes. "If you have a college degree, you can at least try to impress people with that fact." In short, there is a perceived difference in current income, but even more so in one's prospects for the future. A service worker can look ahead, expecting to move up and earn

Profile: Wellsville, New York

Wellsville, New York, is a village of forty-six hundred nestled in a valley along the Genesee River eighty-five miles southeast of Buffalo. A visitor here would observe aging storefronts near the town center, some of them now vacant, and quiet tree-lined streets, vivid with color in the fall. An observer would also witness the inevitable diversity that exists in towns like these, most noticeably in differences between the modest frame houses along Broad Street that cost less than fifty thousand dollars and the newer brick ones at the northern edge of town and across the river to the south that cost three times that much.

The index of household income diversity here is exactly the same as the national average for towns of this size. The probability of any two households falling into different income categories is 96.5 percent. At the bottom, 868 of the town's 2,280 households exist on less than twenty thousand dollars a year, while at the top, 192 households enjoy incomes of more than a hundred thousand. Wellsville is also a town of considerable diversity in employment. A quarter of its population are retired, nearly one in ten are unemployed, and of those who are employed, one-third hold professional or managerial jobs, one-third are employed in service occupations, and one-third work at construction or manufacturing and similar hourly wage jobs.

What is it then that gives Wellsville residents a sense that they are all the same, or at least similar enough to feel that they are part of a community? One reason is simply the place: a physical location, compact in size, and set apart from the farms and hillsides that surround it. Rich or poor, Wellsvilleans share this space, walk the same sidewalks, and shop at the same stores.

Over the years, they have also filled the space with organizations that facilitate community interaction. First there were the churches, Catholic, Methodist, and a few others that have been here since the town was founded in the mid-1800s. Later came the American Legion, Rotary, and Veterans of Foreign Wars. More recently, townspeople have organized the Wellsville Community Kitchen to provide food for families in need, the Wellsville Volunteer Ambulance Corp, a hospital auxiliary, a rural health network, a council on alcoholism, and a baseball league. And each summer there is the Great Wellsville Balloon Rally, founded in 1993, that draws local residents and tourists together for a day of fun and festivity.

more, send their children to college, move if it becomes necessary, and count on a decent retirement plan. A wageworker may be fine in the short run, yet has a limited horizon that not only restricts future earnings but can also focus one's attention too much on the struggles of the moment. As one resident observed, "It's a tough lot."

Thorstein Veblen, who a century ago famously coined the term *conspicuous consumption*, argues that ostentatious displays of wealth—and even displays of middle-class as opposed to working-class status—are more likely to be evident in cities rather than in rural areas and small villages. The reason, he claims, is that in small communities "everybody's affairs, especially everybody's pecuniary status, are known to everybody else." In contrast, urban residents interact more among people they do not know. That encourages them to display their economic status through the goods they purchase and leisure activities in which they engage.[17]

Veblen's assertion is easy to misinterpret. He suggests that real differences exist between city folk and country folk. The former, he contends, spend more of their income on nonessential consumer goods and services, while the latter devote more of their earnings to necessary household items and savings. Veblen does not suggest, however, that status differences are absent in small towns or unimportant. Conspicuous consumption is less significant, he says, only because villagers already know who has more and who has less.

Political scientist Anne Norton has recently extended Veblen's argument by proposing that consumption has become, over the past century since Veblen, more important even than production as the major determinant of social class. Few Americans, she maintains, truly own capital assets of much value. Nearly everyone, men and women alike, is employed. Differences in earnings are evident mainly in what people buy. Norton argues that gender and race play crucial roles in perceptions of what is or is not legitimate to buy. Women are stereotypically known—and criticized—as shoppers. Racial and ethnic minorities as well as the poor are often accused of spending their money improperly and having bad taste.[18]

In a rare ethnographic study of small-town status distinctions, sociologist Carrie L. Yodanis paid special attention to the ways in which women in a small East Coast community demonstrated that they were of higher or lower status. Yodanis found that status was readily identified both in the consumption patterns that Veblen and Norton emphasize and the more subtle manifestations of taste and value that Bourdieu highlights. High status was evident largely through volunteer activities, such as participation on the library or historical society board, holding office in women's clubs, and donating time and money to craft fairs and bake sales. These activities showed that the women involved had free time or flexible schedules, and that they had the social skills necessary to organize and lead meetings. Middle-class women also did volunteer work, but more often did so as mothers or in caring roles, such as visiting the sick, and were known in the community as teachers, nurses, and shop owners. Working-class women seldom had as much time to participate in volunteer activities, did not dress as nicely, and drove older vehicles.[19]

In our interviews, similar marks of distinction were evident. Although the gentry may have tried to hide their wealth, they lived in better houses, drove more expensive vehicles, and went out of town more frequently for shopping trips and vacations. If there was a local newspaper, their leisure and leadership activities were often noted. Neighbors knew who was in the service class because they were their teachers, agricultural extension agents, registered nurses, bank officers, and store managers. In interviews, they usually reported having had conversations with their neighbors about experiences during college, college sports events that interested them, and what their college-trained children were doing. Those conversations as well as the jobs they held and volunteer work they did marked them as members of the service class. Wageworkers more generally discussed vocational and mechanical activities, such as the shed they had built in the backyard, the antique car they were repairing, the gardening they were doing, or the meals they had cooked. Like the Yeagers, they often worked long hours and commuted to work, which gave them less time to be involved in local volunteer activities.

One of the more interesting studies that additionally sheds light on status distinctions in small towns is a national survey in which interviewers who met with people in their homes were asked to rank the quality of each interviewee's house in comparison with other dwellings in the community. The interviewers were free to say that nearly all the houses were about the same, or rate some above average and others below average. The result is particularly interesting because townspeople say they frequently have little idea about one another's incomes or family finances, but are clearly aware of differences among homes. In communities established before modern zoning laws, a stately well-kept Victorian mansion may exist on the same block as a run-down bungalow. In other communities people talk about houses "on the wrong side of the tracks"—that is, "if we had a railroad track," as one man quipped—or residents distinguish places like "McMillan circle," "Country Club Estates," or "the new West end" from houses in the poorer sections of town. In the survey, interviewers ranked 2 percent of homes in small towns "far above average" compared to other homes in the community, 20 percent "above average," 57 percent "average," 18 percent "below average," and 3 percent "far below average." There was as much diversity in small towns as there was

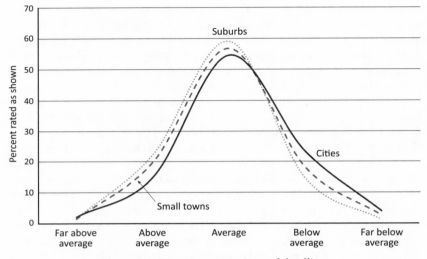

Figure 2.3 Interviewers' ratings of dwellings

in cities and suburbs (as shown in figure 2.3). In other words, the results confirmed that status differences are evident in easily perceived variations in quality of housing.

But this study also suggested a reason why residents of small towns feel an affinity with one another, sometimes even to the point of reckoning that everyone is nearly the same. Level of education is one of the important ways in which people in small towns differ from one another because occupations, lifestyles, and interests vary accordingly. In large metropolitan areas, having a college degree is considerably more common among people who live in better homes than among people who live in homes of lower quality: 48 percent of metropolitan residents who lived in "far above average" homes had college degrees, while only 4 percent of those in "far below average" homes did—a difference of 44 percentage points. In contrast, the differences were not as great in small towns. Thirty percent of those whose homes were "far above average" had college degrees, compared with 6 percent of those whose homes were "far below average"—a difference of only 24 percentage points. In short, the status differences townspeople would have known about because of the quality of their houses were not as likely as in cities to also reflect differences in education-based lifestyles and interests.[20]

The other interesting result from the survey is from questions about membership in voluntary associations, such as parent–teacher associations, service clubs, farm organizations, fraternal associations, veterans groups, and churches. In small and large communities alike, people living in above average homes were more likely than those living in below average ones to hold membership in these organizations. But in small towns, those in above average homes were even more likely than their counterparts in large communities to be members of most kinds of community organizations— consistent with examples like Janssen, Schnell, and Grimshaw all actively contributing to their towns through community organizations.[21] In other words, high social status in small towns carried stronger expectations about contributing to the community through volunteer work.

The larger story from talking with people in small towns is that the status distinctions are quite real, and yet grounded in perceptions that reflect expected contributions to the community. The gentry are expected to fulfill their community obligations by chairing committees at church, serving on the library board, showing up regularly at the Kiwanis and Lions clubs, and perhaps standing for election as a town or county commissioner. The service class is not a bland category of managers and businesspeople but instead is defined by occupations locally considered to be of benefit to the community: teachers, health workers, accountants, bank employees, retail store owners, and the like. Members of the service class are visible to the community as a result of the work they do. Wageworkers are less visible to the community, but are considered good citizens as long as they hold steady jobs, care for their children, keep up their property, and behave as good neighbors. Pensioners have free time and energy, depending on their health, to serve in community organizations and help their immediate neighbors. These at least are the expectations, whether they are always realized or not.

I was struck with the extent to which these expectations are embedded in everyday life as I listened to Felix Helder describe his seaport community of six thousand. The town had been populated by shipbuilders early in its history, had served as a fishing village and small naval post over the years, and was now mostly dependent on seasonal revenue from tourists. Despite the changes it had experienced, the community was unique, according to Mr. Helder, in that it bred hardy people who were especially devoted to helping one another. I discounted some of what he said; he was the town manager, and his descriptions of the town were almost too good to be true. And yet there was a grain of truth in how he said people should behave in a town like his. "You go into the local coffee shop and have your coffee. The richest person in town could be on one side of you and the poorest on the other side. It doesn't mean you are going to their house for dinner on Saturday night, but you know who everybody is." That awareness, he felt, makes it more likely that people's needs in the community will be known. For example, "you know if someone needs oil in their tank."[22]

I kept thinking about Mr. Helder's remark for a long time. Something about it bothered me. If you went to the local café and the richest person in town was sitting there, wouldn't you simply be *more* aware of social differences? Wouldn't your experience be like that of the proverbial peasant family happily living in your hut until the wealthy landowner built a mansion next door? What Mr. Helder was trying to say, I think, is that it is the personal encounter in the restaurant that matters. Being there together and knowing each other by name makes it impossible to be rude or indifferent—perhaps not impossible but at least awkward. You speak. You say hello. You find something to talk about that you have in common, such as the weather, a football game, or the family down the road whose mother died.

Beyond the norms that influence individual behavior in these ways, there are also social mechanisms that help to promote the collective well-being of the community. In one of the communities we studied, for instance, a manufacturing plant had recently relocated to another country, a school had closed, low-income families were suffering from unemployment, and wages were too low to cover the rising costs of health insurance and transportation. But there was an infrastructure in place of elected and appointed officials along with lay volunteers who persuaded another company to take over the abandoned plant and create new jobs. One of the wealthy families in the community purchased the vacant school and developed plans to reopen it as a learning center. And the United Way and local churches stepped up their programs to provide food. Nothing truly overcame the problems that the community was experiencing, but the efforts helped. When a few jobs became available, applicants were screened in terms of needs as well as skills. Because the town was small enough (about forty-five hundred), people had a sense of who was helping and who needed help.

The system of implicit norms and social networks in which small town status distinctions are embedded works reasonably well at persuading townspeople that everyone has something to contribute. Few townspeople actually say, as earlier studies suggested, that everyone is exactly the same or they are all equal. What they do say, in Mr. Parker's words, is that you have to deal with everybody. That is literally true in his case because of the hardware store that he and his wife operate. For most townspeople it is only true metaphorically. You have to deal with everybody, as one community leader explains, because "we are very interdependent." People fulfill the various roles that contribute to their collective well-being. This is one meaning of community.

- 3 -

Going to Be Buried Right Here
How Residents View Their Towns

"OH, WE'VE TALKED ABOUT MOVING SOMEPLACE WHERE IT'S warmer or to a larger community. But we have always said no to that. We were born here. Even our kids have stayed in the area. We're going to be buried right here in this local cemetery and we're very comfortable with that." It just made sense to this man that his midwestern community of fifteen hundred was where he was meant to be—now and forever. He and his wife were the sixth generation of their families to live here.

But is that typical? Certainly it is unusual in contemporary America to find anyone whose family has lived in the same small town for six generations. Even in small towns the average length of residence is only nineteen years, and one of every five residents has currently lived in their community for fewer than five years.[1] What about the typical resident who has resided in their town for only a generation or two? Or is a newcomer, or has lived elsewhere and moved back? How do they understand the choices they have made? What are their reasons for living where they do? What do their perceptions tell us about the changing meanings of community?

As I listened to people talking about their towns, I realized that many of the perceptions promulgated by television as well as in movies and books need to be examined more carefully. Some of the stereotypes about small towns are consistent with how people who live there think about their communities. They may perceive the pace of life to be slower, for example, or cherish the town because it reminds them of the warmth and security they experienced as children. But the specific attractions—and drawbacks—of small towns cannot be understood without listening closely to residents' descriptions.

From residents' accounts, we learn more precisely what it means when people say that the pace of life is slow. We see more clearly what counts as neighborliness, and why that is both an appealing part and a drawback of living in a small community. A person who anticipates being buried at the graveyard in their hometown is expressing something more than resignation. It is not surprising that people who have settled into a life in their community have many good things to say about that choice. And yet the firsthand remarks are surprisingly candid about what is not so desirable.

Perhaps because they fear civic loyalties are declining, social scientists have become increasingly interested in better understanding how communities function. Residents of small towns are keen observers of their communities, and frequently offer rich insights into the social relationships that strengthen—and at other times weaken—their ties with neighbors and fellow residents. We learn how networks govern what can and cannot be said, why newcomers feel uncomfortable, and what provides a sense of community spirit. To an outside observer, small towns may seem static, but a closer consideration shows how they are changing, and why some changes are welcomed more than others.

Ever present in residents' minds are comparisons between small towns and larger places. These comparisons are replete with information about the values Americans think can better be found in small communities than in metropolitan areas, and what they feel is being lost as more and more people live in cities. Urban residents provide insightful contrasts. Age-old distinctions between country and city are still very much alive. These distinctions, though, are continually adapting to new realities. Residents of small towns worry that their communities are losing timeworn values, while residents of suburbs and cities hope their communities can retain some of what was desirable in small towns.

More than a century ago, Tönnies, the German scholar whose discussion of the distinction between the terms *gemeinschaft* and *gesellschaft* has held continuing resonance among social scientists, argued that community that transcends kinship (a community of blood) should include a meaningful combination of place and spirit. Neighborhoods, villages, and towns typically involve both. Place implies proximity, and thus mutual familiarity among coresidents as well as common interests driven by their relationship to the natural and built environment. The "rooms and cellars and their furniture," "groups of buildings," and "the roads and streets between them," Tönnies wrote, provide a dwelling place that gives residents their "common habitation." Spirit inheres in common memories and mutual understanding, a kind of tacit consensus as well as repertoire of shared values that may at times involve something akin to worship or a sense of sacredness about the collectivity of which all are members.[2]

Tönnies's discussion remains a useful starting point for understanding the contemporary meanings of community in small-town America. Place and spirit are integrally connected. The fact that a small town seldom covers more than a few square miles means that residents not only live within close proximity of one another but also share a common visual horizon of natural topographic features, buildings, streets, and fields. Proximity influences time as well as space. Distances and temporal relations shrink. The spiritual connections that are forged through neighborly visits, looking after the safety of one another's children, shopping at the same stores, and participating in community events inscribe meanings into the commonly experienced environment. It is a circumscribed space with a name and identity. To be "buried right here" literally symbolizes the deep connection between place and spirit.

And yet community, even in the smallest towns, is never realized as an entirely self-contained enclosure. Residents participate in the wider world too, commuting, visiting, and vacationing. The consciousness of living in a small town is always divided between what is here now in the present and what lies elsewhere as well as beyond. For contemporary residents at least, the meaning of community is expressed in the language of choice. What an inhabitant prefers is an indication of how community is perceived and an expression in turn of how it is valued.

THE FAMILIARITY OF CHANGELESS PLACES

Ann Gautier lives in a town of four hundred that offers a beauty salon, tavern, American Legion post, post office, and not much else. The nearest city of any size is two hours away. Mrs. Gautier runs a farm supply store and teaches school part-time in another town during the winter months, which seem to last most of the year in her part of the country. Her husband died a few years ago, and none of her children live in the area. She has been thinking lately about her mother, who also died recently. It was her mother who encouraged her to live in a small town. Small towns were just healthier, her mother always told her, because the air was fresh, and you could buy meat and vegetables from local farms.

But Mrs. Gautier's mother also believed in seeing the world. Her mother and father traveled extensively, and on one occasion lived abroad for a year. The summer after high school Mrs. Gautier lived in Mexico and after that left her hometown for good to attend college in a city several hundred miles away. She did her practice teaching in the suburbs of a large city, and then applied far and wide for teaching jobs. There happened to be an opening in the town where she now lives. She was glad it was in a rural area where she could buy natural foods, like her mother advised, but was worried about not being accepted as a newcomer. Had it not been for meeting the man she married, she would likely have moved on.

Like Mrs. Gautier, hardly anybody we talked to indicated that they had no choice about where they lived or had never considered living elsewhere. They did acknowledge that their choices were guided by circumstances.

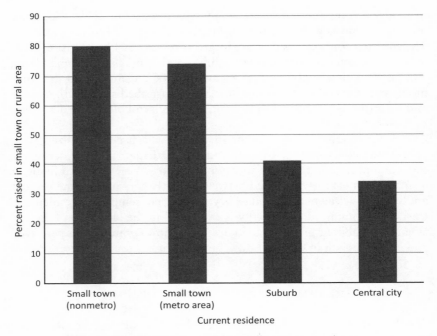

Figure 3.1 Residents raised in small town or rural area

They said they chose to live in a small town because they had enjoyed living in one as a child, felt close to their parents who still lived in a small town, had been financially dependent on their parents at some point in their adult lives, had not been successful or happy living in a city, or had married someone from a small town. Those who left the small town of their youth said they had always wanted to live in a city, liked to travel and see the world, were set on a career that required living in a larger place, had been bored growing up, did not like their classmates in school, or met and fell in love with someone from another place.

Comments like "to be honest, I came back after college and was bored," "I never kept in touch with any of my high school friends," "I always wanted to move to a city," and "my boyfriend wouldn't have been happy here" were typical of people who had grown up in small towns and left. One woman who had moved away, for example, was particularly candid about her hometown. "It was the same twenty people I went to school with from kindergarten until high school graduation. Looking back, even as a little kid, I didn't really have much in common with them."

It is not surprising that influences, such as childhood experiences, family crises, marriage, and jobs, shape people's preferences about where they live. National data show that one of the strongest determinants of where people live is where a person was raised. For example, four-fifths of the respondents in one survey who were currently living in a small nonmetropolitan town had grown up in a small town or rural area, compared with only two-fifths of those currently living in cities or suburbs (see figure 3.1).[3] Although respondents may have been raised in a different town from the one in which they currently live, these data suggest that a large majority of small-town residents live where they do because of circumstances during their youth that either reduced their opportunities to live elsewhere or positively encouraged them to remain in a small community (the large minority of urban and suburban residents who grew up in small towns and rural areas is also impressive). It is important to understand, though, that the people we interviewed talked freely about such background influences, because this information puts their comments about what they like or dislike about small towns into perspective.[4] The attractions are not principally the main reasons they live in a small town. Having chosen to live there because of circumstances, people point to these attractions as some of the benefits of their choice. It is, in effect, a matter of saying that one can be happy anywhere. These are the reasons to be happy in a small town.[5]

Small communities are often viewed by the people who live there as places that do not change much from one decade to the next. Towns may lose or gain population, but these shifts usually occur slowly. Among all nonmetropolitan towns with fewer than twenty-five thousand residents in 1980, for example, the majority were smaller three decades later, but only 18 percent lost population at a rate averaging more than 1 percent a year over the next quarter century, and only 20 percent gained population averaging more than 1 percent a year during that period.[6] Unless towns happen to be located near a rapidly expanding city, or in the path of a new airport or highway, residents' way of life is unlikely to be dramatically disrupted. For residents of rapidly growing cities and people who move around a lot, change is the spice of life. For people in small towns, just the opposite is generally the most compelling aspect of the community. They like the fact that things stay the same. As one of the town leaders we talked to noted, only half in jest: "There's a mural in city hall that got painted in 1900. Sometimes I look at that mural and I think there are a lot of people here who would like the town to remain exactly that way, just completely unchanged."

A case of someone who likes the changelessness of life is Mr. Parsons, the man we met in the last chapter who works at a bank in a town of six hundred and does hobby farming on the side. He says straight-out that he hates change. He would still be raising hogs on his father-in-law's farm if he hadn't been forced to pursue a different line of work. So living in a small town similar to the one near his childhood home has been to his liking. He enjoys tinkering with his old tractor as well as going to a little league game now and then better than traveling to someplace new. He loves the hilly wooded landscape surrounding the town. One of the best things about living here, he says, is the familiar smell of a farming community. "When they cut the hay, there's a smell that is just unreal," he observes. "It just gives you shivers." He likes the smell of cattle barns, straw, fresh paint, and even fly spray and manure.

This is an extreme example, but it is not that atypical of the way many townspeople describe their communities. They like the familiar sights, sounds, and smells of where they live. "It's the same talk, the same activities, the same festivals every year," explains a woman in her thirties who lives in a southern town of three thousand. "Everything's the same." That is how she likes it. Being a "creature of habit," "predictable," and wanting to know what's going to happen seems right to her.

"Oh, I'd really miss the familiar faces," a woman in a town of sixteen hundred replies, when asked if she has ever thought about moving away. The phrase "familiar faces" seems to have special meaning to her, more so than plain words such as friends or neighbors. "I love the smell of fresh dirt around here," a man in another small town remarks. The farms and fields give him a sense of security. Comments like "it's pretty stable here" and "we're not changing much" are common. Townspeople revel in the daily sameness of it all—seeing the same neighbors, living in the same house they lived in as a child, and enjoying the same landscape. "I'm looking out on a big lush green pasture with cattle grazing off in the background," a woman says, describing the view from her front window in a town of two hundred. "The only sound I'm hearing is the air conditioner running." Except for that, things are pretty much as they have been for two generations.

The perception that nothing ever changes in small towns is of course contradicted by the fact that things do change. Populations increase or decrease, people move away and newcomers arrive, stores close and others open. But even residents who acknowledge these changes—sometimes celebrating them and often bemoaning them—insist that they like the fact that things remain the same. What they mean is that life in a small town can be—indeed, has been for them—stable, at least compared with what they imagine city life to be. An older man who has lived all his life in a small community explains, for instance, that his brother moved to a city and made a lot of money. Yet his brother, the man says, has "traveled all over the country," lived in a number of different places, and gotten caught up in "the rat race." His brother's children are "very unsettled," he adds. They are latchkey kids. In this man's view, it is not just that cities change more than small towns but also that getting along in a city requires people themselves to change more frequently by moving around and thus becoming unsettled—to the detriment of their families.

This emphasis on stability is illustrated in a different way in the remarks of another man, a professor who teaches at a community college in a rapidly growing suburb of a large midwestern city but who grew up in a small town. He feels that unlike many of his suburban neighbors, he has been able to lead a stable family life, pointing to thirty years of marriage as proof. He says several of his closest friends have enjoyed stable lives as well and ventures that this is probably atypical of the larger metropolitan area. He attributes this stability to the fact that "they all came from environments like I did. They weren't real city dwellers. They were mostly from farmland backgrounds and small communities. They're more down to earth."

On the surface, the language townspeople use to depict the changelessness of their communities mostly suggests a sense of rootedness. Being down to earth means feeling grounded. Not traveling all over means staying in one place. Feeling settled is the opposite of being up in the air. These are the metaphors through which the attractions of being attached to a particular place are expressed. The language also emphasizes the advantages of familiarity. A person who lives in a small community knows it, and knows what to do and how to get around. That knowledge is the basis for a sense of personal security. It depends on a lack of change, but paradoxically can accommodate change to a degree. A person may never have had occasion to visit a resident on the other side of town or contact the local attorney, yet knows how to get there and probably knows someone else who has done so.

An interesting study by psychologists Walter Perrig and Walter Kintsch examined how this sense of familiarity may work. Subjects were presented with two different descriptions of a hypothetical small midwestern town called Baldwin. In one portrayal, which the psychologists called the Survey version, the town was described as it might appear on a map—for example, "The general store is on the southern end of Main Street" and "A few blocks north on Main there is the Lutheran Church on its east side." The other description was termed the Route version, and consisted of statements such as "Going left on Main after a few blocks you see the Lutheran Church on your right" and "Returning on Main Street to the other end, you come to the general store." Using various structured and open-ended measures, subjects' recall of the town was tested. The main result was that subjects' recollection was much better for the Route than for the Survey version.[7]

Why might this have been the case? One reason may have been that the Route version used more personal pronouns and therefore drew subjects into the picture more effectively than the other version did. The words invited them to identify with the places mentioned ("you see," "you come to," or "on your right") and described what to do ("drive east," "cross the river," or "come to the general store"). Although the subjects had never been there and the town did not exist, they could visualize themselves being part of it.

In real life, this is also what townspeople experience and what they imply in their descriptions of what they like about their community. They not only know where the Lutheran Church is located; they have walked or driven past it, have probably been inside or talked to someone who attended there, and they know how to get there. When people spoke about the hayfield south of town or hardware store that used to be on the corner, they could visualize themselves in the picture. It was easy to recall the hardware store even if it had been gone for years or even if they no longer lived in the town. This was the meaning of familiarity. Feeling at home in a community means in the first instance being an active participant in any description of it and knowing one's way around.

THE SLOW-PACED LIFE

Closely related to the perception that small towns offer changelessness and stability is the perception that life in small communities moves at a slower pace than anywhere else, and thus is more relaxed.[8] "The slower pace is quite an advantage," a man in a town of three hundred says. "It's restful, less distractive." "It's just a relaxed way of living for people," a shopkeeper who lives two blocks from his store in a town of a thousand remarks. Another man says he walks most mornings to the post office, which is just two blocks from his house, chats with a couple of neighbors along the way, and thinks to himself, "This is such a nice place to live." Yet another man, who lives in a town of six thousand, muses after a recent visit to Los Angeles, "I just didn't like the pace there. We're more laid back. Things are slower. You can take a breath here. In the big cities, you hardly ever seem to be able to take a breath."[9]

A resident of an even smaller town likewise voiced an almost-physiological response. With hardly any trees and situated on terrain flat as a pancake, the town gives her a sense of being able to see. She likes that because it helps her feel at peace with the world and herself. She says that when she lived for a few years in a city, she felt claustrophobic. "I felt like I couldn't see anything. I didn't know what was going on." For her, space and time are closely connected. The city was both crowded and frenetic. She simply experiences less anxiety in a smaller place. The smells that people associate with small towns clearly have a physiological basis, too.

In the same way that a person from a mill town may be reminded of home by the smell of sulfur in the air, a person like Parsons feels at home smelling cow barns and hayfields. Another man in a farming town says he loves driving past a freshly plowed field. It is the "smell of fresh ground," he says, that sticks in his mind.[10]

Emphasis on a slow-paced way of life can conjure up images of lazy, slow-witted people who get up late, spend their mornings drinking coffee with friends, and then take long naps during their afternoons. A woman we talked to in a larger community, for example, expressed this view in criticizing her mother-in-law, who the woman said lived in a small town where people gathered at the coffee shop every morning at 9:00 to share gossip, continued gossiping over lunch at 11:00, and returned at 3:00 p.m. for more of the same. Survey results sometimes reinforce these impressions. For instance, 95 percent of the residents of small nonmetropolitan towns in one survey described their communities as "comfortable," 92 percent said their communities were "quiet," only 18 percent said their communities were "exciting," and 38 percent admitted that their towns were "dull" and "boring."[11]

Researchers, noting that people often associate small towns and rural areas with a slower-paced life, have tried to determine if life actually is slower in these places. In a classic study, psychologists Marc H. Bornstein and Helen G. Bornstein found evidence that people walk faster in large cities than they do in small towns. The reason, the psychologists suggested, is that crowding, feelings of being somehow personally restricted in one's movements or the use of one's time, and increased social stimulation lead to a sense of overload in larger places that people try to adapt to by walking faster.[12]

Among several follow-up studies, psychologists Robert V. Levine and Ara Norenzayan conducted one of the most ambitious in thirty-one countries, and included observations of pedestrian velocity and the length of time it took postal clerks to fill a standard order for stamps. Undertaken only in large cities, the study did not include an adequate test of the effects of population size, but did suggest that individualism—as measured by a subjective assessment of the local culture—might be more prevalent in larger places and seemed to be associated with a faster pace of life.[13]

The most extensive research on walking speed and related measures that actually compared small towns and cities in the United States was published some years ago, and was based on relatively sparse observations of approximately two hundred people in six East Coast cities and about fifty residents of small towns in the vicinity of Ames, Iowa. It showed that people, on average, walked slower in the small towns than in the cities, and that post office and gas station transactions took longer in small towns than in cities.[14] While these results are suggestive, the lack of more recent research comparing residents in more towns and cities of course makes it difficult to draw broad generalizations.[15]

The other obvious weaknesses of these studies is that none of them asked subjects if they were aware of walking slower or conducting business transactions less rapidly than in other places, or if it mattered to them how quickly or slowly these activities occurred. There was no indication if these measures of pace were related to other possible sources of variation, such as subjects' age or occupation, or other uses of time, such as minutes spent in traffic or relaxing over a cup of coffee. Nor was there any evidence to suggest that residents who say they prefer a slower pace of life are thinking about how quickly or slowly people in their community walk.

Thus it is important to consider what people actually mean when they talk about enjoying the less frenetic pace of small-town life. The single theme that emerges repeatedly is the convenience of living in a community free of the complexities associated with large populations. As one man explains, "We don't have the burdens of living in a city." Or as the man who says the slow pace is "less distractive" mentions, "You don't have ambulances and emergency vehicles going by." "Not a lot of congestion," a neighbor of his adds, "not the problems you have in urban areas." These residents are rather pleased that there is not a single stoplight in the entire county. A woman who lives in a town of twenty thousand where the population has been growing and where there are numerous stoplights offers a similar view. She has lived in a city and currently works in a high-stress managerial job, so in noting the slow-paced life as an attraction of her town, she quickly adds that she is capable of dealing with a quicker tempo. What she likes is that living close to her work, having shops and basic services nearby, and not having to fight traffic every morning and evening all supply her with more time to relax. The slow pace literally gives her the chance to stop and chat with someone on the sidewalk, or wave to a neighbor from her car, whereas she figures in a city she would be too busy negotiating bumper-to-bumper traffic.

Almost more than anything else, it is the absence of traffic in small towns that serves as a metaphor of the slow-paced life. "Oh, today was very stressful," an old-timer in a town of six thousand likes to tell visitors from the city. "I had to wait for a car to go by before I could pull out of my driveway!" When people mention walking, it is not that a person is expected to walk slow or fast but rather that walking and not driving is possible. They may put more miles on their automobiles than someone in the city, especially if they commute from a small town to a city to work or shop. But being able to stroll down the sidewalk is a symbol of the carefree life. It means having to make fewer decisions, being less dependent on technology—"unplugged," as one woman put it. A project can unfold over a longer period. A person can take time getting somewhere.

Townspeople like these typically associate the slow pace of life with simplicity. They view small towns as places where the basic necessities of life can be attained without the hassles of large metropolitan areas. Going to the post office is not a half-hour drive through heavy traffic and another twenty-five minutes standing in line. That is the example given by a longtime resident of a town of ten thousand. "We get spoiled by the convenience of a small town," he observes. "We expect to drive right up to the front door and go in and be waited on immediately." Others speak of being able to walk to work in a few minutes or living close to their children's school. Still others mention safety, not meaning a low crime rate particularly, but instead less risk of being killed in heavy traffic on a major highway.

The common denominator in comments about the slow pace of small-town life, familiarity of a changeless ambience, and convenience of not having to wait in long lines is being in control. Community implies a social arrangement that helps people get along with daily tasks, much like a home does, as opposed to a large-scale social space in which everything is dauntingly complex. Small towns feel right to their residents because the size of the community is relatively free of confusion. Small towns are in this respect like an extended family that takes care of its children. Mildred Ferguson, a homemaker in her fifties who has lived in several different countries and in cities as well as in small towns, puts it well when asked what she likes about her current community of six hundred. "Oh, I don't know how to explain it," she replies, "but you can walk down the street and you don't have to worry about something happening." Or as Sharon Sandler, who lives in a coal-mining town of seven thousand and travels frequently, says in describing what she dislikes about being in a city, "I feel like a little fish in a huge pond, just swimming in circles, and I don't know what I'm doing, where I'm at, or what to do."

BACK IN THE DAY

For people who did not grow up in a small town but who have chosen to move to one, the attraction is often that small-town life reminds them of something pleasant from childhood. Their memory is of a simpler time that no longer exists in most places yet is still present, they believe, in smaller communities. "It's sort of like the neighborhood I grew up in the fifties," one woman who had been raised in a middle-class suburb of a large city and who now lives in a small town explains. The neighborhood she remembers was "trusting" and "comfortable." It seemed like a "big family." She recalls leaving home in the morning as a child on her bicycle, playing all day with friends, and roaming the neighborhood. The small town of a thousand people where she now lives is like that. "The world is just so troubled," she says. The small town gives her a "day-to-day haven in a very troubled world."

Other townspeople view their communities similarly. In a town of two thousand, a newcomer in his early forties says the community takes him back thirty years to his childhood home in a town of about the same size. "I went the other day to the little mom-and-pop movie theater on the corner. I thought how quaint. I haven't seen one of these since my childhood. It reminded me of my youth when everything was locally owned, when people were friendly and nice."[16]

Besides reminding them of their childhood, small towns where people have lived for generations also provide a tangible link with the past through the presence of those family members from previous generations. These are the "ghosts of place," as sociologist Michael Mayerfeld Bell has colorfully termed them. They inhabit the cemetery that is near enough to be visited often. The memory of their lives is tangibly associated with the field they farmed and stores where they shopped. Their presence is felt on Memorial Day and at funerals, when families gather at the cemetery where parents, grandparents, and great-grandparents are buried.[17]

There is more intergenerational mixing among the living as well. "We are pretty family oriented here," a woman in her twenties says of her community. "It is not uncommon to see three-generation families in this area. People make an effort to spend time together with their grandparents, grandkids, and parents." She comments that this is important to her because there are not a lot of people in the community her own age. She especially likes to sit with older people and hear their stories. A man in his fifties who is part of a multigenerational family echoes her sentiments. His grandfather came to town a century ago, his father still lives here, and his daughter and son-in-law do too. This is where "all my growing up memories" are, he says.

The following is another example.

"He just looked at me. He was wearing an old cowboy hat and jeans and so on. I noticed him when I was visiting my grandmother down the street at the nursing home. There was something familiar about him. I kept looking at him every time I would go. He would just be looking out the window, just staring out at the sunset. One day I said, 'Is your name Don Pedro Milagro?' "

This is Ramon Segundo explaining why he would never live anywhere else. His town is an arid place of five thousand not far from the Mexican border, with barely enough moisture to keep the mesquite trees that grow along the arroyo alive. Several of the ranchers irrigate a few acres to grow hay for their livestock. Mr. Segundo, now in his sixties, works for the sheriff's department. He has lived here his whole life.

"'Is your name Don Pedro Milagro?' I asked him a second time, thinking perhaps he was hard of hearing.

"'Who wants to know?' he replied. Of course we were talking in Spanish.

"'My name is Ramon Segundo and I think I know you. You look like Don Pedro Milagro. I have a good memory of him. You used to live on Walnut Street. I used to work in the fields.'

"During the roundup season, Don Pedro was a cowboy, but during the agricultural season he used to work in the fields. He had a prestigious job because he was older. He was the person who sharpened the tools. He got paid maybe ten cents more an hour than everybody else.

"'You're him, aren't you?' I said.

"'Yeah, but how'd you know?'

"It was the hat. You have to understand cowboys here. Their hats are like their fingerprints. The way they wear it, the headband, just old cowboy hats, get it?

"I told him my grandmother lived on Walnut Street. I used to visit her and watch him across the street.

"'You used to sit on the front steps of your house and you would braid horsehair into key chains. You wore your hat just like you do now. You'd push your hat back and then you'd roll a cigarette with one hand.'

"Anyway, every time I went to see my grandmother I would visit him, and we would talk. I'd walk him around the block in his wheelchair and sometimes I would sneak him a cigarette. One day he started talking about his mother, and I could see he was getting emotional, like he was seeing her.

"'Do you see your mother with us?' I asked.

"'Yes I can.'

"He started making this noise like click, click, click. I said, 'What is that? What's that noise?'

"He said, 'It's my mother.'

"'What is she doing?'

"'She's making tortillas.'

"'What's the noise?'

"'It's her ring hitting the rolling pin.'

"And then I remembered hearing that as a kid with my grandmother. I had forgotten all about it.

"Then I asked him a question. 'Was your mother a pretty lady?'

"He asked me to get closer and he hit me with his hat. 'What was that about?'

"'Don't worry, get closer again.'

" 'No, you're going to hit me.'

" 'I'm not going to hit you,' he laughed. There was a twinkle in his eye. 'Why would you ask such a stupid question?'

" 'What's stupid about it?'

" 'Well, have you ever seen an ugly mother?' "

This is the kind of story that could plausibly be told anywhere: at a barbershop in an urban neighborhood, on an airplane, or in a book of folklore. It conveys special meaning in this context because of its small-town location. It illustrates the local knowledge that comes from living in a community for a long time and includes knowing the fingerprint of an old cowboy hat. It underscores the slow passage of time and continuities of life.

The story points to another feature of small communities as well. Research on memory suggests that it is somehow bundled into mental packages that can be triggered into consciousness by the right stimuli. The stimuli that work best are sensual: smells, tastes, tactile impressions, sights, and sounds. This is why detectives take eyewitnesses back to the scene of a crime, hoping that a forgotten memory will surface. It is the reason abstract concepts are more difficult to remember than an experience of a place rich with sounds and smells.[18]

Mr. Segundo tells the story to show why places have special meaning. When he walks down Walnut Street where his grandmother used to live, he can hear the click, click, click of her ring on the rolling pin. He can see Don Pedro across the street pushing his hat back and rolling a cigarette. Visualizing Don Pedro in his mind's eye, he is reminded of hot days as a boy working in the fields and the smell of fresh-cut hay. "I walk past a vacant lot. It's not just any vacant lot. It's where I played as a kid."

If we are to understand the meaning of community, we must include the mental associations that connect experiences and places. This is why we decorate our homes with photos and memorabilia. To do otherwise is to live among mass-produced items that speak only of consumption. Community extends the principle of home to include its wider surroundings. The old school and park are meaningful because they have been there for a long time, and because one's personal experience is intertwined with their meaning.

The experiences that familiar places bring to mind are not always pleasant. The park that Mr. Segundo is now able to visit was once restricted to the Anglos who lived on that side of town. Walking through it reinforces his views about the possibility of change as well as his memory of the past.

Reminiscing is an important part of small-town life. Telling stories of the past keeps the past alive. Having the places nearby that prompt the stories helps associate them with the community. A town seems like a community because of this mixture of places, memories, and people with whom these memories can be shared.

GROWING UP AUTHENTIC

Apart from the fact that intergenerational mingling and reminiscing is possible, residents often argue that small towns are the ideal place to raise children—a further connection with the idea of communities needing to be the right size to be nurturing. Child rearing is clearly a matter of practical significance for the many residents of small towns who are in fact raising children. Its larger symbolic significance is evident as well, especially in the frequency with which residents who no longer are parents—and perhaps have never been—mention it. Childhood connotes both innocence and vulnerability. For a place to be conducive to child rearing, it must afford an opportunity for innocence to be expressed and safeguard against threats to vulnerability.

At first blush, this emphasis on child rearing usually means that small towns are safe. Children can play in the yard without supervision and wander to a friend's house without parents worrying.[19] Residents point out that crime is low, traffic is sparse, and schools are within walking distance. And their perceptions are warranted, judging from uniform crime statistics, which show that crime rates are lower in smaller towns than in larger ones, and lower still among small towns in nonurban areas (figure 3.2).[20] Of course this impression of safety is tempered by the fact that children in small towns can get in trouble just as easily as in cities and suburbs. And for that matter city parents would argue that opportunities for cultural enrichment, ballet, art lessons, ice skating, lacrosse leagues, gymnastics, and almost everything else are greater in larger places.

But small-town parents often refer to something deeper that they see in small places. This is the freedom they think children need to explore as they grow and develop: getting outside, roaming through backyards and over fences, collecting toads, leading a kind of Tom Sawyer and Huck Finn existence, rather than having structured activities, fixed schedules, and adult supervision. These are the ideals. Collectively, they constitute a definition of authenticity. Children who develop an authentic self, residents contend, have had the freedom to spend time playing, being outside close to nature, being by themselves, and learning without close monitoring who they are.[21]

One parent quotes the adage, "The work of childhood is play," and stresses that play "has to be without adults." That could happen in suburbs, and the saying probably described life in urban neighborhoods a generation or two ago, this parent feels. And yet the seeming lack of organized

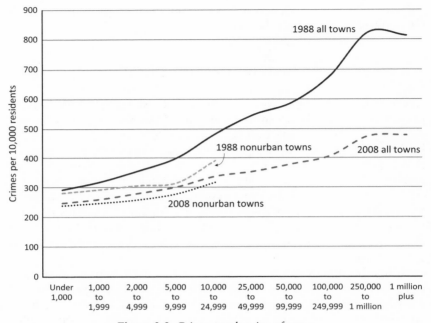

Figure 3.2 Crime rate by size of town

opportunities in small towns appears to be an advantage. It provides the space in which play can happen—literally, in fact, since the average person has considerably more square footage in a small town than in larger communities (figure 3.3).[22] The further advantage of growing up with freedom to play and space in which to roam, small-town residents argue, is that children grow up to be better rounded and more genuine. They are imagined to be more in charge of their lives, better able to make their own decisions, more self-sufficient, and less influenced by the pressures of large institutions that necessarily weigh down on an individual.

It is interesting, certainly, that townspeople and the researchers who study them have varied and even conflicting views of exactly how—and whether—small towns promote authenticity in children. During much of the nineteenth century, it was commonplace to assert that fresh air, hard work, and room to roam resulted in healthier children being raised on farms and in small towns than in squalid urban contexts. But by the start of the twentieth century, that perception was changing. Cities were thought to be attracting the best and brightest, leaving behind uneducated, unmotivated, and perhaps intellectually inferior children in smaller places. In 1915, the renowned sociologist E. A. Ross declared that whole sections of rural America were left with "communities which remind one of fished-

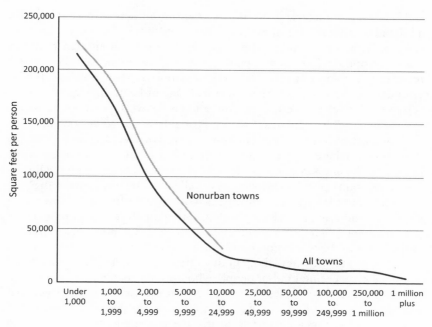

Figure 3.3 Ambience by town size

out ponds populated chiefly by bullheads and suckers."[23] Naturally, that comment does not sit well with researchers who observe better developments in small towns. "Those bullheads and suckers left behind in Midwestern rural communities spawn smart and capable youth, generation after generation," rural sociologist Sonya Salamon concludes.[24] The question is why.

On the one hand, freedom to explore and play without adult supervision is indeed one possibility. Some research suggests, for instance, that "downtime" is essential to childhood development and more effective learning among adults, whereas too much structure and time that is too thoroughly programmed can be detrimental to creative thinking.[25] Authenticity may be nurtured in those moments when self-reflection happens without conscious thought. On the other hand, researchers like Salamon suggest that the informal monitoring that happens in small towns matters more. As residents themselves observe, children are mentored by not only their own parents but also neighbors who watch out for them, teachers who also live in the community and perhaps are neighbors, and opportunities to participate with adults in community activities, such as local improvement projects. Rubbing shoulders with multiple role models may be the source of a better-rounded personal identity.

If children somehow grow up to be more authentic in small towns, adults insist that relationships with other adults are also more authentic. It is the scale that matters, they say. "Well, it's small enough that you know a good deal about the people who live in town," a resident of a town of two thousand says. "It's very neighborly." Mr. Grimshaw, the investment banker, observes that the advantage of living in a smaller place is that one's circles of activity are more likely to overlap. "If you're working in the city," he explains, "you're probably going to get out to work and then get back to your community where you live, so you're living in two worlds, whereas here you're living in both your worlds at the same time. Your business contacts and your social contacts and your neighbors are all the same people." He says that makes the relationships more personable and meaningful. Similarly, a woman who lives in a town of a thousand and regularly visits people in other small towns as part of her job comments, "They just seem to be more genuine, more helpful, more caring. I mean the whole community is a caring community. I travel in six counties, so I see the same thing in the other small towns. People are good and they are a caring kind of people who are easy to get along with most of the time. And the times that I've been in the city, you don't get that feeling. And I don't know why it's that way, but the people are different."

Part of what it means to be authentic, in these residents' views, is being sufficiently well rounded to take care of oneself. Of course this definition of authenticity is arbitrary. Authenticity could just as well mean that a person knows when to depend on others. But in small towns, residents have the sense that in the past, people were somehow more authentic because they lived close to the land, raised their own food, cooked their own meals, and were less dependent on the marketplace. One woman provides this illustration. She says there wasn't a good grocery store in her hometown, but that was good because most of the townspeople raised some of their own food. She had a garden and kept some chickens in the backyard. Most of her neighbors, she notes, cut their own firewood and had wood-burning fireplaces. It made her feel good that if something happened in the world, like the electricity going down, people in her town would probably be OK.

What people like about small towns becomes clearer when contrasted with the remarks city dwellers make about their communities. Consider how a lifelong resident of a city of two million describes her community. Although the suburb in which she lives has a population of only twenty-two thousand, she thinks of her community as the larger metropolitan area. She portrays it as a "friendly, open" city, but dwells at greater length on its "good amenities." She says these include good sports teams, a sophisticated level of fine arts, and music. It is a good place to live, she explains, because it is "easy to fly in and out of," and "lots of people here are well traveled." She says that the traffic isn't bad, but backtracks to acknowledge that there are lots of cars and suburban sprawl. When pressed to explain what she means by friendly, she says "family friendly" is what she has in mind. To her, that means that there are "many activities, many options for families to do."

Or consider the comments of a forty-five-year-old banker who lives in a metropolitan area of half a million three hours from the town of two thousand where he was raised. Having lived in a small town, he is able to draw the comparison and even sees some similarities. He confesses that he sometimes wishes he were still in a small town, but it is unlikely that he will ever live anywhere besides a city. He has made a success of his career, and says that he and his family live comfortably. He likes his community. But his relationship to it is instrumental rather than one of deep emotional attachment. He explains that his reason for living there is that he was looking for a job after college and happened to find one in this place. What he likes best about his community is that it has been growing lately. Somehow, he is proud of that. Even though he dislikes the added traffic congestion and noise, it affirms his own sense of worth knowing that other people are coming to live in his community. His thinking does not venture far down that path. Instead his mind turns quickly to the instrumental benefits of living in an expanding community. Population growth is good for the tax base, he says. "There is a lot of stuff going on. There is more shopping."

Discussions of what is authentic and what is not are always rich with irony. The special irony that attaches itself to the statements townspeople offer is that they are effectively turning one of the most familiar stereotypes about small towns on its head. In that view, attaining an authentic self—which means somehow finding the "real you"—is impossible in a small community because of its oppressive demands for conformity. Instead, residents argue, a small community is a place of freedom. Or more precisely, a secure space patrolled at the edges by attentive, caring adults (parents and neighbors) who give children sufficient freedom to explore, play, and be close enough to nature to discover who they really are. The city, in contrast, inhibits the search for a true self. A person there, bombarded by advertising and the cacophony of competing voices, more easily succumbs to self-deception.[26]

A SPACE FOR FAMILY

When small-town residents contend that their community is a good place for families, they usually have in mind raising children, but relationships with parents and responsibilities toward them frequently matter as well.

These relationships are part of the reason people remain in small towns or return to live in these communities. It may be that the family farm or business has been in the family too long to be abandoned, or the decisive consideration may be a parent's death or ill health. An adult child may give up plans for a life elsewhere in order to care for a parent's needs.

The sacrifices that parents make for their children or their parents are probably no greater on average among residents of small towns than among inhabitants in cities and suburbs. The community nevertheless figures into the meaning of these sacrifices. The family obligation becomes part of the story of why a person has chosen to live in a small community. The story reinforces the connection between community and family. It dramatizes the importance of family, and in some instances encourages people to behave in ways that strengthen that value. Family ties then matter not simply as a belief but also as an activity that is considered significant enough to work at in order to maintain.

The thinking that goes into decisions about family and community are always complicated. A good way of teasing out some of this complexity is to consider the story of Arlan Harding, a postal worker in his early fifties. He lives in a town of fewer than four hundred people nearly a hundred miles from the closest city. The average age of residents in his community is considerably older than in the rest of the state. Not a single new house has been built in the last decade. Mr. Harding is one of the few who graduated from college. In fact, he has five years of college and majored in prelaw in hopes of going on to law school. He had just graduated, however, when his father was diagnosed with cancer. Mr. Harding put his plans on hold, and returned home to be with his dad and help his mother with the little newspaper his parents were putting out each week. His father died two years later. Mr. Harding stayed on and continued to assist his mother, who outlived her husband by nearly two decades. He never pursued his dream of becoming an attorney and living in a city.

A story like Mr. Harding's can be interpreted in several ways. As an only child, he felt a special responsibility to be with his father and help his mother. They had no one else. It was uncertain how long his father would live. His mother was still in good health, but had no place else to go after her husband died. Still, Mr. Harding figures in retrospect that the decision to stay was entirely his. "I never felt pressured or tied down," he says. He could have sold the newspaper and persuaded his mother to move or do something else. "I felt like I could have gotten out of it, sold it, done whatever at any time." Instead, he settled down, got married, kept the newspaper going, and worked at the post office because the newspaper was hardly breaking even. "You get comfortable," he adds. "You get complacent, and the longer you're in it, the easier it gets."

Whatever a person thinks about it later, the path not taken is always there in the shadows of one's imagination. "At first I kind of resented being back here," Mr. Harding acknowledges. "The idea was to get away. You go to college not to move back to a town of 350 to use your degree." Yet as the years passed, he realized that he was using his college training, especially in editing the newspaper and advising his children about their own futures.

If the small town was not what he had hoped for, it at least had its own advantages. Despite their meager incomes, he and his wife purchased a big old house that they love, and have invested their time and energy into restoring it. The workdays are long, starting at six each morning with the newspaper, sorting and delivering mail from eight to four six days a week, and working again on the newspaper until ten or eleven each evening. "I don't want to sound like Garrison Keillor," he says. "If I could, I would rather live in a town of maybe ten thousand than here. But this is comfortable. You know people. It's a slower pace, almost to the point of dozing."

Dozing perhaps, although it is difficult to see that in Mr. Harding's case. He and his wife hardly ever have time for a nap. The reason is mostly the long hours they both work. The slower pace is less evident in their daily schedule than in their sense of not being overly stressed. "Going postal" might be an appropriate phrase for a harried postal worker in a large city, but not in a small town. Mr. Harding believes that the life he has made for himself has provided the time and space in which to behave as a responsible son as well as father.

Saying that a small town is a good place to raise children is too clichéd to sound quite right to Mr. Harding. "We're not *Father Knows Best* or a Norman Rockwell painting," he says. The "we" refers to the hundred or so families who populate his town. It is all too common for people in his community to pop a slice of frozen pizza into the microwave and call it dinner, he thinks. It takes more time, but he and his wife maintain that the extra time is worth it to have family meals that take longer. "I guess we're old-fashioned. Believe it or not, we actually have sit-down meals with meat and vegetables. And we have a garden. Our kids actually know what vegetables are."

Undoubtedly Mr. Harding's neighbors would each have a slightly different story to tell. He does not consider his typical, and it probably is not. What his story illustrates is one of the many ways in which thoughts about family responsibilities and living in a small town come together. Having sacrificed a more prestigious career as an attorney to deliver mail and run a small-town newspaper, his feeling of having done the right thing in helping his mother is strong. It is sufficiently strong to reinforce the value he attaches to having sit-down dinners with his children. It worries him that more children are not learning about vegetables. He fears that families are just "kind of disintegrating."

Drawbacks of Living in a Small Town

Although people in small towns generally say they like living where they do, they are not Panglossian enough to say that everything is to their liking. Many of their complaints have nothing to do with the size of the town itself. People in the Midwest, for example, talk about the harsh winters, and people in the South and Southwest say they hate the hot summers. Their complaints about the town itself are seldom specific to the town, but reflect problems common to many small towns. As much as residents may talk about liking the open spaces or being near farms, the truth is that most towns are located in spots that would hardly have been selected for their beauty or the comforts they provide.

A few years ago, the Economic Research Service of the US Department of Agriculture developed a natural amenities scale that scored places in terms of the environmental qualities most people find attractive, such as mild winters, winter sun, temperate summers, low summer humidity, topographic variation, and water area. Most nonurban small towns—and the majority of the population living in them—were in locations that scored below average on the amenities scale (see figure 3.4). There was also a notable contrast between the scores of nonurban small towns and those of larger cities. For instance, only 8 percent of nonurban small towns received scores higher than "1," whereas 42 percent of cities with populations of fifty thousand or more did.[27]

Other than bad weather or a lack of natural amenities, one of the more commonly mentioned drawbacks of living in a small town is the lack of cultural activities. As one community leader chuckles, "If you like high school athletics, this is a great place to be, but in terms of concerts, artists coming here, lecture series, we just don't have that." At first I was surprised that this came up as often as it did. My assumption—naive in retrospect—had been that people in small towns probably do not care much about such highbrow activities as orchestra concerts, the opera, and viewing fine art in museums; if they did, they would have lived elsewhere. I realized, though, that townspeople frequently visit concert halls and galleries in cities, and they may have relatives who live near such amenities, or they at least have an appreciation of the arts because of television or high school programs. When this was the case, they do miss the fact that cultural activities are not available in their own communities.

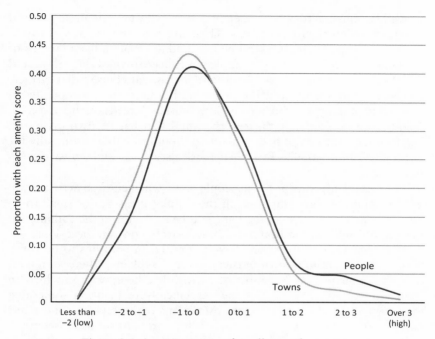

Figure 3.4 Amenity scores of small nonurban towns

Besides cultural events that people in cities and suburbs can more easily attend, the broader cultural atmosphere of small towns is disappointing to residents who long for the kind of interaction they experienced in college or imagine exists in other places. "We are college educated," a sixty-year-old businessperson in a town of five hundred says, mentioning his own background and that of his wife. "We miss the interaction with other college-educated folks and the professional people we lack out here." He says the Internet and email have made it easier to feel connected to a community of better-educated people, but he regrets not having the opportunity to visit face-to-face.

If the lack of cultural activities is a drawback, it is nevertheless one that many townspeople manage to overcome. Middle-class people in small towns take advantage of cultural opportunities when they are on vacation or visiting relatives in cities. Some take in concerts and museum exhibits by driving an hour or two. They figure it is no harder to enjoy the arts than if they lived in a metropolitan suburb and had to drive or take public transit into the heart of the city.

We also came across a number of people who participate in cultural activities within their own towns. These are usually residents of towns of at least three to five thousand people, and more often live in towns of ten to twenty thousand. One example is a college town of three thousand that has a major art gallery along with an annual concert that attracts audiences from throughout the region and is home to a nationally renowned photographer who has a gallery on Main Street. Another is a community of approximately thirteen thousand that has its own orchestra. Yet another is a town of fewer than two thousand known regionally for its productions of popular Broadway musicals, such as *Oklahoma* and *My Fair Lady*.

The mental adjustment townspeople make when cultural activities are truly lacking involves emphasizing the simpler pleasures of small-town life, such as the joy of working hard and being useful to the community. For these residents, the beaux arts are desirable on rare occasions, but unnecessary most of the time. "If you're a person who has to be entertained," a resident of a town of two thousand explains, "there's not a lot of entertainment here. For most of us who live here, we know how to entertain ourselves." Thus, if asked specifically to mention something their town lacks, they point to the absence of a major museum or concert hall, but from day to day these are hardly sources of serious discontent. Indeed, survey responses show that on average, residents of small towns are just as satisfied with the cultural events available in their communities as are residents of cities and suburbs.[28]

What cannot so easily be compensated for are the advantages for children of living in a place with a larger school that offers a wider range of educational opportunities, including orchestras, dramatic productions, dance ensembles, and visits to museums. Although consolidated school districts have broadened these possibilities in many small towns, residents still point to disadvantages. The quality of smaller districts in rural areas is sometimes relatively good because of the property taxes supporting the schools, and yet there are limitations on the variety of science courses that can be taught, for example, or availability of music and arts programs. We talked to some parents who had driven their children to larger towns and worked out arrangements for their children to take advanced placement courses at high schools in those towns. We also spoke with people who had been frustrated because the small-town high school placed so much emphasis on sports compared with academic achievement.

Naturally, many of the townspeople we talked to recognized that unemployment, low wages, a lack of jobs, and inadequate social services were a serious deficit in their community. Although the extent of these concerns varied, and were often mitigated by inexpensive housing and government transfer payments, we found numerous instances in which residents were troubled by local economic conditions. This was especially true when the only manufacturing plant in the community had closed or mines in the area had been shut down, but was not limited to these circumstances. In one of the towns we visited, residents were able to find steady employment at an automobile assembly plant thirty miles away, but rising fuel prices and a dearth of day care facilities were making it difficult for residents to commute. In another town, community leaders were keeping ahead of the grass that grew through the cracks on sidewalks along Main Street, but were unable to pay for a water treatment plant that the community desperately needed. In yet another town, unemployment was low and median household incomes were close to the state average, and yet the community's remote location made it difficult for residents to find fresh produce. In fact, a committee that monitored the situation discovered that even canned goods at the local grocery store were sometimes a year or two beyond their posted expiration dates.

The other drawback townspeople frequently mention is the ease with which gossip spreads. "I call it the small-town disease," a resident of a town of sixteen hundred observes. He says farmers in his community are always watching what the other guys are doing. For example, he was thinking about buying a piece of land and knew from long experience word would spread at the coffee shop before the deal was ever consummated. Knowing that, he asked a friend to be a mole at the coffee shop and report whatever was said. "There's just too many people watching what you're doing," he sighed. This is the downside of people knowing and caring about one another. "I was at the local restaurant," one woman recalled, "and I overheard people in the next booth talking about what a scandal it was that my parents were getting a divorce." A man in a town of eight hundred related a similar incident. He seldom got his hair cut in town, but did one day and within a few hours heard from two neighbors what exactly he had said to the barber.

If gossip is the small-town disease, it is nevertheless one that warrants caution in interpretation. An earlier generation of social scientists, writing at a time when all things progressive were considered to be happening in cities, sometimes described small-town gossip more as a plague than as a simple disease. In a study of a town in Colorado published in 1932, for instance, Chicago-trained sociologist Albert Blumenthal found gossip to be a pervasive feature of community life—so petty as well as so often false and scandal ridden that it shaped public opinion, and frequently constituted a serious invasion of privacy. Another sociologist, drawing on Blumenthal's study concluded that small-town gossip "makes every person's tongue a whip to discipline his neighbor and, at the same time, puts every neighbor at his mercy." Yet it was the residents themselves who informed Blumenthal that gossip was petty and false, and who often singled out the town's gossips for ridicule. That was evident in our interviews as well.[29]

Because they recognize it as a problem, residents do find ways to push back against gossip. One way is to keep silent about business dealings and other private matters, such as how much money a person makes or whether the corn crop was as good as expected—easier now than in Blumenthal's time because of changes in business practices and information technology. Another way is simply to shop out of town. Townspeople also respond by criticizing someone who develops a reputation as too much of a gossip. As one woman explained, a gossip who claims to know about everybody's business is "a major turnoff" and soon would not have many friends. Implicit norms exist as well about what can and cannot be gossiped about. For example, it is more acceptable to gossip about someone being in the hospital than about seeing something illicit through a neighbor's window. Despite its problematic aspects, gossip also serves valuably to spread useful information and maintain social ties. Residents we talked to mentioned, for instance, helping neighbors whose needs became known through the grapevine, and newcomers gained information about where to shop and who to call on for home repairs.[30]

One might expect the drawbacks seen by city dwellers to be the exact opposite of those described by small-town residents, and to some extent that is the case. Urban residents bemoan traffic, congestion, and noise. They list rapid population growth and not knowing anyone among the main disadvantages of living where they do. Yet it is important to note that the standard of comparison for city residents is often not the small town but rather other cities. Indeed, city residents frequently seem defensive about how their communities compare with cities that are larger or more prominent. Comments such as "Of course, we're not New York or Los Angeles, but we're more sophisticated than people might think" are not unusual. Or, "People come here and it's better than they expected. We're not provincial. We're knowledgeable about the world." Or, "We are more genuine here, not like some of that pseudocosmopolitanism you find in other cities." Unless they had actually lived in a small town, they had in mind that the crucial comparisons were other cities, and not unrealistically so because their friends and coworkers, and often they themselves, had lived in other cities. The comparisons dealt with size, weather, jobs, sports teams, and airports.

The comments of people who live in suburbs offer a more nuanced comparison with those of small-town residents. In many ways, suburbanites identify so many of the same attributes as townspeople that it almost seems that suburbanites are trying to replicate small-town life in these larger, more metropolitan communities. For example, they insist that their communities are safe, friendly places in which to raise children. By safe, they do not mean safer than in small towns but rather in comparison with inner cities, where they assume crime is higher. By friendly, they do not suggest, as small-town residents often do, that they are acquainted with nearly everyone but instead that they have found a few like-minded people with whom they could be friends. If they had children, suburban residents say less about children being free to roam the neighborhood, and more about excellent schools, fine after-school programs, ample parks and recreation facilities, and other young families.

Somewhat more surprisingly, many of the people we spoke to in suburbs described their communities as self-sufficient, meaning that everything a person could possibly want was readily available. It was unnecessary, they said, to venture beyond the confines of their own community. A woman in her forties who had lived in cities as well as the suburb in which she and her husband were currently living, for example, said her neighbors frequently remarked that "they have everything they need right here. There isn't a need to go anywhere." That was similar to the way residents of small towns talked. It was not literally true in either case, by people's own admission. They did drive to airports, go shopping some distance away, and fly to visit loved ones. But what they liked to feel was that their community had all the basic essentials nearby.

The clearest contrast between suburbanites and townspeople is in how they understand their community's authenticity. Whereas townspeople insist that their community exemplifies authenticity, suburbanites more often say something is inauthentic about theirs. "It's not reality," one suburban resident explains. "It's not even a dose of reality." Says another, "Look at things around here very long and you realize everything is artificial. Even the buildings aren't quite what they seem." Among those who make comments like this, several reasons become evident. One is that the suburb's residents seem too ethnically and racially homogeneous. "People are the same here and they like their sameness," one resident comments. People in small towns are homogeneous, too, and they recognize that sameness. But suburbanites live next door to inner cities and perhaps even other suburbs that make them aware of greater diversity, so they are more likely to say that homogeneity is not reality. A second reason suburban life is regarded as inauthentic is that the suburbs are usually newer and change more rapidly than small towns did. People point to recently constructed malls and housing developments, and contrast those with older downtown areas in cities or farming communities. That contrast is evident, too, in comments about people. In small towns people are viewed as natural lifelong friends, whereas in suburbs friends are chosen and thus are understood to be somewhat arbitrary.

The other reason suburbs are viewed as artificial is that residents there look at neighbors who live in mansions and drive fancy cars, and wonder about those neighbors' values. One hears remarks such as "I see people driving eighty thousand dollar SUVs," "I was in somebody's house, and they had twenty-two bar stools around their bar," or "There's a family with a full movie theater in their house. How much do you need? I mean, come on!" In contrast, residents of small towns usually know their neighbors well enough to vet their neighbors' values or have stories of caring that vouch for the community's wholesomeness. They also claim that neighbors mostly do not engage in conspicuous consumption. That makes the small town seem authentic whereas suburban life seems unnatural.

An important caveat to the contrasts between small towns and suburbs is that life as it is actually experienced in small towns is sometimes more diverse than in suburbs or even cities. We heard this especially in towns that had at least five to ten thousand residents. What people mean when they say their town is diverse is that they personally know and interact with people who are different from them. "You are more likely to know and be friends with a wider variety of individuals than you might in a larger city," a resident of a town of about ten thousand asserts, "because you are going to recognize and acknowledge people in the store and the bank and church. You are going to have more contact and have a better chance to develop a relationship with them." Whether that could be proven true is difficult to say, but it does make sense. In this man's town, which probably is not atypical, zoning laws have been established only in the last few years. During most of the town's history, it was possible for a mansion to stand side by side with a shack—literally. Rich and poor were neighbors. That did not mean they spent much time together. They did, however, know one another by name and could greet each other on a first-name basis at the grocery store. Friendship was somewhat less selective, people said. They were thrown together by virtue of living in the same small community, whereas in a suburb or city they would have chosen friends because of similar interests and lifestyles. Other people that someone may have seen at the bank or grocery store would have remained strangers.

How Small Towns Are Changing

The question of change in small towns, as I have suggested, is easy to misread. This is partly because of the sense one acquires both from talking to residents and hearing outsiders' remarking that nothing ever changes in small towns. It also stems from the more general perception so often promulgated in the media and fiction that small towns are a thing of the past, and thus must surely be declining. This view corresponds closely with that gnawing fear—the one that never seems to quite go away—that community itself is on the verge of collapse.[31]

The truth is that many of America's smallest towns have in fact been losing population—at least a little. In addition, many towns have been affected by economic difficulties, and have lost jobs and population for that reason. This is especially true of towns that are heavily dependent on agriculture and mining.[32] Perceptions and reality do not always match, but both are important. It makes no sense to dismiss the perceptions held by residents of small towns as a kind of false consciousness. My interest here is only partly in the fact that population may be declining or growing. I am more intrigued by how townspeople themselves perceive the changes taking place in their communities.

Residents in towns of fewer than two thousand people frequently mention that the first thing someone who had lived there twenty-five or thirty years ago would observe now on returning would be a smaller population, a quieter Main Street, and less business activity. "They would notice that there weren't as many people," a man in a town of nine hundred says. He is right. In 1980, the population of his town was fourteen hundred— half again its present size. "They would notice that there weren't as many shops," he adds. "Thirty years ago on Saturday night, you could drive down Main Street and see cars. Now you won't see cars." In a similar vein, another longtime resident of a small town says that even when most of the people in his community lived on farms, they all knew each other because Saturday was the big shopping day. Her family came to shop, she remembers, and often stayed into the evening just talking with people. That no longer happens in her town.

Nationwide, 62 percent of all nonurban towns with fewer than a thousand residents in 1980 became smaller during the subsequent three decades, and even among towns with populations between five thousand and ten thousand in 1980, 42 percent declined in population between 1980 and 2010 (figure 3.5).[33] Many of these towns had been losing population for a long time—some for most of the twentieth century. They had been founded in team-and-wagon days when farmers considered it a major outing to travel three to five miles to the grocery store and lumberyard. Many of the towns were established by railroads that needed stops every seven to ten miles for coal and water to power the steam locomotives. As farms became larger, fewer farmers lived in the vicinity of these towns. Better vehicles and improved roads made it possible to travel ten to twelve miles to a larger town instead of five to the nearest village. Much of that population decline in rural communities occurred in the 1940s and 1950s when marginalized farmers left to take jobs in other sectors of the economy. Further decline occurred in the late 1970s and 1980s when

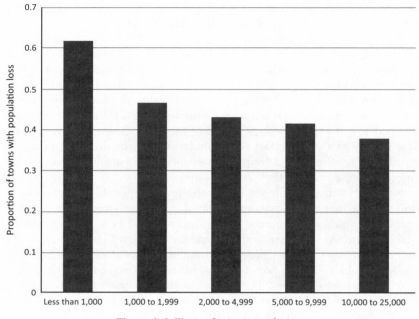

Figure 3.5 Towns losing population

government policies restricted grain exports, and low prices for grain and livestock forced additional reductions in the number of farmers.[34]

In the past quarter century, further changes in agriculture have contributed to the decline of small rural towns. As agriculture has become more specialized, the self-sustaining diversified family farm has declined, and is now replaced by contract farming that involves networks among large feedlots, trucking companies, and meat-processing plants. A farmer we talked to describes the changes this way. "Twenty years ago if you drove by a farmstead nice and slow, you would see cattle, hogs, sheep, and chickens. You might see guineas, dogs, and cats. You don't see that anymore. You see sheds and equipment. Diversification is no longer there. The farmer still may hold an interest in cattle, but they are in a feedlot in another part of the state. He buys cattle he's never seen and has them trucked to a feedlot." The man says this is true in his own case. He has three hundred cattle he has never seen in a feedlot two hundred miles away. They are being fed a scientific diet that gives them just the right number of daily calories and keeps their electrolytes in balance. This arrangement means increased population in the community with the feedlots because of a growing demand for low-wage workers, but it contributes to population loss in the cattle owner's community.

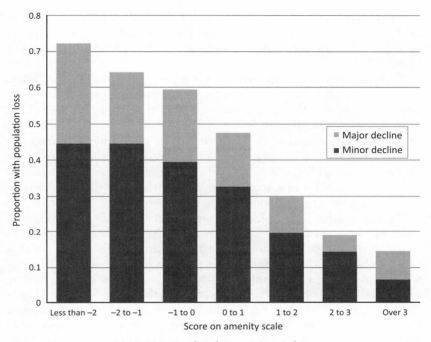

Figure 3.6 Decline by amenity ranking

The towns that are particularly at risk of losing population not only are small but also are located in places with natural amenities that hold few attractions (see figure 3.6). Upward of 70 percent of towns with the lowest scores on the US Department of Agriculture's natural amenities scale have lost population, compared with fewer than 20 percent of those with the highest scores. The difference reflects the fact that the latter can attract tourists and retirees, whereas the former cannot. The fact that the majority of small towns have low amenities scores is part of the reason that so many have lost population.[35]

Population trends illustrate another critical shift in small towns. Traditionally, small towns existed largely to support farming communities. Then, during the latter half of the nineteenth century, towns increasingly supported the mining and manufacturing populations that played an important auxiliary role in urban industrialization. But in recent decades, mechanization in agriculture, mine closures, and the relocation of manufacturing to other countries all have meant that small nonurban towns are no longer as significantly sustained by these sectors of the economy. The most serious population losses have been in small nonurban towns located in counties that are farming dependent, mining dependent, economically nonspecialized, or manufacturing dependent, while the least significant declines have been among towns located in counties that are dependent on federal or state government employment or in services (as shown in figure 3.7).[36]

The states that were most seriously affected are North Dakota, where 90 percent of small nonurban towns with no more than twenty-five thousand residents in 1980 were smaller in 2010 than they had been thirty years earlier; West Virginia, where 84 percent were smaller; Nebraska, with a population decline in 79 percent of its small towns; Kansas and Pennsylvania, each with 75 percent having become smaller; followed by Illinois, Iowa, and Montana, each with smaller populations in 74 percent of the state's small towns. In all, a majority of the small towns in twenty-four states had lost population during this period.

The sense of loss that residents express when describing the changes in small rural communities is sometimes acute. An example is the remarks of a man we talked to in a town that is one-third the size it was when he was a child a half century ago. He says he would never want to live anywhere else and probably could not afford to move even if he wanted to, but he and his wife own their own home, and they have friends and family here, so they are happy. And yet he mentions that he really misses how the town used to be. Thirty or even twenty years ago, a person could drive around the edge of town and see prosperous farms with farm families living there, clothes on the line to dry, children playing, and hogs and chickens in the barnyard. Now most of those farmsteads are gone. He recalls with fondness the little school he attended. It no longer exists. The children in town are now bused to another town. Several of the churches no longer function, he says, because there are not enough people to support them. "There used to be two grocery stores," he recalls. "It was a busy little town." People would gather on Saturdays. It was hard to find a parking space on Main Street. "Today there's a post office and that's it. There are no stores."[37]

Nostalgia for a lost world is especially prominent among older residents. "When I was a kid," Lex Thompson says, "there was a farm on every quarter section, and we had rural schools every three or four miles. Now there isn't one rural school left. All our schools have consolidated. The farmsteads are gone. In many cases there aren't even any trees or any indication that a farmstead was there. It's sad." Mr. Thompson is in his late seventies. He and his wife live in a century-old house on Main Street within easy walking distance of the county courthouse and local hospital. He remembers when there were seven grocery stores on Main Street and at least that many farm implement dealerships in town. Now there is only one grocery store and no implement dealers. On balance, Mr. Thompson is philosophical about the decline of his community. "It's a changing

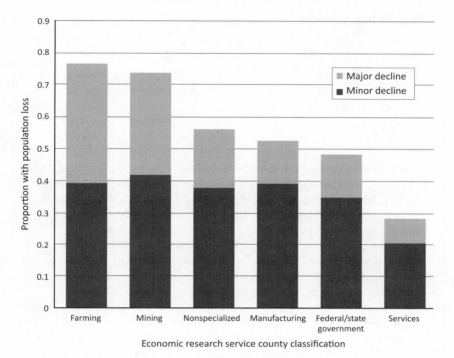

Figure 3.7 Decline by economic type

world," he says. "You have to adjust. You have to roll with the punches." And yet he regrets how his community has changed.

ANGER GROUNDED IN LOSS

Amid the longing, anger swells in the musings of some of the residents whose towns have declined. It focuses on the large corporate enterprises they blame for having undermined the vitality of their communities. Not only the Walmarts but also the corporate farming interests that have driven out the small farmer and depleted the local population are held accountable. Especially to blame are the franchise corporations that undercut the mom-and-pop shops and then moved on to larger locations. "My dad and his brother owned a hardware company here," an elderly gentleman explains. Then John Deere came in and forced them to give up the dealership. "There was bitterness toward John Deere," the man recalls. "I don't like the way our economic system is going to where you constantly have to get bigger and bigger," he adds. "We're just losing the local-

Profile: Millen, Georgia

Just as in large cities, small towns frequently experienced the effects of declining jobs in manufacturing. In 2001, the average county in which one or more small nonurban towns were located employed 4,731 people in manufacturing. By 2009, that number had fallen to 3,590.

The decline in Jenkins County, Georgia, where Millen, a town of 3,100, is located, was much worse. In 2001, 1,189 Jenkins County residents held jobs in manufacturing. That was a third of all nonfarm employment. By 2006, 1,166 people were still employed in manufacturing. But three years later, that number fell to 121.

At the time, policymakers were worried that the entire national economy might be in free-fall because of problems with subprime loans on Wall Street, layoffs in the auto industry, and massive mortgage defaults in housing. As a small rural town—Savannah was eighty miles away—Millen should have been insulated from those problems, which were happening mostly in large Rust Belt cities and Sunbelt suburbs with bloated housing markets. But Millen took the full brunt of the larger economic crisis.

In late July 2006, the company that manufactures Jockey underwear announced plans to cut jobs at its plant in Jenkins County, which had been in operation since the 1950s and as recently as the 1980s had employed as many as 600 people. Two other plants cut jobs at the same time. A year later, Cavalier Homes, a company that produced prefabricated housing components, also announced plans to shut down its plant in Millen as part of a merger with Southern Energy, a company owned by billionaire Warren Buffett.

Georgia labor laws required companies to give no advance warning to employees of layoffs, which meant that the plant closings went into effect almost as soon as they were announced. The state labor commissioner did, however, offer to help laid-off workers retrain and seek other jobs, because companies held no responsibility to do that.

At the end of the decade, the population of Millen had declined by only 10 percent, but unemployment in Jenkins County stood at 21.5 percent. The future looked brighter, though, because the state was building a new prison in the area. Somehow things seemed to have come full circle, locals said. Millen had been the site of a notorious Confederate prison during the Civil War.

owned businesses all the time. They're just being bought out by the big corporations. That's a pet peeve of mine."

Anger is especially evident where the entire community has been adversely affected by a decision somewhere in a distant boardroom or legislative chamber.[38] In one of the mining towns we studied, the largest mine in the area ceased operating a few years ago. Fourteen hundred workers who previously held union jobs and earned an average of sixty thousand dollars a year were suddenly unemployed. That put a huge dent in the economy of a town of seventeen hundred as well as several neighboring communities. Some of the miners moved away, but talk of reopening the mine and retooling to search for precious metals kept others from leaving. Their wives looked for work or tried their hand at managing small businesses. The pastor of the Lutheran Church remembers organizing a project for some of the local high school youths. Of the seven who showed up, three had dads out of work, a fourth "had been living in poverty for a long time without a father much in the picture," a fifth was the son of a man who was about to lose his job, the sixth was from a family that was "not economically secure," and the seventh was being raised by a great uncle and great aunt. The pastor says poverty and unemployment on this scale was evident throughout the community.[39]

Mary Remmert was operating a hair salon at the time. She had quit high school at fifteen at the insistence of her stepfather, who believed there was no point in girls being educated. She learned hairstyling, worked at a salon each morning, worked a second job as a nurse's aide in the afternoons, and when she was old enough served in the National Guard on weekends. Her military service led to a tour of duty in the US Army, which ended when she was injured in an accident. Married by this time, she found out shortly after she filed for divorce that she was pregnant. Determined to succeed on her own, she returned to the mining town where her mother, also divorced, now lived. Together they operated the hair shop, worked at second jobs, and raised Mrs. Remmert's daughter. Everything went well for several years. Mrs. Remmert bought a small commercial building that was being sold cheaply, and opened a consignment shop and pet-grooming salon.

Then the mine closed, and the bottom fell out of the local economy. At about the same time, Mrs. Remmert's daughter was diagnosed with a potentially fatal illness that required regular medical treatment. As a self-employed store owner barely able to pay her bills, Mrs. Remmert had no employer-paid health insurance benefits and not enough income to purchase insurance on her own. She took yet another job working as a maintenance supervisor for the railroad. But when we spoke with her, she had been laid off. With the mine closed and a new ethanol plant failing to live up to expectations, the railroad had no business.[40]

This was the kind of story we found increasingly in small towns that were hit by the Great Recession following the collapse of several of the nation's leading banks and near bankruptcy of the nation's automobile industry. Although residents in many rural communities said things were not so bad because they had never been good, they suffered because the only manufacturing plant in town had shut down or a mine had closed. Others faced layoffs from jobs as teachers or in law enforcement because state legislatures were cutting back on government programs. Still others were living on pension funds that had deteriorated significantly in value. When they described a sense of loss, it was more than a yearning for a mythical past. They were experiencing the real difficulties of demographic and economic decline.

MAKING DO WITH CHANGING CIRCUMSTANCES

In larger towns of at least five thousand, there was less likelihood than in smaller towns of hearing comments about declining populations and dwindling business. One reason is that fewer of these towns have actually lost population.[41] The other reason, we learned, is that shrinkage of smaller neighboring towns has helped these somewhat-larger communities. When the grocery store in a town of five hundred goes out of business, these residents drive ten miles to a larger town to buy groceries. Retired people move to the larger towns to be closer to a doctor or hospital. Farmers live in the larger towns and commute out to their farms, because they have more land that is scattered over wider distances and spend more of their time in town doing business. School consolidation is another important factor. As country schools and schools in small towns have consolidated into larger districts, the remaining schools are in larger towns. This shift results in more parents spending time in the larger towns. We also met several families who had moved to larger towns so their children could avoid long bus rides as well as participate more easily in after-school and evening activities.

Towns of three to five thousand are nevertheless faced with increasing competition from larger regional hubs. People who commute twenty or thirty miles to work in one of these larger communities of forty to fifty thousand residents more often do their shopping there after work. "I can remember when going there was an event," a man who lives in a town of two thousand says about a town of forty thousand that is twenty miles away. "That has changed," he adds, noting that more people in his town are working in the larger one. "We are now less self-contained. We also do not have the variety of merchandise here that we used to have." He says some of the stores in his town have gone out of business as a result and others are closing on Saturday afternoons because everybody is out of town. A resident of another small town observes that it is quite different shopping in a larger place. There is more variety, she explains, but you also get used to not speaking to anyone while you shop. You go shopping for the day to get away and entertain yourself. She thinks there is a subtle shift in how people communicate with one another. "I blame part of it on the Walmart thing," she says.

Walmart is a perplexing issue for people in small towns. On the one hand, residents of small towns report with considerable regret that Walmart has hurt the businesses on Main Street. A former grocery store owner in a town of sixteen hundred, for example, estimates that business at his establishment dropped 14 percent when a Walmart opened fifteen miles away. The owner of a hardware store in another town describes in bitter detail how Walmart draws customers by advertising low prices, but in fact charges twice as much for some items as he does. Walmart has had "a tremendous effect on Main Street," he says, "and it's not good." Residents in smaller towns say they try to buy at the older established stores to help them stay in business, even when prices are high and the selection is poor. On the other hand, residents mention that they are glad to have a Walmart within driving distance when nothing much else is available—and as shown in figure 3.8, the proportion of Americans who say they shop regularly at Walmart is much higher in nonmetropolitan counties with smaller populations than in metropolitan counties with large populations.[42]

Towns where Walmart has located have frequently gone through serious debates between opponents and promoters. In one of the towns we studied, for example, customers of the local grocery store secured a pledge that Walmart would not stock food, but several nurseries were forced out of business by Walmart's garden shop. "I can't believe how many people shop at Walmart," a local businessperson complains. "They're all over the fricking place." He says he was anti-Walmart at the start, but nevertheless has more recently changed his tune. Walmart is bringing growth to the community because of business from smaller towns in the area.[43]

A Walmart Supercenter just ten miles away was one of the changes that Clarence Brown, an attorney in his late sixties, said was affecting his community of six thousand in the Deep South. It was handy having the store that close, he commented, but fewer residents were shopping in town, and that had caused several of the local businesses to close and the community to lose revenue from sales tax. Yet these were hardly the largest concerns for Mr. Brown. He had seen changes before and knew the town's history well enough to figure it could survive Walmart. Before the Civil War, when slaves worked on nearby cotton plantations, the community had been the site of one of the largest cotton mills in the South.

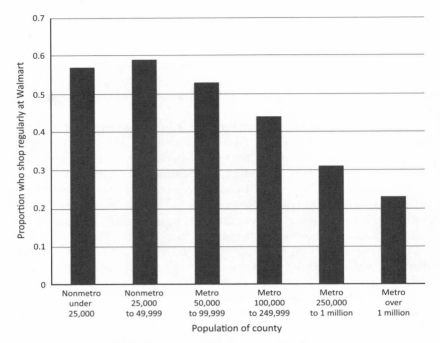

Figure 3.8 Walmart shoppers by size of county

By the end of the nineteenth century, cotton had largely been replaced by truck farms growing vegetables for shipment by rail to southern cities. By the late 1960s, most of the truck farms had gone out of business, unable to compete with farmers in Mexico, southern Texas, and California, where the growing season was longer and labor was cheaper. Logging companies and poultry plants are now the main sources of low-wage employment.

But like many of the people we talked to in the South, it was not the economic ebb and flow that was foremost on Mr. Brown's mind; it was the changes his town has experienced in race relations. As an African American growing up in a small southern town in the 1950s, Mr. Brown knew firsthand about segregated schools and discrimination. After the landmark 1954 Supreme Court decision in *Brown v. Board of Education*, the white-dominated political system in Mr. Brown's community did everything it could to keep schools segregated and prevent blacks from voting. "There were endless court battles and all kinds of terrible things going on with the Ku Klux Klan and other groups that were violently trying to preserve racial segregation," Mr. Brown recalls. "I watched all that as a child." The 1965 National Voting Rights Act was an important, though incomplete, turning point. African Americans gained the right to vote, but local officials still found ways to deny them that right. "We had an old circuit court clerk who was the registrar of voters," Mr. Brown remembers, and he would "come down to the courthouse at 6:30 in the morning" [by special appointment] to register a white voter, but the rest of the time "stayed at home feigning illness." It took years for the situation to improve. Currently three of the five alderpersons in Mr. Brown's community are African American and two are Caucasian. There is still a long way to go.

The "overriding, though subliminal, factor," as Mr. Brown puts it, is still race. Since the Reagan revolution of 1980, nearly all the national officials elected from Mr. Brown's state have been Republican. Despite efforts through popular referenda to change it, the state flag still includes the stars and bars of the Confederate battle flag. The white flight from schools that began in the 1960s in Mr. Brown's community has continued. Although the local population consists of only slightly more blacks than whites, blacks make up nearly 90 percent of the enrollment in public schools. Nearly all the white children attend private schools. If he could change one thing about his community, Mr. Brown says, it would be to somehow remove the racial rancor—"the vestiges of racism that remain here."

Despite the white flight and economic uncertainties it has experienced, Mr. Brown's community has about the same number of residents it did four decades ago. But that is because of another change that many towns are undergoing. Whether declining, stable, or growing, many small communities are challenged by the fact that fewer of their inhabitants work there. Mr. Brown drives thirty to forty minutes every morning and evening to work in a small city. An increasing number of the other residents in his town do the same.

In other communities, limited job opportunities force residents to work elsewhere and better four-lane highways have, in some instances, eased lengthy commutes. Commuting is especially evident among residents in the smallest towns, where the proportion who worked outside the county increased from 24 percent in 1980 to 35 percent in 2000, but is also the case in larger towns, where the comparable figures rose from 10 to 19 percent over the same period (see figure 3.9).

Ms. Clarke's husband, for example, is a college graduate whose training is more specialized than any employer in their small town can use. She needs to live in the community where she works, and housing is cheaper there than in a city, so her husband commutes seventy-five miles each way to a job in a large city. Residents like this are seldom in their community during the day on weekdays, and their significant personal networks may be with people at work rather than in their neighborhood. The upside of

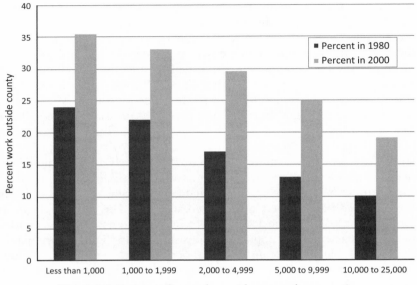

Figure 3.9 Percent who work outside county by town size

such ties is that small towns are better connected with the outside world; the downside is that fewer residents know one another, and fewer are available to participate in community activities.[44]

Jacob Steuben, a man who has just turned sixty, illustrates the transient connections that have characterized some residents of small towns for decades and have increased in recent years. His grandfather owned a small farm that is still in the family, but when the Depression came Mr. Steuben's father had to find employment off the farm to supplement its meager income. Mr. Steuben's father and an uncle began hiring themselves out to help other farmers during harvest. In 1936, the brothers formed a threshing crew that went from field to field working for farmers who could not afford their own equipment. After World War II, the brothers purchased a self-propelled combine. Each May they loaded the machine on the back of a truck and hired themselves as custom cutters, starting in Texas, and then made their way north, following the harvest twelve hundred miles to Manitoba, before returning in the fall. Mr. Steuben says his first trip with the crew was when he was six months old. He says he literally grew up in a wheat truck or on a combine with wheat chaff down the back of his neck. The crew slept in grain bins and haylofts, did their laundry by hand, and ate meals by the side of the road.

As a teenager, Mr. Steuben figured he would become a teacher and put his athletic ability to use as a coach. He went to college and earned a degree in education. But he could earn more money as a custom cutter than as a teacher, so he borrowed money to purchase a combine, and joined his father, uncle, and a brother in the family business. They lived in a small town, which served conveniently as a place to repair equipment in the winter, but were gone six months of the year. Unlike his mother, who traveled with the crew, his wife stayed at home after a few years. She was a social worker responsible for working with the older adult population in a five-county area. After two decades of being on the road, Mr. Steuben sold his part of the combining business to his brother and hoped to settle down. He liked the town. It was home, and he wanted to become more involved in the community. Yet he was used to traveling, enjoyed meeting people, and knew people from Texas to Canada. He learned how to be an auctioneer and sell real estate. He still travels extensively, organizing seventy to eighty auctions a year that include everything from farm equipment to precious antiques. The small town where he lives is truly his home base, and he loves being part of the community, although he is seldom there for more than a day or two at a time.

Although the Steubens' lifestyle is unusual, it is not so different from the long-haul truckers who make their homes in small towns, or the railroad workers, pilots, flight attendants, construction workers, and traveling salespeople who live in small communities. In all these cases, being away is as common as being at home. The Steubens highlight another connection between small towns and the wider world. They have three children who live out of state. One is a social worker like her mother. One is in law school at an Ivy League university, and has spent considerable time in Africa doing humanitarian and development work. The other is in medical school, also at an Ivy League university. The Steubens travel a lot to see their children, and although Mr. and Mrs. Steuben are devoted to their community, they have interests in many places outside the community.

As this example reveals, residents of small towns are integrated into wider social contexts through kin and friendship networks. Nearly everyone we talked to had children, siblings, or close friends who lived in cities. Of course this phenomenon is not new. As the agricultural population declined and cities grew, people raised in small towns went to cities to seek employment. The difference now is that many small towns are in the vicinity of larger metropolitan suburbs, travel is easier, and electronic communication is cheaper and faster. These links influence how townspeople think about themselves and the larger world. For some, the connections result in a cosmopolitan outlook that includes beliefs and values absorbed from friends and relatives living elsewhere. For others, ties to people in larger communities reinforce the conviction that small towns are truly distinct.

In considering these external networks as well as the fact that many residents of small towns commute to jobs in other towns, it is nevertheless important to keep in mind that one of the features residents most cherish about small towns is that most of what they need from day to day is near at hand. Jobs may increasingly be out of town, but are still easier to get to than for people living in large cities. This is especially true for people who live in small towns that have not become too small to provide work nearby. For instance, the proportion of workers whose daily commute each way is fewer than twenty minutes rises from 47 percent in the smallest nonurban towns to 66 percent in nonurban towns of ten to twenty-five thousand residents, but falls to only 29 percent among urban residents in cities of a million or more.[45]

Racial and Ethnic Diversity

The other change that small communities are experiencing is increasing racial and ethnic diversity. Compared with cities, small towns other than in the South have been relatively homogeneous for a long time, but this feature is shifting as a result of immigration and in conjunction with businesses locating in small towns where labor is cheap. Mr. Steuben's town, for example, is 12 percent Hispanic, 5 percent Asian American, and 2 percent African American. The Hispanic population has been there for more than a century because of employment on the railroad, but has grown in recent years, as has the Asian American population. Both groups have done well economically, although strong cultural differences from the Anglo population remain. The Hispanic population also retains strong ties with Mexico and Central America. Even in Mr. Brown's divided African American and white community, the population now includes Hispanic and Vietnamese families that have come to work at the area's lumber mills and poultry plants.

Nationally, small towns have remained relatively homogeneous, with the white Anglo population on average declining only from 91.3 percent in 1980 to 86.5 percent by 2010, and the black population remaining constant at approximately 6 percent. The Hispanic population, however, more than doubled during this period from 2.5 to 6.1 percent. The largest proportions of Hispanic residents were in Arizona, California, New Mexico, and Texas, but the greatest percentage change occurred in Minnesota and North Carolina, where the rise in Hispanic population represented a fivefold increase. In 1980, the population of only 454 small nonurban towns nationwide was at least 20 percent Hispanic, but by 2010 this number had grown to 1,102. Overall, it was true that small towns were considerably less diverse, racially and ethnically, than cities, where the

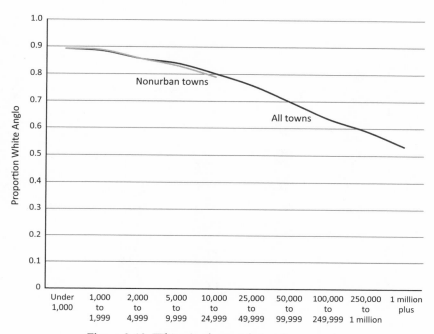

Figure 3.10 White Anglo population by town size

nonwhite population on average was nearly 50 percent. Yet the nonwhite population in small nonurban communities ranged on average from about 10 percent in the smallest towns to more than 20 percent in towns with populations between ten and twenty-five thousand (figure 3.10).[46]

An indication of how small towns are being affected by immigration is shown in figure 3.11. Nearly 70 percent of small nonurban towns of under 25,000 currently include some residents born in other countries. Forty-three percent of these towns include residents born in Europe, with the largest numbers coming from England, France, Germany, Italy, and Russia, and for this reason are unlikely to be recent immigrants. Nevertheless, 40 percent of small towns include immigrants from Latin America, 32 percent from Asia, and 7 percent from Africa. By far the most important sending country has been Mexico, the source of more than 800,000 immigrants living in small nonurban towns in the United States, followed by a distant 40,000 from the Philippines, 34,000 from India, 32,000 from Guatemala, 27,000 from China, 26,000 from El Salvador, and 25,000 from Korea. In addition, small nonurban towns collectively account for more than 10,000 residents from each of the following: Columbia, Cuba, Honduras, Jamaica, Japan, and Vietnam. With the exception of Mexico,

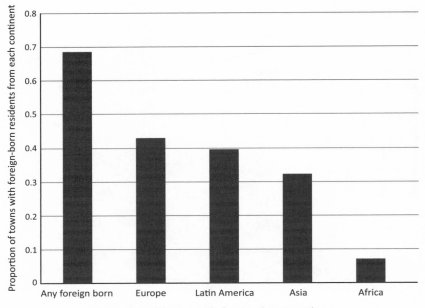

Figure 3.11 Towns with foreign-born residents

for which the number living in each small nonurban town in the United States averages nearly 175, the number from most countries averages between 15 and 20 in towns where any immigrants from that country are living. In only about 20 percent of these towns do immigrants from a particular country live among fewer than 5 coethnics from the same country. That means opportunities to find community among kindred spirits, but except in larger towns and among immigrants from Mexico, limits possibilities for larger ethnic organizations of the kind found in cities.[47]

A town of ten thousand that had doubled in size since 1960 exemplifies one of the more notable instances of immigration and rising ethnic diversity. By the beginning of the twenty-first century, fewer than half the local population was white Anglos. Besides a large Spanish-speaking population from Mexico and Central America, the community had attracted immigrants from Southeast Asia and several African countries. Most of the newcomers found employment in a meat-processing plant. Many of the Anglos fled, and those who remained described the community as a miniature United Nations. Some regretted the loss of the ethnically homogeneous town in which they had lived as children. Others noted with pride that a new library, improved schools, and a Walmart had accompanied the town's growth.

Hispanic residents, some of whom had lived in the community for several generations, also described the changes in ethnic relations and perceptions associated with the arrival of new immigrants. Earlier assimilation patterns characterized by ethnic blending were now being replaced by greater acknowledgment of ethnic differences. Part of the change was what social scientists refer to as a shift from straight-line to segmented assimilation—meaning that newer immigrants, who make up a larger share of the population, or their children, are finding it harder to move up the socioeconomic ladder to better-paying and more prestigious middle-class occupations.[48]

But the change is also cultural. Earlier ethnic minorities assimilated into the Anglo culture to avoid discrimination. As Manuel Ortega, a third-generation Mexican American whose grandfather settled in a small town to work on the railroad, explained, "I regret not having learned Spanish, but we didn't want to because it was a time when we had to sit in the balcony at the movie theater and were not allowed in the swimming pool." With a larger number of recent immigrants, his community is now finding it necessary to teach some classes in Spanish and offer bilingual tutoring, which in turn reinforces a stronger sense of ethnic identity.[49]

Because immigrants come to take low-income unskilled jobs, the long-term residents often regard them with a degree of suspicion. "You definitely see it," one man remarked. "Racism. They think Hispanics don't belong here. They think Hispanics are stealing their jobs." This sentiment was even more pronounced in a town where a quarter of the population was Hispanic and Anglos were angry because a local manufacturing plant's decision to relocate to Mexico had put people out of work. In another town, community leaders held a meeting to discuss how to keep immigrants out. They decided not to build any low-income housing in hopes that the absence of affordable homes would be a deterrent.[50]

Hispanic, African, and Asian immigrants were more welcome in other towns, but only because they were willing to take the least desirable jobs, such as working on the killing floor at meatpacking plants or doing stoop labor on truck farms. That pattern has notable exceptions, however. In one of the agricultural towns where we conducted interviews, we learned that immigrants from Mexico had arrived mostly in the 1980,s and since then had purchased homes, educated their children, and steadily moved into the middle class. The new immigrants, German Mennonites from Canada, were now doing the low-skill agricultural labor. These were old-order Mennonites who had large families and did not value formal education. As a result, boys as young as fifteen were hiring themselves out as farmhands. They were now on the bottom rung of the social ladder. Established residents criticized them for not staying in school and assimilating into the community. Rumor had it that they married their own

Profile: Lexington, Nebraska

One of the towns that experienced a dramatic change in ethnic composition around the start of the twenty-first century was Lexington, Nebraska, a community of approximately 10,000 residents in the south central part of the state. Lexington's location on the main line of the Union Pacific railroad and, later, along Interstate 80 facilitated steady growth in population from 1,392 in 1890 to 7,040 in 1980. The town's population declined in the 1980s, however, falling to 6,601 in 1990. The principal reason was the closing of a plant that manufactured farm machinery.

The vacant plant was purchased by Iowa Beef Processors and later sold to Tyson Foods, one of the nation's largest meat-processing companies, which was moving into new locations as the industry expanded to produce freezer-ready packaged meat and poultry for direct sale in supermarkets as well as to fast-food chains such as McDonald's and Burger King. These plants relied heavily on employees who were recent immigrants from Mexico and elsewhere in Central America.

Between 1990 and 2000, Lexington's Hispanic population climbed from 329 to 5,130, or as a proportion of the total population, from 4 to 51 percent. By 2010, that proportion had risen to 60 percent.

Unlike towns with longer histories of racial and ethnic diversity that made them better prepared to adapt, Lexington experienced the impact of diversity almost overnight. A journalist who visited Lexington in 2000 observed concerns about overcrowding, drug use, and crime. Rather than staying put and dealing with change, he wrote, "the majority of Lexington's white inhabitants moved elsewhere."

That was not quite true. The white Anglo population declined by only 26 percent between 1990 and 2000, partly because deaths outnumbered births. But it did continue to fall over the next decade, from 4,626 in 2000 to only 3,174 in 2010. The possibility that long-term residents of small towns would flee in the face of rising ethnic diversity became widely discussed.

So did the question of ethnic segregation within towns. In Lexington, houses vacated by white Anglos were acquired by newly arrived Hispanics—meaning that the two were more often neighbors than may have otherwise been the case.

Nevertheless, as was true in other towns, there was considerable ethnic separation. Fifty percent of the Hispanic population lived in the two neighborhoods closest to the meat-processing plant, compared with only 32 percent of the white Anglo population.

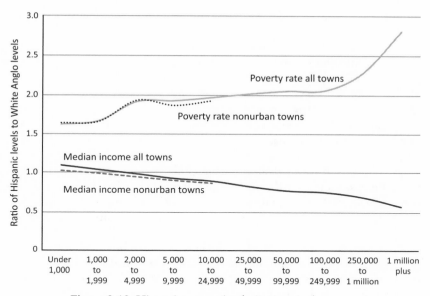

Figure 3.12 Hispanic versus Anglo income and poverty

cousins and might be mentally deficient. Even other Mennonites criticized them.

National data underscore some of the challenges that residents of small towns describe. Poverty rates among Hispanics in small nonurban towns are between 60 and 90 percent higher than among White Anglos in small nonurban towns. Yet those differences are not as great as in cities, where poverty rates among Hispanics range from 100 to 180 percent higher than among white Anglos. Also important is the fact that median household incomes among Hispanics in small towns are nearly indistinguishable from those among White Anglos, whereas in cities the former are from 25 to 45 percent below the latter (figure 3.12).[51]

Immigrants not only change the ethnic composition of small towns but also are an important way in which native residents of those communities are forging wider connections with the rest of the world. A man who operated a truck farm and ran a store in a town of only several hundred people offered one of the most vivid examples of this influence. He remembered hiring a couple of men from Mexico to work on the farm, and then being impressed not only with their work but also with the fact that their presence was good for his family and the community. Over the next decade he hired other men from Guatemala, Samoa, and South Africa. His family also hosted an exchange student from Poland. The man felt these visitors contributed a lot in helping his family and neighbors understand the world outside their otherwise-isolated community.

For immigrant families, settling in small towns is often a mixed blessing. On the one hand, housing may be inexpensive, and nonunion jobs in meat or poultry processing, construction, and agriculture may be available. Steady work even at low wages makes it possible to send remittances home to relatives who may be living in extreme poverty. On the other hand, meat and poultry processing is dangerous work that can fluctuate from season to season, and may be at plants that are guilty of human rights violations or get raided by immigration officials. Seasonal work and a lack of English-language skills make assimilation into the community difficult. Furthermore, the homogeneity that deters even newcomers of white European descent from feeling at home can make adjustments especially difficult for immigrants of different ethnic backgrounds. At the metal-fabricating plant where Mr. Dallek works, for example, the company made a special effort in the late 1970s to hire Vietnamese refugees. Only one of the families stayed. They were from a Catholic background, and a nearby parish helped them assimilate. The other families were from Buddhist backgrounds. After a few years of gaining skills at the plant, they moved on to a city where there were several Buddhist temples.[52]

Living in small towns remains attractive for many Americans because they were raised in a small community or on a farm, heard stories from parents or grandparents who lived in small places, and value the familiarity of changeless places. The scale of a small community makes it possible to conduct daily life at a slower pace, which residents interpret to mean convenience along with the ability to avoid the hassles of complex traffic patterns and large organizations. Living at a slower pace may involve time for a nap or casual evening on the front porch reminiscing with neighbors about the good old days, but usually has less to do with time itself than with the perception of living simply and being in control. That also means feeling, despite the pressure for conformity in a small community, that a person is somehow more authentic and freer to cultivate personal interests. As we will see again in chapter 9, this desire for personal autonomy and control runs afoul of regulations and constraints that residents deem to be unnecessarily imposed by government agencies.

Although it is common in small towns to talk as if life is idyllic, the drawbacks are seldom far from mind. A well-stocked supermarket may be an hour away, and local health care may be pitifully weak. Job opportunities are scarce, rising fuel prices makes commuting difficult, and bad weather generates as much consternation as it does anywhere—more, if the community's finances depend heavily on good crops. Adverse conditions diminish community participation, especially when work and shopping are increasingly conducted outside the community. The disadvantages of small towns nevertheless reinforce community participation in other ways. Having few alternatives, residents gather more often at the local café and regard the high school play as a cultural highlight of the year.

The changes that are taking place in small towns make them an interesting location for thinking about the much-discussed decline of community in US society. The fact that many small towns are losing population can be taken as further evidence that community is indeed declining—at least if it is assumed that residents of small towns do attach special value to participating in their community. Those who have grown up in small towns and now live in cities and suburbs may feel especially that community is not what is once was. We also see from talking with people in small towns, though, that feelings about decline are complex. They cannot be understood simply in terms of population decline, and probably cannot be explained as a function of declining participation in community organizations.

The sense that community is not what is once was is, above all, an interpretation of events, which means that some events count more than others. Highly visible public events in a small town become the grist for stories that in the telling and retelling shape how residents think about decline. Population loss is seldom completely invisible because census results and estimates are reported from time to time in local newspapers. Yet it is noteworthy that in towns that have declined by as much as a quarter over the past quarter century, residents can report that nothing much has changed. The reason is partly that the town's population may have been declining for much longer than that, meaning that residents are used to it by now. And for that matter, population decline of only 1 percent per year may not be noticeable. Other developments are more visible.

The events that residents associate clearly with decline are the ones that are easy to see and talk about—such as the family-owned drugstore that goes out of business after seventy-five years, the vacant storefront on Main Street where the hardware store used to be, or the school building that stands empty now that consolidation takes children to another town. These are places that carry important symbolic connotations well beyond their economic significance. There is always a hint of nostalgia as residents talk about the neighbors who died or moved away as well as the crowds that used to gather in town on Saturday evening. Nostalgia is balanced by the sense of optimism that occurs when residents take note of counteracting developments, such as a new firehouse or even a new flower bed in front of the police station.

How residents think about community decline has much to do with whether they consider themselves still in charge of much that happens in their towns. It is difficult to get over the feeling that a big company closed down the mine and put people out of work unnecessarily. Anger lingers against the school officials who forced consolidation, and politicians in Washington, DC, or the state capital seemingly intent on favoring cities and suburbs rather than small towns. It is much easier to accept decline if it means only that life is simpler and the streets are quieter.

Changing racial and ethnic relationships are widely presumed by outside observers to be causing the most difficulty in small towns. This is because racial and ethnic prejudice is hard to overcome, and because highly publicized events, such as raids against illegal immigrants, have in fact occurred. But residents' views about racial and ethnic relationships are more nuanced than might be imagined. While there are blatant expressions of disdain toward new immigrants by some old-timers, optimism is common as well. Difficult adjustments notwithstanding, immigrants are increasingly the lifeblood of many small towns.

- 4 -

Community Spirit
Small-Town Identities That Bind

ALTHOUGH THEY LIKE THE SLOW PACE OF LIFE and small scale of their towns, residents most often say the best thing about living in a small town is simply the people. They know one another and regard one another as good neighbors. They appreciate seeing familiar faces and waving to people they know on the street. It is a kind of storybook existence, as people describe it—like a scene from a 1950s' television program. But folksy depictions wrapped in half-hour segments for family viewing are hardly reality. We need to move the camera in for a closer look.

Myrna Zlotnik lives in a coastal community of six thousand that is seventy-five miles from the nearest city of any size and a seven-hour drive to the closest large city. She and her husband live in a small cabin-size house that is heated by an old-fashioned woodstove. Hauling wood keeps them busy during the long winter months. She savors the smell of the Douglas fir that grow tall along the Pacific coast. When she thinks about the future, she asserts that she would never live anywhere else again. She says she would be dead by now if she had stayed in the city where she grew up. The slow pace here—"no apparent urgency to get from point A to point B"—keeps the stress level low. If a town gets too large, she explains, people become pushy and, well, you just "start bumping into stuff." She especially values the friendly atmosphere of the community.

There is some truth to the view that small towns are friendly places in which people know their neighbors and generally get along with one another. In a national survey, for example, 44 percent of respondents living in small nonmetropolitan communities said they knew almost all their neighbors, whereas that was true of only 14 percent in larger metropolitan areas.[1] But community spirit involves more than simply knowing one's neighbors—especially when one's neighbors, even in the smallest communities, constitute only a fraction of the town.

Mrs. Zlotnik believes that the clichéd saying about everyone knowing everybody else is a true description of her community. She is a gregarious person who relates easily to friends and neighbors. But when pressed, she says she probably knows only about 10 percent of the town's six thousand residents by name. She has about thirty close friends who share similar enough interests that they get together for dinner parties once in a while or just socialize at the café, telling stories over plates of pasta and keeping the conversation light.

In this respect, her social circle is an affinity group, just as it probably would be if she lived in a city. Two important aspects of small-town life make her social relationships different, however. One is that everybody—rich, poor (like herself), or in between—eats at the same café and buys gas at the same filling station. The faces she sees at the café and gas station are familiar enough that she regards these people as neighbors, even though she may not know them by name. She also feels that living in the same place and seeing one another this frequently is a leveling experience. She thinks of her neighbors as her equals. They also talk about watching out for their neighbors' children, keeping their eye out for one another, and participating in community projects.

This example illustrates that community is a concept that people construct and maintain through the ways they talk about it. Its existence depends only in part on the fact that people actually get together at dinner parties. It does not require that everyone literally knows everyone else. Community is reinforced by the place that throws people together and the discussions that occur in these places. No individual person knows everyone, but it may seem as if they do because they talk about the ones they know, and emphasize the commonalities and norms of neighborliness that they consider important.[2]

Community spirit resides in activities and organizations along with the resulting perceptions and narratives that arise. Making and sustaining these activities and organizations takes effort. Community spirit depends not only on the fact that people live in small out-of-the-way places with tight networks and scant populations. It also relies on residents working together, sharing common interests, and celebrating their shared ideals. As one community-minded resident puts it, "It is an action and a feeling. I feel it when I'm doing something for the town." Community spirit also inheres in unspoken codes of behavior that govern social relationships. This is why newcomers often find it awkward adjusting to small-town life, but also why newcomers are an important source of insights about the nature of camaraderie in these places.

Residents of small towns talk passionately about the social ties that forge solidarity in their communities. Many say they have stayed in small communities or moved to one because they were looking for close neighborly social relations—and are pleased to have found them. They worry about the potential loss of community as times change and they resent decisions that seem to undermine the most basic sources of community spirit. At the same time, there are surprises. For many residents, it is not the camaraderie that instills loyalty to their community as much as it is their attachment to the place, their love of the familiar ambience (however modest it may be), and the feeling they have of being close to the natural environment. For some, small towns are appealingly devoid of social constraints, offering freedom, individuality, and even anonymity.

It is no accident that the word *spirit* is so often appended to references about community. Spirit implies culture—an emotional attachment expressed in and reinforced by a repertoire of symbols. The town's name and location, its school, the school's mascot, the community's history and its commemorative festivals, the unwritten norms that govern routine sidewalk encounters, and the symbolic boundaries that differentiate newcomers from old-timers and townspeople from urban residents all contribute to the spirit of community. With slight modification, what anthropologist Benedict Anderson famously observed of nations pertains equally to towns. Community is *imagined* "because the members of even the smallest [ones] will never know [all] of their fellow-members, meet them, or even hear of them, yet in the minds of each lives the image of their communion."[3]

To say that community is imagined is not to say that it is only a mental fabrication. The fact that a small town occupies a particular place on the map, has a name and a history, and is defined geographically well enough to be easily recognized is important. When respondents in a national survey were asked what came to mind when they heard the word *community*, the top choice among suburban and city residents was their "neighborhood," but among residents of small towns, it was their "town."[4] That is crucial because conceptualizing social categories does not come naturally. In an interesting study of community service organizations, sociologist Paul Lichterman found that even the most dedicated volunteers usually thought of their recipients as individuals, whereas only with effort did they conceptualize themselves and their recipients as representatives of larger social categories.[5] For townspeople, "town" is a social category that comes easily to mind but is also reinforced through events and public discourse.

Much of the social science literature in recent years has highlighted social capital. Social capital consists of network ties with specific individuals, either with ones who are similar to oneself and thus constitute relationships of bonding, or with different others with whom bridging occurs. This view lends itself to enumeration. If people visit frequently with their neighbors over dinner, and if they see one another at club meetings and bowling alleys, community is said to be strong. If those social ties weaken, community is considered to be weakening. Those kinds of participation are significant in small towns, as I have suggested. But they are by no means all that make a small town a community. It is important that residents are able to conceptualize their town as a community, and not simply to visit or email their closest friends. The town as a social identity is preserved and made real through symbols that represent it, and through the narratives that blossom around these symbols.[6]

SCHOOLS AS SOURCES OF COMMUNITY SPIRIT

In all but the smallest towns, nothing serves so effectively to instill community pride as the local school. "Our school is central to everything," a resident of a town with only a thousand people and hardly any stores left on Main Street asserts. "We have one school K through 12. Old-fashioned school. Wonderful, wonderful school. It makes us proud." This is a man who has no immediate connection with the school. His children are grown, and he is retired, but like many residents of small towns, he regards the school as the focal point of the community. People gather at the school for games and plays, town meetings and holiday events. "It isn't perfect," he acknowledges, "but it is a very good school, and our whole community revolves around it. Nobody plans anything in this community without checking the school program. Everyone gets the school calendar, and that is the social calendar for the community. Everything revolves around it."[7]

If a school closes because of declining population or consolidation, the blow to the community is more than simply having to see the remaining children bused to another town. It strips the town of a critical piece of its identity. "You jerk the school out of there," Mr. Steuben says, "and you just cut the town's throat." He remembers the little towns in Montana, Oklahoma, Texas, and Wyoming that he traveled through as a custom cutter. They had a couple of grocery stores, a hardware store, a telephone office, and a school. But then, he figures, two-thirds of them lost their schools. He is all for good education and is glad to live in a larger town with strong schools. But for the small towns, he thinks losing their schools is like a cancer creeping through town.

Data compiled by the National Center for Education Statistics (NCES) in 1987 and again in 1999 show the reality behind residents' worries about school closings. Although school consolidation had been taking place for more than half a century, during these twelve years the number of schools in small towns fell from approximately 18,000 to approximately 11,000, and in rural areas from about 19,000 to approximately 16,000. During the same period, total enrollment at schools in small towns fell from 9.5 to 4.8 million, and in rural areas from 6.7 to 4.7 million.[8]

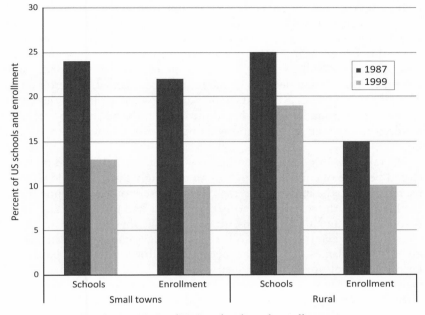

Figure 4.1 Decline in schools and enrollment

Meanwhile, the school-age population grew more rapidly in cities and suburbs than in small towns and rural areas, which meant that the nation's schools included a declining share of these smaller communities. As shown in figure 4.1, the proportion of US schools located in small towns fell from 22 percent in 1987 to 10 percent in 1999 and in rural areas from 15 to 10 percent. School enrollment as a proportion of total US enrollment declined in small towns from 24 percent in 1987 to 13 percent in 1999 and in rural areas from 25 to 19 percent during the same period.

If school-age population was any indication, there was a good chance of small towns losing a school or already having lost one. Among all nonurban towns with fewer than twenty-five thousand residents in 1980, 81 percent had fewer than five hundred school-age children, 70 percent had fewer than three hundred, and 37 percent had fewer than a hundred. Most of the towns with small numbers of school-age children had total populations of under two thousand, but among towns with populations between two and five thousand, 27 percent had fewer than five hundred school-age children, and that proportion rose to 34 percent over the next two decades.[9]

It is difficult for an outsider to truly appreciate what having a school means to a small town—or the effect of losing one. In one of the mining towns we studied, there were two school buildings now vacant because the children were being bused to a town ten miles away. The buildings were crumbling hulls, waiting against hope ever to be reopened. They were a constant reminder, one of the residents explained, of better days. The silence was too. Residents remembered when children's laughter from the playground could be heard throughout the town. They recalled children riding their bicycles and walking to school. Now the town was quiet.[10]

We talked with people in another town where the school had recently closed because of consolidation. "It's an ugly, ugly thing," a resident told us, referring to the merger process. "When the school leaves, it just sucks the life out of the town." In another town that had lost its school more than a decade ago a man told us, "It was just like they took the heart out of our town when they did that. People no longer had a regular place to go." He still blames the school superintendent for not fighting harder to keep the school open. "It was just a smoke job," the disgruntled interviewee said. "They spent more money closing the school than keeping it open. That's really when the town started going downhill."

Teachers and many parents talk with pride about how good the school in their town is, frequently lauding its graduation rate and the standardized scores of its pupils. But the most publicized community-wide aspect of the school is usually its sports program. If the town has a local newspaper, at least a quarter of it is generally devoted to the week's athletic events. A good student who performs well academically may get their name in the newspaper once a year, but a star athlete receives regular publicity. If the home team has a winning season, the entire community turns out for its games. Towns in rural areas typically have a highway sign at their edge stating the most recent year of winning a state championship. "I've said for years that the only identity small communities have is through their children," an older man in a town of seventy-five hundred explained, referring to the importance of football and basketball tournaments. Communities just lose their entire identity, he said, when the school closes. Another resident told us, "There's a huge sense of pride, and it kind of brings the community together when we win a basketball championship." But he said the town's football team was known as the worst one in the region and had been for fifteen years. "It really makes the community feel bad during football season," he lamented.[11]

Because of the symbolic importance of schools to the community, coaches and teachers occupy a special position that can work to their benefit in gaining friends as well as respect, but can also make them uncomfortable when the spotlight shines too brightly. A winning coach is likely to be the toast of the town. In one community we studied, for example, the coach was especially beloved for having won several state championships. There was even a street named in his honor. Teachers and school principals we talked to usually said they knew a lot of people in town and enjoyed being in a friendly community. But that was different for those teachers who had lived in the community a long time than it was for the newcomers. The old-timers were often women who had grown up in the area or had married local men. They had family ties in town as well as professional connections. The newcomers found it harder to assimilate. They had been raised elsewhere, gone to college in a larger community, and come to town because of a job opening. Some purposely isolated themselves because they had family and friends elsewhere, and expected to move on after a few years. "They are sort of a lost group if they don't have a family connection here," one parent noted of the teachers in his community. "They just sort of do their own thing. They're in the background and very quiet." Even the ones who tried to assimilate sometimes acknowledged that it was difficult to feel accepted. They knew community spirit revolved around the school, and yet it did not always include them personally.

Some of these towns had distinctive school traditions that went back many years, but in other towns we learned of new efforts being made to invent activities that townspeople hoped would eventually become traditions. One idea is fall homecoming, which typically is the same weekend as the traditional homecoming football game at the high school, but is now a more extensive celebration that lasts the entire weekend and is billed as a *town* homecoming. If the town still has a newspaper, a sufficient number of former residents may subscribe, so announcements of the town homecoming can be circulated this way. Increasingly, Web sites, list serves, and emails are also used to spread the word. The homecoming festival may include a sidewalk sale, community picnic, parade, and antique show as well as class reunions and family gatherings. "People come back from all over the country," one resident notes. "The town homecoming is a big deal," reports another.

SMALL-TOWN FESTIVALS

One of the most popular events in small towns is an annual festival, usually held in conjunction with the homecoming weekend, or at another time when residents and former residents gather to promote community spirit plus remind themselves of the community's traditions. These events are seldom evident in towns of fewer than a thousand residents, but were nearly universal in the towns we studied that had populations of at least two thousand. Fall harvest celebrations, county festivals, and rodeos are common examples. In most instances the festival celebrates something distinctive about the community, whether that consists of commemorating its founding or drawing visitors from the region because of its ethnic traditions. The Oktoberfest in a prairie town of twenty-three hundred surrounded by pastures and soybean fields is typical. Timed to coincide with the homecoming football game, the festival runs for three days, involves costumes and prizes, includes a dance, and reminds everyone of the community's heritage. Another town calls its festival Old Home Week. Still another has an annual Blueberry Festival, and yet another hosts the best-attended Salmon Festival in its vicinity. Less typical is another town that celebrates its religious heritage with a festival topped by a parade of citizens dressed as biblical characters. One town we visited called itself the German capital of its state, another Little Sweden, another was known as the nylon capital of the world, and yet another billed itself as the start of the Chisholm Trail. Each had festivals commemorating its heritage. A dinner theater with special performances during the annual festival was the regional attraction in one town, an annual outdoor musical concert in another one, and a tractor pull in still another. Other festivals included Daniel Boone Day, Fun Day, Dogwood Day, Hot Dog Day, Frog Leg Day, Tomato Day, Carrot Day, and Daisy the Cow Day.[12]

Residents spoke glowingly of these events. The people we talked to in one small town boasted of having the best Mardi Gras festival anywhere— that is, anywhere that celebrates Mardi Gras in the fall. A leader in another community said his town was the inspiration for the famous *American Gothic* painting. Indeed, nearly every community in which we conducted interviews considered itself special in some way. One town conceived of itself as the birthplace of rock and roll, and another—two, in fact—as the birthplace of the blues. Yet another boasted of being the *real* home of the first rodeo (in contrast to faux competitors), and another as the location of the first Red Cross chapter.

In other towns, residents reported with pride that their community currently produced more irrigation sprinklers than any other place, that theirs had shipped the most ammunition during World War II, and that their town was where the police had spotted a UFO some years back. They knew about these distinctive features of their town because of hearing about them at the annual festival. A community nestled along a winding river billed itself as the best hiking spot around, a community near a lake claimed to have the best birdwatching anywhere, and another one claimed to be near the most scenic covered bridges. It may only have been that the town had the oldest Halloween parade on record, the largest ball of twine, the most colorful ceramic jack rabbits, the largest tomato ever grown, an exceptionally large oil storage tank, or the best attended gun

Profile: Shepherdstown, West Virginia

Shepherdstown, West Virginia, is a community of eight hundred, not counting the four hundred students who attend Shepherd University, located on the Potomac River seventy-five miles upstream from the nation's capital. Its location as well as the university has given it the opportunity to become a popular weekend getaway for visitors interested in the arts, music, and history. With Harpers Ferry just twelve miles to the south and the Antietam National Battlefield across the river three miles east, Shepherdstown has little difficulty attracting visitors, but does find it necessary to put on special events that draw them specifically.

Unlike towns that have one festival during the year, Shepherdstown has five. Each July it hosts the Contemporary American Theater Festival. In October its calendar includes the Sotto Voce Poetry Festival. And in November the American Conservation Film Festival comes to town. The theater festival is held at the university and venues in town. The film festival is also held at the university and the Opera House. In addition, the Mountain Heritage Arts and Crafts Festival is held each June and again in September. Each of these events attracts hundreds of tourists for an afternoon, evening, or longer.

Smaller events include the Back Alley Garden Tour and Tea, held each year in May, and the Shenandoah-Potomac House and Garden Tour, usually in late April.

As if these were not enough, the town hosts community-wide celebrations on holidays as well. Santa's arrival and the lighting of the town Christmas tree occur in late November and December. The Easter bunny oversees an Easter egg hunt each spring. May Day includes a parade and traditional dance around the maypole. And July 4 includes a parade and community picnic.

These events have worked well to bring revenue to Shepherdstown, but residents worry that the community may have grown too dependent on hosting tourists. Most of the regular retail business is now located in Martinsburg and Hagerstown. A small but growing number of residents commute to jobs in Washington, DC, spending little time in Shepherdstown except on weekends. As a result, housing prices have increased. Some residents complain that the community is becoming "yuppified." Others enjoy the festivals that clog the town with swarms of people and block the streets from week to week, but say it is harder to get acquainted and feel that people really care about the community.

show, but residents knew about and made a point of mentioning it, half in jest, half seriously.

If there was any way to weave its distinctive historic identity into an annual celebration of some kind, residents did so. Several towns hosted annual reenactments of Revolutionary or Civil War battles, and a few commemorated local skirmishes with outlaws and renegades. One town took pride in calling itself the Indian or, more recently, Native American capital of its region. It was true that Indians populated the region before white settlers came. But that was more than a century ago. There had been no significant Indian population in the town for many decades. Yet the town had been named for an Indian chief, and so over the years all the streets were given Indian names as well. Each year on a Saturday in May the town hosts a well-publicized Indian festival. A high school boy is elected chief, and a high school girl is elected princess. The two dress in Indian garb and preside over the event. It is all done lightheartedly, but residents say it is the one thing that gives their town an identity.

A community leader in another town agreed that something like this was important enough that a festival just might save a dying town. "The only way you're going to survive is to make the community unique, different, even odd," he observed. "Make it an antique capital. Restore the old opera house. Offer the best fried chicken. Have an Oktoberfest." That view was generally shared, although occasionally we heard mixed opinions. These came from town leaders who worried that festivals were taking the place of more serious discussions about their community's future. It was good that the festivals were happening, they said, because organizing them brought people together and sparked conversations about the town's history. But coming up with a comprehensive plan for the future, including something about historical preservation along with applying for grants or raising money locally were much more difficult. As one town manager noted, "Those are great things to talk about, and everybody feels good doing it, but implementing things becomes very hard."

Small-town festivals are largely organized and staffed by local volunteers, which means that the meetings during the year at which planning occurs provide occasions for sharing information about other community developments and exchanging gossip with neighbors. As is true of other aspects of small-town life, festivals are changing as a result of demographic shifts and different means of communication. The towns we studied with declining populations were finding it more difficult to organize festivals, but other communities were attracting visitors by advertising on the Internet and in state tourism magazines, and were supplementing local traditions by hosting antique car displays, tractor pulls, and craft fairs. Small towns are also benefiting from regional celebrations in which they can participate, such as festivals that combine events up and down a river, or commemorations of an early expedition or along a pioneer trail.[13]

At their best, festivals spark community spirit because emotions run differently than on other days, and because people physically come together and participate in common activities. The lightheartedness plays an important role. Men sport top hats and beards, and women don prairie dresses or wear Victorian-era jewelry. Children wear costumes, much like they would in any community on Halloween. The difference is that the town is symbolized as the focus of the event. Beneath the fun is a layer of serious commemoration. These are our war heroes, first settlers, volunteer fire company, teachers, or youths.[14]

Just as national holidays do, small-town festivals provide opportunities to define and redefine the community. In emphasizing the town's first settlers and early citizens, residents who have lived there for generations can imagine that the community especially values its old-timers—and perhaps feel that it should pay more attention to preserving its past. Festivals also serve as occasions for assimilating new citizens. In our research, we saw this especially in towns with large numbers of recent immigrants. On the one hand, old settlers' picnics and pioneer days permitted one definition of the community to be remembered. On the other hand, Cinco de Mayo festivals, celebrations of Mexican Independence Day, performances by Mexican American dancers and Guatemalan marimba groups, and tables with eastern European and South Asian food suggested a changing definition of the community.[15]

For better or worse, community festivals selectively emphasize some aspects of reality and neglect others. Just as weddings and funerals do in families, they present the community in its most favorable light. Acrimony is temporarily set aside. Festivals are not the time to worry that the town's population is diminishing or be reminded that growth is significantly altering its ethnic composition. Whole sections of the community— minorities, the poor, and newcomers—may be left out. Celebrations work because they are clearly demarcated from everyday life. They punctuate time with levity, lifting spirits above the ordinary humdrum, adding color, drawing people loosely together, and perhaps most important, giving them something to talk about. This is why festivals so often commemorate the town's history. In collective memory, the festivals both retell and become part of that history.

The one caveat that emerged from talking with residents is that community festivals sometimes become so popular that they overwhelm the town—and indeed define it in unanticipated ways. The clearest example was a town of two thousand that decided a few years ago to host an annual motorcycle rally. As publicity spread, the crowd grew to nearly twenty thousand bikers, biker babes, and spectators. Residents said the event was mostly helping local liquor dealers. It put the community on the map, so to speak, but not in the way many of its citizens wanted.

OF TRAGEDIES AND CARE

Caring behavior serves in much the same way that festivals do—when they work well—as symbols of community spirit. Residents of small towns feel that they can rely on one another for help in the event of a tragedy or some other adverse situation. In my Civic Involvement Survey, nearly two-thirds of the respondents in small nonmetropolitan towns said they could count on their neighbors if someone in their immediate family became seriously ill. That was twice the number who felt that way in central cities, and was significantly higher even than in suburbs and small towns in metropolitan areas. It was five times the number in any community who felt they could count on social welfare agencies for help (see figure 4.2).

This sense of being able to depend on one's neighbors is what sociologist Robert J. Sampson identifies as the source of *collective efficacy* in a community. When neighbors trust one another and experience a sense of

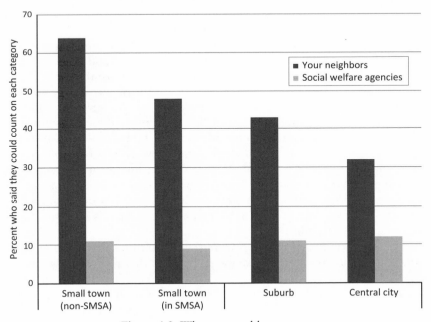

Figure 4.2 Who you could count on

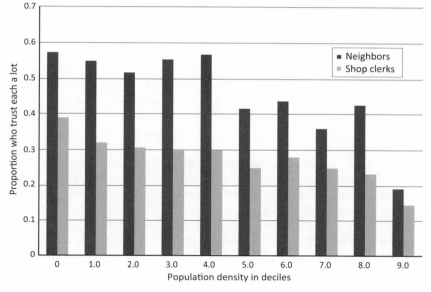

Figure 4.3 Trust of neighbors and shop clerks

cohesion that involves solidarity and shared values, they also feel more capable, Sampson argues, of controlling their lives as well as facing the challenges that confront them. In his research on inner-city neighborhoods in Chicago, Sampson found that collective efficacy was strongly associated with lower crime rates and lower fears of violence.[16]

Collective efficacy crucially means being able to rely on informal networks rather than impersonal bureaucratic agencies. But it does not stop there. It also means feeling more confident about the business transactions that make up such a significant share of our social interaction. Some interesting evidence of this is shown in figure 4.3, which summarizes results from a national survey conducted by political scientist Robert Putnam. Although the data that were released for public use did not permit an exact comparison of residents in small and larger towns, it did report variations in the population density of the communities in which respondents lived, which as we saw in the last chapter are significantly lower in small towns than in larger communities. As population density increases, the proportion of residents who say they trust their neighbors "a lot" declines—from almost 60 percent in the least densely populated areas to less than 20 percent in the most densely populated ones. The proportion of people who say the same about shop clerks is lower in all comparisons, but also declines significantly, from almost 40 percent down to about 15 percent.[17]

In our interviews, it was the fact that shop clerks and local business proprietors were known personally that resulted in their being trusted. Fellow residents knew them by name and saw them in other settings, such as at school functions, church, or civic events. This, as much as the sheer inconvenience of having to drive to another town to shop, was one of the reasons residents mourned when a local business closed. Their sense of efficacy was stronger when they could do business with someone local who they could trust.

Further emphasizing the importance of collective efficacy, a longitudinal study conducted among residents of nearly a hundred small towns in Iowa examined the extent to which shocks to the community, such as natural disasters and the loss of a major employer, affected community life. Contrary to expectations suggested in some of the social science literature, the study showed that shocks were not associated with declines in residents' perceived quality of life. The reason possibly was the sense of collective efficacy that came from townspeople's feeling of being cared for by their fellow citizens. What the study did not examine is how significantly caring behavior in response to local misfortune and tragedies— small and large—figures into residents' understandings of their communities.[18] It may be that these stories of caring—the narratives residents tell about how they helped one another and overcame adversity—develop within days or weeks after a tragedy, such as a destructive tornado or flood, and play a significant role in residents' sense that their town is a good place to live after all.

When asked what is good about their towns, residents characteristically tell stories that illustrate how the townspeople work together—often in modest and yet meaningful ways—to help one another and promote the good of the community, especially during times of personal hardship. As a small example, an elderly woman in a town of two thousand recalls, "I had a backyard with a wooden fence and it was getting in bad shape, and the local men came up and tore all that out and rebuilt the fence, labor free. They didn't expect anything." A neighbor of hers chimes in, "I know a young couple that was expecting a child and were trying to remodel their house and get it back together and some men went up there and helped them do that, again as a charitable donation. They didn't take any payment or anything of that nature." One of their friends was not to be outdone. "The other day I had a vehicle that wouldn't start," she said, "and I just called the neighbor down the road and said, 'Can you come over and pull it so we can get it off the street?' 'Sure, I'll be right over.'"

Mr. Parsons and his wife tell the following story. They were at the little league game only a few weeks before we talked to them. A tornado struck a farm not far from town that evening. They called the lady whose farm had been damaged the next day and offered to bring some food. The lady said townspeople had already brought her more food than she could eat in a month. "That's just what happens in these small towns," he observes. "Everybody will do what they can to help out. It's just the way we do things. That's the way we live."

Another man told us about his son, now seventeen, who was diagnosed with lymphoma at the age of eight. "This town did things for us that I cannot to this day believe. I mean they did fund-raisers for us in the community to help with our medical expenses. They set up special funds for us and just bent over backward for us. I would walk into a barbershop downtown and say, 'I need a haircut,' and the stylist would look at me and say, 'I've been wanting to do something for your family to help you through this time; this is on me.' That kind of thing is just absolutely common."

In a manufacturing town of six thousand on a major river, residents' minds turned to instances of flooding when asked what was distinctive about their community. "Being a river town, we've had flooding," one resident explained. He recalled a flood when he was in high school. Everyone pitched in to sandbag the power plant. "There were hundreds of people helping fill sandbags. You'd look up, and somebody was bringing cold water or bringing sandwiches and potato chips or cookies. That went on for days. It's your neighbors helping your neighbors." Flooding like that happened about once each decade, but for this man the community pulling together during emergencies was testimony to the town's basic virtue. "It's the Golden Rule. That's just the way our community is. At the drop of a hat, they'll come and help you."

Other examples include the story of a man who operated a greenhouse, in which he grew flowers and vegetables. When he was in the hospital after an automobile accident, the football team came over and planted his tomatoes, and some church ladies potted his flowers for him. A woman in another town says she and her husband keep several cows in a pasture a few miles away. Every so often a neighbor calls. "Your cows are out. I tried to put them in, but didn't quite get it done. We got several of them." She is grateful for the neighborly assistance.

Stories like this function in public discourse as warrants—supportive evidence that sticks in residents' minds as proof that the people in their community are good caring individuals, and that the town somehow attracts and encourages such behavior. Such stories do not prove statistically that small towns are any more caring than larger communities or that residents necessarily feel better about their towns when caring occurs. They are best understood as community lore. When residents talk about their towns, these anecdotes are what they associate with the meaning of community.[19]

Profile: Picher, Oklahoma

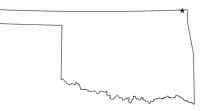

Why do small towns die? Fifty-two percent of nonurban towns of under 25,000 had fewer residents in 2010 than in 2000. But decline is seldom dramatic or fatal. Only a fifth declined by more than 10 percent, and out of more than 16,000 only 57 declined by more than 50 percent.

Sometimes death is precipitated by a plant closing or decline in farming. That happened in Lily, South Dakota, when the railroad that had led to its founding in 1898 shut down service in 1979. Lily's population dropped from 37 residents in 1980 to only 4 in 2010.

Towns also die from natural disasters. Church's Ferry, North Dakota, fell from 138 residents in 1980 to only 12 in 2010 when a series of wet seasons increased the size of nearby Devils Lake. McMullen, Alabama's all-black population of 66, fled from Hurricane Katrina in 2005 and only 10 people returned.

The story of Picher, Oklahoma, was different. Located in the far northeast corner of the state, Picher was founded in 1913 when lead and zinc were discovered in the area. As mining boomed, its population grew to 14,252 in 1926. With a gradual reduction of mining in the area, the population eroded steadily, from 7,773 in 1930 to 2,180 in 1980. In 2000, the town was still doing reasonably well with a population of 1,640, and as recently as 2007 was estimated to have approximately 1,600 residents. But three years later the number had fallen to only 20. Mining took away what it had previously provided in jobs for its employees and profits for its owners. The residents who remained in Picher after most of the mining activity ended in 1967 were living amid 14,000 abandoned mine shafts, 70 million tons of mine tailings, and 36 million tons of contaminated sludge. In 2006, plans were finally made to evacuate the town, but before they could be carried out, a tornado struck the area in 2008, causing extensive damage to what remained. In 2009, the school and post office closed, and with federal assistance the remaining residents moved away.

Although the Picher story was extreme, it was not unique. Dependent on single industries for employment and with meager political clout, towns have died from mining disasters, chemical spills, and toxic-waste pollution like the one that led to Picher's demise.

To make the contrast vivid, residents also tell stories about city life suggesting that a caring spirit is lacking there. The woman who talked about her cows above, for example, says her daughter lives in Washington, DC, where "it's hard to even know who is in your apartment complex." Ms. Clarke, the county extension agent, notes that she was riding her bicycle in a city a few years ago and took a spill. "I went head over heels over the handle bars, and the only person who checked on me, even though there were four people walking within visual sight of me, was the person I was with. Whereas here, if I were to have a bicycle accident and there were four people there, I really feel they would immediately try to help. There just is kind of an interest in that."

Residents of large metropolitan communities sometimes are in fact less sure that acts of kindness characterize where they live. The comment of a man who himself does volunteer work at the Salvation Army in a city is revealing in this regard. He says that "we like to think that we help one another" in this community, but is unsure if that is true. "In my dream world, I would say yes, but in reality, who knows?" Who knows indeed; the implication is not so much that the community is uncaring but rather that people live anonymously. Nobody would know if people were or were not helping one another.

The strangest story of small-town caring we heard was told by a man who lived on the edge of town near a wooded field. He and his neighbor were digging a hole one day to put up a fence. A big rabbit came along and sat within about five feet of the two men. When they looked at it, the rabbit ran away a few feet and then returned. The men thought maybe the rabbit was sick or even rabid. But when the strange behavior continued, the men followed the rabbit into the brush and after about a hundred yards came to the rabbit's nest. A big snake was threatening the rabbit's babies. Clearly, the rabbit was seeking the men's help, the speaker concluded. He said he came home and told his wife the story—and it was probably a story he had told many times. What made it unusual was that he volunteered the tale in response to a question about possible criticisms of his community. He said there had been a newcomer who had nothing good to say about the town, but after a few months she was sold on it because everyone was so caring. He thought the story of the rabbit revealed just how caring the community was. Even the animals knew it.

If caring behavior is grist for apocryphal stories, it nevertheless reinforces community spirit in tangible ways. Besides the obvious benefits of people working together to solve their problems, charitable activities promote conformity to community norms. In an interesting study of a small isolated town in northern California, sociologist Jennifer Sherman found that low-income residents who otherwise had few opportunities for economic advancement were extensively engaged in informal caring activities, such as caring for one another's children and helping neighbors with home repair. These activities supplemented other survival strategies, such as hunting and fishing, applying for food stamps, and in a few cases selling drugs. But they also served, Sherman argued, as a kind of moral capital. By engaging in charitable behavior, poor residents demonstrated that they were responsible members of the community.[20]

That sense of moral capital was evident in my interviews as well. Lower-income residents distanced themselves from riffraff and welfare chiselers by describing small acts of neighborliness in which they had engaged as well as telling stories about similar activities among fellow residents they admired. Besides living frugally and keeping up their property, they tried to be good citizens by keeping their eye on an elderly neighbor, taking a Jello salad or casserole to a bereaved family, or fixing a broken shutter on a widow's house. Neighbors who noted these activities concluded that the town was community minded.

Nor was it only lower-income residents who earned moral capital in these ways. Many of the tales of neighborly caring that people portrayed in interviews occurred among middle-class residents. The events were sometimes minor enough to seem trivial. For instance, Mr. Segundo, the man who recalled his conversations at the nursing home with Don Pedro, described his neighbor, Johnny, on one occasion helping him chop down a tree, and on another occasion, spoke of the local hardware dealer coming over in the middle of the night to help install a new water heater. These acts of neighborliness were ones that Mr. Segundo could easily have paid for—and he did in fact offer to pay. Had he lived in a large metropolitan area, he likely would have hired someone to do the work. But in a small community, where even the nearest McDonald's was fifty miles away, neighbors depended on one another. It was how they got to the doctor in the absence of public transportation. It was where they got hamburger buns when none could be had at the grocery store.

The Unwritten Code of Being a Good Neighbor

Charitable acts, such as helping an elderly neighbor or pitching in to save the town from flooding, stand out as symbols of community spirit. They become the stock of local lore; they are part of the stories repeated at the coffee shop or related to strangers to show that small towns are good places to live. In more subtle ways, community spirit in small towns is maintained through behavior so common that hardly anyone notices it unless someone fails to conform or a social scientist comes along asking questions about it. These small acts of neighborliness convey implicitly that small towns are friendly places.

The most important rule of being a good neighbor is to abide by the etiquette that demonstrates in token ways that the town is a caring community. A key part of this etiquette is the rules that govern ordinary sidewalk behavior. There is a good chance of knowing people you meet on the sidewalk, so the proper thing is to acknowledge their presence. That can be done simply by making eye contact, but is more likely to require a visible or verbal greeting as well as perhaps a brief conversation—as one man emphasized by mentioning that he typically has at least five conversations on the way to the post office. Anything less would be rude. Not speaking or looking away is enough to mark a person as a stranger, and probably a shifty-eyed one at that. "I almost wondered if people had something wrong with their hands," one newcomer jokes, "because every time I met someone on the street, it seemed like their hand automatically waved."[21]

It is not only necessary to wave; it is incumbent on townspeople to signal in just the appropriate manner, as determined by the time of day, how well the parties know each other, and whether they are related by blood. If their meeting occurs while driving, the appropriate wave is further determined by the speed at which they are traveling, whether the greeting happens in town or the country, and how rough or smooth the road may be. For instance, a one- or two-fingered wave with palm resting firmly on the steering wheel may be appropriate at higher speeds, while an arm out the window wave at slower speeds may indicate a moment to stop entirely for a brief chat.[22]

Sidewalk and other public encounters are also the time to mention some piece of information that shows a behind-the-scenes connection. "You don't just say, 'Hi, how are you?'" a lifelong resident of a small town explains. "You say, 'So, I understand your daughter broke her leg. Is there anything we can do to help?'" That kind of remark shows that people have been talking. It says, in effect, that even in this era of health information privacy rules, your friends know something about your family. I know this because my friends know your friends.[23]

Perhaps because the likelihood of knowing someone on the street is high, the custom of smiling and waving extends to strangers as well. Mr. Segundo, for example, says his son-in-law who visits from another state has remarked on more than one occasion, "People wave at me and I don't even know them." Mr. Segundo laughs. "Yes, that's the way it is." It is not that townspeople are unable to distinguish a stranger from someone they know. Rather, it is that their sense of community necessitates waving at everyone.

Another rule is to send greeting cards on birthdays, anniversaries, and holidays, and shower a sick neighbor with get-well cards and a bereaved family with cards of condolence. Card sending is expected even when townspeople routinely see each other in person. An elderly man reports with pride in his voice that his wife is "very, very good about sending out cards even to people who are pretty well outside the perimeter of knowing them but are in the community." An older woman says she keeps a large supply of cards on hand for every occasion in case something happens when she cannot get to the store. Younger people say sending greeting cards is not nearly as common among their generation as the practice is among older people. But one young woman mentions that her mother constantly reminds her to send greeting cards. "The idea," her mother explains to her, "is that as you get older, you plan to send out more cards than you receive." In this instance, even though the younger woman says local customs are changing, there is intergenerational pressure to keep the old ways alive.

Beyond the simple etiquette of greeting one another properly and sending cards, the most important rule for being a good neighbor is to not be a burden on the community. In the first instance, this means being independent and self-sufficient. In fact, a kind of paradox is involved. Being a good neighbor means not depending on your neighbors for much of anything unless you are truly in desperate straits. At one of the home gatherings we convened, we asked people to say what was distinctive about living in a small town. "Less tolerant of riffraff," one person in the group volunteered. She explained, "A small town is made up of a lot of very independent people. They don't suffer well those who just lay around and expect someone else to take care of them." What she was pointing to is a key principle of community life. If a town prides itself on caring for its own, that can only work to the extent that the caretaking required is limited. And the way to limit those needs is by everyone doing as much as they can for themselves.[24]

Social scientists would call this emphasis on self-sufficiency a way of dealing with the free rider problem—taking and not giving back. Norms have to be established to discourage free riding. Formal organizations can deny benefits to anyone who is not officially a member. In colonial America, towns would literally deport an indigent who was not an official resident. The current practice in small towns is less formal. Free riding is discouraged by calling a lazy person riffraff. "We don't approve of riffraff who just don't want to help themselves and who expect a handout," this woman comments.[25]

Judy Quandt was a single mother with three children and only a high school degree when she moved to a town of five thousand that was suffering from high unemployment after the only manufacturing plant in the area closed its doors. She was hardly riffraff but experienced the norms that operate when residents fear someone may be expecting to benefit from the community's generosity. She secured a cheap rental house and found a job as a nurse's aide, yet soon began hearing rumors that she was not the kind of resident the community wanted. That was five years ago. She is now married and has found a better job. She likes living here because the rent is cheap, she can walk to work, and it is a safe community for her children. But she mostly keeps to herself. It has been hard to avoid feeling ostracized.

Being self-sufficient is such a critical part of being a good neighbor that a number of people we talked to report not having sought help at times when they could have used it. Or they tell stories about neighbors who refuse help because these extreme examples show that people really are expected to be as independent as possible. One case is Old Chuck, as he is known in the community, a retired widower who lost his house and everything in it when a forest fire swept through the area. The man telling the story belongs to a civic group that raised five hundred dollars to help Old Chuck. "Took the money to him. He turned around and handed it right back. Said, 'I've never taken anything from anybody my whole life, and I'm not going to start now. Give it to somebody who really needs it.'"

Being reluctant to take charity is part of the code that governs behavior among recipients. To spare them the potential embarrassment of accepting charity, the matching rule is for donors, if at all possible, to give anonymously. A woman in a town of about a thousand recalled her husband falling from a roof, shattering his heel, and being out of work for months while the doctors did reconstructive surgery. "I got anonymous cash in the mail," she says. "People would just put cash in an envelope and send it to me." The same woman voices the discomfort that arises when charity is not anonymous. One of her daughters had recently been married. The church wedding included four hundred guests. The woman said a friend at her church who lives in a big house and is married to a banker put on a beautiful bridal shower plus provided the decorations for the wedding. That was a nice example of small-town caring, the woman reported. But as soon as she said it, her voice trailed off with something about not being financially well off. "You don't want to feel like you're a welfare case," she said.

Her story is similar to an event that a woman in another town describes. "It was when the kids were little," she recalls. She and her husband were working, but the family budget was so tight that there was no money to buy the children Christmas presents. They told the children not to say anything, but word got out at school. On Christmas Eve, they all went to the Christmas program at the school. When they came home, they found a box on the kitchen table. In it was a gift for each member of the family and an envelope with eighty dollars. "We never knew who brought it," the woman says. She also admits that it hurt her pride to have been the recipient of charity. It helped that the charity was anonymous.

But if charity has to be anonymous, how does that affect personal relations in situations where a neighbor cannot hide their need? One possibility is that donations of time need to be handled as delicately as monetary assistance, but in a different way. Social scientists who study the meanings of money argue that financial transactions invoke special rules that usually do not apply in other relationships.[26] A cash handout has to be anonymous because it would otherwise communicate to the recipient that the donor knows something about their financial situation. Talking about personal finances is generally a taboo topic, perhaps especially in small towns.[27] But donations of time are different. Although hours and minutes can be translated into dollars and cents, as anyone who has dealt with lawyers knows, contributions of time for charitable purposes are usually exempt from these implicit calculations. The reason is that charitable time is popularly regarded as a voluntary activity that occurs in a person's leisure hours, which we commonly refer to as free time. This means that people can volunteer their time for civic organizations or help needy neighbors and be more public about it than they can in giving money.

What may be distinctive about caring behavior in small towns is that neighbors actually claim to know one another and thus find it harder to escape helping one another than would be true if they knew less about each other. In a suburb where people stay to themselves, a needy neighbor can live right next door and never receive help, whereas a situation like that would be more awkward in a small town. Women who are not gainfully employed outside the home, and who therefore are thought to have plenty of free time on their hands, are especially at risk of being called on to volunteer. We heard about this from many of the women we talked to. They felt obligated to assist with everything from school committees to caring for the sick and elderly. They enjoyed being helpful, but sometimes wished they were called on less frequently.

We caught up with Linda McKenzie, a stay-at-home mother of four children ages five to fifteen in a town of thirty-three hundred, as she was dashing from one obligation to another. She and her husband live in a nearly new brick house in one of the better neighborhoods on the edge of town. Both have college degrees. He works as a commodities trader in a larger town fifteen miles away. That morning Mrs. McKenzie had been up since five, and gotten her children dressed, fed, and off to school by eight o'clock. She had also picked up a neighbor's boy and watched after him while his mother was having chemotherapy for breast cancer, and had driven her youngest home from preschool plus delivered flowers to a friend in her community who was sick. That afternoon she drove her children and several others home from school, hosted an after-school 4-H club meeting, and then cooked supper, and in the evening took her oldest son to tennis practice and walked her daughter down the street to visit friends. When asked what she liked best about her town, a slow pace was not something that crossed her mind. It was the caring that went on among neighbors and friends every day.

She confessed it was often difficult being a good neighbor, though. The eighty–twenty principle applied, she said. Eighty percent of the volunteer work was done by 20 percent of the people. She helped the woman with cancer by watching her son and frequently by driving her to the hospital. This had been going on for four years. Another neighbor took turns driving the woman, and still another cleaned her house. "Right now," Mrs. McKenzie observed, "I have the friend with cancer, a friend who lost a little boy to a drowning, and several neighbors who are having financial difficulties because of losing their jobs." She sometimes wonders what more she could possibly do. But the "outpouring of support" that people give and receive continually amazes her.

Perhaps the subtlest aspect of being a good neighbor is simply demonstrating civility whenever a person is tempted to engage in conflict or express anger. Not everyone we talked with agreed about this. Some argued that people in their town were all too willing to voice disagreements and hold grudges. Yet most agreed that it was important in their community to get along and work out differences. A resident in a town of nine hundred described a junk dealer who annoyed his neighbors by feeding stray cats. Eventually one of the neighbors persuaded the city council to pass an ordinance against this behavior. For the storyteller, this was the exception that proved the rule. For the most part, he explained, people in his town try to get along. "These are your neighbors. These are the people you work with, you go grocery shopping with, you go to the sport activities, and it's your kids and their kid's best friends on the field. You may disagree with each other, but on all but the rarest occasions, you've got to get along. And they do."

"We just aren't very confrontational," is the way another resident puts it. "We learned when we were young, don't go looking for trouble. You don't create conflict with people unless your basic values are challenged. Most things really aren't that important. Why make a big deal out of them?" "Yes," another man laughs. "We're kind of restrained. We just think, let's suffer through this." The editor of a small-town newspaper says it differently. In his job, it is not always possible to avoid confrontation. Readers come to him angry about a story. They think he is biased, or has given someone too much publicity and someone else not enough. He remarks half seriously that he worries sometimes about the safety of his family. The conflicts are that big. "Then you find yourself sitting next to that person at a soup supper benefit that evening," he says. "You have to be able to set things aside. You have to have good people skills or you'll just be miserable."

Civility in small towns is perpetuated by the simple fact that if someone treats you with respect, you are more likely to treat them likewise. There is, however, more to it than that. The network structure of small towns is also a key factor. We asked some of the people we interviewed to say how many close friends they had and indicate how they knew their friends. Most said there were between twenty and thirty people in their community who they regarded as truly close friends. The ways in which they knew them varied—by living next door, going to the same church, participating in club activities, serving on committees, having met through business dealings, or being related to one another. These different points of intersection notwithstanding, most said that their friends also knew each other. They were members of overlapping networks and participated in mixed gatherings, such as community picnics and town meetings, rather than only in more restricted settings. This was an aspect of community life that residents understood and considered important. The fact that your friends not only know you but also know each other means that the chances of them talking about you behind your back are greatly increased. If you are rude to one friend, there is a good likelihood that your other friends will hear about it. You risk alienating more than one person. "You're always connected with somebody" is how one person explains it. "It's always someone's cousin."[28]

Whether people talk about you behind their backs or not, the scale of life in small towns encourages at least a facade of civility in public relationships because people know they will have to continue dealing with each other the next day and the one after that. A clear illustration of this aspect of social relationships is a story that a businessperson who lives in a town of twelve hundred tells. He runs a truck farm that manages to get along with two full-time employees besides himself during the winter, but hires two to four temporary laborers from Mexico each summer on a temporary visa program that functions with government approval. A store manager in town refused to serve the Mexicans because they could not speak English, and the manager complained to the man telling the story that he should not be hiring people from Mexico. The man said this incident made him furious. He wanted to tell off the store manager, who clearly did not understand the program through which the Mexican workers were being hired. Instead, he held his tongue. "It's a small community," the man explains. He sees the store manager almost every day. "I have to talk to him. So you just let it fly. Unless it's something really important, you're not going to push it."

The other aspect of small-town life that affects civility is the fact that onstage and backstage behavior is different than in cities and suburbs. In those larger settings, more of life can be backstage. What happens inside your home is backstage. Even the interior of one's automobile is backstage.

People play loud music in their cars, sing along, polish their lipstick, and yell rude remarks at other drivers. In a small town, all these activities are more likely to be considered onstage. That makes for a greater sense of accountability.

But in the final analysis, the norms of civility and conviviality that govern sidewalk behavior in small towns would be inconsequential were in not for the fact that sidewalks actually exist and are used. When townspeople report that they live close enough to walk to work or the post office, it is critical not to overlook the fact that they *walk*. In a city or suburb, they might walk the dog, but would scarcely think of trekking on foot to the mall or work. It is, once again, the scale of small towns that matters.

Furthermore, sidewalks are by no means the only spaces in which neighborly behavior occurs. Sociologist Ray Oldenburg has coined the phrase "great good places" to describe the cafés, coffee shops, community centers, beauty parlors, drugstores, stores, bars, and corner hangouts that he believes constitute the essential fabric of community life. In these public spaces, Oldenburg argues, people share in the joy and stimulation of fellowship with respected peers. The need for sociability, he says, has encouraged such places to emerge wherever people live and congregate, whether in cocktail lounges in upscale neighborhoods, or inner-city pool halls, or at day-care centers and fitness clubs.[29]

On a per capita basis, small towns may have no more of these public spaces than cities do, but it is impressive that almost no town seems too small to have at least one, if not half a dozen or more, of such places. In nearly every community we studied, a VFW, American Legion, or community building provided indoor space for small community gatherings. Larger events were held in school gymnasiums and auditoriums, at fair grounds, and in churches. It was a matter of pride in some communities to have constructed a roller-skating rink or swimming pool where children, teenagers, and their parents could gather, and in others, to have an agricultural building or picnic ground that served a similar purpose. Because people knew one another or were expected to act as if they did, the post office, café, and convenience store served as public space as well.

There were specific spaces in which community issues that may have been divisive were hammered out. School board hearings and town council meetings served this purpose. But conflicts that may have been evident in those settings, or were expressed behind closed doors among relatives and in law offices, were seldom reported to have occurred in these other public spaces. They were great good places that preserved the spirit of local conviviality by keeping conversation within the accepted norms of congeniality. It would have been embarrassing to have a heated political argument in such settings and quite out of place to shout an obscenity.

The Difficulties That Newcomers Face

Nearly everyone we talked to in small towns admitted that it is difficult for newcomers to feel comfortable in their towns. Even though long-term residents usually claim to want newcomers, and many towns even have programs to attract people, it seems that moving into one of these communities is not easy. A woman who herself had moved to a town of twenty-five hundred people four years ago expresses the prevailing view: "It's a bit cliquish. If you weren't born and raised here, you're an outsider even though you've lived here for thirty-five years. That's just kind of typical in small communities." Ms. Clarke, the agricultural extension agent, says this was certainly true of the small town in which she had been raised. "If you didn't grow up there, it's very hard to commingle and truly become part of it," she remarks. "You're a new person for far longer than you would be a new person in a larger area." She has been actively involved in her present community for five years and still feels like a newcomer. Long-term residents agree that they probably are not as welcoming toward newcomers as they should be. "It takes courage to get out of your comfort zone and go introduce yourself to them," one man explains.

People who lived in towns dominated by a single ethnic or nationality background say it is especially difficult for newcomers to assimilate into their communities. Language is rarely a barrier, but ethnic distinctiveness has been maintained over the years through other means. People go to the same church and marry within their ethnic group. The old-timers who are honored at community events for having operated a business a long time or hold large family reunions at the town hall are from the dominant ethnic group. Outsiders from a different ethnic background feel the subtle ways in which food, values, and habits of deference and demeanor are unfamiliar. "It is a very closed community," a resident who moved to a predominantly German town of two thousand two decades ago observes. "They have close-knit families here and that is who they socialize with. To really get to know people here is hard. It is very definitely a German community, and Germans have a very different way than I was used to growing up."

What facilitates assimilation into small towns is the same thing that smoothes the transition for newcomers in cities and suburbs: children. As one man who has lived in several small towns puts it, "Kids help the most. If you have kids, there are a lot of kids' activities and a lot of family activities. That's very easy to work your way into." Even people who do not have children sometimes have found that children's activities, such as ball games or scouts, are so central to community life that these events are the best way of meeting neighbors and making friends. "You go to football games and sit by somebody on the bench," a woman in a town of two thousand explains, "and then maybe after the game you get together."

Civic clubs help as well. "If you really want to grab the bull by the horns," one man advises, "join Rotary, join Kiwanis, join Lions." That usually works best, though, for married men. Single men and women say they have found it hard to assimilate. Small-town bars are not exactly where most say they want to hang out. Without children or spouses, they feel isolated. A man I met through a mutual acquaintance and knew only as Alejandro drove this point home one day. He was telling me how much he loved living in a city of two million. "It's a great place," he said. "Lots of bars and stripper clubs. I go out with a different girl every weekend." Then he told me about his cousin who lives in a small town and is unhappy. His cousin happened to live in one of the towns I had been studying. "He should move to the city," Alejandro said. "You just need to be happy. The bars and the stripper clubs make me happy."

Because they know it is difficult for newcomers to fit in, many of the townspeople we met volunteered advice for anyone who might be considering moving to a small town. One suggested going next door for a stick of butter or cup of sugar just as an excuse to meet neighbors. In a small town, she says, that would be something neighbors would do. Another advised watering the lawn or planting a garden at times when neighbors were out, and by all means going over to chat if someone else came along. The bottom line is that a newcomer has to plan on making 90 percent of the effort to meet people, they said. Volunteering for committee work was often mentioned as well, but newcomers themselves expressed misgivings about this strategy. They said committees were frequently governed by such strong traditions that only old-timers were allowed to serve. A newcomer who volunteered might be regarded as pushy.

Townspeople say it is hardest for newcomers from the city to fit in. The difficulty is failing to recognize and understand the subtle cues governing behavior in small towns. "If they were from a small town and they understood small-town life," a man who headed the welcome committee in his community noted, "they would tend to fit in pretty well most of the time." In contrast, city people seemed to come with an "attitude," he reported. They did not know exactly when and how to be neighborly, and that somehow was interpreted by the locals as dismissive or arrogant.

Members of the welcome committee have a story they like to tell, this man says. "A guy is moving into town, he stops at the gas station and says, 'Is this a friendly town or not?' and the guy at the gas station says, 'Well, what kind of town did you just come from?' 'Oh, it was a miserable place, the people were unfriendly, unhappy, they didn't treat you well; it was just a terrible place to live.' And the guy at the gas station says, 'I'm sorry, this is exactly that kind of town.' Another guy comes by and says,

'What kind of town is this?' 'What kind of town did you come from?' 'Oh, greatest, friendliest people in the world, wonderful place to live, to raise your kids, couldn't ask for anything better.' He says, 'Guess what, you found that town again; it is great here.'"

This is a comforting story for the welcome committee. The message is that whatever difficulties newcomers have adjusting are their own fault. Not only do they have to learn the unspoken rules of being a good neighbor. They also have to put themselves out. They need to show themselves willing to get involved in civic activities. "If you want to get involved," the man telling the story explains, "then this is a great place to live.

It would be mistaken, however, to argue that newcomers are deterred principally by the treatment they receive from established residents. Small towns attract their share of people who come expecting to leave as soon as they can. We found this to be true especially among younger college-educated professionals. The smallest towns were good places to start when a teacher or health worker was fresh out of college. With no experience, new teachers were sometimes unable to secure a position in a larger school system. The small town was desperate to find a teacher. Classes were probably small and less intimidating. The teacher would come for a year or two and then move on. The same was true of health professionals, some of whom came because of loan-forgiveness programs requiring a few years in a rural community.

The clearest contrast between small towns and cities with respect to newcomers' adjustments is that choice plays a much greater role in cities. The recurrent theme among small-town residents is that newcomers have one choice: they can choose to become part of the community or not. In cities and suburbs the emphasis is on choosing among a variety of possibilities. A woman whose daughter-in-law recently moved to a large city offered a good illustration. "She found other young moms," the woman said. "She found people who think like she thinks, people who want to raise their kids like she does." Generalizing from this example, the woman said the adjustments necessary were "just finding the kind of activities you like, finding the kind of friends you like, concentrating on that." Those choices were more available in the city where her daughter-in-law lived than they would have been in a smaller community.

DEALING WITH SCORN

With the vast majority of Americans now living in cities and having done so for several generations, it is easy for small-town residents to feel ignored and even second rate, as if they missed the train somewhere along the way and are having to stay behind as a result. If they feel attached to their community, it is still easy to consider themselves inhabitants of a second-class place. Perceptions of this kind are evident in occasional remarks about the advantages of living in cities and defensive comments about residents' decision to live in small towns. Although the sense of being looked down on by city people can be understood in psychological terms, it functions mainly as a further symbolic distinction through which community is defined. Townspeople and residents of large cities may watch the same television programs, eat the same breakfast cereal, and shop at the same chain stores, but stereotypes of the differences persist. Small towns are places where village idiots reside, country bumpkins gather, and rednecks tell bigoted jokes. In defending themselves against the negative views they assume city people hold about them, residents of small towns assert what they believe is actually of value about their communities.[30]

The distinction between small towns and cities manifests itself in the stories townspeople tell about city people who looked down on or did not understand them, and their own rebuttals of these negative or ignorant perceptions. A woman who lives in a small town and does not herself have much education, for example, says she has been called a redneck and her sons, who are both in college, have felt looked down on by students from urban backgrounds. A woman in a mining town seconded that observation, saying that visitors look down on the locals for being uneducated and poor. She has heard comments about residents dressing poorly, not carrying themselves properly, and burping too loud. Another woman who is well educated and grew up in a small rural town says her current friends in the city ask if her hometown has electricity, and figure everyone there is a racist or right-wing fanatic. A businessperson in a town of about a thousand who deals with customers and suppliers from cities notes that a common response from these city people seems to be, "I've got this guy out in the prairie, a country bumpkin," who they can take advantage of. "They don't realize that, gee, we do have telephones here." In a town that attracts tourists from cities because it is near a national park, a resident says she has gotten used to strange remarks from city people. "I'll greet them, and they will slow their speech down and raise their voices, and say, 'Do you have a bathroom?'" Sometimes city people ask her how a literate person can live in a small town like hers.

But the comments people in small towns remember from city folks more often are interpreted by the townspeople as reflections of urban ignorance than of scorn. City people likely have not heard of their town, sometimes even have no idea where the state is located, confuse it with another state, and ask if it is like something they have seen in a movie. One resident recalls being asked if her town has the Internet. She thinks it funny that anyone in a city would think her town of less than a thousand does not have the Internet.

Townspeople's reaction to ignorant and derogatory remarks by city folks is usually to laugh off such comments, and counter them with assertions about their community actually having telephones, cable television, the Internet, indoor toilets, and other amenities, such as good neighbors, a nice coffee shop, or a low crime rate. There is nevertheless an edge to townspeople's comments about urban dwellers. Residents of small towns do not exactly dislike city people but they are seldom reluctant to withhold criticism, either. If inhabitants view their own small towns as bastions of stability and down-to-earth commonsense self-sufficiency, townspeople describe cities as frenetic places in which moneygrubbers with rich tastes and shallow values live. Urbanites talk too fast, are rude and abrupt, speak with accents, and do not fit in well when they visit. "I suppose there are good people who live in a doggone city," says a man who lives in a town of sixteen hundred. "They ride a cotton-picking train two hours every morning and the same thing every night. That isn't living!" Townspeople like this man especially have misgivings about residents of cities making decisions that affect small towns. They worry that environmental policies, agricultural programs, school consolidation plans, and tax laws are all coming too much from city people who are ignorant of small-town ways.

Residents of small rural communities take special pride in having commonsense ingenuity—what they refer to as horse sense—and figure this is something city people lack. A horse would be smart enough not to stand in a blizzard with its head facing into the snow, townspeople say. A city person might not be that intelligent. "My group of friends out here kind of laughs at the East Coast establishment or the West Coast," a man in a small midwestern town explains. "We think those guys couldn't fix a carburetor on a car if their life depended on it. We grew up doing that stuff. We say, 'Boy, those guys on the coasts don't know what they are doing.' "

As this example suggests, perceptions of being looked down on and ridiculed often have as much to do with region as with community size. While people in small rural communities mention being perceived as hicks and rednecks, people in cities sometimes do too because they live in regions to which such stereotypes have been applied by the media. Midwesterners and southerners are most likely to say their regions are perceived this way. They may not have actually been called rednecks, but they worry that people in coastal cities see them this way. They try to counter these images by arguing that well-educated people who have moved there from other places and lived in other parts of the country populate their city. It is evident that these negative self-perceptions reflect media portrayals of state and regional politics. People in red states, for instance, are quick to describe their city as less conservative, less bigoted, and less racist than someone from the outside may have imagined.

There is also a new kind of scorn, people in rural areas told us, which differs from the proverbial imagery about hicks and hayseeds. It is the view that farmers and people in farm communities are rich, lazy schemers, like welfare chiselers, who are living off the government at taxpayers' expense, and worse, are profiting by producing bad food that is fattening the public, creating health problems for everyone, and polluting the environment. It is this image that makes people in rural communities especially angry. They laugh off the perception that people in small towns are rednecks or illiterate. That view is one they no longer hear expressed often or openly. But the idea that farmers are bad for the United States is one they can easily read about in newspapers or hear on television. "The farm life is really a hard life," a farmer says, "and you have to be very smart these days to be good at it. It's a huge investment. The combines they use to harvest the grain cost a quarter of a million dollars. That's as much as a home. A good used tractor costs sixty thousand dollars. If your crops are hailed out or get a bug, you can't make the payments. Then they take the equipment away." It makes her mad that people in urban areas think government is unfairly helping farmers. "People in cities sometimes don't even know where milk comes from. Until you've lived [the farm life], until you've worked it, you don't understand."

Does this woman really believe city people do not know where milk comes from? Or is a remark like this better understood as make-believe that nevertheless communicates an element of perceived truth? It is the same question that realistic fiction poses. Consider Pulitzer Prize–winning novelist Annie Proulx's best seller *That Old Ace in the Hole*, which describes small-town life somewhere in the panhandle region of west Texas and Oklahoma. Proulx visited there from the East Coast while writing the book. Reviewers praised it as an accurate—and even sympathetic—description of the place. They said it succeeded brilliantly in capturing the residents' irascible gullibility, strange vernacular speech, and eccentricities. Traditional ways of life are nearly extinct, writers concluded, as inhabitants struggle with the harsh ecological realities of parched land and stinking hog farms. National Book Award winner Timothy Egan visited the region a few years later and saw it the same way. The towns were dying. An outsider might admire the locals' courage, but wonder about their sanity.[31]

Our interviews with people in the town where Proulx located her story as well as farmers and residents in neighboring towns revealed a rather-different picture. It was true that language sounded different than in Maine or New York, but the largest distinction was the frequency with which Spanish or a mixture of Spanish and English was heard. Although the smallest towns were becoming smaller, they were hardly dying, and the larger towns were growing. A few of the long-term residents were nostalgic, but it was more common to hear nuanced opinions about hog processing and immigration. Townspeople insisted they had good reason to be skeptical of outsiders who came with fancy business deals, yet took pride in the new biofuel facility, remote-controlled center-pivot irrigation systems, and modern no-till farming methods. One of the residents reported a recent conversation with a lady in New York City about his satellite radio subscription. She "didn't even know where her food came from," he said.[32]

Feeling criticized and misunderstood by city people, then, is an opportunity for townspeople to assert not only that their communities are special but also that they are different in particular ways. Some of the distinctive values that emerge in these real and imagined exchanges suggest, in effect, that there are no fundamental differences at all, for instance, in literacy and access to the Internet. But others assert that townspeople are friendlier, harder working, and more neighborly than city people. It is probably significant that older stereotypes of small-town and rural life, such as perceptions about country folk being unwashed and incapable of speaking clearly, are seldom mentioned or are easily laughed off. Terms such as hick, hayseed, bumpkin, and yokel rarely come up at all. The positive values that are mentioned may also be changing. Although neighborliness remains as one of these values, social connections with the outside world seem to be an important part of the discourse as well. The subtext in stories about encounters with city people is that the storyteller travels frequently to the city, and has friends, relatives, and business connections there. Stories about the Internet, satellite radio, commodities markets, and GPS-guided tractors also underscore these wider links.

Escape from the Built Environment

There is an old saying about small towns that if you are driving through one and blink at the wrong time, you can miss seeing it entirely. That was never literally true for most towns, and it is less the case now than in the past. The simple reason is that a traveler would have no opportunity to blink and miss the town because bypass highways and interstates do not pass through small towns at all. Yet the implication of the old saying remains. Small towns are indeed small. They are so small that city people who visit them talk of the emptiness they feel there. A kind of sadness envelopes them because the built environment is so miniscule against the vast nothingness that surrounds it.

For many townspeople, it is precisely the lack of an extensive built-up environment that most attracts them. They appreciate being close to open land, which they consider part of their community. It is unnecessary to drive for miles through sprawling suburbs and overcrowded turnpikes to get into the countryside. It is right there, minutes and perhaps only seconds away. The surrounding land is a special part of the community's ambience. The townspeople see, talk about, and spend time in it.[33]

"I just crawl into my old pickup. Within a block, I can be out in the country," a man who has lived in a small town all his life says. "People drive out from the city to see a deer. I see deer almost every day, pheasants, quail, turkeys." A woman who was born and raised on a farm and now lives in a town of two thousand says that what she likes is living in town, "but you can be out in the country in five minutes." One of her neighbors expands on the point. "You've heard you can take the farm kid out of the country, but you can't take country out of the farm kid." He was a farm boy who moved to the city for a decade, but has returned to a small town to raise his children. He likes to drive into the country. Seeing the farms reminds him of his past. For others, living near the land carries no childhood memories, yet is an aesthetic experience they enjoy. They speak of rolling hills, wooded fields, and roadside ditches with wildflowers. Others say small-town living gives them a greater respect for the land. They see it not just as raw nature or a playground but also a place where people work hard to earn a living and grow food.

The aesthetics of small-town living are worth considering because they are truly important to so many of the people with whom we talked. Admittedly, many small towns are not much to see. Houses are often small and old. Modest buildings, many of which stand empty, occupy Main Street. Unsightly automobile repair shops, convenience stores, and gas stations are frequently the most visible signs of life. A community with quaint flower beds and charming shops is rare. There are no architectural wonders or lavishly landscaped gardens. And yet it is the beauty of the place that residents so often remark on as one of its most enjoyable aspects.

"I drive down in the valley from the north coming off the interstate and go, 'Oh, my goodness, this is breathtaking.'" This is a man who has lived in his community of two thousand for ten years. His town is certainly not a vacation spot and would never attract tourists for the scenery. But he says, "I love just driving around and looking into the bluffs and the ravines and going down roads I've never been on before and seeing things that are absolutely beautiful. I have such a love for the land out here and I don't farm it or anything. I just drive through it, and it is beautiful."

In another town that a stranger would likely dismiss as barren and uninteresting, a man offers a similar comment. "Maybe I grew up simple," he begins, almost apologetically. "I don't know what it is, but you know what's really enjoyable is to be out there in the hills, and it's about this time of the year in June, and I walk around, and look at all the different wildflowers, the grasses. You know, just the birds sitting on the trees. When I hunted, I bow hunted deer a lot. And sitting out there in the fall, I didn't need to see deer or even kill anything, you know. I liked to see the little finch birds that would hop up and down the tree. I like to watch squirrels jump across trees. I've actually seen two squirrels fall out of trees. Did you ever think a squirrel would fall out of a tree?"

Of course it is the human association with the land that gives it special meaning, just as is true for people who claim a special attachment to a skyscraper or urban condominium. For many people in small towns, the land is special because their parents or grandparents settled in the area and farmed. A person who may have grown up on a nearby farm can point to a low spot where they used to get stuck in the mud or a path through the pasture where they walked to go fishing.

Staying in one place over a long period gives residents an opportunity to attach memories to local places. "See that hill overlooking the valley," a man in his late twenties who grew up in this particular town says. "That's where I proposed to my wife." A woman in her sixties says the land near her community is special because her grandparents on both sides "poured out their blood and sweat" trying to make a living there. A man in his eighties says simply, "Most of my friends are over there in the cemetery."

Although it is rare, a few people who never lived in small towns or farmed move to small communities because they wish to live close to the land. This back to the land movement, as it was known in the 1960s, was part of the counterculture that emerged after the civil rights movement and as a response to the Vietnam War. Fed by questions about the fundamental meaning and purpose of life, it motivated people to look at alternative careers and lifestyles. Some turned to communes and religious movements, and others to political activism or drugs. Many of those alternatives received scrutiny in the press and among scholars. Less well known were individuals and couples who struck off on their own to live in small towns and farming communities. Often without much money and even less hope of making any, they farmed, pursued artistic interests, and worked at odd jobs to make ends meet.[34]

David Cranfield's story illustrates the search that has led people to small towns in quest of closeness to the land. Growing up in a large city, he never imagined he would live anywhere else. He went to college expecting to graduate and embark on a career in business like his father. But in college he participated in a Great Books program that exposed him to Greek and Roman literature, Virgil, John Milton, Saint Augustine, Saint Francis, and others. He remembers well memorizing the lines from William Wordsworth:

The world is too much with us; late and soon,
Getting and spending, we lay waste our powers;
Little we see in nature that is ours;
We have given our hearts away, a sordid boon![35]

The poem and other readings that he did in the humanities, he says, "ig-nited a desire in me to do something tangible and worthwhile, and also to be close to nature." The next year he transferred to a university with an agricultural college where he could earn a degree in agriculture and crop protection. After graduation, he moved to a small town that a friend told him about and rented an untended apple orchard. Barely making enough to live on, he and his wife managed to raise a family, turn the orchard into an apple business, and eventually purchase the land.

After more than twenty years, Mr. Cranfield's business has expanded, and he makes a decent living. He says there are always ups and downs because of weather and price fluctuations, but he has done well enough to send his children to college, and beyond that, says he doesn't care about money and just wants to have time to be with his family plus do what he loves. Having come here to be close to the land, he has fallen in love with the town. Like so many others, he tells a story about commu-nity involvement to capture what he likes best. It is about a storm a few years ago that ripped through a neighboring town. He immediately drove over to see how he could help. When he arrived, nearly everyone from his town was there too. "You couldn't find a place to park," he recalls. "Guys with chainsaws. Just a beehive of activity." He says it would be impossible for someone in a witness-protection program to live in his town. "Every-one would want to know who the hell you were."

Having chosen to live in a small town, and having friends who live in cities, Mr. Cranfield muses about the similarities and differences. He rec-ognizes the opportunities that cities provide, but considers small-town life fundamentally more wholesome. In a city, he says, you can "throw people away." He means that if you get into a dispute with someone, you can simply choose not to deal with them again, whereas in a small town "you don't have that luxury." He thinks social relationships are less selective, too. Living in a smaller place is "healthier," he comments. "It's like being an extended family."

He sees a parallel between balanced social relationships and living close to the land. Being able to mingle only with your own kind and avoid people with whom you disagree, he says, is a way of feeling in control, but strikes him as being unnatural and somehow not the way things should be. By the same token, being surrounded by a human-built environment strikes him as an artificial source of control. In a small town, he remarks, you are surrounded by nature, and everyone in the community is aware of that fact. "You feel the weather. It's something we talk about. You're all in kind of a cosmic dance with nature." It has always interested him that the words *humus* and *humility* are connected. Dealing with humus, with dirt, he says, has a "tendency to ground you in the realities of life."

The other thing that Mr. Cranfield emphasizes is the sense of wonder his relationship with the land provides. "We have incredible sunsets. We see sunrises that just knock your socks off. We have incredible displays of thunder and lightning. It's like a symphony. You start off with some percussion, some distant rumbling of the kettledrums. You hear a little bump of thunder off in the distance, just barely. You see a cloud starting to form. Then the different movements of the symphony proceed, one after another."

COMMUNITY SPIRIT AS CULTURE

Viewed from these various perspectives, small-town community spirit, then, turns out to be rather different than a casual observer might imagine. True, it involves knowing people who live nearby, and are valued as friends and neighbors. But much of the activity that generates community spirit is symbolic. It involves the school, its mascot, and the home team—the school as an expression of the community's identity. Townspeople take pride in the school's academic and athletic performance, its presence, and their contributions to it as taxpayers. They lament its decline or the consolidation plan that sends children to another town. The school, though, is not an activity that requires regular and extensive participation by the majority of the town's adults. The same is evident in community festivals. They occur once or twice a year, giving the town an identity without requiring much in the way of day-to-day participation. Responses to local disasters and family crises function similarly, drawing the community together by necessity in their immediate aftermath, and then serving much longer as retrospective narratives about community solidarity.

Sidewalk behavior illuminates a somewhat-different and yet-related aspect of community. People who actually know one another well because of family and workplace ties may stop on the sidewalk for an extended conversation. But the more interesting sidewalk behavior involves the expectation that people will act *as if* they know one another, even if they do not. This kind of make-believe behavior reinforces the cultural assumption that, yes, we are all part of a close-knit community without requiring that people necessarily spend a great deal of time indulging in one another's business.[36]

The reason that newcomers find it difficult to fit easily and quickly into small-town life has little to do with their actual levels of participation. They can show up at the occasional school board meeting and invite the neighbors over for dinner—and still feel that they somehow do not quite belong. This sense of distance from the community reflects its local culture more than anything else. They feel mildly uncomfortable because the norms governing sidewalk behavior are new and they are unfamiliar with unwritten aspects of the town's history.

Being looked down on by visitors from the city further reinforces the cultural identity of small communities. It is not that life is so different in small towns than in cities or that city people actually ridicule the residents of small towns. Scorn works as much in the imagination as in actual behavior. As townspeople mentally rebut the negative stereotypes they think may be directed toward them, they affirm the values they hold dear by associating them with their community. It is in these lines of demarcation, to invoke Anderson again, that community is imagined.

The fact that community spirit stems from symbolic activities makes it no less real. Townspeople still feel good about their community knowing that people with whom they may not be intimately acquainted are neighborly, hearing stories about pulling together, and greeting one another with a wave and a friendly "hello." The fact that solidarity is imagined nevertheless reduces the amount of interaction that is actually required to maintain a strong sense of community spirit. Busy residents sometimes complain about having to stop for a long conversation with a loquacious neighbor, but for the most part they manage to carry out the rather-hectic work and family schedules that would be expected anywhere, and yet insist that theirs is a slow-paced life. As one lifelong resident of a small town explained, "It's not what you might think of as constant chitchat or running over to the neighbor's for a cup of sugar all the time. Not that at all. But if something does happen and you need help, your neighbors are there."

It is this particular symbolically expressed meaning of community that makes possible the paradoxical sense of self-sufficiency that is also so deeply engrained in small-town culture. It is mistaken to imagine that "small" is understood and valued only as the scale of acquaintances that makes it possible to have relatively intimate knowledge of one another's affairs. Small does not mean that the village somehow functions as a deeply supportive network of intimate social relationships. Small is valued because a person can more easily be self-sufficient in that context than in a larger one. This is one of the reasons that residents of small towns relish having escaped from the built environment. Sparsely settled communities connote an absence of people as much as their presence. In large backyards, open spaces along Main Street, and surrounding fields, residents experience a sense of freedom, an opportunity to be alone and do things their own way.

At one extreme, the association of smallness with self-sufficiency involves deliberately living in a small town, running a small business, or operating a small farm in order to avoid the complications of large-scale organizations. The owner of a print shop in a town of twelve hundred put it well when she explained that she and her husband "have never had an employee, and that's exactly the way we wanted it." In a small community, she said, people learn to do things for themselves. You paint your own house, mow your own lawn, and take care of yourself. Or as another resident put it, "You fix things and make do with what you have."

Smallness seldom means quite that level of personal autonomy. It implies mostly that life in a small town is simple enough that problems can be solved locally. Hard work and a proper understanding of personal responsibility should in most instances carry the day. When neighborly assistance is needed, it is supposed to be done in ways that do not undermine self-respect. When all this works well, living in a small community provides a secure sense of being at home among kindred spirits without seeming oppressive.

- 5 -

The Frog Pond
Making Sense of Work and Money

A STANDARD INTERPRETATION OF THE AMERICAN dream holds that it is all about achieving success. The path to success involves getting as much education as one can, finding a rewarding career, and moving up the ladder as one gains greater skills and matures. A successful person is expected to move from place to place in search of career opportunities, rather than becoming too attached to their community, and work hard and attain specialized knowledge that is rewarded in a competitive market. Success may not come in the form of an extremely high salary or powerful position but instead is attained, usually in comparison with one's parents, by taking advantage of the opportunities at one's disposal, wherever they may be. When asked to account for success, people usually tell stories about working hard, knowing the right people, and being willing to take risks. Apart from the occasional military hero or explorer, people who attain the American dream usually pursue it in cities. These are the locations of the most specialized organizations, largest markets, and best job opportunities.[1]

Small towns are the place to examine a different kind of story. People in small towns know it is unlikely that they will ever become rich living there. Job opportunities are limited.[2] Many lines of work that might be interesting are simply unavailable. This is especially true for people seeking employment in the professions or managerial occupations. The likelihood of being employed in those occupations is significantly lower in small towns (and even lower in small rural towns) than it is in larger communities (as shown in figure 5.1).[3] Choosing to remain in a small town or deciding to move to one is tantamount to saying that some other goal in life is valued more highly than becoming a huge success. Instead of pursuing all possible opportunities to get ahead, the person makes other choices, perhaps intentionally settling for less. The person who stays in a small town is in this respect deviant, perhaps not in happiness or even earnings, but in bucking the national trend of living in cities and suburbs.

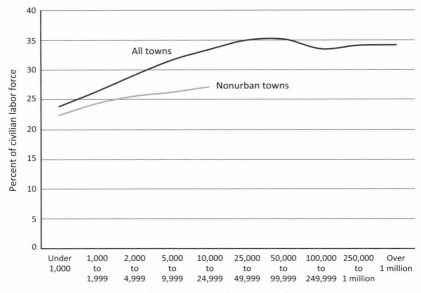

Figure 5.1 Employment in professions and management

A small-town person's siblings, children, and childhood friends are likely to include people who have moved to a city or suburb.[4] Thus, the interesting question to ask is how people explain their choice not to pursue the American dream the way those relatives, friends, and indeed many other people do. How do they account for living in a place that likely offers them fewer opportunities than if they had opted for a larger community? Do they feel they missed the boat somewhere along the way? Did they make the wrong choices? Were there overweening circumstances? Were other values—perhaps the desire for a more intimate community—more important?

As I reflected on people in small towns discussing their work and livelihoods, the first thing that struck me was that their aspirations were often rather modest. I was used to teaching Ivy League students who wanted it all. Many of them had been striving earnestly ever since they were in preschool to be the best at everything: spelling, math, soccer, and violin. They were programmed to achieve. They had in mind that when they graduated, they would do whatever it took to continue getting ahead. They would specialize, get into the best graduate programs or law firms, and move anywhere to attain the best job possible. This was not the way people in small towns talked. They were not driven to become the smartest chemist in the country or most successful trader at Goldman Sachs.

Their stories were quite different, focusing as much on families and communities as on competition and success.

In reality, few Americans actually attain the proverbial dream of moving up from rags to riches. Whether they live in small towns or large cities, about 99 percent of the public know they are never going to be rich. Success comes in smaller doses and is measured differently. It involves adjusting to the unexpected circumstances of life, the situations that a person cannot control, and learning to find happiness amid these situations. In this respect, the stories people in small towns tell about their livelihoods are probably a better window on US culture writ large than the accounts given by the rich and famous who we so often hold up as models of what success should be.

It is probably wrong, when one considers it more carefully, to think that people in small towns differ fundamentally from people elsewhere in how they decide on careers. Nevertheless, it is the case that the scale of one's community can have a decided effect on the scope of one's aspirations. The influence can be understood as a frog-pond effect. For some people, being in a small frog pond works to their advantage. They can be the best student in their class or the best football player in town, and that sense of achievement gives them greater confidence than if they were in a larger place. In many instances, people in small towns insist that they chose their line of work because it indeed fulfilled their aspirations and utilized their talents. There are instances, though, where being in a small town discourages such pursuits. People say they did not have good role models or could imagine only a few occupations because those were the only ones evident in their town.

In effect, their frog pond limited their horizons. They became involved in their line of work less because it enabled them to realize their talents and more because it seemed like the only thing they could do. "I wanted to be a teacher," a man in his sixties recalls, but in college he tried to explain calculus to some of his fellow students and immediately became frustrated. Blaming himself and suffering from self-doubt that he associates with having grown up in a small town, he says, "A light went on one day, and I realized I couldn't explain anything to anybody. How could I ever be a teacher?" From that moment on, he shifted his sights toward returning home and working at something else. He has enjoyed living in a small town. And yet his understanding is that it was the default option left to him because he was unable to teach. His small-town background figures into his account at several levels, providing a reason for his self-doubt and an explanation for his choice of career.

This example illustrates the kind of thinking that needs to be considered to make sense of the relationship between living in a small town and residents' attitudes toward work and money. The issue is not only that people in small towns earn less money on average than they might by living in a city. It is not that they are more likely to be employed in agriculture or small businesses than in large corporations. It is rather that community is an important part of their story.

"We always have options in telling a life story that makes sense to us," philosopher Seyla Benhabib writes, but these options are "inflected by the master narrative of the family structure and gender roles in which each individual is thrown."[5] And by the places in which one lives, I might add, especially if that place is a community where narratives of why its residents have chosen to live there walk the streets and fill up gatherings on rainy days at the grain elevator.

Townspeople tend not to talk about work and money solely in the idioms of career interests, job security, or opportunities for advancement. Choosing where to live is a significant part of how they tell their story. Individualism in the sense of freely making choices and independently pursuing happiness is very much present, as observers of US culture so often emphasize in other contexts. But being part of a community also matters to these residents. How exactly they factor it into their thinking is the question I want to consider here. For example, do they view their commitment to living in a particular kind of community as a significant sacrifice? Or do they find ways to reconcile individual interests with living in small places? And what special issues arise for women, people whose lives have been significantly disrupted, and the offspring of farmers?[6]

RESTRICTING THE RANGE OF OPTIONS

The frog pond performs the key function of limiting choices. An abundance of opportunities to choose from may be desirable, but its downside is that having so many choices can be overwhelming. Identifying with a particular frog pond narrows the options. Deciding on a college major does that. Choosing to follow in a parent's footsteps does so too, as does living in a small town. A good example is a twenty-two-year-old who lives in a town of about a thousand where the best excitement on weekends is at the quilting shop and fishing pond. In high school he imagined himself going away to college, learning textile management, and pursuing a career in the city working in the fashion industry. But in college, he suddenly found his horizons widening to include a dizzying array of possibilities. Performing well in all his courses, he realized many career options were possible. The question of what to do with his life was so acute that he began having panic attacks and decided to come home for a semester to figure things out. Some of his mother's friends in town were renovating an old building and hoping to turn it into an antique store. Without thinking much about what he was doing, he started helping them and found it enjoyable. Now two years later, he thinks he will stay in his hometown, work at the grocery store, and see if he can start a nonprofit business. He repeatedly mentions the "handful of people" there in his hometown who seem to share his values. It feels good to him to have settled into something he likes rather than having to think about so many different possibilities. "Every once in awhile you think, 'Well, what if,'" he says. "But you can't 'what if' all your life. You have to go forward." At least at this point in his life, he is able to go forward because his hometown has limited the choices he has to think about.

The decision to return to one's hometown is quite different for other people than it was for this young man. In other cases, the familiar frog pond serves less to restrict a perplexing array of possibilities in the wider world than as a safety net when other options prove unworkable. A man who is now in his forties and still living in the town of twenty thousand where he was raised recalls his decision after a year away at college. Growing up in a town where the dominant Anglo population often discriminated against Hispanics, he had struggled in school. His parents nevertheless understood that education was the ticket to a better life and insisted he go to college. Unable to make passing grades, his only option was to return home. After working at several different low-paying jobs, he tried going away to a junior college, but again failed to make the grade. Back in his hometown, he got a job at an electronic goods and appliances store. The owner offered to pay his way at a nearby vocational technical school where he could learn to repair electronic items if he would promise to continue working at the store for seven years. Seven turned into fifteen, and what had begun as a safety net turned into a life. He has married, raised a family, and shifted to a larger store. In his spare time he does volunteer work to help improve relations between the Hispanic and Anglo population.

Many of the residents we talked to in small towns have had limited career options because they grew up on farms or in working-class families, and were raised by parents who could not afford to send their children to college or set them up in business. In rural communities, the transition is often from marginal farming and part-time off-farm work into full-time wagework as an unskilled or semiskilled employee. Mr. Yeager, the factory worker we met in chapter 2 who lives in a town of thirteen thousand with his wife and three children, is an example. His father grew up on a farm, and struggled to keep the farm in the family by tending crops and livestock in the evenings and on weekends while working full-time at a plant that manufactured telephone wire. Mr. Yeager is in a sense following in his father's footsteps by working full-time at a manufacturing plant. The difference is that Mr. Yeager has no ties to farming. His life is also similar to his parents in that both his wife and mother worked outside the home.

As manufacturing has diminished in small towns like Mr. Yeager's, a more typical pattern is for sons and daughters of marginal farmers and working-class families to move directly into service jobs. If they were fortunate, they married someone who could be employed in a profession, such as teaching or accounting. An example would be Delores Barnes, a woman who grew up in a town of two thousand people. One of four children, she was raised mostly by her mother, who worked as an aide at the local hospital. Her dad was an oil field worker who drank too much and abandoned the family when she was in junior high. Her mother struggled to make ends meet but never took assistance from anyone. When Delores graduated from high school, she worked her way through a secretarial course and managed to finish a year of college before quitting to get married. Her husband became a teacher. His parents had not been to college either, but were a little better off than hers financially. His dad worked for the utility company and his mother was a nurse. Delores's husband finished college, and took a job teaching and coaching. Over the next twelve years they had three children and moved several times before settling in their present location. They now live in a town of seventeen hundred.

Mrs. Barnes works at the bank and sells insurance on the side. Initially she figured she had two choices. She could be a hairdresser or secretary. The former appealed to her artistic side, but she opted for the latter because it paid better. She worked part-time when the children were little and then started at the bank when the youngest was in school. It was the perfect job. She was through at 3:30 p.m. when the children came home from school. It was a block from her house, provided health insurance, and she could take the day off if one of the children was sick.

The small-town frog pond has worked well for Mrs. Barnes. She says she could have lived in a city, and in fact, she and her husband did live in a city one year when he was going back to school to get more education, but they preferred a smaller place. They like the "slower-paced way of life," she says, and the schools are good. Coming from a family with a meager income, she figures she would likely have wound up working in a clerical job similar to the one she has even if she had finished college and moved to a city. The one dream she knows she will never fulfill is to own a business of her own. The dream she is proudest of is raising three children who are now happily married.

Between her husband's salary teaching and hers at the bank, Mrs. Barnes feels they live comfortably, even though they might have earned more living in a city. Housing is cheap, and there are not many diversions that require a lot of money. Nothing about the small town has stood in the way of pursuing her hobbies, now that she has more time. Working at the bank and being a teacher's wife means she has plenty of opportunity to make friends. She serves on several community-wide committees and is active at her church. As an expression of her artistic interests, she hosts jewelry parties for women in town. The one challenge is that she is starting to learn to play bridge. That is a challenge because the bridge players in town are all much better than she is, but she has found a solution. She plays bridge with other beginners online.

Mr. Keller, the medical clinic director we met in chapter 2, tells a similar story. In the town of twelve hundred where he grew up hardly anyone had been to college. Certainly nobody in his family had. His father worked long hours on the maintenance crew for the state highway department. His mother's family members, he says, were "gypsylike folks" who moved around and took whatever jobs they could find. He was more fortunate than many of his high school classmates in being able to go to college. Coming from a lower-income background did not hinder his opportunities in that respect. But it did make it harder for him to know what to do in college or think about a career. Unlike college students who had relatives and family friends in science and engineering, or worked for large corporations, he had no way even to think about such possibilities. His frame of reference was the small town. Deciding that he might be able to work at a health clinic in a small town was an idea within his reach.

Ironically, young people whose small-town parents most seriously want them to go to college—and indeed, who make significant sacrifices to provide these opportunities—sometimes confront an unexpected limitation. What their parents want most is simply that their children get a college education. Naturally they are supposed to major in something practical. But their parents, who probably have not gone to college themselves, have bought into the idea that college, period, is the path to a better life, and thus have little sense of how to think more specifically about choices among colleges and possible majors. As one woman explains, her parents "felt that college education was the way to go and urged all of us to go to college," but she adds, "The choice of college and the choice of curricula were totally up to us." At the time, that seemed terribly liberating. Yet in retrospect it was a disadvantage. Unlike youths whose parents worked in the professions, understood the intricacies of different college majors, and lived in communities with larger high schools and better career counseling, these young people were left with little specific guidance.

A small hometown can serve in such instances as a psychological refuge. Although it is rare for small-town residents to say straightforwardly that they were afraid to live elsewhere, they sometimes acknowledge that they found it easier emotionally to stay than to leave. Paul Genessee, a man now in his forties whose education stopped in twelfth grade, is a case in point. He is unmarried, lives in his hometown of twelve hundred, and drives twenty miles to a larger town where he works as a typesetter at a print shop. He says he planned to go away to college, but backed out at the last minute. "I was a little bit afraid of leaving, of getting too far away from home, so I just started working instead," he recalls. In retrospect, he wishes he had moved out of state and gone to college. "Finding out what it was like elsewhere and being glad to be back," he says, would have been better than "wishing I had done it back then." He feels it would have been difficult, though, at eighteen to adjust to some other location. He was not much of a people person, he notes, and his mother pressured him to stay home a lot. What he likes most about his hometown is feeling peaceful, quiet, and safe.

The sense, as Mr. Genessee puts it, that a person living in a small town is happier having tried living elsewhere reflects the broader value that Americans place on moving away from their parents, becoming independent, and seeing the world. It is more acute for a man like this who lives in a small town because he feels himself having failed to be as competent as he should have been. Had he lived elsewhere, he could persuade himself that his decision to return to his hometown was made from strength rather than from weakness.

The contrast is evident in the remarks of Sheila Wilkes, a woman in her forties who lives in her hometown of six thousand. While she was growing up, she wanted to marry someone from her hometown and spend her life there. She especially identified with her mother, whose ancestors were among the town's earliest settlers. It was comforting being among aunts, uncles, and cousins. After two years of college, she came home and worked at the local radio station. But she moved to a city in another state after a few years and there met her husband. Now, back in her hometown, she feels no sense of weakness for having returned. She simply feels that this is where she is meant to be. "It's the way I was raised," she says. "These are my people."

For residents like Mrs. Wilkes, it matters to be able to say that they tried living elsewhere and *chose* to return. Having made this choice, they are also able to compare how they felt living in a city with how they feel now. The frog pond figures into this thinking as well. A person living in a small town might feel that what they do is insignificant—at least compared to the movers and shakers who exercise influence in large cities. But as frog pond, the reference point becomes the town. A sense of personal efficacy is the result. "You get involved in things and feel you are making a difference," one woman explains. "In a small town you get to see the final outcome." The outcome may be babysitting a neighbor's child and being present years later when that young person graduates from high school, helping plant flowers at the library, running a small store, or working at the courthouse. Living and working in the town as well as spending most of one's time there reinforces the conviction that what one does matters. Being involved in the community means that a person's story is interwoven with those that neighbors tell about who does what in the community. People may not "blow their horn," as the saying goes, but they know that word spreads about what they do.

Although few people say they would live differently if they could do it over, a number of the older people we talked to did register some regret as they reflected on the decisions they had made early in life. They feel that they were probably too cautious back then and passed up opportunities for fear of taking risks. True, they often had not had many opportunities and they did the best they could. But they blamed themselves for thinking too small.

I introduced the Bradfords in chapter 2 as an example of a couple living comfortably in a small town on a teacher's pension and some rental income from a farm. Mr. Bradford says his parents struggled to make ends meet during the Depression and passed that sense of insecurity on to him as he was growing up. Mrs. Bradford's father, the cowboy, was more successful financially, but he worried a lot about the possibility of losing everything. Both Mr. and Mrs. Bradford are proud that they have worked hard all their lives and have lived frugally. Like many people with modest incomes, they say it is better not to have been rich because wealthy people are no happier than they are. In fact, they point to a rich family they know whose children were spoiled and now as adults are lazy. Despite being content with their lives, the Bradfords nevertheless wonder if they limited themselves unduly by narrowing their horizons. "I took life as it was and didn't really dream," Mrs. Bradford says. Mr. Bradford remarks, "I had a lot of opportunities that I let slip by because I was afraid to try some things. I was afraid to fail." "We both have been guilty of being in our little rut," Mrs. Bradford adds, "of not expanding our lives more than we have."

An attorney we talked to in a town of twenty-five thousand expressed ambivalence similar to the Bradfords even though his income was much higher than theirs. Although he was one of the more prominent citizens in his community and had experienced reasonable success in his career, he thought his imagination had been limited by growing up in a small town. His parents had actually lived in several states while he was a boy, and the family had even lived in a large city for a couple of years. Looking back, he remembers neighbors in the city who had never been anywhere, but he thinks he might have explored wider opportunities had he spent more of his life in a city. "I'm not a bumpkin," he says, "and I don't mean to frame myself as one. But I'm a little concerned that maybe I haven't branched out as much as I could have or perhaps should have."

The common factor in these stories is that the frog pond has defined the range of career options people considered. This influence is more than strictly psychological. It is rooted in social networks. Studies of how people find jobs show that social networks are a decisive influence. Weak ties, such as a friend of a friend or a distant relative, are especially important.[7] The people we talked to who stayed in small towns generally did so because of social networks. Sometimes these networks involved weak ties, such as hearing about a farm for sale from a distant cousin or attaining a job at a local business through the parents of a high school friend. More often the ties were strong, such as taking over farming from one's father or wanting to live close to one's widowed mother. When people moved away, networks played an important role as well. For instance, a doctor who grew up in a small town says he was able to live rent free during his first year of medical school with a friend that his father had known in college. Others from small towns tell of visiting relatives in the city to learn about jobs, receiving help from neighbors while they were pregnant or their children were small, and following in the footsteps of older siblings in going away to college. It is the fact that these networks are shaped by their communities, which in turn stamps not only the aspirations of residents but also their opportunities.

In Quest of a Balanced Life

In social science terminology, the American dream is a cognitive framework or schema that arranges bits and pieces of experience into an intelligible pattern, much like the simple unconscious schema does that allows us to recognize faces. The difference is that facial recognition schemata are hardwired, rooted in simple perceptions, and learned early in life, while the American dream is picked up over a longer period through cultural exposure, such as hearing parents, teachers, and guidance counselors talk about success.[8] Much of the imagery of which the American dream is composed consists of vertical metaphors. A person moves up the corporate ladder, earns a higher salary this year than last, and achieves above anyone's expectations. Failure is described in opposing metaphors. The lack of success is tantamount to falling below expectations, earning a lower income, and in the worst case being down and out. It is almost impossible to talk about success without using these metaphors. A vertical scale makes for ready comparisons between ourselves and others, and between the present and past.[9]

But vertical metaphors also are how we think and talk about balance. Justitia, the blindfolded Roman goddess of justice whose image can be found in many US courtrooms, holds a scale that serves as a measuring device to weigh the relative merits of opposing values. Balance is indicated by the height of the pans on either side of the fulcrum. Height on one side may suggest that value has been sacrificed on the other side. To bring about equilibrium it may be necessary to give up some of what has been accomplished on the high side to bring up the lower side. Similarly, the American dream implies that gain in one area of life is accomplished by incurring a deficit in another area. Earning a higher salary means expending energy by working hard and thus giving up leisure time. Moving up in one's job may mean lowering one's expectations about living close to one's parents or taking long vacations. The narratives used to make sense of work and money include such images of trade-offs and balances.[10]

The frog pond is a horizontal metaphor, flat, defined by length and width more than by height. An understanding of balance requires paying attention to the horizontal dimension as well as the vertical scale. An aspirant for an Olympic medal competes in a global frog pond. Among Olympic competitors balance in life is likely to be heavily tilted toward practice, strength, proper training, and a good diet. Institutions of higher education function similarly as large frog ponds, recruiting staff and students nationally and internationally in the name of excellence as well as diversity. Small towns establish a delimited frog pond in which the range of career options is necessarily restricted, leaving room for clearer considerations about alternative values.

The quest for balance is the key to understanding how residents of small towns frequently think about their communities in relation to their work and money. Consider what Mr. Parsons, the loan officer we met in chapter 2, says about his choices. "I can tell you I have been offered a lot better positions and a lot more money in the banking industry to go to bigger communities, and I've turned them all down. My wife and I decided way back when we got married that we were not going to live in a larger community." The trade-off he describes is completely straightforward. The value that he and his wife place on where they live justifies the sacrifice of a higher income. Exactly why that trade-off makes sense is clarified by what he says next. "We were going to raise our kids in a small community." It was not the small town per se that mattered for the Parsons but instead their sense that children would be safer, happier, and better rounded in that context.

If it is the quest for a balanced life that motivates people to give up something in order to live in a small town, then it is important to understand in closer detail what makes that trade-off attractive. Mr. Parsons's emphasis on family fits well with results of other research showing that it is not the American dream of success as much as it is the ideal of being a responsible breadwinner that shapes popular thinking about work and money.[11] The breadwinner works to provide for their family rather than to achieve success for its own sake. Breadwinning suggests a focus on money that will secure a comfortable home and good education for one's family. A broader view of breadwinning, though, would have to include location. A breadwinner might choose to work at a high-paying but frustrating job in order to live in a good school district, for example. In Mr. Parsons's case, the decision was to work at a less remunerative job in order to raise his children in a small town.

The breadwinner is sometimes described by social scientists as a person who sacrifices personal aspirations for the sake of their family. In this view, the breadwinner grudgingly gives up the chance to pursue a more fulfilling or remunerative career, and maybe even passes up opportunities for enjoyable avocational interests to feed and clothe the family.[12] Psychologically, there is not much to be said for it. But consider the story that Mr. Parsons tells about why his life is fulfilling. "I hired a friend of mine who was a contractor." This is how the tale of building his garage began. "He's a farmer but he's got a degree in, I think he could be a shop teacher, or whatever, and he did a lot of construction. And between my sons and him and I, we built it ourselves. I wanted to experience that. I wanted to be able to go out and buy the materials. I enjoyed that. I just didn't say, 'Build me a garage.' I was involved with a lot of the planning, a lot of the purchases, and stuff, but that's the way I wanted to do it. It took us a long time to get it done, but we really enjoy what we have." He likens this to the satisfaction he receives from his family as well as living in a small community. Balance in life is not just about sacrificing an interesting career for one's family but also is achieved by scaling back on specialization and efficiency. It involves developing multiple skills, working with one's family and neighbors, and accomplishing something of modest proportions slowly and deliberately.

Mr. Cranfield, the man we met in the last chapter who values the balanced social relationships of a small town, is illustrative of a similar logic. In his case, it was a considered decision to live poor and grow apples in order to have a simpler life. That is the trade-off he values. But he also thinks living in a small town helps in trying to achieve that balance. Because nobody in his town has much money, and indeed quite a few are poor, he finds it easier to feel comfortable about what he has. He thinks there is less conspicuous consumption than in cities. Townspeople would look askance at someone who flaunted their wealth. It also helps, he supposes, that consumer goods are simply less available. "You can't buy stuff," he says. You would have to drive fifty or a hundred miles to buy something that would be more readily available in a city or suburb.

The scale of a small town establishes a kind of symbolic boundary around a person's aspirations. It says, realistically, this is what I think I can achieve. Within this orbit of accomplishment, I will be content with whatever happens because other sources of satisfaction are present as well. I can enjoy my family and neighbors, learn new things, avoid becoming overly specialized, and escape the pressure of always striving for more. This is how the American dream is understood at the grass roots—at least by many of the residents we talked to in small towns. It may be nice to imagine that anyone can join the ruling class, but in reality we know that time, health, other values, financial constraints, and accidents of birth establish the parameters of success. It is not so much a matter of setting one's sights low but rather of being realistic.

Ms. Clarke, the county agent, expresses this notion of being realistic particularly well. "I was born somewhat of a realist," she says, "so there were certain things that I really enjoy that I just knew never would be. I like vocal music. If I could have been anything in the whole wide world, I would have been a country music star. I don't think I have the body or probably even the voice or definitely the drive to want to scrape by for that particularly long and maybe never make it." She enjoyed vocal music in high school. The state competitions served as a kind of frog pond in which she could compete, but also showed her that she probably would not do well in music on a wider scale. Now she is content singing in her church choir. She thinks about money the same way she does about music. As high school valedictorian, she could have opted for a career in which she could make a lot more money than she does now. "If money were a big issue," she laughs, "I certainly wouldn't be a county extension agent here in this town." But the community gives balance to her life. She enjoys being connected with agriculture, living within an hour or two of her parents and siblings, and having a prominent role in her town.

Lives Interrupted

If people who stay in small towns or move to one in quest of a balanced life constitute one category, a different trajectory is represented by the many people who wind up in small towns through unexpected circumstances. An unplanned pregnancy, a divorce, an illness, losing one's job, lacking money to finish college, the death of a parent, or simply not knowing which direction to take in life are all among the unexpected circumstances that shape where and how a person lives. Much is written about the unanticipated setbacks that cause families in cities to fall into poverty. Usually the story is about mothers and children on welfare or existing on minimum wage jobs. Often the story is of families living in substandard inner-city housing.[13] But there is another category of people who are frequently overlooked. These are people who might well have pursued ordinary middle-class careers from homes in suburban housing developments had it not been for some unexpected event in their lives. The college major they planned on proved ill suited to their interests. The marriage they vowed to keep for life fell apart. A widowed parent needed their help. They did not end up in unemployment lines or welfare offices. They instead found themselves living in a small town where housing was cheap and a job was available. Perhaps they returned to their hometown where they could rely on help from parents and siblings. Perhaps they retained ties to the city, commuting there for employment. These are people who by all objective accounts failed to achieve what they set out to be. Living in a small town was Plan B. And yet through a series of adjustments, they came to make a small town their home.

US Census data and surveys do not begin to tell the story of how unanticipated events channel people into jobs and places to live they never expected. In our interviews, we encountered numerous instances in which happenstance events of this kind played an important role. Tragedy struck. A business closed. A child died. People changed course because they had no other choice. Or they moved seeking refuge from painful memories. The point is not that small towns are any more likely than cities to be populated by people whose lives were interrupted. It is rather that small towns include people who never expected to live there and really would have preferred to be somewhere else. For them, adaptation is often difficult. The small town is appealing because of family ties or as an escape from an even harder situation in a city. And yet the drawbacks are fully apparent. The possibility of what might have been tugs at people's hearts.

The story of Allison Willard is fairly typical of people we encountered in small towns whose lives had led them there by a circuitous route. She lives in a community of a thousand people more than a thousand miles from the city where she grew up and expected to spend her life. As a teenager, she planned to become a mother after high school with a traditional woman's job as a secretary or nurse. "But then all of a sudden everything changed," she remembers. "I really didn't have a clue who I was going to be." She quit school, found a job, and got married. At twenty-seven, she was a divorced mother without a college degree struggling to earn a living in a low-paying office position and caring for her infant son. One night a woman was abducted from the parking lot of the townhouse where Mrs. Willard lived. "That was the final straw," she recalls. Her parents and sister had moved to a city in the state where she now lives. She decided it was time to join them. When she got there, she hated it. "I thought I had moved to hell," she says. "It was just hideous." But one evening she met a man at a party for divorced adults, then fell in love with him, and got married. They lived in this city for most of the next two decades. In her late forties, she finished college and got a job as a newspaper correspondent. Life, though, remained complicated. Her father was in and out of the hospital dying of cancer. A teenage son was in rehab for addiction. Two elderly relatives were ill and required care. Then came the terrorist attacks on September 11, 2001. She and her husband had often talked about moving to a small town. The attacks jolted them into doing it. The transition took four years. During that time they commuted and switched jobs several times.[14]

Mrs. Willard says her small town is like a "great big dysfunctional family." The part she likes is that life is simple. "It's like moving back to our childhood," she says. When her children grew up and moved away, and when her parents died, she found herself "really missing family." The town provided that. People knew and cared for one another. They also knew everyone else's business, which was what made it seem dysfunctional. "Every day is like a great theatrical production finding out what everybody is talking about," she explains. "If somebody gets a nosebleed, you know about it." Those aren't the only problems. Lots of little arguments occur among neighbors, like someone's dog chasing someone's cat. She also says her finances are horrible. She earns half as much as she did in the city and works just as hard. Her husband runs a small gift shop that barely covers expenses. She has to drive fifteen miles to buy fresh fruit and vegetables. Yet she doubts that she will ever leave this town. She isn't sure she would want to. But she does have regrets. She fantasizes about traveling and living other places. "Oh God," she says, "wouldn't we all like to have a do over? Oh my God, it would be so wonderful!"

Another person who lives in a small town because of unexpected circumstances is Mark Ingram, a man now in his sixties. He and his wife currently live in a town of six thousand where they draw on Social Security, and he works part-time at a local accounting firm, devoting as much of his spare time as possible to charity work, such as collecting toys for children whose dads are incarcerated at a medium-security prison in a neighboring town. In college Mr. Ingram hoped to become a pilot, but on graduating he was drafted, served his time in Vietnam, and then got a job in another state at a retail store operated by a regional franchise corporation. The company moved him from state to state, and after several years he was working in a large city at the regional headquarters supervising credit and collections for three hundred thousand customers at 150 stores. Then the company went bankrupt and he lost his job.

Mr. Ingram found employment in the finance division of a large software company, lived in cities in several other states, and then became unemployed again when the company closed its finance division. After that he took a job with another regional retail franchise chain and was transferred to the small community where he and his wife now live. That company experienced such difficulties supplying items to its stores that he decided to quit. In his fifties at the time, Mr. Ingram was less employable and less willing to move. He accepted a job selling cars and then was glad to find work filling out tax reports at the accounting firm.

Despite the many setbacks he has experienced, Mr. Ingram has become philosophical about it all. When he was growing up, his dad always put him down, he says, and told him he would never accomplish anything in life. He feels he has achieved quite a lot. Although his career has been filled with unanticipated twists and turns, he decided long ago that money is not everything and he is happy to have raised three lovely children. Still, he has mixed feelings about living in a small town. He says it is nice to know everyone and not have to fight rush-hour traffic. But he mentions that the city fathers are narrow minded, and dislikes the fact that everybody knows everything about everyone.

As this story illustrates, there is a point at which people may opt to stay in their community rather than seek greener pastures elsewhere. For Mr. Ingram, it was the realization in his fifties that the chances of finding a better job in another town were slim. There are also residents in small towns who make this decision much earlier, not because they are returning to their hometown or have been unable to find work elsewhere, but instead because they have come to realize that community is essential to their well-being.

Pete Latham, a car salesperson who has just turned forty and lives in a town of ten thousand, provides an interesting example. By the time Mr. Latham went to college, his parents had lived in eight different towns in several different states. He grew up feeling he had no friends and did not fit in anywhere he lived. He says college was like going to a candy store. He hoped to become an attorney like the ones he saw on television, but drinking, using drugs, and hanging out with his new friends proved more appealing. "I really went wild," he remarks. "I was the type of guy who would go to a bar and pick a fight just to see if I could do it." He doubted that he would live past thirty.

After college Mr. Ingram spent four years in the navy, got a job selling computers, married a woman he met at work, and had a son. Soon after, he and his wife quit the job over a labor dispute and moved to another state, where he began managing a rental storage company. His marriage was going downhill rapidly. Separated from his wife, he and his son moved to the town where he now lives. He worked at a meatpacking plant slaughtering cattle and hogs until he decided the job was making him into a more vicious person than he wanted to be. That was when he started selling cars. The reason he did not move on was that he "hit a wall," as he puts it. He had always felt he "wasn't really grounded in anything." Some friends persuaded him he needed to settle down. He had custody of his son, so began working on reviving his relationship with his estranged wife. With the help of his friends and a local church, his marriage is working

again. For the first time in his life he feels grounded—in no small part because of his community.

In considering people in small towns whose lives have been interrupted,
we should of course not assume that all of them have experienced downward mobility or are necessarily unhappy. Many residents of small towns
are pleased to be where they are, even though life has not turned out as
they expected. Especially if they grew up in low-income families, saw their
parents struggling to make ends meet, and had few opportunities themselves, the hard knocks they may have experienced are all too familiar.
Although they may have dreamed about a better life, they know that
things could be much worse. Compared to their parents' lives, theirs may
seem reasonably comfortable. Two brief examples offer illustrations.

Thelma Thompson is in her late sixties. She is African American, divorced, and a lifelong resident of a racially mixed southern town of about
five thousand. Her twelve brothers and sisters have all moved away. Most
of them live in cities. She married young, devoted her time to being a
mother, and then worked for years as a cook. A few years ago after several bouts in the hospital, her work became too strenuous. She now works
part-time for the school district as an assistant, helping handicapped children get on and off the school bus. The median income in the community
is about a quarter below the state average. Hers is less than one-third of
the state average. "I'm able to manage," she says. "It's all in managing. I've
learned how to budget." Her tiny three-room house with a sagging front
porch was a fixer-upper. Her son did most of the work. Her wages cover
the mortgage. One of the neighbors mows the grass. She has a few flowers and tomato plants out along the curb. "I love getting out there in the
yard," she says. The slow pace of life suits her. She recalls her childhood,
fetching wood for the old potbellied stove, picking cotton, walking to the
fields on a hot dusty road, and being told to sit at the back of the bus. It
amazes her that things have changed so much.

The second example is Doris Bunting. She also lives in a racially divided southern town, but is white. The community once had more than
thirteen hundred residents, yet over the past fifty years has declined to
half that number. The school closed a few years ago. So did the drugstore
and grocery. The nearest doctor is twenty-five miles away. A good house
can be purchased for forty thousand dollars, or less than half the state
average. Mrs. Bunting got married right out of high school against her
parents' wishes, although there was little chance of her going to college
anyway. Her dad held a low-paying job at the local sawmill and traveled
seasonally as a construction worker. Now in her fifties, Mrs. Bunting is
divorced. Early in her marriage she moved from place to place, living
temporarily in five different states as her husband's work in construction
required. She tried running a gift shop for several years, but the store failed.

She now works part-time at the community library. She says it is almost impossible for women to find work. Labor at the sawmill is too hard for women, and besides, the sawmill has scaled back to one shift. Some of the women used to drive thirty miles to work at a poultry-processing plant, but it shut down a few years ago. Mrs. Bunting feels fortunate. Life is much easier than it was for her parents. At least she has steady indoor work. She has a "paid for" house and two cars. Her daughter lives nearby.

These two stories capture the realities of life for low-income residents in small towns. Divorced and existing on meager wages from part-time jobs, neither woman would be able to live in more expensive housing in a city. At their age, they have few opportunities to improve their standard of living. Mrs. Bunting, for instance, says her experience as a shop owner and in dealing with people should qualify her for a better-paying job, but she would have to move, and she thinks her age would make it difficult to find employment. Despite the lack of better incomes, both women have actually experienced upward mobility compared to their parents. The fact that housing is cheap and neighbors look out for each other makes small-town life a desirable option.

Among the people we talked to, stories like those of Thompson, Bunting, Latham, and Ingram were fairly typical of residents for whom a small town served as a refuge. It offered them an island of stability to which they could return after struggling with personal difficulties elsewhere. In that respect, the changelessness of small-town life was key. The frog pond itself was a constant.

But there were interesting exceptions in which the frog pond also changed, sometimes for the worse. I was reminded of these situations as I listened to Yolanda Jones describing how she had come to live in a nine-thousand-person industrial town seventy miles from the nearest city. She had grown up in a town of ten thousand about twenty miles from her present community. After high school she went away to college at a large state university, where she majored in business and met her future husband. They married, moved to a city of two million, and found jobs. Neither liked their jobs, though, and her husband, who had grown up in the town where they now live, was suffering from a serious case of homesickness. They quit their jobs and moved to his hometown.

It was a good decision at the time. Over the years, the town had become the regional headquarters of a large manufacturing firm. Its middle class was large for a small town because of the managers employed by the company along with the local economy's ability to support good schools, several medical clinics, and a hospital. The community's wageworkers mostly held decent-paying union jobs at small plants that served as suppliers of industrial motors and aircraft parts. Mrs. Jones and her husband found white-collar jobs, and considered the community an ideal place to raise children. Unlike smaller towns in the area, the community was large enough and its economy was strong enough to have attractive cultural amenities. These included its schools, a library, a citizens' organization devoted to historical preservation, a small art gallery, and occasional concerts and plays. The town was even becoming a destination for tourists.

That all worked well for the Jones and their two children for about a decade. Then the manufacturing firm that was the mainstay of the community moved its headquarters. Within a few weeks, the managers who had made up the local gentry relocated. Simultaneously, one of the smaller manufacturing plants shut its doors and the other two cut their workforce by half. One of the nation's largest Internet merchandizing firms seized the opportunity to set up a call center and distribution facility, hire unemployed workers part-time, and pay them minimum hourly wages with no benefits. Within a few years, the community still had the highest unemployment rate in the state and more than half the children were on subsidized school lunch programs.

Mrs. Jones was one of the fortunate few who retained her job. It is reasonably secure because she works in social services, administering programs for the elderly who no longer have money from pensions as well as the homeless who have experienced bankruptcies and foreclosures. She will stay, but the cultural amenities are gone, and the community is recasting its self-image. Her story illustrates that safe havens are not always as secure as residents might wish.

GOOD WIVES AND MOTHERS

Judging from the people we interviewed, it may be the case in some communities that women living in small towns are more likely than men to have moved there from somewhere else because of their spouse's family or work.[15] This difference is an item of comment even on blog sites by women in small towns warning other women of the dangers of being attracted to plainspoken honest men who would lure them back to their hometowns where the unsuspecting woman would soon experience regret. The men stay local because they farm with their fathers, work at a family business, or hold jobs attained through family networks. Or they return to their hometowns because they enjoy fishing at the old pond and drinking beer at the local tavern. Their wives are women they met in college, while traveling, or during some interval working in a city. That means the wives are newcomers. Wives of men who had grown up elsewhere usually are newcomers as well. In both instances, the wives follow their husbands to a place that holds few career opportunities for women. If they are teachers or nurses, they are fortunate. Otherwise, they help contribute to the family budget by cleaning houses, waitressing, working as para-professionals at schools and nursing homes, or finding employment at an office or store. Pay is low, opportunities for advancement are limited, and a seemingly secure job can disappear overnight. Their satisfaction in life, they say, comes mostly from being good wives and mothers. This is not to say they are unhappy. They have nevertheless made choices or found themselves in situations that involved sacrifice.[16]

"Sometimes I feel like I went to college for no good reason." This is Janice Kemeny talking. She has three children under the age of six and lives on a farm ten miles from the nearest town. The town is too small to need a stoplight. For anything besides gas and a few groceries, she has to drive fifty miles each way to a larger town. That includes trips to the pediatrician whenever one of the children is sick, regular forays to Walmart for household necessities, and frequent runs for parts and repairs when one of the farm machines breaks down. In between, she cares for the children, cleans the house, and does the laundry. During busy seasons on the farm, she drives a tractor, hauls hay, and helps her husband and the hired man keep the irrigation pumps running. Busy as her life is, she does not feel what she does is interesting or important. "It's like you work all day, go to bed tired, and the next morning you wake up and it's the same thing all over again. That's how I feel. It's sort of frustrating."

Mrs. Kemeny did not expect to become a farm wife spending her life in the country near a small town. Growing up in a town of twenty thousand that, compared to her present location, seemed almost like a metropolis, she planned to go away to college, become a pharmacist, and live in a city. Instead, she fell in love and got married right out of high school. She and her husband, who was from another state, moved to that state and tried to find work. Barely surviving hand to mouth, they decided to move back to her hometown, where they could get help from her parents and she could take classes at the community college. Within a year her husband filed for divorce. Devastated, she made up her mind to pursue her dream of getting a college education after all, and the next year moved to a city with a large university. Still struggling with the emotional damage from her failed marriage, she did not do well. Chemistry proved so difficult that she abandoned her hope of going into pharmacy. She graduated with a degree in accounting and passed the certified public accounting exam. "I was pretty proud of myself," she says.

Deciding what to do next was a struggle. She was dating the man who is now her husband, but she was unsure if marrying him was what she really wanted. He was farming with his dad in the middle of nowhere. She had thoughts of pursuing her career in a big city. She was good at accounting, and figured that in a city she could attain advanced certification, move up the corporate ladder, or perhaps work on a graduate degree. At least accounting was something she could also do in a smaller community. To see what might work out, she took a job in the town she now commutes fifty miles to, not in accounting, but instead doing office work for the school district. It was not what she wanted. But she did decide to go ahead and get married. Her husband was doing well enough with farming that they could get by without her income. She decided to stay at home and start having children.[17]

Mrs. Kemeny has been relatively fortunate because the farm has been large enough to support the family. Brenda Morawska's story includes elements that are more typical. She went to college in her home state, earned honors, and then went off to another state, where she earned a master's degree and became a research statistician at a research and development firm in a large city. Her husband also had a postgraduate degree and worked in the city. But he was from a farm background, and when his father died, his mother asked if he wanted to come home and farm or if she should sell the land. Mrs. Morawska and her husband moved to the town of seven thousand where her husband had been raised. The farm was too small to support them. After a professional job that her husband was counting on fell through, he wound up working as a part-time maintenance person. Mrs. Morawska worked whenever she could as a substitute teacher at the elementary school. There was "no demand for research statisticians," she says, stating the obvious. After a few years teaching, she got a job at a sporting goods store in another town. After that, she used her knowledge of computers to manage the office for an electric contractor.

Mrs. Morawska has just turned sixty. She works as a secretary at a nonprofit organization in a town that requires her to commute fifty miles a day. Her husband commutes forty miles each way to his job. The nearest community of any size is two hours away. On the rare occasion when they go there to shop for groceries or clothing, the gasoline bill makes them wish they had stayed at home. She remembers vividly how difficult it was adjusting to the rural life. "Moving down here was just a terrible, terrible thing for me," she says. "It was culture shock to move from the big city to a town at least a hundred miles away from anything."

For women like this who have given up a promising career that could have been pursued more successfully elsewhere, living in a small town is at best a mixed blessing. On the one hand, they find fulfillment from being good wives and mothers, and consider themselves fortunate to live where children can play safely and have friends. Mrs. Kemeny happily uses her accounting skills to keep track of the farm's finances. Some mornings she sits at her home computer doing tax reports for a couple of clients she knows from college. She believes in spending as much time with her children as she can, teaching them early and not expecting the schools to be their main source of learning. On the other hand, she misses the other path that she chose not to take. "When you work really hard for something and achieve it," she says of her college degree, "it changes who you are." She would like to go to law school if she could. "I have a lot of dreams," she adds, "but I don't think any of them are realistic." Mrs. Morawska has concluded that dreaming is overrated. She advises against believing that happiness comes from achieving your dreams. "You have to have goals," she says, "but they have to be realistic. The ability to change and adapt is just about the hugest thing anybody can have."

Being a good wife and mother in a small town involves more than simply switching emphasis from a career that might have been fulfilling to the humdrum daily round of doctor's visits and laundry. Women who have made that choice in small towns report the same joys and sorrows that women in cities and suburbs do. They say it is enormously rewarding to be present for a child's first steps or first day at school, and appreciate living close to a good school and being able to help with after-school programs and committees. But they also worry about the lack of opportunities in small towns. The school may be too small to have an adequate music program. There may be no piano teacher in town. Not having grown up there, women may feel the old-timers treat them as outsiders. If they pitch in and volunteer for civic activities, they can soon be overwhelmed because they are among the few willing to do so. Meanwhile, they at least have to be creative in finding ways to pursue their goals.

A pattern of adjustment that is becoming more evident in small towns than would likely have been the case a few decades ago is maintaining a dual residence. For women with careers that require employment in cities or suburbs, but who are married to men who farm or have jobs in small towns, dual residence offers a solution. For example, Lenora Vickstrom, a married farmer we talked to in a town of nineteen hundred, told us she intends to take a job in a city when their son graduates from high school, live there during the week, and commute home on weekends. That will probably work out for her because they have only the one child and she has been able to keep active in her career by working as the chief financial officer for the local hospital. In the meantime, though, Mrs. Vickstrom has had to make a difficult transition to small-town life. She grew up living in cities and has always wanted to live in one. But one summer when she was in college, she visited her grandparents in a small town about thirty miles from where she now lives and a friend there invited her to a rodeo. At the rodeo she met her future husband. She wanted him to follow her career, but since he owned land, she followed his. Although she loves the peacefulness, safety, and simple fun of living in a small town, she still prefers the city. "When you are from the city," she says, "you are used to diversity and many different cultures. When a city girl is placed in a small town where there is one culture, one way of doing things, it is truly hard."

It was like going back in time twenty-five years, she explains, because small-town women were expected to find their place in the home, work hard, raise a family, and keep quiet, whereas she had grown up thinking a woman should use her education to get ahead and speak up if she had an opinion. "But what do you do?" she muses. "You choose your life and you make the best of it."

One of the most remarkable stories of adjustment we encountered was that of Rosemary Case, a mother of four who lives in a town of eleven hundred located more than two hundred miles from any major city and more than a thousand miles from the city in which she was raised. As a girl growing up in a middle-class family with well-educated parents who earned a good living in the professions, she dreamed of being a ballerina and somehow combining that with her interests in writing. After high school, she went to college intending to further her interests in writing by majoring in English and taking psychology classes as a form of self-exploration. That spring her world was shaken by the killing of four students at Kent State University in Ohio. The hippie lifestyle of the campus counterculture beckoned her to embark on a cross-country journey of further self-exploration. Somewhere along the way she met a man who said he loved her. He was fresh out of the navy and had no money, but figured he could earn a living in construction. They settled in the small town where her husband had been raised. The rent on their little house was thirty dollars a month. They heated it with wood. Soon their first child was born. Her husband's family helped him find jobs and assisted her with babysitting. Money was so tight she needed to work. The only work she could find was cleaning motel rooms. She applied for a job at the local newspaper and was turned down. There was no way she could continue going to college.

"It broke my heart," Mrs. Case recalls about being turned down for the newspaper job. "It was just devastating. My self-esteem just crashed." But a year later, the man who ran the newspaper died and his widow was struggling to keep the paper in business. The woman hired Mrs. Case as her assistant. It was part-time work and did not pay much, but it was something. It fit well with having children, helping them with homework, and having time to be involved in their after-school activities. Over the years she became a Cub Scout den mother, served on school committees, organized a Students against Destructive Decisions chapter in the high school, and was active in one of the local churches. She remains an oddity in the town, as a woman who still cherishes the freedom of the hippie culture, thinks it would be nice to live in a commune, and dreams of writing a book someday. But she has become a firm believer in the value of living in a small town. She would never move back to the city where she grew up and hopes her children won't either. The problem with cities, she says, is that "everything is transient." She thinks it is unnatural and unhealthy for families to migrate so much. "What we have here," she explains, "is the generations. I think that is what God intended—families should stay close."

For women without college educations, the disappointment of not being able to pursue a career in a small town may be less, but their lack of education further restricts their opportunities. An example is Calida Rawlins, a woman we met in a town of about a thousand who is in her early sixties yet still spends most days cleaning motel rooms. She grew up in a city, recalls having few aspirations in high school other than becoming a wife and mother as well as perhaps working as a secretary, and got married soon after she graduated. Her husband's life had been disrupted when he was drafted to fight in Vietnam, and he wanted nothing more than to return to his hometown. They did. His parents owned a motel, and the newlyweds settled into being assistant motel managers. "It took me awhile to work my way into the community," she recalls, "because I thought very differently than most of the people here." After her children were in school, Mrs. Rawlins took a job at a local preschool program. The motel business was hardly thriving, located as it was in one of the poorest counties in the state, and she and her husband were having trouble paying their bills. She enjoyed working with the preschoolers. That job continued for twenty-three years. But then preschools came under state certification requirements, and with no education, she lost her job. She has been back at the motel ever since. Each morning she tallies the income and expenses, fills out government reports, and then goes from room to room with her cleaning cart. She seldom gets out of town. "The motel business," she says, "was not my choice. It was my husband's choice." She adds, "Business doesn't float my boat."

In cities and small towns alike, women's lives are shaped not only by their husbands and children but also by the needs of their parents. One case of this is Georgene Partridge, a woman we talked to who lives with her husband in a comfortable brick house in a town of about twenty thousand people. Mrs. Partridge has a college degree and expected to use her education as a teacher, but she has never held a position in teaching. The closest she has come is teaching Sunday school and helping her children with their homework. At first she stayed home because she wanted to focus as much of her time as possible on her children. Her husband felt the same way, and switched his job as an accountant to a small firm that offered nine-to-five hours and no work on weekends. But by the time their children were old enough to be on their own, Mrs. Partridge's mother died and her father needed her help, so they stayed in the community for that reason, and she did not teach. Then her husband's mother died, and she helped care for his father as well. She has no regrets, but her life did not turn out exactly as she expected it would.

Mrs. Partridge's experience is a story that happens in communities of all sizes, and affects lower-income families more than ones whose parents can afford retirement homes and assisted living facilities. What is perhaps distinctive about the people we talked to in small towns is that their sense of obligation to their parents was strong enough to keep them in the community to help their parents even when they could have afforded other arrangements. In many instances, the people who stayed had siblings who had moved away. The ones who remained said they liked small-town life, but they also were especially convinced that someone needed to be close to their parents.[18]

Although it is most common for women in small towns who have moved there because of husbands or parents to say they have sacrificed careers, the other issue women in this situation sometimes face is dealing with unpleasant relationships among neighbors and with in-laws. This is the more general problem that people in small towns refer to when complaining about everyone knowing everyone else's business. If they were in a larger community, it would be easier to escape, but here it is impossible.

Marcy Prescott is a case in point. She is a mother in her early thirties who lives in a town of twenty-three hundred. Although her story is largely upbeat, her voice falters on several occasions as she describes her life, and it is clear that one issue in particular troubles her deeply. Having grown up in a city and gone to college, she expected to spend her life in a large metropolitan area, perhaps working as a teacher, married to someone from an urban background, and living close to her friends. But after college, she was surprised to find herself falling in love with a man from a small town, and he insisted on living there when they got married. Mrs. Prescott has been able to teach school there and likes the town as a place to raise children. The problem is that she has had a falling out with her husband's sister, who also lives in the town, and whose circle of acquaintances necessarily overlaps to a considerable degree with hers. "Living in a small community," Mrs. Prescott says, "everybody's very aware of everything. In a city, if your sister-in-law doesn't agree with what you do, it doesn't have a big effect. Nobody knows and nobody cares." Here in such a small town, though, it matters a great deal. She has tried and tried to build a better relationship, but nothing has worked. She has begun to give up hope of reconciling with her sister-in-law. "I think that would really change the chemistry in our family," she sighs. "It just makes me sad."

Farming's Legacy

As early as the 1930s, policymakers and agricultural economists expressed concern about the rate at which children from farm backgrounds were leaving farms for better jobs in cities. It seemed clear that mechanization was reducing the need for farm labor. During the Depression, sagging crop yields and prices further reduced the chances of young people being able to stay on farms. And yet well into the post–World War II era, when many young people did in fact pursue different careers, farm life seemed to be a deterrent to higher aspirations.[19] The question was why. Was it because people loved the family farm that much? Was it that they lacked skills or were afraid of living in larger places?

Some insight comes from the career trajectories of people who had been raised on farms in the 1940s, 1950s, and 1960s. The career paths range from easy transitions to college and urban jobs in the professions to much-slower and more arduous shifts out of farming. For people in this second category, a visceral attachment to land that had been in the family for several generations is often evident. But the clearest conclusion has to do with the family social ties that farming entailed. The farm was a family business as well as a place to live. For marginal farmers, it was a business that was not fully self-sustaining. In that respect it was like a small business in town, such as a grocery or hardware store. Marginal farmers kept the business going by working part-time at jobs in town that provided a steady income. Young people, usually boys, filled in for their fathers by doing chores and field work before as well as after school and on weekends. The transition from doing that to a full-time career elsewhere was frequently slow and uncertain. The uncertainty was driven by fluctuating farm incomes, indecision about whether a new career could be combined with part-time farmwork in conjunction with one's parents, and by the health and longevity of parents. Younger people who stayed in rural communities or returned to them did so partly to sustain the family farm, but also because of needing to be near a parent with failing health or who was widowed.[20]

A transition of this kind is well illustrated by Leon DeSoto, a man who grew up in a town of two thousand in the 1950s. The town had been settled by French Canadians, many of whom still spoke French and had large families, which Mr. DeSoto looks back on fondly because he always had plenty of playmates in the neighborhood. His grandfather had run a bulk fuel delivery service along with a store that collected cream and eggs from farmers. His father farmed. In high school, Mr. DeSoto helped his father on the farm before and after school as well as during the summer. After college Mr. DeSoto returned to his hometown, got a job selling cars, and continued helping with the farmwork. Those years were difficult because he would work full-time in town and then work in the fields until nine or ten at night. For a while it looked like the farm income might improve, but increasingly the reason Mr. DeSoto stayed was that his father was in poor health. By the time his father died, Mr. DeSoto had worked in several different jobs in town and his children were going to college. His wife had been teaching most of the time to supplement the family income. With his father gone and no children in the area, the DeSotos finally moved away. They relocated to be closer to their children. Mrs. DeSoto teaches school, and Mr. DeSoto works in a car dealership. They still live in a small town, preferring it because housing is dirt cheap. It took them thirty years to fully sever their ties to the family farm. Their children all have professional jobs in cities.

The transition the DeSotos made from farming took a long time, but they were fortunate enough to have been to college, and find employment in teaching and sales. For others the transition has been more difficult. I introduced Mr. Dallek in chapter 2. He is the eighty-seven-year-old man who grew up on a farm, worked as a farm laborer, ran a hardware store, and then earned a modest living in a metal-fabricating plant. The farmer he worked for after he returned from the Korean War was his father. Mr. Dallek says he would have loved to spend his life farming. He stuck it out for a decade. But his father always treated him as a hired hand and refused to let him make any of the decisions about how to manage the farm. That was the main reason Mr. Dallek left farming and tried to run a hardware store, despite not knowing much about the business. He says what he has enjoyed most about the small town he lives in now, and even about the manufacturing company he worked for, is that people know him and treat him with respect. "That's really nice," he says, "when you've grown up with a father who never complimented you for anything."

With so few of the US labor force still employed in agriculture, it is easy to conclude that farming no longer matters much, even in small rural communities. Most of the people who live in these towns work at other jobs. But farming continues to play an important role in many of these communities. Its direct role is in shaping the local economy. In good years, townspeople do well because crops and livestock are the main items that bring outside revenue into their communities. In times of crisis due to weather or weak agricultural prices, businesses in town suffer. These effects occur through the market transactions in which local farmers engage, but also because of the fact that townspeople may hold part interest in local farms, especially when landownership and farm management are shared among extended families.[21]

Figure 5.2 provides an overview of the ups and downs that farming communities have experienced in recent decades. The data are from annual information compiled by the US Bureau of Economic Analysis at the county level. In order to specify the information for towns most likely to be affected by farming, the 20 percent of counties for which the overall income was most dependent on the value of sales from crops and livestock in the late 1960s were selected. Farm income refers to the mean net income received per farm proprietor, and is shown here adjusted first for inflation using the Consumer Price Index and then computed as variation from the mean value across all years. The category "farmers" refers to the

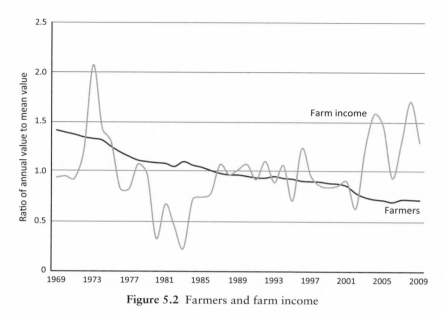

Figure 5.2 Farmers and farm income

mean number of farm proprietors in these counties per year and computed as the ratio of that number in each year to the mean value across all years. As variation from the mean across all years, the two indexes thus appear on the same scale.[22]

The most noticeable aspect of the data is the degree of annual fluctuation in net farm income. Unlike salaries in the professions and among skilled hourly wageworkers, annual incomes for farmers are highly unpredictable. They vary not only because of local weather conditions that affect crop yields but also because of global markets and the effect on those of weather in other countries. For example, the sharp rise in net farm income in the United States in 1973 was largely a function of a spike in the prices of agricultural commodities, which was in turn driven by a steep decline the previous year in grain production in Russia.[23] Other factors, such as the rising demand for corn used in ethanol production in recent years, have also affected farm income, but have not overcome annual fluctuations. The farm income data also reveal that when adjusted for inflation, the amount received per farm proprietor has not risen except for the increases evident in several of the years after 2003.

The trend in the number of farmers in these agriculture-dependent counties has been steadily downward from a mean per county in 1969 of 995 to a mean per county in 2009 of 501, or an overall reduction of approximately 50 percent. That reduction is an important part of the reason that farm incomes per farm proprietor have not declined. The data also indicate a weak but noticeable relationship between short-term declines in farm income over a several-year period and the rate at which the number of farmers declines. The three periods in which this rate of decline was greatest were 1975 through 1978, 1984 through 1987, and 2001 through 2004.

One other piece of information that is helpful for understanding the changes in farming communities is the evidence shown in figure 5.3. From information collected at five-year intervals by the US Department of Agriculture, it is possible to compare changes in the number of farms of varying sizes. Contrary to the view that small farms have simply been absorbed into larger ones, the data suggest a somewhat more complicated story. On average in farming-dependent counties, the number of small farms with fewer than 50 acres actually increased, from 107 per county in 1978 to 143 per county in 2007. The sharpest decrease was in medium-size farms of 180 to less than 500 acres, which declined over the same period from 224 to 128 per county. The number of farms with between 500 and 1,000 acres or more also declined, from 114 to 74 per county. And the largest farms with more than 2,000 acres increased from 41 to 60 per county.[24]

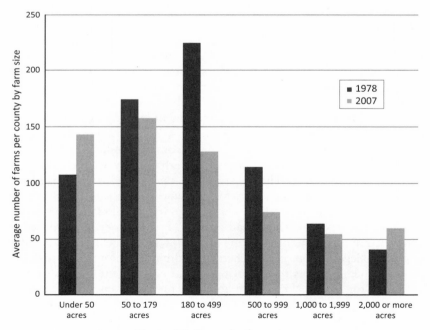

Figure 5.3 Farms by farm size

The pattern suggested by these changes, then, is one of small farms continuing to be significant, perhaps as hobby farms or specialized operations, such as organic farms, and probably held by owners whose income derives only partly from farming. Midsize farms that were more likely to have been the principal source of farmers' incomes were the ones that may have proven marginal and were located in areas that could be absorbed into larger farms.

In our interviews, we found that in farming areas, the culture of small towns was profoundly affected by these patterns in farm incomes and the number of farmers. Despite the fact that relatively few farmers may have been living in or near the towns, townspeople were aware that local business and trends in population were influenced by downturns in farm income as well as the number of farmers declining. It was also evident that people who had grown up on farms and may still have been involved in farming part-time, or because they expected to farm someday when the older generation retired, were influenced by the uncertainties associated with farming. The legacy of farming shaped their thinking about themselves, their career choices, the options available to them, and their values.

Tom Fenster, a man who drives a road grader for a living, says that "running a grader is about the closest to farming I could get. I enjoy seeing the equipment run. I still feel part of the farm community that way, so I get a great deal of satisfaction. I get a sense of accomplishment just running the machine and trying to make the road better than it was." His parents, grandparents, and great-grandparents were farmers. Growing up on a farm, he wanted to become a farmer. He learned how to repair machinery in high school and worked during the summers as a farm laborer. Becoming a farmer proved financially impossible, though. With few other options available, he was happy to find a steady job that resembled farming.

For residents like Mr. Fenster, the shadow of farming extends in memory to earlier generations who settled in the area, or in some other region, worked bravely to carve out an existence from the land, made good, and then failed during the Great Depression. Perhaps they are the grandchildren of that generation. They heard about their grandparents losing the farm, and then having to take low-paying work on the railroad or in construction, as one man recalled. Losing the farm had long-lasting consequences. The next generation had nothing. Perhaps they also worked in construction or at a manufacturing plant. Finally their children were able to go to college and become teachers or health professionals. But they still think of themselves as the offspring of that earlier generation who had done well for a time. "I'm a farm boy," one man explains, "even though I grew up in town." He had never lived on a farm. Neither had his parents. But his grandparents had. Those were the better times that he cherished even though he had never experienced them directly.

Profile: Crystal, North Dakota

The two regions most affected by the changes in agriculture during and after the 1980s were the Southeast, where small cotton and tobacco farms were absorbed into larger operations, and the upper Midwest, where large wheat farms became even larger. Between 1979 and 2009, the number of farmers in North and South Carolina along with Georgia fell by 84,198, for a decline of 45 percent, and the number in North and South Dakota, Nebraska, and Kansas dropped by 78,258, or a decline of 35 percent.

On average, these declines affected the population of small towns less in the Southeast than in the upper Midwest. In the Southeast, only 16 percent of small towns in counties with high rates of farm decline also experienced significant population decline—about the same as in counties with less farm decline—while in the upper Midwest, 47 percent of small towns in counties with high rates of farm decline suffered population loss. Towns that were already small experienced the worst decline.

Crystal, North Dakota, in Pembina County, illustrates these changes. Between 1979 and 2009, the number of farms in Pembina County declined from 944 to 521, the average farm size increased from 720 to 1,246 acres, and the number of farm proprietors fell from 1,063 to 428. The eleven towns in Pembina County all lost population as a result. Crystal fared the worst. Its population fell from 255 in 1980 to 138 in 2010, for a decline of 46 percent. There was at least a 40 percent decline in five other towns with fewer than 200 residents in 1980.

In contrast, Cavalier, the county seat, which was also the largest town in Pembina County, declined by only 13 percent, from 1,505 in 1980 to 1,301 in 2010. Cavalier fared better than Crystal and the other small towns for several reasons. More than 800 residents of Pembina County worked in federal, state, and local government jobs. The majority of these residents lived and worked in the county seat. That meant better opportunities for retail stores and service shops as well.

The number of farmers who lived in the county seat held steady, while the number who lived in smaller towns declined. The smaller communities also ceased being as attractive to older residents. Only 6 percent of Crystal's residents were sixty-five and older in 2010—down from 19 percent in 1980. In contrast, the proportion in Cavalier increased from 20 to 33 percent.

As this example suggests, the lure of living on or near a farm is one of the attractions that draws people to rural communities. Even though they could be earning more in another location, they opt for a small town because it reminds them of their parents or grandparents. Some become hobby farmers, tilling a few acres on weekends or tending a large backyard garden. Others are content to be in the vicinity of farms despite the fact that they have no personal connection to farming. Still others turn to farming—even in an era when agriculture is often regarded as a mere holdover from the past—because they view it as an attractive business opportunity.

Lawrence Burgess and his wife, Margaret, were in their late thirties when they decided to move to a small town on the West Coast and try their hand at farming. He had a graduate degree from one of the nation's leading business schools and had moved up the executive ladder at one of the largest petroleum companies. She had graduated from an elite university and also held a well-paying job in corporate America. With some encouragement from his dad, who had farmed in addition to doing other things, Mr. Burgess decided that farming might be his best opportunity to run his own business. Today, the Burgesses farm three thousand acres, and earn a decent living growing truck crops and organic rice while leasing the paddies during the off-season to duck hunters. They miss the intellectual stimulation and cultural diversity of living in a city, but have no regrets about moving to a small town. They treasure the serenity and security of their community, and spend much of their spare time volunteering for civic activities.

But there is another legacy of farming that has not been so generous to small towns. Recall Mr. Janssen, the third-generation farmer who tends more than nine thousand acres at age seventy and has no intention of retiring anytime soon. We were unable to talk with his son, who farms with him, but can imagine some of the issues that may be present in this arrangement from the interviews we conducted with others farming in partnership with fathers and fathers-in-law. The difficulties they mentioned ranged from disagreements about who was in charge to financial strains. The Janssens' acreage was large enough to easily support two families, but in many instances that was not the case.

Research shows that the stress involved in two-generation farm families is often particularly acute for mothers and daughters-in-law. Especially if the younger woman has moved there from another community, she may be treated as an outsider and not be fully integrated into the farm's decision-making process. Possibilities for overt confrontations about exclusion and hurt feelings may be limited because of the younger couple's economic dependence on the older couple. The daughter-in-law may also have given up a career and find herself having to care for aging in-laws.[25]

Reports from the US Department of Agriculture have noted for some time that the median age of farmers is rising.[26] Data from the US Census Bureau shows that among all males age eighteen and over who listed their occupation as farmer (either as an owner or tenant), the median age rose from forty-five in 1950 to fifty in 2000. Median age, though, does not reveal the full picture or its consequences for farm communities. A clearer sense is given by the percentage of farmers who are over age sixty. That figure rose from 19 percent in 1950 to 36 percent in 2000. For the children of farmers who were in line to take their place, 81 percent in 1950 would, on average, have been able to do so by the time their fathers were sixty and they themselves were about age forty. A half century later, that proportion would have fallen, on average, to 64 percent. Their fathers were living longer, enjoying better health, and able to continue farming longer because of mechanization. Instead of simply retiring when the work became too arduous, the older men stayed in charge by gradually scaling back, hiring help, and shifting more of their attention to management.[27]

"What we see here," one community leader in a farming town observes, "are young people who would like to stay and farm moving away because the farm isn't capable of supporting them *and* their parents—and sometimes their grandparents as well." What this leader might also have mentioned is that even if the parents or grandparents were no longer directly involved in farming, their longevity was postponing transfer of ownership to the younger generation. As tenants, the younger generation would have been paying approximately a third of their earnings to the older generation who still held title to the land.

Greater longevity among the farm population is thus a factor in the life of small rural communities by virtue of the pressures it imposes on the younger generation to seek opportunities elsewhere. Even if farms were not becoming larger as a result of greater mechanization and economies of scale, farm communities would have difficulty retaining the offspring of farmers. The younger generation might aspire to continue the family tradition of farming, but find it necessary over a longer period to live elsewhere until the older generation retired or died. In the meantime, community leaders would notice that the resident population was aging and fewer young people were staying.

Getting by with a Little Help

"My goodness, honey, I've been so many places. When I finished school, I couldn't wait to get away from home. I had a boyfriend who wanted to get married. He was in the army, and I thought, hee-haw, get away from home. So we got married, and I went to Texas. First time I'd been away from home in my life and I cried my eyes out." This is how a woman who is typical of many people in small towns' lowest-income strata begins her story.

Nellie Tavers lives in a crumbling two-story house in a town that would have to count all the dogs and cats to declare a population of a thousand. "Here we were in Texas, far away from home, me seventeen and pregnant, him in the army. We didn't make any money back then. I couldn't work, so we just nearly starved to death. After I had the baby, I came back home and stayed at home." Her mother helped with the baby and got her a job at a packaged-food-processing plant nearby. The work was backbreaking. The pay scale was minimum wage. After a few years of that, she quit and tried to run a hairdressing shop. "My husband was a truck driver. He said the only way we are going to get along is for you to just get out of the shop and get on the truck with me. So I drove semi with him for a while. I always say I didn't think I liked him when I got on there driving the truck, and I was sure of it when I got off."

"So I got off the truck and moved back to mom's and married a guy that had a band." She'd always loved music. Growing up, she'd learned to play the piano listening to Jerry Lee Lewis albums. "I thought I was a big singer, so we went around with this band just playing local places. I realized, no, this ain't going to work, and then the roof fell in on him one day and he couldn't work anymore. So we moved and lived there about ten years. Then we moved back here, and my mom was in this house that I am in now."

Mrs. Tavers is now in her sixties. Looking back on her life, she wishes some of her decisions had been different. It would have been nice to get more education. Her mother worked at a shoe factory during the Depression, and the Works Progress Administration employed her father. Her parents wanted their children to have a better life. But after the fire that took their house one night, her parents couldn't afford to send any of them to college. Losing everything sort of destroyed their will to live. Her dad died a few years later. "I've been through the ropes, so to speak. I'm older and wiser," she says. "I know a little bit about everything, but not enough to be worth a flip."

Mrs. Tavers has cancer. It started in her lungs and spread to her colon. Now the doctor is keeping his eye on a small tumor on her pancreas. At the moment, she is in remission. She has three children. Two live in other states, and the third lives in Europe. They don't come often for visits. She drives a rusty twenty-year-old car. "It's going to poop out one of these days and then I don't know what I'm going to do." Her daughter offered to buy her a better one, but Mrs. Tavers couldn't afford the insurance. Her Social Security check is six hundred dollars a month. Her only major purchase has been the new chair she sits in while recovering from her last surgery.

Her frog pond is the town. She tried living in an apartment in a larger town where she could be closer to the hospital, but was unable to pay the rent. This old house where she and her mother had lived had been empty for four years when she returned. It was in pretty bad shape after the flood that came through and washed mud almost to the ceiling, but at least it was hers. "I have wonderful neighbors," she says. "When I've been sick, they've come and done my yard, cut my dead flowers down, took care of everything around here for me." One of her neighbors drives thirty miles to Walmart about once a week, and brings her back groceries and supplies. "Nellie, here's some food for you," the lady across the street says, leaving a dish on the kitchen table. A farmer in the community prunes her trees. Another neighbor takes her to the little Baptist Church, where the congregation prays for God to heal her cancer. They dragged in an old overstuffed chair when she could no longer sit in the pew. "Without good neighbors," she comments, "I don't know what I would have done."

For someone like Mrs. Tavers, the frog pond is less about money and work than balancing neighborly obligations. Although she is mostly on the receiving end these days, she tries to fulfill the timeworn neighborly expectations of giving back and being as self-sufficient as she can. One of her neighbors offers to drive her to chemo, but Mrs. Tavers drives herself whenever she is able. She hates to think of a neighbor having to sit there for two hours with nothing to do. She still plays the piano at church when she is feeling well enough. Mrs. Tavers is making a quilt for a raffle to be held next month at the nursing home. At Christmas she bakes banana nut bread in coffee cans, ties ribbons on them, and takes them to the neighbors on her street.

THE COMMUNITY AS REFERENCE GROUP

Mrs. Tavers and the other people whose stories I have shared in this chapter have one thing in common: the community serves not only as a place to live or a social unit that commands some of their time and interest but also a point of reference. The community is part of these people's personal story, figuring into their accounts of why they chose their particular line of work, and how they have succeeded or in some cases failed to achieve their aspirations in life. A person's self-narrative becomes enmeshed with the town's.

Usually, mention of reference groups comes up in the context of competitive situations. The competition is with one's siblings as a child and classmates while going to school, and comparisons with them are continuously made, formally and informally, in terms of academic performance, athletic accomplishments, friends, clothing, and nearly everything else. Later on, the reference group inevitably widens to include others in the same occupation and within a kind of pecking order based on information about salaries, promotions, awards, travel, the price of housing, and where a person lives. If where a person lives is a small town, it is difficult to avoid the community being one of a person's reference groups.

Reference groups and evaluations of achievement go hand in hand. Indeed, the two are almost synonymous. Relative to a person's reference group a person can be ranked near the top, somewhere in the middle, or near the bottom. That is one way to think about small towns as a reference group. Relative to others in the community, a person may be closer to the top or bottom. As we saw in chapter 2, those distinctions exist in small towns and are well known in the community.

The examples I have considered, though, suggest other important ways in which communities function as reference groups. For better or worse, small towns serve as frog ponds that define a reasonable range of options to consider in life. They do not entirely rule out even the most ambitious options—there are enough instances of celebrities and successful business leaders from small towns to serve as examples. But it is certainly easier to ignore certain options if those are unrepresented among any of the people who live in a town. In that respect, the frog pond eliminates some of the confusion of having to make choices when all possible options are on the table.

Beyond the psychological security it may provide, the frog pond can also serve in reality as a fallback option when other possibilities do not pan out. The narratives in which this aspect of the frog pond is emphasized involve a refreshing element of candor. Why do I live here and do the kind of work I do? Frankly, because I tried somewhere else and I failed. I came back to my hometown and moved to another small town because I need the support. I had family there who could help me. I knew someone in business who gave me a break. It was easier to get a job in a small frog pond than in a larger one.

Stories about making a life in a small town, even as a fallback, however, are complicated. If the grass is greener elsewhere, few of us go through life thinking only that things would have been better had some other path been taken. What we see in stories about the relationship between living in a small town and choices about work and money is that community does imply settling in. Being in a place means that the community is integrated into one's life. It becomes home in the sense that the taken-for-granted realities of daily life are here.

We have also seen here the particular challenges that are sometimes faced in making a small community a home. For some, the sense of having failed in a wider context or having to live in an out-of-the-way place for lack of better opportunities remains difficult. It is at least harder to reckon with having lost a job or failed in a marriage than with viewing small-town life as the ideal place in which to live in harmony with nature as well as oneself.

The challenges that women face who have been unable to fulfill personal aspirations in a small town, I have suggested, are especially worth understanding. Theirs is a delicate balancing act that involves trade-offs between careers and family along with adjustments to living in a community in which they may not have been raised as well as shouldering heavy caregiving responsibilities. These are challenges that the community sometimes helps to mitigate, but that can also be difficult to resolve in the fishbowl environment of a small town. Sometimes equally difficult are the intergenerational dynamics among families in small towns with farming connections, and the issues that may arise among siblings and in-laws in small communities. These are challenges that again underscore the diversities of experience that exist in otherwise seemingly homogeneous places.

If someone like Mrs. Tavers depends wholeheartedly on having neighbors she trusts, the conclusion to be drawn is not that small towns are cozy places where community works as well as idealized depictions of it suggest. She is too self-sufficient and takes too much pride in doing things herself to suggest that community is a matter of being buddy-buddy with a close cadre of friends. The better conclusion is that communities are the places in which the struggles of daily life occur, which may include losing one's job or fighting cancer. The frog pond shapes personal horizons, not in the strict sense of preventing anyone from having connections elsewhere or jumping from pond to pond, but rather as the place in which one's life is lived most days and through which one's story is inflected.

- 6 -

Leadership
Earning Respect, Improving the Community

IN A TOWN OF EIGHT HUNDRED PEOPLE, surrounded by cornfields and chicken hatcheries, and located more than a hundred miles from the nearest city, a man in his early thirties could easily become discouraged. But John Owens has lived here for only a year. He is still high on the small-town values that drew him here as a high school social studies teacher with two young children of his own. Although the town's population has dipped slightly in recent years, the local farm economy has been strong. The John Deere dealer just finished constructing a new building, and there is a recently opened medical clinic. Having escaped the housing bubble that put people in many parts of the country in financial jeopardy, the town's bank is doing well. Mr. Owens says housing in the community has always been amazingly affordable. That was one of the reasons he decided to move here.

Mr. Owens acknowledges that many of the high school students he teaches will move away in search of better jobs and never return. But he says there are a surprising number of opportunities for those who stay. "The ability to network," he says, is the key. "You move up to a large city and you decide to become a carpenter there, for example, and you really have to advertise hard because nobody knows you. People don't know if they can trust you. They've never heard of you before. But in a small community, people know you and your family. If you're respectable people, they'll say, 'Well, we'll have him come and do our work for us.' Now the reverse also happens. If you come from a family that is not so respectable, you may want to move out of town."

This same principle of being known, networking, and being respected as a person that people can trust is central to community leadership. Mr. Owens singles out the banker in his town as an example. The banker is a man who is "involved in the community a lot." The banker "doesn't just sit back in his office and never talk to anybody." Mr. Owens's impression of the city council members is similar. Somehow they contribute to the town's pride in itself.

Bureaucratic organizations, such as corporations and government agencies, have formal leadership structures based on a hierarchical model of authority. Someone is officially in charge and commands authority by virtue of that position. In contrast, communities operate through a mixture of formal and informal authority. Formal authority resides in elected and appointed offices, such as mayor, councillor, and town administrator. Informal authority accrues to wealthy residents, philanthropists, clergy, and residents who volunteer for important committees. Community leadership is for this reason harder to define and more difficult to evaluate than leadership in formal organizations. It is no less significant. Leadership is essential to good government and the rational planning in which communities are now expected to engage. Leadership guides the process of seeking government funding, building infrastructure, attracting business, and securing population growth or hedging against the ill effects of population decline.

Much of the literature on community leadership has emphasized formal aspects of local politics and planning. For instance, how school boards are elected as well as how they deliberate have been the focus of studies, as have inquiries into the formation of coalitions among local interest groups and political parties. Political scientists have been interested in communities as laboratories in which to study the functioning of democratic procedures. Students of social movements have examined how grassroots pressure groups shape local policies on such topics as school bonds and water fluoridation. In recent years, greater attention has been given to questions about the effects of tax abatement policies and government funding on such issues as land use, sprawl, and industrial innovation. As valuable as these studies of formal governmental processes are, they reveal little of what the average resident thinks about leadership or how these views contribute to the positive social atmosphere that communities hope to encourage.[1]

The critical aspect of community leadership, as Mr. Owens's comments illustrate, is respect. Respect is the basis for the exercise of legitimate authority. For formal officeholders, it is the necessary qualification for securing votes along with attaining and retaining appointed office. Respect is equally essential for informal leadership. It is the basis on which consent is given and from which cooperation is secured. Respect is similar in popular understandings to prestige, but differs in the sense that prestige connotes an elevated status that may be the object of envy or modest misgivings, whereas respect suggests genuine appreciation, even toward someone whose status may not be especially high. For example, a person who is hardworking but poor might be respected, yet would probably not be considered a person of high prestige.

Respect is especially important as a criterion for leadership in small communities. When people know one another as well as they claim to in small towns, and often over a long period of time, respect is conferred through diffuse associations, such as a conversation here, a shared committee assignment there, and a task accomplished on some other occasion. In a national study, respondents were asked how much or how little they would admire various people in their communities. In small nonmetropolitan towns, 79 percent said "a lot" toward a "person who helps the poor," 66 percent said this about a "person who gets things organized," and 61 percent gave the same response for "a person who volunteers." At the opposite end of the spectrum, 72 percent said they would "not admire" someone who was "too busy to get involved." These percentages were significantly higher in small towns than among respondents in cities and suburbs.[2]

Respect earned through such varied roles as community volunteer or neighborly citizen is different than the respect a person gains by performing well in a specialized role, such as being a good surgeon or excellent teacher. It is the community through its various networks and activities that confers respect. The conferral of respect is the means by which the community, so to speak, rewards good behavior. It is for this reason that something of how communities sustain themselves can be learned by examining the bases on which respect is given. The behavior that is rewarded with respect should be behavior that contributes to the good of the community.

.   WHO LEADS?

In fictional portrayals of small towns, leadership is usually embodied in a colorful character who is either loved by all, such as the sheriff or a country doctor, or an object of ridicule or contempt, such as a bumbling town boss or corrupt lawyer. In real life, it is more common to imagine that town leadership rests with an elected body of town council persons or county commissioners. But townspeople themselves seldom mention these officials as the true leaders of their communities. For example, a teacher in a town of fifteen hundred says, "I would like to say members of the county commissions, city council, and board of education." He notes that they "should be looked up to," but doesn't think that's true. Residents in towns like his point instead to prominent members of their community who serve in a variety of formal and informal capacities. Leaders are known and admired because of who they are and what they do. They come in contact with the rest of the community through the functions they perform.

Even in the smallest towns leadership revolves around the activities that fulfill particular community needs. People are seldom immodest enough to nominate themselves, but they do not hesitate to identify leaders in the sector of the community they know best. For instance, Mr. Parsons, the banker in a town of six hundred, says bank officers play a crucial leadership role in his community and the neighboring towns. "They're kind of thrown into it," he says, "maybe because of their education or experience." People come to him not only for loans but also for personal advice. "I've had a wife in here talking about her husband drinking," he says. "Why me? I don't want to hear this stuff. But you listen. You try to console. That's what you have to do." Mr. Steuben, the auctioneer, echoes this view. "You know, the bankers, people in business like that who are visible," he says, "they are looked to as leaders, as people who are doing things the right way." Others that people identify as leaders include prominent doctors, lawyers, and wealthy farmers or business owners. "It's the business owners," Ms. Clarke explains, "the financially successful ones."

But townspeople just as often say they do not respect the richest people in their communities. "Success seems to breed more envy than it does respect," one community leader observed. The perception is that those upper-income people "either screwed the community to get the money," he says, "or somehow underhandedly came about their wealth from the backs of others." That impression is evident in other communities where lower- and middle-class residents point to people who are "filthy rich," or those who had just inherited their wealth, benefited from owning an oil well or a mine, or struck some business deal with government help and then failed to spread the wealth around. That perception extends to founding families that are known to have dominated local politics and business over the years. "Their families have been here for a very long time and they hold themselves with dignity," a man of more recent vintage observes. "That's what sets them apart from us ragpickers." Even greater disdain is evident toward wealthy people who are deemed to be arrogant, such as "people who have money and show it off," or "people who are cocky" about their wealth—those are the ones residents say are not held in high regard.

For a businessperson to be considered a leader, it is of considerable advantage to be homegrown or have other long-standing loyalties to the town. Not just any businessperson can qualify. It has to be someone who owns a local business and has been there for a long time, or at least long enough to have become involved in civic activities and perhaps have demonstrated commitment to the townspeople by keeping the business open against competition from the outside. It may be the owner of the hardware store, lumberyard, or bank, for example. In conversations, nobody is quite sure about it, but they figure people like this who live in town and have a business there care about the community's future, and probably invest their money locally.

The contrast that worries townspeople is the store manager who simply works for a company headquartered somewhere else. "The grain elevator's not owned locally anymore," a farmer says in explaining why there are few respected leaders in his town. "The gas station would be the same way. It's an outside influence. It's a branch of another area." As more of the local businesses are franchises of large corporations externally owned, townspeople worry about the consequences. They are happy to have the stores. And yet the managers of these stores are known to be newcomers or they are thought to be transients who will move on when better opportunities appear. At the least, these managers are thought to have mixed loyalties that might prevent them from being fully involved in the community.

This skepticism toward leaders who may move on in a year or two reflects some of the inherent distrust of newcomers that so many residents say is part of their local culture. Even though a newcomer may be planning to stay, long-term residents are suspicious of someone who tries to be a leader by importing ideas from some other place. "Some people come in and try to be leaders who have just moved here," Mrs. Bradford notes as she describes her community of six hundred. Mr. Bradford picks up on the remark. "They just want to be in charge and kind of take over. I kind of resent those people who come in from the city and say, 'Well, we did it this way.' Well, why didn't you stay there?"

It helps, too, if a business leader is known for having worked on some community improvement project. For example, a resident of a town of thirteen hundred singles out a businessperson who renovated a building on Main Street to be used as a theater as well as turned an old restaurant into a mini-mall with a coffee shop and beauty salon. She holds this businessperson in high regard. In contrast, she does not admire another business owner who campaigned against a bond issue to improve the local schools.

GAINING RESPECT

In all but the smallest towns, community leadership has become increasingly professionalized. The day-to-day business of town administration is more likely to be in the hands of a full-time salaried town manager than a part-time mayor who essentially functions as an elected volunteer. Both the town manager and mayor are more likely to shoulder responsibilities that require specialized training. A leader who at one time may have been comfortable appearing among friends and neighbors in informal garb is more likely to dress as an executive when representing the town. Appropriate training and apparel are especially needed when dealing with the growing number of issues that involve meetings with representatives from external government agencies. As one leader observes, "You have to bring more professionalism to this position. I don't go to meetings in jeans and flip-flops. If I am going to a county meeting, I put on my suit and my heels."

One would think that people serving their communities in professional roles, such as a school or town administrator, or a doctor or business owner, would need to do little else to gain respect. But in some ways their formal position of leadership in the community makes it harder. They have to do something in addition to their work to earn respect. Otherwise, they are likely to be viewed as arrogant or self-serving. Or as one local official put it, "People think the government workers just sit there and draw a paycheck." The best way to avoid being perceived that way is to serve voluntarily in community organizations.

Consider Jocelyn Brown, the city administrator in a town of six thousand. She is a busy woman in her late forties who has an aging mother in a town thirty miles away who needs her care. Most mornings Mrs. Brown is at work before eight, and she is often still there until six in the evening. At least one night a week there is a community task force or town council meeting she is required to attend as part of her job. Yet she is also a member of the Rotary club, Chamber of Commerce, Parent–Teacher Association, oversight committee for a local fine arts center, and new economic development organization. About the only local organization she is not active in is her church.

Of course, much has been written about the decline of voluntary community organizations. The reasons include hectic schedules among two-career couples, residents moving to and from their communities, and people commuting longer distances to work.[3] These difficulties are affecting community organizations in small towns as well as suburbs and cities, especially when declining populations make it difficult to sustain traditional organizations and when larger proportions of the remaining residents work outside the community. But small towns often have more of these organizations for their size than do larger communities. For instance, when the more than 1.5 million nonprofit associations registered with the Internal Revenue Service are classified by the population of the zip code in which they are located, there are more than 10 associations per 1,000 residents in the least populated areas, and that number declines to about 2 per 1,000 residents in the most populated areas (figure 6.1).

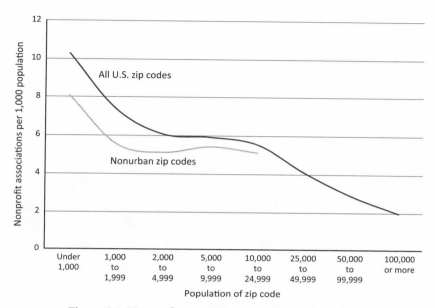

Figure 6.1 Nonprofit associations per thousand residents

This does not mean that residents in smaller communities are neces-sarily more active in nonprofit associations than inhabitants of larger com-munities. Indeed, one reason for the larger number of such organizations in smaller places is that many nonprofit organizations, such as a hospital board, parent–teacher organization, scouting troop, or veterans associa-tion, exist at the county or town level, regardless of how small or large the population may be. It does appear, though, that the greater number of nonprofit associations per capita in smaller places is one of the reasons that residents of small communities talk about the local importance of these organizations.[4]

Community organizations in small towns differ in emphasis from groups in larger places as well. Some of the most notable differences are evident in figure 6.2, which compares residents in small nonmetropolitan towns with residents in suburbs, taking into account differences in race and ethnicity, gender, age, and levels of education. The two kinds of orga-nizations that are underrepresented in small towns are ethnic, racial, or nationality associations along with political clubs or organizations. The other organizations are all better represented in small towns than in sub-urbs. Not surprisingly, farm organizations are the most disproportion-ately represented in small towns, but so are labor unions and youth groups, and three of the organizations—church-affiliated groups, fraternal groups,

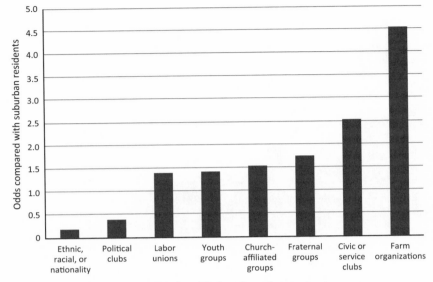

Figure 6.2 Membership in selected organizations

and civic or service clubs—are traditionally the ones that have been most active in community betterment and community-wide charitable activities. Although the larger populations of suburbs have been conducive to specialized groups, it is also notable that membership in many of these is as common in small towns as in suburbs. For example, no significant differences are evident in these data between small-town residents and suburban residents in the likelihood of holding membership in environmental organizations, sports clubs, health and fitness centers, hobby or garden clubs, literary or music groups, or professional associations.[5]

A particularly important aspect of membership in civic organizations in small towns is its visibility. People in a small town know if the town administrator is present at the Rotary club meeting and involved in the fine arts council. Civic organizations help maximize that visibility. Other members see the councillor or local physician there at the regular meetings, whereas an individual act of kindness or charitable donation could go unnoticed.

The specific activities that earn respect are ones that either directly benefit the community, or indirectly show that the community is composed of decent and caring individuals. Dixie Longren, an elderly woman in a town of twenty thousand, says a man in her Sunday school class is the kind of leader everyone in her community respects. "He's just a good old farm boy," she chuckles, "but if I needed something, I would not hesitate to call him. I feel sure he would take care of it." A woman in a town of nine hundred singles out "the lady who runs the dime store here" because she "does so much for this community." She says the dime store lady makes small donations to the nursing home and the Sunday school children. A woman in another town of about the same size mentions her neighbors, a couple in their eighties, explaining that they have been involved in "every single volunteer effort and every single community organization." A man in another small town nominated a teenager as a rising young leader in the community, explaining that the boy goes around voluntarily mowing lawns for some of the community's elderly widows.

It is notable how often townspeople mention voluntary service even when talking about fellow citizens who hold formal leadership positions in the community. "We've got a couple guys here who are CEOs of the bank and other businesses," says a resident of a town of twelve hundred, "who put a lot of time into the community. They volunteer a lot." A councillor in a town of twenty-five hundred says respect goes to leaders who are "very generous toward the community." Ms. Clarke shares this feeling. She says the financially successful business owners in her town are respected because they are "real givers to the community." In another small town, one of the long-term residents offers a similar view somewhat more pointedly. "They don't necessarily have high positions in the community, but they're caring people. They're genuine people." She says the mayor is not one of them. He is regarded locally as "a bit of a scoundrel," as someone who is not considered a caring person.

Here again it is the scale of small places that matters. "You see people every day," is how one man puts it. "You see those little things that people do." It helps if someone is known as the bank president or chair of the Lions club. But it is still necessary for that person to do little things, such as showing up at a picnic fund-raiser or helping an elderly person across the street. In a large community nobody would have noticed. Or if they had, they would have had nobody to tell. In a small place word spreads. In interviews, people recount stories that have circulated through the gossip mill. They have heard that someone assisted a neighbor, that another person regularly visited the sick, and so on.

The way respect works is that people who do contribute to the community feel rewarded for doing it and thus are more likely to continue being involved. As one woman explained, she really liked the respect she earned by serving on the local school board, and this appreciation was one of the reasons she ran for city council and served a term as mayor. But equally important is the fact that people who have not done much to help the community see how things work and decide to become more engaged. A good example of someone becoming more involved is a woman who says she did not grow up thinking that community service

Profile: Mayville, Wisconsin

Approaching Mayville, Wisconsin, from the south, a traveler on Highway 67 passes a well-kept public park on the right, two cemeteries on the left, and several large road signs. One of the signs includes the emblems of many of the town's established community organizations. German Lutherans and Catholics, arriving in the 1860s, mostly settled Mayville. The town is surrounded by farms with fertile fields as well as large dairy herds that contribute to the state's abundance of milk and cheese. Mayville itself is home to several tool-and-die firms that have been in business here for more than a century as well as a growing number of commuters who travel fifty miles each way to jobs in Milwaukee.

Like many small towns, in Mayville, the elected and appointed officials rely heavily on voluntary community organizations to look after the town's many civic activities. In all, more than fifty of these are organized as formal tax-exempt associations and there are at least a dozen more that function informally. This is in a town of only slightly more than five thousand people. Many of these organizations are familiar landmarks in communities of this size. Besides the two Lutheran churches in town, there is one nearby in the countryside along with the larger Catholic Church in the center of town and the smaller Methodist Church a few blocks away. Well-established civic organizations include the Lions club that meets on Wednesday evenings at a local restaurant and the Veterans of Foreign Wars that meets at the VFW Hall the first Thursday of every month. Other traditional organizations include the Knights of Columbus, Rotary International, Kiwanis International, and the Parent–Teacher Association.

Although membership in these traditional organizations has declined nationally, newer special interest groups flourish in Mayville, as they do elsewhere. Some, like the American Bowling Congress chapter that came to Mayville in 1974, and a bikers' group that formed in 1976, are no longer new. Others, like Women's Aglow, an evangelical fellowship, and True Men Ministries, its male counterpart, are of more recent vintage.

And in Mayville, as in many small towns, what was once an informal alliance between voluntary organizations and local government has resulted in new forms of public–private interaction. A local chapter of the Wisconsin Association for Home and Community Education, for example, conducts leadership seminars in grant proposal writing, and Main Street Mayville seeks public funding for neighborhood development and community improvement.

was important. "My parents didn't focus on volunteering in the community, so I didn't have that sense of needing to help your community." But in the small town where she now lives things are different. "This town has taught me that community is important and you need to volunteer. There is a strong sense of needing to help each other. We have Christmas suppers and Thanksgiving dinners for those who don't have family close. We have a lot of volunteers in our nursing homes and at the school." She personally volunteers for a civic organization, at the school, and in her church.

Volunteering, caring for one's neighbors, and working together on community projects are clearly of benefit to the community's well-being. Civic involvement in these instances does not depend solely on the altruistic motives of the individuals who participate. It is encouraged by the reward system of the community itself. Civic involvement is rewarded with respect. People who contribute to the life of the community are looked up to, while those who do not are punished with a lack of respect. "It's the people who reach out to people and treat everybody as an equal," a councillor in a town of two hundred says. "They do things for other people, but not for recognition. They do it because there's a need."

Disrespect is directed especially at people who do not take care of themselves. "Oh, we have people here who don't even keep their grass mowed," one man observes. "You can be poor, but you don't have to be dirty," says another. "We have people here who just sit around and complain and don't do anything," a woman who describes her community of twelve hundred as a hardworking town says. People who keep too much to themselves are looked down on as well. "They're kind of like cockroaches," Mr. Steuben says. "You never see them, but they're always around. This community is exactly what you make of it, I tell them. If you want to stay in your dog-gone house and not interact with anybody, you're allowed to do that. But don't turn around in a year and bitch about nothing going on in the community." The specific attributes associated with disrespect underscore what is valued in community leaders. Disrespect inheres especially among those who are "self-centered and selfish," as one woman puts it. It is the altruistic virtue of the community that must somehow be upheld. In the simplest terms, that means helping to make the community better and caring for its needs. In broader terms, a leader must be upstanding, someone who cares for their property, and is sociable and clean.

Civic participation elevates individuals in the eyes of fellow residents, and yet ironically, community involvement also levels the playing field, as it were, and thus eases the tension that might otherwise exist in small towns between the haves and have-nots. A woman who serves on the city council in her town of eight hundred makes a revealing comment in this regard. She says she is respected because of her position on the council, but adds, "I don't put myself above them on a pedestal or anything like that. I just do what I was born to do." Working alongside farmers, waitresses, and retirees cleaning up a vacant building as well as putting on a potluck dinner shows that she is just a member of the community like everyone else.

CULTURAL LEADERSHIP

Although community leadership nowadays even in the smallest towns generally implies an office worker who oversees budgets and implements planning (with voluntary civic work on the side), an important and frequently overlooked leadership role is performed by the person or persons who might aptly be called the village folklorist. Not to be confused with the academic study of folklore, the village folklorist is the keeper of local traditions, the resident who knows the town's history, remembers what happened when, and can repeat the stories to anyone interested in listening. Sometimes the village folklorist is officially associated with the local historical society and may even be the curator of a small museum in which the community's prized artifacts are kept. If the position were in a larger community, it might be held by a faculty member at the state or municipal university, or an employee of the metropolitan museum and cultural center. In a small town, it is likely to be a resident who has earned a reputation for storytelling, perhaps at the local hardware store or as editor of the community newspaper. It is just as commonly a person who developed a sideline interest in town lore that has become of value in preserving the community's heritage.

I emphasize the village folklorist because the sense of community that prevails in small towns is greatly indebted to the leadership this person provides. It is wrong to imagine that residents of small towns identify with their communities only by virtue of living there. The community is also a story that people know. The narrative includes a myth of origin—usually grounded in historical fact, but generally with apocryphal elements—that says something about the town's first inhabitants, perhaps starting with settlers of European descent or including Native Americans. The community story is likely to include the larger-than-life exploits of a hardy pioneer, early town promoter, teacher, or doctor. There may be the memory of a devastating fire or flood, or a tragedy that befell an unfortunate family.

These stories are not the shared experiences that residents know firsthand. The tales that give their community a distinct identity are known because someone has handed them down, repeated them at a town meeting, printed them in the local newspaper, and filed them away somewhere at the library or courthouse. They are the stories of the United States *writ small*. Nearly every small town of a few thousand residents has called on its local folklorists to put together a commemorative pamphlet describing its history or an event with the same purpose. Walk the central streets of any town, and the artifacts that have been preserved are not hard to locate—such as the mural on a business wall, a statue of a Civil War soldier, a plaque at the entrance to the town park, or the names inscribed in church windows.

Vera Gruenling is one of the more colorful village folklorists we met. She lives in a farming town that has grown over the past twenty-five years to more than twenty thousand, which means a large number of newcomers who are unfamiliar with the community's history and traditions. Now in her seventies, Mrs. Gruenling has lived here all her life and was a teacher for nearly four decades. A typical morning finds her at the YMCA for an hour of exercise, and then tutoring fourth graders who are struggling with math and English. She knows the town's stories by heart, having so often taught her elementary school pupils how the first settlers struggled to build houses and plow the land. She tells of the town's founders, how they secured a railroad, and where their pictures can be found in the town's museum. The stories are not only about rugged individualism but also about the community's efforts to help one another and protect itself from outsiders. In the early days there were bands of gypsies who stole food; later, the community competed with neighboring towns for good highways and better stores. She recalls the flood of 1965 that wrecked the park and required the community to build a new zoo. From time to time, the editor of the local newspaper calls her for information about the town's past. Recently, she has been participating every Wednesday in a Living History group at the senior citizens' center. The group is recording oral histories and writing memoirs. "We ramble on about things that happened in the past," she says, and help the community "learn more about the place." She also volunteers at the local historical society, entering biographical information into its computerized database. The historical museum has recently opened a new wing that includes an impressive visual display of the town's history.

Mrs. Gruenling is typical of other village folklorists we met in several respects. Being a lifelong or at least long-term resident, and being among the community's older citizens, is a natural advantage for knowing the town's past. Having been a teacher, shop owner, or elected official generally means a large network of local acquaintances and opportunities to have heard as well as told community lore. We talked with antique dealers, waitresses, and hairdressers who were known especially as fonts of local lore. Being retired like Mrs. Gruenling is another advantage insofar as it makes time for volunteer activities. Other amateur folklorists we talked to included residents who volunteered at the local library, school, church, or club. In the smallest towns, neighbors sometimes knew simply by reputation who to ask for the best stories or latest gossip, but volunteering at the library and other local centers of culture meant that even a stranger could benefit from the folklorists' information.

As local government offices have expanded and become more formalized, the village folklorist in some communities is a person whose official functions require knowledge of local history and traditions. Sara Porterfield is an example. For the past decade and a half, Mrs. Porterfield has been the director of park facilities and services in a southern community of six thousand that prides itself on preserving its antebellum charm while adapting to the changing social and economic realities of the twenty-first century. Her job includes publicizing information to attract tourists as well as handling the technical details of park usage and maintenance. Having recently updated the community's Web site, she can recite almost word for word the story of the town's founding and its more recent developments. She knows the year the first textile mill was founded and when the last one closed, where the old shirt factory was located, which famous writer visited in the 1950s, and how the art deco movement reshaped the town square. Her repertoire includes stories about an early gristmill, an influential preacher, a large peanut farm, and how the railroad was built. Not surprisingly, she believes the community's strength depends on knowing its past. That means that "everybody knows who you are, and who your mom and daddy were." It also means a fall festival when the community's history can be recalled, and shopkeepers who can tell tourists colorful stories of the town's past. "We think that's our niche," she says.

In many communities, the village folklorist serves not only to instill pride in the town but also to preserve critical aspects of local ethnic culture. A leader in a predominantly Finnish community, for example, told us stories about the settler's difficulties learning English and the ridicule Finnish children sometimes were exposed to in school. He described with some amusement the tradition of the Finnish sauna in which extended families and neighbors participated each Saturday in preparation for Sunday worship services. Non-Finnish neighbors imagined promiscuous behavior occurring and on several occasions filed lawsuits seeking injunctions against the practice, he said, but in reality the norm was to be as "pure in the sauna as in church," where strict gender segregation prevailed. In other towns, keepers of local legends told of Germans being persecuted during World War I, Swedish ancestors settling as a colony, Spanish-speaking forebears working as migrant farm laborers, and Italian immigrants working in the mines.

Native American leaders play a particularly important role in preserving both the ethnic and village traditions of their communities. Mato Tanka lives in a town of seven hundred people on an Indian reservation composed of Oglala Sioux, some of whose ancestors were veterans of the battle at Little Big Horn and others whose relatives were at Wounded Knee.[6] Fluent in Lakota and English, Mr. Tanka grew up on the reservation and dropped out of school in tenth grade, but through the insistence of his grandfather got a job immediately doing custodial work, graduated a few years later from the police academy, and eventually earned a law degree from one of the nation's most prestigious law schools. He currently serves as the tribe's attorney, dealing with litigation involving land and gaming regulations, and is a principal keeper of Lakota narratives, songs, and sacred rituals that extend for at least nineteen generations. In this capacity, Mr. Tanka is the head singer for the Lakota Sundance, performs at wakes and on other ceremonial occasions, and teaches classes in traditional singing. The Lakota understanding of history, he says, is not linear but rather is about who you are. "The essence of what I want to do with my life," he stresses, "is to be a good relative." That means especially participating in local service activities but also being related to everybody, whether through blood, in the community, or via the Lakota understanding of the grandfather great spirit.

Mr. Tanka lists the issues that come across his desk as an attorney: estate settlements, divorce, an arrest for drunkenness, someone needing financial assistance, a jurisdictional dispute with the state or federal government, or a new or cold-case murder investigation. All too often, litigation results from poor planning on the part of one or the other of the disputants. Mr. Tanka wishes more of his community understood the true meaning of Indian time. "My grandfather taught me about Indian time," he says. "It means you buy your snow shovel in the summer." He thinks frequently of his grandfather and his grandfather's grandparents. They are the models of what it means to be a good relative. "They gave their lives for the people," he explains. "I think they're watching."

Although they are often wise in their own right, village folklorists are not to be confused with the proverbial village oracle or sage. Folklorists are known locally for their knowledge of local affairs. They represent and convey information about the past plus present activities of the community. In contrast, the village sage speaks from personal wisdom, gained perhaps from reading or travel. A sage who writes or speaks to an external audience may acquire a reputation outside the community that becomes identified with the community. "Yes, so-and-so lives here," community residents may say about a well-known essayist in their community. But they may also be chagrined about a self-styled sage who writes a newspaper column or Internet blog. The local folklorist is more likely to be regarded by fellow residents as a community asset.

In social science jargon, the village folklorist is a central node in a social network that produces and reproduces cultural capital. Usually cultural capital means the knowledge a person uses to get what they want, such as a high-paying job in a prestigious occupation. Because social scientists tend to think about the whole society as the relevant unit, rather than local communities, the cultural capital that matters is readily exchanged in the society-wide stratification system for money and status. An advanced degree, training in a profession, technical skills, and familiarity with haute couture are the best kinds of cultural capital to have.

But in small towns it also matters to have locally specific cultural capital. Some of what is important to know is instrumental. When resources are scarce and perhaps geographically limited as well, it matters to know who in town is best at welding together a broken trailer hitch and who to call when the septic tank overflows. Cultural capital also consists of expressive information that is good for social networking. Gossip can be exchanged for instrumental information. Knowing the town's history and being able to tell its stories serves similarly. An insider knows the traditions or who to ask. Being an insider feels better than existing on the margins of a small community. This is why the village folklorist fulfills a valuable role.

HOLDING OFFICE

"Being the first female mayor here," Margaret O'Brien says, when asked what goal in life she is most pleased to have accomplished. This is her ninth year, the first of her third term. "Even though we're a small rural town, I'm proud of what it is like today, the progress we've made. How do I say this and not sound sexist? I'm proud that I can work with a male council, and work right up there with the males and feel comfortable."

Mrs. O'Brien's story is not so different from that of many elected officials in small towns. She came here as a young bride forty years ago. She had grown up in a different state, living near an air force base, and dreamed of joining the military when she was old enough. She wanted to serve her country and see the world. Her father said no. That might be fine for her brothers, but not for her or her sister. She decided to find another way to travel. She became an airline stewardess, as they were called in those days. It was fine for a while, but having to be thin, pretty, and wear a uniform with a little blue cap got old quickly. "I was just a waitress in the sky," she recalls. Soon after, she quit, got married, moved to the community where she has spent her life, and became a mother. She begged her husband, couldn't they move, couldn't they go live somewhere else, anywhere? But this was his home. He had a good job with the utility company. He wanted the children to live near their grandparents. She took courses at a nearby community college and got a job as a social worker.

Over the next three decades, Mrs. O'Brien's job as a social worker provided a steady income that supplemented her husband's salary and made it possible to send their children away to college. Although she was still regarded as a newcomer by many of the townspeople, the job put her in contact with the local residents and gave her an opportunity to learn valuable skills. State and federal regulations governed what she could and could not do. She worked with families on welfare and in need of medical assistance, applied for grants, and interfaced with doctors and the police. She also did volunteer work. Having learned from her parents that a person should give back to her community, she tried to do just that. Being mayor is a way of continuing to serve, even though she is technically retired.

On most occasions, the daily life of a small-town mayor is not strenuous. Mrs. O'Brien sips hot water with lemon while listening to the morning news on a regional radio station and reading the only daily newspaper available in her part of the state. She exercises for a half hour on the treadmill and then heads over to city hall. This morning she interviews a candidate for a city job, and is pleased to discover that they have experience working in a similar-size town, then handles some other business and staffs the phone so her assistant can run errands. She attends a Rotary luncheon, makes some calls about a Republican caucus meeting she plans to attend in another town on Saturday, and has time by midafternoon to do a crossword puzzle and catch up on some reading. Still, there always seems to be something needing her attention. A local lake and the cemetery both need improvements. The highway that runs through town is being repaved. Grant writing still takes up much of her time. She points to new light poles and trash receptacles, and mentions a new water storage facility and recycling center—all these projects required grants from the state.

The expertise required of public officials in towns like Mrs. O'Brien's is constantly changing. Although her grant-writing skills developed over several decades, the reading she does on slow afternoons is often concerned with new funding opportunities along with state-mandated programs. For instance, she suggested recently that the local library purchase used car seats for infants that could be loaned to low-income families, only to learn that the idea would put the town in legal jeopardy if an accident happened. In other communities of fewer than five thousand people, town administrators described master's degrees they had earned in public administration and continuing education classes they were required to take.

But it is the intrigue of local politics that small-town officials find most interesting and especially challenging. Marvin Bencke is a longtime county commissioner in Mrs. O'Brien's town. He is a third-generation farmer, a college graduate, and has taught school. Because of having to deal with government agricultural programs, he became interested in questions of public finance and tax policy early in his career. That prompted him to run for public office. Being a lifelong Republican, he ran on that ticket, won, and served two terms. Although he was planning to sit out the next election, a fellow commissioner died and Mr. Bencke offered to run for that seat. But the Republican Party had another candidate in mind. Mr. Bencke ran instead as a Democrat, won, and served for eighteen years on that ticket. He says it made life interesting, to say the least.

When scandal erupts, it can be especially devastating in a small community. Carol Mason, an appointed official, recalls the former mayor in her town of five thousand. When her mother died, he came to her house dressed in overalls, picked a spot in the backyard, dug a hole, and planted a tree in her mother's memory. She thinks of him whenever she looks at the tree from her kitchen window. A few years later, she stopped at his office with some papers to sign. He said he had something to take care of first and asked if she could come back in an hour or two. When she returned, she learned that he had gone to the rural cemetery where his parents were buried and shot himself. She learned later that he had mistakenly authorized the city to purchase some property. The town council agreed it was a simple mistake, but the newspaper picked up the story and turned it into a major scandal.

Scandals aside, it is seldom easy to hold an elected or appointed office in a small town. Doing so exposes public officials to squabbles that can simmer for years. Every local official we talked to had stories to tell. In some communities, residents were angry years later because their school had undergone consolidation. In others, there were lingering disputes about the town having to rely on the county sheriff's department for law enforcement instead of having a police force of its own. Or there was resentment because a neighboring town had a better health clinic, or faster emergency medical and rescue services.[7]

Mrs. Mason's community is surrounded by coal mines. At least it was until the 1980s, when the coal mines shut down. Now the community is surrounded by abandoned pits. There used to be a manufacturing plant in town that employed a thousand workers, but that too has closed. She describes the community as a "friendly town" that takes special pride in its basketball teams. But with the economic setbacks the community has experienced, her job is not easy. It depends both on technical expertise in writing grant proposals to state and federal agencies, negotiating with environmental agencies, and utilizing informal interpersonal skills. Mrs. Mason has been instrumental in securing funding for a new hospital and bargaining with the state to locate a medium-security prison in the area. But she could lose her job at any time if she fails to maintain the approval of a majority of the deeply divided town council. She is the buffer between the council and the public. If she could wave her magic wand and ask for anything, she says she would wish for greater harmony. "People make something really big out of something that could be handled much easier," she remarks. Small problems too often get blown out of proportion. Her constant motto is "Be careful what you say."

Given the potential for significant misunderstandings, it is surprising that anyone runs for public office in small towns—and in some of the towns we studied, residents said it was difficult to find good leaders. But usually community pride is sufficient to override such difficulties. There were public officials like Mrs. Mason who had gone to college and graduate school, secured formal training in public administration, and returned to their hometowns because of spouses' employment or needing to be close to parents. Others, like Mrs. O'Brien, held jobs in their communities that made it hard to say no when asked to run for elected office.

There are also public officials for whom their small towns function as a frog pond in which to cultivate aspirations for wider public service. Craig Baker holds an appointed administrative position in a foothills county of ten thousand populated mostly by farmers and ranchers. The son of a local rancher, Mr. Baker never imagined himself following in his father's footsteps. As a teenager, his interests turned increasingly toward government. He recalls one year at the county 4-H fair being assigned to clean one of the exhibit buildings and meeting a state representative whose table was in the building. In college Mr. Baker majored in political science, volunteered for political campaigns, and seriously considered going to law school. But shortly after graduation, while working in the state capital, the position he now holds opened up. Although he was young and inexperienced, his political connections worked to his advantage. "I'm not an educated expert," he says, but he feels he has an "instinct" for local politics. He knows the back roads and people of his county. He understands that government moves slowly here and that it takes a lot of patience to move people out of their comfort zones. His dream is someday running for the state house of representatives. Meanwhile, it gives him a great deal of satisfaction to help people in his community both on and off the job.

COMMUNITY BETTERMENT

Besides caring for one another in small ways, community leaders are expected to initiate projects that actually improve the community. In interviews with leaders and nonleaders alike, we found this expectation to be nearly universal. Residents of declining towns describe plans to make the place look better by tearing down or renovating old buildings, starting new businesses, and attracting jobs. As the mayor of one town explained, "Our Main Street isn't what it used to be, but we keep it from looking like it's falling apart." Towns that are growing often have plans to maintain the small-town feeling by starting a historical museum, initiating a festival, or having a community barbeque. People admit that the community gets to looking seedy if nothing is done. They worry when the town square begins to deteriorate, trees die in the park, and vacant lots are not mowed. They speak with pride about plans to fix up an old bridge or build a new fire station. These activities have important symbolic as well as instrumental value. They are a point of central identity for the community and a visual reminder of something that residents hold in common—the courthouse, municipal building, public library, park, school, and renovated post office on Main Street.

In our interviews, we found town leaders and residents engaged in a delicate dance between tearing down decaying structures so that new ones could be built and seeking to preserve historic buildings. On the one hand, townspeople understood the significance of keeping things from looking as if they were falling apart. Just as in urban neighborhoods, broken windows and abandoned buildings signaled disorder plus seemed to invite crime.[8] On the other hand, efforts were made to preserve and restore the best historic buildings. As a community leader in one of the southern towns we studied explained, her community was having success in attracting tourists who enjoyed weekend excursions to a bygone piece of vintage Americana. "We have these beautiful old homes, beautiful streets with trees, the town square, and antique shops," she says. Urban planners had even visited to learn how to replicate the small-town feeling evident there.[9]

This was not an isolated example. Many of the towns we studied were attempting to promote tourism as a way to secure jobs, retain population, and increase tax revenue. Several had launched formal tourism committees. One had copyrighted the town's name as a brand that could be printed on souvenirs. The efforts ranged from small-scale projects, such as opening an antiques mall or hosting an annual motorcross rally, to more ambitious ones, such as building a visitors' center and historical museum to opening a casino. The smaller efforts had reasonable success in attracting visitors from the immediate vicinity as well as taking advantage of such amenities as a lake that could draw fishing and boating enthusiasts, an ethnic heritage that served as an excuse for an annual festival or crafts show, and proximity to a city, so that agrotourists could be attracted by events at local farms. The larger projects usually occurred in special locations, such as in towns adjacent to national parks or near Indian reservations. Sometimes a town benefited from having been the birthplace or childhood home of a president, or the gravesite of a famous pioneer or cowboy.

Profile: North Stonington, Connecticut

Unlike many small towns, the leaders of North Stonington, Connecticut, faced the challenge not of promoting growth but rather of controlling it. Located near Interstate 95 in the corridor between New York and Boston, North Stonington was an attractive prospect for corporate expansion and new upscale housing developments. Its population of 3,748 in 1970 grew to 4,991 in 2000, prompting concerned residents to consider steps to preserve the historic small town character and rural beauty of the community.

In 2003, a steering committee of resident volunteers produced a comprehensive Plan of Conservation and Development for the community. The plan called for preserving existing farms and attracting new agricultural businesses, improving roads, and ensuring a variety of housing choices. It also identified as high priorities the need to set aside limited areas for commercial growth, reduce the overall density of residential development, protect natural resources and open land, keep municipal and recreational facilities in their present locations, and promote energy conservation.

A follow-up evaluation six years later showed that much remained to be done but that a number of actions had been taken. New zoning regulations had been passed, a water supply and quality-management plan had been adopted, a plan to control noise pollution had been implemented, and regulations were in place for energy-generating wind facilities. There was a lengthy list of ideas still under consideration. The 2010 census showed that the population had edged up to 5,291, or an increase of 6 percent in ten years.

That was all to the good, as was the fact that numerous public meetings had been held and community spirit had been facilitated in the process. The goal of preserving a bucolic ambience, however, came increasingly into conflict with concerns about high taxes. Despite relatively high household incomes, residents incurred rising commuting expenses and some experienced layoffs. Community meetings turned increasingly toward discussions of economic development that might alleviate tax burdens or generate sufficient revenue to improve the school system.

Community spirit was evident in the fact that residents proudly celebrated North Stonington's bicentennial, commemorated the community's fallen heroes each Memorial Day, and happily promoted the local basketball and soccer teams. Being a community meant taking part in those activities. It also meant exchanging hard words from time to time at town meetings and voting in hotly contested elections for town leaders who held varying views of community priorities.

Residents frequently expressed ambivalence toward these tourist-seeking ventures. The small efforts that had limited success were usually regarded with mild amusement as something that gave the town a bit of flair and drew a few outsiders without fundamentally changing anything. The larger projects often made more of a difference and generated greater controversy. For example, in one of the towns that had become a regional gaming center, residents complained that they no longer knew one another and had to lock their doors. They conceded, however, that revenue from the casinos was paying for an improved water and sewage system, and buildings were being preserved that otherwise would have fallen into disrepair.

The key to managing residents' ambivalence in this case was to use the new revenue not only for water and sewage projects but also to maintain the town's historic identity. In other communities leaders expressed hope that a new county museum, a restored courthouse, renovation of an old warehouse, a small theme park, hitching posts, or traditional-looking lampposts would simultaneously attract visitors and commemorate the community's past. In the process, it was of course not the actual past that was being preserved but instead an imagined one that selectively shaped and reframed the town's identity.[10]

While community betterment projects make an actual difference to the quality of life, they also serve a symbolic role. They do this in two ways. One is by enlisting the community's involvement in making them happen. When people have worked together on a beautification project, circulated petitions and raised funds, or even voted for a public bond offering, they renew their sense of collective ownership of the community. The other symbolic function is the tangible mark that the project bestows on the town. For example, "We have a huge new water tank up on the hill," one resident exclaims. "It's awesome." For her, the water tank with the town's name emblazoned on the side is an identifying feature. And when community betterment projects fail, the blow is symbolic as well. The same woman, for instance, laments the fact that year after year, the community's finances and depleted school enrollment prevents it from building a new music room in the high school to replace an earlier one that was torn down after being declared structurally unstable. "Any other school would just build a new facility," she says, "but no, not here. Money is so tight. You have to go through conniptions to get anything done."

If tearing down old buildings and mowing vacant lots are important to a community's sense of well-being, infrastructure and essential social services are vital. Much of the discussion in national media about infrastructure and services has focused on striking an appropriate balance through state appropriations and tax measures between rural areas and cities. But for people who actually live in small rural towns, the issue is frequently about competition with other small towns than about trade-offs between rural areas and cities. Community leaders know that there is a limited supply of state and federal funds along with a limited number of doctors, dentists, and pharmacists willing to live in small towns. So if one town lands a grant or lures a physician, another town may be at a loss not only for health care but also to attract a new business or keep residents from leaving. In some ways, this is no different than it has been for a long time. When towns began, they competed with one another to secure a railroad or become a county seat. The difference now is that health care, schools, and government services have become the principal activities subject to such competition. The other difference is that distances have shrunk. When transportation was more difficult, towns ten miles apart could compete successfully. Now the competition occurs between towns thirty or fifty miles apart.

Mr. Keller, the medical clinic director who lives in a town of five thousand, has been centrally involved in the competitive struggle for health services in small towns. In his administrative role he constantly skirmishes with the hospital, in the newspaper, and with other clinics in the area that could damage business at his clinic. The newspaper, he says, seems to dislike his clinic and favor the other one in town. He organized a women's health fair at the local Walmart recently and the newspaper refused to publicize the event. He still fumes about that. Sometimes the competition with the other clinic is only good-natured rivalry, but at other times it becomes so intense that people refuse to speak to each other or make angry remarks.

At one level, securing health services for the community is simply a matter of writing grant proposals and lobbying with state officials. Mr. Keller says it is no different in that respect than getting a new bridge built or finding money for a new fire truck. But schmoozing matters even more. He wound up going to a lot of golf tournaments. He meets doctors, businesspeople, and faculty at medical schools and colleges at these tournaments. When he finds someone who might be interested or knows someone else who might be interested in moving to a small town, he makes his pitch.

Community leaders have also been doing more to target the young. The pitch to young people is that small towns may offer more job opportunities than someone oriented only toward cities might assume. Teaching, social work, and health services are common examples. Keeping in contact with people who leave is difficult, although community leaders say it has become easier because of email and the Internet. The idea is similar to the one used by colleges to secure donations from alumni and recruit children of alumni as students. High school reunions and homecoming festivals function in the same way in small towns. Another strategy that has had some success is economic development directors keeping in touch with their former classmates.

INNOVATION

Although the social sciences have seldom regarded small rural communities as likely venues for innovation, many of the leaders we talked with said innovation was precisely what was needed if their towns were to attract jobs and retain population. Skepticism about small-town innovation stems from theories of modernization, which associated new ideas with the industrial, technological, and scientific advances that took place in cities. Network studies have reinforced this view. If small towns are literally places in which everyone knows everyone else, it is easy to assume that residents are too busy mingling with one another to cultivate ties outside the community. Dense, closely bounded networks circulate familiar—and sometimes stale—ideas, but seldom draw in new information. Open, loosely tied networks are more conducive to creative synergy.[11]

But small towns are not inherently inhospitable to innovation. Network studies also suggest that dense networks are sometimes necessary to implement new ideas, and resources and leadership may matter more than social ties. Small towns are in reality quite different from stereotypical closed networks in which only stale ideas can circulate.[12] Many of the leaders we interviewed were well connected with the outside world. They participated in regional and state governmental associations, agricultural extension networks, farmers' cooperatives, trucking companies, foundation grant programs, and clergy councils, and more generally, were linked through travel, the mass media, and the Internet. "To quote the book by Thomas Friedman, the world is becoming flat," explained a farmer who also served as town manager in a community of thirty-five hundred. "You can sit and work anywhere, assuming you have some Internet capability. You don't need to be on the fortieth floor in some city." Small towns are also the location of innovative manufacturing firms, experiment stations, and start-up companies.[13]

Small businesses are sources of innovation, whether in experiments with new technology, consumer products, or marketing. The most innovative small businesses usually benefit from being in or near metropolitan areas where colleges and universities, an educated labor force, and good distribution channels are located. That edge has put small towns in isolated areas at a disadvantage. Yet that situation may be changing as a result of easier communication through the Internet and wireless service, better transportation, and new developments in agriculture and biofuels.

In town after town with populations of three to ten thousand, innovative experiments are now evident.[14]

One example is a small manufacturing plant that specializes in the use of precision laser and plasma cutters to produce parts for large machinery companies. Through computerized ordering and inventory controls along with greater incentive at large corporations to minimize costs through outsourcing, small plants like this one have become more competitive. In other towns, state and federal community reinvestment programs as well as enterprise zones provide tax abatement and interest-free loans to start-up firms. Many towns have municipal or county-level economic development directors whose salaries are subsidized by the state. Town Web sites with information about the available labor force, wage rates, housing costs, and schools have become common. Web sites, blogs, and listserves are being used to keep in touch with high school alumni.

The best ideas, according to experienced community leaders, are not far-reaching leaps of imagination—ideas like persuading a major corporation to build a new headquarters in town or inventing some basic new gadget. The innovations that work best are those that build on existing resources. In one town of fewer than two thousand people, a young woman nicely illustrates this point. She is one of seven children, all the rest of whom went away to college, including one to Harvard and one who taught in Japan. But this woman fell in love with a man from her home-town. She has a degree in Latin American studies, and he has one in architecture. Their educations were not the best suited for life in a small rural community. But her dad was trying to start a small business there. She put the practical skills from college to use, working with her father to develop a computerized bookkeeping system and launching a Web site. As the business expanded and began hiring Spanish-speaking workers, she was the natural person to provide translations. Meanwhile, her husband has used his architectural training to start his own business specializing in general contracting. Besides working with her father, she now serves as the county's economic development consultant. She works with other small start-up businesses to provide reduced utility rates, county property tax exemptions, and low-interest revolving loans. Two of the new businesses she has attracted specialize in welding and metal fabrication. The skills required are ones that people in the community already have or can acquire through evening classes at the high school. About two-dozen new jobs have been created.

In another town, the village manager exemplified the kind of innovation he thought was characteristic of small communities in his part of the country. Interested in saving money on heating costs but wanting to avoid the mess of bringing wood into the house, he installed an external wood-burning furnace that consumed about five cords of wood each winter at a fraction of what oil or gas would have cost. Noting the heat being lost by the outside furnace, he then surrounded it with a greenhouse and began growing spinach for a local farmer's market. Lately he has been selling unused greens to a farmer who feeds pigs. He says other residents are finding ways to turn personal interests into moneymaking enterprises. A neighbor with wooded acreage is making biodiesel in marketable quantities. A newcomer with a background in chemistry has a small gas chromatography laboratory, which tests for contaminants on food, paper, and textile samples. The lab has clients from around the globe. Another resident runs a small firm that makes specialized apparel products for the military. The town has helped these businesses by renovating old storefronts, upgrading the water system, and applying for grants to improve health care facilities.

Although innovation more often than not connotes new business ventures, it also involves creative efforts to meet needs for social services. Communities with aging residents have benefited from subsidized senior citizens' housing programs along with programs to provide assisted living, medical care, and prescription medications for the elderly. Other towns face needs for social services because of increasing numbers of new immigrants. In one such town, the community obtained a grant from the state to provide health screening at the local elementary school and expanded its visiting nurse program. It cleaned up a pond that was a public health risk and held meetings for residents interested in participating in a community gardening program. Not having a local newspaper, let alone one in Spanish, it sent information about community services to residents in mailings of monthly water bills and posted notices in local stores.[15]

These projects cost relatively little, and the more expensive ones were subsidized by the state. Other examples included partnerships between towns and the state to house prisoners, build small solar energy production units, and recycle wastewater for irrigation. With small grants from the state, towns were rehabilitating the facades along Main Street, adding English-as-a-second-language courses at the high school, and subsidizing transportation for the elderly. At relatively modest cost, towns were installing solar energy panels on public buildings, putting up cell phone towers, and finding locations for wind energy units.

Many small communities, though, face needs for social services and infrastructure that require significantly larger expenditures. Hospitals and schools are among the most expensive. Aging gas mains and water lines may need to be replaced. A juvenile detention center needs to be built or an industrial loan has to be provided to keep a manufacturing plant from relocating. State coffers may be too depleted to help. The only way to fund these projects is by raising local taxes—seldom a popular idea.

Angela Lorenzo is the town clerk in a community of thirty-five hundred that was facing the difficult task of having to raise local taxes in order to proceed with the improvement projects that the community needed. The state was in deep financial difficulty, so most of the funding had to be secured locally. The residents took pride in being known as a progressive community, but were less than eager to approve any project that increased local property taxes or required a local sales tax. "We wanted to remain progressive," Ms. Lorenzo recalls, "and yet not chase people out because of the tax base."

The solution was an idea that would work in a small town or neighborhood, but would be much harder to implement in a city. The town's development committee initiated a series of roundtables that met once every six months, were widely advertised, and were small enough that residents turned out to talk about community needs. Then every eighteen months, a community summit was held that drew together the ideas from the roundtables as well as enlisted the participation of business leaders, educators, clergy, and elected and appointed officials. As a result of these meetings, residents felt they had a say in deciding what projects deserved their support. When we talked with Ms. Lorenzo, the community had recently passed a six million dollar bond issue to renovate the local nursing home and a twenty-four million dollar bond issue to construct a new hospital.

Communication is another aspect of infrastructure that requires creativity. Emergency 911 phone services are accommodating the fact that a growing number of rural residents use cells phones rather than landlines. When a 911 call comes by landline, the caller's location appears on a computer screen, but that does not happen if the call is made from a cell phone. Towns have been working with state officials and telephone companies to circumvent this problem by installing GPS chips in cell phones, and in other areas, experimenting with voice-recognition text-messaging systems. Another challenge involves arrangements for videoconferencing and Web-based learning in small-town schools. A gifted high school student in a small isolated community wanted to take advanced placement calculus via videoconferencing, for example, but the telephone company offered only audio conferencing. Regional planning commissioners worked to arrange service through a different telephone company.

Regional planning efforts are facilitated by Web-based networks and state agencies that mandate cooperation, for instance, through participation in county sales tax programs, or for distributing state funds for street and highway improvement. The possibilities for formal and informal cooperation are reinforced by the fact that towns are often located in close proximity to one another. For example, nearly two-thirds of small nonurban towns are located in counties in which there are at least five other

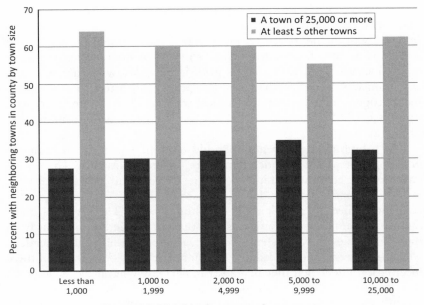

Figure 6.3 Neighboring towns by town size

towns. A third of small nonurban towns are also located in a county that has at least one town with a population of twenty-five thousand or more (see figure 6.3).[16]

While the proximity of other small towns makes it possible and sometimes even necessary to cooperate on projects, town leaders just as often talk about these neighbors as competitors. Competition may have historic roots in conflicts over the location of railroads and county courthouses, and it likely is perpetuated by athletic rivalries. As we have seen, residents also bemoan the fact that fellow residents are commuting to another town to work or shop, or that a larger town's Walmart or shopping center is taking business from local merchants.

Nearest-neighbor analysis provides a method for assessing the effects of competitors with various characteristics, whether that involves competition between rival automobile models or towns that literally are close neighbors. Using latitude and longitude coordinates, nearest-neighbor analysis facilitates identifying the town that is closest geographically that has particular characteristics. One of these characteristics is population size. Town leaders we talked to frequently speculated that the population of their own town was being adversely affected by the presence of a larger town nearby.

In figure 6.4, the effects on the probability of towns declining in population between 1980 and 2010 when the nearest town of at least twenty-five hundred is of varying size are shown. The figure compares these effects for small towns of fewer than a thousand residents in 1980 and slightly larger towns of between two and five thousand residents in 1980. For the smallest towns, the probability of losing population is better than 60 percent, and it makes little difference whether the nearest neighboring town has only a couple thousand residents or more than ten thousand residents. Only when the neighboring town has more than twenty-five thousand residents is there a slight reduction in the probability of the small town losing population.[17]

For the somewhat larger towns of two to five thousand residents, the probability of losing population is lower in each comparison than it is for the smaller towns of under one thousand residents. The probability of losing population is slightly higher if the neighboring town is slightly larger, i.e. has between five and ten thousand residents. But then the probability of losing population decreases as the nearest neighboring town's population increases.

These results make intuitive sense. Towns of under a thousand residents are unlikely to have schools and professional services, such as doctors and

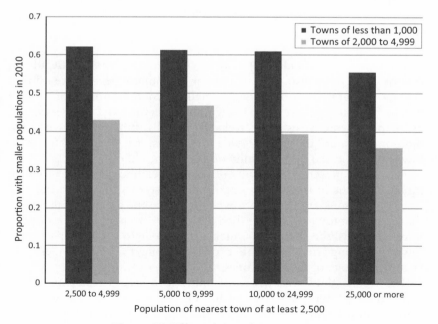

Figure 6.4 Effect of size of nearest town

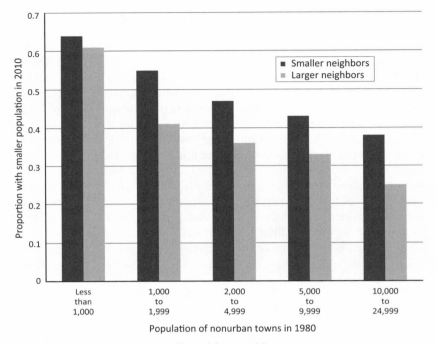

Figure 6.5 Effect of five neighboring towns

dentists, of their own. Housing may be cheaper, but there is little advantage of living there instead of in a larger community nearby, even if that larger community is still relatively small. In contrast, towns of at least two to five thousand are more likely to have services and businesses that make them attractive as places to live, especially if there is a town of ten thousand or more that can provide jobs. Thus, it is beneficial for these towns to be located in the vicinity of a larger neighbor.

Figure 6.5 presents the results of nearest-neighbor analysis in which the populations of the five geographically closest towns are considered. The comparisons are between towns for which the mean population of the five nearest towns is *smaller* than the town's own population, or *larger*. In other words, the comparison makes it possible to ask for a particular town of varying size whether that town is among the smaller ones in its vicinity or is one of the larger ones.[18]

The results show that towns of under a thousand residents have a better than 60 percent chance of having declined no matter how they compare in size with their five neighboring towns. The chances of having lost population are only slightly improved if their neighbors are larger—

similar to the result in the previous figure. But for towns that have at least a thousand residents, all the way up to towns that have between ten and twenty-five thousand residents, having larger neighboring towns is actually beneficial. Towns with larger neighbors are consistently less likely to lose population than those with smaller neighbors.

Of course, there are many other factors that determine whether a town loses population, holds its own, or grows. But this evidence counters the impression that it is disadvantageous to have larger neighboring towns. True, the chances of losing population are reduced if the size of one's own town is larger. And yet taking that into account, those chances of declining are further reduced if there are some larger towns in the vicinity. In those cases, residents of the smaller towns can more easily find jobs in the larger towns.

Resistance to Innovation

Community leaders we spoke with generally considered it important to adapt as best they can to changing circumstances. As one leader observed, "We're progressive in the sense that we're not afraid to try things." They point to having economic development programs, good wireless service, and technology classes at the high school or junior college. They also acknowledge that residents sometimes resist innovation. "We have an aging community," an official in a town of a thousand explains. He says residents like to have a "safe, warm, friendly community," which means they are not especially interested in any new technology or economic development programs. The inability to welcome newcomers coupled with hostility toward immigrants is a problem other leaders mention.

Resistance is not always the best word to describe townspeople's reluctance to innovate. A better term might be apathy. It stems from the feeling that efforts to attract new residents and businesses in the past have failed. It grows from the sense that what happens to the community does not matter. Young people who doubt they will stay beyond high school may be in this category. So also may be people near the end of life. If their children and grandchildren live in the community, feelings may be different. But when children and grandchildren have all left for other places, the community's future becomes less interesting. "You just don't have the same sense of urgency to keep the community thriving," one resident remarked. "I'm going to die. There's really nothing left here for me."

Resistance may also stem from opposition to seeking outside help from government. One community leader we talked to said that the ranchers and ranch hands in her area were especially leery of outside help. Her view was that the community was paying taxes, and if it did not receive the assistance, some other community would. But the townspeople had a different view. "We don't want to apply for that because we're not taking care of ourselves" was how she described it. "Somebody else might have the right to tell us how to take care of something. We'll stand on our own. If we need a new roof on the courthouse, we'll figure it out." She thought it was good to be self-sufficient, but not to be arrogant about it. Or stupid.

Absent organized resistance, town administrators face thorny questions about how best to innovate amid limited opportunities. We found this to be true not only in one-industry towns but also in communities with diversified economies. For example, in one of the coastal towns we studied, logging and fishing had been the mainstay of the local economy for more than a century, but were currently employing significantly fewer of the local labor force than the tourism industry, a nearby casino, and a large state prison. Generally, diversification was beneficial to communities' economic and demographic trajectory. Town administrators, though, frequently mentioned difficulties arising from conflicts among the various constituencies involved. In this community, the town council was wrestling with trade-offs between protecting the environment and clearing land for a new medical facility, and between catering to the high-end tourism market and providing services to employees at the casino as well as families of inmates at the state prison. With unemployment at 14 percent, school enrollment declining, and county-funded social services nearing bankruptcy, the trade-offs were difficult to resolve.

Mostly what governs attitudes toward innovation is plain old-fashioned pragmatism. One of the towns we studied provides a vivid example. A group planning to build a small college that might expand into a university had recently purchased land a few miles from the town. The townspeople were nervous not only because the plan might bring traffic, cause taxes to be raised to pay for new roads, and burden the water supply but also because the town was a conservative, ethnically homogeneous community and the newcomers were members of a religious organization that few of the locals knew much about. There were hastily called town meetings and efforts to pass zoning laws to keep the newcomers out. Rumors flew about all kinds of damage and inconvenience that might be anticipated. But without any of their misgivings disproven, longtime residents gradually realized that the potential benefits would probably outweigh any of the risks. The campus would possibly boost local business. Nobody was quite ready to view the venture in purely economic terms, or at least to say so. They instead applied the familiar language that they used in other circumstances. They figured that the community took a down-to-earth attitude toward most things. They knew how to roll with the punches. It was live and let live. Things usually had a way of working themselves out, people said. "I feel like they are not going to hurt anything," a lifelong resident mentioned. "They aren't doing anything illegal. They aren't a drug group. This is America. If they want to be here, they have a right to be."

Community leaders who had been most actively involved in efforts to repopulate small declining towns acknowledged that many ideas that might sound good at first, simply were not practical. The possibility of attracting a new manufacturing plant or some other large business that would employ several hundred people, for example, was a dream that was never going to come true for most rural towns far from cities and off the beaten track. In the few instances in which a large new plant was built, moreover, the results were mixed.

An example of this kind occurred in a remote town of twenty-seven hundred that had been declining for twenty years as a result of weak performance in the neighboring oil and gas industry along with the closure of a carbon-extraction facility. Things began to turn around when plans were announced to construct a nuclear-enrichment plant adjacent to the community. Although there was some resistance from antinuclear groups and some of the local citizens who wanted their community to remain unchanged, state and federal officials pushed the deal to completion, partly in expectation of significant revenue from uranium extraction and ad valorem taxes. That part never materialized. The European company that owned the plant decided to import uranium instead of mining it locally. The town, though, benefited at the start. Unemployment fell as laid-off workers from oil and gas companies found jobs in construction. Housing prices rose, and local businesses found themselves catering to new customers with French, German, and Dutch accents. Population edged up by several hundred, and with predictions of further growth, residents passed a bond issue for a new forty million dollar school, put in new water and sewer lines, made plans to build a senior citizens' center, and contracted with a national housing developer to construct new homes. Then the nationwide foreclosure crisis that happened in 2009 forced the developer to cancel plans. Most of the subsequent growth took place in larger communities a half hour away. The town manager told us he still expected the town to benefit in the long run, but "it seems like every time we take two steps forward, we take two or three steps back."

Leaders in other communities suggested that a better idea than hoping to attract a sizable manufacturing firm was to encourage small businesses wherever that may be possible. At least that is the view we heard from some of the most thoughtful community leaders we talked to. They had learned this the hard way, one town manager explained, when the one big plant in the area was sold six or seven years ago and moved to another state. Overnight, four hundred jobs were lost—a devastating blow to a town that had only three thousand residents. Since that time, the town has held annual economic summits focused on helping people in the area start smaller companies. "Lots of small businesses are probably a healthier model for us than one great big guy," he observed.

Townspeople hoped especially for small businesses that would bring young families with children and thus boost school enrollments. That aspiration was expressed particularly in communities facing the possibility of losing their school. One person even decried the arrival of retired people because he feared every one of those meant a house no longer available for a family with children. But it was much more realistic, leaders said, to anticipate retirees being attracted than young families. Retired people were often looking for a slower-paced community with cheap housing and less traffic, and they were not as likely to need employment. They would need medical services, but if they were on Social Security or had pensions, that would be new revenue for the community.

Leaders were also realistic about the limited contributions that older people would make to their communities. If older people had lived elsewhere and had investments, there was a good chance those investments would not translate into added business for local banks. If someone was used to shopping online or at a mall, they would not transact that same business locally. "They come back here to live," one community leader in a town of two thousand noted, "and they realize they have gotten used to the fast pace and the amenities they had in the city. They end up buying a house here because it is cheap and then spend most of their time traveling." People who did that, she explained, seldom became involved in local community organizations.

Meth Labs and Alcohol

Even more than declining population and a lack of attractive jobs, the problem that perplexes small-town leaders is drugs. What was once regarded as a feature of the urban ghetto now seems to have become present in out-of-the-way rural communities. Contrary to the image of small towns free of crime, law enforcement officials are being called on to deal with drug-related theft and domestic violence. Methamphetamines appear to be the drug of choice, although cocaine, marijuana, and prescription drug abuse are also common.[19]

In his case study of Oelwein, Iowa, a rural town of six thousand, journalist Nick Reding chronicled the human tragedy that can affect small-town America from methamphetamine use. Violence and fires occurred. Overextended fire and police forces struggled to keep up. Teenagers were arrested or dropped out of school. Families were torn apart. One young man lost his fingers and part of his face.[20]

Reviewers of Reding's book saw the Oelwein tragedy as an instructive example of the wider decline of small-town America. With population plummeting, institutions failing, tax receipts falling, and young people losing hope, it was hardly surprising that small towns were drowning their sorrows in drugs. "What's clear is that the golden rolling heartland that Americans used to think symbolized stability," a reviewer concluded in the *New York Times*, "beats fitfully and irregularly still and almost certainly remains inclined to seek out sources of chemical optimism."[21]

In reality, the situation in Oelwein was complicated. Like many small towns, its population had indeed been declining—by nearly 50 percent since 1960. The farm crisis of the 1980s hit area farmers especially hard, and after two decades, adjustments to new agribusiness ventures were still being made. Yet the community's institutions were hardly falling apart. Other than an uptick in burglaries around 2005 and 2006, the crime rate was not particularly high. It in fact never exceeded the national average, and on several occasions was less than a third of the national average.[22] None of that was of much comfort of course to the families whose lives were being destroyed by methamphetamine or the community leaders seeking solutions.

Our research found considerable variation in the extent to which small towns were compelled to deal with methamphetamine use along with other problems related to drugs and alcohol. A few town leaders said that to the best of their knowledge, drug abuse was nonexistent in their communities and alcoholism was rare. Those were the exceptions. The most common response included candid acknowledgment of local problems. Indeed, nearly everyone knew of drugs being sold or manufactured and used in their communities. Just as in Oelwein, there were tragic incidents.

"My sister, God rest her soul, was raised in the same household as I was, and for some reason, she just decided to go that way." This is how a leader in a town of four thousand responded when asked about drugs in his community. Drugs destroyed his sister's liver. In another community of about the same size, a middle-aged couple told of having their son sent away permanently to an institution. He had become so dangerous from using drugs that they were afraid to be near him. "It was in our family," another parent said. A resident of a rural community of seventeen thousand where the crime rate was routinely at least 50 percent above the national average insisted that "there was probably not anybody who wasn't affected by somebody cooking meth."

In other communities, residents who had not been personally affected knew of neighbors who were. "We're just hoping to make it through prom season," one woman said. It seemed that at least one teenager a year in her community died driving under the influence. "We had a couple of young kids who had been drinking die in a car accident," a woman in a town of two hundred recalled. In another town of two hundred, a resident confessed that he knew of three places locally to buy drugs. "We've had several meth labs raided here," a man in a town of eight hundred reported. A resident of a town of only seven hundred said there were "a couple of blocks in town" where drugs were readily available. "They busted a meth lab just a few miles from here," she said. In another town, a drug dealer killed one of his teenage customers.

I was curious how residents accounted for these problems. After mostly putting a good face on their communities, they were a bit chagrined at having to acknowledge the presence of drugs and drug-related crime. The topic seldom came up voluntarily. Only when we asked did townspeople venture their observations on these subjects. I wondered especially if they would read a larger story of small-town decline into their accounts, the way journalists did, or whether they would understand it differently.

The man who said everybody in his town of seventeen thousand had somehow been affected by meth was one of the few who explicitly associated drug use with the cultural climate of small towns. He identified three aspects of small-town culture that he thought were responsible: "there was nothing to do," which he regarded as the reason so many young people in small towns were on drugs; "the redneck mentality" encouraged everyone young or old to consume alcohol in abundance; and "nobody in the community wanted to admit it," which meant denying that problems existed.

The more common way of associating drug problems with narratives about community was by referencing the decline of community *in general*. Residents did not mean community decline in the specific sense of their own community or in terms of people not participating in civic activities. They instead meant a kind of cultural decline in which parents no longer disciplined their children as rigorously as they should, children grew up expecting instant gratification, and adults were too often oriented toward unfulfilling material pursuits.

"Parents just want to be their kids' friends," says the man whose sister died because of drugs. That's not how it used to be. "When I was growing up, I had to be home no later than midnight. I believed my dad would kick my tail." "There was no use me dragging Main Street and squealing the tires," another resident recalls. "Before I even got home, four people would have called [my parents]." That kind of monitoring is still present, he says, but may be diminishing. Others point to cultural trends that locate the problem on someone else's doorstep. For example, teenagers who have more money nowadays means a greater opportunity to travel to cities where drugs are sold, television commercials glamorize wine and beer, and the Internet brings new temptations from the outside. It is not uncommon to blame strangers, immigrants, and gangs.

The closest residents come to identifying something particular about their communities that may result in drug use is low self-esteem. Although this can be a problem anywhere, it may be exacerbated in a small community where opportunities are few. "When you look in the mirror every day and don't like what you see," a man in a town of three thousand says, "you take a shot of something and you think you look a little better." "They have to feel validated and important," a mother in a town of twenty-three hundred says.

These understandings figure into the solutions that community leaders consider in dealing with drug and alcohol problems. The answer is not somehow to redress a weakness of small-town life itself but rather to focus on the same remedies that can be useful anywhere. These include the following. For one, primary emphasis should be placed on education, especially early knowledge about the dangers of drugs and alcohol (teachers and parents we talked to see no reason why this could not be done as effectively in small towns as in larger communities). Second, work with parents through churches, schools, and community organizations to encourage their efforts to train children appropriately. In addition, provide programs to keep young people busy and instill a sense of accomplishment. Sports programs, music, and community service also come frequently to leaders' minds. And fifth was the notion of relying on effective law enforcement.[23]

Residents we talked to supported these efforts, although there were mixed feelings. In several towns where drug abuse was known, residents criticized the sheriff for not providing better law enforcement, and in one community the sheriff himself had been arrested. Some of the older residents felt the problems would simply be resolved if parents and neighbors monitored children the way they used to. In one community, the people we talked to at a neighborhood gathering mentioned the local "AA House" with some pride. It was a small house behind the Congregational Church that the townspeople had purchased to host Alcoholic Anonymous meetings. There are a lot of cars there most evenings, one of the neighbors said. She knew exactly whose cars they were.

Whether serving as a volunteer at the local history museum or heading the county transportation department's crew of several hundred, small-town leadership requires both the technical skill that training and experience can provide along with the knowledge of local customs that residents argue is especially valued in small communities. The respect on which effective leadership depends accrues from going out of one's way to know the specific needs of the community as well as uphold its expectations about neighborliness and common sense.

The special problems that leaders say are distinctive to their communities hinge on the delicate balance of preserving the past while also adapting to economic and demographic challenges. Emphasis on the past arises from the fact that residents have remained in the community or moved there because they prefer to live as they imagine Americans used to live. Although the past sometimes becomes a source of resistance to innovation, it may also be one of the community's most important assets.

Opportunities for innovation are facilitated both formally and informally. Formal programs include local, state, and regional economic development plans, grants for infrastructure upgrades, and tax incentives for small businesses. Informal facilitation occurs through loosely structured networks that bring town managers, farmers, and small business entrepreneurs together with one another as well as interested parties in other communities and cities. These networks increasingly characterize small towns as open systems that are integrated into wider economic and cultural fields through business transactions, travel, tourism, and the Internet.

Although good leadership is sometimes considered the key to small-town population growth, the structural factors that determine the likelihood of population growth or decline must be acknowledged. As we saw in chapter 3, towns are more likely to lose population if they are already small than if they are somewhat larger. We saw, too, how the likelihood of growth or decline is affected by the natural amenities of counties in which towns are located. There is not much that good leadership can do to change these natural amenities. Nor is there much that leaders can do under most circumstances to nurture the effects of being located in the vicinity of larger towns.

In my research on population change among approximately fifty-five hundred towns in the Midwest, I identified several additional factors. Towns that lost population in the quarter century after 1980 were significantly more likely than other towns to have already declined between 1950 and 1980, and indeed to have lost population between 1910 and 1950. Towns that lost population were likely to have been affected by a decline in the number of farms and the profitability of local agriculture. There was a "crowding" effect in which towns—especially smaller ones—in counties with a larger number of other towns were more likely to lose population. In contrast, towns that grew or were less likely to lose population benefited mainly from being located closer to cities as well as in counties with an interstate highway. They also benefited from being a county seat or the home of a college.[24]

To pin too much hope for population growth on community leaders is thus a recipe for disappointment. Leadership nevertheless matters for reasons that have more to do with day-to-day life in small towns than with long-term growth or decline. Residents care that their leaders are trusted individuals who are engaged in civic activities and interested in promoting community spirit. They want competent leadership in fiscal matters and handling complex relationships with state and regional government. They care about infrastructure, how the community looks, and especially whether the community provides good educational opportunities and health services.[25]

Leadership that can be considered progressive is valued, despite cautionary tales about leaders who try to change things too rapidly. The good thing about small communities is that progress can be measured in small doses. If a huge new manufacturing plant is unlikely—and for that matter, undesirable—progress can be evident in the fact that a crumbling building that nobody cared to look at any longer was torn down, the elementary school has been renovated, and Main Street has recently been repaved.

- 7 -

Habits of Faith
The Social Role of Small-Town Congregations

VALLEY VIEW UNITED METHODIST CHURCH occupies a spacious corner lot conveniently located just a block from the town square which surrounds a modest two-story county courthouse constructed of native limestone. The church's stately red-brick building with a tall bell tower rising above the front door was erected a century ago to replace the small frame church constructed in 1870, two years after the congregation was organized by a circuit rider. The sanctuary with curved wooden pews easily holds two hundred worshippers, but on most Sundays attendance at the eleven o'clock service is fewer than half that number. This morning, the preaching service and Holy Communion are being conducted by candlelight. Heavy rain on Saturday afternoon flooded the river that runs through the south end of town and knocked out the area's electricity.

It is not uncommon in small towns to find several aging churches within a block or two of Main Street or the town square. One was probably founded by the Disciples of Christ, another by Presbyterians or Congregationalists, and another by one of several Baptist denominations. There may be a Lutheran church and probably a Roman Catholic one. In addition, at least one newer church building of modern design is likely to exist on the edge of town, several modest storefront or residential congregations are tucked along side streets, and perhaps a metal-frame edifice or two with a church sign in front are located on the outskirts of the community. Filmmakers and writers still depict small towns with church spires rising above the trees along with hymns emanating from white-clapboard edifices. Those images may be dated and stereotyped, but religious congregations are still a vital feature of small-town America. Ask almost any small-town resident, whether they are personally religious or not, and the answer is nearly always that religion is an important part of their community.

When they talk about religion, moreover, townspeople hardly ever mean anything other than Protestant, Catholic, or other denominations in the Christian tradition. Although there may be an occasional Jewish, Muslim,

Buddhist, or Hindu family living in the community, it is more likely that those families will travel to a larger metropolitan area to worship than to have a worship center associated with their own faith in the community itself. A study conducted in 2009, for example, identified 3,376 Jewish congregations nationwide, but only 15 were located in counties with populations of fewer than twenty-five thousand people. The same study identified 513 mosques nationwide, but only 3 were in counties this small. Of the 625 Buddhist temples identified in the study, 6 were located in small counties of this size, as were only 2 of the 183 Hindu temples in the study.[1]

The Valley View ministerial alliance recently canvased the community to see what could be done to increase church attendance. At the Congregational and Christian churches, both founded in the nineteenth century, attendance on Sunday mornings has fallen below a hundred. The Southern Baptist Church up the street from the Methodist Church is barely holding its own. Attendance at the new Lutheran Church on the edge of town and the Catholic Church is stable. Eleven other churches, mostly fundamentalist, Pentecostal, and nondenominational Bible congregations, are faring better, although none has more than a hundred members. Religion is nevertheless quite important in the community. The flagging attendance is partly because members more often spend their weekends visiting children living in cities and suburbs than was true a generation ago. The more serious source of decline is that the town is economically depressed and losing population. More than half the stores on the town square are vacant. After rising to four thousand in 1920, the population settled back to thirty-two hundred through the 1950s and since then has declined by a third.

Studies of churchgoing demonstrate that people's habits are significantly influenced by their surroundings. When people move to a different region of the country, their religious participation increases if that part of the country has high rates of religious involvement. It decreases if the rate of involvement there is low.[2] Research shows that religious participation among new immigrants to the United States is similarly affected. It rises in communities where churchgoing among the native-born population is high. It declines where native-born religious participation is low.[3]

The puzzle is how do people know? How do they know whether religious participation in their community is high or low? Especially if religion is as private as many observers say it is, how would someone determine that religion is or is not important? Is it because of particular individuals they meet? Is it because of reading statistics from surveys, canvasing the community, or some other information? Is it that people actually talk about their religious activities more often than might be supposed even in secular settings, as a study of volunteers at a soup kitchen found? Is it that people draw conclusions from viewing cars in church parking lots, as one team of observers tried to do?[4]

In a city, the information that shapes public perceptions of religious activity is probably a function of geographic region. Atlanta may be regarded as a religious place because it is in the South, whereas Boston may have the opposite reputation because it is in the Northeast. Small towns have a reputation of being more religious than big cities, perhaps correctly judging from surveys. But it is interesting to ask residents of small towns why they think religion is important in their communities. Doing so provides a window into the social role that small-town congregations play.

Townspeople usually do not try to judge the significance of religion by estimating how many people believe in God or attend church regularly. One of the few exceptions in our research is a man who figures that 95 percent of the townspeople in his community believe in God and at least 50 percent are at church on any given Sunday. This man happens to teach social studies at the high school. Another exception is a member of a Nazarene church in a town of about nineteen hundred. She is sure that nearly everyone in her community is affiliated with a church. The reason she knows this is that her congregation recently completed a survey of the town. I mention these because they are indeed exceptions. They illustrate that it is rare for townspeople to think about the importance of religion the way that social scientists do.

The common way of indicating the importance of religion in small towns is by pointing to the number of churches. "There are a lot of churches in town," a man in a community of thirty-three hundred says. He isn't sure just how many, but notes that three of them are different kinds of Lutherans. A lifelong resident in another town offers a more precise figure. "There are twenty-two churches in this county of about six thousand people. So I would say it's more important here than in the bigger cities." He conjectures the reason for the difference is that in cities, nobody knows whether you go to church or not, whereas in a small town "you have more accounting to the audience." Churches are a visible part of his community because of their buildings. "Let me see," a woman in another town says, "one, two, three, four, five, six." She pictures the churches as she counts. "It's pretty important," she concludes. The membership at some of the churches is usually small, yet townspeople seem to take pride not in the size of any particular building but simply in the fact that there are a lot of them.

Churches are indeed more visible in small towns than in larger communities not merely because it is easier in smaller places for residents to visualize its main buildings but also because there are more churches per capita in less populated areas than there are in more heavily populated places. The data shown in figure 7.1 are drawn from two national studies,

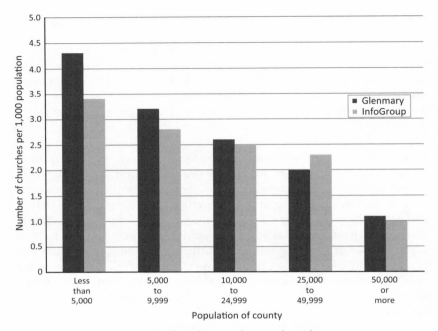

Figure 7.1 Churches per thousand residents

the first conducted in 2000 under the auspices of the Glenmary Research Center, and the second in 2009 by a commercial firm called InfoGroup. The studies provide somewhat-different results because of the methods used, but both demonstrate that churches are more abundant, relative to population, in smaller areas than in larger ones. In counties with fewer than five thousand residents, for example, there are approximately four churches for every thousand residents, but that number declines to about one church for every thousand people in counties of fifty thousand or more.[5]

In addition to the fact that church buildings are a more visible part of the community in sparsely population places than in urban areas, it is also more common for the average resident to be affiliated with a congregation. As shown in figure 7.2, the rates of adherence at churches range from more than 60 percent of the population in the least populated counties to fewer than 50 percent in the most populated ones. Similarly, actual membership in congregations is around 50 percent in counties with fewer than five thousand residents, but declines to 34 percent in counties with more than fifty thousand residents.[6]

The other tangible marker of religion's importance is the fact that in many small towns, one evening a week is still customarily thought of as

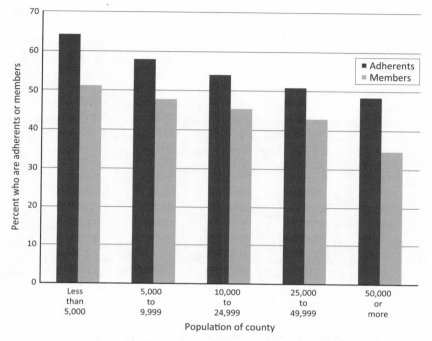

Figure 7.2 Religious adherence and membership

church night. This is the evening when cars are parked in front of churches and community leaders know not to schedule other events. "Oh, Wednesday nights," one woman explains when asked to say how she knew religion was crucial in her town. "That's our church night. Everybody knows, every organization, the school, everybody knows to never try to plan anything for Wednesday night. That's church night."[7]

People who estimate the importance of religion in their communities in other ways are usually residents who have lived elsewhere. If they have lived in cities, they say religion in their small town is more significant in comparison. This judgment is mostly from knowing friends and neighbors who do or do not participate in religious services. Occasionally the perception is based on some personal incident that is considered especially revealing. An interesting example is given by a woman who is Catholic but married to a Lutheran. After attending the Lutheran Church for several years, she decided to attend the Catholic Church some of the time. People were shocked, and several actually questioned her about it. "If you are Catholic here, you just don't go somewhere else. And if you are Lutheran, you stay within the church. So the Lutherans kind of shunned me for a while because I was going to the Catholic Church, and the Catholic

Church didn't accept me because I hadn't been going there all along." This was her evidence that religion is key in her community.

Nearly every study of small communities conducted between the 1920s and 1950s suggested that religion played a crucial role in those decades. If residents of small towns still argue that religion is important, does that mean little has changed? Is religion a way of preserving the past in small towns, perhaps even more so than it is in cities and suburbs? Or is religion adapting to the changes taking place in small towns? The best answer to these questions comes from townspeople themselves. They talk glowingly of their congregations giving them a sense of continuity with the past, but also show that congregations are adapting to new challenges.

HABITS OF BELONGING

"Somebody asked me if I was a born-again Christian. I said I went to church every Sunday from the time I was out of the womb. I had to be darn sick if I ever got to stay home." This is Emma Wilkins. She is a spry eighty-two-year-old who grew up in a town of eight hundred, married her high school sweetheart, and has been living in her hometown ever since. "You just do those things," she says, describing churchgoing in the same way she talks about cleaning house and canning her own tomatoes. "They are just a way of life, I guess."

Habits are much of what small-town congregations are about. Weekly services are routine, starting at the same hour, meeting in the same space that has been used for decades, singing familiar hymns, and seeing familiar faces. The worship service may not be as lively or exciting as those at a big church in the suburbs, but longtime members appreciate the familiarity of it all. The weekly services give a sense of regularity to the passage of time. Mr. Steuben, the auctioneer, and his wife attend a Mennonite church that has about six hundred active members—making it one of the larger congregations likely to be found in a small rural community and yet one that continues to exhibit decades-old customs. "One Sunday is not any different from another Sunday," he says. "Oh, somebody will raise hell about something every once in a while, but that's just a hiccup. Basically it's a steady deal. It's always there. You've got active members who keep the deal alive."

Izzy Jorgensen, a member of a Lutheran church where about fifty people attend regularly, makes a similar observation. She notes that "every Sunday morning, somebody brings snack items and there's coffee time, fellowship time before church ever starts." That happens at nine o'clock, and then the service is from 9:30 to 10:30 a.m., and after that people break into groups of eight or ten to discuss the sermon. Committees meet promptly at 7:30 every Wednesday evening in the fellowship hall, and once a month the men get together for breakfast at the café while the women meet as a group just to talk and have a short Bible study. The steady deal, as Mr. Steuben would put it, is just as predictable at her church as at his.

When habits are this ingrained, just being there each Sunday is a mark of loyalty, especially if the sermons are dry and the music is bad. This is one of the reasons that people show up, even though they may be less than thrilled about what then happens. A lifetime Lutheran in a predominantly Finnish congregation, for instance, says his church has been putting on a dinner of sauerkraut and bratwurst for the Germans in his community for as long as he can remember. "I can't stand either one," he complains, referring to the sauerkraut and bratwurst, yet it is difficult not to participate. It says something good about people that they will stick with a congregation over a long period. A member of a Catholic parish in a town of ten thousand puts it well when he notes that what he likes best about the parish is its "continuity." Many of the parishioners, he says, have been lifelong members. They have "stood by the parish through thick and thin." That gives him a sense of history along with a feeling that people really care for the parish and one another.

As much as the continuity, it is the visibility of public behavior that facilitates regular participation in small-town religious activities. When people know one another in town as well as in church, churchgoing becomes part of their public reputation and this fact puts social pressure on them to be present at church services. People know that the car dealer goes to the Methodist Church and the bank manager is an elder at the Presbyterian Church. Parents' public reputation affects their children's behavior as well. People talk if the bank manager's children are out drinking on Sunday night instead of participating in the youth group. Again, Mr. Steuben provides an example. His children were brought up in the same church that he was. When they were teenagers, they went through a phase when they did not want to attend Sunday school or go to the youth fellowship. Mr. Steuben told them in no uncertain terms, "That's non-negotiable." In fact, his opinion of other parents who did not hold their children to the same standard went down. It made him "real hacked off about the doggone deal" when parents weren't pushing their kids' "butts out the door" to get to church. The habit of going to church is simply ingrained, not only because parents believe this is the right way to live, but also because the community expects it.

The fact that churchgoing in small towns involves habit and depends on social pressure does not mean, of course, that everyone faithfully attends week in and week out. National surveys show that 36 percent of inhabitants in nonmetropolitan communities of fewer than twenty thousand residents claim to attend religious services weekly or nearly every

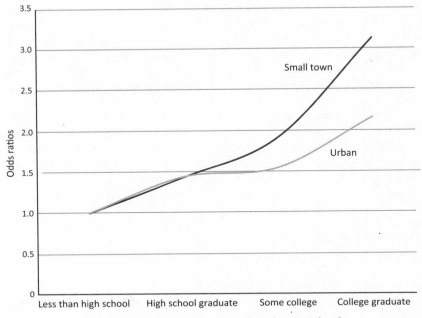

Figure 7.3 Church attendance by education level

week. That figure is only 5 percent higher than the national average for the whole US adult population. A quarter of small-town residents say they attend services less than once a year or never—a figure that differs little from the national average.

But what is notable about small towns is the extent to which church involvement is expected among the community's leaders and other up-scale residents. As shown in figure 7.3, the odds of someone attending religious services regularly are higher if that person has more education, but those odds increase more dramatically among people living in small towns than among those living in cities or suburbs.[8] This pattern is consistent with the fact (as I noted in chapter 2) that residents who live in "above average" homes, as judged by interviewers, are more likely to be involved in community organizations if they live in small towns than if they live in larger places. This difference pertains to religious organizations as well. In small towns, 54 percent of upscale residents belonged to a specific religious group of some kind, such as a fellowship group or Bible study, compared with 39 percent of upscale residents in larger communities.[9]

It is also evident from our qualitative interviews that church attendance and nonattendance are matters of public discussion in small towns. Residents talk about the religious affiliations of their friends and neighbors, and whether some neighbors do not attend at all. Clergy periodically canvas their communities to invite residents to church and discuss the results with their congregations. Clergy also serve on the boards of community organizations, and see members during the week at the post office or grocery store. They mention members apologizing for having missed the latest worship service or potluck dinner. Residents themselves volunteer in interviews that poor health prevents them from attending services often, they have to work on Sundays, or in a few cases, they have quit going because of a falling out with the pastor.

For those who do attend regularly, churchgoing is often reinforced by the fact that small congregations feel like families. "We've got a tremendous church family here," a town leader in a community of two thousand explains. "We're not terribly large. I suppose we have sixty or seventy people who come regularly. That's our family. It's terribly important." His view is shared by a woman who attends a Congregational church of about a hundred members in a town of a thousand. "If you come to choir practice, it's a family, and we've bonded. It's an uplifting time, and you go home and say, 'Boy, I'm glad I went to choir practice. I feel so much better.' " A Lutheran member in a town of thirty-six hundred chuckles, "It is a lot of family. The people who aren't blood related to me, well, my church family is like they are."

Although church leaders in large congregations in cities and suburbs also like to say that their churches are like a big family, the secret to this claim actually being a reality in small towns is the limited scope of a small community. Socializing occurs within the community. People share more than just the fact that they see each other for a few minutes on Sundays or sit together on a committee once in a while. They can talk about how the weather is affecting the local agriculture or how the proposed bypass will hurt the businesses on Main Street. People mention that their next-door neighbors also go to the same church, they go with fellow church members to a movie, meet someone from their church at the coffee shop, or spend time together on Sunday evenings at the Dairy Queen.

As an example, one man says that he and his wife have taken dance lessons with three other couples from their church. Another man mentions by name the two other couples that he and his wife know from church, but also play cards with and see during the week at school functions. There are still affinity groups, like there are in large urban churches. Mr. Parsons, for instance, says he and his wife belong to a couples' group at their church of a hundred members. "In fact, last night we went out to one of our members' farm pond and had a potluck out by their farm pond. Potlucks are great. I mean that's the only way to eat, in my opinion, because you get a great variety and everything's good." But in small churches, affinity groups are less likely to separate people than is often true in large churches. The congregation remains intact as a single community. In the Parsons's case, the whole church comes together routinely to organize a soup-and-sandwich dinner, host a pancake breakfast for the town, and have a cleanup day at the church.[10]

Data from a national study highlight the differences between small and large communities in churchgoers' friendship patterns. Among active churchgoers nationally, those who attend larger congregations are more likely to report having more than ten close friends in their congregation—presumably because there are more people with whom to make friends. In small nonmetropolitan communities, though, nearly half of active church-goers participate in congregations of fewer than two hundred members. That contrasts with only 18 percent of active churchgoers in metropolitan areas. Yet despite belonging to smaller congregations, 43 percent of churchgoers in small nonmetropolitan communities report having more than ten close friends in their congregation, compared with only 33 percent in metropolitan areas. Why? It is probably because they see one another not only on Sundays but also during the week.[11]

In addition to the fact that congregations forge bonds among their own members, they also serve as bridges across the wider community by sponsoring broader events open to the public. These activities are especially common in smaller towns of five hundred to a thousand. In one town of this size, for instance, several people note that there is a fund-raiser or benefit dinner for the community at least once or twice a week. One woman says with some pride that it is possible to get a wonderful home-cooked meal for five dollars at these events. In another town, the Catholic Church's bingo night with all the popcorn you can eat is a popular attraction for Catholics and Protestants alike. In some communities, the churches actually seem to compete with one another in sponsoring events for the entire public. In others, the church leaders say they are trying to keep up with school activities that would otherwise draw people to ball games. Examples include churches renting the high school auditorium for a guest musical performance or hosting a town festival during homecoming week.

Although school activities may pose the most common source of competition for churches, another source that townspeople sometimes mention is the availability of attractive recreational activities, such as boating, fishing, gardening, and playing golf. This may be the reason for the pattern shown in figure 7.4. Average weekly church attendance is lower in areas that rank highest on the natural amenities scale than in areas that rank lowest. Generally, attendance declines as amenities scores increase. Attendance, however, is higher in small nonurban towns than it is in large urban towns at each level of the amenities scale. And attendance is highest in small nonurban towns located in areas with the lowest amenities scores.[12]

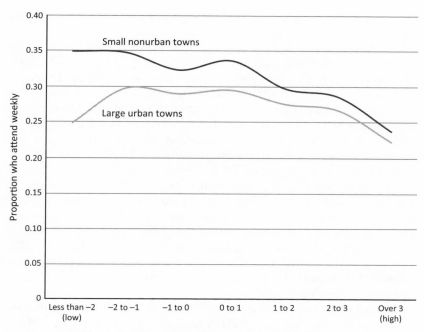

Figure 7.4 Attendance by town size and amenities

Of Life and Death

Social scientists have long observed that modern society insulates itself from having to think very often about illness and death. Hospitals and nursing homes segregate the dying from the wider community. Funeral homes are tucked in out-of-the-way places far from the shopping malls that residents visit regularly. Churches are the one place where births, deaths, and illnesses are regularly acknowledged. Praying for the sick, hosting baby showers, and holding memorial services are part of the routine. Even in churches, though, the grim realities of life are sometimes shielded from view. Happy uplifting praise choruses substitute for paeans about suffering and solitude. Residents of small towns insist that things are more traditional there. Deaths, farm accidents, a boy drowning in the local lake, a teenager killed in an automobile crash, a mother struggling with breast cancer—these are harder to hide from in a small town. News travels quickly. People see one another at the grocery store. The family affected includes people they know. The churches provide a patterned way of responding. "If you have a death in the family, people stop by and bring food over," a resident explains. "When my father and mother passed away," another says, "they didn't live here, but food was brought to us, memorials were given, people stopped by and just expressed their sympathy."

In large suburban communities, church members experience similar expressions of sympathy within their congregations or neighborhood Bible study group. The difference in small towns is that when illness and death occur, faith transcends particular congregations. A vivid example is the story that a man in a prairie town of two thousand tells. His daughter, the youngest of four children, was born hydrocephalic. The doctors determined that she was educable, although she was paralyzed on one side and half her brain was atrophied. She went to kindergarten and first grade, but died just before her eighth birthday. The Presbyterian Church that the family attended was extremely supportive. But what the man recalled most clearly was how supportive the Catholic Church was. So often in towns like his Catholics and Protestants went their separate ways, sometimes perpetuating generations-old doctrinal animosities. In this instance, however, the death of an eight-year-old girl bridged the gap. The man was impressed with Catholics' respect for life and understanding of suffering. He recently threw a birthday party for the priest, now retired, who became his closest friend.

Another important connection with death and suffering in small communities is established through the liturgical calendar. In his rich ethnographic study of a rural village in England, Michael Mayerfeld Bell observes that awareness of life and death was kept in the villagers' minds through constant references to the cycle of nature.[13] This is true in many small towns in the United States as well. Harvest festivals, roadside stands selling sweet corn and tomatoes, and maypole dances are examples. The churches participate as well. "There are lots of Bible references to sowers, to seed, and growing," a pastor in a farming community says. He makes frequent use of these references in his sermons. "We talk about the difficulties of trying to raise crops during droughts and have lots of prayer requests along those lines. People in farming understand that." On Sunday mornings one can hear hymns about seedtime and harvest, bringing in the sheaves, or gathering at the river. The message is that life is filled with ups and downs. Like the seasons, much about life is not within human control.

Caring for the Community

Lucille Pulliam wanted a better life for her three children. Soon the oldest would be in high school. In the city where they lived, drugs and gangs were a constant threat. The monthly rent took most of her meager income. Like a growing number of people living in poverty, she was intrigued by the possibility of moving to a small town where housing was cheap and crime was low. A foreclosed house was being auctioned for taxes in a town of thirty-six hundred an hour away. She bid, won, moved, and found a job. But she had nobody to fix it up. It turned out that the house was in such poor condition that it should have been condemned. Somehow the pastor of the Methodist Church learned of her plight and asked the six-member ministerial alliance at its next meeting if they thought the town's church people could help. Over the next six months, people from all the churches got together and basically redid the house.

The remarkable thing about this story was not that the church people pitched in to help a needy neighbor. They were used to doing that for one another. It was rather that they were willing to help this particular woman. People in the community were wary of newcomers who were there simply because housing was cheap. These newcomers were known as the type who "want to sponge off the system," as one old-timer put it. That was anathema in a town that prided itself on its work ethic. Even though Mrs. Pulliam had a job, people wondered if she would keep it or would soon be on welfare. Had it not been for the church connection, they likely would have done nothing to help. The ministerial alliance made the difference. Its imprimatur said in effect that this was a legitimate case for Christian charity. It helped, too, that the Baptists and Presbyterians did not want to be outdone by the Methodists.

Cooperative programs like this are not uncommon in small towns. They sometimes date to the town's earliest years when fledgling congregations helped each other get started and often shared the same building for a time. Ministerial councils became popular during the first quarter of the twentieth century, and frequently continued through informal arrangements involving joint worship services, jointly sponsored holiday festivals, and community projects. In small towns with declining populations those traditions are again becoming more important.

In a town of about five hundred, as one example, the Christian, Presbyterian, and Methodist congregations merged a few years ago to form a single mainline community church, thereby leaving one evangelical Protestant church and the Catholic parish, which shared a priest from a town thirteen miles away. In a community of this size it was already common for churches to hold get-togethers because people knew one another as neighbors. The Catholic Church, for instance, sponsored a tea every so often for ladies from the Protestant churches. Sometimes it was a salad luncheon. One of the Protestant churches puts on musical programs for the whole community. "We go over there for fellowship," a Catholic woman says. "You know everybody, so it isn't like you're afraid to go there."

Besides cross-denominational church socials, cooperative projects to help families in need are fairly common. "All the churches get involved," says Mr. Parsons about an annual project in his town of nine hundred. "We'll find a family in need of house repair. It might be as simple as cleaning the gutters or something larger like painting a house. If it's a large project that might take two or three different weekends, we assign each church a time." Besides spreading the work around, what makes these programs successful is adapting them to the particular needs of different communities. Whereas food pantries, Christmas baskets, and Thanksgiving dinners for the needy are fairly common, other programs reflect greater creativity. One of the more interesting cases is a rural community of sixteen hundred that includes widows and single mothers with little knowledge of automobile maintenance, but farmers and mechanics with such abilities. The ministerial alliance paired need with skill by organizing a "car ministry" consisting of free oil changes and car washes one Saturday a month.[14]

The cooperative relations among churches may be changing, though. In many of the towns we studied, independent fundamentalist churches had emerged since the 1980s and become a significantly greater influence relative to old-line churches, such as Methodists, Presbyterians, and Lutherans. Community leaders in some of these towns said the result had been less cooperation across denominations. Some attributed it to fundamentalists' tendency to adhere to strict distinctive beliefs that separated them from other churches. "We would almost be giving the idea that the teachings of the other churches are of equal weight to what we are teaching," one fundamentalist pastor said in explaining why his church did not participate in community services with the town's other churches, "and we don't believe they are." Other pastors said there was simply a more competitive sense among churches than there had been in the past. It may have been the result of pastors at independent churches needing to work harder to attract and retain members. It may have been simply that pastors were working such long hours among their own members that they had little time left for community-wide activities.[15]

This trend toward more conservative churches, compared with the historic influence in small towns of mainline Protestant churches and Catholic parishes, is part of a larger phenomenon observed frequently in studies of US religion. National surveys show that mainline Protestants significantly outnumbered evangelical Protestants in the 1970s, but in more recent years have dwindled in comparison. In these surveys, the proportion of residents in small towns that belonged to mainline Protestant denominations fell from 38 percent in the 1970s to 20 percent since the start of the twenty-first century. During the same period, the proportion of small-town residents holding membership in evangelical denominations increased from 29 to 34 percent (Catholics held steady at approximately 20 percent, as did members of historically black denominations at 8 percent).[16]

Among the people we talked to, a majority belonged to Catholic or main-line Protestant denominations, but there were also members of evangeli-cal denominations, such as Southern Baptists and Assemblies of God, and independent fundamentalist and charismatic churches with names such as Courts of Praise, Revival Tabernacle, Covenant Promise, and Living Hope. These members were quite dedicated to their fellow believers, but varied in the extent to which they were connected to other churches and com-munity organizations.[17]

Even among members of well-established churches we encountered in-stances in which loyalties to the congregation were in tension with other churches or the town itself. A Catholic woman we talked to described feeling "out of it" in high school because most of the other students in town were Protestants. She often had activities at church that conflicted with events at school. Others reported similar experiences. One noted that his church did not approve of dancing, which left him out of the high school's most popular weekend activities. Another said her family did not have a television because of the morally questionable influences they feared. That made her a laughingstock among fellow students. Among adults, tensions between church and town sometimes occurred over theo-logical disputes. One resident recalled an incident that split her church and strained relations with townspeople who could hardly avoid seeing one another on the street. She figured that in a larger community, it would have been easier for people simply to go their separate ways. Pastors and priests reported conflicts arising from misunderstandings about zoning and church maintenance. It was not uncommon for ill feelings to divide communities when church memberships coincided with ethnic and kin networks. In those instances, German Catholics or Swedish Lutherans would mention that it was still difficult to marry across religious lines or conduct business together. Those divisions were more evident in smaller towns than they likely would have been in larger places.

Whether they are performed cooperatively or by single congregations, many of the caring activities in small towns have become routine, such as sponsoring a food pantry or deacon's fund. One of the pastors we met described a food pantry that purchased bulk groceries from a state-run food bank and had been operating for decades through regular donations from families at his church. Another pastor mentioned a Vietnam veteran who needed gas money for a doctor's appointment. The pastor phoned the gas station and told them to charge the purchase to the church's discre-tionary fund. He said heating oil in the winter was a common request.

Although caring activities were routine, they were frequently stretched thin in communities with low wages and high unemployment. This was especially true when a mine closed, a factory shut down, or a crop failure occurred. Families scraped by, helping each other in small ways and only turning to the churches as a last resort. "How can you get by?" a priest in a town where the mine had closed asked a member whose husband had been out of work all winter. "Well," she said, "my parents will call us up and they don't want to make us feel bad, so they'll say, 'We made a bit too much food. Can you please come over and share some of it with us?'"

We also learned about creative ways of helping that reflected the special skills and needs in small towns. The Methodists in one community where farming and construction work were prominent purchased a run-down house for next to nothing, fixed it up, and made it available rent free on a short-term basis for families that may have lost their homes because of foreclosures or natural disasters. In another town that was too small to have a separate Alcoholics Anonymous organization, the adult Sunday school class at the main church started fulfilling the same function. As people began to open up, it turned out that nearly everyone was affected in some way personally or by a family member with an addiction. Other examples included church people in rural communities helping sick members plant or harvest crops, and there were still some instances of old-fashioned barn raisings. It was almost funny, a middle-aged farmer laughed. Her husband was so independent that he tried twice putting up a barn alone, and both times the wind blew it down before it was finished. At that point, their small church of about fifty people decided to step in and put up the barn whether he liked it or not.

In the smallest towns, churches are sometimes the only places in which civic functions can be held—another way in which churches serve their communities. The Methodist Church we encountered in one small community is the only building in town that can accommodate the town's entire population of around 150 plus an equal number of out-of-town visitors. That makes it the location of choice for any funeral that draws a sizable crowd. It is also the venue for the annual harvest festival along with a moneymaking dinner and craft sale that attracts farmers and tourists as well as townspeople. The local residents who are not Methodists include Catholics, Lutherans, and Presbyterians who drive to other towns for church, but they work shoulder to shoulder with the Methodists to put on the harvest festival and host dinners after funerals. The Methodist pastor is a member of the city council and serves on a community improvement committee that is attempting to turn the vacant schoolhouse into a community center. Church members drive fellow members and other neighbors to the doctor when their help is needed, check in on neighbors who may be ill, and host benefit dinners at the church if a tragedy befalls a local family. If it were not for the church, these activities would probably diminish.[18]

Where emergency fire and rescue services are limited, as is true in many towns, churches are also likely to play an especially important role when disaster strikes. In a town of twenty-four hundred, as one example, a flood shut down the electric grid, and the town was left without its pumps to provide water plus had no cable television service. "People in the outside world," a resident recalled, "knew more about what was happening here than we did." The mayor was faced with the challenge of getting information to the community about what to expect, and what steps they should take to protect themselves and their homes. One of the churches had been working on a plan to do door-to-door evangelism. The pastor, in cooperation with other pastors, volunteered to organize a door-to-door information campaign using the same plan. They divided the town into "care pods," worked up an information sheet, and canvased the town, telling people how to take care of themselves. They repeated the effort daily for a week until the electricity and water supplies were restored.

Pastors and lay members naturally are eager to tell heartwarming stories about times when their congregations have made a difference in the community. Unfortunately, the picture is not always this positive. Declining membership, loss of population, and depressed economic circumstances in small towns can discourage civic involvement rather than motivate it. Consider the experience of four churches in a southern town of six hundred. The Assembly of God Church shut its doors for lack of participation, the white Baptist Church had no interaction with the African American Baptist Church, and the Methodist Church was basically in survival mode with about forty-five members and shrinking finances. Although efforts had been made earlier in the town's history to form a ministerial council, each of the churches went its own way. There were no joint services or cooperative programs. The downtown area was completely boarded up. Farming in the area was depressed, and a mine that had previously provided some employment had closed. The only remaining employer was the public school, and it was struggling. Each of the three pastors tried at various times to initiate after-school programs, tutoring, and other activities for children, but none was successful. Even getting the church members to come to anything besides Sunday morning services proved difficult. "They just had other things they felt were more important," one of the pastors explained. "About the only thing they would come out for was a football game."

Church Conflicts

In her study of congregational conflicts, sociologist Penny Edgell Becker found that disagreements emerge and escalate over the smallest incidents. A pastor visiting one family and failing to visit another when someone is in the hospital can trigger lasting resentment. Church people notoriously fight over hymns they do or do not like, and whether the organ should be at the back of the church or the front. Conflicts, Becker discovered, were more severe when a congregation was already losing members, struggling with finances, displeased with the pastor, or failing to meet the expectations of a growing community. These were common issues in the suburban churches she studied. In a subsequent study conducted among congregations in upstate New York, she found that family issues were especially important. Although her study did not focus on church conflicts, the congregations in these smaller rural communities were especially oriented toward ministries involving families with children, and this emphasis increased tensions that arose periodically over questions of homosexuality, abortion, and gender roles.[19]

Like so many aspects of small-town life, church conflicts have been the grist for humorous accounts that illustrate the old-fashioned and sometimes-wise common sense that prevails in these settings. One of radio entertainer Garrison Keillor's Lake Wobegone monologues describes a rural Lutheran church that split over the question of whether women should be ordained. Those opposed said women's ordination was against God and contrary to scripture. They would have left and formed a new church, but the church they belonged to controlled the cemetery. They wanted to be buried there alongside grandma and grandpa. So they stayed, and when the congregation called a woman pastor, the only pastor who would come, they decided, what the hell. It may be contrary to the Bible, but we like her.[20]

Although clergy and lay members who actually live in small towns usually portray their congregations as caring communities, conflicts do occur—indeed, a quarter of pastors in rural churches reported a conflict causing some of their members to leave within the past two years, according to one national study, or the same proportion as in urban or suburban congregations.[21] When conflicts happen they can be devastating, particularly in smaller places where people see one another regularly and possibly have few other church options. Disagreements within and between extended families are one of the most common sources of tension. At one of the churches in our study the pastor described an incident between two men, one of whom accused the other of saying something insulting to the first man's wife. The accuser left the church over the incident. That was more than a decade ago. He has never returned, even though he still lives in the community. Having no other local options, he and his family drive to a town half an hour away to attend church.

As another case in point, the pastor of an evangelical church in a town of about a thousand told of an incident several years before he arrived that nearly destroyed his congregation. The church operated a state-accredited elementary school for about fifty of the town's children, but enrollment was dwindling and the accreditation standards were stiffening. Amid these difficulties, the pastor at the time became discouraged, left, and the school closed. Most of the families with children left the church and have never returned. The current pastor says it is almost impossible to attract any families with children.

The tension was even more severe in another town with only one congregation. Members took different sides toward the denomination's position on homosexuality. Half thought the denomination should do more to welcome gays and lesbians into full membership, while the other half were adamantly opposed to anything that might encourage or legitimate what they viewed as a wicked lifestyle. The latter half pulled their membership from the congregation, stayed at home on Sundays, or drove to another town. But in a town of fewer than two hundred people, it was hard for the two factions to avoid seeing one another. It was awkward to run into someone at the café and not feel like speaking to them.[22]

Because churches are located in small communities, it should not be assumed that conflicts are more acute than in other locations. We found plenty of instances in which people remembered intense conflicts and yet by all indications had put them to rest. At a church of fewer than two hundred in another small town, the congregation had divided into two warring factions over the church parking lot—one side wanted to pave it, and the other did not. Both sides became quite outspoken in defense of their view. But when the pavers won by a narrow vote, the opposition accepted the decision and nothing further was said. That was true in other situations as well, such as conflicts about plans to replace or renovate the church building, and decisions to hire a new pastor.

Two aspects of these controversies were key to their being resolved. The first aspect was when neither side regarded the issues as fundamentally about biblical interpretation or moral principles but instead about budgets, relationships, and families. In that sense, the concerns were important, yet they were different from questions about abortion, homosexuality, or whether to oppose or support some major theological policy of their denomination. And second, the small-town ethic of keeping one's mouth shut kicked in. Members knew that if they were going to continue living in the same community, seeing one another at the post office and shopping at the same grocery store, there was a time to quit fighting.

In towns of three to five thousand or more it is not uncommon, though, to find churches that have emerged because of splits in older established congregations. In a town we visited that had fewer than four thousand residents we noticed there were two Methodist churches five blocks apart. They were among the twenty congregations in this small community. Why was there a need for two Methodist churches? "Congregations start fighting," one of the pastors explained. People say, "Well, you know, this is important enough to me that here is where I stand, and if you don't see it that way, we'll go start our own church." The second Methodist Church and several of the other local congregations had begun that way. In another town the thousand-member population was served by eight churches, two of which were small Pentecostal congregations in makeshift buildings located, respectively, at the opposite edges of the community. Judging from their names, it appeared that one favored more direct revelations from the Holy Spirit than the other. But a longtime resident explained that the pastor of the older congregation had an affair with a woman in his congregation in the 1990s, precipitating the split, and half the members left to start the new church.

Sociologists of religion view congregations forming because of disputes in established churches as an example of the religious marketplace.[23] Religion flourishes, according to this interpretation, when competition exists among churches and when congregants are free to choose some other church, or start a new one, if the spirit moves. There is plenty of evidence that competition of this kind is present, even in small communities. One church adds a new educational wing, and pretty soon another church renovates its sanctuary. Less often noticed in the academic literature, though, are the efforts that church leaders make to suppress overt competition.

In small communities it is important for clergy to get along with one another, just as it is for lay members of different congregations. Clergy face the prospect of seeing one another at the bank and football game, and may anticipate having these regular interactions for years. It does Pastor Smith no good if he and Pastor Jones cannot get along. To keep strained relationships from happening, pastors find ways to work together despite differences in liturgical style and theological interpretation. A striking example is evident in a rural community of less than a thousand in which there are seven churches, including Catholics, mainline Protestants, and evangelical Protestants. Although there are significant doctrinal differences and occasional incidents of members of one church defecting to another one, the pastors have a ministerial association that maintains good relations among all the churches in town. It helps that they have a common commitment to serving the community. Behind the scenes, the pastors take turns being on call with the sheriff's department in case an accident occurs, or a family needs gasoline or a place to stay overnight. The community's Thanksgiving and Good Friday services are jointly sponsored. Whenever one church hosts a concert, guest speaker, or some other special event, the pastors usually advertise it as a ministerial association event just to show that one church is not trying to outdo any of the other ones.

LINKS TO THE WIDER WORLD

The perennial criticism of small churches in small towns, including among members themselves, is that they become so focused on their own needs and interests that they lose sight of the wider world. Although watching television, traveling, and having relatives in other places mitigates this insularity, the churches believe they have an obligation to expand their horizons. The gospel mandate to spread God's love beyond Judea, as the Bible says, to Samaria and the uttermost ends of the earth requires a wider vision. Large churches in cities and suburbs can more easily do this. Their size makes it possible to hire special global ministries staff, and members may have business contacts abroad. Still, it is notable how many small congregations in small communities have established links to the wider world.

In town after town, we found small churches with ties to other countries through members and former members who had become missionaries and international humanitarian workers. These links are present even in the smallest rural congregations. A Baptist church with only twenty-five regular members in a town of eight hundred had connections with a ministry in Brazil because of a man who had grown up in the church and gone there as a missionary. The church not only supported him financially but several of the members also went on occasion to help for a week or two with the ministry there. In rural communities, farmers whose work was seasonal were often the ones who participated in such trips. Residents with skills in construction, teaching, and health services were also among the volunteers. In another town, the Catholic Church had sent several missionaries to Brazil and had kept in close touch with them over the years. These connections with homegrown missionaries depended on family ties, but formalized links have also become more common.

"Recently one of our ministers went to Tanzania and lived there for three months," a Lutheran member in a remote farming community of fifteen hundred says. She appreciated learning about churches in Tanzania from the minister's sermons. Her experience was similar to the members of a Lutheran church in an even smaller community whose pastor had served as a short-term minister in eastern Europe and frequently reported to his members about conditions there. In a town of twelve thousand where separate weekly masses were conducted in English and Spanish, a visiting priest from India provided information about his home parish and raised money for the ministry there. At a nondenominational church in another community, the pastor had done evangelistic work on several occasions in Central America and Africa. He was trying to instill a global perspective among the youths in his congregation. In other instances, pastors were among the few in their community who had ever traveled outside the United States. The pastor of a mainline Protestant congregation in a town of twelve hundred, for example, had been to the Soviet Union during seminary. The trip left him with a continuing interest in peacemaking and international social justice.

A second connection occurs through denominational programs. Catholics, Methodists, Lutherans, Southern Baptists, Presbyterians, Assemblies of God, and smaller denominations all have international evangelistic and humanitarian aid ministries in which the smallest congregations participate. These programs provide information about needs in other countries or other parts of the United States, and facilitate opportunities to be of assistance through financial gifts, donations of food and clothing, and volunteer time.

An example is the United Methodist Committee on Relief. Following the 9/11 attacks on New York City and Washington, DC, the committee was one of the first relief organizations on the scene. That was true as well when Hurricane Katrina struck New Orleans, a tsunami devastated Southeast Asia, and a massive earthquake took place in Haiti. Members of Methodist churches in small towns far from any of these locations were able to assist financially and by sending volunteers. Besides responding to emergencies, churches worked with denominational agencies to develop longer-term arrangements. At one congregation, for instance, a relationship with a mission church in Haiti involved filling boxes with toys, supplies, and mosquito nets, regular correspondence, and periodic visits. This had been happening for almost forty years.

Other congregations were involved in similar programs through Catholic Relief Services and Lutheran Social Services. It seemed especially important to members of these congregations to feel that they were crucial participants in the larger programs. A lay member at a Lutheran church in a town of twelve hundred says he and a few other volunteers from the congregation go to Africa once a year to help with an educational program. "You're living out here," he says, "and you just have that feeling of, well, that you're doing something to help on a grander scale." In another rural community, members of the Catholic parish took special interest in a partner parish in Kenya with which they exchanged news, letters, photographs, and emails.

A third international tie occurs through short-term mission trips. These connections are facilitated by denominational and interdenominational agencies that specialize in such ministries, but they also require the initiative of a local leader. A church member in one small town, for instance, mentions "a hometown boy who is an itinerate speaker with an international ministry," and says that the town still serves as this man's "home base" and helps him with financial support. The same congregation participates in short-term mission trips to Mexico. Each year, two or three teenagers or young adults join a group organized with other churches in the region to spend several days in Mexico doing volunteer work. "It just opened their eyes," the pastor says, "to the fact that we are a blessed people."

These programs are seldom cheap. A short mission trip to Peru can cost as much as seventeen hundred dollars just for airfare, not to mention the time involved in organizing the trip. Pastors and lay leaders in economically depressed areas say they have had to rethink their priorities and find less expensive ways to be involved in the wider world. They drive to Mexico instead of flying to Peru or do volunteer work in a US town hit by a natural disaster. The people involved nevertheless feel they have been able to serve and have had their horizons broadened as a result.

Leaders say that good communication and careful planning are the keys to a successful program. One of the clearest examples of good planning happened when a church was destroyed by fire in a small southern town. Needing outside assistance to rebuild, the members got together and poured a concrete slab to serve as a foundation for a new building, and then scheduled two workdays for volunteers coming from several states to construct a prefabricated building. Information about hookups for volunteers' recreational vehicles was posted on a Web site along with tool needs and arrangements for meals. In another community, a retired pastor regularly visits churches in a half-dozen surrounding towns to collect clothing and small household items, and then drives a van loaded with the material to churches in central Mexico. Each summer lay volunteers from the US churches spend a few days in Mexico providing tutoring and health screening. As much as the help is needed in Mexico, the benefits accrue more to the US volunteers, who gain a different perspective on their own lifestyle and faith. That may be especially critical in small towns. "When you're in a small town," one pastor explains, "you seem to think small and maybe even feel insignificant." But being involved in projects in another country or even in another part of the United States, he says, "lets you see from a broader perspective that you are significant."

There is also an emerging international connection in many rural communities through immigration. In a town of ten thousand that had been predominantly white Anglo, for example, more than a quarter of its population is now Latino or Asian American. The change has happened because a large meat-processing plant opened in the community in the 1990s. The influx has caused churches there to initiate Spanish-language services and provide temporary housing for immigrant families. In another town, an Anglo woman who learned to speak Spanish in college and figured she would have no use for it is now working with Hispanic immigrants in her community. Her interests in cross-national ministry had been sparked in high school when she and her sister along with their dad spent three weeks in Mexico working at an orphanage affiliated with Mother Teresa's Missionaries of Charity. That trip led her to return to Mexico another summer to work at a home for boys. She says these experiences in high school opened her eyes to what was going on in other countries and helped her know what it was like to be a foreigner. They also deepened her interest in human rights. Although she lives in a safe community that has not changed much in a hundred years, she is keenly interested in human rights issues facing people in places like Darfur.

A national survey suggests that international connections like these may be fairly typical of small communities. Among active churchgoers who attended congregations in small towns or rural communities in nonmetropolitan areas, 39 percent said their congregation had sponsored a short-term mission trip to another country during the past year, 40 percent said their congregation had hosted a speaker from another country, and 50 percent claimed that at least a few of their fellow church members were recent immigrants. Other connections were even more common. Three-quarters said their congregation had taken up a hunger relief offering in the past year. Three-quarters also said their congregation had helped to sponsor one or more foreign missionaries.[24]

Mission trips and partnerships with congregations in other countries broaden perspectives in a way that merely watching news on television seldom does. A vivid example occurred at a Catholic parish of five hundred members in a town of about five thousand that learned of a priest in Central America who was seeking to establish a partnership with a North American parish. The Central American priest was serving fifteen rural villages, rotating among them over a two-month cycle. The area was extremely poor and badly in need of medical assistance. The US parish sent a medical team. It proved to be an eye-opening experience in more ways than one. During the trip the team's vehicle broke down, forcing the group to walk an hour and a half through driving rain back to the nearest town. On arriving, they learned the mountain road had washed out and they likely would have been killed had their journey continued. Shortly after their return, news came that their interpreter had been murdered.

CHALLENGES FACING SMALL TOWN CONGREGATIONS

Barbara Raines is the pastor of two Methodist churches twelve miles apart. One is in a town of thirty people, and the other in a community of fewer than two hundred. Both towns have been losing population—a trend that has been going on for more than fifty years. Farms in the area have grown larger and fewer, the railroad is gone, and businesses and schools have closed. Only a trucking company, fertilizer plant, couple of beauty shops, and bank are left. The larger of the two congregations averages thirty-five to forty regulars, and the smaller one never exceeds twenty. Rev. Raines preaches a 9:30 a.m. service each Sunday at the smaller one and an 11:00 a.m. service at the larger one. There are few young families or children at either church, and in recent years more of the aging members have been moving to a nursing home in a larger town twenty miles away. The obvious question, one that even the Methodist district superintendant asks, is why the two congregations do not consolidate. The commute from one to the other is an easy fifteen or twenty minutes along a paved road. But neither congregation is willing to shut down. In fact, a few years ago the smaller congregation was down to ten members and in such poor financial shape that it seriously considered closing, but members started a newsletter, canvased their neighbors, and kept the congregation going. Both churches have their own buildings and are the only congregations in their respective towns.

This is a pattern widely evident in rural America. Methodist circuit riders started churches by the thousands during the nineteenth century as the frontier expanded. Baptists, Catholics, Disciples of Christ, Presbyterians, and other groups started churches in many of the same locations. The practice was a good one. When frontier towns died—as many did—for lack of rail service, drought, fire, or failing to be selected as a county seat, the fledgling churches in those communities closed, while the ones in towns with rising populations flourished. Over the years, nearly every small town came to be the location of several churches. Yet the decline of population that began in the 1920s in many small towns, and that continued through the twentieth century, left churches that were too small to support themselves and yet were reluctant to close. They had a building and cemetery that commemorated the history of the community and its families.

Rev. Raines illustrates one arrangement that has played an important role in staffing small declining rural churches. She is in her early seventies and a widow. Her husband was a Methodist minister. During his career, he had worked his way up from small churches in small towns to a choice position in a community of fifty thousand that was one of the larger towns in the district. Although it was customary for Methodist clergy to be assigned a new location every three to five years, the district superintendent kept him in this community for twelve years. Like nearly all pastors' wives, Mrs. Raines had always been an active lay volunteer in her husband's congregations. During the twelve years in this community of fifty thousand, she served as youth coordinator for all the Methodist churches in the district and a Sunday school teacher in her local congregation.

With only a high school degree, there was no way Mrs. Raines could go to seminary and be ordained as a regular paid clergyperson. The denomination, though, had always included a provision through which laypeople could become unpaid local pastors and serve in congregations staffed by occasional visits from regular clergy. A recent provision that pertained to Mrs. Raines was that anyone past a certain age, usually fifty, was not required to attend seminary full-time to receive a license but instead could attend classes from two weeks to a month in duration and accumulate sufficient credits over a five-year period. It was through this process that she became Rev. Raines and was hired as a youth minister. After serving in that capacity for nine years, she and her husband were moved by the district superintendent to a small congregation in a town of fifteen hundred. She did not work, and after two years her husband retired and they moved to another state to be near their children. Her husband began preaching again almost immediately, and they decided to return to the state where he had spent most of his career. He filled vacant pulpits for five years, including the two that his wife now has, and when his health made it impossible to continue, she took his place. Since his death five years ago, she has served full-time at the two congregations.

The parts of this story that are representative of broader trends in small communities are that Rev. Raines is an older woman and earned her license as a pastor later in life. It is also increasingly common for pastors in small communities to serve more than one congregation, and for husband and wife teams to serve as copastors, or one to be paid and the other to be an unpaid volunteer. These arrangements have made it possible for small congregations to remain open. In most instances, younger clergy intent on working their way up would not find small congregations like this attractive, but for older clergy who may have family ties in an area and be interested in a slower pace, one or two small congregations in small towns can be attractive. As another example, a woman who pastors two rural Lutheran churches in a similar context but in another state says she is happy to be able to serve these congregations because both are within a few miles of the farm she and her husband own. She went full-time to seminary, but only after having held other part-time jobs and doing volunteer youth ministry work while her children were growing up.[25]

Catholic churches in small rural communities have adapted to sparse populations and a scarcity of priests by closing parishes, shutting down parochial schools, delegating more of the routine administrative tasks to lay volunteers, relying on immigrant priests, and asking priests to serve more than one parish—a pattern called clustering. Father Tom Malone is currently serving in one of these clustered arrangements. Although he could have served a larger urban parish, he says he preferred a smaller place where he "could be a bigger fish in a smaller pond." He lives at the rectory in a town of eighteen hundred, serving the parish there and commuting to two other parishes in neighboring towns. The three parishes include approximately five hundred families. Members have become accustomed to not having a full-time priest in each parish, but Father Malone says the adjustment has not been easy. For years, parishioners went to Mass at the same hour each Sunday. Now there is a rotating system that keeps people on their toes. If they prefer to worship in their hometown, they may have to attend on Saturday evening instead of Sunday morning, of if they prefer Sunday morning, drive to another town. The decisions about schedules and locations have been accompanied by some resentment as well as frustration. "This community feels very hurt," Father Malone says. "Their priests have been taken away from them. The people do not feel valued or appreciated."[26]

Declining population and economic setbacks also force congregations to postpone repairs to church buildings, scale down programs, freeze or reduce pastors' salaries, and require pastors to rely more on spouses' income or second jobs. "My family has felt the pinch very hard," the pastor of an evangelical congregation in a declining town of a thousand says. His story is not atypical. Prior to becoming a pastor, he had been in secular employment and took a huge pay cut to enter the ministry. Five years ago his move to the present location involved another salary reduction, and he has not had a raise since then. The church shut down a radio program it used to cosponsor on a Christian radio station in the area, cut back its community-wide programs for children by 50 percent, and has not replaced a worn-out lawn mower or broken video projector. The pastor has taken a second job as a clerk in one of the town's few remaining stores. The difficulties have partly been caused by a drought that has hurt agriculture-related incomes and business in the region. The trouble also illustrates small congregations' vulnerability to population shifts. The congregation lost twenty-six members in one year. Several died, others moved away because of health or a loss of jobs, and still others grew disillusioned and switched to a different church in town. "When you lose people like that, it obviously has an economic effect on the church," the pastor says. "It also has a psychological effect. You are friends with these people, and they are suddenly gone. That's a hole in your life."

Church closings in small towns are difficult for many reasons. In some of the towns we visited, the churches were doing fine financially—usually because of a few families who supported the congregation generously—but were too small to attract a pastor. Members were often proud of the building that they and their forebears had lovingly maintained. They hated to see the building empty, torn down, or put to other uses. In other towns, the threat of a church being shut down seemed like a slap in the face to the remaining members. They knew the decision was in the hands of a bishop or regional board, but could not help feeling betrayed.

Perhaps because it is difficult to completely shut down a church, it is more common for churches to shrink in membership than to actually

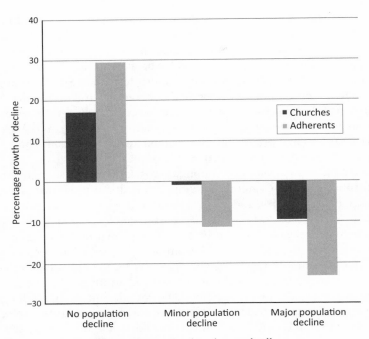

Figure 7.5 Change in churches and adherents

close. This tendency is evident in county-level data collected nationally in 1980 and again in 2000. In counties where the population grew or at least remained stable during those two decades, the total number of church adherents rose at a higher rate (29.5 percent) than the total number of churches (17.2 percent). In other words, congregations on average became larger. The pattern was different in counties that lost population. In counties experiencing minor population loss (that is, a decline of less than 1 percent per year), the total number of church adherents dropped by 11.2 percent, but the number of churches declined by only 0.8 percent. And in counties with major population loss (a decline of more than 1 percent per year), the total number of adherents dropped by 23.2 percent, but the number of churches fell by only 9.4 percent (see figure 7.5).[27]

Although church closings in declining areas are relatively rare, and undoubtedly influenced by many considerations, one aspect of the local social circumstances that matters is the number of towns in the immediate vicinity. Taking account of differences in total county population, the data collected in 1980 showed that the number of churches per county was larger when there were more towns in the county. That made sense because historically the founding of churches usually went hand in hand with the founding of towns. In fact, the 1980 data showed that each additional town in a county was associated with an average of 2.8 additional churches in the county, taking account of differences in the total population. But having more towns and thus more churches also meant that it was easier during the next two decades for churches to be closed in those communities—apparently because the remaining members could more easily travel to an adjacent town. Statistically, there was a negative relationship between the number of towns per county and the number of churches per county in 2000, taking into account the number of churches and the population in 1980. Each additional town in the county was associated with a decline on average of approximately 1.2 churches.[28]

If closings are hard for the members who lose their church, questions arise as well for the churches that remain. An example is a Methodist church in one of the towns we studied that had a population of about three thousand. As the county seat, the town's population had been stable over the past quarter century, partly because more farmers in the area lived in town and partly because more of the town's younger residents commuted to jobs in a city forty miles away. Countywide, there were nine other towns, only one of which had more than a thousand residents. All these towns were smaller than they had been a generation ago. The Methodist Church in the county seat had about 150 regular members, down from 200 in the 1980s. It was faring better than the four Methodist churches in neighboring towns, at least two of which were expecting to be closed in another year. The questions that the county seat church was facing included the prospect of welcoming new members when these sister congregations closed. Its members were mostly old-timers who had belonged to the congregation and made friends over a number of years. How would they respond? They would of course welcome new families. But they wondered if the new families would feel at home. Would they resent their own church having been closed? Would they be a clique that kept to themselves? Would they truly feel welcome? These were the issues that the county seat church was pondering.

A contrasting example—one that shows the possibilities for growth even in remote rural locations—can be found at the Central Mission Church, which is also located in a small community with a declining population. The town has no industry, and farmers in the area have been suffering from drought for the past seven years. Statewide the average age is thirty-five, but here it is forty-eight. The farmers' sons and daughters nearly always move away, at least temporarily. The older generation hangs on to the farm because it has been in the family for five or six generations. The farmers hope that one of their sons will come back when they retire. In the meantime, they go to the church that their family has

attended for decades. Most are Methodists, Lutherans, or Congregationalists. These churches are losing members and struggling to attract new
pastors when one leaves. In contrast, Central Mission has been growing.
Its membership is a hundred, up from fifty a decade ago when Pastor
Frank Newland arrived. Today he is at the hardware store making a small
purchase. A woman who usually attends another church but has visited
his comes into the store. "I'm going to visit your church again one of
these days," she tells him. "We always love to have you," he says. "God is
in your church," she says. "I go to my church and I like my church, but
God is in your church. He shows up when you have church."

"That was a great compliment," Pastor Newland reflects later. He attributes it to the fact that his church is not just a country club but instead
a place of genuine worship. But pressed to say more, he explains that it
is the love the church tries to show that really matters. "We are a very, very
economically depressed area," he explains, "so financial concerns among
our families are always an issue." They are especially an issue for the
families at his church. They are the poorest of the poor, the "riffraff" who
are seldom welcomed with open arms by the established residents. They
come because average housing costs are 70 percent cheaper than the state
average. Indeed, it is not hard to find a vacant house that can be rented
for next to nothing. The newcomers include abused women on welfare
who are fleeing husbands and boyfriends in the city. There are jobless
workers who came when times were better and have been unable to locate
work elsewhere. Pastor Newland says there is a surprisingly high rate of
turnover among the members at his church. The newcomers feel more at
home than at one of the older churches in town, but then they move on
or perhaps the husband does find a job, leaving the women and children
behind. He says the financial strain on marriages is acute. Alcoholism is a
chronic problem.

The challenge that Pastor Newland's ministry faces is how to help
these low-income families, given the fact that everybody in town is suffering from hard times. He gives out approximately a thousand dollars during the year in direct aid to families needing help with utility payments
and medical bills. But his main emphasis is on teaching families to handle
their money well. "We try to teach them to live within their means and
how to stretch their money," he says. Almost everyone who attends has
taken a training course in family finances within the past year. He emphasizes programs for children as well, especially since the ones at his church
are often from single-parent families. There is a program on Wednesday
evening as well as Sundays. The goal is to build close relationships with
the children and their parents. It is a struggle, but Pastor Newland finds
the small gains heartening. "My mom says I need to come to church be-

cause I'm a better person when I do," a girl in her teens told him recently. All he could say was "wow."

Whether they are in declining or growing communities, small-town churches usually face the challenge of having mostly older members and thus finding it difficult to attract young people. The problem is partly that young people move away to find better jobs, meaning that the few who remain may be in congregations with insufficient numbers of children and other young adults to be appealing. An added problem is that older members may be resistant to new ideas that might be of interest to younger people. Rev. Raines says she frequently encounters older members saying her suggestions will not work, even though she knows they have been tried successfully in other congregations. Another pastor makes a similar observation, noting, "You always have a certain number of folks in your church, everybody's got them, they just have a different name and a different face, but they say we only do things one way, and if others don't toe the line, they aren't welcome." A lay member of another church explains, "My children really struggle when they come back and go to church with us. They go to churches that are more contemporary, more lively. They don't want to go to our old traditional church, and sing the old, old hymns." He says his congregation has lost members who now drive to a larger town to find a church that caters more to the younger generation.

Another quandary people in small-town churches face is the question of how much, or how little, to participate in political activities. I will say more about this in chapter 9, but for now it is sufficient to mention that small congregations in rural communities are sometimes quite pleased to feel they are part of a larger political effort, such as a referendum to lower taxes or campaign to recall members of the state school board. Townspeople may join with others in their diocese or denomination to press for legislation, and they may send members to rallies or make treks to megachurches, or encourage fellow parishioners to watch religious television and talk radio programs. But members of small congregations also express misgivings about such efforts. Their congregations are accustomed to helping families in the community and keeping out of political controversies. We noticed that even in conservative parts of the country, townspeople often said they disagreed with church leaders who were pressing strong political agendas. One man put it this way. "We are evangelical Christians," he said, referring both to his own church and the majority of his friends in the community. "But we do not feel at home with the Religious Right. The activities of the extreme right wing are very offensive to us." Asked to explain, he said the church was to be "salt and light in the community," but the Religious Right was trying to gain control through politics. "The Lord intended for the church to be an influence," he said, "not a control."[29]

ADAPTING TO DIVERSITY

Yet another challenge has come, as I mentioned before, as a result of population change that is bringing greater ethnic and racial diversity to small towns. In some instances, this change has also resulted in greater religious diversity. In a town of eleven hundred, a woman in her fifties who has lived previously in a city provided an interesting example. She says her community is having a hard time adjusting to the presence of non-Christians. For decades, the high school hosted a vesper service of church music as part of the community's celebration of Christmas. But now there is a Jewish family in the school district and two Muslim families. "You have to change," she says, "and it's been very hard for people to understand. As long as nobody questions the legality of things, you just go on doing it." She thinks the town will adapt, yet she worries because the town has not confronted its feelings about racial diversity, either. "Yeah, we have our little white Christian community," she sighs.[30]

The challenge of diversity has been especially acute in towns that have grown because of large meat- and poultry-processing plants and related companies, such as feedlots, sugar factories, and biofuel plants. Two examples illustrate the different ways in which churches have attempted to respond. In one community, the population doubled from five to ten thousand in a twenty-four-month period, and the nearly all-white Anglo population suddenly found itself in the minority as most of the newcomers were Hispanics and Asian Americans. The meat-processing plant responsible for the population explosion was controversial from the start, not only because of the dramatic impact on the community, but also because the work was dangerous and the firm resisted all efforts by the workers to unionize. At the same time, the company paid decent wages, offered steady employment, and carefully avoided hiring immigrants who were not documented. Several Hispanic and Asian American congregations developed, yet shift work made it impossible for employees to attend regularly. There were also Muslim workers from Africa, but the nearest mosque was miles away. The firm hired Rev. Juan Lopez to work as a company chaplain. Rev. Lopez says his job is not to replace independent congregations or hold worship services but rather to counsel those workers who may be having marital or financial problems, refer them to social service agencies that can be of assistance, and hold prayer meetings. Critics view him as a lackey that management is using to avoid costly labor disputes, but he feels the company is demonstrating a pathbreaking approach to bringing faith more actively into the workplace, even in small towns.

The other community has grown from ten thousand to more than twenty thousand over the past fifteen years as a result of several large food-processing firms that mainly employ Hispanic immigrants. More than half the population is now Hispanic. Rev. Mike Toland moved here a decade ago as pastor of a Southern Baptist congregation with an average weekly attendance of about 150. Rev. Toland is a thoughtful, articulate person who amply illustrates the complex adjustments necessary for churches in rapidly diversifying towns. He tried unsuccessfully a few years ago to start a Hispanic ministry at his church. The effort failed because the church was located on the opposite edge of town from where most of the Hispanics lived. The congregation also faced a huge chasm in attempting to bridge language and cultural differences. Although he does not admit to having misgivings about the Hispanic presence, he does report with some sense of empathy that the white population, as it calls itself there, expresses dissatisfaction with the changes it associates with rising diversity. The white community believes the Hispanics are responsible for drugs and gang violence, that many are in town illegally, and that the Hispanics soak up social services and place added demands on the schools at the white population's expense. Rev. Toland says his children have sometimes been the only Anglos in their classes at school. He believes the community has lost Anglos who simply moved away rather than deal with changes taking place. While he understands these negative reactions, he also finds them troubling and wants to do something to facilitate better relationships.

Ironically, the path to greater cross-ethnic understanding for Rev. Toland did not come from interacting with Hispanics in his own community but instead from organizing short-term mission trips to Mexico. For many years, his congregation has given small monthly donations through the Southern Baptist Convention to help churches in India. It still does, but Rev. Toland decided it might make more of an impact on his own members to take volunteers to Mexico. Each summer a handful of church members drive across Texas into Mexico and conduct a Bible school for children at a local mission. One big insight was that something similar could be done back at home. Initially the congregation spent a thousand dollars fixing up the building, and purchasing special supplies and equipment, but after being in Mexico the volunteers realized they could use a different approach. Now they organize activities in the town park closer to where the Hispanic children live. The cost is less, and the results are better. Seeing the living conditions in Mexico proved to be an eye-opening experience as well.

Rev. Toland's congregation has been working on two small fronts, besides holding Bible classes in the park, to bridge the gap between itself

Profile: McCamey, Texas

With early settlers including large numbers of Baptists from the South, Texas has long been one of the nation's most religiously active states. Among the nearly nine hundred small nonurban towns in Texas, the counties in which these towns are located include an average of ninety-two churches, and of these, sixty-two are affiliated with conservative evangelical Protestant denominations. Nearly every one of these towns has a Southern Baptist congregation.

McCamey, a town of sixteen hundred in West Texas, has three Baptist churches and six other congregations. These churches illustrate the challenges that church leaders in many small towns face.

Founded when oil was discovered here in 1925, McCamey experienced a short-lived boom that brought its population to more than three thousand in 1930. It survived the Depression better than many towns in the region, and by 1960 still had more than three thousand residents. It has declined steadily ever since. Nevertheless, its Hispanic population has grown from 35 percent in 1980 to 59 percent in 2009. Median household income is 20 percent below the state average. Independent oil and gas companies are still the major employers.

McCamey's nine churches play an integral role in the community. Among longtime residents, being affiliated with one of the churches is a major part of their identity. Over the years cliques have formed among church people, who meet after church for lunch or on weekdays for breakfast. Several of the pastors hold services at the nursing home. The Ministerial Alliance organizes volunteers to help at the Friendship Center, where needy families receive food and clothing. The alliance also sponsors an occasional rock concert by a Christian band in hopes of attracting more of the community's young people. The Catholic parish, Assembly of God congregation, and Jehovah Witnesses Kingdom Hall appeal to both the Anglo and Hispanic populations, and one of the Baptist churches has assisted in founding a Spanish-language congregation.

But the town's decline and weak economy has left all the congregations struggling financially. Attendance at several of the churches has fallen below forty. Although the Ministerial Alliance facilitates cooperation among its member congregations, tensions remain between Protestants and Catholics as well as between the fundamentalist and moderate Protestant churches. Drinking and drug abuse pose recurring problems. When a pastor leaves to take a more attractive job in a larger community, it is often difficult to recruit a replacement.

and the Hispanic population. One is to participate in an interfaith alliance that provides financial support for a Spanish-language congregation. That idea emerged from being unable to organize a Hispanic ministry on its own. The other is to provide volunteer labor to help poor families that come to the congregation's attention. For instance, the congregation recently rebuilt a house for a mother with four children whose father had in effect deserted them. These experiences and the trips to Mexico are also changing the congregation's views. "If I was born in Mexico," Rev. Toland says, "I could understand the draw that America would have, and the hope that America would give a husband and a father. I could see that. These families are coming from such terrible places, such poor areas, that to be able to have the hope of America would be amazing. Who am I to say that if I was born in Mexico that I wouldn't do everything I could to get here by legal or illegal means? That is always an undercurrent for me. I always keep that in mind." He says the congregation shares this perspective, at least to the extent that members provide help to people who need it without asking any questions about documentation. He has also become an advocate for a nationwide work-card system and more efficient program though which immigrants can become citizens.

These are issues that few church leaders in small towns or anywhere else have fully figured out. Some leaders come down on the side of halting immigration altogether or cracking down on illegal immigrants, while others stress the value of churches helping the needy, whoever they are, and working harder for social justice. "As a Christian, I struggle with this," Rev. Toland says. "I just am asking God to give me his heart for this issue because it is not easy." The reason it is not easy is that preachers and their congregations, even in small towns where incomes are often low, enjoy the comforts to which Americans are accustomed, and are content with the security of familiar friends and fellow churchgoers. It is hard enough to follow Jesus's command to help the poor and feed the hungry, and yet even harder to figure out what an appropriate public policy toward immigration and poverty should be.

In the meantime, churches face difficult questions about what their responsibility should be toward both legal and undocumented immigrants. Father Jose Espinoza, a priest in his early forties who grew up in Mexico and became a US citizen two years ago, says that if he could tell officials in Washington, DC, one thing, it would be to pass a reasonable immigration law. "I mean, how long have we talked about immigration? The government has made promises and nothing has happened." He serves two parishes, one in a town of nine thousand and the other in a town of three thousand two miles away. The population is 80 percent Hispanic and mostly employed as farm laborers. "A lot of the people here," Father Espinoza says, "are suffering by not having papers, just being scared of being deported, and looking for secure jobs. They work here for a while and then move some other place because they don't have papers."

In the town where Father Lopez was serving as a company chaplain, several of the churches were quietly helping undocumented workers avoid deportation and obtain needed emergency services. What are they supposed to do, one of the pastors asked, if the authorities try to split up the family because one of the children has been born here and the other has been born in Mexico? Or what happens with a sick child if the parents do not have papers and the hospital is not allowed to treat the child? What stand does the church take? In another community, the churches celebrated when an immigrant family attained citizenship, but worked behind the scenes to help undocumented workers. In yet another community, church activists found it more effective to partner with service agencies from other towns and seek legislative reforms.

A better immigration law would solve some of the problems, but others would remain. Father Espinoza feels discouraged many Sunday mornings as he looks out over the heads of his weary parishioners. During cherry- and apple-picking season hardly anyone is there. Work at the orchards continues seven days a week. Then during the winter months, attendance drops again as families return to live with their relatives in Mexico. He worries about single mothers who come to him asking for food and the teenagers who are tempted to join gangs. The local Native American population is no better off than the immigrant community. Hardly anyone earns enough to support a family. The town's finances have sunk to the point that the municipal swimming pool is facing closure. For a while, Father Espinoza was trying to organize events for his families in the community park, but now that the town is charging a hefty usage and cleanup fee, he has had to suspend these events.

Economic Disruptions

Besides immigration-fed diversity, small-town congregations are sometimes dramatically affected by sudden shifts in economic conditions over which they have little control, and that go well beyond the usual fluctuations of agricultural markets or long-term decline in population. These are the disruptions that result from a major mining accident, the closing of a large manufacturing facility, or the relocation of an air base or government installation. The challenge for local congregations is adjusting to a community with new needs and divided interests.

A town that might have aptly been named Gold Rush underwent just such a series of disruptions. Founded in the nineteenth century when gold was discovered in the surrounding mountains, the community grew to eight thousand almost overnight and then gradually fell to about half that size, becoming a company town of miners and their families. When the mine closed in the 1990s, the older miners and their families stayed, but nearly all the younger families moved away. The local churches adjusted to smaller memberships composed of retirees who wanted to preserve as much of the past as possible. But within a decade, four unanticipated developments occurred: a large casino opened nearby, the federal government opened a scientific laboratory in the abandoned mine, tourism flourished, and a wealthy celebrity initiated an upscale real estate development that attracted well-to-do retirees from several of the nation's largest cities.

Clergy and lay leaders in Gold Rush experienced something as close to the loss of community as any town we studied. Up and down Main Street, each congregation dealt with a different aspect of the town's new realities. A fundamentalist congregation took a strong stand against the casino, maintaining its theological opposition to gambling, working on the Sabbath, and drinking alcohol. One of the mainline Protestant churches attracted members among the new upscale residents, but these newcomers mostly attended on Christmas and Easter, skipped services on other Sundays, and argued for tolerance, diversity, and progressive politics. Another mainline Protestant congregation doubled its membership and expanded its facility, yet was divided between members clinging to their traditions and members who hoped to minister more effectively to newcomers. The Catholic Church grew the most, but found itself struggling to meet the needs of low-income workers at the casino and in the tourist industry. In the past, low-income workers were usually employed by the mining company and had family ties in the community; the newcomers were seasonal workers who hailed from several different countries and seldom stayed in the community more than six months at a time. The ministerial alliance operated a food bank, sheltered women from domestic abuse, and provided financial help for families low on fuel, but the clergy were uncertain where the community was headed. "There are so many different people coming and going," one pastor sighed. "It's hard even to do the usual 'meet and greet,'" said another.

The disruption in Gold Rush was extreme although not unique. Towns devastated by floods and tornadoes, towns in the path of major exurban development, and those with similar experiences of mines closing and casinos opening faced similar challenges. Churches within a few blocks of one another responded differently. They were affected not only by the changes in the community but also by the tacit division of labor in which they participated.

CONGREGATIONS IN TRANSITIONAL COMMUNITIES

If economic hardship and population decline are the most common challenges that small-town churches face, the situation in an increasing number of communities is quite different. These are communities located close enough to metropolitan areas to be affected by suburban sprawl. Churches in these areas and towns that are growing may not face the prospect of declining memberships. They nevertheless may experience new competition from suburban megachurches, and in any case, are having to consider what it means to be in transition.

Hope Springs is a rural community of fewer than a thousand residents that is anticipating major growth over the next ten years as a result of its location just fifteen miles from a large state university and thirty miles from an expanding city of more than a million. As new telecommunications and bioscience companies have moved to the area, housing developments have sprung up within twenty miles of Hope Springs. The seven churches in Hope Springs are facing an interesting dilemma. On the one hand, their members are mostly long-term residents of the community who farmed, or worked at government offices or in stores in the area. They recall a time several decades ago when three of the churches consolidated for lack of new members. The churches currently draw an average attendance on Sunday mornings of between eighty and a hundred. The prospects for growth are there in the presence of some new families and an uptick of enrollment at the local elementary school, but for the most part, things are not changing rapidly. On the other hand, the pastors who meet with one another once a month at the ministerial council luncheon wonder if they should be doing more to plan for the future. It seems that they have two choices. Their churches could remain small, attract a new family now and then, and retain the intimate fellowship that has long characterized their members. That scenario makes sense for one important reason. Just thirty miles away there are two large megachurches, each with massive physical plants and more than ten thousand members. As Hope Springs grows, chances are good that new families will drive thirty miles to attend one of these megachurches. There is no way a small congregation of a hundred members can compete. The other scenario, though, is to compete. Perhaps the churches in Hope Springs will never grow larger, but they can accommodate to the new realities of the community.

Rev. Erin Montague-Morgan is the twenty-five-year-old pastor at Hope Springs United Church of Christ. Having interned at two small congregations with dwindling memberships, she is happy to be here, where the opportunities to grow the current number to above a hundred are good. Hope Springs United Church of Christ is a perfect example of a transitional congregation. Its older members are concerned that Pastor Montague-Morgan is moving too quickly. They are the bedrock members who show up for every service and generously support the congregation financially, but they are also high maintenance. They expect visits when they are in the hospital and when someone they know dies. Pastor Montague-Morgan, being of a different generation, has recently been to college and lived in a city, and she wants the church to minister to young families. The new residents in town are seldom there. They commute to work and have not yet joined a church.

The conflict at Hope Springs United Church of Christ illustrates how transitional churches sometimes face difficulties that might seem trivial to an outsider. The issue is not that people gossip at the post office about what they do and do not like, although that happens. It is rather that churches are small democracies in which real decisions have to be made. In this case, the burning issue is the ramp—from the sidewalk to the front door. For elderly members, the ramp is too steep for the average wheelchair or walker, and there is no access to the basement at all. To solve the problem, the members voted recently to build a one-story ground-level fellowship hall behind the church. The elderly members saw this decision as an important victory. But the fellowship hall will also be a good way to attract new families by hosting scout meetings for the children who attend school just across the street. On the surface, it is a win-win situation. And yet thorny concerns are now being raised about who will have access when and under what conditions. Who will schedule meetings at the building? Who will clean up? What fire and safety regulations have to be met?

It is easy to imagine that churches in transitional communities are conflicted over deep theological and moral questions. That may be the case, but the situation in Hope Springs may be more typical. Pastor Montague-Morgan learned about homiletics and biblical interpretation along with evangelism in seminary. All she can do sometimes, she says, is laugh about how poorly her training prepared her for the real world. She has been surprised at how much of her time is taken up with seemingly mundane questions about wheelchair ramps and zoning regulations. These are the day-to-day questions that keep her up at night.

In a number of the towns in our research, the churches thought of themselves as transitional congregations. It was an apt description not because of economic shifts of the kind that happen in transitional inner-city neighborhoods but instead because the community was literally betwixt and between. It was no longer a small town where nothing much ever changed. Nor was it a suburban community where things were definitely changing. These transitional churches are in communities like Hope Springs that are twenty to fifty miles from a metropolitan area—too far to be drawn directly into urban development and yet close enough to be influenced by it. The churches have to plan for a future that is likely to be different, although in ways that are hard to predict.

Interestingly enough, being a transitional church is not always a welcome idea. The resistance would seem most likely to come from long-term members, but can come from forward-looking pastors as well. In communities where population is increasing and is expected to continue increasing, the self-perception of being a transitional church can be an impediment to taking more serious steps to grow. Every pastor, it seems from our interviews, has growth in mind as a possible objective. The possibilities for growth, however, vary considerably from congregation to congregation even within the same community. The differences can be seen in the following comparison.

South Park Community Church is a sleek, open-beam brick-and-glass structure that can accommodate a crowd of two hundred when every one of its padded pews is filled. In 1958, its leaders decided the old building that had stood at the center of town for half a century would no longer suit the congregation's needs. The present church was constructed on several acres of country land a year later. Slowly the town grew in its direction. Today it is surrounded by upscale four-bedroom homes on wide tree-lined lots. A school, the community park, and a shopping mall several blocks away make the neighborhood a desirable location for families with children.

The town in which South Park Community Church is located is one of the larger ones in the area. Between 1950 and 1980, the population doubled, and since 1980 the population has increased by another 50 percent. Approximately twenty thousand people currently make the community their home. Over the past few decades the town has benefited from the presence of a regional airport, a community college, a large food-processing plant, and several small manufacturing firms, and being close to a productive field of oil and natural gas. The community has never been particularly prosperous, although a few of its families have done well in business and agriculture. The median household income is about 20 percent below the state average, as are the median housing prices. As the community has grown, the population has become more diverse. Most of the families are white Anglos, but a sizable minority of the population is Hispanic, and a smaller minority is African American.

Although the town has been growing, the membership at South Park Community Church has barely changed in recent years. Most Sundays, fewer than seventy people show up for the eleven o'clock worship service.

That number is slightly higher than it was a decade ago, when a conflict occurred that nobody wants to say much about except that several families left, but membership is still lower than it was in the 1980s. The congregation thinks of itself as a small church, which it is, and does not anticipate that it will ever be much larger. Enough of its members have lived in the community all their lives that they have a more vivid image of the church's history than they do of what its future might be.

Pastor Glen Fisher is trying to change that. He arrived four years ago, still working on his seminary degree through an online program that allows him to take most of his classes from home. He turned thirty just last week. At first he was thoroughly discouraged. As the excitement of being in charge of his own congregation wore off, he realized how difficult it was to initiate any of the ideas he had in mind about making the church grow. He knew he could move on at some point, perhaps to a younger congregation in a city or suburb, but felt called to invigorate South Park as much as he could.

Over the past two years, a group of twelve has emerged that shares Pastor Fisher's vision of a more vibrant church. The group did not form overnight or without effort. They were members of various ages who mostly had known each other already, but who came together as a leadership team from doing committee work, talking individually with Pastor Fisher, and reading and discussing some material about church planning and church growth. At first, they thought of the congregation as a church that would experience ups and downs, and always remain small. Now they believe the congregation will grow. One thing they have decided for sure is that a lot of people in the community do not attend church regularly, if at all. They figure the congregation would grow if some of these people in the community could be persuaded to take their faith more seriously.

Pastor Fisher thinks three important insights can be drawn from what is happening at South Park. First, attitudes matter and can change. That has been evident at South Park in the shift from thinking that the church would always be small to the vision that it can grow. Whether it does in fact grow, moreover, is less critical than members having a positive attitude about the congregation. They are learning that sometimes they will fail. Plans will go awry. An idea will crash and burn. But that's not a big deal. Things will still move forward. Second, members are learning that the church's future is up to them. Rather than looking to the pastor to solve their problems, which they did when Rev. Fisher started, they are realizing that things are more in their hands than in his. And third, the leadership group has come to think of itself as an incubator. They pride themselves on generating new ideas that can be implemented.

One of the books that proved helpful to Pastor Fisher and the leadership group at South Park Community Church was *Turnaround Strategies*

for the Small Church, by Ronald Crandall.[31] By contacting denominational leaders, Crandall identified and studied a hundred congregations of
fewer than two hundred members that had experienced a significant turnaround of some kind in the last two to five years. Among other things, he
found that the turnaround involved intentional leadership that held forth
a positive vision of the future, and were guided and sustained by the Holy
Spirit. Through prayer and Bible study, fellowship, and special events,
participants came to view the small size of their congregations as an asset
instead of a liability. Turnaround was also furthered by an emphasis on
mission and evangelism, and by learning to seek and welcome newcomers
rather than focusing on the more comforting aspects of the past.

It was evident in Crandall's research that the biblical mandate of wit-
nessing was key. Small churches that experienced a significant turnaround
were ones in which members learned how to explain the Bible to friends
and neighbors. That required Bible study and prayer. It necessitated that
the congregation engage in neighborhood visitation, and be open and hos-
pitable toward newcomers. Crandall terms this *adoption*. It was like a
family adopting a child. The congregation had to embrace newcomers and
make them feel at home.

In follow-up research, Crandall also identified something important.
A majority of the churches that had initially been identified as having experienced a positive turnaround of some kind had undergone a significant
setback in subsequent years. More often than not, the setback occurred
when the pastor left and was replaced by another one. That suggested
that pastoral leadership was key, but that it was also important for pastors to cultivate lay leadership.[32] This was what Pastor Fisher was aiming
to do. "You're leading other people to do ministry so that they don't feel
inferior to what you do," he says. "Their prayers are just as good as yours,
and their visits to the hospital are just as good as yours. It's empowering
them to do ministry."

There is no doubt that lay as well as pastoral leadership matters.
Whether an organization is a business or church, leadership is necessary
for planning new programs and implementing them. Another point that
Crandall emphasizes, though, is equally significant. That is the need to
adjust methods to the particular situation. These are the demographic,
social, and cultural aspects that loom large in sociological research. Demographic aspects—population trends—are especially important. South
Park Community Church has a reasonable chance of growing because the
population of the community has been growing. Five years ago, a third of
the town's population was living in a different county, and one-quarter
was living in a different state.

But South Park's future is less certain when the community's social
characteristics are taken into account. Over the past quarter century, the

town's total population has increased by approximately six thousand. The Hispanic population has increased by about seven thousand, while the white Anglo population has shrunk by about a thousand. Of the seventy churches in town, five are predominantly Hispanic and hold services exclusively in Spanish, the Catholic parish has grown the most and offers masses in Spanish as well as in English, and nearly a dozen small Pentecostal and evangelical nondenominational churches have been started in ethnically mixed neighborhoods. South Park's membership and the neighborhood in which it is located are ethnically homogeneous.

The importance of the community's changing ethnic composition is clearly evident in the experience of another congregation. West Side Church is also located in an upscale, predominantly white Anglo neighborhood. It is affiliated with a different denomination but otherwise is similar in theology to South Park. Like South Park, it stresses evangelism and church growth, and has had greater success in that effort, at least if comparisons are made over the past ten years, when the congregation was initially in a slump and has now doubled to nearly two hundred regular members. But like South Park, its membership has remained ethnically homogeneous. Its leaders decided that it made more sense to help two of the independent ministries that were starting among the Hispanic population. One now has a hundred members, and the other has seventy-five. West Side Church might not be termed a turnaround congregation. Nevertheless, it has been forward thinking in adapting to the changing needs and interests of the community.

Apart from the ethnic factor, the comparison between South Park and West Side illustrates another crucial aspect of the social dynamics in this community. South Park's immediate neighborhood was built in the 1980s, which means that it includes fewer newcomers and fewer families with children. West Side Church was constructed only a decade ago, and its neighborhood is still growing. The pastor at West Side says most of its new members already knew someone from the church before they joined. They met at school meetings, while tending children at the playground, and at neighborhood gatherings, and some of them were blood relatives. South Park is not as well located in that sense. Its incubating group will have to reach out further and more intentionally to meet newcomers.

The cultural aspects of a community include the attitudes and congregational outlooks that Crandall's research discusses, and that Pastor Fisher says are so important at South Park. "Forget about the past," he cautions. "Get that attitude out! Move forward. We can't do anything about the past. We can only do stuff about the future." He thinks a kind of collective psychology had settled over the congregation at South Park. They were so afraid of failing that they were unable to take the risks necessary to succeed.

Pastor Fisher's comments are especially candid. He is hopeful about the changes he sees taking place among the leadership nucleus at South Park and yet he remains frustrated. He thinks the congregation is timid. It annoys him that they expect him to do so much of the work instead of them shouldering it.

Among the church members we talked to at South Park and West Side, there was a rather-different perception of what the church should or should not be doing than among the pastors. The clergy were far more interested in how the church was faring and whether it was growing than the lay members were. For the pastors, the church was their life. Their career and whether they were perceived as being successful or not depended on how well the church was doing. That was not the case among even the most regular members. They cared more about their jobs and families. The church was a place to worship, be nurtured, and serve, but it was not their home.

Besides the fact that it was a job for the clergy and not for lay members, the clergy differed in other essential ways. Many of the clergy we talked to were newcomers in their communities. Pastor Fisher did not live in the community where his church was located. He commuted four days a week from another town an hour away. The differences sometimes revolve around age as well. As a thirty-year-old, Pastor Fisher looks easily to the future. He encourages the congregation to forget the past. He has nothing invested in the congregation's history.

The history of a small congregation in a small town, though, is important to many of the people who belong to these congregations. They may have grown up in the church and been married there. The building may have been constructed and lovingly maintained by their parents. The cemetery out back of the church has the graves of their ancestors. The church is a marker of the community's continuity and a symbol of where it stands in the passage of time. For these reasons, planning for the future generally requires paying close attention to the past.

As the examples presented in this chapter demonstrate, congregations in small towns face varying challenges that reflect the demographics and economic circumstances of the local community. Religion is visibly important in small towns and plays a significant role in social service provision. It is seldom entirely free of conflict, but usually reinforces residents' perception that their community is a place of neighborliness and caring. There are few generalizations that pertain to all churches in all small towns, other than the fact that most of these congregations are indeed small, and many of them are in transition as a result of population change.

They do of course differ significantly from large congregations in large metropolitan areas. If a small congregation can occasionally help support a missionary who grew up in the community, a large congregation can have a global ministries specialist on staff who organizes short-term trips and assistance to dozens of missionaries. The people we interviewed in large contexts mentioned friends and warm fellowship at their churches, just as the ones in small towns did. But the church members in metropolitan areas also spoke glowingly of the concerts they had just attended at their church, its fine choir, a recent evening of poetry readings, and the menu of interesting Sunday school classes. If they were at churches with inner-city ministries, they described the challenges they faced in keeping up with urban poverty. They seldom worried that their church might be closed for lack of members.

The necessary caveat in considering the distinctive challenges small-town churches face is that these congregations also struggle with many of the generic issues of concern in any community. However they may be likened to business entities that focus on numerical growth or decline and financial viability, churches are basically organized to nurture spirituality. Whether small or large, and whether located in declining towns or burgeoning cities, the principal challenge facing congregations is facilitating members' relationship with the sacred. A pastor with a congregation of sixty that becomes smaller by one or two members each year makes this point forcefully. He worries about the needs of aging members who move away to nursing homes and the lack of young people. But his greatest concern is cultivating the prayerful awareness of his members of their relationship to the divine. "We can't do anything without God," he says. Sunday after Sunday he tries to drive home this notion. Most of all, he labors to give his congregation an experience of divine presence in worship through neighborly service and in small study groups on Wednesday evenings.

Contentious Issues
The Moral Sentiments of Community Life

"I DRIVE DOWN THE INTERSTATE, and there are billboards advertising all these places with totally nude dancing. Just going down the interstate! So now you've got a six-year-old saying, 'Hey dad, what does that mean, totally nude?' I'm concerned where all this is headed. Or has already gone—this 'anything goes' mentality." This is the moral corruption that worries Gene Fazio, a high school basketball coach in his early fifties who lives in a riverfront town of ten thousand. On all sides, the high school is surrounded by well-kept working-class bungalows, and down the street a few blocks are the small manufacturing plants and retail stores that have been operating here for more than a century. It isn't just the blatant sexuality that bothers Mr. Fazio. There just seems to be something wrong with the world these days.

"The moral climate of our country has decreased precipitously over the last thirty or forty years," complains Rev. Terry Thompson, a sixty-three-year-old pastor of a fundamentalist congregation called God's Word Bible Church in a town of twenty-five hundred. On any given Sunday, nearly a quarter of the town's population hears him preach. He works closely with two other fundamentalist preachers in town who share his beliefs. The mainline Methodist and Lutheran congregations also lean heavily toward conservative convictions about morality. "I graduated from high school in the 1960s," Rev. Thompson explains, "and the teachers' main complaint then was chewing gum and talking in class. We've seen that change tremendously. Kids are no longer taught that there are absolutes as far as right and wrong is concerned. There's grave danger in the constant teaching that we are nothing more than glorified animals. There's nothing special about us then. Kids have to find their sense of being special somewhere else. And very often for young girls and boys it's in sexual fantasies."

Living in a small town, it is easy to feel beleaguered by the outside world. The town is like a haven, but one that is threatened, a life raft adrift in a sea of change over which it has no control. Nobody in the town makes decisions that matter in the wider world. Influential business tycoons in New York, Washington, Los Angeles, and Hollywood make those decisions, which are crafted by media moguls and government lawyers who have little understanding of small-town America. Meanwhile, a local business dies, a family moves away, a homecoming queen gets pregnant, and a promising athlete succumbs to a meth addiction. Even if the town is growing, it seems insignificant compared to the tens of millions who populate large cities. So a person thinks about all the forces over which they have little control and seizes on the few where some grasp is still possible.

"One of the prophecies in the Bible is that in the latter days, you will see people doing what is unnatural, such as women turning to women, and men turning to men. That was almost unheard of when I was a child. But today it's very prevalent." This is a man in his late sixties who lives in a town of nine hundred surrounded by cornfields. "America has fallen away from the Bible," he asserts, pointing to an epidemic of greed, dishonesty, and a lack of caring. "I think the United States is going to see some serious consequences." He fears these problems are spreading out of the cities and now contributing to the demise of his own community.

A middle-aged couple living in a town of fifteen thousand that has become racially and ethnically diverse in recent years sees "a decline, a disintegration of the family." The wife points to kidnapping, molestation, pornography, and sexual deviation as evidence. The husband describes the decline as a problem of people being too tolerant about moral issues as well as experiencing "real confusion" about right and wrong. He anticipates increasing "havoc in our system."

Since the late 1980s, social observers have argued that a cultural war is increasingly evident in US values. On one side are self-styled progressives—liberals who believe that values are contextual, and moral decisions must be made with a relativistic understanding of varying circumstances and constraints. On the other side are the traditionalists—conservatives who believe in firm distinctions between right and wrong, and whose convictions are often understood as being grounded in divine revelation. Progressives live in places like San Francisco and New York City; conservatives reside in small towns like Tyndall, South Dakota, and Brinkley, Arkansas.[1]

Of course, many of the stereotypical notions about a US culture war are overstated—and some are plain wrong. It is not true, for example, that the most outspoken traditionalists are country bumpkins. Many are well-educated, thoughtful, and articulate spokespersons for conservative moral principles. They live in upscale suburbs, teach at elite universities, earn handsome salaries as corporate executives, and express their opinions on popular radio and television programs.

Most of what we know about contentious culture war issues comes from surveys that broadly map national opinion as well as investigations of movement activists who mobilize money and influence on behalf of political candidates and legislation. While some of this research has been conducted in small towns, little of it has considered how living in a small community shapes the ways in which moral sentiments are expressed. As a result, it is easy to imagine that small towns are simply bastions of moral conservatism—or that they are as fraught with cultural conflicts as anywhere else.

What we know from decades of sociological theorizing is that a community's sense of itself is closely intertwined with its perceptions of good and evil. Communities reinforce their defining values by mobilizing against external forces that are deemed to threaten the community's vitality. Residents identify positions on social issues that they believe to be shared in their community—and in talking about these positions reinforce the sense of indeed being a community. Townspeople define themselves over and against strangers, deviants, and alien lifestyles of which they disapprove.

It is from this theorizing that notions about the peculiarities of small towns arise. A town that promotes and defends conformity can be a dangerous place for someone who inadvertently deviates. An African American who strays into an all-white community of southern racists can be in big trouble. So can a gay person who stops for gas in a town of bigoted rednecks. The enforcers of community values may be the local sheriff, a popular preacher, or a vigilante committee.

But the stuff of which scary lore about small towns is made fails to take account of the fact that small towns are well integrated into the national culture. It is precisely this integration—the ease with which interaction occurs between residents of small towns and people as well as ideas from other places—that sparks concerns about billboards advertising nude dancing, stories of child molestation, and evidence of an "anything goes" mentality.

People who live in small towns understand that whatever the circumstances may have been that led them to live where they do, their communities are in a tenuous position with respect to the wider culture. On the one hand, these small communities reflect the nation's larger economic and demographic trends, and participate in the same environment of media and entertainment. On the other hand, living in a small town is tantamount to going against the grain, and thus having reasons to think and behave differently from people elsewhere.

The net effect of this ambiguity is to inflect discussions of contentious moral issues with special significance. How a person thinks about abortion and homosexuality—or the position one takes toward teaching evolution or combating drugs—is partly a way of defining oneself as a member of a community. Moral convictions convey the shared sense of what is good about a community. They suggest how a small town may be threatened, and what should be done to preserve its cherished way of life.

A SENSE OF DECLINE

Hardly anyone we talked to in small towns felt that the moral life of the United States is improving. To the contrary, they were pretty sure it was declining. That response is probably not surprising. National polls suggest that many Americans are concerned about moral decline. People may be especially likely to feel this way living in a community that prides itself on preserving the past—a community in which the population is declining. A few of the people we talked to drew a direct association between the two kinds of decline, arguing, for example, that their town would be better off if people nowadays were obeying the Bible.

But the connection between one's community and a person's sense of moral decline is usually not this direct. Instead, the link must be understood by considering what exactly the problem is when someone says morality is declining. Usually it is something about the family, including promiscuity and divorce, or how children are being raised, the work ethic is declining and people are becoming greedy and materialistic, or people are focusing too much on themselves and not enough on others. If we recall what people in chapter 3 said they like best about their communities, these specific kinds of decline will sound familiar. They are precisely the values that people appreciate most about their communities. Inhabitants regard their small towns as places where families are strong, children can be raised properly, people work hard and are not materialistic, and residents care more about others than themselves. If these values are in decline, the decline is a threat to what people in small towns hold dear. A few examples will show what I mean.

Denise Hedron, an accountant who lives with her husband and two teenage daughters in a Sunbelt town of eight hundred, says the worst moral problem in the United States is people not being willing to work hard. It is understandable that she might feel this way. She grew up on a farm, helped with chores after school, and worked her way through college. But when asked to say more about her views, she asserts that the underlying problem is "the destruction of marriages," which she traces back to the permissiveness of the 1960s and 1970s. "People getting pregnant and not getting married, [and children] not having a father in the household to provide direction and leadership," she says, are the reasons children do not learn to work hard. "I know people don't want to hear it, but when you look at the cold hard facts, you see that one of our biggest moral failings as a country is letting people feel it's OK to divorce and remarry and have sex and just do whatever makes you feel good. It's ruining our children." She also connects the dots between this general problem and her community. "I look around our community and I see the children who are struggling in our school system" she explains, citing these children as an instance of the failure of marriage. She adds that her church's youth group is trying to step into the gap and teach children better values. Sometimes even this is a struggle, she says, because you always have to avoid "stepping on someone's rights."

The basketball coach I mentioned earlier who is troubled by billboards advertising nude dancing illustrates a somewhat-different connection between moral concerns and community values. At one level, he draws a fairly simple contrast between corruption in cities and goodness in his small town. The billboards offer nude dancing in Saint Louis and Chicago, he says, whereas "we don't have those kinds of whatever you call them—clubs—in this town." At another level, nude dancing is just a symptom of a larger problem that again is more acute elsewhere, he feels, than in his community. "I would categorize this as a sharing community," he observes, noting that the largest company in town is locally owned and gives money back to the community. "They aren't outsiders taking and not returning," he explains. He also believes there is a broader "downward spiral" in our country. Drugs are beginning to show up where he teaches, and he figures guns will be next. Ultimately, he thinks the root problems are "bad parenting" and "the greed factor." These are the precise opposite of the good parenting and sharing that he feels have made his community strong.

It is perhaps easy to read comments like these and conclude that small-town residents are overly pessimistic, maybe fearing too readily that their way of life is eroding. If they had a better grasp of the wider world, a critic might argue, they would realize that things are not so bad. A different interpretation, though, is possible. Set aside the fact that people are often nostalgic about community and a family life that never really existed, at least not in as rosy a way as they imagine. Consider instead the change that many residents in small towns have in fact experienced. They grew up in small towns or urban neighborhoods that seemed warm and comforting, perhaps because they were children and not faced with the harsh demands of adult life. For whatever reason, they wanted to replicate that sense of living in a secure friendly environment. They stayed in a small town or moved to one. But they sacrificed something as a result. The big company they could have worked for was not located there. The corporate ladder they could have climbed required them to move from city to city. Their childhood friends and siblings mostly chose that route, as have their children. Daily life now consists of friends and neighbors who share their values, and news from the outside world, commercials, and television programs about people who do not share their values. Little wonder that they feel the society is not going in a good direction. "It's not just the breakup of the family," notes one man, serious as he thinks that is. "We as a culture, as a community, as churches, as governments aren't doing things like we should."

The point is not that moral decline is felt more acutely in small towns than anywhere else or only because of living in a small community. There are many reasons to feel that things are not what they used to be—including promiscuity on television and drugs on the street, not to mention a middle-aged person's own fading sense of youthful vigor. The point is rather that moral decline takes on distinct meanings in small communities. What a person cherishes there—the chance to raise a family, feel secure, and feel cared for by neighbors and friends—is precarious under the best of circumstances. A sense of broad moral decline hits home. It makes one's community all the more important.

PROTECTING THE UNBORN

Besides general concerns about moral decline, residents of small towns closely follow the contested issues of the day. Just as it is in cities and suburbs, abortion is one of the topics that surfaces repeatedly when people in small towns discuss moral issues. Especially if they are Catholic or members of a conservative Protestant church, and also are deeply invested in raising children, they are likely to stand firmly on the prolife side of the issue. A Catholic woman in her thirties who is a full-time mother is a good example of the thinking that goes into taking this position. Hers is by no means a formulaic response that could easily be reduced to slogans. "I am an independent person," she says, "and I don't want to hear that I don't have a choice about what I do with my own body." And yet she is opposed to the prochoice position because she is convinced that abortion is devastating to women. The reason, in her view, is that it is contrary to women's nature. "Women have a sense of being a mother. Maybe they are a twenty-one-year-old who says, 'I do not want to have kids.' But they go along, and the doctor tells them they will never be able to have kids. That woman is going to mourn." By the same token, she says, "When a woman chooses to have an abortion, to end a life, there is a strong emotional part there—something that a woman has to deal with for the rest of her life." It is for this reason, the woman explains, that her feelings about abortion definitely influence how she votes.

When asked what the most serious or troubling moral problem in the United States is, people in small towns more frequently than not say it is abortion. Some of the reason that opposition to abortion is strong in

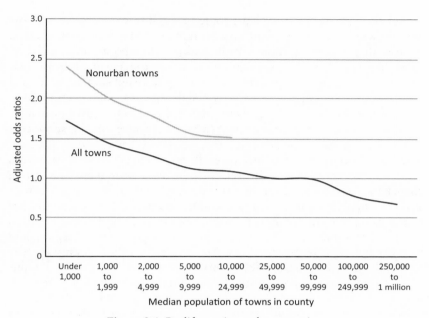

Figure 8.1 Prolife sentiment by town size

these communities is that residents of small towns differ from those in larger towns and cities in ways that relate to attitudes toward abortion, such as age, gender, education, and region. But taking these factors into account, *where* a person lives still appears to make a difference (see figure 8.1). Compared to someone living in a metropolitan county in which the median town size is between twenty-five and fifty thousand, the odds of being against abortion under all circumstances, or only with the exception of rape or incest, are 1.7 times greater among people living in an area with only small towns of a thousand residents, and decline to 0.7 among people living in an area with towns averaging more than a quarter-million residents. In addition, the odds of holding prolife views in each size community are about 1.4 times greater among people living in nonmetropolitan areas than in metropolitan communities.[2]

In qualitative interviews, many of the people we talked to held sentiments about abortion that they were eager to express. "If a child in a mother's womb is not safe," a man in one small town told us, quoting Mother Teresa, "nobody is safe." In his view, abortion is tantamount to the idea that "man can manipulate life, and decide when it begins and when it ends," and that makes it a "grave moral crisis." What he means is that there is corruption eating away at the moral fabric of the whole society. It is rarely the case that people in small towns personally know anyone who has actually had an abortion. But abortion goes hand in hand with perceptions about riffraff and people who are lazy and irresponsible. The idea that a woman might choose to have an abortion suggests that she is not living according to the purported standards of hard work and moral obligation that are the hallmarks of small communities.

A pattern that underscores these small-town orientations is evident in the results of another set of national surveys that have asked respondents if they think it should be possible for a pregnant woman to obtain a legal abortion under various circumstances. If the pregnancy has resulted from rape, puts the mother's health seriously in danger, or there is a strong chance of a serious defect in the baby, upward of three Americans in four say having an abortion should be possible, and the odds of saying this are nearly as high in small nonmetropolitan towns as in larger metropolitan communities—taking account of differences in age, sex, race, region, and level of education (as shown in figure 8.2). But under other circumstances— especially ones that suggest deviations from small-town norms—the differences between attitudes in smaller and larger communities increase. If a married woman merely does not want any more children, the odds of saying an abortion should be possible are only about three-quarters as great in small towns as in larger communities. If a woman is poor and cannot afford more children, or is unmarried and does not want to marry the man she got pregnant with, the gap between small-town residents and people in larger communities is greater. And the largest gap in attitudes is toward a woman who simply wants to get an abortion for reasons of her own—the response that connotes "abortion on demand."[3]

Town leaders we interviewed usually had particularly strong opinions about abortion. Those who considered it a moral abomination were likely to have spoken against it during community-wide political campaigns and at church meetings. Such admonitions could be regarded as preaching to the choir, at least in settings where there was little disagreement about abortion, and yet talking about controversial subjects on which people agree can function as a community-building practice in much the same way as backyard discussions of local weather and sports. The implied interlocutor against whom residents can vent their displeasure is Mother Nature, a rival sports team, or the strangers who are presumed to take the other side on abortion. These outsiders provide the occasion for arguments against abortion to be expressed until they are known by heart.

Consider what Mrs. Gautier, the store owner we met in chapter 3 who lives in a town of four hundred, says when asked what social and moral issues she feels strongly about. "The biggest one is the prolife issue," she says. "If we don't have respect for life, what is there?" Without prompting, she repeats a conversation she has had on the topic. "My daughter is

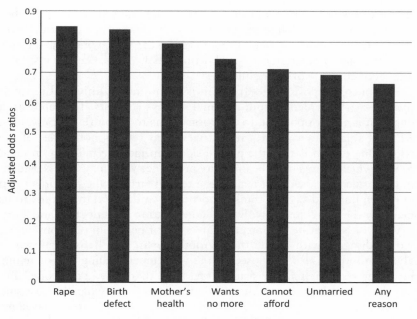

Figure 8.2 Attitudes toward abortion

a Democrat, and she says to me, 'But you Republicans believe in capital punishment.' And I said, 'Yes. Capital punishment isn't the best thing in the world, and I'm not going to say that I approve of that. But that person did something to be getting punished. That baby never had a choice. That baby never had a chance unless somebody helped it along.' " It is as if she is having the conversation with her daughter all over again.

Mrs. Gautier has more to say on the topic, this time offering another quote from a previous conversation. "It's like somebody said, 'How come God didn't send us somebody who was smart enough to figure this all out?' And he said, 'I did. You aborted him.' I'm really strong on the pro-life issue. And I'm sorry, but if these political parties can't get that straight, what can they get straight? We don't have the brains and the wonderful human intellect that we could have had. We don't have it because we got rid of it. We destroyed it."

These are ideas that Mrs. Gautier has herself thought about, yet it is also important to understand that they are part of the public moral discourse that ties her family and community together. At the Catholic Church she attends, the members pray regularly for the unborn. She is glad to have people there who "can talk and inform" others about the issue. The church group rejoiced with her when her sister became pregnant at age forty-seven and had a healthy baby. Mrs. Gautier likes to quote her deceased mother who had ten children. "My mother always said, 'Well, which one of you do you think I should get rid of? Which one of you wants to be the one to be sacrificed?' " Aborting a baby, Mrs. Gautier insists, is like sacrificing one of your children.

Of course, opposition to abortion is by no means universal in small towns—as the evidence from national surveys suggests. The interesting question is why opposition to abortion seems to be more the prevailing ethos in small towns than a mixed view that reflects both sides of the issue. One reason is that the prolife side is in fact the majority in most towns, which means that the minority prochoice view may be less evident or less often expressed. For example, a retired farmer who lives in a town of fifteen hundred says he thinks abortion is "a decision that needs to be made by the individuals involved in consultation with doctors and spiritual advisers," but he volunteers that "a lot of people in our community would disagree with me on that." Another man says he is "opposed to abortion," yet is also "opposed to the government telling me, or telling my daughter, or telling my sister if I had one that she can't get one." But he adds, "I can't go out in the public forum and say what I've just said without running a real risk of just getting my brains beaten in as some kind of an immoral baby killer." He keeps quiet because the prolife activists in his community are so vocal. In addition, the prochoice side frequently tends to be framed in terms that render it less amenable to public expression. This tendency is evident in the ways in which people who favor choice describe their position.

Mrs. O'Brien, the mayor we met in chapter 6, is a mother who is Catholic and has three decades of experience as a social worker in her rural community of eleven hundred. She provides a good example of someone who is strongly prochoice. "Abortion, to me, should not be in the government," she says. "Abortion is a personal issue, strictly personal. I would like to see it stay that way. I don't believe that it's right of me to tell someone else their rights. I've got my personal feelings and I've given those to my children. But they are adults now and they have their own decisions to make. So for me I don't have a strong opinion one way or the other. It's just simply a matter of leaving it up to the individual."

Two things stand out about the way she describes her position. One is the heavy emphasis on the word *personal* and related references to herself ("to me," "I've," "feelings," "the individual"). She means that decisions about abortion are up to the individual, but also implies that how one thinks about the issue will simply be different from person to person, depending on their experiences and outlook. The other is the lack of what sociolinguists call quoted speech. Unlike Mrs. Gautier, for example, Mrs. O'Brien does not quote conversations she has had, nor does she repeat

Profile: Ellis, Kansas

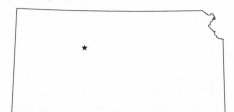

Surrounded by flat, open fields of wheat, corn, and soybeans, Ellis, Kansas, is a town of two thousand situated along Interstate 70 in the western part of the state. Like most towns in the area, its population is smaller than it was in 1950, but over the past decade it has grown slightly. Although a rail stop existed as early as 1867, Ellis County was largely unsettled until the 1880s, when German Catholic immigrants from Russia arrived in large numbers. Their influence remains evident in the county's religious composition, which is 54 percent Catholic, 22 percent mainline Protestant, and 18 percent evangelical Protestant, with the remainder adhering to several small denominations. Saint Mary's Church on Monroe Street is by far the largest church building in town.

Abortion has long been an issue of interest among Ellis residents, as it has been statewide. In 1973, more than twelve thousand abortions were performed in Kansas. That number fell to a low of sixty-four hundred in 1987, but increased to more than ten thousand in 1991, and has remained at roughly the same level. Although Ellis County is sparsely populated, as many as ten or twelve abortions are performed among residents of the county each year. In addition, more than a hundred out-of-wedlock births are recorded annually, with up to a third of those among teenagers.

Pregnancy counseling is provided locally by the Planned Parenthood Health Center and the Mary Elizabeth Maternity Home, both located in Hays, the county seat, sixteen miles from Ellis. Besides supporting the antiabortion-oriented Mary Elizabeth Maternity Home, opponents of abortion have posted road signs throughout the county warning against abortion and have urged the elimination of federal funding for Planned Parenthood, which supports the choice to have an abortion or not.

Ellis residents have mixed opinions about abortion, ranging from believing that it is always morally wrong to saying that it should be a matter of individual choice. Some believe the issue has received too much attention, especially in view of the murder of abortion provider Dr. George Tiller in Wichita in 2009. In 2010, US senator Sam Brownback, a conservative Republican who was an outspoken opponent of abortion, ran for governor, including among his campaign promises efforts to further curb abortion in Kansas. Statewide, Brownback won 63 percent of the vote, and Democratic candidate state senator Tom Holland received 32 percent. Ellis voters gave Brownback a 72 to 24 percent victory over Holland.

arguments she has heard others make. Indeed, her emphasis on individual choice begins as a strong assertion, yet ends with the statement that she does not have a strong opinion either way. When pressed to say more about why she holds these views, she refers to her experience as a social worker. She says she sees abortion being abused as a means of birth control and in other instances abortion being used to prevent the birth of badly brain-damaged fetuses, but in none of these cases does she feel it appropriate to offer advice. "Leave it to the individual," she says. In comparison, a person in her community who holds strong beliefs against abortion would be more likely to articulate those views as judgments that should apply authoritatively to the entire community.

One might also wonder if opposition to abortion helps in some communities to shore up their collective identity, perhaps like the witch hunts did in colonial Massachusetts. When the colony felt threatened, scholars have argued, witch hunts became a way of affirming loyalty to the colony's basic values, especially because accusations against witches drew the community together and gave the colonists reason to declare their faith in correct religious teachings.[4] A similar assertion has been made about the temperance movement in the late nineteenth and early twentieth century when rural communities presumably promoted Prohibition as a way of protecting the traditional values residents felt were threatened by immigration and urbanization.[5]

Research suggests that the most vocal and best organized opposition to abortion has been in cities and suburbs where electoral clout is greatest and large meetings can be held.[6] But in small towns, as we have seen in considering sentiments about moral decline, there is sometimes a sense of being besieged by an alien world, and this feeling is evident in comments about abortion as well. It surfaces especially in remarks about abortion being a problem in cities, unlike in small towns, where people presumably hold stronger values about the sanctity of life.

An example of perceived differences between cities and towns is evident in the comments of Mr. DeSoto, the man we met in chapter 5 who grew up in a community of immigrants from French Canada and now lives in a town of about eight hundred. He places great value on living in small places. He enjoyed the community in which he was raised because several generations of close relatives lived there and he could roam the neighborhood with his friends. He selected his present community not only because housing was cheap but also because the town was small. He worries, though, that small towns are beleaguered. The town he grew up in has lost population, and few of his generation have stayed. On social issues, his preference for small-town virtue influences how he explains his attitudes. He expresses his convictions about abortion not initially by stating his own view, which he says later is that abortion is "murder pure and simple," but instead by asserting, "I don't know why we kill babies in this country," and then mentioning an "abortion butcher" he read about who lives in a city. The implication is that "we" who kill babies are people in cities, not residents of small towns like his. This is a theme that runs through his comments about other social issues as well, such as drunkenness and political corruption. Small towns symbolize how the world should be, and cities evoke disconcerting thoughts about where the world may be headed. Comparing the two, Mr. DeSoto states unequivocally, "People in these little towns grow up with a better set of values."

It is one thing to imagine that small towns are a breath of moral purity in an otherwise-toxic world, but much worse to fear that town life itself is threatened. I can illustrate this point by quoting a woman in her early thirties who describes herself as a "very conservative Republican." She is an active churchgoer who says it is important not only that people believe in God but also that they trust in the Lord Jesus Christ as their savior. She has several children and was raised as a natural-born child in a large family that included several adopted siblings. So she has multiple reasons to be opposed to abortion, the strongest of which is her faith. "Abortion is murder," she asserts, quoting God as saying, "I knew you before I put you in your mother's womb" and "I knew you before I put a star in the sky." She offers an implicit reference to city life by claiming that it was sad for the nation to "cry over the four thousand people or so who died on 9/11," yet not to mention the forty-five hundred babies murdered the same day, and the next, and the next. She also believes the larger moral malaise of which abortion is a symptom is threatening her own town. "I've watched small-town American women who have been in deep, dark depression over aborting their baby at age fourteen," she says. Underscoring the point, she adds, "This is in small-town America as much as in the big city." She feels small towns are in big trouble because they are "not sharing the way God would want us to." Besides abortion, the other indication of rampant moral demise that worries her is sexual promiscuity. "It's happening in small-town America as much as in big cities," she says, noting sexual experimentation that stops short of intercourse. "We're exchanging lower pregnancy rates for the throat cancer coming out of blow jobs that children are doing."

This woman's concerns about abortion are more extreme than those of many people living in small towns. In indirect ways, however, other residents draw connections between abortion and the moral rot they feel is weakening their towns. A typical example is evident in the way a man in his late forties who works as an auto mechanic in a town of twenty-five thousand discusses his concerns. The community has been growing, and as a result he has enjoyed steady employment over the past two decades, unlike mechanics he knows in small declining towns, so he has reason to feel good about his life. Although his community has become racially and ethnically diverse, he says it is foolish to mourn the past because the "good old days were never really that good." He describes himself as a practical person who does not become interested in social issues unless something practical can be done about them. Yet he is adamantly opposed to abortion even in cases of rape and incest. The only exception, he says, would be if a pregnancy truly endangered a woman's life. The reason he is so strongly against abortion is not only that it is, in his view, taking the life of an innocent baby but also because it indicates the more pervasive decline of family values in United States and even in his own community. "Life has gotten so busy," he says, "that people don't have the time to sit down together like they used to. The family isn't as close as it used to be." He thinks the family used to be the source of "strength and nurturing and love," but "we're getting away from that." He comments, "This town has struggled for a long time with finding family-friendly things to do." But the community's efforts have had only mixed results. It isn't that he is thoroughly depressed by the direction things are headed. He just worries about his children's future and doubts that any practical solutions can be found.

The sense of near futility evident in this man's remarks is a key to understanding both the activism and lack of activism in small towns toward abortion. Activists feel that abortion is a particularly heinous evil that they can do something about. For example, the basketball coach I mentioned earlier is proud that some of his students join an annual bus trip to the nation's capital to protest the Supreme Court's 1973 decision in *Roe v. Wade*. Overturning the decision would be an important victory that he and his students feel they can help bring about. In contrast, most of the people we talked to said they were against abortion, and personally would not have one, or want their wife or daughter to have one, and yet they expressed reservations about the more aggressive prolife activism they had heard about. As one woman observes, "When you have an unwanted pregnancy, none of your options are good"—which means abortion may be wrong, but she dislikes activists turning it into a hot-button issue. She thinks activists' play on people's concerns "because it is not something that affects most people personally. They can think this is a big deal, and I don't do it, so that makes me feel better about myself, but if someone else does it, they are a terrible person."

This woman's perspective stops short of supporting activism because it identifies implicit or even intentional manipulation of people's concerns by activist leaders. Then there is the view that abortion is morally wrong, and yet not an issue that should become a matter of judgment or criticism among good friends and neighbors. A live-and-let-live attitude of this kind leaves the door open for differences of opinion while retaining faith in one's own convictions. "I am antiabortion," a Presbyterian woman in a rural town of a thousand says, adding, "I personally can't take exception with the person who makes that decision." She is "not fanatically against abortion" like some of the groups she regards as staunch prolife activists. She just feels that abortion is not good for the country.

Not surprisingly, there are also people in small towns who resist pro-life activism, even though they are basically opposed to abortion, because small-town culture itself exposes them to several crosscutting currents of thought. A good example is a woman in a town of fifteen hundred who attends a conservative charismatic church. She believes abortion is fundamentally wrong, and finds support for this conviction in the teachings of her church as well as from most of the people she knows at church and in her community. She is conflicted, though, because she does not feel the government should be "telling someone about a personal decision like that." This skepticism toward government intrusion is also a strong motif in the culture of her community. In addition, she thinks of herself as a feminist—an identity she regards as a distinguishing feature of her generation. "I think my generation really did help to wake up women to take charge and to respect their bodies," she says. "Rape is not the victim's fault," she asserts, implying that understanding this fact has to be part of any discussion of abortion. Ultimately, she holds firmly to her view that abortion is wrong, but wishes that the debate, which she regards as unfortunately explosive, could be more nuanced.

The conclusion to be drawn from instances like these is that opinions about abortion vary considerably even in small towns that otherwise might seem to be remarkably homogeneous. Although outspoken support for prochoice policies is rare, the prolife position is far more complicated than news stories and surveys usually suggest. Nor is it satisfactory to conclude that the public in small towns is simply part of the muddled majority. The reason opinions may seem muddled is that observers have not stopped to pay sufficient attention to the multiple factors shaping opinions. In our interviews, the most important of these factors include the basic and widely shared conviction that human life is precious and that taking a life in the womb is wrong, the perception that fellow townspeople generally share and support this conviction, an us versus them mentality that often perceives small town virtue over and against as well as indeed threatened by big city and mainstream media disrespect for basic values, misgivings about government intervention into personal life, doubts about extremist antiabortion activism, an emphasis on personal decisions that not only argues for individual responsibility in sexual behavior but also acknowledges the right of people to form their own opinions, and awareness of crosscutting social influences that may include gender and age cohorts as well as church and town, or even more personal experiences such as having been adopted or having had a baby out of wedlock.

How people sort out these complex influences cannot be understood by suggesting that people have a cultural tool kit that pretty much lets them do whatever they deem to be in their self-interest amid a world so fragmented that values hardly matter. That throw-up-your hands approach runs counter to what people actually say and believe about their deep convictions, and fails to illuminate the influences that town life and other social factors have in shaping attitudes. It especially falters in shedding light on the behavior that results. Weighing complex considerations about abortion encourages people to take a pragmatic approach toward dealing with it. While it is true that many people do not think enough about this particular issue for it to matter much one way or the other, those we talked to who do care about it are seldom engaged in activist movements. Getting involved to that extent requires a rare combination of interpretative frameworks, such as believing so strongly that abortion is always wrong and feeling so threatened by alien values that government intervention seems essential, and is as much attributable to social network connections, as studies have shown, as to convictions.[7] The more likely response is to take action that is deemed helpful, and at the same time does not bring in government too directly or violate principles of individual freedom. Concretely, the action that best fits these considerations includes voluntary contributions of money or time to support crisis pregnancy clinics. Townspeople we talked to saw that as a pragmatic solution. It provided counseling, information about adoption, and in some instances community support for mothers who decided to keep their babies. Crisis pregnancy clinics also served as vehicles for antiabortion activists to heap guilt on expectant mothers for considering abortion, but that was not how most supporters of these clinics in small towns understood their purpose.

The pragmatic approach toward reducing abortions fits well with small-town residents' emphasis on common sense and ingenuity. It seems practical to do a little that helps one woman through a crisis pregnancy, rather than expending a great deal of energy on movement activism that may or may not accomplish anything. A critic might argue that saying something like "we need to help mothers have their babies" is an after-the-fact justification for doing little, but in reality it is a statement that also motivates action, such as contributing money or time to helping at a crisis pregnancy clinic.

HOMOSEXUALITY

In national surveys, conservative attitudes toward abortion usually go together with negative views toward homosexuality. And in reality, many of the states with constitutional bans on same-sex marriage—such as Ala-

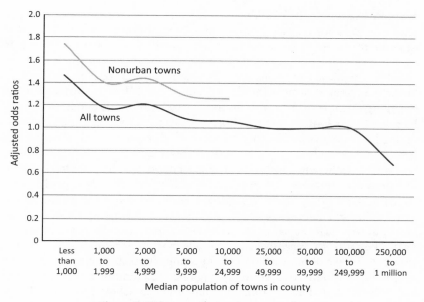

Figure 8.3 Support for antigay amendment

bama, Arkansas, Kansas, Nebraska, and North Dakota—are ones that have large numbers of small towns and have also sought to restrict access to abortion providers. Thus, it is not surprising that the data summarized in figure 8.3 shows support for a constitutional amendment banning gay marriage, were one to be proposed in the US Congress, among respondents in a large national survey, with comparisons among those living in nonmetropolitan and metropolitan counties in which the median population of towns ranged from less than a thousand to more than a quarter million, and with differences in gender, race, education, age, and region taken into account.[8]

Most of the variation in the figure, however, occurs at the lowest and highest values of town size—meaning that among most towns in between it matters relatively little on this particular issue whether the respondents live in an area comprised of smaller or larger towns. There also appears to be a wider range of opinion about homosexuality than there does about abortion, even in small towns, and on some survey questions the responses given by people in small rural communities are indistinguishable from those of metropolitan residents when factors such as age, region, and level of education are taken into account.[9] In some ways, this is surprising because small towns are often regarded as places where gossip and peer pressure discourage nonconformity, and where images of rural masculinity promote homophobia.[10] Unlike in large cities, small-town residents whose sexual orientations differ from those of the majority may find it more difficult to escape attention. Yet when asked if they personally know someone who is gay, close to 90 percent of people living in small nonmetropolitan areas say they do, and about half of these say the person they know is a member of their family or a close friend.[11] As a consequence, an emerging attitude in small towns appears to hold that homosexuality can be tolerated as long as it stops short of disrupting the local community—or leads to behavior like that "bunch of idiots in California." Among heterosexual residents who consider themselves relatively well informed and tolerant, this view expresses itself in support for gay rights, but usually does not condone gay marriage. Residents say they personally know someone who is gay or have a gay person in their extended family, and believe that gay people should be permitted to teach, join churches, and hold public office the same as anyone else. Just don't flaunt it, is the caveat. The more conservative stance holds that homosexuality is a sin and that gay people should not enjoy the same rights as everyone else. The reasoning is usually that some damage to the community will follow if rights are extended. Heterosexual families will somehow lose control over their children's morals and worse things may follow, such as child abuse, pornography, and sexual addiction.

Mrs. Saunders is one of the people whose views toward homosexuality fall toward the more tolerant end of the spectrum. She says that she has a gay acquaintance, although he doesn't live in her town, and has no problem being his friend. Nevertheless, she insists that she does not want homosexuality to be "in front of me"—meaning that it should stay out of the public eye. "As long as they're respectful and not trying to advertise it," she says, "I don't mind. It's your deal." She even believes homosexuals should be allowed to marry. Her reasoning is that marriage is pretty much a private matter and that what counts should be a person's happiness. "If it's going to make them happy," she remarks, "who cares. I don't see it as a problem. They're not hurting anyone." She underscores the same principle in arguing that homosexuals should not be denied membership in churches. Even though that would probably have a public aspect to it, she thinks the psychological harm from exclusion would outweigh the possibility of any damage to the collective good of the congregation. "God has the right to judge," she says. "We don't."

Mrs. Barnes, the woman we met in chapter 5 who works at the bank in a town of seventeen hundred, expresses a contrasting—but generally tolerant—perspective. She is a lifelong Catholic who regards herself as a conservative Christian. She is adamantly against abortion and generally votes Republican for that reason. But she is not as opposed to homosexuality as one might imagine. Although she opposes gay marriage, she be-

lieves gay people should in other ways enjoy the same rights as anyone
else. "I have not been around it a whole lot," she acknowledges. Most of
what she knows about it is what she has seen on television. She says it is
important to respect how people lead their lives. "Years ago, I don't think
that the average person in a small town would have accepted it," she says.
"But I think it is becoming more acceptable." She does not think there are
many gay people in her town, but she knows it is more common in some
cities. She has personally known people who were gay, she notes, and that
has affected her views more than anything else. "You just can't be a person who says I will not accept your way of life."

One of the reasons Mrs. Barnes emphasizes respect and acceptance is
that she feels her church has been relatively silent about homosexuality,
unlike its aggressive condemnation of abortion. Although she assumes
the Vatican is against homosexuality, she has heard few denunciations of
it in her parish. That view is one we heard from other Catholics as well.
As one remarked, the church is not trying to "fix homosexuals," and in
the absence of that, she figures "that's just how a person is, that's how
God made them."

At the opposite end of the spectrum are townspeople who definitely
believe that homosexuality is morally wrong. Among residents who hold
this view, some do try to apply the same norms of small-town civility to
homosexuals as they do to heterosexuals. For example, a Presbyterian
woman who regards homosexuality as a violation of God's law says she
wants to avoid being hateful and "come to a good place" in her thinking
on the topic. "I'm not there yet," she admits, but "I'm working on it." A
Lutheran woman in her community struggles as well. She says her church
is quite conservative on the issue, but people are reluctant to say much
about it for fear that someone's son or daughter might be gay. She is relieved that her church does not condone the ordination of gays and lesbians because there would be a ruckus if it did. Other townspeople are less
charitable. They are convinced that homosexuality is condemned in the
Bible and, equally troubling, represents a worrisome cultural shift in the
wider society. These concerns are evident in comments such as "they're so
pushy it makes me sick," "you see a lot of this in big cities," "the [gays]
are really trying to take over," "television seems to glorify them, and I'm
really sick of that," and "they are being treated like saints because of their
sexual preference."

With opinion divided about homosexuality, a number of states with
large rural populations have passed constitutional amendments banning
gay marriage, and as we saw in the last chapter, congregations have felt
strongly enough about the issue to split or withdraw from their denominations.[12] One reason for these events is that statewide referenda and
congregational policies represent public goods—laws and decisions that

affect everyone, or seem to, whether people are gay or straight—and thus force residents to take sides. A related reason is that the opinions of those who oppose gay rights and same-sex unions are often articulated more forcefully than the views of people on the other side. As is true of arguments about abortion, townspeople with moderate or liberal perspectives about homosexuality feel they are in the minority in their communities, feel uncomfortable speaking out, and believe the issue is private enough that it should not become a matter of public discussion or policy.

How a live-and-let-live attitude of this kind works itself out is evident in the remarks of a pastor who regards himself as open minded and tolerant, and yet is unwilling to take a strong stance in favor of gay ordination or same-sex unions. "I do not have any great zeal about same-gender relationships," he says, "except that I think the making and keeping of commitments is important." For him, honesty and fidelity are critical enough that he emphasizes them rather than becoming an activist on either side of issues about homosexuality. Ms. Clarke makes a similar observation. "I think it's important to commit to something or to someone," she says. "If your choice is to commit to someone of the same sex, I don't really have a big problem with that." In her case, she also believes that being this open minded is "pretty darn rare" among people with rural backgrounds similar to hers. Her comment suggests that she probably would not say much about her views among the people she works with in her community.

The fact that residents of small towns who consider themselves moderates or liberals on homosexuality are reluctant to talk publicly about it does not mean that they haven't been thinking about the topic. Especially if they belong to congregations or live in states where gay marriage has been discussed in the media, they probably have heard views they liked or disliked. But their opinions are guided by a mixture of rational arguments, emotions, personal experience, and views about what is good for their community. How these complex considerations come together is clearly illustrated in the comments of a man in his sixties who lives in a town where churches and government officials have discussed homosexuality on a number of occasions. He is rather tired of thinking about the issue, and his exhaustion stems as much from mixed sentiments as anything else. He became convinced several years ago that the idea of homosexuality being a choice was not a defensible argument. He just thinks, "When did you choose? Do you remember when you made that choice? Do you remember standing in the school yard, and there's the quarterback and there's the head cheerleader, and you decided which one had the cutest fanny?" He thinks people do not choose but instead are born with one sexual orientation or the other. And yet his emotions are not in the same place as his rational arguments. "I'm not ready to be sitting in church and see Bob put his arm around Frank," he says. "I'm not going to bash them, but I'm not ready for that either."

For most of the people we talked to, homosexuality was a topic they knew was generating new understandings that were either leaving them upset or feeling that they would eventually have to adopt new attitudes themselves. A man in his fifties who lives with his wife in a tiny rural community, for example, says homosexuality is something nobody would have been aware of in his area twenty or thirty years ago, but now it is just one of those changes everyone is getting used to. "I guess if that's what you want and you're not bothering me, I can live with it," he says, mentioning two gay couples in the area. "They don't seem to bother nobody. Everybody kind of knows what's going on." This man attends a conservative Baptist church that does not condone homosexuality, and yet his strong sense that everyone should be free to be themselves is more influential than the church in shaping his thinking. As for homosexuals marrying, he says, "I guess you ought to have the right to choose that way of life if that's what you really want." Others made similar comments, noting friends they knew in high school who are now known to be gay or saying that their children have challenged them to think more deeply about the issue.

School Controversies

Small towns and rural communities have been the location of some of the most contentious battles in recent years over school curricula. The widely discussed 2005 Kitzmiller case in which a judge ruled against teaching intelligent design as part of high school biology lessons, for example, occurred in Dover, Pennsylvania, a town of fewer than two thousand people.[13] Controversies about evolution have been played out in states with large rural populations, such as Alabama, Kansas, and Louisiana, while questions about teaching the Ten Commandments or having them displayed in public buildings have taken place in small communities, such as Maumelle, Arkansas, and Stigler, Oklahoma. Polls show that the US public at large is divided over these issues, but residents of small nonmetropolitan towns are generally more favorably disposed than people in larger communities toward prayers, Bible reading, and lessons about creation or intelligent design in their schools. Indeed, one survey suggests that an avid small-town proponent of evolution would likely be outnumbered nearly ten to one by fervent creationists.[14]

The notion that small towns are filled with people who want Christian dogma promulgated in public classrooms, though, is false. While it is the case that small homogeneous communities find it easier to encourage prayer, Bible reading, and creationism in schools than cities with religiously diverse populations do, it is rare for townspeople to argue that public school curricula should include explicit religious teachings. Residents have read or heard too much about church–state controversies to be in favor of that. Instead they contend that the Ten Commandments, for instance are universal moral teachings that will have a salutary effect on the community and need not be taught as biblical doctrine.

As immigration brings greater ethnic and religious diversity to small towns, it is certainly conceivable that some communities will react by arguing all the more forcefully that traditions such as school prayer or teaching the Ten Commandments in school should be preserved. For example, one of the pastors we interviewed in a town of eight hundred that was beginning to feel the effects of immigration asserted in no uncertain terms that the Ten Commandments should be posted in public schools and taught as regular parts of the curriculum. "The words 'separation of church and state' are not in the Bill of Rights or the Constitution," he said in defense of his view. Or as a church member in another community complained, "We [Americans] exaggerate the Jewish holidays, Buddhism, and of course Islam, but are not allowed to teach the Christian viewpoint." Yet it seems more likely that communities wanting to preserve moral traditions will find other ways in which to do so. The pastor of a conservative evangelical church in a town with several recent immigrant Hindu families, for example, says he would not want his children learning Hinduism in school if they were living in India, so he figures it best to preserve his community's spiritual traditions through the efforts of his church. In other interviews, people draw sharp distinctions between religion and morality.

Consider the position articulated by a woman who says it would be difficult to teach the Ten Commandments as religious doctrine in her community's school. "We have Islamic kids, we have Jehovah's Witnesses, we have Jewish families," she says, so despite the fact that she would like the Ten Commandments to be taught, she feels they should be distilled into moral principles and not taught as religion. She happens to live in a city where the population is in fact quite diverse. But a woman in a small town who understands that even Protestants and Catholics may have different views offers almost the same reasoning. "Even if you don't believe in the God that I believe in," she says, "a logical person could agree that it would be wrong to put something first in life that is not God." And if people could agree in principle on the first commandment, she believes they could probably see the value of other commandments as moral ideals.[15]

Lars Johansen is a fifty-year-old newspaper editor—a Lutheran whose wife is Catholic—who has raised six children in a small town. It is interesting to contrast his views about the Ten Commandments and prayer in public schools with the woman I just quoted. While she illustrates the fairly common view that some basic underlying truth can be found in the Ten Commandments that would elicit agreement from almost everyone, Mr. Johansen considers it more prudent to recognize the differences among religious traditions. Some of the Protestants in his community, he says, think Catholicism is evil. If those Protestants wanted the Ten Commandments taught in public schools, they might also have to tolerate prayers to the Virgin Mary. "I believe in the wisdom of the Constitution," he says. He thinks the people who are trying to force their own religion down other people's throats had better think twice. "You allow the camel's nose under the tent," he explains, "and you get the other end too."

The orientation toward such curricular controversies that seems to outweigh strong ideological positions is the same small-town pragmatism that we have seen in previous chapters. This view is evident when townspeople say they would like to see the Ten Commandments taught or prayer allowed back in the schools, but figure there are better ways of "skinning a cat," as one man put it, such as encouraging parents to do a better job of instructing their youngsters, or having the schools teach honesty, fidelity, and generosity as moral principles. Although there have been activists on both sides, this is also the stance most evident at the grass roots about the teaching of evolution.[16]

Without a doubt, there are residents in small towns who feel strongly that evolution should not be taught at all, or if it is, should be exposed as false doctrine. This view is well represented by the woman I mentioned earlier who talks about the danger of children getting cancer from giving blow jobs. Although her thoughts on that issue are unusual, to say the least, she is not the type who spews right-wing invectives on talk radio. She is a college graduate who held a position as a banking executive before focusing full-time on raising her children. She says she was taught evolution in sixth grade and made up her mind at that point that the idea was nonsense. For a long time she had no cause to think further about it, but now that her children are in school, she has been revisiting the topic. She has found a number of reasons to believe that evolution is not just scientifically wrong but also damaging to human society. One reason, she says, is that the theory of evolution was responsible for slavery. People were taught that "the black man hadn't evolved like the white man," she says, "so was inferior. That's how slavery came about." A second reason is that according to evolution, death would have happened before sin, but that contradicts the biblical view of sin being the cause of death. A third reason is that the big bang theory, as she understands it, suggests that everything is spun off clockwise from a single dot, and yet there are planets going counterclockwise in the solar system. A fourth problem, she says, is that an evolutionist would have to believe that the moon used to be part of the earth, which she believes could not have been the case. And a fifth reason evolution is wrong, she thinks, is that the biblical story of the flood explains the Grand Canyon better than eons of evolution. Above all, she thinks it is demeaning to imagine that a human could have ever been a monkey.

A knowledgeable scientist would find these assertions ludicrous. They are extreme even among the fiercest opponents of evolution, but they do illustrate something important about the relationship between living in a small town and holding radically conservative positions on social issues. This woman did not believe in these arguments because she had heard them articulated in her town. Even though she lived in a predominantly Republican community and went to a conservative church, she had never expressed her views about evolution publicly because she figured they would not have been shared. Instead, she quietly read on her own—and consulted Web sites on the Internet—to find support for the conclusions that she had arrived at in sixth grade. She was more atypical than typical of the way opinions are formed and discussed in small towns.

The more common approach in small towns—and probably in larger communities as well—is to search for practical ways to reconcile science and faith. The solutions that people come up with are nearly as varied as the people describing them. For example, a man whose wife teaches science in their small community's high school portrays her as the "believer" in the family and himself as the guy who wants facts, so as a couple they mostly have an ongoing debate about evolution and creation. A woman who learned science in high school says the matter is pretty simply resolved as long as you remember that science tells us how and religion tells us why. She interprets the distinction to mean that evolution should be taught in school and creation should be promoted in church. Another woman gives a fairly typical answer when she says she is just confused and hopes someday to get it all sorted out. Yet another resident asserts that the Bible depicts God as a progressive deity whose relationship with humanity changes, which leads her to believe that evolution is simply God's way of doing things.

But whether they feel confused or have it all figured out, few of the people we interviewed felt it was necessary for school boards to keep going back and forth in efforts to revise science curricula. When required to choose, these townspeople say they would vote for a school board candidate who is critical of evolution or a different one who is not, but they mostly want the issue to go away. "Nobody is going to win the argument," one man laments, telling how creationists in his state brought in a big gun who had a gift of gab and the other side mustered the support of top scientists. "Just back and forth, it's never ending," echoes a fellow resident. Or as another man says, noting that his wife is a staunch believer in evolution and he still prefers the creationist view, "I won't stand on a fence post and preach it or anything," adding that the best way to approach the topic in schools is "carefully."

The reason they want the issue to go away is not that they consider it unimportant but rather because they figure the obvious solution is to be open minded—or as one woman says about evolution, "You learn it like anything else in science. You learn it for what it is and go on." For some, like one of the men we interviewed who described himself as a "literal six-day creationist," it made sense that evolution should be taught in the interest of knowing all perspectives, and for others, it seemed like a good idea for students to know about intelligent design in case there were holes in scientists' evidence for evolution.[17] As one of the science teachers we interviewed put it, "I've tried to maintain a fair balance in my classroom. In education we're not there to preach to people. We're there to get them to think. I'm not one of those who say everything is black and white."[18]

AN ETHOS OF COMMON SENSE

There are other moral issues that townspeople said were important enough that they should receive more attention than they do—problems such as drug use and alcoholism, job training, school improvement and consolidation, the gap between rich and poor, and protection of the environment. But the most contentious issues—abortion, homosexuality, and teaching the Ten Commandments and creationism—were ones that residents of small towns portrayed quite differently than an outside observer might have guessed from watching stories on Fox News or CNN.

Whole communities were sometimes divided between factions that supported or opposed a revision to the school curriculum, or because a local pastor declared themselves to be in favor of gay marriage. Had they known such fights were brewing, cable news producers would have sent reporters to record the most incendiary statements from both sides. Having watched these segments, viewers would have missed understanding what was truly the case in most small communities.

Polls are useful reminders that sentiments on such issues as abortion, homosexuality, and evolution are usually more conservative in small non-metropolitan towns than in larger metropolitan communities. At the same time, polls must be interpreted clearly if they are to be taken seriously at all. When aggregated nationally, surveys show that residents of small towns register opinions that are mixed, nuanced, and heavily dependent on how questions are asked. Aggregation also fails to adequately reflect the fact that sentiments in one community may be quite different from those in another one.

Townspeople are good observers of the processes that shape the discussion of contentious issues in their communities. The fact that interviewees share ideas that span the ideological spectrum and, in interviewees' own view, deviate from local norms is an indication of the candor with which they describe their opinions. What comes through repeatedly is the fact that discussions of controversial issues take into account residents' expectations of how others with whom they associate may react. People refrain from expressing their views about abortion or homosexuality for fear of offending a neighbor or fellow church member, and they withhold commentary even when they may have strong opinions because they feel the issue is complicated, confusing, or requires tolerance and respect. It is not uncommon for statements of absolute moral conviction to be couched in personal language ("my personal persuasion," as one man puts it)—not because people are moral relativists or because their opinions are private, but instead because they reflect community norms of getting along and respecting differences. What people want to believe is that their communities are fair minded—places where "we can live and get along, disagree, yes, but not try to force others to accept our views."[19] In this regard, inhabitants of small towns are like other Americans who generally abide by norms of civility, but are probably more attuned to these norms because so much of small-town life is public and is communicated both in direct interaction and in behind-the-scenes conversations among neighbors and friends.

The extent to which discussions of moral issues are implicitly monitored by community norms is, I have suggested, an important consideration in understanding why conservative opinions seem to predominate as often as they do despite the fact that sentiments actually are divided and nuanced. The few who may be most agitated about abortion, gay marriage, or some other issue are more likely to speak out as well as frame their arguments as absolutes. When one side implicitly appears to be in the majority, residents whose views are in the minority are less likely to state their opinions publicly. This is why church votes about gay ordination or local school board elections sometimes produce surprises. What was popularly assumed to be the majority view, turns out not to be when secret ballots are counted.

Above all, interviewees in small towns seem intent on demonstrating that a commonsense, pragmatic, open-minded orientation to contentious issues prevails in their communities. It is they who are the guardians of this spirit, which they believe to be profoundly American and indeed responsible for much of the good that has been accomplished since the nation's founding. A can-do attitude that also respects common decency, considers both sides of a controversial issue, and finds a way forward is one that small-town residents believe is fundamentally transmitted in strong two-parent families along with schools and churches, and is maintained from day to day and year to year by other-regarding neighborliness as well as community involvement. Residents worry that the same traditions are not being upheld in cities and fear that their communities may be threatened by corrosive tendencies in the wider culture. These concerns help to reinforce the conviction that living in a small community is a good choice. And at the end of the day, reactions to perceived threats are less critical than the belief that open-mindedness and fair dealings will prevail.

- 9 -

Washington Is Broken
Politics and the New Populism

DURING THE 2008 PRESIDENTIAL CAMPAIGN, Republican vice presidential nominee Sarah Palin drew widespread praise from part of the electorate for suggesting that Americans who live in small towns—like her community of Wasilla, Alaska, population nine thousand—were somehow more authentic, harder working, and more committed to honesty, sincerity, and dignity than the rest of the country. Pundits had a field day arguing that a candidate so distant from the action in urban and corporate America was incapable of understanding the true challenges facing the nation. In any case, they noted, too few of the population still lived in small-town America to make much of a difference in a national election.[1] But this was hardly the first time that small-town values had been touted—or criticized—in national elections, nor was it likely to be the last.

The populist movement of the late nineteenth century attracted hundreds of thousands of voters in small towns and on farms, especially in the Midwest and South. It emerged at a time when rural America was suffering from low crop yields, tariff and currency policies that reduced opportunities to sell in foreign markets, high freight costs charged by wealthy railroad magnates, and exorbitant interest rates levied by eastern banks. Although the movement was successful in electing a few of its members to the US Congress, it mostly earned the scorn of city pundits and then faded within a few years after having accomplished scarcely any of its goals.[2] What remained of it was a lingering antigovernment sentiment expressed in calls for fiscal conservatism.

Despite a declining population relative to urban America, small towns and rural communities retained enough of a voice that political candidates through the remainder of the twentieth century periodically claimed to represent the values of small towns in the United States, even when their qualifications for office were largely attained in other venues. After Franklin Delano Roosevelt's extended tenure in the White House, many in small-town America saw Harry Truman as more closely one of their own. They subsequently viewed Dwight Eisenhower, whose roots were in Abilene, Kansas, in the same way. Following the terms of John F. Kennedy, Lyndon Baines Johnson, and Richard Milhous Nixon, not to mention the divisive war in Southeast Asia and the Watergate scandal, voters turned to Jimmy Carter to exemplify what they hoped would be a return to the simpler values of rural America. Ronald Wilson Reagan's career on the silver screen and as governor of California did not stand in the way of his cultivating a cowboy image reminiscent of the frontier, and interrupted by the single term of George Herbert Walker Bush, William J. Clinton became another president with small-town roots. His two-term administration was followed by the election of George W. Bush, who promised that the small-town values he learned in Midland, Texas, would guide his presidency.[3] Thus, it was scarcely novel for part of the electorate in 2008 to be attracted by Palin's small-town background and observers to again note the seeming strength of populist appeals.[4]

The possibility of a new populism was as much the idea of journalists and political operatives hoping to fan controversy with stories of outraged citizens mobilizing to protest the national debt or defend their right to carry guns as it was about anything truly new or well organized. To be sure, themes from earlier populist agitation were resurrected, including allegations that Washington, DC, was broken or in the pocket of Wall Street financiers, and arguments that ordinary people were capable of solving their own problems if merely left alone. Rallies with boisterous crowds calling for a new direction in Washington attracted considerable media attention and posed questions about the sources of such sentiment. Was it rooted in insecurity fed by a faltering economy, home foreclosures, and high taxes? Was it a manifestation of lingering white racism? Did it reflect an underlying sense of moral malaise?

There was no particular reason to suspect that residents in small towns were any more likely to be the instigators of a new populist movement than people in larger communities. The number of potential activists living in small towns was too small to become the driving force. It was more likely that townspeople who wished to be heard would do so by joining with grassroots protagonists in cities and suburbs. Enough was said about small-town values being resurrected, though, that it made sense to ask what those values actually were. An emphasis on community and family, a sense of geographic and emotional distance from Wall Street and Washington, and a commonsense orientation accompanied by concern about moral decline were all certainly present—but what else?

NUANCED ANTIPATHY TOWARD BIG GOVERNMENT

Talk to almost anyone in a small town, and sooner or later some invective about government ineptitude and waste spews forth. Residents complain of bureaucrats in state and federal office who allegedly have never visited a small town, and hence would be shamefully out of place if they did. "Don't get me started," sighs a resident in one community. "Washington is broken," declares a leader in another small town. He says that view is shared by 90 percent of the people he knows. Feeling left out and left behind is common. And yet opinions vary. Like everything else about small-town America, every generalization that seems indisputable from a distance turns out to be more complicated when examined at closer range. The most dyed-in-the-wool opponents of big government acknowledge that some aspects of what it does are completely reasonable. In the same communities, neighbors can be found who hold positive views toward government. And when comparisons are made with larger places, the differences in attitudes toward government frequently are negligible.

Surveys provide a glimpse at some of the complexity. When asked if they think "we're spending too much money," "too little money," or "about the right amount" on various "problems in this country," fewer than 10 percent of the residents in small towns think too much is being spent on education, health, or law enforcement. These percentages barely differ from those in the United States as a whole. The contrast is on problems that respondents can imagine are more significant elsewhere than in their own communities. These issues evoke greater concern about overspending. A third of small-town residents think too much is being spent on "assistance to blacks," and more than 40 percent believe this about "assistance to big cities" and "welfare." On these topics, small-town residents are significantly more likely to say too much is being spent than are respondents in the nation generally. These problems, however, elicit the largest percentages expressing concern about overspending from the general public as well (see figure 9.1).[5] In short, the survey responses suggest that townspeople are by no means overwhelmingly or uniformly opposed to the kinds of social programs that require government spending. This conclusion is further confirmed by responses to another question asking people if they "consider the amount of federal income tax which you have to pay as too high, about right, or too low?" Not surprisingly, a majority of the public (61 percent) thinks that its federal income taxes are too high, and yet the percentage giving this response in small towns is no greater than elsewhere.

But surveys that ask standardized questions designed to elicit quick responses from the general public on an assortment of topics offer little insight into the ways in which residents of small towns actually think and

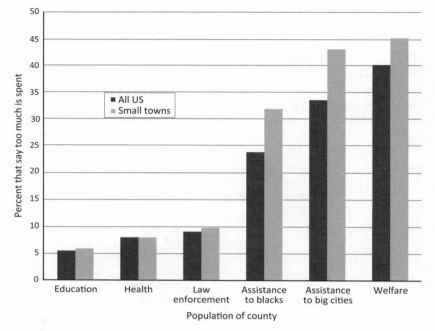

Figure 9.1 Concern about government spending

talk about government when given the opportunity to express themselves in their own words. Although it is the case that some of the townspeople we interviewed had little to say about government's role in their lives, the vast majority were more than willing to describe their opinions in some detail. It is evident that they had been thinking about what they liked or disliked about government, and probably had discussed these opinions with their neighbors and friends.

A view that is hardly unique to small towns, but that has special resonance in these places, holds that big government is deplorable principally because of its size. "The federal government is so big and so bureaucratic that they don't even know where they're at," says a registered nurse in her early fifties who lives in a town of seventeen hundred. She adds, "I'm in favor of local people helping local people and having as much local control as possible." What makes her comment typical of the way in which many residents of small towns express their views is the distinction she draws between big bureaucracy and local control. Unlike the sentiment sometimes expressed in political commentary, such dislike of bureaucracy is rooted in a desire for an intimate relationship—such as the ones found in a family—in which personal needs are nurtured lovingly; the "us" that townspeople contrast with the "them" of big government is their town. Bureaucracy is alien in the same way that a stranger is: it lives in another place, somewhere outside the community, and threatens the normal relationships to which townspeople have grown accustomed. From this perspective, local government is a natural and necessary emanation of the needs as well as interests of the town, whereas state, regional, and national bureaucracies are beyond the pale. As a longtime resident of a town of two thousand explains, "Of course you need some services," referring to "your lights and your water" that are provided through local government, but the other government agencies that try to come into his community, he says, "should stay home."

When big government is regarded as alien to the local community, the added difficulty is that misunderstanding is assumed to be almost inevitable. Being part of a small town, as we have seen in previous chapters, is about presuming to understand the local culture—the appropriate way to greet passersby on the sidewalk, first names and family histories of store clerks, contributions of town leaders to community projects, and especially, narratives of neighborly assistance during times of personal and community tragedy. A stranger does not intuitively share these understandings, which is why it takes so long for newcomers to feel fully at home. In the same way, government that resides somewhere outside the community cannot understand its local culture, either. Especially the state and federal government, as one resident of a small town puts it, "are just so out of touch."

Townspeople less often admit they do not understand government as say it does not understand them, and yet that perception follows occasionally. It, too, is similar to the view expressed about strangers. If strangers do not share the familiar stories that implicitly bind the townspeople together as a community, it is partly because they have beliefs and values that are difficult to comprehend. They somehow find it attractive to live in noisy places with heavy traffic and confusing highways, and they take pleasure in pursuing careers that rob them of time to be with family. Government is similarly incomprehensible, not only because it is big, but also because its size suggests rules, regulations, and requirements that are ultimately confusing plus beyond the reach of ordinary common sense.

The fact that big government is a stranger to the local community means that the politicians who run it may be perceived as untrustworthy, just as a newcomer may be viewed who is suspected of being riffraff, a drug dealer, or a person on the run from the law. "I really feel politicians are bought and paid for," Mr. Parsons says, exempting local officials from that generalization, but asserting that it includes "even a lot of your state people." Mr. DeSoto's stance is similar. "It used to be you voted for the person you thought was best," he explains. "Then you voted for who you thought was the lesser of two evils. Now it doesn't matter who gets in. They are all scoundrels." The best thing government can do, he contends, is to "get out of people's business." Others express the same view in succinct remarks, such as "less is more" when it comes to government, and rhetorical questions, such as "Have you ever seen [government] actually fix a problem?"

Sentiments like these are sometimes knee-jerk reactions, rooted in emotion as much as in reasoned analysis, but residents of small towns who otherwise trust public officials do worry that these politicians seldom have the interests of small communities at heart. As a homemaker in a town of nineteen hundred says, "Hey, this is our small community. It makes me sick when millions of dollars are spent on campaigns, and we can't even get help to have a good factory put here." The cities, these residents maintain, necessarily drive political decisions, and that means anything from sparse funding for local projects to poor representation to regulations that may be necessary in cities yet make no sense in small towns. The specific topics residents complain about are sufficiently varied—from unfilled potholes to the need for better Internet service to school closings to a lack of jobs—and sometimes so seemingly minor that they obviously carry symbolic as well as material weight. For example, community leaders in a town of nine hundred that had been losing population for several decades were convinced that their town's very survival was being threatened by the fact that politicians in their state were beholden to residents in large metropolitan areas. The reason they felt imperiled was that state law disallowed roadside advertising. If only they could put up a sign, they said, tourists would surely stop for a meal at the local restaurant and see what a lovely town it was.

Being in the numerical minority, residents of small towns understand that cities have more political clout than they do. The concern, though, is less about representation than about politicians misunderstanding the workings of small communities. Several of the people we interviewed, for instance, selected regulations about babysitting, day care, and elder care to illustrate how policies oriented toward large metropolitan communities are ill suited to small towns. At one level, they understood the need for state licensing and regulation of these services, but at another level, they considered it a matter of government interference when neighbors were no longer able to freely help one another. As one woman explained, the licensing "got so picky that people who babysat for years and did a good job weren't able to do it." For her, this reflected badly on politicians' ability to understand the realities of small-town life. "Sometimes you just need common sense," she sighed.

This view that common sense should be sufficient bridged into a kind of antielitism among townspeople as well. As one man put it, "[The government should] have some confidence in the American people. Don't think we're stupid. That's the feeling I get. The government has to come in and rescue us because the American people are pretty stupid. So a few elite people have to figure out how to fix us."[6]

We encountered a stronger criticism of state and federal government policy, too. This one blames big government not just for favoring cities now but also for a long history of programs that have been devastating to people in small towns. It is most evident in towns and counties that have lost a significant share of their population. These are rural communities in which farms have grown larger, leaving fewer farmers in the area and thus fewer people in the towns as well. An explanation for farms becoming larger is that government policy has dictated it. Of the people we talked to, nobody could quite articulate how this had happened. They just felt that big agribusiness lobbies governed farm policy and that benefits to ordinary farmers were so meager that they could not survive, while large farms, feedlots, and hog and poultry conglomerates were better able to withstand temporary setbacks in the market.

A related and more cynical interpretation held that government leaders had intentionally formulated policies to deplete rural areas. In this view, as one community leader described it, Roosevelt's New Deal had been designed to help people in cities more than in rural areas and therefore depopulate those areas. Social Security and health insurance programs, according to this criticism, were examples of programs that helped employers and employees more than farmers. Then during World War II, military expenditures went disproportionately to coastal cities. And since then, wealthy interests in big cities had worked government to their advantage and the detriment of small towns. As one man who held these views put it, "It was more by design than by accident."[7]

Townspeople also say that big government cultivates dependence rather than allowing people to do things for themselves. "You encourage people to think they deserve something instead of doing things on their own and finding their own solution to problems," one community leader explains. A similar view is expressed by a retired oil refinery worker who lives in a town of seven hundred people who pride themselves on being fiercely independent. "Anymore, when something goes wrong we expect the government to come down and fix it for us," he observes. "That's the mentality of a lot of people. Uncle is supposed to come in here and take care of it for me. Well, Uncle can't take care of everything." His concern about dependence does not mean that he thinks government should do nothing. For example, he feels that the government's drug plan for senior citizens has worked well and should not be cut. And yet he holds government responsible when he sees people not taking sufficient responsibility for themselves.

Concerns about welfare chiselers and riffraff prompt townspeople's most direct criticisms of government. In this view, it is the down-and-out who have become most dependent on government and indeed have learned to take advantage of government programs. "I think government is a disgrace," asserts a skilled laborer in his early sixties. "People want it, though. They want government to take care of them so they don't have to be responsible. It's like [Hurricane] Katrina. They expected government to come in and take care of them. One old gal had a breast implant with the money she got." An insurance agent who lives in an isolated rural community of fifteen hundred offers a similar observation. "We've got welfare trash out here just like they do in the cities," he says. "That's another thing that is grossly wrong with this country. Everybody thinks the government owes them something." It rankles him to hear people "bitching" about not having enough to live on. "They are the ones who go walking down the street with a pregnant wife and a can of beer smoking cigarettes. And we're paying for it. It's a danged aggravation." The town manager in a low-income community with high unemployment coined the term "mailbox payroll" to describe the people he wishes would leave. Such types just sit around waiting for their government check to arrive, he says. Some of them even wear designer clothes. "They've figured out the system and abuse it." To be sure, negative sentiments such as these are directed mostly toward the perceived moral imperfection of riffraff themselves, but government is thought to aggravate the problem by doing things—usually at an unreasonable cost to taxpayers and with limited effectiveness—that individuals and families should take responsibility for themselves.[8]

For people who are already convinced that big government is impersonal, incapable of understanding ordinary people's needs, perhaps corrupt, and in league with riffraff, they require only a small leap of imagination to believe that the United States is on a slippery slope toward socialism. They view federal government intervention in the affairs of financial institutions and other businesses not as necessary steps to forestall economic collapse but instead as socialist incursions. "I don't know how much time you have for me to talk about this," a community leader in a town of eight hundred says as he warms to the topic of what he dislikes about the government, "because I think our whole country is moving into socialism. We're buying the banks and the auto companies, and if that isn't socialism, I'm not sure what socialism is." In his view, the American way of life, insofar as it is rooted in free enterprise, is sorely endangered. "We're becoming more socialist all the time," another resident laments, "and it's going to ruin this country." Although they probably would not refer to it as populism, they favor efforts not only to return control over the lives of individuals and families to the small communities in which they live but also to roll back the ever-expanding grasp of big government.

Town hall meetings are attractive as a forum for expressing such concerns. A meeting of this kind had recently been held in one of the towns in which we conducted interviews—an ethnically diverse community with an expanding population of about eighteen thousand. The electorate was bipartisan and included a large number of independents, but generally went Republican. "I think a lot of people in our area, the majority, simply tend to feel like the political process is a waste of time," a man who attended the meeting explained a few days later. His view, he said, was that "when they become involved in our lives," government programs are "detrimental." Health care, which had been the focus of the town meeting in his community, was the example he had in mind. "Who wants somebody in the government making a decision that a doctor should make for your health care?" he asked. "When government gets involved, they have a tendency to take over." Everyone in his community, he thought, was against any kind of government health care bill. It was just another symptom, he felt, of the spending that just goes on and on. Medicare had been a disaster, in his opinion, because of all the laws and tax forms that a person had to fill out. Even the post office, he averred, would be much better if it were run by private enterprise. The mayor of a nearby town said she shared these sentiments. Although she was actively involved in local politics, she was deeply concerned about what she saw happening at the national level. "I'm certainly not for socialized medicine," she said, "and we certainly don't want our government to get involved because most of the programs that they're in are going broke financially. They can't even run the post office." Government, she felt, is just "taking too much control of our lives."

The sentiment that government is incapable of running anything appears frequently as a blanket condemnation of big government. Nothing it does seems to work efficiently or effectively. Yet it also seems that antipathy toward government more typically arises from a specific complaint or two, and then is generalized to other areas. For example, some of our interviews, conducted at the height of public concern about US military intervention in Iraq and Afghanistan, produced strong statements about the wars taking too long or not being waged aggressively enough.[9] These opinions were then followed by equally pessimistic statements—from Republicans and Democrats alike—about government lethargy toward environmental protection, crime, and foreign competition. Different concerns emerged in interviews conducted later during the time that became known as the Great Recession. As assistance from federal and state programs declined, townspeople found themselves left with costly mandates that they were having difficulty funding. These included school buildings, emergency response units, streets, water systems, and other infrastructural items for which towns had taken out loans. Even the most thoughtful town managers who understood the specific nature of the problem were sometimes eager to condemn everything they saw happening in Washington, DC.

The same tendency to jump from one criticism to another was evident in comments about health coverage, education, and energy independence. It mattered little whether people thought government should be doing less or more. What came through most clearly were the values that residents also emphasized when talking about their towns. They liked the fact that in small communities, life seemed to be manageable; the problem with government was that everything was "out of control." The fellow residents of their town worked hard and took responsibility for their lives. Government officials, in contrast, were "piddling around," "wasting our time," and "not getting much accomplished."

The Good That Government Does

But for every person who complains that the United States is on a path toward socialism, there are residents who concede that some—even much—of what government does is beneficial. They mention state and federal grants that have brought a new hospital or police station to their community, subsidized a medical clinic and provided transportation for the elderly, and kept a local factory in business or paved the highway. They often regard these programs with some ambivalence—as an office worker in a town of twenty-two hundred did in asserting that "we work to help ourselves"—and at the same time recognize that applying for government grants is the way to help themselves.

Ambivalence is especially evident in the opinions expressed by farmers and people in farm-related occupations. They hated government controls that limited the acreage they could plant and required them to report in detail about farm business to agricultural agencies. As the manager of a large ranch put it, "We have so darn many regulations that we can hardly make a living anymore." He said ranchers and farmers in his community constantly complained about regulations governing everything from the uses of animal waste to the purchase and spraying of pesticides. They nevertheless acknowledged that government subsidies were necessary to tide farming communities through periods of slack markets and poor crops. Without these payments, "there wouldn't be any farmers and ranchers left," a woman in an agricultural community observed. "There just wouldn't be." She admitted that farm policies were always a "touchy subject," but saw little alternative to price support programs and market regulation.

Acknowledging the necessity of government programs is evident among townspeople without farm connections as well. Mr. Ainsley, the retired man I introduced in chapter 2 who lives with his wife in a town of sixty-five hundred and spends his afternoons playing golf, puts it this way in talking about state and federal government officials: "They're not perfect by a long shot, and they waste all kinds of money and resources, but at least they try to do good." As examples of government programs that are helpful, he mentions breakfast and lunch programs for schoolchildren along with food stamps for the poor. Mr. Ainsley illustrates one of the reasons that residents of small towns see the good that government does as well as the problems. He is one of many such residents who have held a government job—in his case, as a financial administrator. In that capacity he was painfully aware of the inefficiency of government bureaucracy, but naturally believed that the work he and his colleagues were doing was useful.

School administrators are another case of local administrators whose jobs and organizations depend on government. Like Mr. Ainsley, they understand from the inside how government works and why public funding is necessary. The superintendents and principals we talked to were generally appreciative of governors who supported public education, having little to complain about other than concerns that one part of the state—especially cities—might be getting more than its share of public funds. Administrators in small towns recognized that the quality of their schools depended heavily on state budgets as well as local bond issues. Like other citizens, they disliked federal regulations. "We've already been audited twice this year," one superintendent complained, "and now they want to do it again."

Having worked in government inflected the manner in which residents spoke about politics and the content of their opinions. Although they often knew more than their neighbors about local, state, and national politics, they were sometimes cautious about expressing their views. This was especially true of appointed officials, such as school superintendents, city managers, and county clerks. They said that they had learned to keep the peace by keeping their opinions to themselves. Like religion, politics was a topic they felt should not be discussed in polite company. Even in confidential interviews, they were sometimes reluctant to say which party they preferred or what they thought about the current presidential administration.

Others, though, took just the opposite view. They felt it best to state their opinions forthrightly and took some pleasure in doing so. These were more frequently elected officials who were used to taking sides on partisan issues. For example, a man we interviewed who lived in a town of fewer than five hundred people and had served one term in the state legislature as well as many years in county government joked that he got "foot in mouth disease" once in a while, and was one of those people about whom suspicions of being an idiot were confirmed when he opened his mouth, yet he took pride in speaking his mind. Others felt the same way about themselves and their neighbors. They said stereotypes of small-town residents being too polite to disagree with one another were untrue of their community. People were more than willing, they said, to express themselves and to do so with passion. And that was true whether it was an issue that really mattered or merely a topic of conversation. Ms. Clarke, the county extension agent, observed that in her community of thirty-three hundred, government mostly "gives us something to yell about."

Town Politics

With such prevailing skepticism toward big government, the fact that sweetens townspeople's attitude toward local government is mainly that it is local. The division between "us" and "them" that separates townspeople from state and federal officials does not apply. Local officials are, as one resident says, people "we can talk to" and "they understand." Or as another resident says about the elected officials in his community of three thousand, "They treat me pretty well." So he regards them as "square shooters," notwithstanding the general suspicion he feels toward politicians. In the abstract, the result is trust. More concretely, being able to communicate on a firsthand basis amounts to working out practical solutions that make sense for specific persons in particular situations.

A good example is the story told by a pig farmer who lives in a town of about five thousand people. "One of my friends came home drunk one night," the man recalled. The friend was a paraplegic who had driven home drunk and was now crawling across the grass from his car to the front door of his house. "The cops came along and were trying to arrest him, but he was very strong in his upper body, and they were having a real tussle. When they called the station, the dispatcher said, 'Don't arrest him, just put him to bed.' " The man telling the story said it illustrates the "mind-set" in his town. He knows all the cops by name. If he were driving drunk, he knows they would arrest him and he would deserve it. But if it were something minor, like not having his seat belt fastened, they would probably just give him a warning. The point, he says, is that in a town of five thousand, people treat each other the way they do because they know each other. "When you have an issue that needs to be resolved, you go to the city council, and they listen to you." The electric utility and zoning boards operate the same way, he says. "You get to know the people and what's going on here," he concludes, and "it works better" that way.

In another town of about the same size, a resident who has served on the town council offers an observation that sounds similar. He has little patience for big governmental bureaucracies, but local government, he feels, knows the community well enough to figure out what it needs and be effective in making improvements. Little things, such as zoning laws and rules about mowing lawns, keep the community attractive and yet do not require heavy-handed enforcement. "It's all part of the civil order," he says. "[We] do a good job at it. But the state and federal [officials], they just get in the way."

The town leaders we talked to emphasized that they spend a great deal of time making residents feel as if programs are personalized to particular situations. The ones who felt successful in doing this often ran unopposed in local elections or had held appointed office for an extended period. They were trusted because the community sensed that whatever laws and regulations were in force, could also be tailored—not bent but adapted—to particular needs. It was their familiarity with the distinctive aspects of the community that mattered.

A rough sense of the differences between trust of local officials and trust of the national government can be seen in figure 9.2, which shows the proportion of respondent's in Putnam's national social capital benchmark survey who said they trust their local government to do what is right "just about always" or "most of the time," and who said the same about the national government. In the absence of direct information about community size, the figure shows comparisons for respondents living in less and more densely populated areas. The proportions of respondents who trust their local government decline (with some variation in between) from almost 50 percent in the least populated areas to about 30 percent in the most populated communities, while the proportions of people who trust the national government rise slightly as population density increases from just under 30 percent to slightly more than 30 percent. Thus, as was also the case in our qualitative interviews, there was a considerable gap in the least populated areas between trust toward the local versus national government.[10]

The appointed officials we interviewed were especially aware of the need to cultivate trust by tailoring their efforts to particular situations, and at the same time avoiding the appearance of favoritism or partisanship. Of all the people we talked to, they were the most relieved to know that their names and the identities of their towns would not be disclosed. They did not want to be viewed as too closely associated with one party or another, and indeed disliked the partisan conflicts they saw on the national

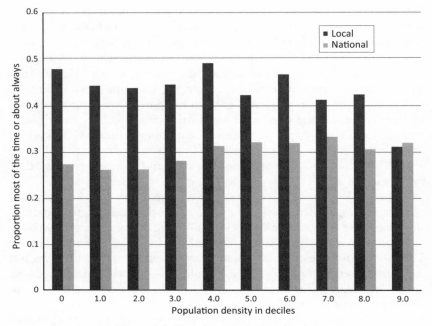

Figure 9.2 Trust by population density

stage. As one town manager explained when asked about national politics, "People have gotten away from being statesmen, and they rely on the same old posturing and ideologies." For that reason, he tries to avoid becoming identified with either party. "Locally, we get things done," he says, "because people know people and just want to do the right thing."

Mr. Helder, the town manager we met in chapter 2, took the job as a short-term interim replacement and has now held the position for fifteen years. He says he learned in school that town government was sort of OK, state government was better, and the federal government was best. But he now thinks local government is about as good as it gets. He is frustrated with state and federal government because of decisions in which he has little say. Lately, regulations governing utility companies have become a thorn in the flesh. "We could be 100 percent for something, and they could say 'no,' and we could be 100 percent against something, and they could say 'yes.'" But like many of the local officials we talked to, his views were nuanced. He says thinking that state and federal government can make magic happen leads only to disappointment. Instead, he tries to cultivate trust by inviting representatives to come and mingle over coffee with ordinary people. "[We] have an open talk where people can just come over and talk to them." He believes firmly in democracy from the bottom up. That means spending a lot of time soliciting ideas from local residents. He knows they are all busy working, so instead of organizing committee meetings, he visits with them at their places of work.

Howard Collins is the city manager in a coastal community of eight thousand that depends heavily on the oil and gas industry for its tax base. For decades the community was solidly Democratic, but since the 1980s it has been solidly Republican. That has not eliminated the need to cultivate trust to get anything accomplished. Mr. Collins recently succeeded in getting a comprehensive strategic growth plan approved and a ten million dollar public bond offering to construct a new municipal building. Most of the effort involved meeting with small groups to make them feel that the idea was theirs. "We got over two hundred people involved in the process," he recalls. Initially there was a lot of negativity, but eventually people started to believe that things could happen. "I don't want to sound like I'm bragging," he says, "but trust is a lot bigger than it was."

This level of trust and cooperation does not mean that local politics are free of controversy. As we saw in chapter 6, community leaders earn respect by serving voluntarily and helping their neighbors, and just as easily lose respect when they are viewed as selfish, lazy, or overly ambitious, or when an issue such as school consolidation or tax assessments becomes divisive. A leader in a town barely covering a single square mile, for example, described the situation in his community as one of constant bickering. Of the three town council members, one of them was usually voted off every year. The townspeople are "never happy," this leader says. The result was so much instability that nothing much was ever accomplished. This was a town of six hundred, so the local residents were content to leave anything important, such as fire and police protection, to the county. In another town residents portrayed their local government as being in utter turmoil as a result of an out-of-town leader deliberately trying to shake things up. In yet another town, all hell broke loose when the council decided to save the community of three thousand some money by turning the job of police dispatching over to the county.

Although they were generally far happier with local officials than with state and federal government, many of the townspeople we interviewed sensed that local government was not as accommodating as it used to be—and this concern aggravated fears that community life as they knew it was fading. Mr. Grimshaw described the change this way: "When I was young, the attitude was, 'You elected us and we're here to serve you.' You'd go into the city hall, and it was 'What can I do for you?'" Now there is a different attitude, he thinks, that says in effect, "We're in charge of you and we're going to tell you what to do." A man in another town complained of a similar shift in government, noting that he was always being told about some new ordinance the town council had passed. Yet another man thought the problem was the growing professionalization of local officials. He felt it would be better if all the officials had regular jobs instead of being employed full-time by the government.

These comments reinforce impressions that can still be found in some textbooks on local government that small-town politics are mostly driven by personalities and cliques.[11] While it is certainly important that local officials are known personally and relate well with other influential persons in their communities, this impression is far less accurate than it may have been in the past. In all but the smallest towns, appointed administrators with advanced education or on-the-job training in public administration carry out most of the day-to-day tasks of supervision and planning, and elected officials are increasingly expected to be knowledgeable about complex legal and fiscal issues. In our interviews, we were impressed with the professionalism and technical knowledge of local officials, far more than with evidence of encrusted parochialism. Nor was it true that residents were obsessed with personalities—any more than is true of major media coverage of national politics—at the expense of interest in substantive issues. When asked about local politics, residents typically commented, both positively and negatively, about issues of substantive concern, ranging from school bonds to property taxes, and from police protection to streets and sewers. They may have disliked what they thought was going on in Washington, DC, but it was local issues that interested them more. Animal control, potholes, crime, vandalism, ambulance service, the park, and the nursing home—these were the issues that mattered.

TENSIONS IN THE SOCIAL FABRIC

The slow pace of change that many residents appreciate about their small communities generally augurs well for local politics. When things stay the same, the tried-and-true methods that have worked well in the past can be counted on to work well in the future. We have seen, though, that small towns are frequently the locations of natural disasters and other traumatic events. A cyclone rips through the community, a flood devastates the town, or a fire destroys a significant portion of Main Street. What effect do these events have on local politics?

We previously considered instances in which catastrophic events became the occasion for narratives about the strength of community spirit. Although their lives may have been profoundly disrupted at the time, residents are able in retrospect to construct stories about coming together, feeling close to their neighbors, and cooperating to overcome temporary hardship. As the tale is told and retold, it becomes an important part of local lore. The response to a catastrophic incident demonstrates that the townspeople are helpful and the community is resilient.

These narratives usually leave out the seamier side of what may have happened. Collective trauma generates multiple interpretations of what happened, how it occurred, what went wrong, and what should be done better next time. Frequently the most obvious culprit is government. Allegations emerge about how the federal government should never have built the dam that failed, government scientists and engineers missed the toxic chemicals that seeped into the local water supply, and local officials were slow in upgrading the emergency weather-warning and fire equipment. As time passes, some residents are able to secure insurance payments and rebuild more quickly than others. Whatever tensions may have already been present are exacerbated.

One of the more candid illustrations of this kind of community conflict took place in an agricultural town of about a thousand people. The town was located in a relatively prosperous area with rich flat fields that generally yielded above average crops of corn and soybeans, and provided sufficient income to keep local stores in business and support excellent schools. In 1995, the worst tornado that had ever happened anywhere in the state ripped through the town. One person was killed, and scattered farmhouses and outbuildings over a twenty-mile span were damaged or destroyed. One end of town was completely unaffected, but the other end sustained heavy losses. The fire station and one of the oldest church buildings were completely torn apart. The elementary school that was almost new and symbolized the town's prosperity was leveled. The cleanup effort took months. Some of the displaced residents never returned. A decade later much of the town had been rebuilt. Compared with neighboring towns, a large majority of the houses and stores were new. But scars remained, especially in residents' views of local politics.[12]

The lingering conflict was best described as a division between those who thought the community was better for what had happened and those who did not. The optimists pointed to the new stores and houses, and emphasized the town's resurgent prosperity. They mostly saw the tornado as the start of a new era. They credited the mayor and town council with excellent forward thinking. The other side thought too little of the town's history had been preserved. They wanted to tell a longer story in which the tornado was just the latest of hardships that had also been experienced by previous generations. They faulted the mayor and city council for selfishly exploiting the crisis to their own advantage.

We talked to residents who years later still considered themselves on one side of the controversy or the other. Several recalled the tenth anniversary of the tornado as having been almost as troublesome as the event itself. Those who thought the rebuilding had been done successfully celebrated, while many of the rest refused to participate. Accusations of lying and mismanagement were still being voiced. On several occasions, incumbent town leaders had been replaced in local elections. "The longer you're in office," one disgruntled leader complained, "the more people you tick off."

This community's experience was atypical, both in the extent of the damage it sustained from the disaster itself as well as the duration and severity of the political fallout, yet it nevertheless highlights a crucial point about local politics. Unlike in large communities, where annoyance with local leaders may be resolved through prevailing apathy, it is harder for residents of small towns to ignore what they may dislike about the local leadership. Once the respect and cooperation that normally buttresses local politics is lost, it may be difficult to regain.

WHY REPUBLICANS WIN

Antipathy toward big government, a preference for fiscal conservatism, and an emphasis on small-town self-sufficiency and local autonomy have generally been regarded by political analysts as the stuff of Republican politics more than of Democrats. Many of the leaders and residents I have quoted identify themselves as Republicans. In national data, residents of small nonmetropolitan towns are in fact more likely than those of larger communities to identify as Republicans. This tendency is evident in figure 9.3, which shows the odds of small-town residents identifying as Republicans (or Democrats) relative to the odds of residents in larger communities saying the same thing. Since the start of the twenty-first century, the odds of being Republican are approximately 30 percent higher for small-town residents as for people living in larger communities. And the odds of being a Democrat are about 20 percent lower. The figure shows that preference for the Republican Party among small-town residents diverged sharply from the comparable preference in large communities in the 1970s, but nearly disappeared during the Reagan era in the 1980s, and has diverged again in more recent years. In fact, the spread between preferences for Republicans versus Democrats is wider in recent years than it was in the 1970s. The figure also estimates what these odds would be if differences between residents of small towns and people living in larger communities were taken into account—such as differences in age, gender, race, region, and level of education. Most of the divergence remains when these differences are taken into account (as shown by the "adjusted" odds ratios). In addition, less of why small-town residents disproportionately identify themselves as Republicans in recent years can be explained by these other factors than was true in the 1970s.[13]

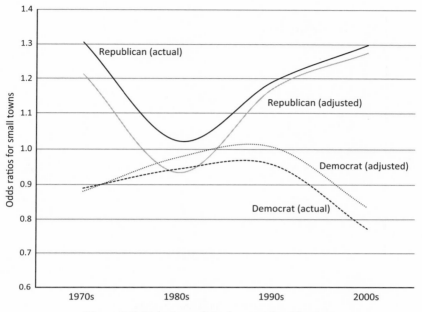

Figure 9.3 Relative political party identification

Despite the fact that Republicans are relatively better represented in small towns than Democrats are, a sufficient number of Democrats and independents live in small towns for the question to be posed, Why are small towns so often regarded as bastions of Republicanism? One reason is the winner-take-all way in which election outcomes are determined. This means that a town or county that gives a majority of its votes to a Republican candidate comes to be regarded as a Republican stronghold, even if a large minority in that location vote Democratic. For example, in the 2008 presidential election between Republican John McCain and Democrat Barack Obama, voters living in nonmetropolitan counties composed mostly of small towns did in fact vote in larger percentages for McCain than their counterparts did in larger metropolitan areas (figure 9.4). And yet the proportions for McCain in the smaller nonmetropolitan areas averaged less than 60 percent. That had also been the pattern in 2004, when smaller nonmetropolitan counties averaged 59 percent for George W. Bush (compared with 42 percent in the largest metropolitan areas). As political scientists Morris P. Fiorina, Samuel J. Abrams, and Jeremy C. Pope observe in their book *Culture War? The Myth of a Polarized America*, the extreme divide between red and blue states is not so extreme when actual voting practices are taken into account.[14]

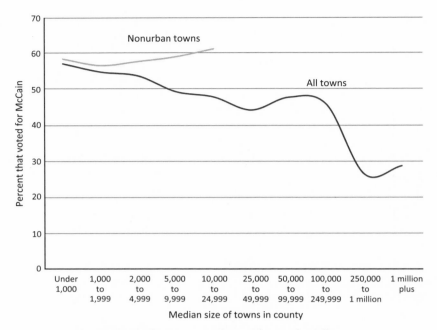

Figure 9.4 Red state voting by incidence of small towns

There is another dynamic in small towns, however, that analysis at the state or national level fails to take into account. At the local level, especially when a large segment of the voting population considers itself independent, elections depend heavily on candidates' and party operatives' ability to shape local opinions. In our interviews, we found three factors that worked decisively in favor of Republicans. These factors are evident in town after town, regardless of region, and especially in communities that are predominantly white.

One factor that favors Republicans in many towns is enjoying at least a small edge over Democrats in local party affiliations. Although local candidates are not always from the same party as state and national winners, the local candidates win often enough on the Republican side to be in charge of town councils, school boards, and county commissions, and enjoy political patronage in appointed jobs, such as road maintenance or agricultural support. With a slight edge in the popular vote, Republicans can be more visibly involved in local community activities, and at times influence state and national elections in small ways. For example, polling stations can be set up in prolife churches, and the town council members can escort older voters to the polls.

A related factor is that voters in states in which Republican candidates often win may be more likely to register as Republicans, even if they are Democrats or independents, in order to participate in Republican primaries. Ms. Clarke, for instance, says she is a Republican mainly because she lives in a Republican state, which is "very different from being Republican," she notes, than actually being a Republican. "If I want to vote in any primary elections, most of the time I need to be a Republican." A resident of another Republican state says nearly the same thing. "I'm definitely a Democrat," he asserts. "But I am not a registered Democrat. As a matter of fact, I am a registered Republican because of the primary issue. We don't have Democratic primaries here because there are so few of us. I like to be able to vote in the primaries." A woman in another town explains, "I've been a Democrat ever since I began to vote, but I changed my affiliation a few years ago so I could vote in the primaries, and have an effect on local elections for sheriff, county attorney, and the like. So I changed and I just haven't seen a reason to change back. So what does that say? I don't know." Another woman who is still a registered Democrat says almost the same thing. "If you're not a Republican, you really don't have choices," she comments, referring to the primary elections. "How crazy is that?"

Dominance of the primaries can of course backfire. We found voters who were registered as Republicans but were deeply unhappy about Republican policies. This was especially true during the last years of George W. Bush's presidency, when the war in Iraq was sinking his administration's popularity. "Don't get me started," says James Jefferson, an eighty-six-year-old Republican who lives in a town of five hundred surrounded by cotton fields. He had served in the navy during World War II and hated seeing lives torn up by the fighting in Iraq. "We have no business there. The CIA information was manipulated by the president to get us into that war." That made him mad. Lately, it seems to him that the Republicans are just trying to help the wealthiest top 4 or 5 percent. In his view, the war had been fought for money and oil. That was Mr. Steuben's reaction as well. He remembered attending a Republican rally that was so "frickin' scary" he almost became a Democrat. He would have, too, except the Democrats seemed to be "ass wimps" who just sat around bitching.

A third factor is the intensity with which positions on particular issues are held. As we saw in the last chapter, abortion is one such concern for many residents of small towns. It is the one issue that they say influences how they vote. They may be an independent, but they always choose a prolife candidate over a prochoice one, and that nearly always means voting Republican. Intensity may be especially important in small towns where people know they are likely to be dealing with one another for a long time—as neighbors, as fellow members of the coop, at the grocery store, when a tire needs fixed, to file a deed, or for their insurance. When disagreements about politics arise, they have two choices. One is to openly take sides and talk through the issues. That happens often enough. But the other is to avoid making waves. That can be the preferred option, especially on issues deemed to be moral as well as political. As we saw in comments about abortion, people on the prochoice side mentioned that their opinion was in the minority, emphasized that theirs was just a personal view, and admitted they did not express it publicly very often.[15]

The tendency for prochoice residents to keep quiet is evident when people talk more generally about their political views. Some take pride in being among the town's few Democrats, occasionally running for office themselves on the minority ticket or championing their views to rankle the local Republican establishment; others retreat. A case in point is Lorraine McBride, a woman in her fifties who grew up in a small mining community, lived in Massachusetts for two decades, and now lives in her hometown. Having gone to college and having lived in a more liberal part of the country, she describes herself as a liberal Democrat. That puts her in a minority. She is also divorced, which sets her apart from many of the local residents. "I have very different viewpoints from the people who live here," she acknowledges. "I'm still clinging to the East Coast. Most of my friends have liberal viewpoints, and I'm in a very conservative community here." She maintains those opinions not by making a public show of them in her local community but rather by keeping in touch with friends elsewhere. She is in a good position to do so because she still has business clients on the East Coast.

We encountered a surprising number of people like Mrs. McBride. They held liberal views on social issues, prided themselves on being independents yet usually voted Democratic, and seldom said much about their views locally. Their profile varied in terms of age, gender, race, location, and occupation, but usually included something that caused them to feel different—socially as well as politically—from their small-town neighbors. Like Mrs. McBride, they had lived in another part of the country and made friends with whom they remained in contact. Or in other cases, they had children who lived elsewhere and provided a reason to identify with political opinions uncommon among their local friends. In still other instances, they had experienced a falling out with the local Republican establishment over a matter as small as a zoning regulation or school controversy. For example, one woman recalled her high school biology teacher being "run out of town" for teaching evolution. She has never felt quite at home since then.

For people who felt at odds with the local political climate, the simplest recourse was to draw a sharp boundary between a private space, in which they could talk as little or as much about politics as they might wish, and a public space where they knew they would be in the minority. Mrs. Zlotnik, the woman we met in chapter 4 who enjoys the smell of Douglas fir in her coastal town of six thousand, illustrates how a boundary like this may work. The community, she says, is very, very Republican, but she considers herself a progressive and votes Democratic. Her private space includes her thirty or so closest friends in town. To keep on amicable terms, they keep things light and never discuss politics. They probably know that she is more liberal on some issues than they are. And yet the tacit taboo against talking about politics limits her potential influence at the same time that it eases her social relationships.[16]

GRASSROOTS ACTIVISM

By nearly all indications, small-town America has relatively little to offer in terms of actual muscle for political operatives who might wish to organize a populist movement. Despite the fact that as many as thirty million Americans live in small towns, they do not represent a majority of registered voters in any state, and are scattered too widely to be easily organized in one place—at least much less so than people who are concentrated in populous metropolitan areas. Residents of small towns may be more conservative on average than people living in larger communities, but they are by no means overwhelmingly conservative. The most promising ideological appeal that a populist movement might make would be to the antigovernment sentiment that prevails in many small towns. And yet this sentiment includes suspicion toward both of the major political parties along with much that happens in state capitals and Washington, DC. As we have seen, townspeople hold strong opinions on some issues, and are willing to speak up if they feel that their local officials are not serving them well, or their churches and schools are being threatened, but prevailing community norms emphasize getting along, being friendly with fellow inhabitants, keeping quiet about issues that might escalate into community conflicts, and using common sense to work out disagreements.

The possibility of a new populism emerging with widespread support in small towns and rural areas has nevertheless been widely discussed, largely in conjunction with the Tea Party movement. Loosely organized in scattered locations around the country, and publicized through conservative talk radio and cable television, the Tea Party was composed of fiscal conservatives who opposed what they saw as dramatically rising federal government bureaucracy, regulation, and deficit spending. The movement included arguments favoring grassroots activism and traditional values.[17] Polls showed that popular support for the movement was strongest in predominantly white rural communities (figure 9.5).[18]

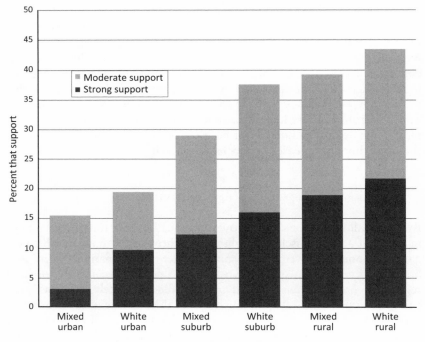

Figure 9.5 Tea Party movement support

Some of the people we interviewed were strongly in favor of the Tea Party's activities. "I absolutely love Sarah Palin," one woman who voted for McCain in 2008 and was deeply troubled by the Obama administration told us. "I love Sarah Palin because she is really not afraid to speak her mind. She stands for a lot of things that American people feel but don't necessarily voice. I think people have a right to speak and I think it is about time they do so." This woman, whose community of seven thousand was suffering from high unemployment and low wages, felt that her fellow residents had been complacent too long and had "just let government take over." The Tea Party, in her view, has brought awareness to that fact and given the people a voice.[19]

Mr. Collins, the city manager in a gas and oil town of eight thousand who we met earlier, says there is a lot of interest in the Tea Party movement in his community. Although the population where he lives is racially and ethnically mixed, he says that the people he talks to are generally upset with the federal government. "They're disgruntled with the Democrats and they're disgruntled with the Republicans," he says. "They don't know who they like." He thinks the trouble is partly that the federal government tries to make "one size fit all" instead of letting local communities tailor programs to their own needs. The No Child Left Behind education program was a disaster, in his view. Lately, the threat of higher taxes and disgust about the government bailing out large companies seems to be driving popular unrest.[20]

Mr. Helder, who is also a town manager, keeps his political views to himself. As an appointed official in a community that prides itself on tolerance of diversity, he has to. But in private, his distrust of Washington, DC, comes through. He credits Obama with rallying people and giving them hope, but does not think people in Washington truly care about creating jobs. He likes Palin. He figures that anybody who became a governor without going to Harvard or Yale, and who is constantly being derided by the media, cannot be all that bad. Besides, he says, "she's one gorgeous woman." He isn't sure he would actually vote for her. His point is rather that somehow the public needs to regroup because Washington has gotten completely out of touch.

Yet the relatively sparse population of small towns leaves open the question of how people in these communities might become mobilized in sufficient numbers to support a populist movement. One critical factor in all such previous efforts is communication, whether in the small discussions that took place in eighteenth-century taverns and town halls, in the newspapers circulated by nineteenth-century populists, or on the cassette tapes used by insurgents in late twentieth-century uprisings in other countries. While studies note the importance of intimate discussions in coffee shops and church basements, they increasingly emphasize the value of long-distance communication that links leaders, constituents, and donors across regions.[21] The current inhabitants of small-town America are better connected with one another as well as like-minded citizens in metropolitans than ever before. Cable news channels, which research shows to be far more given to expressions of opinion and commentary than network news, have long been available in even the remotest rural communities.[22] More recently, the Internet of course connects to Web sites about social and political issues as well.[23] The woman I mentioned in the last chapter who found the arguments she needed to dispute evolution is one example of the Internet's ability to connect people with similar views.

Besides communication, a second critical factor in mobilizing social movements is frequent elections and an abundance of public offices to be filled in these elections. The United States has one of the largest numbers of local governmental units of any late industrial society when consideration is given to the existence of village, town, township, county, and state legislative districts, and school boards, water districts, park commissions, and regional planning committees.[24] In most small towns, voters are asked to go to the polls at least once every two years to elect a state governor as well as a representative to the US Congress, and in many instances elections are held more frequently for school bond approvals, special referenda about taxes, amendments to state constitutions, and revisions of local law enforcement codes. Even in communities dominated by one or the other of the major political parties, primaries are often hotly contested. The frequency with which elections occur has two crucial consequences. One is that citizens have to make up their minds: despite having nuanced views or thinking of themselves as independents and wanting to get along with their neighbors, they have to choose and thus become part of the majority or minority. The other consequence is that the many elected and appointed officials gain experience in governing, and thereby are drawn into the political process.

The other factor that a social movement must have is leadership. In small communities leadership depends, as we saw in chapter 6, on networking and serving the community in formal or informal capacities to earn the respect of fellow residents. That means opportunities for elected officials to gain respect by serving in volunteer roles, and other residents to gain and maintain local visibility by showing up regularly at town meetings, engaging in service activities, and being involved in social networks and community organizations. Not just anyone can come in and achieve this kind of standing in the community, but opportunities for leadership are open to those who may have long-standing family ties in the town, and occupy important roles in local businesses and churches.

In our interviews, taking place as they did prior to and during a major national election as well as a subsequent midterm election, we talked with community leaders who were strongly supportive of candidates from one or the other of the major parties, but also who were sufficiently troubled by what was happening in their state capital and especially Washington that they were eager to throw their weight behind almost anyone who promised a new direction. Conservative clergy were often the most outspokenly supportive of a clean slate because they had been frustrated in efforts to roll back laws allowing abortion or restrict the rights of gays and lesbians, and were now convinced that liberals were taking over the country. These clergy were upset that school prayer had been disallowed and were concerned that sexual immorality was weakening the nation, and willing to speak on these issues to their congregations and in other forums.

These concerns are well illustrated in the work of Rev. Todd Buchanan, a Baptist pastor who graduated in the 1980s from one of the nation's most conservative seminaries and currently preaches each Sunday to a flock of seventy-five people in a town of twenty-four hundred that has lost nearly a third of its population in the time he has been there—and yet continues to support twenty churches. Rev. Buchanan says there is no political topic too large or controversial for him to preach about, and it annoys him to no end that African American churches seem to get away

Profile: Sheridan, Wyoming

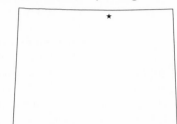

With a population of more than seventeen thousand, Sheridan is one of the larger towns in north-central Wyoming. In recent years, it has become a magnet for tourists interested in dude ranch vacations, fishing, and hunting, and has continued to serve as an important supplier of the nation's coal.

In 2008, Sheridan County went for John McCain and Sarah Palin in the US presidential election by a 68 to 30 percent margin. That was a weak victory in the region for the Republican ticket. To the south, 77 percent of voters in Johnson County opted for the GOP, and to the east in Campbell and Crook counties, 80 percent did. Sheridan voters went with Lyndon Johnson in 1964, but had been solidly Republican ever since. In 2010, Republican candidates for the House of Representatives, governor, and secretary of state won by a decisive three-quarters majority. Republican candidates for state legislature and county offices ran unopposed.

The Sheridan Tea Party held its first meeting at Grinnell Plaza in front of the city hall on April 15, 2009. Its supporters called for a decrease in government spending and reduction in the size of the federal government. "We're fed up with redistribution of wealth," one of the speakers said. "We want free markets, not freeloaders." A year later, the movement's rally drew a crowd of 260 and was co-sponsored by Wyoming Gun Owners, a grassroots organization promoting states rights and opposed to federal legislation mandating health insurance.

A statewide poll in 2010 showed widespread support in Wyoming for the Tea Party movement. Fifty-one percent of those surveyed said they agreed or strongly agreed with the movement's aims. Eighty-four percent of Tea Party supporters had misgivings about the federal government, 85 percent were skeptical of claims about global warming, and 90 percent were concerned about immigration.

Ninety-five percent of Tea Party supporters thought President Barack Obama was doing a fair or poor job, compared with 30 percent of those who disagreed with the movement.

Thirty-five percent of those favorable to the movement thought Obama was a Muslim, and 40 percent doubted that he had been born in the United States. "He's off-the-charts liberal," one voter explained. "He's a socialist. That just scares me. I don't think I've ever been almost physically sick as when Obama got elected." It was just the "anomaly of electing a black man that got him elected."

with hosting and endorsing political candidates, while white churches like his are threatened with losing their tax-exempt status when they do the same thing.

Rev. Buchanan has a ready audience every Sunday when he preaches against abortion and what he calls the "pornification" of the United States. He has yet to attend any of the protest rallies that have been happening in a nearby city, but he could easily become a spokesperson in his community for any conservative candidate seeking to move state and national politics to the Right. In 2008 he supported McCain, but without enthusiasm. "I don't think he was really a conservative," he says. "Now Sarah Palin, yes, she would have been ideal, or [Governor Mike] Huckabee."

In the ensuing months, Rev. Buchanan became increasingly troubled by what he heard coming out of Washington from the Obama administration. "The president is selling out America through sin," he says. "He's promoting it just like the abortion issue. He made the first statement out of the box that he would do all he could to push abortion. The health insurance that he's promoting is going to destroy the baby boomers of my generation. When I get ten or twelve years older, I won't be able to have open-heart surgery or a lung transplant because I won't be able to afford it. He's trying to change it from being run by the people to being run by socialism."

For Rev. Buchanan, the thought of dying for lack of affordable medical care is merely an example of the wider peril he envisions overtaking the United States. He watches Fox News faithfully because "they of course tell you the whole story." The more he watches, the more he learns about abortion, euthanasia, mercy killings, and unreasonable lawsuits against doctors that drive up the cost of health care. These problems bring to his mind biblical warnings about evil in government. "Whenever you have a righteous man in office," he remarks, "the people rejoice, and when you don't, it's just the opposite." The Obama administration is doing everything it can, he believes, to undermine his ability as a pastor to speak against evildoers, such as the homosexuals who are "trying to destroy the American family."

"The world's in a mess," Rev. Buchanan says. "We're fulfilling the Bible. The Bible said there'd be a charismatic guy [who would] come on the scene, and people would vote for him, and we have that charismatic leader. He's been voted in. I'm not saying he's the anti-Christ, but he has some of those tendencies. I've never seen anybody get up on public television and tell so many lies." It disturbs Rev. Buchanan that President Obama has deluded so many Americans into liking him. "He's doing the same thing that Hitler did, and the sad thing is that people are just sitting back and letting him do it. Nobody's saying a word other than a few conservatives."[25]

- 1 0 -

Keep Your Doors Open
Shaping the Future

HOW ARE ORDINARY RESIDENTS OF SMALL TOWNS shaping the future of their communities? Are they encouraging their children to stay—if not in their own town, then in some other community like it? Or are contemporary residents—like previous generations—instilling aspirations in their offspring that can only be realized in cities and suburbs? Essentially the question is one of basic values. It may not be surprising that people who have chosen to spend their lives in small places make the best of it—talking about how much they enjoy their friends and neighbors, reveling in the warm greetings of passersby, showing up week after week at the same place of worship, and basking in good-spirited agreement about moral and political issues. But do they value small-town life enough to tell their children they should stay?

The answer, frankly, is no. If small-town residents were successfully arguing that the next generation should stay close by, these communities would be considerably larger than they are. Current residents themselves, as we have seen, seldom say they opted to live where they do because of pressures from parents or grandparents. One does not have to read too closely between the lines to see that residents were guided by circumstances as much as deeply held values. This was where the family farm happened to be located. It was the place that had an opening for a teacher or doctor. An aging relative became ill and needed care. This was where a boyfriend lived. Housing was cheap.

Enough of these circumstances work in their favor that most small towns will survive. Population growth nationwide has been sufficient to repopulate small towns, even if most of this growth occurs in large metropolitan areas. That does not mean small towns can move successfully into the future without strategic planning. The adage that standing still means moving backward holds true. For good reason, town leaders work at attracting new jobs and workers, better roads, and community improvements.

But in this chapter, I want to focus on the future that small-town residents are encouraging the coming generation to seek. If loyalty to the community itself is not that important, what is? Is it simply that the individualistic American success ethic prevails? That would be the most likely explanation. After all, social observers have long held that however much Americans might talk about community spirit, they are nearly always willing to sacrifice that spirit on the altar of getting ahead. Or is there something subtler at work? Are there perhaps understandings of what is significant in life that are not so different in small towns than anywhere else, and yet that cast the relationship between individuals and their communities in a different light?

From listening closely to residents of small towns talking about what they would do over if they could—and from considering what parents, grandparents, teachers, and clergy say they consider important to advise young people—my conclusion is that the continuing role people envision themselves and their communities playing is more complex than commonly supposed. Parents want to rectify the shortcomings of their own decisions, even if they do not regret the lives they have made for themselves. They recognize the constraints as well as advantages of living in small towns. Higher education is generally valued, as are hard work and good planning. And yet the aim of it all is less to get ahead—at least if that means the usual rewards of success in a career—and more to experience as much as life has to offer. That means taking risks, experimenting, moving out of one's comfort zone, and gaining maturity. On the way, a sojourner does not leave the community behind as much as take it along. Its values are internalized, just as the childhood habits instilled in home and hearth have always been. But crucially, as learning and maturity are understood to take longer, and parents and grandparents live longer and more easily stay in communication, the community literally remains active whether close at hand or at a distance.

THE IMPORTANCE OF COLLEGE

To begin to see how what I have just described gains expression in real life, the place to start is with the most commonly understood means of getting ahead: going to college. Whether they themselves went to college or not, nearly everyone we talked to in small towns thinks it is a good idea these days for young people to go to college if they possibly can. This is sometimes true of residents who were unable to attend college themselves, and is especially common among people who did attend college.[1]

What residents recognize is that young people who go away to college are less likely to return than those who do not seek college training. An

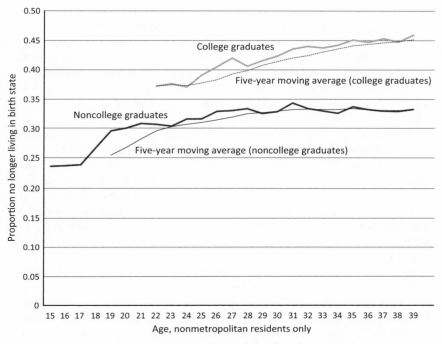

Figure 10.1 Geographic mobility by education

indication of the difference is evident in figure 10.1, which shows the probability of young people living in a different state from the one in which they were born. Among fifteen-year-olds living in nonmetropolitan areas, the probability of having moved from their birth state is about one in four. The probably rises to about three in ten by the time young people who have not graduated from college reach age twenty-two, but it is seven points higher for young people of the same age who have graduated from college. Furthermore, the probability of having left one's birth state continues to rise among college graduates, reaching 45 percent by the end of people's thirties, whereas the probability stabilizes at 33 percent for young adults who have not graduated from college. In all likelihood, the differences would be even larger if comparisons could be made including residents who grew up in nonmetropolitan settings and currently live in metropolitan areas.[2]

For those who have been to college and have been able to remain in a small town, it is at least conceivable that the next generation may be able to do the same. I was struck by this possibility when listening to Olaf Hennink, a fifty-year-old chemist, talking about his experiences and the advice he would give. Mr. Hennink was raised on a farm but knew by the time he started high school that he wanted to go to college. He majored in chemistry and went immediately to a master's program at a university in another state. Being away from his home community and ambivalent about his plans, he returned home and farmed for several years with his father. When the farm economy went south, he found a job working for a large chemical-processing company in a small town about twenty miles away.

The advice that Mr. Hennink says he would give someone graduating from high school in his town is to "go to a good college and get at least a master's degree in a scientific field." The reason to do this, he explains, is that a person "needs the credentials to get a good job and be satisfied with it." He has two sons and a daughter. The oldest son has followed his father's counsel, majoring in mechanical engineering and now working at a manufacturing firm in his parents' hometown. The second son has gone off to another state to college. His return is more doubtful. The daughter is still in high school.

Others were less certain that a college-educated young person would be likely to live in a small town, but considered higher education imperative nonetheless. A teacher in an unincorporated village of fewer than a hundred residents observed that neither of his parents had gone to high school and it had taken him more than a dozen years attending classes part-time to finish college. His dream for his three children is that they all complete at least a college degree.

In few instances are there any explicit concerns that a young person from a small town might be incapable of succeeding in college. There is, however, recognition of the difficulties that might be involved. For example, a teacher living in a town of six thousand notes the tension that a young person in her community might face between wanting to start a family and taking the time to get an education. "I would advise getting as much education as you can before you settle," she says, "because once you settle down, then you have other obligations." Psychological issues, such as doubting one's capabilities, might also pose difficulties. A financial consultant in a town of seven hundred, for instance, emphasizes the need to "have self-confidence to go forward for an education." She considers it important not to be intimated by the fact that there are "a lot of very smart, well-educated people in this world."[3]

There are of course exceptions to the view that young people should go to college. Parents and educators in small towns are realistic enough to know that college is not for everyone. "For some people, trade school is going to be the answer and probably more useful than college," observed a farmer in one of the towns we visited. That was especially true in his community, which was too small to employ more than a handful of college graduates. A school superintendent in a town of four thousand had the same opinion. "Not everybody needs to go to college," he said. "There are a lot of good jobs out there, opportunities that technical schools and trade schools can provide. A woman who ran an art studio and gallery in another town felt a person nowadays should think twice about going to college because the cost is so high. Her husband thought spending a few years in the military learning to be subservient was a wise choice.

None of these people explicitly offered the view that college is less important for someone growing up in a small town than for a person living in a city. They likely would have denied that notion. Implicit in some of their remarks, though, was the fact that they themselves knew it was possible to make a good life in a small town without a college education, and that knowledge filtered into their perceptions of what it might take for a young person to be happy. Their frame of reference simply focused on the value of other experiences and skills besides college.

A further example is Betty Lundberg, a sixty-year-old mother of two who lives in a town of eight hundred and is married to a farmer who raises cattle. Mrs. Lundberg's dream growing up was to become an airline stewardess and see the world. She never imagined becoming a farmer's wife. But she and her husband-to-be started dating in high school, married soon after, and then worked for a few years in a town of thirteen thousand before taking over his father's farm. If she could have, she says that the one thing she would have done differently is grow up on a farm instead of in town. She thinks farm children learn more skills and gain greater self-confidence. But she is basically satisfied with her life, and feels that the sewing and cooking classes she took in high school along with what she has learned over the years being a wife and mother have been sufficient.

Mrs. Lundberg's thoughts, when asked what she would do now if she were graduating from high school and thinking about the future, turn back to what she actually did. "I'd probably do the same thing again," she says. She would go to town and earn money to get married. Unlike many of the people we talked to, she does not say that she would go to college, even though her parents had lived in a college town and her dad's income would have made tuition possible. The one thing she would have done differently would have been to save more money. That would have come in handy, she comments, because "farming isn't very profitable."

Later on, after talking more about her family and community, Mrs. Lundberg's views about why she would do things pretty much the same become clearer. She loves her town, and being able to walk up and down the streets with the knowledge of who lives in every house. She is glad that her children, now grown, live in small towns—one nearby, and the other an hour and a half away. She regrets it when "kids get out of school [and] don't stay." They "go to a bigger town," she says. "Some of them like to go to big towns, but I don't care for a big town."

Pitfalls to Avoid

While it is true that many people in small towns who have not been to college instinctively point to higher education as the ticket to a better future, it is crucial to recognize that going or not going is not, in their minds, simply a matter of making the right decision about getting an education. Life is more complicated than that. Other considerations come more significantly into play. The decision not to go to college may not have been an option at all. If one were to do it over or give advice to a young person, these other considerations would be more important.

Living in a small community, residents contend, is generally favorable in terms of the values and experiences it provides to young people, but— perhaps because they view it as a sheltered space—a small town is also fraught with pitfalls. "You are who you are with" is how a mother in a town of five thousand summarizes it. For a young person, that is especially true. The worst dangers are present in the friends who drink, use drugs, or engage in other risky activities—ranging from merely carousing around and doing poorly in school, to engaging in promiscuous sex or breaking the law. Apart from these serious perils, residents often mention the ill effects of ordinary circumstances that limit young people's opportunities.

The story Sue Pollard, a woman in her early fifties who lives in a town of five thousand, tells reveals one line of thinking in which circumstances dominate. She was one of eleven children. Her parents lived in a small foothills community, where her father worked as a mechanic. Money was clearly too tight for any of the children to consider going to college. Yet perhaps surprisingly, Mrs. Pollard thinks she could have gone to a community college or state university, working and paying her own way, had it not been for the cultural norms that prevailed in her community.

"All of us girls," she recalls, referring to her sisters and friends in school, "worried about what boys were looking at us." During grade school, she fantasized about becoming a rancher or teacher, but those ideas were short lived. "We got interested in boys and that kind of went out the window," she says. By her first year in high school, her dream was "to be married and have two children." She and her future husband began dating her senior year in high school, and then got married a month after graduating.

If she were doing it over, Mrs. Pollard says that she "would have gone to college and not gotten married right out of high school." She did eventually take some college classes, but she adds, "The longer I put it off, the more frightening it was." The advice she would give today, if she had girls, is simply don't plan your life around a man. "Look after yourself first and don't get sidetracked by the boys."

Mrs. Pollard was hardly alone in stressing the importance of thinking for oneself instead of getting married too quickly and following a man around. To some extent, this sentiment reflects the fact that women and men her age did marry younger than is true now. Although early marriage was probably as common in cities and suburbs as in small towns, the fishbowl in which teenagers who went to small high schools lived undoubtedly added to the pressure. When serious dating routinely took place in high school, a young person without a mate by graduation could fear that time was running out.

Small-town norms against having an abortion or acquiring a reputation as a slut may have also encouraged early marriage. In any case, the advice that small-town residents say they would follow if given a chance to do things differently is frequently to focus less on dating and early marriage. "Oh my," a woman in her early fifties who grew up in a small town and now lives in a city says, "I would say, 'Stop messing around with that guy! Slow down a bit. Take it easy.'"

This advice likely stems from more than just personal experience. Living in a small town, it is easier for residents to know about young people in their community who marry early and do not go on to college for that reason. Marrying early is not the norm, but when it occurs, it stands out. US Census data show that 17 percent of women and 7 percent of men ages sixteen through twenty-one living in nonmetropolitan areas are married or have been married at least once. Controlling statistically for differences in age, race, and gender, the odds within this age group of being married or having been married are at least two-thirds higher in nonmetropolitan areas than in metropolitan ones.[4]

The potential effect of early marriage on college attainment is illustrated by the data summarized in figure 10.2. The data are from the US Census, selected to include persons ranging in age from sixteen through twenty-one living in nonmetropolitan areas at the time the census was taken. For comparison purposes, data are shown for the 1960 census, which was taken at a time when relatively few Americans attended college, and the 1990 census, when a much larger number attended college and before the Census Bureau changed its definitions of metropolitan and nonmetropolitan. In 1960, the odds of a young man who was married having completed at least one year of college were only a quarter of the odds of that being the case for a young man who had not been married (accounting for differences in age and race). Among women, being married reduced the odds even further—to about an eighth compared with women who were not married. By 1990, early marriage was less likely to suppress the odds of going to college, but only marginally so. The odds of

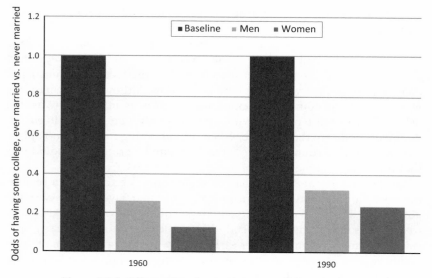

Figure 10.2 Effects of early marriage on college attainment

having some college among young men who were married were about a third as large as among young men who were not married. Among young women, the odds were about a quarter as large among those who were married than among those who were not married.[5]

These data suggest that residents of small towns who worry about the ill effects of early marriage for going to college may not be overreacting by very much if they base their concerns on their own experiences or what their parents said to them a few decades ago. In that era, early marriage dramatically reduced the chances of going on to college, especially for women. The concerns that residents express now continue to be well founded. Although it is relatively rare, early marriage significantly reduces the chances that a young man or woman will go to college, or at least will postpone doing so.

Besides early marriage, the most frequently mentioned pitfall to avoid is narrow-mindedness—a trait that residents associate with living in a small community. As one woman put it, if she had it to do over again, she would try to "not be so narrow minded and not pigeonhole" herself. Another woman said that she had in mind becoming a cosmetologist and never thought about anything else. A farmer's son said he would have liked geology, but never gave enough thought to that as a career option. Some of the people who felt they had closed off their opportunities prematurely blamed themselves. They thought it was their fault, perhaps because they were teenagers with little experience, or were too eager for the security of a job and home. Others, though, attributed their lack of insight to the community. As the woman who said she had pigeonholed herself explained, "I was totally unaware of the possibilities there for my life. I didn't have any female role models doing those things."

We asked people what they thought the best way to avoid or overcome narrow-mindedness or a lack of insight might be. One of the clergy we talked to gave a particularly good answer. Having grown up in a small town, he said he felt as if he had "life wrapped up" because he knew everyone in town and had friends he'd known since they played together in diapers. But going away to college and then seminary jolted him out of his comfort zone. He acknowledges the importance of being open minded, but denies that simply deciding to think broadly is enough. He suggests a threefold approach. First, "pursue your goals and your dreams," which of course implies having a plan in mind. Second, "don't be afraid" and "don't back down, just because you feel uncomfortable or out of place or inadequate"—which is how he felt on leaving the comfort zone of his "Podunk" town. And third, "be careful and go slow," rather than succumbing to pressures to settle into a job or family too quickly.

THE DISADVANTAGES OF LIVING IN A SMALL TOWN

Like this man, most of the residents we talked to in small towns are sufficiently optimistic to believe that a person can do most anything in life, no matter where one has been raised. They believe wholeheartedly that the United States is still a land of opportunity. They do recognize, however, that people are always to some extent products of their environment and that knowledge of the world is shaped by a person's social context. A young person from a small town may be able to achieve anything that they desire, but may have to overcome barriers that would not have been present in a large metropolitan area. That may be especially true for someone from a small town heading off to college with little knowledge of what to expect.

Few residents of small towns think that poor schools are a significant barrier to making something of themselves. The ones who did generally lived in the smallest towns, usually with a sagging economy and declining population, where classes were small and advanced courses were nonexistent. As one young man from a town like this noted, "I really didn't have to apply myself that much." The school, he thought, was good preparation for junior college although not for anything beyond that. But he was not typical. Most small-town residents have heard enough about the problems of inner-city schools to consider themselves fortunate. They often take pride in their local schools, as we have seen, and consider them one of the community's best assets. Frequently they have good reasons for thinking this way. Despite the town's meager size, the school may have a decent tax base or receive enough financial support from the state to accomplish its goals. Test scores and graduation rates are likely to be respectable, if not higher than in many urban locales.[6]

The disadvantages that parents and educators in small towns identify resemble what we considered earlier in discussing the frog-pond effect. A young person may do reasonably well, or even excel at earning good grades or performing in sports or music, and yet feel incapable of succeeding in the wider world. It is all too apparent to this young person that the action is elsewhere. A good student in a high school of two hundred, it seems, would be less competitive in a high school of three thousand, and would be lost at a university of thirty thousand or in a city of three hundred thousand. That might be the self-perception of a reasonably good student. A less talented student could feel even more compromised.

Descriptions of these effects of growing up in a small frog pond vary but usually identify a lack of vision as a central problem. Vision to imagine fruitful opportunities may be lacking because of a realistic understanding of one's limitations. Family financial resources may be limited. It may be impossible to leave one's hometown for greener pastures. A restricted vision may also stem from low self-confidence or simply a lack of role models capable of sparking the imagination.

Bill Sykes is the guidance counselor at a high school of two hundred students in a town of just over three thousand. For the past ten years he has been struggling to enlarge the vision of the students he counsels. Although he feels he is making progress, the task remains challenging. The community prospered when lead was discovered in the hills nearby in the 1870s. By 1900, the population soared to more than ten thousand. But over the next half century it declined by 50 percent, and then fell to its present size when the mines closed in the 1970s. All that is left of the mines is extensive pollution that the Environmental Protection Agency is still trying to clean up, not to mention lingering health problems in families suffering from lead poisoning. Less than one adult in ten has graduated from college.

Math and science scores at the high school have improved over the past five years to the point that they now resemble the state average, Mr. Sykes says, and the dropout rate has fallen. But 60 percent of the students are on free and reduced-cost lunch programs, and the school's per capita expenditures on students is the second lowest in the state. It is difficult to inspire even the best students to believe in themselves. "Probably where we are most restricted here," he says, is that "we don't see the opportunities that are available." If he could say only one thing to the students, it would be simply, "Go out and look."

The students here have trouble gaining a clearer vision of the opportunities available because of both the poverty they experience and the small frame of reference that their community provides. Poverty has little effect on how well they do in school, but limits their ability to travel and participate in activities outside the community that might widen their horizons. The small town focuses their attention inward to the point that possibilities even at a metropolitan area seventy-five miles away where colleges and employment opportunities are plentiful seem frighteningly out of reach. "No matter how much talent they are gifted with," Mr. Sykes explains, "their environment may still bring them down because they don't have a vision of anything better than what they've had all their lives."

He understands the problem from his own experience. Growing up on a farm in a neighboring county, he figured that he would follow in his father's footsteps and saw little reason to be interested in what he was being taught in high school. His father had not gone to college, so hoped his son would, but encouraged him to major in business as preparation for returning to the farm. Had it not been for an uncle who was a teacher, Mr. Sykes probably would have stayed on the farm instead of becoming an educator.

Yet for most of the students here, the frog pond consists of uncles and aunts, parents, and neighbors who have never been to college. Morale in the community is low. Most of the houses are old, and many are run down. Few of the stores are new. Vacant buildings and aging vehicles line Main Street. "The mentality affects everyone," Mr. Sykes says. In small ways, it has even influenced his behavior. Citing his yard as a small example, he says he used to take pride in keeping it looking immaculate, but yard maintenance is not much valued in the community. "So my yard is not what it once was," he remarks.

Still, it is his job to counsel students, so Mr. Sykes does what he can. He tries to emulate the beneficial effects his uncle had on him. Even in a small town, he thinks, role models can be found to give young people a broader vision. Teachers have been away to college and could serve as role models if only the gap between them and the students that typically prevails in the classroom could be overcome. "We try to get our kids involved in extracurricular activities, such as band, athletics, or some kind of club," Mr. Sykes notes. "That's where kids see teachers in a different light, not just as an authority figure." Sometimes relationships develop, he says. Sometimes the kids begin to imagine wider possibilities.

Part of the difficulty that Mr. Sykes has experienced in challenging students to think more broadly is indeed attributable to the poverty in his community. Young people whose families lack the finances to send them to college may, in effect, be saying that there is no reason to dream bigger dreams. That lack of vision is more troubling to educators in more prosperous communities. In those contexts, the problem is more likely to be viewed as one of young people feeling so comfortable with small-town life that they decide on careers they can pursue without ever having to move away. While it might be better for the town's population if they stayed, educators who see talented students limiting their options worry about the long-term consequences.

Karen McFarland is the high school principal in a prosperous community of about twenty-five hundred that has managed to stay at about that number over the past half century despite a general decline in the local farm population and major expansion in the nearest city, which is an hour away. The high school is only two blocks away from a small liberal arts college that does a reasonably good job of preparing students for careers in teaching and business, and prepares a few for law school and medical school. There are several community colleges within thirty miles and a large university in the city that is fifty miles away. Yet as she counsels the seniors at her school, Mrs. McFarland finds it is difficult to push them to think outside the box. They say, "I could be a city employee or work at the bank, or get a job at the grocery store." She says, "Sometimes I think that's all they see. It's a very restricted vision of the kind of jobs and what life is really like."

Mrs. McFarland adores her community. "I live here. I love it. I'm not trying to put people down here in the community," she says. It hurts her to think about the kids who move away and then never come back, but the kids who never think about leaving worry her more. "Don't be closed minded. Give it a try," she tells them. "If you think outside the box, then you can never look back and say, 'Gosh, I wish I would have done this or that.' Keep your avenues open." One of her former students, a woman now in her twenties, says much the same thing. She does not regret staying in the community, but she wishes that she had been less plagued by self-doubt.

For students who do go on to college, the other disadvantage of coming from a small town is the one I discussed in chapter 5: college is often a new experience, both socially and intellectually, making it a time of uncertainty and ambivalence. Besides the usual challenges of being away from home for the first time and having to study hard, the small-town background can mean never having had to associate with large numbers of people. The decisions to be made in choosing classes and friends as well as thinking about career possibilities can be unnerving.

Mr. Hennink, the chemist, tells of going to a small college near his home town because it was small and familiar, despite its limited courses and majors, and then trying a large state university for a semester. He felt so out of place that he returned to the small college. His master's training was frustrating as well. Knowing little about the field or university before he arrived, he was disappointed in the classes that he was required to take. This was part of the ambivalence that prompted his return to the small town.

Mrs. McFarland says that students from her high school sometimes go off to a big university out of state and survive for only a semester. "They feel defeated. They're not the top dogs like they were in high school. They get lost and they're thinking, 'Oh my gosh, something is wrong, this is not a good fit for me.'" She tells them, this is reality. "You're not the big dog all the time. You're going to have struggles." Then she challenges them to be tough. "Prove to yourself that you can have a little hardship and survive. Prove it to yourself. Prove it to your classmates. Prove it to your community."

REAL REASONS TO ATTEND COLLEGE

If residents of small towns understand that higher education is the key to a more prosperous future, they are not quite that instrumental when they describe its benefits. There is still some of the old sentiment that provided reasons in an earlier era to attend high school. Education was a way to become a better citizen as well as a more knowledgeable person who would remain in the community and work for its benefit. College carries similar connotations, especially now that further training may be required beyond college if a person is to be successful in a profession. The difference is that college is less likely than high school was to be a contribution to the home town. The benefit is more like bread on the waters, effecting good in the wider world wherever a person may eventually live. One of the clearest expressions of this view came from a Vietnamese immigrant who was grateful for the help that he had received as a refugee and felt the importance of giving back. His advice, which both of his daughters have heeded, is to "finish college" and "be more active with the community." For him, community meant both the town in which he lived, which included a large number of immigrants, and US society more generally.

The shifting nature of these potential civic benefits also suggests that college is understood, perhaps increasingly even in small towns, as a contribution to the person's individual development. In our interviews, people talked about college as a way for the coming generation to gain maturity, acquire a sense of accomplishment and self-confidence, bide time until they are older and more capable of making good decisions, and simply explore their options. These aspects of personal development seemed to overshadow the idea that college was preparation for a career. "You need a college education," a parent explained in describing the advice he gives his children. "It may not be so much the things they will learn, but having those four years to mature emotionally and to try out some different things." Or as another parent observed, "It gives you a time to grow up." The logic is similar to what columnist David Brooks has termed the odyssey years. Unlike the proverbial farm child, who worked alongside their parents and was a full-fledged adult by age sixteen or seventeen, the contemporary cohort of young people take their twenties—and perhaps their early thirties as well—to tinker with this and that, and discover what it means to be an adult.[7]

The connection with living in a small town is that residents sometimes felt it was all the more crucial to spend a few more years gaining maturity because the community itself was not a good incubator for adulthood. The town may have been good for small children, yet it was somewhat infantilizing for older ones. The small community was too insular; the church was too chummy. There were no opportunities for the kind of summer programs and internships available to middle-class youths in cities. Compounding the problem, youths raised in small towns lacked self-confidence. If they went away to college, it might take them longer to find their niche.

A school superintendent in a small district of approximately four hundred students said his thirty years of teaching, coaching, and working with teenagers had taught him one thing: be true to yourself. A person who followed that dictum, he said, would have no regrets in life. That was more important than pursuing success in a career. The difficulty in a small town, he had learned, was that teenagers' usual lack of confidence was more acute when the community in which they had been raised was so isolated and sheltered. He tells them, "Don't be afraid to fail. Don't be afraid to experience things just because you may fail. Be true to yourself. Get after it." He thinks too often young people take the road of least resistance. If they live in a small town, they can be a success in their own little world. But if you "haven't ever failed," he says, "you haven't really done much, quite honestly."

As if echoing this man's philosophy, another superintendent said the goal that he tries to achieve working with students in his community of eleven hundred is getting them to challenge themselves with new experiences and ideas. That begins in kindergarten and continues through twelfth grade. For those who continue on to college, the aim that he hopes they keep in mind is experimenting with new things. "Be more willing to try things. Try different things. Give different classes a chance. Try something that you wouldn't expect you'd be good at, and see how you do."

Yet another superintendent—a veteran educator in a town of six hundred—cast a similar idea in slightly different language. He says he is definitely a believer in education and thinks a good liberal education is especially critical. But he adds, "I'm not real sure it takes a college education to do what one may want to do. Colleges are on the verge of being even less relevant than high schools in some respects." Instead of assuming that the purpose of college is to gain technical skills, he believes a person should take a different approach. The purpose of education should be the "broadening of one's thoughts and mind." A person should spend the time figuring out what one loves to do and should look closely at all the options.

WHAT TO AIM FOR IN LIFE

As these examples suggest, educators in small towns think a lot about the future that resides in the hearts and minds of the next generation. While it is not surprising that they stress education, it is important to observe closely what they consider to be the aim of education and how that relates to the rest of life. They seldom emphasize purely technical skills or academic achievement for its own sake. Nor do they identify life goals that would sharply distinguish a person living in a small town from anyone else. What they do underscore, though, involves lessons honed from their own experience of living in a small town and interacting with families who do.

Not surprisingly, the small-town ethic of hard work, good planning, and self-sufficiency comes through clearly as an ideal to emulate no matter where a person eventually lives. The disrespect that residents express toward riffraff in their communities is an indication of what they want their offspring to avoid. They can usually point to someone they know who is on welfare or the lazy people they imagine living in urban slums as examples. More often, townspeople point to some of their own mistakes. They say it is fine to have fun in high school or college, but if they had it to do over again, they would work harder and establish clearer long-term goals, and yet try to anticipate being open to change.

The ability to adapt and be flexible enough to change—whether that means a change of careers, a shift in financial circumstances, or the need to move to a new location—is a trait that educators in small towns mention repeatedly. They have seen the value of adaptability as they have moved themselves, and have witnessed fluctuations in local agriculture and business. "Don't be afraid to change," the high school principal in a town of five thousand says. "If you get into something and it is not necessarily what makes you happy, you need to go ahead and strike out and try something different." He says this is especially true given today's uncertain financial conditions.

Closely related to being flexible is an understanding of the need to constantly ask questions and seek advice. Educators stress this not simply because it is a classroom habit but also to counteract the culture of self-sufficiency they see in small towns. The same high school principal, for example, says his community seems to be composed of "rugged individualists" who are "too proud" to ask questions and try to do everything on their own. "Make sure you get help every step of the way," he advises. "If you don't know the answer, make sure you find somebody who does. Ask questions. There is no such thing as a stupid question."

Lifelong learning is another emphasis. The idea that a person needs to continue acquiring knowledge and being interested in learning new things after graduation has become clichéd in educational circles, but it is not limited to those venues. The manager of a small manufacturing plant that employs 130 workers in a town of 1,400 was adamant about the need for lifelong learning. He says that even the college graduates who he hires to do engineering and marketing are not trained as well as he would like them to be. "They've been given this belief that they have been educated and have an inherent right to an outstanding income," he complains. "They want to be coddled and feel good all the time." He thinks this is a problem in cities, too, not just in his small town. To remedy the problem, he tries to train the young people who work at his company that "they have not been educated, and the only solution is to start from day one." He tells them, "If you're not getting a half percent better every day, you're automatically getting a half percent worse." He has instituted a reading and study program at the company, and requires his employees to participate in it.

This man's view of the need for lifelong learning was more cynical than most. Others saw it more as a necessity in today's economy. "What are we looking at now?" a farmer in a town of fewer than a thousand residents asked. "Changing professions seven or eight times in a lifetime." A young woman who had been reared in his community and now lived in a city said this was true. In her experience—having already pursued three different professions—the key was always to stay flexible and learn enough to "be able to make choices," rather than getting into a situation where you don't have choices.

INTERNALIZED SMALL-TOWN VALUES

Being flexible, keeping one's options open, and continuing to learn and change—these are values that can be embraced anywhere. They suggest, for that matter, that someone growing up in a small town should be prepared to move away. It is as if parents are training their children to leave.

Perhaps the security of small-town life is all the more precious for this reason. It cannot last. The community is a good place to raise children, and then they depart.

"The likelihood of my kids moving back here," a man who has a good job as a bank officer in a town of seventeen hundred says, "is pretty well never." His oldest son lives in a city two hundred miles away. He loves it there and has only fleeting thoughts of ever returning to the small town. The man admits, too, that the town has been less attractive for his wife than for him. She has a master's degree in education and would like to be a school principal, but there are no opportunities in town. "It was great here for raising kids," he says, but otherwise, women in the area face limited career opportunities. Even the social activities available for professional women are sparse unless they happen to love hunting and fishing. "I hate to say it," he observes, "but this is almost a man's world out here, and for my wife, she has complained about it for years."

What parents more often seek to instill in their children are portable small-town values. Rather than encouraging them to spend the rest of their lives in town, they stress ongoing personality traits that reflect the town. Loyalty to the community is exemplified less in expectations about working there for a lifetime than in the ceremonial aspects of community that I have explored in previous chapters. The small-town festival symbolizes community spirit, but can be celebrated once a year and by visitors as well as residents. The school is a source of community loyalty, yet schools are for children who grow up and do other things. Participation in community associations is done as a volunteer and can be continued in other places. The quaint town square can be visited, remembered, and imitated in suburban housing developments.[8]

The most portable values are aspects of the inner self. These include the values that small-town residents like to imagine are strongest in their communities, but in reality are widely shared in metropolitan areas as well. Hard work, honesty, and personal integrity lead the list. So do the desire for self-sufficiency and need to be neighborly. Religion's public persona along with the frequency with which conservative moral and political views are expressed may be more distinctive of small towns, although they are by no means absent in other places. Residents worry that even the younger generation in their own small communities may not be as faithful to these values as was true in the past. There is tacit awareness that neighbors can quietly vote Democratic and be welcoming toward gays and lesbians.

Values that are portable are nevertheless inflected with small-town meanings. The idea that a person should be flexible enough to try out new things, overcome a lack of self-confidence, and be willing to fail casts the usual meaning of achievement in a different light. Flexibility does not imply self-interested status attainment measured in career success, and gained by compromising one's values and manipulating one's friends. Flexibility is instead an outlook that anticipates failure. It says in effect that bad decisions are expected, and the person who makes them and winds up in a small town is still OK. A person can fail, but still have a positive attitude because of the support that is present in a small community.

Maria Sanchez is a good example of someone who believes in the ability to keep picking oneself up with the help of small-town neighbors and friends. As an immigrant who could not speak English, she struggled in school. Her parents did stoop labor in the fields, working hard to earn a living and find their way through the complicated process of becoming citizens. She recalls coming home from school and crying because of the prejudiced comments of her Anglo classmates. Eventually she made it through college and became a teacher. The advice to the children of immigrants she now works with is to not be afraid. "Grow a thicker skin. Ignore the negative comments. Quit crying. Keep going. Dream. Dream big." She keeps a file of stories about people who have overcome the obstacles facing them. She tells the tales to her students to counter the negative comments they may hear. It sounds like a pull-yourself-up-by-the-bootstraps philosophy. But it is deeply communal. Staying optimistic, she says, requires support from one another.[9]

The meaning of happiness is similarly infused with small-town nuances. Living in a small community out of the limelight is a reminder that happiness does not depend on glamour and success. The frequency with which residents with meager incomes describe their financial situation as comfortable is telling in this regard. When asked about their advice for the coming generation, they seldom highlighted pursuits for the sake of earning more money. As one man observed, "The money aspect is highly overrated." They emphasize happiness and service more often. People in larger communities do, too. The difference is that in small towns, there is a more explicit denial of the relationship between wealth and happiness. The wealthy are respected to the extent that they mingle with ordinary folks and serve the community. Happiness is said to come in small doses, especially through one's association with fellow residents in good times and bad.[10]

CONTINUING COMMUNITY TIES

If residents of small towns implicitly understand the future of their communities to exist in the internalized values that young people carry with them, the ties that remain are not entirely mental and emotional. Tangible connections remain. Even for those who never return as full-time residents, social attachments to the community continue. They are facilitated, as many of the examples I have offered indicate, by temporary returns to work at the family store or live on the family farm, visits to parents and siblings, the need to help aging parents, and the desire for support and advice. The school of hard knocks tethers some to their home communities. Immaturity in facing the wider world along with the normal uncertainties of jobs and marriages send former residents back to their places of origin.

We talked to a school superintendent after he had just given the high school commencement address in his town of three hundred. He has no illusions about the town's ability to keep its youths. Eighty-five percent of the recent graduating classes have gone on to a four-year college. Most of the remaining 15 percent of the students continue the vocational training they have received in high school at a community college. This superintendent nevertheless believes that many of the graduating seniors will stay connected to the town. He knows this from experience, despite what the students may think when they graduate. In his commencement speech, he advised them to acquire skills to do something they enjoy and save their money. He also advised them, "Don't forget your roots. As you grow older, those people you can't wait to get away from—so you can go to the city and be your own man or woman—don't forget them. Don't forget your roots, because as you get older, you're going to need those people more."

Some of what may draw people back to their roots is the sense of authenticity that I discussed in chapter 3. Not only the residents who remain in small towns but also those who have left or merely visited sometimes entertain the idea that people there are more authentic than people elsewhere. What they mean includes the opportunity that children have in small towns to play, roam freely, and live close to nature. The haystacks in surrounding fields, animals giving birth, family barbeques in the park, and having to deal with everyone in the community are all part of the picture.

The magnetism of this pull toward small-town authenticity was clearly evident in the remarks of a prominent film producer we interviewed who had spent her childhood summers with grandparents and cousins in a small rural community. She tells the students she teaches in New York and Los Angeles about how "incredibly important" it is to get a college education. Yet she adds, "What's funny is that with all my educational experience, I find myself constantly coming back"—back to the small town where she spent her summers. "That's where I find my meaning."

The likelihood that young people who move away will remember their roots is increased by a philosophy we heard on several occasions as "learning from the school of hard knocks." The idea is similar to the adage that "you can lead a horse to water, but you can't make it drink." It suggests that parents and educators can teach children only so much. Then children have to grow up and experience setbacks in order to truly understand the realities of life. "I've done plenty of dumb things, and they were costly, but you learn by the school of hard knocks" is how one man—a cattleman with a history of failed investments—put it.

One interpretation of the school of hard knocks emphasizes rugged individualism: leave home, strike out on your own, and take your licks. That view was certainly present in small towns. It was part of the notion that people should take responsibility for themselves. It was balanced, though, by the notion that a person experiencing a rough time always has a safety net back home in the town. It means the prodigal child going away, making mistakes, and returning to their parent's embrace. The cattleman went off to college, discovered he was too young to pick a career, and changed majors seven times. His son no longer lives in the area. The cattleman knows, however, that the small-town values are deeply implanted in his son's personality. His son comes home for visits and advice. He recently said to his dad, "Man, parents are pretty smart!"

Leaving the Doors Open

What does all this suggest about the future of small towns? The parents, educators, and town leaders who live in these communities are not exactly telling the next generation to pick up and leave. The unwritten emphasis on small-town security remains. It is inscribed in the fact that residents turn out faithfully for school plays and athletic events as well as in the camaraderie that manifests itself at the hardware store, if one still exists, or the VFW pancake breakfast. Parents tell their children that this is a good place to grow up, raise children, work hard, and lead a simple life; the young people may not appreciate it now, but will later. The small town is an enclosed space, like a house in which to make a home.

But it is a house that functions best when the doors are left open, not merely unlocked, as residents mention so frequently in signaling the safe neighborliness they feel. Openness suggests more appropriately the opportunity to come and go, to leave and come back. It is the possibility for fresh air and new ideas. The boundaries are permeable. The space is a home, not a fortress.[11]

"Keep your doors open," John Laughlin says. He is a businessperson in his early seventies who has lived nearly all his life in a town of six thousand. Life has been good for Mr. Laughlin and his wife, Julia, who is now retired from teaching and still does tutoring on the side. Neither would want to live anywhere else. But as they look back on their lives and think about what it would be like to be young again, they know there are paths they could have taken and did not. Mr. Laughlin earned top grades and was a member of the honor society in college. He could have worked anywhere. Mrs. Laughlin thinks how interesting it would have been to spend a couple years in the Peace Corps.

"Get a little bit uncomfortable," Mr. Laughlin advises. "There's a comfort level that you can come back to, but don't be afraid to get out of that comfort zone and see what the world has to offer." For him, leaving the doors open means being willing to try new things and take risks, even if that results in failure. Mrs. Laughlin says it means following a person's basic passions, even if that means putting oneself in scary situations some of the time.

Doors are significant features of life wherever a person lives. They seem to have special meaning in small towns. Perhaps it is because of talking so often about doors that do not have to be locked. Or because doors are the familiar entryways to the homes that provide comfort, the school at which town meetings are held, and the coffee shop where neighbors gather to exchange gossip. Closed doors indicate a space that soon becomes stale. Open doors point to an image of greater freedom.

Small towns have always been communities with open doors, despite prejudices to the contrary that view them only as parochial enclaves. Sometimes the doors are not as open as at other times. Newcomers who squeeze in through half-open portals register the difficulties of truly feeling at home. New immigrants whose presence sometimes arouses xenophobia among established residents feel the difficulties acutely. Yet in reality, small towns were mostly founded by immigrants, welcomed new settlers in hoping of becoming larger towns, sometimes succeeded, and always depended on trade and transportation with other places.

Leaving the doors open is an invitation to vulnerability. Young adults will leave through those doors in hopes that college, service in the military, and jobs in urban places will open other doors. Others will take the opportunity to stay, but travel more often and stay in contact with people elsewhere via electronic communications. Population trends in the nation at large will likely be sufficient to prevent all but the smallest towns from disappearing. Open doors, though, will result in change, just as railroads and highways have in the past. It will be increasingly important for community festivals to be staged and newcomers to be welcomed.

- 11 -

Concluding Reflections
Community in Small Towns

GENERALIZATIONS ABOUT SMALL TOWNS—even when those towns are all located in the United States in the twenty-first century—bump unsteadily into bothersome exceptions almost as soon as they are made. Small communities vary in size, history, and location. They range from isolated villages on the open prairie to hilly mining communities set in dusty valleys, and from seaport towns on rocky coasts to small manufacturing centers surrounded by cornfields and cow pastures. They are not quite as diverse as they once were, having been incorporated into the national culture of discount stores and fast-food chains, and having in most instances lost their distinctive ethnic traditions. Much of that diversity has nevertheless been kept alive in community festivals and reanimated by new waves of immigration. About the only generalization that can safely be ventured about small towns, it might seem, is that they are indeed small compared with most cities and suburbs.

Community, however, is a different matter. Although its specific manifestations vary in degree and from place to place, the characteristics that surface as people describe their experiences and understandings of community do so with considerable regularity. Indeed, most of the characteristics that observers have remarked on in broad theoretical discussions of community are evident here, and yet are refracted in ways that illuminate the special meanings of living in a small town and demonstrate how residents find community—or at least hope it can be found and thus lament when it seems to elude their grasp.

One of the more useful attempts to identify the elements that must be present for a community to achieve something close to a workable and sustainable ideal is found in the work of sociologist Suzanne Keller, mentioned earlier in this book. She taught for many years at Princeton University, and during that time conducted a lengthy and thorough investigation of a community called Twin Rivers located eleven miles from the

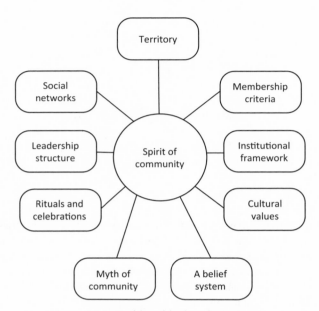

Figure 11.1 Building blocks of community

center of that campus. Keller's research began in the 1970s, and concluded a few days after the attacks on New York City and Washington, DC, on September 11, 2001. The ethnographic research, qualitative interviews, and surveys she conducted convinced Keller that community could not be reduced, as some scientists have tried to do, to a network diagram or mathematical formula. Instead, she found that residents' experiences and interpretations of life in Twin Rivers resonated with insights gleaned from Alexis de Tocqueville and Martin Buber along with studies of early American villages and ethnic enclaves. She identified the ten building blocks of community shown in the diagram (figure 11.1).[1]

> *Territory* or turf, Keller argues, is figuratively, if not also literally, the bedrock of community, serving as the bounded site in which it exists, and providing it with a spatial signature, physical identity, and perhaps sense of security and closure.
>
> *Membership criteria* specify who belongs to the community and who does not belong. These are the stated and unstated symbolic boundaries as well as cognitive classifications that distinguish "us" from "them," "insiders" from "outsiders," and constitute a rationale for inclusion or exclusion.

An institutional framework consists of the formalized laws along with
   informal rules and sanctions that govern in routine circumstances,
   and maintain order in response to crises and conflicts.

Cultural values that particularly facilitate the social cohesion of the
   community emphasize cooperation, mutual responsibility, and sharing. These values undergird the prevailing local consensus about
   priorities and goals.

A *belief system* offers justifications and explanations for the demands
   that a community may place on its members, and suggests the ways
   in which they should behave to attain their goals.

A *myth of community* tells how it originated, who founded it, and the
   reasons why, and weaves together its stories about progress, failure,
   hard times, and notable events.

Rituals and celebrations bring people together, punctuating the daily
   rhythms of their collective life with times for emotional expression,
   remembrance, and joy.

A *leadership structure* serves vitally to guide and govern. It consists of
   not only individual leaders but also the expectations that reward
   them with respect and command loyalty from those they lead.

Social networks are the actual relationships that tie people together in
   bonds of family and friendship, and radiate to include neighborly
   behavior along with acts of charity, benevolence, and community
   service.

The spirit of community, finally, Keller argues, is that sense of inter-
   dependence that arises from all the foregoing, and ultimately transcends individual interests so that people identify with and willingly
   assume responsibility for their community.

In reality, each of these characteristics may be present in varying degrees, and together specify different aspects that give communities their
distinctive identity and constitute strengths or weaknesses. A community,
for example, may have a well-established annual festival that ritually
commemorates its founding, but lack an effective leadership structure
to conduct routine business, while another community may have a dense
network of interpersonal relationships yet seldom generate a sense of responsibility that extends to the whole community.

In what follows, I want to draw on these characteristics to summarize
what can be learned about community from the observations and interviews we conducted in small towns. This is not meant to suggest that all
small towns effectively provide a sense of community to their inhabitants,
or do so any better than urban or suburban neighborhoods do. My view
is rather that community manifests itself in distinctive ways in small
towns along each of these ten dimensions.

Territory as Community Space

The importance of its physical place and location can hardly be emphasized enough in understanding the sense of community that exists in small towns. When residents talk about their community, they typically have mental images of how it looks, and these images conjure up personal memories of experiences in that location and feelings about those events, and are often accompanied by a physiological response, such as a sense of being able to see or breathe more easily than in unfamiliar places. Residents—the appropriate term for members of a community who inhabit its space—can describe the buildings on Main Street and count the number of churches by picturing them in their minds. One of the most common features that residents say they like about their town is its "familiarity," which means knowing where things are and how to make one's way around. If the town is familiar, residents observe, you can picture yourself in it, getting to the grocery store, for example, by turning left at the post office, driving past the school on your right, and going two blocks past the Lutheran Church on your left. Except in larger towns, residents seldom describe where they live by referring to a specific neighborhood or housing development. The reference point is the "town." They live in the center of town, the old part, the new part, on the edge, the West side, or perhaps a few miles away.

In many instances, townspeople are keenly aware that their town's existence and future well-being depend on its relationship to the terrain it occupies as well as that surrounds it. The community was founded because farmers moved into the area, the railroad made it a stopping point, there was a river, or a mine was opened. Its location is not accidental, and townspeople's own location is thus grounded. Whether they farm, work in the mine, run a retail store, or teach at the school, residents know that the local economy, which depends on the physical space, is what matters most. Population is declining because farms in the area are becoming larger. Business is in the doldrums because the mine has closed.

An interesting distinction can be made between the direct attachments that exist between an individual and a place, on the one hand, and the indirect attachments that imply a connection between a place and the community of which an individual is a member. The former is evident when a farmer feels a special attachment to a parcel of land that has been in the family for generations or when a homeowner notes the pleasant view from her front window. A connection between a place and community is more evident when a resident worries about the empty buildings on Main Street, or takes pride in the fact that everyone keeps their lawn looking nice. In these latter cases, how the space is maintained and how it looks reflects on the community's image of itself.

The scholarly literature disagrees as to whether a physical space is necessary for a community to exist or is only one of the ingredients important to some communities. Examples can certainly be given of social networks that are called communities despite having no particular territorial location. The "astrophysics community," the "Hispanic community," and the "Facebook community" are instances. Although the various members of these communities exist in particular locations, the community itself cannot be identified with any specific location. When communities do have a physical space, that place contributes a crucial dimension to its collective identity.[2] Americans consider themselves to have something in common because of the particular part of a continent they occupy. They sometimes call it their "homeland" and feel the need to defend it. Similarly, townspeople identify themselves as residents of a specific place that gives them something in common with their fellow residents and is the space in which much of their daily life is spent.

Besides the space literally configured by the town's physical borders, the "great good places," as Oldenburg calls them, that exist within these borders contribute significantly to residents' sense of community.[3] Some of these places actually belong to the collectivity. They are the town halls, community centers, schools, parks, fire stations, clinics, and hospitals that the townspeople collectively support plus consider their own. Others become great good places even though they are privately owned because residents gather there, mingle over coffee on rainy mornings with their neighbors, and exchange greetings that help them to remember that they are part of the community. Taverns, pubs, the local café, a farmers' coop, the barbershop, and the beauty parlor are typical examples. Traditionally, these places were concentrated in the center of town, serving as a symbolic core for community activities and providing easy access for multigenerational interaction. It is not surprising, therefore, that residents describe the loss of a school or closing of a store on Main Street as ripping the heart from their community.[4]

Territory may be the space in which sharing takes place, but it is also space to which residents have differing levels of access, and for that matter, may be contested turf that generates conflict more than community spirit. The coffee shop is more likely to be the turf of small-town pensioners than of busy parents and commuters. Its denizens may be known as the village gossips. The private territory that constitutes most of the space that a town occupies is heavily stratified between high-end and middle-income housing as well as between spacious homes on large lots and modest dwellings for low-income and aging residents. In racially and ethnically diverse communities, these distinctions are likely to be inscribed in patterns of de facto housing segregation.[5] The land surrounding the town may be scarred with abandoned open-pit mines or controlled by multigenerational farm families. The tensions that may exist in multigenerational families, or emerge in connection with decisions about schools and taxes, as the familiar saying acknowledges, "come with the territory."

DISTINGUISHING WHO BELONGS AND WHO DOES NOT

The criteria that define membership in a small town include, in the first instance, residence. A small town is a community, to a large degree, simply because people live there, just as a neighborhood is, or a city or nation. In legal terms, residence involves establishing a permanent address, having one's mail delivered there, listing that address on one's tax forms, and in some cases proving that one is a citizen or has entered the country legally. All these legalities provide periodic reminders that a person indeed belongs to a community. An address is an important aspect of membership in a community, but of course not the only one, and not always the clearest evidence of who belongs and who does not. A person can have an address yet spend so little time there that the person hardly feels part of the community at all or is not regarded as a member by other residents. Or as we have seen, a person can live in a community and still be considered an outsider because of somehow failing to meet the expectations of other residents.

In small places, residence more easily becomes common knowledge than in larger places. When townspeople say they know everyone in town, they mean that they have some idea of who lives there, who does not, and who is an old-timer or newcomer. They likely have never spoken to all of the five thousand or ten thousand people who live in their community. Yet they somehow have a sense of who belongs and who does not. This sense of membership and nonmembership has more to do with subtle cues of behavior than with simply having an address in the town. People who belong are seen often enough at the filling station to be considered as residents. They have explained to someone at the coop who they are, and that person relates the information to others at the café the next day. Although it helps to have an actual residence, a person who is away at college or gone most days driving an eighteen-wheeler can still be a part of the community. They belong because of their background and continuing family ties. Someone else may live in the town, but be regarded as a stranger, outsider, riffraff, or someone merely passing through.

Michele Lamont and Virag Molnar usefully distinguish between symbolic boundaries, which are the shared cognitive classification schemes that people use to make sense of their world, and social distinctions, which are the institutionalized mechanisms that actually sort people into separate groups.[6] Racial categories that divide people into "blacks" and "whites" are a familiar example of the former, while Jim Crow laws that segregate housing, transportation, and social services on the basis of race would be an illustration of the latter. To some extent, small towns reinforce the overlap between symbolic boundaries and social distinctions through legal mechanisms. Being a member of the community is partly determined by paying local property taxes and voting in local elections.

Symbolic boundaries come to be matters of shared public information when private tacit conceptual categories are threatened or in some other way transgressed to the point that discussion emerges and action is taken. In small towns, the symbolic boundaries that define residents as legitimate members of the community are dramatized in several ways. At the simplest level, the small scale of a town makes it possible for visitors to be easily identified and tagged as strangers because they deviate from some well-known aspect of local behavior. For example, their vehicle is marked by an out-of-state license plate, or in some states, an out-of-county license plate letter or number. Their gaze may be directed at the towering grain elevator for a few seconds too long whereas a local resident would pay no attention to the storage facility's existence.

A complicating fact is that most people are members of more than one community, at least if "community" is broadly defined. Their neighborhood is one of these. Others may include their coworkers, the church or synagogue they attend, and their friends on Facebook. Residents of small towns have these multiple, overlapping communities, just as people in larger places do. One difference that stands out in our interviews, however, is that townspeople rarely identify themselves with more than one geographic community. They talk as if it is taken for granted that their geographic community is their town. They do in fact participate in other geographic entities, such as voting precincts, counties, school districts, congressional districts, enterprise zones, agricultural belts, and regional planning areas. But with the exception of people we interviewed who actually worked for some of these other entities, residents spoke only of their towns as their community.

The reason for this identification of community with town is significant. It points to the importance of the multiple ways in which membership is symbolically communicated. Not only does the town have a name (counties do, too) but the name is also likely to be marked on road signs at the edges of town, on its water tower or grain elevator, in its newspaper (if it still has one), on many of the local businesses, and of course as part of most residents' postal address. It helps, as we have seen, if the town has a school, and if the school's athletic teams compete with other towns. While it is harder to say, it also seems to matter that towns are geographically separate from one another. Not that a resident of, say, Evanston, Illinois, is unable to tell where the line between it and Skokie or Wilmette runs, but the distinction blurs in day-to-day transactions to a greater extent than for someone whose nearest neighboring town is ten miles away through open country.

THE INSTITUTIONALIZED FRAMEWORK OF LAWS AND RULES

Keller's use of the term "institutional framework" is meant to specify the laws, rules, sanctions, and rewards that provide governance to a community. These are the officially codified statutes that tell the members of a community that they are required, for example, to pay annual dues or have the right to vote in periodic elections. They include regulations governing motor vehicles, the maintenance of property, and personal safety. They also include unofficial but commonly understood norms of interpersonal behavior, such as the expectation that a resident will wave or smile at a fellow resident when their paths cross on the sidewalk or at the post office. They remind us that being a member of a community is more than simply being regarded somehow as belonging or not belonging. Members are also subject to the formal and informal expectations that govern behavior.

Like territory, residents share institutionalized laws and rules, and for that reason may associate with being part of a community merely by being governed by the same regulations. Also like territory, laws and rules pertain differently to different residents. Sundown laws that prohibited African Americans from being in town after dark are an example. According to one estimate, these laws were in effect in as many as a thousand towns in the early part of the twentieth century and were still evident in some communities seeking to restrict Hispanic immigrants. Other illustrations include regulations against loitering as well as differential enforcement of drug laws and documentation of citizenship.[7]

In my interviews, the legal codes and formalized government regulations to which townspeople were subject came up mostly when residents were unhappy about them. New certification requirements for day-care providers, a new leash law, or lax enforcement of drug laws were common matters of concern. Otherwise, residents pretty much took for granted that there were in fact laws and it was important to abide by them. Part of their town being a good community was that neighbors in fact regarded each other as being law-abiding citizens. Townspeople also considered it advantageous to live in a place that was small enough to accommodate special circumstances. They appreciated the fact that they could meet personally with the mayor or perhaps ask the sheriff to give someone a warning instead of making an arrest.

What came through repeatedly was the assumption that formal and informal regulations should be pragmatic, and could generally be decided on the basis of common sense. This was a key part of what people meant when they said everybody in their community was equal or at least nearly the same. While recognizing status distinctions along with understanding the value of specialized expertise for managing a farm or teaching at the high school, they believed that issues of common importance could mostly be decided through common sense.

By its nature, common sense is local knowledge that can simply be taken for granted rather than having to be defined clearly. It manifests itself after the fact by tacit agreement that a decision is the correct or only practical one, given the circumstances. This is why intrusions on local common sense from the outside, especially from state and federal government, play an important symbolic role in defining loyalty to the local community. These intrusions are subject to public ridicule. The lesson is that outsiders cannot possibly understand what members of the local community already know.

COOPERATION AND SHARING AS COMMUNITY VALUES

The cultural values that are particularly conducive to a sense of community emphasize cooperation, mutual responsibility, and sharing. In small towns, these values surface repeatedly in residents' descriptions of what they value about their communities. Interviewees tell stories about neighbors helping one another along with events such as natural disasters that they say brought out the best qualities among their fellow citizens. Sharing occurs in small, seemingly trivial ways, such as exchanging gossip at the gas station or after church, and thus maintains casual acquaintanceships that facilitate interaction when more serious cooperation is needed. A relatively high number of voluntary associations on a per capita basis also puts residents at risk of being asked to participate in community projects. Residents happily pitch in with their neighbors to beautify the park, care for widows and orphans, host pancake breakfasts, take casseroles to the sick, and organize bingo nights.

If all this sounds a bit too good to be true, it is. Residents' stories are instances of selective memory in which a charitable activity or particularly altruistic event stands out, while moments of selfishness and indifference are forgotten (or withheld when talking to a stranger conducting research). We seldom heard reports of outright callousness, but townspeople do speak candidly about conflicts and disagreements. They generally agree with the old saw that good fences make good neighbors and sometimes have compelling tales to tell about border disputes that literally involve fences. There is also a pervasive feeling among community leaders that the eighty–twenty principle applies. Twenty percent of the residents, they say, are responsible for 80 percent of the volunteer activity that takes place. Moreover, volunteering rarely benefits the entire community equally and directly. While residents regard volunteering as an admirable characteristic of the local population, their narratives about such activity reveal that its benefits are selective. Just as in larger places, residents volunteer at the school because they have school-age children, the nursing home where their aging parent lives, the church of their choice, and the VFW pancake breakfast because it benefits fellow veterans. The scale of small towns nevertheless enhances the likelihood that these specialized volunteer associations will be linked to one another through overlapping memberships—a characteristic that has been shown in other contexts to promote community cohesion.[8]

In simplest form, sharing is best understood as a reciprocal relationship, such as one student helping another with math, and that student in return helping the first student with history. Townspeople mention reciprocal relationships of this kind—for instance, when neighbors exchange recipes or watch each other's children. Serial reciprocity extends the relationship, such that A helps B, B helps C, and eventually what goes around comes around and benefits A. Small towns facilitate this kind of sharing as well. Indeed, the chances of the circle eventually being complete are increased by the fact that people in the community know each other and routinely interact with many of their fellow residents. Word spreads. Weeks, months, or years later a good deed is repaid.

The people we talked to also made it clear that good deeds are repaid in another important way: through respect. Especially those who are well off may be in little need of in-kind gifts, but if they have served the community, they are rewarded with respect. Similarly, residents most in need earn moral capital by helping their neighbors in small ways. In both instances, the respect earned has a leveling effect. People in the middle stratum feel better about those above and below when it seems that everyone is chipping in to assist in small ways. The rumor mill can be devastating for those who violate expected norms, but serves valuably to spread word about good behavior.

There is also the interesting expectation that townspeople will be self-sufficient—a norm that seems initially to contradict the spirit of sharing, but actually complements it. Being self-sufficient means doing everything in one's power to avoid becoming a burden to the community. Mow your own lawn. Clean out your own gutters. Drive yourself to the hospital for chemotherapy. A person who accepts help from a neighbor should do so reluctantly, the norm says. In practice, self-sufficiency thus reduces the demand for caring and sharing to the point that it can more easily be managed. It probably contributes to the esteem in which caregivers are held as well. To accept charity too easily is a good way to lose respect.

BELIEFS THAT VALIDATE A COMMON WAY OF LIFE

The difference between "cultural values" and a "belief system," as Keller uses the terms, can be illustrated with two examples. The statement "I should go over and visit my neighbor because she has been in the hospital and maybe I can cheer her up" is an instance of a cultural value, as the term is defined in Keller's discussion. The statement expresses the importance that a person attaches to being a helpful, cooperative member of a community. In contrast, the statement "This is a good place to live because housing is cheap, there is no traffic, and I can get to work in five minutes" is a case of a belief system. It provides an explanation of why living here in a particular community makes sense. Instead of reinforcing a sense of community by arguing that people should help one another, it expresses the idea that members of the community have something in common. They tacitly share an outlook that involves a similar lifestyle. The unstated agreement is that residents of the community consider it is nice to live in an inexpensive house close to work where there is little traffic.

In practice, values and beliefs are of course intertwined. The fact that neighbors help one another is a value that encourages them to pitch in when needed, and is at the same time part of the lifestyle they share and a justification they may give for living where they do. It is critical, though, that community in small towns is not entirely about sharing and caring. Although some of that happens, associating small-town life with inordinate levels of sharing and caring paints a picture that does not square with reality. Residents of small towns are no different from anyone else in devoting a lot of their energy to their own work, families, and leisure activities.

The beliefs that validate small-town life have mostly to do with the distinct personal advantages that residents perceive in living there. They appreciate knowing people, having friends, and being able to spend time with their families—and thinking that this is something that their coresidents appreciate as well. Other frequently mentioned beliefs emphasize that life is simpler in a small town than it would be in a larger place, the pace is slower, children can be more authentic, the cost of housing is lower, and neighbors are less materialistic. Calling these "beliefs" is a good way of describing them. In reality, towns and the experiences of residents living in them vary, and for that matter, may not differ much from those of people in larger places. These, however, are how townspeople perceive their communities.

If one tangible aspect of small-town life has come to have central symbolic importance, it is probably townspeople's perception of traffic. When asked to explain what they mean by the slow pace of life in their town, they talk about not having to sit in traffic or deal with rush-hour congestion. Living in a "quiet" community means an absence of traffic noise and loud sirens. Liking their community because it is "familiar" is something they illustrate by saying they get lost driving in a large city. As they see it, small towns are better in these ways than large cities. Otherwise, townspeople deny many of the differences that they fear have been applied to them by outsiders. The distinctions are not to be counted in access to the Internet, cultural interests, or knowledge but rather in the number of noisy vehicles clogging the nation's arteries.

The residents we talked to seldom regarded themselves as victims who had somehow been left behind when friends and relatives moved to better-paying and culturally richer lives in cities and suburbs. Yet there is an undercurrent in residents' beliefs that depicts themselves as survivors. Their way of life is threatened, they sometimes explain, by government bureaucrats who have no appreciation of small-town values or by wealthy corporate executives who live in cities. The stories they tell are of harsh winters, store closings, and small churches struggling to remain open. The narratives underscore that small-town residents incur costs for upholding the values they cherish.

Community Mythology

Community mythology refers to the stories that members of the community share about its founding, subsequent history, changes, and the high and low points it has experienced. Usually the tales have been sanitized to the point that they tell about a glorious past while leaving out the seamier details that residents would just as soon forget. For this reason, community legends bend easily into images of a golden age when things were better than they are now. But heroic incidents in the past are sometimes used as well to argue that progress is still being achieved. In small towns, the good old days include stories about pioneers who overcame hardship, early settlers who brought civilization, later inhabitants who hunkered down during the Great Depression, soldiers who fought and died defending their country, and other citizens who started families, ran businesses, and held leadership positions. The golden age was a time when streets were filled on Saturday evenings and children played happily on the school grounds. Connections to continuing progress are imagined in stories about new immigrants, new businesses, and new agricultural technologies.

In anthropologist Mircea Eliade's classic work on myths of origin in tribal societies it was evident that these narratives were transmitted by specific individuals who bore special responsibility and to whom distinctive status accrued for being knowledgeable of the past, being able to tell or enact the stories on special occasions, and perhaps having been the recipients of privileged esoteric information passed to them through the generations.[9] In small towns, as I have noted, a similar kind of cultural leadership is typically institutionalized. The village folklorist is usually a longtime resident who is called on to tell how things were in the early days, relate the history of the community's founding, and perhaps reveal little known or half-forgotten legends about traumatic historical events and community scandals.

Community legends should not be understood as stories that strengthen communities merely by generating agreement. Among the people we interviewed, some of the stories they told were almost sacred, for example, in relating how the farm or their house had been in the family for generations. Many of the stories, though, were the kind that people tell in jest, as if the characters are truly taller than life and yet interesting enough to reveal something about the community's lighter side. Bizarre incidents, shoot-outs, grasshopper attacks, and tales of colorful ancestors were told in this way. Myths were also the occasion for dramatizing, reliving, and perhaps resolving long-standing disputes. The narratives sometimes included tales of swindlers, wealthy residents taking advantage of the poor, racism, hostility toward immigrants, and disagreements about efforts to rebuild following a natural disaster.

RITUALS AND CELEBRATIONS

Community spirit in small towns is reinforced through periodic rituals that draw people out of their homes and away from work long enough to enjoy one another's company, engage in celebratory activities that involve sharing, and do something that explicitly reminds them that they are residents who have something in common. My interviewees identified two basic kinds of rituals that served these purposes. One was the community-wide event—such as a Fourth of July celebration, homecoming weekend, or Fall Festival—conducted on behalf of the whole town and open to anyone who wished to participate. These rituals were nearly universal in small towns, occurring at least once or twice a year, commemorating something distinctive about the town, and giving residents an opportunity to spend time relaxing together. In many communities, athletic events fulfilled similar functions on a more regular basis. The other was the kind of event that happened on a smaller scale, such as neighbors gathering to help an ill resident or bereaved family. Although these smaller events do not involve the whole community, the people we talked to regarded them as expressions of the community's full identity and commitment to helping one another. The event qualified as ritual because it conformed to certain well-institutionalized rules, such as taking food to a bereaved neighbor's house or gathering at a wake, drew people together, and resulted in stories being told about its importance to the community.

Emile Durkheim, in discussing rituals in the *Elementary Forms of the Religious Life*, distinguished between the behavior of which rituals were constituted and the collective representations or consciousness that was associated with these activities, but insisted that in practice, the two should be considered together.[10] It is abundantly clear in small towns that both the activities and interpretation of them contribute to the sense of community that residents derive. The activities punctuate time by giving residents something unusual to do or enlisting them in response to an exceptional event, such as a natural disaster or automobile fatality. People actually come together and exhibit emotions like joy or grief that would seldom be expressed in public on other occasions. The subsequent interpretations of these events are equally significant. People recall the events as evidence that their town is indeed a community of residents who care about one another, enjoy each other's company, and pitch in when help is needed.

Recent scholarship on rituals has returned to Durkheim's emphasis on people being in one another's physical presence, and thus experiencing an emotional charge that would otherwise be less likely or absent. Randall Collins in *Interaction Ritual Chains*, for example, argues that the key to an effective ritual is bodily copresence—a shared focus of attention, shared mood, and some barriers that restrict involvement from outsiders.[11] A sense of community is reinforced, even if it involves only two or three people, Collins says, because they are in fact sharing some activity together and feeling special emotions. Community festivals, athletic events, weddings, and funerals clearly qualify. The difference in a small town is that the "community" that is dramatized in the ritual is also the community in which people live, work, and conduct business. In comparison, the crowd at a wedding feels the temporary rush of excitement and good will, dances and drinks toasts together, and thereby ritually commemorates the value of family, but the celebration may have little to do with the community in which they live.

Rituals are especially relevant for understanding how definitions of who belongs and who does not belong are constructed as well as revised.

In towns with significant immigrant populations, community celebrations usually included symbolic gestures of inclusion, such as ethnic music and tables with ethnic food. At the same time, commemoration of towns' founding tacitly excluded new immigrants. Besides festive events, ordinary town meetings also provided ritual occasions for discussing inclusion and exclusion. In several towns, these conversations arose in conjunction with proposals for annexing additional territory. More common discussions occurred at town meetings in which proposals were considered for attracting newcomers, providing necessary infrastructure, and determining which newcomers would be welcome and which would not.[12]

Although the rituals that come most readily to residents' minds are formally organized community-wide events, the daily interaction that happens on sidewalks and at the café function with equal importance as informal rituals. They are for the most part convivial encounters that take place in neutral public space and consist of talk about safe topics, such as the weather, athletic events, local happenings, and family outings.[13] They convey to bystanders that residents get along and provide occasions to reinforce implicit agreement about common values. An angry daughter-in-law would not dare shout invectives at her mother-in-law in these public venues. Were she to do so, she would become the focus of community gossip—the twenty-first-century version of the village shrew.[14]

A LEADERSHIP STRUCTURE

The necessity of a leadership structure reminds us that communities are more than aggregations of like-minded people who merely happen to live in the proximity of one another and enjoy one another's company. That view is sometimes rooted in the distinction between gemeinschaft and gesellschaft, in which community is identified by the former and thus connotes warm, collegial, intimate relationships among undifferentiated coequals, whereas only the latter implies formal organization, hierarchy, and a well-defined division of labor. Small towns are amply constituted by gesellschaft-type relations as much as they are by gemeinschaft.

Our interviews with town leaders demonstrate that special training and experience is required for performing the many administrative tasks that are needed in small towns. Leaders earn respect by participating in voluntary associations such as the Lions and Kiwanis clubs, a chamber of commerce, or their respective places of worship. Leaders are expected to maintain the basic infrastructure of the community, enforce its laws, protect the public safety, and facilitate social service provision.

There is some truth to the observation that small-town leaders function on the basis of personal relationships and charisma. The leaders we talked to spent part of each day keeping abreast of local events, attending community meetings, and taking calls from constituents. Residents appreciated leaders who performed competently, but also wanted to feel that town leaders were their equals rather than lording it over them.

Town leaders currently spend an important share of their time participating in wider regional and state activities that focus on economic development along with fulfilling regulatory mandates. In these roles, town leaders play a key brokering function that defines the local community in relation to the wider social environment.

SOCIAL NETWORKS

In addition to the more formalized structures that guide and govern the community, informal social relationships among individuals are a critical part of what it means for people in small towns to feel that they belong to a community. These relationships include working together, talking to a neighbor over the back fence, greeting a fellow church member on Sunday morning, meeting for coffee at the local café, arranging a business deal, going fishing with a buddy, visiting a relative in the hospital, and myriads of other examples. Thinking of these not only as relationships between two individuals but also as networks that directly and indirectly connect any number of people has the value of showing that a community is tied together in multiple ways.

My interviewees provided ample evidence that even in the smallest towns, the closest personal relationships are selective, and based largely on affinities and shared interests. When respondents were asked to talk about the people in their community that they knew well enough to invite to their house for dinner or to share a meal at a restaurant, they explained that they knew these people because of specific subcommunity-level groups and activities. Dinner guests, they said, would include a couple who went to their church, a next-door neighbor, a friend they had known since high school, a coworker, someone they had worked together with on a project sponsored by the Lions club, or a member of their extended family. In these ways, their relationships differ little from ones that have been studied in cities and suburbs. The sense of sharing and togetherness that is expressed probably has more to do with dining, worshiping, reminiscing, working, or volunteering than it does with the community itself, at least if community means the town. The distinctive feature of social networks in small towns pertains more to the fact that these particular relationships overlap with other networks and situations. The next-door neighbor is also a person one sees at church, meets on the street, and runs into at the ball game.

Social networks in small towns are structured by the fact that people live in relatively close proximity to one another and for this reason have opportunities to interact in multiple settings. The chances of knowing someone's name or having spoken to them in the past are greater among people who live in the same small town than among people who live in different towns or different parts of a metropolitan area. The likelihood of mutual recognition in small towns reinforces the sense of "we-ness" that already exists because of coresidence. But it is also important to remember that social networks in small towns are shaped, as they are elsewhere, by factors that divide the community and reinforce alternate identities. In our interviews, we found numerous instances of fellow church members knowing and identifying with one another better than with members of a different church as well as evidence that social networks are structured by landownership among farmers, age, the presence or absence of children, occupations, and gender. Residents considered it appealing to sit at the local coffee shop with someone of a different socioeconomic class and recognize nearly everyone in town, but their relationships varied in duration, intensity, and content.[15]

The likelihood that neighbors, fellow church members, and coworkers know one another suggests that social relationships in small towns are closed networks (or using other terminology, have high "clustering coefficients"). This possibility indicates that residents of small towns may also be closed minded, not from deficient intelligence, but rather simply because their networks fail to expose them to new and different ideas. The evidence from my interviews suggests that this argument is not supported. Despite purporting to know quite a large number of their coresidents, interviewees claimed a much smaller number of coresidents as truly close friends with whom they spent a great deal of time, and most spoke about having regular relationships with people outside their community. They kept in touch with friends in other towns or cities where they had previously lived, had grown children or other relatives who lived in other parts of the country, traveled, emailed, obtained information through the Internet, and had business dealings with people from other places.

The possible exception had to do with politics and discussions of politically inflected social issues. Leanings toward the Republican Party and conservative views on social issues characterized many of the towns in which we conducted interviews. I suggested that several reasons for these leanings were probably at work. One is that a majority view can be perpetuated by the simple fact that those people have more of an opportunity, given equal involvement in local social networks, to have their opinions reinforced. Another possibility having to do with networks is that residents said they often did not talk openly about politics, especially in situations where they expected disagreements. Even if networks are fairly open and diverse, then, politics in those settings may not be discussed. In addition, people with liberal views were more likely than those with conservative stances to express their opinions as personal opinions and use tentative, conditional language.

As social networks have expanded through electronic communication, some of the literature has questioned whether geographic proximity is still important, or whether community can be found just as easily in cyberspace as in real places. Keller's framework in which multiple building blocks of community are included is helpful in this regard. A certain kind of community may be possible strictly through network ties in cyberspace, but the contributions of territory and rituals in which people are physically copresent would be missing, and it would probably still be necessary to invent collective myths and establish a governance structure of some kind.

Caution is also suggested toward efforts to identify community only through evidence about the extent and configuration of network ties. Although networks have advantages for investigation through mathematical models, the empirical reality is usually messier than these models indicate. Networks can be simulated by, for example, asking people to name their close friends or investigating their email contacts. But in real life, we find that people have difficulty identifying who exactly is a close friend and who is not, and they exchange information of many different kinds through many different channels and attribute significance to the relationships involved that often have little to do with the frequency of these exchanges.

The Spirit of Community

The spirit of community in Keller's discussion is the result of all the other activities and beliefs that facilitate it. At the same time, community spirit can be distinguished as an awareness on the part of individuals of something that transcends their self-interest and for which they feel responsible. In a family, for instance, members know that each person has a distinct personal identity and pursues particular individual goals, but members also recognize that they are part of a family and feel responsible for one another's well-being. In small towns, this meaning of community spirit is perhaps most easily seen in the expectation that a good member of the community will contribute time and energy to the collective well-being by, say, participating in community projects or at least being self-sufficient so as not to burden the community.

There is perhaps a more subtle way in which community spirit is evident as well. If the idea is that a person somehow feels responsible for the community, then the feelings must be considered and not only the tangible activities that constitute community projects. Repeatedly in our interviews we heard people talking as if they personally felt sad or happy about how their town was faring. They wished that they could find a way to forestall declining population, mourned the loss of their school, felt bad when a business closed, took pride in a new fire station, and were happy about the new gutters being installed along Main Street. True, they were personally affected in a way that might be understood in terms of self-interest. They had to drive further to shop or they less often had to wade through water on rainy days when parking on Main Street. But that was not all. Self-interest alone did not capture how they felt. These developments reflected how they felt about the community. The town was worse or better off. Something bad or good had happened in which they participated as members of the community.

Afterword

IMPLICIT IN ALMOST EVERYTHING that small-town residents say about their communities is a comparison with big cities. According to people who live in small towns, their communities are friendlier, safer, more familiar, more neighborly, more caring, and better places to raise families than a large metropolitan area. Residents of cities and suburbs are naturally less inclined to agree with negative assessments of their own communities. Although the primary point of reference for residents of big cities seems to be other large metropolitan areas, part of what they say resembles the comments of people in small towns. It is the friendly, neighborly atmosphere they especially appreciate. A resident of a medium-size city, for example, talks warmly about the "little neighborhood get-togethers" on her street. "We take cookies and little gifts to each other at Christmas time," she explains. "We choose to get together sometimes for dinner." She says this is what happens on the "self-contained" cul-de-sac of eight houses where she lives. A woman in her seventies who has lived all her live in suburban Minneapolis comments that the best thing about her community is its "small-town atmosphere." Similarly, a resident of Chicago says she likes the fact that it is quiet on her street and there is a "nice neighborhood feeling" on her block. From comments like these, one might conclude that urban planners and landscape architects who have tried to promote a small-town atmosphere in larger places have been successful. One might suggest doing more to build outdoor malls that resemble old-fashioned town squares as well as constructing townhouse developments to include wide verandas, porch swings, and potted geraniums.

But being able truly to replicate all the characteristics that people find desirable about a small town in large cities is, frankly, a losing proposition. Everything that I have explored in the foregoing chapters indicates that scale matters. It isn't just that people in small towns are inherently friendlier, easier to get along with, or more civically oriented. The difference is that smallness shapes social networks, behavior, and civic commitments. Some of these influences can be duplicated in cities. The fact that the Chicago woman, for instance, mentions her block is not surprising. It is on that scale that she feels a sense of quiet neighborliness. Most everything else about her life is fundamentally different than if she were living in a small town. She speaks of walking with her boyfriend through Millennium Park during a free concert. It was enjoyable for them, but they didn't know anyone else in the park. Asked if she liked Chicago well enough to stay, she said the city was "great," but she figured she might move in a year or two to San Francisco, or maybe to Spain. People in suburbs give similar responses. They like their immediate neighborhood because it is quiet and friendly. Some have yards and gardens that connect them with nature. They enjoy being outdoors. For example, the woman in suburban Minneapolis says that the cornfields disappeared decades ago, but "we're still close to the wide-open spaces." These suburban residents, however, seldom work or shop in their neighborhoods, go to church there, or actually see many of their neighbors on a regular basis. The Minneapolis woman says her suburb "is a good location to come and go from."

Closer inspection of the language that residents use to describe their communities suggests further differences in orientation and outlook. Inhabitants of suburbs emphasize that their communities are family friendly, just as small-town residents do. But that means something different in suburbs than in small towns. Family friendly more often connotes diversity, which suburban residents say is a good thing because children need to mingle with people from racial and ethnic backgrounds different from their own. Whether suburbs are actually as diverse as residents claim is, of course, debatable. But suburban residents know that diversity is something they should value. More often a family-friendly suburb implies amenities—schools that are not only high in quality but also large enough to offer a wide range of academic, athletic, and artistic programs, plus access to organizations providing entertainment and recreation. As a parent who lives in a rapidly growing suburb of eighty thousand observes of his community, "It was planned really well in terms of residential development and recreation parks and trails."

A family-friendly suburb also means a convenient place in which to live. Convenience is a value stressed by residents of small towns as well, so once again it is important to understand the differences in what counts as convenience. In small towns, it means being within a few blocks of the bank and living close to school, but it also connotes knowing the banker and teachers well enough to cut through the bureaucratic formalities required in a larger place, and implies a circumscribed array of opportunities that simplify the kinds of decisions a person has to make on a daily basis. The suburban definition of convenience differs because of the larger scale in which social relationships occur. Convenience means being able to drive to "workplace destinations," as one suburban resident puts it. It is living sufficiently close to an interstate to get to where one wants to go in twenty or thirty minutes.

The sense of place implied by these different nuances of meaning can be described metaphorically as a circle in small towns and an arrow in larger metropolitan areas. Although people in small towns spend plenty of time elsewhere, especially if they have to drive to another town to buy groceries or see the doctor, the community strikes them as a bounded space, like a circle that coincides roughly with the town's municipal limits. The community is a space in which social relationships occur, whether at work, the school, the farm supply store, or the American Legion post. An arrow serves as a better description of suburban space because residents' homes are places to which they come and go. A person literally drives in one direction to work, another to the shopping mall, and yet another to church or school. Social relationships are scattered in those different directions.

Despite the fact that residents of small communities regard themselves and their neighbors as somehow more authentic as well as truer to such traditional values as personal integrity and altruism, there is no reason to believe that small towns are morally superior to large cities, or the reverse. Each has its advantages and disadvantages. The one promotes neighbor-liness that sometimes becomes stifling, while the other provides opportu-nities that sometimes become overwhelming. The issue is rather one of recognizing the extent to which small towns actually are different from metropolitan places. Small communities do have some advantages. How-ever much they may be changing, and becoming more fully influenced by national advertising, business patterns, and politics, they are and will re-main different from cities as long as their populations remain small and social interaction within them is relatively self-contained.

People who move from large metropolitan areas to small rural com-munities in the hope of having the best of both worlds quickly discover that they can enjoy some of the benefits of small towns, but that many of the other potential advantages can be attained only at a cost they are un-willing to pay. A good example is John Meyers, a fifty-year-old business executive who moved with his wife and three sons a decade ago to a ham-let of a hundred people twenty-five miles from a large city. Mr. Meyers is an executive vice president of an international insurance company that was recently purchased by a firm in Switzerland. From his home study, he spends an hour early every morning communicating via a secure email link to the firm's employees in India who have been processing accounts during the night. He checks in with his boss who lives in a suburb of New York City and stays in contact via email from his bedroom office. To this extent, Mr. Meyers is part of the new electronically linked global work-force that can also enjoy the benefits of living in the country. He and his wife own several acres. They take pleasure in being able to plant a gar-den, wander into the nearby woods where wildlife can still be found, and take in fresh air and beautiful sunsets. None of the other traditional attributes of small-town life are within their grasp, though. They know none of their neighbors because the neighbors, as near as Mr. Meyers can tell, are seldom at home. His home office is good for the first hour of the day, but then he has to commute twenty-five miles into the city because his boss insists he be there to interact personally with other employees. In fact, his boss monitors exactly where he is at all times through the GPS locators on his cell phone and computer. Mr. Meyers is a sociable person, so he makes a point of visiting with friends twice a week, yet to do this he has to meet them at a bar somewhere in the city. At least four times a month, he drives to the airport forty-five minutes away and then flies to another city to give workshops. He and his wife are part of a church fellowship group that they have to drive fifteen miles to attend.

This example returns us to the question I posed at the outset of whether small towns are somehow characteristic of what the United States is really like, even though only a minority of the public lives in them. The answer is no. Small towns are instead what many people think the United States should be like, and indeed, what they would like it to be. Small towns are neighborly and impose high expectations on residents to be involved in the community. There is a homey, secure connection with the past along with a rewarding sense of camaraderie for those who want it. For those who do not want it, small towns are stifling. Those who live in larger places have to find comforting social relationships in different ways. It is no accident that writers look to Tocqueville, who was impressed with the small communities he visited in the 1830s, for insights into the continuing success of US democracy. It is understandable that populists sometimes call on citizens to reject big government and fend for themselves the way people do in small towns. Those are dreams that work to some extent in small communities, but miss the complex realities of social life on a larger scale.

As much as small towns are changing, they do have a viable future. It is unlikely that refugees from cities and suburbs will heavily repopulate them. But the depopulation that happened as a result of large-scale farming has slowed. Easier transportation and better communication, the aging of the US population, and a continuing desire to live closer to the land and among friendly neighbors are among the factors keeping small towns alive. They are places in which the slower pace and smaller scale of the past is preserved. They are also communities in which leadership and innovative ideas are poised expectantly toward the future.

METHODOLOGY

Apart from growing up in a small town and living in communities that seemed small most of my life, the research that led to this book began in earnest in 1996. As part of a project on civic involvement, my research team and I conducted 250 qualitative interviews in 18 states with community leaders and ordinary residents, about a third of whom lived in small towns, and the remainder of whom resided in cities or suburbs. In 1997, we also conducted a representative national survey among 1,528 randomly selected respondents. Those data became the basis for my book *Loose Connections: Joining Together in America's Fragmented Communities*, published by Harvard University Press in 1998. That book, including a chapter on small towns, focused on changing patterns of civic involvement amid the increasingly porous institutions of which the United States is composed. It left me with many unanswered questions about community life in small towns as well as a great deal of unanalyzed data.

A decade passed before I was able to return to these questions about small towns. In 2007, I initiated a project on social change in the Midwest that included an analysis of statistical data collected by the US Census Bureau among approximately 5,500 towns from 1890 to 2005. To supplement the statistical data, my research assistants and I conducted interviews with approximately 200 residents and community leaders in towns selected to illustrate the changes taking place in rural farming towns and rapidly growing metropolitan areas. That project resulted in my book *Remaking the Heartland: Middle America since the 1950s*, published by Princeton University Press in 2011. Faced again with a great deal of unanalyzed qualitative information, I decided to expand the focus of my research to include small towns in other parts of the United States. In 2008 and 2009, my research assistants and I conducted approximately 250 additional interviews, and in 2010 and 2011 approximately another 150 interviews. Besides the qualitative interviews, I also drew on data collected by the US Census Bureau for incorporated places between 1980 and 2010, reanalyzed the data from my 1997 survey, and examined data from several other national surveys conducted between 1998 and 2008. The census data from which the principal analyses were conducted were obtained from the Missouri Census Data Center and socialexplorer.com, and included the 1980, 1990, 2000, and 2010 decennial censuses as well as estimates from the aggregated 2005 to 2009 American Community Surveys. Urban area variables were used in the various data files to identify towns in which any portion of the resident population was within an urban-fringe area. As discussed in chapters 1 and 3, the total number of towns varies slightly depending on whether only 2010 data were analyzed or trends were analyzed for towns present in both the 1980 and 2010 files.

During the course of the research I personally visited more than 100 towns, where I talked informally to residents, clergy, and other community officials, collected information at courthouses and libraries, and took photos. Of the formal interviews, approximately 120 were conducted in person at interviewees' homes or places of work, and the remainder were conducted by telephone. Trained professional interviewers conducted all the interviews. The interviews lasted an average of an hour and a half, with some ranging up to three hours. Eighteen of the interviews were conducted jointly with husbands and wives. All the others were conducted with one individual, although in several cases husbands and wives were interviewed separately, and in several other cases interviews were conducted with siblings or two generations from the same family. In addition to the individual interviews, several focus groups were conducted involving multiple residents from communities.

Respondents for the qualitative interviews were selected using a purposive quota design. The aim of the design was to maximize diversity among respondents by selecting approximately equal numbers of men and women, younger and older people, and college-educated and non-college-educated respondents, and then within these larger categories to select people from different occupations, religious backgrounds, and racial and ethnic backgrounds, and from towns varying in size, patterns of growth or decline, region, and principal basis of economic activity. Town characteristics were determined primarily from census data along with additional information about housing, community histories, and local economic conditions. Individual respondents were identified in most cases by conducting an interview with a community leader, such as an elected or appointed official, school superintendent or principal, county extension agent or county commissioner, or clergyperson, and asking for referrals to other residents in the community, and then asking these interviewees for additional referrals. Small towns in which interviews were conducted ranged in size from 43 to 25,000, with a median population in 2008 of 1,443. In addition, 150 respondents were interviewed for comparative purposes in cities or suburbs with populations ranging from 40,000 to 2.8 million. Interviews were conducted in 43 states, and included small towns in which the dominant industries were farming, livestock and meat processing, sulfur mining, open-strip coal and copper mining, deep-shaft gold and salt mining, oil and natural gas production and processing, traditional manufacturing and metal fabrication, electronics, call centers and information processing, tourism, gambling, biofuels, and advanced technology. Mean household incomes in the communities ranged from slightly above the national average to 30 percent below the national average, and unemployment varied from as low as 4 percent to as high as 20 percent. In many of the smaller communities, health services and educational facilities were the principal employers. Respondents worked in 85 different occupations, ranging from custodian, short-order cook, and office assistant to bank president, doctor, and lawyer. The most common occupations were housewife, teacher, farmer, and salesperson. Among the community leaders interviewed the most common were elected or appointed officials, such as mayors, town administrators, and economic development directors, along with school superintendents and principals as well as Protestant clergy or Catholic priests.

The interviews were conducted using semistructured interview schedules that included fixed-stem questions asked verbatim of all respondents and flexible follow-up questions to probe for greater detail and more specific information. The aim of the questions was to encourage interviewees to tell their stories as well as talk about the meanings, understandings, and interpretations they associated with their communities, their own work and family experiences within the community, and some of the larger issues facing their communities, ranging from economic issues, such as job training and the availability of educational opportunities, to social and moral issues of concern, like drug use or abortion. The majority of respondents were interviewed using an initial version of the questions, and during the final year of data collection, respondents were interviewed using a modified version in which questions were included to probe more deeply into topics that arose in responses to the earlier interviews. Special interview schedules were designed for respondents who were interviewed as informants about particular issues, such as the changing character of schools, Catholic parishes, and political leadership in small towns.

All the interviews were professionally transcribed, and each interview was analyzed qualitatively for content and variation pertaining to the main themes that became the chapters of this book. Particular attention was given to variation associated with occupation, age, gender, size of community, and location. Where it was possible, the qualitative interview information was supplemented with census data, responses from national surveys, and information about local communities available to the public through online Web sites and research documents. Although many interviewees gave permission to be identified along with their communities, we abided by strict Institutional Review Board rules governing human

subjects research and have kept all such information confidential. Pseud-
onyms are used for individual respondents, the names and locations of
communities are not disclosed, and some characteristics have been withheld or altered to prevent individuals and communities from being identified. The interview guides used in the study are as follows.

Small Town Resident Interview Guide: Version A

1. For the tape, then, have I explained the purpose of the study, and do
   you give permission to record this interview?
2. Before we begin, I need to fill in some background information; for
   instance, I will say for the tape that you are (male/female).
3. In what year were you born?
4. So that makes you how old?
5. What was the highest year you completed in school?
6. If any college: Where did you attend college, and what was your
   major?
7. If any postcollege: What was your graduate work in?
8. What is your occupation? [If retired, ask what it was.]
9. Are you married?
10. If married: What is your spouse's education?
11. What is your religion?
12. And for the tape, you live in (name of town or county and state).

To begin, then, ...

1. We are especially interested in hearing people's stories about how
   they got involved in the line of work they are in, whether that means
   their work, homemaking, or what they used to do if they are retired.
   Could you tell me your story, maybe starting with when you finished being in school? How did you get into what you wound up
   doing?
2. Were there any other influences or events that shaped the kind of
   work you wound up doing? Can you say a bit about those?
3. What kind of influence did your mom and dad have on the kind of
   work you went into? For example, did they want you to do what
   they did? And if so, how did they let you know that, or how did
   they guide you? Or did they encourage you to do something else?
4. How did your parents feel about college? Did they want you to go
   or not, or what did they say?
5. How did your parents feel about where you lived? And how did
   you feel? For instance, some parents really want their children to
   live close to them and feel bad if their children move away. How
   was it in your family?

6. As you were getting your start (in your job, farming, setting up a household, having your own children, etc.), tell me about that. What did you do? What kinds of challenges did you face? What was the hardest part?

7. Here's a different kind of question. Suppose you were just about to graduate from high school and were thinking about your future. What advice would you give yourself about what you should do or not do?

8. Tell me how doing these things would help you get what you wanted out of life.

9. I have several questions about your immediate family, which means the people currently living with you in your household. So who would that be? [Probe especially for spouse, children, and any other relatives.]

10. And who would you identify as the main breadwinner—that is, the person most responsible for the family's income—or are there more than one?

11. I'm not going to ask any personal questions about finances, but I have a general question, which is: Would you say that your finances right now are very tight, fairly tight, fairly comfortable, or very comfortable?

12. And tell me a bit more about that; for instance, what does (tight or comfortable) mean? What are some of the ways in which things are tight or not so tight?

13. What things would be really helpful to have, but are things you can't afford right now?

14. Have times been better for you financially in the past than they are now, or how would you describe it?

15. What are some of the main factors that keep your finances from being better than they are now?

16. If you were going to make a significant improvement in your finances, what would you have to do? For instance, would you have to get more education, change jobs, move to a different area, or what?

17. Why would that be necessary, and how would it help?

18. Would you say your life has been easier in terms of finances than your parents or harder, or what would you say about that? In what ways has it been easier or harder?

19. Did your parents ever live through some really difficult times, like people experienced back in the 1930s during the Great Depression, or just some time when they didn't have much money at all?

20. If yes: What kinds of things did they say about that? How did it affect them? How did it affect you?

Next are some questions about your community ....

1. Now, are you the first in your family to have lived in this community, or did earlier generations live here as well?
2. If earlier generations: So tell me the story. Which of your family came here first? Where did they come from? When did they come? And why did they settle here?
3. If no earlier generations: Tell me the story of how you came to live here. When did you come? Where had you been before? And why did you come here?
4. What are some of the things you really like about living in this community?
5. Can you give me an example—something that would illustrate what is really nice about living here?
6. Why is that special to you?
7. And what are some things you don't especially like about living here? Or maybe something you would change if you could?
8. Give me an example about that?
9. Could you ever imagine yourself living someplace else? And whether it was realistic or not, if you had to live someplace else, where would it be? Or what kind of community would it be?
10. If you had to move away for some reason, what would you miss the most? Your friends, of course, but what else? What kinds of things are you attached to here that you know you would miss?
11. This next question may be one you will need to think about for a moment. City people sometimes say things about people who live on farms or in small towns in the country that aren't very favorable. For instance, they will call country people "hicks" or say they talk funny, or wonder why they live in out-of-the-way places. I imagine you know what I'm talking about, right? Or maybe these things will be said on television or in a movie. Did you ever hear anything like that? Could you give me an example? Did you ever feel like somebody was looking down on you because of where you lived? How did that happen?
12. Now on the other hand, people who live on farms and in rural communities often feel proud of where they live. What are some things that make you proud of where you live? And what else?
13. Is it the case that people in your community are really friendly, neighborly, and helpful? How would you describe it? Put it in your words for me.
14. Give me some examples of how people are neighborly.
15. You have probably heard the saying "good fences make good neighbors," which means that sometimes there are disagreements, or some-

times neighbors don't get along. Sometimes they are nosy or gossip too much. Talk to me for a few minutes about that. I'm sure it happens in your community some of the time. What would be some examples?

16. I don't know if you've heard the term "small-town nice," but it means that people in small towns are really nice and polite, but sometimes don't say what they really think. For instance, they will say, "well, I don't know" instead of "no, I disagree." You've probably noticed this kind of thing, so tell me about that. Where does that show up in your community? [Use alternative wordings for different regions.]

17. On a slightly different topic, people in small towns and rural communities are known for being self-sufficient. They don't ask for help unless they really need it. They stand on their own two feet, as people say. They are good at fixing things and finding ways to solve their problems. Does that describe some of the people in your community? Can you think of an example? Does it describe you?

18. What is an example of how you like to be self-sufficient, fix things, or solve your own problems?

19. If someone had lived in your community twenty-five or thirty years ago, and came back today, what would be the main changes they would notice?

20. And what other changes would they notice compared to thirty years ago?

21. What are some of the main reasons for these changes?

22. Have these changes been good for the community or not so good?

23. Why have they been good (or not so good)?

24. Some people we have interviewed talk about a "sense of loss"—or feeling that maybe things were better in the past. That can happen in communities that are declining or not growing. Do people you know say that sometimes, or how would they put it?

25. In most communities, there are people who are looked up to and respected. In your community, what kinds of people are these? What kind of people are looked up to and respected?

26. And then there are people who aren't respected as much. What kinds of people are these?

27. There are also people in most communities who kind of keep to themselves. What kinds of people in your community keep to themselves?

28. Why do they keep to themselves?

29. Is your community doing anything to attract newcomers? If yes: What is it doing?

30. If any newcomers: What kinds of people are moving into the community? Why are they coming?

31. How important would you say religion is in your community?
32. Can you give me an example that would show how important it is?
33. Which religious congregation (if any) are you associated with?
34. If any: What tradition or denomination is it?
35. Is it in your community? If not, how far away is it?
36. About how many people belong to this congregation?
37. What kinds of things do you do with other members of your congregation just to be friendly and socialize? For instance, do you get together for coffee or have dinners together, or what do you do?
38. Has there been a time when your congregation was really helpful to you?
39. Tell me about that time.
40. Let me ask about some of the congregation's activities and programs. Does the church do anything involving churches in other countries, like helping a sister congregation in another country or sponsoring a missionary?
    If yes: Tell me about it. What does the church do?
    Does the church do anything else like this?
41. Does the church have any activities that focus especially on helping the needy in your own community?
    If yes: Tell me about these activities. Who needs help, and what do you do?
    Can you give me a specific example (without mentioning names) of someone or some family the church has helped?
42. Does your church sponsor any short-term mission trips to other countries?
    If yes: Tell me about it. Where do you go? What do you do? Who goes?
    Can you give me an example that would show how this works?
    Why does your church do this?
    How do you think this activity influences the life of the congregation?
43. Have you, yourself, ever gone to another country on a mission trip?
44. If yes: Where did you go, and what did you do? How did you get involved? What kind of impact did it have on you?
45. People often say they have a special feeling about the land. The land is very meaningful to them. Is that true for you?
46. If yes: In what ways is the land special to you?
47. If no: Why do you think the land isn't so special for you?
48. Do you think the land is special for a lot of people in your community?
49. What are some things that make it special?
50. What kinds of things do you do just to get out and enjoy the beauty of nature in your area?

Now we're moving to the last set of questions ....

1. As you know, people have different views on social and moral issues. Are there any particular social and moral issues that you feel
   strongly about?
2. If yes: What issue or issues do you feel strongly about? Why do you
   feel strongly about this issue (or these issues)?
3. If no: Are there some issues, though, that you might care enough
   about to have them affect how you vote?
4. As you think about the way things are going in America, what
   would you say the worst moral problem is in our country today?
5. Tell me how you think this problem is affecting our country?
6. What are some things people in your community are doing about
   this problem?
7. Abortion is an issue that many people feel strongly about. In your
   own words, how would you describe your views about abortion?
8. What are some of the main reasons that you hold these views?
9. Another issue that has been in the news a lot is evolution. What are
   your views about evolution and how it should be taught in the
   schools?
10. What would you say has shaped your views about evolution the
    most?
11. An issue that a lot of communities are facing has to do with drugs,
    alcoholism, and crime. Has this been a problem in your community?
12. If yes: Can you give me an example?
13. If no: Why do you think this hasn't been a problem?
14. What do you think the best way is to deal with drugs and alcohol-
    ism in a community?
15. Here is another question: Is the government generally helping to
    make things better in your community or is it making them worse?
16. Put it in your own words for me. How is government making things
    (better or worse)?
17. Do you generally consider yourself a Republican, a Democrat, or an
    independent?
18. Those are my questions. Is there anything you would like to add or
    go back over?

Small-Town Resident Interview Guide: Version B

1. For the tape, then, have I explained the purpose of the study, and do
   you give permission to record this interview?
2. Before we begin, I need to fill in some background information; for
   instance, I will say for the tape that you are (male/female).
3. In what year were you born?

4. So that makes you how old?
5. What was the highest year you completed in school?
6. If any college: Where did you attend college, and what was your major?
7. If any postcollege: What was your graduate work in?
8. What is your occupation? [If retired, ask what it was.]
9. Are you married?
10. If married: What is your spouse's education?
11. What is your religion?
12. And for the tape, you live in (name of town or county and state).

To begin, then, ...

1. Tell me about your work. What are some of the main activities your work involves? How do you spend your time? What are your main responsibilities? Can you describe your work in some of those terms?
2. How long have you been in this line of work? Give me a brief history, including any other jobs you may have had, and why you switched, if you did.
3. We are especially interested in hearing the stories of how people got into their line of work. Can you tell me your story? Maybe starting in high school or earlier? How and why did you choose your line of work?
4. I'm curious about the connection between living in or near a small town and your line of work. How did where you lived—or where you wanted to live—influence your thinking about the kind of work you went into?
5. If you had gone to work in a city, what would you have sacrificed? What would you have given up that you have in a small town?
6. Why was that a sacrifice you were willing to make?
7. Turn it around now. What have you sacrificed by living in a small town? What have you given up that you would have had living in a city?
8. And why was that a sacrifice you were willing to make?
9. Ever have any regrets? Ever think "what if" you had chosen a different path? Can you tell me how your life might have been different?
10. Do you think you would have had better opportunities to make money if you had lived in a city?
11. So did you choose to live in a small town because money wasn't important, because it was cheaper, or what?
12. If married: One other question about how you got into your current line of work. How was your decision influenced, if at all, by your spouse? For instance, did your spouse's line of work influence yours?

13. I'm not going to ask anything specific about family finances, but compared with other people in your community, would you say your finances would probably be in the top quarter, the top half but not the top quarter, somewhat lower than the community average, or significantly lower than the community average?

14. How would you describe the house you live in compared with other houses in the community?

15. Would you say your house would probably cost more than the average house in the community or less?

16. Most communities have a few families who are quite a bit wealthier than the rest of the community. Maybe they own quite a bit of land, have oil wells, or have inherited money. Tell me about those kinds of people in your community. What do they do?

17. What are some of the things these wealthy people are able to do that other people in the community can't do? For example, do they live in a nice house, travel, or what?

18. Do you ever hear criticisms of these wealthy people? Like, they show off or anything like that? Tell me what you hear people saying?

19. What kind of power do these wealthy people have in the community? Do they influence how the town is run or anything like that?

20. Shifting topics a bit, people in small towns often say they know everybody in town. But of course you know some people better than others. Just as a rough guess, about how many people who live in your town would you say you know on a first-name basis? Either as a raw number or a percentage of everybody in the town.

21. How many people in your community would you say are your close friends?

22. Let's say you were going to invite some people in your community over for dinner or maybe just go out to a restaurant together—so you would be spending an evening with them. Who would they be? How would you know them? What would you have in common? Why would you choose them?

23. To put it a bit differently, of the people you know best in your community, how do you know them? What are the connections? And where do you see them?

24. This next question may be difficult, but let me ask it this way: Of the people you know best, would most of them also know each other? Or would a lot of them not know each other? Maybe they are in different social circles. They know you, but wouldn't know each other.

25. Say a bit more about this. Why would they know each other or not know each other?

26. Are people in your town pretty good neighbors? And if so, can you give me an example of something that would show what it means to be a good neighbor?
27. Suppose I moved to your town and I said to you, I want to fit in. I want to be a neighborly person. Tell me the unspoken rules. What would I need to do to be accepted as a neighborly person?
28. What else would I need to do? What are some of the other rules of neighborliness?
29. Turn it around. What would be something I should not do? What would get me criticized, maybe as somebody who wasn't following the rules?
30. Compared with living in a city, what are some of the things you like best about living in a small town?
31. Why is that something you especially like?
32. When you go to a city, what don't you like about being there?
33. Why is that something you don't like?
34. Now if someone from a city came to your town, they might be critical of it. What would some of those criticisms be, do you think?
35. How would you respond to those criticisms?
36. People we've talked to in small towns sometimes say they like their town because nothing much changes there. Things stay the same. Would you say that about your town? Do things stay the same? And if so, why do you like that? Or don't you like it?
37. Another thing people say is that they like the slow pace of life in a small town. Help me understand that. What does it mean to say that the pace of life is slow?
38. Do you like the slow pace of life? And if so, why do you like it?
39. Tell me about "community spirit" in your town. What are some times when you really feel like there is a lot of community spirit?
40. Help me understand community spirit in your town. Is it a feeling? Or how would people there describe it?
41. We've been talking about small towns. I'm just curious, when does a town start to lose that feeling of being a small town? Is it size? Or what makes the difference?
42. Let's say a town has twenty thousand people. Would you consider that a small town? Why or why not?
43. What would you say the ideal size for a small town might be? What would make it big enough, but not too big, as far as you're concerned? Why that size?
44. Is there anything about the way your town looks that you especially like? For example, some people say they like the way Main Street looks, or maybe it has some quaint old houses or something. Anything? Why is that something you like?

45. What do you like best about where the town is located?
46. Why is that something you especially like?
47. Are there things you like about the immediate location of the town? Maybe it's in a beautiful valley or close to farms. Anything like that?
48. Describe that for me. Put it in your words about why you like it.
49. Next I have some questions about leadership in your community. When I say "leadership in your community," who comes to mind? Who are the important leaders?
50. What is it about these people that sets them apart as leaders? In other words, what makes them leaders?
51. How do you feel about the community's leadership at the moment? What are they doing that is really helping the community?
52. Can you give me an example of something specific that the leadership has done and how that has helped the community?
53. On the other hand, what have the leaders failed to do or not done in a way that helped the community?
54. Why didn't that work out? Or what could have been done that wasn't?
55. Have there been any proposals that were controversial? Maybe part of the community felt strongly one way, and others felt strongly a different way?
56. If so, tell me the story. What happened?
57. Have you, yourself, been involved in any leadership roles in the community? If so, what? What was something you accomplished?
58. Among the community's current leaders, who do you personally know best or feel the most comfortable with? Why is that?
59. What would be an example of something innovative that has happened in your community recently? For example, some towns have gone to sustainable energy, built a new hospital, or attracted a new business. Anything like that?
60. How did that get started? And how has it affected the community?
61. Is your town dealing with any issues having to do with immigration and new ethnic groups?
62. If yes: What are some of the issues? Is the community nervous about becoming more diverse or how do they feel about it?
63. I haven't asked yet about religion, but how important is religion in your community? Is it pretty important or not so important? What would you say?
64. What gives you a sense of whether religion is important or not? What would indicate that one way or the other?
65. Which congregation, if any, are you involved in?
66. What kinds of things do you do with other members of your congregation? For example, do you talk before and after the worship

services, or work together on committees? Can you give me any examples like that?

67. Finally, I have a few questions about politics. Would your community be mostly Republican, mostly Democrat, split right down the middle, or how would you describe it?

68. Does one party or the other usually win in local elections? Or how does it work there?

69. What are some of the big issues that people there care about? Maybe issues that you know are of concern in the community. Or ones that you personally care about.

70. Why are these issues especially important?

71. Is the federal government currently doing anything that helps people in your community? Or how would you describe it?

72. What about the state government? Is it doing anything that especially helps your community?

73. When you get together with people you know there in the community, do you talk about political issues? Or is that a topic you don't talk about so much?

74. What would be some topics that you do talk about? Or would not talk about?

75. If you could tell the president one thing, what would it be?

76. And if you could tell the governor one thing, what would it be?

77. Did you vote in the 2008 presidential election?

78. If yes: May I ask who you voted for?

79. Those are my questions. Is there anything else you might want to add?

Community Leaders Interview Guide

1. For the tape, then, have I explained the purpose of the study, and do you give permission to record this interview?

2. Before we begin, I need to fill in some background information; for instance, I will say for the tape that you are (male/female).

3. In what year were you born?

4. So that makes you how old?

5. What was the highest year you completed in school?

6. If any college: Where did you attend college, and what was your major?

7. If any postcollege: What was your graduate work in?

8. What is your occupation? [If retired, ask what it was.]

9. If employed: What organization do you work for?

10. Where is that located?

11. What is your title or position there? [Elected official may also have other job.]

12. How long have you had this position?
13. Are you married?
14. If married: What is your spouse's occupation?
15. For the tape, you live in (name of town or county and state).
16. And how long have you lived there?

To begin, then, ...

1. Give me a thumbnail sketch of your community. What does it look like? How big is it? What kinds of people live there? What kinds of work do they do?
2. What would be one thing that is distinctive about the community? What is it known for or what sets it apart from other towns?
3. What do you, personally, like best about living there? Anything else?
4. What don't you like so well? What would be something you'd change, if you could?
5. So my main question is this: What do you see as the major issues or challenges currently facing your community? Talk to me about those. Any others? Why is this a challenge?
6. How is the community attempting to deal with each of these issues? And how is that working out? Is there a plan or committee of some kind? Who is involved? Is the state or other jurisdictions involved?
7. Are there any other big issues facing the community? What are they?
8. What would you say is one of the best things that has happened in your community in recent years? Something that has contributed positively?
9. Tell me why that was especially important. Why was that so beneficial?
10. What about something that hasn't worked out so well? Maybe something that has been a setback for the community? Tell me about that.
11. Is this something the community can deal with? Or what's going to be the result?
12. Has the community's population been growing in recent years, staying about the same, or declining?
13. If growing: What are some of the main reasons for the growth? I'm interested in specifics, such as a new industry, an economic development plan, something happening in the area—things like that.
14. If declining or staying the same: What has happened lately to cause decline or keep the population stable? Anything else?
15. What do you anticipate over the next decade or so? Decline? Stability? Growth? What will determine that?
16. How does your location there affect growth or decline? For example, are you affected by the proximity of an interstate or distance to a city?

17. What are some of the main employers in the area? Are there some companies that provide a lot of jobs? What are they, and what do they do?

18. Give me a bit of the history of these companies, if you can. When did these companies come? What attracted them? How are they faring?

19. Now if someone lived in your town but commuted to work someplace else, where would they go? What kinds of work would they probably be doing?

20. What would be the attraction? Why would they live in your community and commute somewhere else? Can you give me an example of someone who does that?

21. If someone had lived in this community twenty-five or thirty years ago, and came back today, what would be the main changes they would notice? Again, I'm looking for specific changes. How about changes in race or ethnicity? Or something like a new school or park?

22. Do you have a sense of what the area was like back then? For example, have you heard people talk about what they liked to do back then? Seen pictures? Heard stories?

23. Have any stores there gone out of business in recent years, and, if so, could you name them for me?

24. What has the community done to try to preserve a sense of its past? What kinds of traditions does it honor? How has it tried to maintain the downtown area?

25. Are there any ethnic traditions being preserved, like a Swedish heritage or German festival? Anything like that?

26. How about an annual parade, festival, or celebration? Could you tell me about anything like that?

27. And are there specific plans for further development in the area— anything like a new corporate center, housing developments, and the like? How about low-income or senior citizen housing?

28. If yes, where will those be, and what impact will they have?

29. How are things financially for people in the community these days? Are people pretty well off, are they experiencing some setbacks because of the economy, or what?

30. Just to pursue this a bit: What influences the local economy there the most? Is it a particular company or industry, and if so, how is that faring? Or is it something else?

31. Every community has some families that are struggling to make ends meet. What about those people? How are they managing these days? How are they being supported?

32. How about agriculture in the area? How is that changing? And how is that affecting the community?

33. Is anything new happening in particular in agriculture? For instance, new crops, new equipment, feedlots, or anything like that? If so, could you talk a bit about those?

34. Of course, agriculture has good years and bad years because of weather and fluctuations in markets. In bad years, what impact do you see there in town? For instance, do you see businesses shutting down or maybe people moving away?

35. I don't know if you would have a sense of this, but from what farmers say there, are government programs helping them or hurting them? And if so, in what way?

36. My next question is about health care in the community. What's the situation there in terms of doctors and a hospital?

37. So is the situation improving, declining, or what? What do you need that you don't have?

38. What about services for the elderly, such as nursing care or assisted living? What do you have, and how adequate is it?

39. What about the schools? What schools do you have, and what are they like? Is the school population increasing, declining, or what? Are there any plans for building new schools or closing old ones?

40. Small towns often pride themselves on voluntary civic associations. Do you have some of those that are especially active? And if so, what do they do? Can you give me an example?

41. Has there been any community-wide civic project, like building a new fire station or library, or anything like that? How did that come about?

42. Tell me about religion there. What are the main churches in town? How are they faring?

43. So what role do the churches play in the community? Why are they important?

44. Are there any religious organizations that are not churches? Maybe a Jewish center, a mosque, or some other group?

45. Is your community making any efforts to get new people to move into the community?

46. If yes: What is it doing?

47. When new people move in, what are some of the adjustments they have to make to start feeling comfortable? Maybe you can think of someone who hasn't lived there all their life and talk about that.

48. We understand that people from cities are moving back to small towns—maybe to retire or because it's cheaper. Do you have some folks like that? Can you give me an example?

49. In some of the communities we've been studying, there is an effort to promote tourism. Things like heritage days, festivals, or picnics.

Is anything like that happening in your community? If yes: Tell me about that. What's happening?

50. In other communities, local, state, and federal government is playing a big role in helping the communities—building roads, providing tax incentives, helping with hospitals, and the like. Are there examples of that in your community? If yes: Tell me about those.

51. Are there any efforts in your community to resist growth, to put the brakes on? If yes: What is behind those efforts? Why are people resisting growth?

52. What about alternative energy—wind, solar, biofuels, and so on? What's happening in your community on that front?

53. Is the community being affected at all by Walmart or anything like that? For instance, are people driving out of town more often to shop?

54. How about the Internet, email, and cell phones? How is all that affecting the community?

Next I'd like to focus on your activities as a community leader ....

1. What sorts of activities and issues are you most involved in? Give me a sense of what you do from day to day.

2. If you had to pick out something that makes your work difficult or frustrating, what would it be?

3. So if you could wave your magic wand and make those problems go away, what would you wish for?

4. On a more positive note, talk to me about some particular issue or project where you've experienced real success—something you are especially pleased to have accomplished.

5. Here's a different kind of question. How is the way you do your job different from the way someone might have done it five or ten years ago? In other words, what's happening that's new, different, or changing?

6. Let me ask about technology. How is new technology affecting the kind of work you do or the issues you face?

7. How about changes in the marketplace? How are you being affected by those?

8. What impact is the economic downturn having on what you do?

9. How about the political climate? How is it there where you are, and how does that affect what you do?

10. How has the political climate in your area been changing, say, over the past five years or so?

11. Are people in your community becoming more interested in certain issues, or how would you describe the hot-button issues today?
12. Which political party seems to be having the most success in your area these days? Why is that? What accounts for their success?
13. What seems to influence how people in your area vote in state and national elections? Are there particular special interest groups that have a lot of influence?
14. In a lot of communities, people are a bit skeptical toward public officials. Sometimes there's a bit of cynicism or mistrust. What kinds of mistrust do you see in your area?

Now we're moving to the last set of questions ....

1. As you know, people have different views on social and moral issues. Are there any particular social and moral issues that you feel strongly about?
2. If yes: What issue or issues do you feel strongly about? Why do you feel strongly about this issue (or these issues)?
3. If no: Are there some issues, though, that you might care enough about to have them affect how you vote?
4. As you think about the way things are going in America, what would you say the worst moral problem is in our country today?
5. Tell me how you think this problem is affecting our country?
6. What are some things people in your community are doing about this problem?
7. An issue that a lot of communities are facing has to do with drugs, alcoholism, and crime. Has this been a problem in your community?
8. If yes: Can you give me an example?
9. If no: Why do you think this hasn't been a problem?
10. What do you think the best way is to deal with drugs and alcoholism in a community?
11. Here is another question: Is the government generally helping to make things better in your community or is it making them worse?
12. Put it in your own words for me. How is government making things (better or worse)?
13. Among people you talk to, are they generally pleased with how things are going in Washington these days, not so pleased, or what? How would you describe the mood there in your community?
14. How about the mood toward the state government? What are some of the issues on people's minds?
15. If you could tell the governor one thing, what would it be?
16. And if you could tell the president one thing, what would that be?

17. Do you generally consider yourself a Republican, a Democrat, or an independent?
18. If I may ask, who did you vote for in the recent presidential election?
19. Those are my questions. Is there anything you would like to add or go back over?

Clergy Interview Guide

1. For the tape, then, have I explained the purpose of the study, and do you give permission to record this interview?
2. The year in which you were born?
3. So that makes you how old now?
4. Your title at the church?
5. How long have you been at this church?
6. Do you serve the one congregation, or do you serve more than one?
7. If more than one: What are the others, and where are they?
8. Before you became the pastor here, what were you doing and where did you live?
9. What was the highest grade or degree you completed?
10. Where did you go to college?
11. Where did you go to seminary?
12. Are you married?
13. What is the name of your church? [If serving more than one congregation, note this and select one, preferably in the pastor's community of residence, as the reference point for subsequent questions.]
14. Where is your church located (town and state)?
15. Just so I'm clear, what denomination or tradition is it?
16. For the tape, let me say that you are (male/female).

To begin, then, I have some questions about your congregation ....

1. About how many people do you have at worship services each week?
2. Is that number growing or declining? For instance, how would it compare with ten years ago?
3. What are some of your main concerns or challenges as you minister to this congregation? Talk to me for a few minutes about those.
   Can you elaborate a bit on why this is a challenge, and what you are doing to face it?
   Are there any other major challenges? What would those be?
4. Does your church have its own building?
   If yes: When was it built?
   If no: Where do you meet?

5. In what kind of area is your church located? For instance, in an older part close to the center of town, in a newer section of town, out in the country, or where?

6. What are the other main churches in your community? (Any others?)

7. Now are there things that all of the churches, or some of them, do together; for instance, do they share any programs, or what kinds of relationships are there among the local churches? Just give me a sense of how the churches interact or maybe some examples.

8. Let me ask about some of your congregation's activities and programs. Does the church do anything involving churches in other countries, like helping a sister congregation in another country or sponsoring a missionary?

   If yes: Tell me about it. What does the church do?

   Does the church do anything else like this?

9. Does the church have any activities that focus especially on helping the needy in your own community?

   If yes: Tell me about these activities. Who needs help, and what do you do?

   Can you give me a specific example (without mentioning names) of someone or some family the church has helped.

   Does the church have a committee to administer these activities, or how does it work?

10. Does your church sponsor any short-term mission trips to other countries?

    If yes: Tell me about it. Where do you go? What do you do? Who goes?

    Can you give me an example that would show how this works.

    Why does your church do this?

    How do you think this activity influences the life of the congregation?

    If no: Would you like your church to do this?

    If yes: What would you like it to do?

    Why would this be a good idea?

    If no: Why not?

11. Have you, yourself, ever gone to another country on a mission trip?

    If yes: Where did you go, and what did you do? How did you get involved? What kind of impact did it have on you?

Next are some questions about your community ....

1. What is your community like? Paint me a word picture of it. Take a few minutes and describe it for me so I can imagine it in my mind.

2. Now tell me a little more about the community. What are some other things you haven't mentioned thus far? For instance, what are the people like?

3. If you were to ask people there in your community to mention three things they like about living there, what would those three things be?

4. For each one, ask: Now say more about that. What would people have in mind when they said that, and why would it be important?

5. If someone had lived in this community twenty-five or thirty years ago, and came back today, what would be the main changes they would notice?

6. And what other changes would they notice compared to thirty years ago?

7. What are some of the main reasons for these changes?

8. Have these changes been good for the community or not so good?

9. Why have they been good (or not so good)?

10. As you know, a lot of smaller communities have lost population, and I believe that may be true of your community. Is that correct? [If they say it isn't, you can perhaps strike an agreement that it at least isn't growing much and tailor the next questions accordingly.]

11. How would you explain this loss of population? Why has the number of people declined? What has happened?

12. Are there any other reasons why the population has declined?

13. How do people there feel about the decline in the community? Do they regret it? Are they happy about it? Do they not think about it? Or what are their feelings?

14. I'd like to know why some people move away. Can you think of somebody like that and tell me why they moved away?

15. And what are some of the other reasons people move away?

16. People moving away often has an impact on a congregation. Can you talk to me a bit about that—about someone moving away and how that has affected your congregation?

17. What about the people who stay in the community? They have reasons to stay. But do they have fewer opportunities than the people who leave? Or how do they differ from the people who leave?

18. Some people we have interviewed talk about a "sense of loss"—or maybe nostalgia. Perhaps a feeling that things used to be better. Do you ever hear people say anything like that? Or something along those lines? What do they say?

19. When communities lose population, they have to "downsize," just like a business does. So I have to ask you to talk about that for a few minutes. For example, communities sometimes downsize by closing the school, or the hospital shuts down or businesses leave, or they

share police and fire protection with another town. What sorts of things has your community been doing to downsize?

20. What are some more ways in which your community has been downsizing? (Maybe mention some of the examples again.)

21. In other ways, life in small towns has gotten easier because of better transportation and better communication. So people may think nothing of driving an hour or two to eat out or go shopping. Or they order things through the Internet. Do you find yourself doing that or hear people saying they do? What would be some examples?

22. How are things financially for people in the community these days? Are most of the people pretty well off, are they experiencing some setbacks because of the economy, or what?

23. Just to pursue this a bit: What influences the local economy there the most? Is it mostly farming, and if so, how is that faring? Or is it something else?

24. Without mentioning any names, can you give me an example of somebody who has been having difficulties lately?

25. Why, would you say, have they been having these difficulties?

26. Overall, would you say that things are getting better financially in the community, getting worse, or staying about the same?

27. Why do you think things are (getting better, getting worse, or staying the same)?

28. What would it take for things really to get better? What would improve things in the community economically?

29. Is that likely to happen? Why or why not?

30. How has your church been affected by the local economy? Has the church had to tighten its budget, and if so, in what ways?

31. In most communities, there are people who are looked up to and respected. In your community, what kinds of people are these? What kinds of people are looked up to and respected? What is it about these people that causes them to be admired?

32. And then there are people who aren't respected as much—maybe people sort of look down on them. Not that they would be criticized in public, but maybe people would privately talk about them. What kinds of people are these? Why aren't they respected?

33. There are also people in most communities who kind of keep to themselves. What kinds of people in your community keep to themselves?

34. Why do they keep to themselves?

35. Some people we've talked to say living in a small community is like being in a fishbowl. Sometimes they would like a little more privacy. I suppose being a pastor you might feel that way yourself sometimes. Can you talk some about that?

36. Not mentioning any names, of course, but how do people get to-gether to socialize? For example, are their groups that meet for cof-fee? Does socializing happen mostly among relatives? Or how does it work? Can you give me some examples?
37. Is your community making any efforts to get new people to move into the community?
38. If yes: What is it doing?
39. When new people move in, what are some of the adjustments they have to make to start feeling comfortable? Maybe you can think of someone who hasn't lived there all their life and talk about that.
40. People often say they have a special feeling about the land. The land is very meaningful to them. Do you hear people saying that the land is especially meaningful, or how do they talk about it?
41. I'm wondering if you ever refer to the land or farming in your ser-mons or worship services? Like, in some churches, they sing about "showers of blessing" or "bringing in the sheaves."
42. I imagine you do preach about "loving your neighbor." Am I right? Again, without mentioning any names, have there been instances of conflicts or disagreements between neighbors that you can think of? Could you give me an example and talk about that a little? For in-stance, what was the trouble, and what happened?
43. Have you ever heard the phrase "small-town nice"—meaning that people in small towns, get along by being really nice and polite, and not disagreeing, even when they do? Have you ever come across something like that, or how would you put it?

Now we're moving to the last set of questions ....

1. As you know, people have different views on social and moral is-sues. Are there any particular social and moral issues that you feel strongly about?
2. If yes: What issue or issues do you feel strongly about? Why do you feel strongly about this issue (or these issues)?
3. If no: Are there some issues, though, that you might care enough about to affect how you vote?
4. As you think about the way things are going in America, what would you say the worst moral problem is in our country today?
5. Tell me how you think this problem is affecting our country?
6. What are some things people in your community are doing about this problem?
7. Abortion is an issue that many people feel strongly about. In your own words, how would you describe your views about abortion?
8. What are some of the main reasons that you hold these views?

9. How, if at all, do your views about abortion influence how you vote?

10. Now some of the controversial issues are complex, so just take your time and tell me what you think. For instance, what is your view about teaching the Ten Commandments in public schools?

11. Another issue that has been in the news a lot is evolution. What are your views about evolution and how it should be taught in the schools?

12. What would you say has shaped your views about evolution the most?

13. An issue that a lot of communities are facing has to do with drugs, alcoholism, and crime. Has this been a problem in your community?

14. If yes: Can you give me an example?

15. If no: Why do you think this hasn't been a problem?

16. What do you think the best way is to deal with drugs and alcoholism in a community?

17. Why is that the best way?

18. Then a rather different issue is providing jobs, job training, and other kinds of assistance for people who need it. Is that an issue in your community?

19. How is your community dealing with this issue?

20. Here is another question: Is the government generally helping to make things better in your community or is it making them worse?

21. Put it in your own words for me. How is government making things (better or worse)?

22. Those are my questions. Is there anything you would like to add or go back over?

NOTES

1. Introduction

1. The history of small towns and the mythology that grew up around them is amply described in a relatively neglected survey, Richard Lingeman, *Small Town America: A Narrative History, 1620–the Present* (New York: Putnam, 1980). Lingeman's book is no longer in print, and because of its scope necessarily paints with a broad brush, but it is replete with interesting details and anecdotes, and provides some useful information about small towns through the early 1970s.

2. Opinion polls offer varying impressions of Americans' attitudes toward small towns. Generally speaking, polls suggest that many Americans would like to live in a small town or rural area, and show that a majority of those who do live in small towns are satisfied with their communities. For example, a poll conducted by the Pew Research Center in 2008 found that 30 percent of those who responded would prefer to live in a small town if they could live anywhere, another 21 percent preferred a rural area, whereas 23 percent preferred a city, and 25 percent preferred a suburban area; of those who said they currently lived in a small town, 55 percent described their community as excellent or very good. The proportion of people who described their communities as excellent or very good was higher, though, among respondents in suburbs (68 percent) and rural areas (71 percent), and only slightly lower (52 percent) in cities (Paul Taylor, Rich Morin, Kim Parker, D'Vera Cohn, and Wendy Wang, "For Nearly Half of America, Grass Is Greener Somewhere Else," Pew Research Center Social and Demographic Trends Report, January 29, 2009, http://www.pewsocialtrends.org). Yet the Pew results are of limited use because the response rate to the survey was only 22 percent for those sampled through landline phone numbers and 20 percent for those sampled through cell phone numbers. Further complicating the difficulties, of the respondents who said they lived in a small town, 33 percent lived in counties that the researchers coded as having high-density populations, and 62 percent were coded as actually living in an urban or suburban area. Earlier surveys generally reported favorable attitudes toward small towns as well. For example, a 1985 Roper Poll found that 61 percent of those surveyed thought a small town was best for "the kind of friends you'd have," compared with only 12 percent who thought a big city would be best (26 percent volunteered "no difference"). Small towns received equally large or larger preferences as places for leading a healthy life, privacy, and raising children (Roper Organization, November 2, 1985, based on a sample of 1,998 personal interviews, http://www.ropercenter.uconn.edu/data_access/ipoll). Nevertheless, a story two years later (William Mueller, "Do Americans Really Want to Live in Small Towns?" *American Demographics* [January 1987]: 60) that drew on other evidence argued that schools and health services in small towns were inferior, gossip and interpersonal conflicts were common,

and it was not exactly healthy to live "downwind of farmer Bob as he gives the crops a blast of some chemical carcinogen." A decade earlier, as census data demonstrated that the population living in small towns and rural areas was declining, or at best stable, a poll conducted on August 19, 1977, by the ICR Survey Research Group for Hearst Newspapers reported that 21 percent of Americans claimed to have moved from the suburbs to a country or rural setting, while only 12 percent had moved from a country or rural setting to the suburbs (http://www.ropercenter. uconn.edu/ipoll). Polls results are difficult to interpret because, as I mentioned in the preface, many Americans who live in large metropolitan areas imagine themselves to be living in small towns. In a 2006 poll conducted by the Pew Research Center, for instance, 26 percent of those who responded said they lived in a small town, 16 percent said they lived in a rural area, and 57 percent said they lived in a city or suburb (51 percent said they would prefer a small town or rural area if they could live anywhere; Richard Morin and Paul Taylor, "Suburbs Not Most Popular, But Suburbanites Most Content," Pew Research Center Publications, February 26, 2009, http://www.pewresearch.org). If those responses were taken at face value, 78 million Americans lived in small towns, whereas the US Census showed that only 52 million lived in incorporated places of under 25,000 (including incorporated places of that size that were in metropolitan areas), and indicated that 222 million Americans lived in urban areas, whereas the poll responses suggested only 174 million (US Census Bureau, *Statistical Abstract of the United States: 2008* [Washington, DC: Government Printing Office, 2008], tables 28 and 29).

3. H. Paul Douglass, *The Little Town: Especially in Its Rural Relationships* (New York: Macmillan, 1919), 3.

4. Ibid., 242.

5. On social capital, see especially James Coleman, "Social Capital in the Creation of Human Capital," *American Journal of Sociology* 94 (1988): S95–120. For one of the most extensive empirical examinations of the changing role of social capital in community life, see Robert D. Putnam, *Bowling Alone: The Collapse and Revival of American Community* (New York: Simon and Schuster, 2000). Helpful attention is also being given to the role of spatial arrangements in relation to social capital. See, for example, Kevin S. Hanna, Ann Dale, and Chris Ling, "Social Capital and Quality of Place: Reflections on Growth and Change in a Small Town," *Local Environment* 14 (2009): 31–44, which emphasizes not only the ways in which space influences social networks but also the attachment to places and spatial arrangements that is important to residents' sense of community. See also the more general argument in Ann R. Tickamyer, "Space Matters! Spatial Inequality in Future Sociology," *Contemporary Sociology* 29 (2000): 805–13. This is a theme that also appears repeatedly in my interviews, as discussed especially in chapters 3 and 4. Readers interested in network approaches to community should consult M.E.J. Newman, "Detecting Community Structure in Networks," *European Physical Journal B* 38 (2004): 321–30; Filippo Radicchi, Claudio Castellano, Federico Cecconi, Vittorio Loreto, and Domenico Parisi, "Defining and Identifying Communities in Networks," *Proceedings of the National Academy of Sciences* 101 (2004): 2658–63; in which community is defined as a subset of

connections in a network that are denser than in other parts of the network. For a readable introduction, see also Albert-Laszlo Barabasi, *Linked: How Everything Is Connected to Everything Else, and What It Means for Business, Science, and Everyday Life* (New York: Penguin, 2003). Defining community strictly in terms of network connections offers attractive opportunities for quantification, but leaves aside important questions about the meanings of community to those involved, the quality of their relationships, and properties of the collectivity that cannot be reduced to relationships between individuals.

6. As background for my research, I benefited greatly from reading memoirs composed by writers who grew up in small towns. See, for example, M. J. Anderson, *Portable Prairie: Confessions of an Unsettled Midwesterner* (New York: Thomas Dunne, 2004); Leslie O. Anderson, *Memoirs of a Country Boy/Newspaper Man* (Elk River, MN: DeForest Press, 2004); Bob Barnett, *Growing Up in the Last Small Town* (Ashland, KY: Jesse Stuart Foundation, 2010); Carol Bodensteiner, *Growing Up Country: Memories of an Iowa Farm Girl* (Des Moines, IA: Sun Rising Press, 2008); Eric B. Fowler and Sheila Delaney, *Small-Town Boy, Small-Town Girl: Growing Up in South Dakota, 1920–1950* (Pierre: South Dakota Historical Society, 2009); Mary Karr, *The Liar's Club: A Memoir* (New York: Penguin, 2005); Dorothy Hubbard Schwieder, *Growing Up with the Town: Family and Community on the Great Plains* (Iowa City: University of Iowa Press, 2002); Karen Valby, *Welcome to Utopia: Notes from a Small Town* (New York: Spiegel and Grau, 2010). Insightful as such volumes are, their value as interpretations of small town life are limited because of focusing on a single community, emphasizing what that community is remembered to have been like during the writer's childhood, and in most instances being written by someone who went on to become a journalist, writer, or educator. As artistic works, the most engaging memoirs tend to exoticize small-town life as well, with characters named Bubba and Clem who make moonshine, and one-eyed grandmothers who shoot holes in the kitchen wall and fend off plagues of fence-post-devouring insects.

7. I discuss population decline and other changes in chapters 3 and 6. The perception that small towns are declining is rooted in the fact that the population of many of the smallest towns is indeed declining. Relative to the growth of large cities and suburbs, small towns are also a relatively smaller proportion of the US population. This sense of decline should not be exaggerated, however. For example, in their book *Century of Difference: How America Changed in the Last One Hundred Years* (New York: Russell Sage Foundation, 2006), 173, Claude S. Fischer and Michael Hout include a chart based on census data from 1900 to 2000 showing a large decline in the proportion of Americans who lived in the "countryside" (presumably on farms and in unincorporated or small villages), but relatively little proportional decline in the population living in "towns" (incorporated places of at least twenty-five hundred people not in a metropolitan area).

8. I have in mind studies such as the following: Nancy Tatom Ammerman, *Bible Believers: Fundamentalists in the Modern World* (New Brunswick, NJ: Rutgers University Press, 1987); Lynn Davidman, *Tradition in a Rootless World: Women Turn to Orthodox Judaism* (Berkeley: University of California Press, 1991).

9. I discuss politics and attitudes toward social and moral issues in chapters 8 and 9. An interesting example of homespun wisdom gleaned from colorful small town residents is Denis Boyles, *Superior, Nebraska: The Common Sense Values of America's Heartland* (New York: Doubleday, 2008). See also Bill Bryson, *The Lost Continent: Travels in Small-Town America* (New York: Harper Perennial, 1990).

10. As the source of sociologists' interest in the distinction between the terms *gemeinschaft* and *gesellschaft* is especially important in this regard, see Ferdinand Tönnies, *Community and Civil Society*, ed. Jose Harris (1887; repr., Cambridge: Cambridge University Press, 2001). In his *The Division of Labor in Society* (1893; repr., New York: Macmillan, 1933), Durkheim presents an argument about mechanical and organic solidarity that should not be taken directly as an assertion about the declining sociological significance of small towns. Some interpretations of Durkheim draw this conclusion, however, especially in suggesting that community in modern society ceases to be based on locality and instead is based on nonspatially grounded social relationships (see, for example, Joseph R. Gusfield, *The Community: A Critical Response* [New York: Harper Colophon, 1975]; David W. McMillan and David M. Chavis, "Sense of Community: A Definition and Theory," *Journal of Community Psychology* 14 [1986]: 6–23). While it is certainly true that ease of travel and electronic communication make possible social relationships that are less spatially bound, the suggestion that locality ceases to be important to understandings of community is clearly false. In a national survey (Robert Wuthnow, *Loose Connections: Joining Together in America's Fragmented Communities* [Cambridge, MA: Harvard University Press, 1998]), 42 percent said their neighborhood comes closest to their definition of community, 35 percent said the town in which they lived comes closest, 8 percent said the larger region in which they lived was the best approximation, only 12 percent said the people they associate with felt closest to their definition, and 3 percent gave other responses. The significance of proximity on a smaller scale is also evident in Suzanne Keller, *Community: Pursuing the Dream, Living the Reality* (Princeton, NJ: Princeton University Press, 2003). In a different context, see also Clive C. Taylor and Alan R. Townsend, "The Local 'Sense of Place' as Evidenced in North-East England," *Urban Studies* 13 (1976): 133–46.

11. A valuable survey of the literature can be found in Thomas Bender, *Community and Social Change in America* (Baltimore: Johns Hopkins University Press, 1978). In retrospect, an important contribution that shaped subsequent thinking about community in suburbs was Herbert J. Gans, *The Levittowners: Ways of Life and Politics in a New Suburban Community* (New York: Pantheon Books, 1967). In the context of popular Cold War concerns about the atomization (an interesting metaphor) of social relationships in so-called mass society (for example, as described in David Riesman, *The Lonely Crowd: A Study of Changing American Character* [New Haven, CT: Yale University Press, 1950]; further examined in William Kornhauser, *The Politics of Mass Society* [Glencoe, IL: Free Press, 1959]), *The Levittowners* produced encouraging evidence that newcomers in large suburban housing developments were successfully meeting their neighbors as well as mingling over coffee and backyard barbeques. For a crucial statis-

tical study that could be interpreted as suggesting that small towns were not distinct from larger metropolitan areas, see John D. Kasarda and Morris Janowitz, "Community Attachment in Mass Society," *American Sociological Review* 39 (1974): 328–39. With national survey data, this article examined whether several measures of community attachment were influenced more by size of place (and population density) or duration of residence. The authors concluded that size of place mattered little compared to the effects of duration of residence. Several aspects of the study, though, limits its usefulness as evidence about the distinctiveness or lack of distinctive characteristics of community in small towns: the study was based on data from Great Britain rather than the United States, the rural–urban variable did not distinguish respondents in small towns from those living on farms or in the open country, or those living in small towns that were distant from or in closer proximity to metropolitan areas, and the conceptual argument did not take account of the fact that duration of residence is greater in smaller communities than in larger ones. Still, the results did show that respondents who expressed greater interest in their place of residence (an attitudinal measure of community attachment) were also more likely to spend time with friends and relatives in the area as well as participate in community organizations.

12. For a notable exception, which includes information about small towns in comparison with urban residents, see Claude S. Fischer, *To Dwell among Friends: Personal Networks in Town and City* (Chicago: University of Chicago Press, 1982). For a more general examination of survey data about friendship and contacts with family, see Claude S. Fischer, *Still Connected: Family and Friends in America since 1970* (New York: Russell Sage Foundation Press, 2011). Ethnographic studies of small towns that are helpful in providing a grassroots sense of community dynamics include Sonya Salamon, *Newcomers to Old Towns: Suburbanization of the Heartland* (Chicago: University of Chicago Press, 2003); Richard O. Davies, *Main Street Blues: The Decline of Small-Town America* (Columbus: Ohio State University Press, 1998); Osha Gray Davidson, *Broken Heartland: The Rise of America's Rural Ghetto* (Iowa City: University of Iowa Press, 1996).

13. For an insightful source of myth and imagery, see Emanuel Levy, *Small-Town America in Film: The Decline and Fall of Community* (New York: Continuum, 1991). This work identifies nearly a thousand twentieth-century films that dealt with small towns and examines approximately eighty of these in detail. For a more limited regional focus, but with insightful historical, literary, and ethnographic essays, see Richard O. Davies, Joseph A. Amato, and David R. Pichaske, eds., *A Place Called Home: Writings on the Midwestern Small Town* (Saint Paul: Minnesota Historical Society, 2003).

14. For additional information about the interviews, see the methodology appendix.

15. The US Census Bureau (2010 Decennial Census, released April 1, 2011, http://www.census.gov) estimates the number of incorporated places (exclusive of census-defined places) in 2010 as 19,505, of which 18,088 had populations under 25,000. The 2010 population in all incorporated places was estimated at 189 million, of which 52.9 million were in places with populations under 25,000. The number of incorporated places with populations under 25,000 was reported as

17,412 in 1960, 17,826 in 1970, 18,152 in 1980, 18,191 in 1990, and 18,221 in 2000; the total population in these places was estimated at 40 million in 1960, 44 million in 1970, 47.8 million in 1980, 48.5 million in 1990, and 52 million in 2000. Electronic data files for incorporated places in 2000 were obtained from the Missouri Census Data Center, supplemented with 2010 population figures from congressional redistricting data (the most recent available at the time of the analysis), and used to sort out towns in urbanized places, leaving 14,548 non-urbanized towns with populations under 25,000 with a total population of 29 million. See US Census Bureau, *Historical Statistics of the United States: Colonial Times to 1970* (Washington, DC: Government Printing Office, 1975), series A73–90. For definitions of urban-fringe places, see US Census Bureau, *Statistical Abstract of the United States: 1982* (Washington, DC: Government Printing Office, 1982), 21. Examples of towns excluded because of being identified as urban-fringe communities are Atherton, California, in the vicinity of San Francisco and San Jose; Chickasaw, Alabama, six miles from Mobile; Elsmere, Delaware, four miles west of Wilmington; Hiawatha, Iowa, seven miles north of Cedar Rapids; Hillside, Illinois, fifteen miles from downtown Chicago; Mission, Kansas, seven miles from Kansas City; Highland Park, Texas, three miles from Dallas; and Rothschild, Wisconsin, six miles from Wausau. Census Bureau data for incorporated places underestimate the number and population of small towns in New England (Maine, Massachusetts, New Hampshire, and Vermont), where township definitions apply. Rural residents served by small towns are not included in population estimates for incorporated places.

16. On the history of New England minor civil divisions, see J. A. Fairlee, *Local Government in Counties, Towns, and Villages* (New York: Century, 1906); James S. Garland, *New England Town Law: A Digest of Statutes and Decisions concerning Towns and Town Officers* (Boston: Boston Book Company, 1906).

17. The information for minor civil divisions is taken from the 2000 and 2010 decennial censuses, drawing principally from county subdivision data compiled by the Missouri Center for Census Data and http://www.socialexplorer.com. The 2010 redistricting files were used to identify minor civil divisions with fewer than 25,000 residents and then merged with the 2010 data to select towns with no population in urbanized areas.

18. The data shown in figure 1.1 combine information from the 2010 decennial census for incorporated places and minor civil divisions (in New England and New York) that had populations under 25,000 and were not located in an urban-fringe area. Analysis of the electronic data files identified a total of 9,054 towns in nonurban areas with populations under 1,000 in 2010, 2,841 towns with populations of 1,000 to 1,999, 2,618 towns with populations of 2,000 to 4,999, 1,131 towns with populations of 5,000 to 9,999, and 663 towns with populations of 10,000 to 24,999. The mean population of these towns, respectively, was 396, 1,428, 3,131, 6,989, and 15,028.

19. The electronic data files for the 2010 census population of incorporated places and minor civil divisions in nonurban areas showed 3.59 million people living in towns with populations under 1,000, 4.06 million in towns of 1,000 to 1,999, 8.2 million in towns of 2,000 to 4,999, 7.9 million in towns of 5,000 to

9,999, and 9.96 million in towns of 10,000 to 24,999. In addition to the 33.7 million people who reside in these incorporated places and minor civil divisions with fewer than 25,000 people, as many as another 30 million people who live in the vicinity of these towns may depend on them as the closest venues for schools, routine supplies, and local government services (US Census Bureau, *Statistical Abstract of the United States: 2010* [Washington, DC: Government Printing Office, 2010], table 29, in which 59 million people as of 2000 were classified as living in rural areas).

20. A reason for incorporating 25,000 as a threshold is that published census data have generally employed this number as a cutoff point in tabular summaries. The most relevant survey data permits identifying respondents in nonmetropolitan communities of 20,000 and under. The historical distinction used by the Census Bureau to identify places of under 2,500 as "rural" has been employed in some studies, but its value for community studies has been limited; see, for example, Irwin T. Sanders and Gordon F. Lewis, "Rural Community Studies in the United States: A Decade in Review," *Annual Review of Sociology* 2 (1976): 35–53. See also Robert R. Dykstra, "Town–Country Conflict: A Hidden Dimension in American Social History," *Agricultural History* 38 (1964): 195–204. This article argues for the importance of distinguishing town from nontown residents in rural areas. In our qualitative interviews, we asked some interviewees directly how large a town could be and still be considered small. Nearly all those interviewees agreed that a town of 20,000 to 25,000 was still small enough to be considered a small town. We also examined when other interviewees volunteered comments about suitable definitions of small town. Several interviewees placed the appropriate size as high as 40,000 to 50,000. For a useful discussion of considerations involved in place-level census data, see Charles M. Tolbert, Michael D. Irwin, Thomas A. Lyson, and Alfred R. Nucci, "Civic Community in Small-Town America: How Civic Welfare Is Influenced by Local Capitalism and Civic Engagement," *Rural Sociology* 67 (2002): 90–113. Because of different data constraints, these authors excluded towns with fewer than 2,500 residents, but included those with up to 20,000 residents, and distinguished between towns in metropolitan and nonmetropolitan areas. They contend that small towns should be where civic engagement is especially notable and suggest that large data units, such as counties, "may mask essential differences in local communities' institutional structures" (ibid., 92).

21. The average distances mentioned here are computed as the square root of the mean number of square miles of land per county in each state divided by the mean number of incorporated towns with populations of less than 25,000 per county in each state; US Census Bureau, County Data, electronic data file for the 2000 census, supplemented with data for the number of towns with a population in 2010 of under 25,000 in each county.

22. Because of the relatively large number of qualitative interviews, it is important not to confuse these data with the kinds of information typically drawn from surveys. The qualitative interviews are not culled from a "sample" and are not meant to represent a predefined population. For those purposes, I have included data from representative sample surveys. The purpose of qualitative interviews is

to examine in greater detail than can be done in surveys the discourse through which ordinary people describe their lives and communities, the cognitive schemata and narratives they use to make sense of their experiences as well as convey the meanings of them, and the variations in these meanings and accounts. For recent thinking in the social sciences about qualitative interviews used in conjunction with surveys, see especially Mario Luis Small, "'How Many Cases Do I Need?' On Science and the Logic of Case Selection in Field-Based Research," *Ethnography* 10 (2009): 5–38. For other works of particular value, see also Kathy Charmaz, *Constructing Grounded Theory: A Practical Guide through Qualitative Analysis* (London: Sage, 2006); Juliet Corbin and Anselm C. Strauss, *Basics of Qualitative Research: Techniques and Procedures for Developing Grounded Theory* (London: Sage, 2007); Steiner Kvale and Svend Brinkmann, *InterViews: Learning the Craft of Qualitative Research* (London: Sage, 2009); Irving Seidman, *Interviewing as Qualitative Research: A Guide for Researchers in Education and the Social Sciences* (New York: Teachers College Press, 2006).

23. These aspects of community life amply demonstrate the importance of the "local context in constituting social worlds," as has been argued in Gary Alan Fine, "The Sociology of the Local: Action and Its Publics," *Sociological Theory* 28 (2010): 355–76.

24. Clifford Geertz, *Local Knowledge: Further Essays in Interpretive Anthropology* (New York: Basic Books, 1982), 92.

25. Having invoked Geertz, it may be appropriate to note here that my approach emphasizes interpretation through a close reading of the discourse, symbols, and rituals of community life in small towns much in the way suggested in Clifford Geertz, *The Interpretation of Cultures: Selected Essays* (New York: Basic Books, 1973). The observation I mention here about not taking community in small towns for granted, but needing to interrogate how it happens and what it means, is similar to the view expressed in Lyn C. MacGregor, *Habits of the Heartland: Small-Town Life in Modern America* (Ithaca, NY: Cornell University Press, 2010). MacGregor concludes her engaging ethnographic study of Viroqua, Wisconsin, by asserting the utility of "remaining agnostic about what community is and focusing instead on understanding how community is made" (ibid., 236).

26. For a compelling account of how a distinctly "American" character developed and spread, see Claude S. Fischer, *Made in America: A Social History of American Culture and Character* (Chicago: University of Chicago Press, 2010). On the effects of food processing and franchise marketing, see George R. Ritzer, *The McDonaldization of Society*, 6th ed. (Newbury Park, CA: Pine Forge Press, 2010). Among empirical studies of the effects of television, see James R. Beniger, "Does Television Enhance the Shared Symbolic Environment? Trends in Labeling of Editorial Cartoons, 1948–1980," *American Sociological Review* 48 (1983): 103–11; Karen A. Cerulo, "Television, Magazine Covers, and the Shared Symbolic Environment: 1948–1970," *American Sociological Review* 49 (1984): 566–70. For advertising, see especially Jackson Lears, *Fables of Abundance: A Cultural History of Advertising in America* (New York: Basic Books, 1995).

27. The point about looking for symbols, rituals, and meanings that undergird a particularly deep, emotion-laden, or valued aspect of a society, and that be-

comes closely attached to persons' identities, follows suggestions in Ann Swidler, "Geertz's Ambiguous Legacy," *Contemporary Sociology* 25 (1996): 299–302; Ann Swidler, *Talk of Love: How Culture Matters* (Chicago: University of Chicago Press, 2001), 220–23; Ann Swidler, "Comment on Stephen Vaisey's 'Socrates, Skinner, and Aristotle: Three Ways of Thinking about Culture in Action,'" *Sociological Forum* 23 (2008): 614–18.

2. YOU HAVE TO DEAL WITH EVERYBODY: THE INHABITANTS OF SMALL TOWNS

1. Glenn V. Fuguitt, David L. Brown, and Calvin L. Beale, *Rural and Small Town America* (New York: Russell Sage Foundation, 1989), 411. I also draw here on US census data from 1970 and 1980.

2. US Census Bureau, 2010, residents of incorporated places and New England towns; household income data drawn from the merged 2005 to 2009 American Community Surveys, http://www.socialexplorer.com.

3. The data in figure 2.1 are from the 2005 to 2009 American Community Surveys, conducted by the US Census Bureau. For the diversity index, see Peter Michael Blau, *Inequality and Heterogeneity: A Primitive Theory of Social Structure* (New York: Free Press, 1977); Thomas Rotolo, "Town Heterogeneity and Affiliation: A Multilevel Analysis of Voluntary Association Membership," *Sociological Perspectives* 43 (2000): 272–89. This index is adjusted for the number of categories, and is calculated as $k / k-1$ $(1-\Sigma \, pi^2)$, where k is the number of categories and p is the proportion of households in each town that fall into the ith census-defined income category, which were: less than $10,000, $10,000 to $14,999, $15,000 to $19,999, $20,000 to $24,999, $25,000 to $29,999, $30,000 to $34,999, $35,000 to $39,999, $40,000 to $44,999, $45,000 to $49,999, $50,000 to $59,999, $60,000 to $74,999, $75,000 to $99,999, $100,000 to $124,999, $125,000 to $149,999, $150,000 to $199,999, and $200,000 or more.

4. James West, *Plainville, U.S.A.* (New York: Columbia University, 1945), 115 (emphasis and colloquial misspelling of "ever'body" in the original); Arthur J. Vidich and Joseph Bensman, *Small Town in Mass Society: Class, Power, and Religion in a Rural Community* (New York: Doubleday, 1958), 40–41; W. Lloyd Warner, *Yankee City* (New Haven, CT: Yale University Press, 1963). Reflecting on ethnographic studies of this era, anthropologist Sherry Ortner observes the stress on social class in sociological studies compared to its relative absence in the work of anthropologists in the 1960s and 1970s; Sherry Ortner, *Anthropology and Social Theory: Culture, Power, and the Acting Subject* (Durham, NC: Duke University Press, 2006), especially 20–21.

5. See also David M. Hummon, *Commonplaces: Community Ideology and Identity in American Culture* (New York: State University of New York Press, 1990), which treats townspeople's emphasis on being equal as an example of villagers' ideology.

6. Pierre Bourdieu, *Distinction: A Social Critique of the Judgment of Taste*, trans. Richard Nice (Cambridge, MA: Harvard University Press, 1984). For the

United States, Bourdieu's insights have been significantly extended beyond observations about taste to include a more general concept of symbolic boundaries that may consist of moral sentiments and values as well. See especially Michele Lamont, *Money, Morals, and Manners: The Culture of the French and the American Upper-Middle Class* (Chicago: University of Chicago Press, 1992); Michele Lamont and Marcel Fournier, eds., *Cultivating Differences: Symbolic Boundaries and the Making of Inequality* (Chicago: University of Chicago Press, 1992); Michele Lamont, *The Dignity of Working Men: Morality and the Boundaries of Race, Class, and Immigration* (Cambridge, MA: Harvard University Press, 2000).

7. US Census Bureau, American Community Surveys, 2005 to 2009, electronic data file, residents in nonurban towns of twenty-five thousand or less in 2010, with median household income in 2009 averaging approximately $40,000; 3.3 percent of households in these communities earned more than $150,000.

8. These stereotypical characteristics are largely confirmed in a study by Donald D. Landon (*Country Lawyers: The Impact of Context on Professional Practice* [New York: Praeger, 1990]), in which more than a hundred lawyers living in communities of under 20,000 were compared with lawyers in a city of 150,000. Landon's interviews are similar to mine in showing that small-town lawyers are heavily involved in local civic activities and at the same time emphasize the freedom from large-scale bureaucratic constraints that practicing in a small community provides.

9. US Census Bureau, residents of incorporated places, 2000, towns in nonurbanized areas; the percentage of adult residents age twenty-five and over who held a professional school degree or PhD, respectively, was 0.9 in towns of fewer than 1,000 people, 1.2 in towns of 1,000 to 1,900 residents, 1.5 in towns of 2,000 to 4,999, 1.8 in towns of 5,000 to 9,999, and 2.2 in towns of 10,000 to 24,999. In towns greater than 25,000, the percentage was 3.2.

10. In his book *Golf and the American Country Club* (Urbana: University of Illinois Press, 2001), Richard J. Moss estimates that there were a thousand US country clubs by 1900 and four thousand by 1930. For an emphasis on status distinctions and exclusivity in these clubs, see James M. Mayo, *The American Country Club: Its Origins and Development* (New Brunswick, NJ: Rutgers University Press, 1998).

11. US Census Bureau, American Community Surveys, 2005 to 2009, electronic data file, residents in nonurban towns of twenty-five thousand or less in 2010. The percentages employed in these various service industries in small nonurban towns do not differ significantly from the percentages in larger communities, with the exception of finance and insurance, which rises from 4 percent in smaller towns to 8 percent in large cities.

12. For a description of the history and work of county extension agents, see Anne W. Van den Ban and H. S. Hawkins, *Agricultural Extension* (Oxford: Blackwell, 1996). On its early development, see Edmund de Schweinitz Brunner, *Rural America and the Extension Service: A History and Critique of the Cooperative Agricultural and Home Economics Extension Service* (New York: Columbia University Press, 1949).

13. US Census Bureau, American Community Surveys, 2005 to 2009, electronic data files.

14. Estimates from the 2005 to 2009 American Community Surveys and data from the 2000 decennial census showed that the mean number of workers employed in manufacturing was 29 in nonurban towns of under 1,000, down from 33 in 2000; 98 in towns of 1,000 to 1,999, down from 112 in 2000; 201 in towns of 2,000 to 4,999, down from 233 in 2000; 423 in towns of 5,000 to 9,999, down from 499 in 2000; and 896 in towns of 10,000 to 24,999, down from 1,033 in 2000.

15. Examples are included in subsequent chapters.

16. The data in the figure are from the American Community Surveys conducted by the US Census Bureau and aggregated from 2005 through 2009.

17. Thorstein Veblen, *The Theory of the Leisure Class* (1899; repr., New York: Penguin Books, 1967), 88–89.

18. Anne Norton, *Republic of Signs: Liberal Theory and American Popular Culture* (Chicago: University of Chicago Press, 1993), 47–86.

19. Carrie L. Yodanis, "Producing Social Class Representations: Women's Work in a Rural Town," *Gender and Society* 16 (2002): 323–44.

20. General Social Surveys, 1982–84, electronic data file, courtesy of the National Opinion Research Center at the University of Chicago. The surveys included 593 respondents who lived in nonmetropolitan towns of fewer than 20,000 residents along with 2,251 respondents who lived in larger cities or suburbs. We asked a subset of our interviewees how they would rate their own home in relation to other homes in the community. As in the survey, most responses were in the average to slightly above or slightly below average range.

21. Among those living in above average or far above average homes, the percentages, respectively, in nonmetropolitan towns of fewer than twenty thousand residents and all larger communities were as follows: church, 54 and 39; literary or arts organizations, 16 and 13; farm organizations, 10 and 5; nationality organizations, 7 and 5; school fraternities, 12 and 9; hobby organizations, 14 and 12; youth organizations, 16 and 11; veterans organizations, 16 and 5; service organizations, 22 and 15; and fraternal organizations, 16 and 13.

22. Mr. Helder summarized his sense of community mindedness by observing that things like helping someone who needs fuel oil "are taken care of because, like I say, it reaches a point where even though it isn't blood family, there are people who recognize that I survive because you survive."

3. GOING TO BE BURIED RIGHT HERE: SMALL-TOWN IDENTITIES THAT BIND

1. US Census Bureau, population of incorporated places, 2000, electronic data file. In nonurbanized towns of under 25,000, 19 percent of the residents on average had lived in a different county five years previously. That compared with 24 percent in urbanized towns of more than 25,000. Among nonurbanized towns, the proportion rose from 18 percent in towns of fewer than 1,000 residents to 24 percent in towns of 10,000 to 24,999 residents. The highest proportions were in Colorado and Nevada, where 30 percent had not lived in the same county five years previously, and the lowest were in Louisiana, Mississippi, and West Virginia,

with 15 percent having moved. Data from the 1980 US Census Bureau showed that 20 percent of residents in nonurbanized towns of under 25,000 had lived in a different county five years previously.

2. Ferdinand Tönnies, *Community and Civil Society*, ed. Jose Harris (1887; repr., Cambridge: Cambridge University Press, 2001), 22–51.

3. General Social Surveys, conducted by the National Opinion Research Center at the University of Chicago, electronic data files, in which 1,143 respondents surveyed between 1998 and 2008 were classified as living in a nonmetropolitan town of fewer than 20,000 residents. Of these, 42 percent had been raised on a farm or in the open country, and 38 had been raised in a town of under 50,000 residents. Comparable results are evident in the Civic Involvement Survey, electronic data file (hereafter referred to simply as the Civic Involvement Survey). I designed the survey, and the Gallup Organization conducted the field research during January and February 1997 among 1,528 nationally representative respondents. For further information about the survey, see Robert Wuthnow, *Loose Connections: Joining Together in America's Fragmented Communities* (Cambridge, MA: Harvard University Press, 1998). For the present purposes, I reanalyzed the data by identifying respondents who lived outside a Standard Metropolitan Statistical Area (MSA) and described their community as a small town. Among the 232 respondents so classified, 77 percent said they had grown up in a small town or rural area, 12 percent said they had grown up in a city, and 10 percent said they had grown up in a suburb. People currently living in a small town inside a Standard MSA were also likely to have grown up in a small town or rural area: 62 percent of these 294 respondents had grown up in a small town or rural area, 17 percent grew up in a city, and 22 percent in a suburb. Among the 642 respondents currently living in a suburb, 29 percent had been raised in a small town, 22 percent in a city, and 48 percent in a suburb. Among the 359 respondents currently living in a central city, 28 percent had been raised in a small town, 50 percent in a city, and 20 percent in a suburb.

4. Information about jobs, marriage, and other circumstances shaping people's choices to live in small towns will be provided in chapter 5.

5. Because an extensive literature has developed in sociology about the distinctions among reasons, warrants, accounts, motives, and related concepts, it is crucial to understand that what people say they like or dislike about their towns *may* be among the reasons they have chosen to live there—or as after-the-fact justifications—but are better regarded simply as straightforward expressions of what they do or do not appreciate about where they live. In pilot interviews, respondents often had difficulty identifying *one* thing they liked or disliked the most, so the standard question asked for three things. To prompt beyond short answers, such as "the people" or "it feels secure," respondents were asked to explain why each of the things they mentioned was important to them. Dislikes were elicited by asking specifically what aspects of the town respondents did not like or would change if they could. For a discussion of some of the most relevant sociological literature, see Stephen Vaisey, "Motivation and Justification: A Dual-Process Model of Culture in Action," *American Journal of Sociology* 114 (2009): 1675–715; Terri L. Orbuch, "People's Accounts Count: The Sociology of Accounts," *Annual*

Review of Sociology 23 (1997): 455–78. For the classic source, see C. Wright Mills, "Situated Actions and Vocabularies of Motive," *American Sociological Review* 5 (1940): 904–13. For a more recent extended theoretical treatment, see Luc Boltanski and Laurent Thevenot, *On Justification: Economies of Worth* (Princeton, NJ: Princeton University Press, 2006).

6. US Census Bureau, electronic data file, population data for 14,232 incorporated towns in nonurbanized areas and having fewer than twenty-five thousand residents in 1980. The states in which the fewest small towns experienced *either* decline or growth averaging more than 1 percent annually over the next quarter century were Maine, New York, and Vermont. Other states with relatively low rates of growth and decline in small towns were Illinois, Indiana, Kentucky, Michigan, Mississippi, New Hampshire, and Ohio.

7. Walter Perrig and Walter Kintsch, "Propositional and Situational Representations of Text," *Journal of Memory and Language* 24 (1985): 511. The authors highlight differences in the coherence of propositions in the text. Also evident in this experiment is the importance of egocentric or viewpoint representation, which develops through performance within a spatial context; see in Timothy P. McNamara, Julia Sluzenski, and Björn Rump, "Human Spatial Memory and Navigation," in *Learning and Memory: A Comprehensive Reference, Volume 2*, ed. Henry L. Roediger III (New York: Elsevier, 2008), 157–78.

8. Poll data suggest that a slower-paced life is preferred by a majority of Americans, no matter where they live, but is especially valued among residents of small towns. For example, a 2008 survey conducted by the Pew Research Center showed that 71 percent of those who responded preferred to live in a community with a slower-paced lifestyle, compared with only 22 percent who preferred a faster pace. Eighty-five percent of those who claimed to live in a small town preferred a slower pace, as did 89 percent of those in rural areas, compared with 71 percent in suburbs and only 39 percent in cities. See Paul Taylor, Rich Morin, Kim Parker, D'Vera Cohn, and Wendy Wang, "For Nearly Half of America, Grass Is Greener Somewhere Else," Pew Research Center Social and Demographic Trends Report, January 29, 2009, http://www.pewsocialtrends.org.

9. The relation between small towns, the air, space, and breathing was mentioned frequently in our interviews. For example, "I've got some room to breathe here," another man said, noting that he could drive two hours in any direction and not be in a city. While he meant that metaphorically, he also felt the air was healthier where he lived than in urban areas.

10. Echoing the sentiments of the woman who felt unable to breathe in a city, a woman in another town explained that her husband was unable to breathe when they visited their son in a city, and she herself missed seeing the sky and watching the clouds.

11. Civic Involvement Survey. While these responses distinguished residents of small nonmetropolitan towns from those in other communities, the differences were most evident with residents of central cities and relatively small with residents of suburbs. For example, 89 percent of suburban respondents and 76 percent in central cities described their communities as comfortable; 85 percent and 66 percent, respectively, said their communities were quiet; 10 and 29 percent,

respectively, said their communities were exciting; and 24 and 23 percent, respectively, said their communities were dull or boring.

12. Marc H. Bornstein and Helen G. Bornstein, "The Pace of Life," *Nature* 259 (1976): 557–58. The research involved measuring the time in which people observed on the street walked a distance of fifty feet; measurements were taken for 309 subjects in fifteen sites in six countries, but were mostly conducted in large cities.

13. Robert V. Levine and Ara Norenzayan, "The Pace of Life in 31 Countries," *Journal of Cross-cultural Psychology* 30 (1999): 178–205.

14. Aaron Lowin, Joseph H. Hottes, Bruce E. Sandler, and Marc Bornstein, "The Pace of Life and Sensitivity to Time in Urban and Rural Settings: A Preliminary Study," *Journal of Social Psychology* 83 (1971): 247–53.

15. For one source of more recent evidence, an electronic data file for a nationally representative sample of 13,038 persons, of whom 2,582 were classified as living in nonmetropolitan areas (no other geographic information was released), see US Bureau of Labor Statistics, *American Time Use Survey, 2005: Respondent and Activity Summary File Codebook* (Ann Arbor, MI: Inter-university Consortium for Political and Social Research, 2005). Among the relevant items, no differences between metropolitan and nonmetropolitan residents were evident in the mean minutes recorded in time-use diaries for time spent with friends or sleeping. From ordinary least-squares regression models, the predicted values adjusted for age differences showed that men in nonmetropolitan areas spent 38 percent more time on lawn and garden activities than men in metropolitan areas (unfortunately, differences between suburban and center-city residents could not be compared), and men in nonmetropolitan areas spent 22 percent less time traveling to work than men in metropolitan areas (no significant differences were evident among women on either measure). The most notable difference between nonmetropolitan and metropolitan residents was on an item labeled "relaxing and thinking"; men age eighteen through twenty-nine in nonmetropolitan areas spent 38 percent *less* time relaxing and thinking than men of the same age in metropolitan areas (the comparable difference for young women was 19 percent less time in nonmetropolitan areas), but for both men and women in their thirties, forties, fifties, and older, nonmetropolitan residents spent *more* time relaxing and thinking than metropolitan residents, with differences ranging from 24 percent among men age thirty through forty-four to 48 percent among women of the same age. Other items, such as waiting time at the bank or time spent traveling to purchase groceries, did not show significant differences, but also were recorded in time-diaries too infrequently to warrant solid conclusions and could not be compared among sufficiently detailed locations. One possible conclusion from this evidence along with psychological experiments is that pace of life has less to do with clocked time than it does with cultural perceptions about the differences among places.

16. We also found people, though, who discovered that moving back to a small town and expecting it to be like their childhood community was disappointing. For example, a woman in California who had recently moved with her husband to the town in which he had been raised after having lived elsewhere for four decades remarked, "He lived here for the first twenty-six years of his life. He

had very close friends who he had been raised with. And when we came back, they had stayed here, but we had zero in common. It was devastating for him. Most of the people we're close friends with now are not from here."

17. Michael Mayerfeld Bell, "The Ghosts of Place," *Theory and Society* 26 (1997): 813–36.

18. On sensory stimuli, see, for example, Alan F. Collins, Martin A. Conway, and Peter E. Morris, eds., *Theories of Memory* (London: Taylor and Francis, 1993). On the role of places and tangible objects, see Eviatar Zerubavel, "Social Memories: Steps to a Sociology of the Past," *Qualitative Sociology* 19 (1996): 283–99; Paul Connerton, *How Societies Remember* (Cambridge: Cambridge University Press, 1989); Michael Schudson, *Watergate in American Memory: How We Remember, Forget, and Reconstruct the Past* (New York: Basic Books, 1992); Barry Schwartz, "The Social Context of Commemoration: A Study in Collective Memory," *Social Forces* 61 (1982): 374–96.

19. Small towns as good, safe places in which to raise children was a theme in many of the interviews. A nice example was this comment from a father of three children who lived in a town of thirteen hundred located more than eighty miles from the nearest city. "My wife's sisters come [out from the city] and say, 'Where are the kids?' and we say, 'I don't know.'" He laughs and continues. "Her sisters are used to having to be concerned about are the kids still out in the front yard and we don't worry about that. Last night I was in the house and my wife said, 'Did you know [name of daughter] wasn't in the yard?' and I said, 'No, I guess I didn't,' but she was over two houses down. I wasn't worried about that."

20. Perceptions of crime in small towns are complicated. Although residents we interviewed generally insisted that crime was low and safety was high in their towns, they acknowledged, when asked, that drug use (especially methamphetamines) and alcoholism were present in their communities, and led to occasional robberies, arrests, and automobile accidents. While crime was not absent from their perceptions, residents were able to think of it as the exception to the rule, rather than the rule. They accounted for it not as some mysterious or endemic and uncontrollable problem but as the work of a drug dealer who had come to town, a sheriff lax in enforcing the law, or a bad seed who needed to be locked up. National data drawn from the US Census Bureau County Data electronic data file and merged with the data file for towns shows that the rate of crime was lower in 2008 than it had been in 1988 for places of all size, and that in the counties in which nonrural towns were located, it varied in 2008 from a low of 240 crimes per 10,000 persons for towns with fewer than 1,000 residents to 320 crimes per 10,000 persons for towns with 10,000 to 25,000 residents, both of which were significantly lower than the rate of 409 crimes per 10,000 persons in cities with 100,000 to 250,000 residents and 479 crimes per 10,000 persons in cities with more than 1 million residents. The data also suggest that violent crime varies more with town size than property crime.

21. Sociological work suggests that authenticity is culturally defined and that its meaning varies from one social context to another, but that concerns about authenticity may also be driven by social change along with the sense that something of the past has been lost in the transition from agrarian to industrial and

from industrial to postindustrial society. For an interesting review of the litera-ture, see Rebecca J. Erickson, "The Importance of Authenticity for Self and Soci-ety," *Symbolic Interaction* 18 (1995): 121–44. On the social construction of seemingly real or false meanings of authenticity, see Dean MacCannell, "Staged Authenticity: Arrangements of Social Space in Tourist Settings," *American Journal of Sociology* 79 (1973): 589–603; Richard A. Peterson, *Creating Country Music: Fabricating Authenticity* (Chicago: University of Chicago Press, 1999). For studies that discuss the quest for authenticity as an attraction of small towns, see Cath-erine M. Cameron and John B. Gatewood, "The Authentic Interior: Questing *Gemeinschaft* in Post-industrial Society," *Human Organization* 53 (1994): 21–32; Japonica Brown-Saracino, "Social Preservationists and the Quest for Authentic Community," *City and Community* 3 (2004): 135–56.

22. US Census Bureau, incorporated places and New England towns, 2010, electronic data file, population per town divided by square miles per town times square feet per mile.

23. E. A. Ross, *Changing America: Studies in Contemporary Society* (Chau-tauqua, NY: Chautauqua Press, 1915), 157.

24. Sonya Salamon, "From Hometown to Nontown: Rural Community Effects of Suburbanization," *Rural Sociology* 68 (2003): 17–18.

25. For a discussion of this research, see Matt Richtel, "Digital Devices De-prive Brain of Needed Downtime," *New York Times*, August 24, 2010.

26. On the conditions underpinning the modern quest for personal authen-ticity, see of course Lionel Trilling, *Sincerity and Authenticity* (Cambridge, MA: Harvard University Press, 1972); and the further development of these ideas in Charles Taylor, *Sources of the Self: The Making of Modern Identity* (Cambridge, MA: Harvard University Press, 1989) and Charles Taylor, *Multiculturalism: Ex-amining the Politics of Recognition* (Princeton, NJ: Princeton University Press, 1994).

27. US Department of Agriculture, Economic Research Service, "Natural Ame-nities Scale," 2004, http://www.ers.usda.gov. The scale provides scores at the county level. I merged the county-level data with the electronic data file for incorporated places and New England towns from the 2010 US Census to obtain an estimate of amenities scores for towns. The scale is especially sensitive to latitude and tem-perature. For example, towns with low scores are located in latitudes such as those represented by Minnesota and North Dakota, whereas towns with high scores are in latitudes such as those represented by Virginia and Oklahoma. The mean Janu-ary temperature of towns with the lowest scores is ten degrees while the mean January temperature of towns with the highest scores is forty-five degrees.

28. In the Civic Involvement Survey, 30 percent of respondents in small non-metropolitan communities said they were "very satisfied" with cultural events in their community, 27 percent of respondents in small metropolitan towns gave this response, as did 30 percent of respondents in central cities and 27 percent in suburbs.

29. Albert Blumenthal, *Small-Town Stuff* (Chicago: University of Chicago Press, 1932), especially 128–43; Nels Anderson, "Review of *Small-Town Stuff*," *American Journal of Sociology* 38 (1932): 294.

30. For an interesting discussion of how the rumor mill works among new immigrants, see Joanna Dreby, "Gender and Transnational Gossip," *Qualitative Sociology* 32 (2009): 33–52. For essays examining the constructive functions of gossip, see Robert F. Goodman and Aaron Ben-Ze'ev, eds., *Good Gossip* (Lawrence: University Press of Kansas, 2004).

31. My own view about the larger question of community collapse is that Americans have always been and remain individualistic, and have been able to reconcile this individualism with a healthy degree of participation in voluntary and other community activities. The form of these activities has changed, but it is hard to assert convincingly that an overall decline has taken place. In this, I mostly agree with Claude S. Fischer's observation in *Made in America: A Social History of American Culture and Character* (Chicago: University of Chicago Press, 2010), 10, that he is "unpersuaded by assertions of revolutionary change .... and [is] more impressed by continuity over the centuries." For my arguments about individualism and altruistic activities as well as changes in the form of community activities, see Robert Wuthnow, *Acts of Compassion: Caring for Others and Helping Ourselves* (Princeton, NJ: Princeton University Press, 1991); Wuthnow, *Loose Connections*.

32. The Economic Research Services division of the US Department of Agriculture has developed a classification scheme that places US counties in one of six economic categories: farming dependent, mining dependent, manufacturing dependent, federal and state government dependent, services dependent, and nonspecialized. By merging the electronic data files from the 2000 census for incorporated places with the county data, the proportion of nonurban towns of less than twenty-five thousand residents that fall into each category is as follows: farming dependent, 11 percent; mining dependent, 3 percent; manufacturing dependent, 29 percent; federal and state government dependent, 10 percent; services dependent, 14 percent; and nonspecialized, 33 percent. Between 1980 and 2008, 29 percent of the towns in farming dependent counties declined in population by at least 25 percent, as did 25 percent of the towns in mining dependent counties; that compared with 15 percent in manufacturing counties, 17 percent in federal and state government counties, 14 percent in services counties, and 18 percent in nonspecialized counties. Respectively, the proportions of towns in each economic category that grew by at least 25 percent during these years was 13 percent, 14 percent, 18 percent, 23 percent, 25 percent, and 20 percent.

33. US Census Bureau, incorporated places in all states and towns classified as minor civil divisions in New England states and New York, 1980 and 2010, electronic data file. The figure shows the percentage of towns outside urbanized areas in 1980 by size that had smaller populations than they did in 2010. The percentages are based on 9,162 towns with populations under 1,000 in 1980, 2,874 towns with populations between 1,000 and 2,000, 2,435 towns with populations between 2,000 and 5,000, 925 towns with populations between 5,000 and 10,000, and 518 towns with populations between 10,000 and 25,000.

34. Although many of the residents we interviewed talked about real or expected population decline in absolute numbers, *relative decline* was of concern in other instances, even when towns were experiencing modest population growth.

An indication of relative decline is that mean population of all nonurban towns with fewer than twenty-five thousand residents in 1980 increased by 19.3 percent between 1980 and 2010, compared with an increase of 30.6 percent for all towns, and 63 percent among towns of under twenty-five thousand that had the good fortune of being in urban areas.

35. In the figure, decline is defined as population in 1980 being greater than population in 2010, and major decline as the 2010 population being less than or equal to 75 percent of the 1980 population. From ordinary least squares regression for 2010 population as the dependent variable, controlling for 1980 population, towns had 354 fewer residents in 2010 for each reduction of one point on the natural amenities scale.

36. The data in the figure are taken from Economic Research Service county classifications conducted in 2004 and merged with the data for towns. Among nonurban towns of twenty-five thousand population or less in 2010, 11.1 percent were located in farming dependent counties, 2.7 percent in mining dependent counties, 32.1 percent in manufacturing dependent counties, 35.3 percent in nonspecialized counties, and 8.9 percent in service dependent counties.

37. For an analysis of the agricultural and geographic factors associated with population decline among approximately two-thirds of the fifty-five hundred towns in the Middle West, see Robert Wuthnow, *Remaking the Heartland: Middle America since the 1950s* (Princeton, NJ: Princeton University Press, 2011). In the Civic Involvement Survey, 26 percent of residents of small nonmetropolitan towns described their communities as "declining," which was higher than the 20 percent in small metropolitan towns and 19 percent in suburbs who gave the same response, but lower than the 41 percent in central cities who said their community was declining.

38. The relationship between population decline and incomes in small towns is complex. In *American Agriculture in the Twentieth Century: How It Flourished and What It Cost* (Cambridge, MA: Harvard University Press, 2002), 113, Bruce L. Gardner writes, "Data are not available on income levels for particular towns, so we cannot compare incomes in shrinking and growing towns." That is not the case, however. The census data used here for incorporated places does include measures for particular towns, including median household income. For the nonurbanized towns with populations of less than twenty-five thousand in 1980, I compared median household incomes in 1979 and 2009 among towns that had declined in population by 25 percent or more, less than 25 percent, no decline but less than 25 percent increase, and 25 percent or more increase. Compared with the average change among all nonurban small towns, median household incomes fell by 4 percent in the towns with major decline, fell by 5 percent in towns with minor decline, remained the same in towns with stable or minor increases, and increased by 10 percent in towns with major growth.

39. Employment in the Minnesota iron ore industry grew from approximately eight thousand in 1972 to fourteen thousand in 1979, but dropped precipitously to less than six thousand in 1982 and was below four thousand in 2005, for an overall drop of 83 percent since the mid-1960s. See Thomas Michael Power, *The Economic Role of Metal Mining in Minnesota: Past, Present, and Future: A Re-*

port Prepared for Minnesota Center for Environmental Advocacy and the Sierra Club (Missoula: University of Montana, Economics Department, 2007). For a valuable case study of the impact of a plant closure on one small community, see Carol D. Miller, *Niagara Falling: Globalization in a Small Town* (Lanham, MD: Lexington Books, 2007).

40. Other residents we interviewed in the same community expressed varying views of the mine's closure and railroad's layoffs. One interpretation was that the mine's equipment was so old that replacing it had become too costly for the company. Another was that the government had not done enough to protect domestic mining companies from foreign competition. Yet another was that the company had been forced into bankruptcy by having to pay high union wages and generous pension benefits. Residents agreed that the community had faced decades of ups and downs with the mining company, and somehow would survive.

41. As I discussed previously, and as shown in figure 3.5.

42. The data in the figure are from my analysis of the electronic data file from the 2006 Cooperative Congressional Election Survey, a nationally representative survey including 35,816 respondents with identifying information available at the county level. For questions, methodology, and information about response rates, see Stephen Ansolabehere, *Guide to the 2006 Cooperative Congressional Election Survey* (Cambridge, MA: MIT Press, 2010). Regular Walmart shoppers were identified by two questions that asked first whether the respondent shopped at Walmart at all, and if yes, whether that was regular or less often. Using 2005 US Census Bureau data, I classified respondents by the population of the county in which they lived, and whether the county was located outside or within a combined statistical area.

43. Although much of the public debate about Walmart has focused on larger metropolitan areas in which Walmart was or was not welcomed, for an insightful discussion of the ways in which Walmart has cultivated small-town values, such as thrift, family, and community, see Rebekah Peeples Massengill, *Wal-Mart Wars: Moral Populism in the Twenty-First Century* (New York: New York University Press, 2013). Massengill also notes the connection between Walmart's public persona and evangelical religious orientations. For more on this topic, see Bethany Moreton, *To Serve God and Walmart: The Making of Christian Free Enterprise* (Cambridge, MA: Harvard University Press, 2009).

44. Although it is true on average that housing is cheaper in small towns than in cities and suburbs, and many of our interviewees mentioned this fact, there were townspeople who said their family budgets were strained because they had made a decision to pay more for housing and earn a lower salary given that they wanted to live in a rural area as well as perhaps purchase a small plot of land to do hobby farming or keep a horse. At the lower end of the housing market, an indication of differences between small towns and cities is that data estimated from the 2005 to 2009 aggregated US Census Bureau American Community Surveys showed that 35 percent of owner-occupied houses in nonurban towns of under a thousand residents were valued at less than $50,000, compared with 17 percent in nonurban towns of ten to twenty-five thousand residents, and only 7 percent in urban towns ranging from as small as twenty-five thousand to as

large as a million or more. In the same data, median values of owner-occupied housing ranged from $87,120 in the smallest nonurban towns, to $142,902 in nonurban towns of ten to fifteen thousand, to approximately $280,000 in urban towns of fifty thousand or more.

45. Data estimated from the 2005 to 2009 aggregated American Community Surveys. Comparable data in the 2000 census was reported as the mean commuting time, which declined from 25.4 minutes in the smallest nonurban towns to 19.3 minutes in nonurban towns of ten to twenty-five thousand, and rose to 29.4 minutes in cities of a million or more.

46. The data in the figure are from the US Census Bureau, incorporated places and New England towns, 2010, electronic data files.

47. These results are drawn from the electronic data files for incorporated places and New England municipal subdivisions from the aggregated 2005 to 2009 American Community Surveys conducted by the US Census Bureau and released in 2011.

48. On segmented assimilation, see especially Alejandro Portes and Min Zhou, "The New Second Generation: Segmented Assimilation and Its Variants," *Annals of the American Academy of Political and Social Science* 530 (1993): 74-96; Min Zhou, "Segmented Assimilation: Issues, Controversies, and Recent Research on the New Second Generation," *International Migration Review* 31 (1997): 975–1008; Roger Waldinger and Cynthia Feliciano, "Will the New Second Generation Experience 'Downward Assimilation'? Segmented Assimilation Re-assessed," *Ethnic and Racial Studies* 27 (2004): 376–402; Alejandro Portes and Patricia Fernandez-Kelly, "Segmented Assimilation on the Ground: The New Second Generation in Early Adulthood," *Ethnic and Racial Studies* 28 (2005): 1000–1040; Alejandro Portes, "Migration, Development, and Segmented Assimilation: A Conceptual Review of the Evidence," *Annals of the American Academy of Arts and Sciences* 610 (2007): 73–97.

49. For a good discussion of these cultural changes, based partly on research conducted in a small community, see Tomas R. Jimenez, *Replenished Ethnicity: Mexican Americans, Immigration, and Identity* (Berkeley: University of California Press, 2009); Tomas R. Jimenez, "Mexican-Immigrant Replenishment and the Continuing Significance of Ethnicity and Race," *American Journal of Sociology* 113 (2008): 1527–67.

50. It might be supposed that residents of small homogeneous towns would be more resistant to immigrants than residents of cities that are already more diverse. Attitudinal data show relatively small differences, though. For example, the Religion and Diversity Survey that I conducted in 2003 found that 70 percent of residents in small nonmetropolitan towns favored a law to reduce immigration, but that figure was only 8 percent higher than the response among residents of metropolitan areas. On another question, 72 percent of small town residents agreed that the United States owes a great deal to the immigrants who came here, only 6 points lower than the response in metropolitan areas. Clearer indications came from our qualitative interviews that showed relatively little affect one way or the other in towns having experienced little direct impact from immigration, and comments ranging from very positive to very negative in towns with high rates of immigration.

51. Data in the figure are calculated from the aggregated 2005 to 2009 American Community Surveys, and pertain to towns that include both Hispanic and White Anglo residents, the number of which was 5,052 for nonurban towns of 25,000 residents or less, and 9,284 for all towns. Median incomes were higher among Hispanics than among White Anglos in 1,831 of the 5,052 nonurban small towns.

52. For evidence of frequent human rights violations in meat and poultry plants, see Human Rights Watch, *Blood, Sweat, and Fear: Workers' Rights in U.S. Meat and Poultry Plants* (Washington, DC: Human Rights Watch, 2005). See also Georgeanne M. Artz, Peter F. Orazem, and Daniel M. Otto, "Meat Packing and Processing Facilities in the Non-metropolitan Midwest: Blessing or Curse?" (paper presented at the annual meeting of the American Agricultural Economics Association, Providence, Rhode Island, July 2005); Georgeanne M. Artz, Peter F. Orazem, and Daniel M. Otto, "Measuring the Impact of Meat Packing and Processing Facilities in Nonmetropolitan Counties: A Difference-in-Differences Approach," *American Journal of Agricultural Economics* 89 (2007): 557–70. For two studies of Postville, Iowa, a meat-processing community of twenty-two hundred people, offering local perspective on ethnic diversity along with conflicts about immigration and undocumented workers, see Stephen G. Bloom, *Postville: A Clash of Cultures in Heartland America* (New York: Mariner Books, 2001); Mark Grey, Michele Devlin, and Aaron Goldsmith, *Postville U.S.A.: Surviving Diversity in Small-Town America* (Boston: Gemma Media, 2009).

4. Community Spirit: Small-Town Identities That Bind

1. Religion and Diversity Survey, a nationally representative survey conducted under my direction in 2003; see Robert Wuthnow, *America and the Challenges of Religious Diversity* (Princeton, NJ: Princeton University Press, 2005). There were 611 respondents in this survey who lived outside a Census-defined MSA and identified their community as a small city or town or rural area, and 1,807 respondents who lived in an MSA and identified their community as a city or suburb. Respectively, 44 and 14 percent said they knew almost all their neighbors, 13 and 10 percent said they knew half their neighbors, 12 and 17 percent knew only a quarter, 27 and 48 percent knew only a few of their neighbors, and 4 and 10 percent knew nobody in their neighborhood.

2. Sociologists have long been interested in the idea that "everyone knows everyone" in small towns. Writing in 1903, Georg Simmel ("The Metropolis and Mental Life," in Georg Simmel, *On Individuality and Social Forms*, ed. Donald N. Levine [Chicago: University of Chicago Press, 1971], 331) took the fact that "one knows almost every person he meets" in a small town as evidence that social relations necessarily were different (reserved and even cold) in larger places. Louis Wirth ("Urbanism as a Way of Life," *American Journal of Sociology* 44 [1938]: 1–24) incorporated this argument into his own treatment of the significance of population size. Offering a somewhat-different interpretation, Claude S. Fischer (*To Dwell among Friends: Personal Networks in Town and City* [Chicago: University of Chicago Press, 1982], 61, citing David Hummon, "Popular Images

of the American Small Town," *Landscape* 24 [1980]: 3–9) emphasizes that "such public familiarity need have nothing to do with people's private lives."

3. Benedict Anderson, *Imagined Communities: Reflections on the Origin and Spread of Nationalism* (London: Verso, 1991), 6.

4. These results are from my Civic Involvement Survey. Among respondents in metropolitan areas, 41 percent said community meant their neighborhood; among residents of small towns in nonmetropolitan areas, 43 percent said community meant their town.

5. Paul Lichterman, *Elusive Togetherness: Church Groups Trying to Bridge America's Divisions* (Princeton, NJ: Princeton University Press, 2005). Lichterman's extended ethnographic research was conducted in a city of approximately 235,000 residents, and was especially concerned with the ways in which various religious service organizations bridged racial and social class differences. He found that social ties that bridged these differences usually focused only on individuals, whereas the one group that deliberately emphasized larger social categories was more effective at addressing underlying issues. See also Paul Lichterman, "Social Capital or Group Style? Rescuing Tocqueville's Insights on Civic Engagement," *Theory and Society* 35 (2006): 529–63; Paul Lichterman, "Integrating Diversity: Boundaries, Bonds, and the Greater Community in *The New Golden Rule*," in *Autonomy and Order: A Communitarian Anthology*, ed. Edward Lehman (Lanham, MD: Rowman and Littlefield, 2000), 125–41. The tendency in US culture to stress charity and volunteering as individual acts of kindness has often been observed in the literature. See, for example, Christian Smith and Michael O. Emerson, *Passing the Plate: Why American Christians Don't Give Away More Money* (New York: Oxford University Press, 2008); Robert L. Payton and Michael P. Moody, *Understanding Philanthropy: Its Meaning and Mission* (Bloomington: Indiana University Press, 2008); Susan Eckstein, "Community as Gift-Giving: Collectivistic Roots of Volunteerism," *American Sociological Review* 66 (2001): 829–51; Robert Wuthnow, *Acts of Compassion: Caring for Others and Helping Ourselves* (Princeton, NJ: Princeton University Press, 1991). Conversely, some of the popular difficulty in recognizing social categories is that these are the bases of inequality that are difficult to acknowledge. See, for example, Douglas Massey, *Categorically Unequal: The American Stratification System* (New York: Russell Sage Foundation, 2007).

6. For the most able development and defense of the argument that community is declining because numerical measures of social capital in surveys show downward trends, see Robert D. Putnam, *Bowling Alone: The Collapse and Revival of American Community* (New York: Simon and Schuster, 2000). Criticisms of this contention have emphasized the replacement of older forms of social participation with newer ones, and changing political, legal, and cultural forms of organization. See, for example, Carl Boggs, "Social Capital and Political Fantasy: Robert Putnam's 'Bowling Alone,'" *Theory and Society* 30 (2001): 281–97. For one of the more interesting studies of changing forms of civic involvement, see Emily Barman, *Contesting Communities: The Transformation of Workplace Charity* (Stanford, CA: Stanford University Press, 2006). The emphasis on community as symbol and narrative that I have in mind here is similar and indebted to the

nicely developed argument in Mario Luis Small, *Villa Victoria: The Transformation of Social Capital in a Boston Barrio* (Chicago: University of Chicago Press, 2004).

7. In the Civic Involvement Survey, respondents were asked if they had attended meetings about community issues in the past year, and among those who had, 69 percent in small nonmetropolitan towns said the meeting had been held at the school; that compared with 59 percent in suburbs and 52 percent in central cities.

8. NCES, Schools and Staffing Surveys, 1987 and 1999, electronic data files, weighted sample results for number of schools and total K–12 enrollment in the United States by locale, where small town was defined by the NCES as an incorporated or census-designated place with a population less than 25,000 yet greater than or equal to 2,500, and located outside a Consolidated MSA or MSA, and a rural locale was defined as any territory designated as rural by the Census Bureau. Between 1987 and 1999, the number of schools estimated in these surveys fell from 18,556 to 11,393 in small towns, and from 19,391 to 16,578 in rural areas, while increasing from 19,482 to 21,895 in large or midsize central cities and from 21,132 to 37,761 in urban-fringe areas of large or midsize cities or large towns. Estimated total school enrollment between 1987 and 1999 declined from 9.5 to 4.8 million in small towns and from 6.7 to 4.7 million in rural areas, while increasing from 13 to 14.3 million in central cities and from 13.3 to 23.8 million in urban-fringe areas. Another way of describing the change is that schools in small towns and rural areas made up 48 percent of the nation's schools in 1987, but only 32 percent in 1999 and 37 percent of total enrollment in 1987 yet only 20 percent in 1999. The 1987 and 1999 surveys were used because the NCES definitions of locale changed in 2003 as a result of data collected in the 2000 decennial census (nces.ed.gov/ccd/rural_locales.asp). For a summary of the study, see National Center for Education Statistics, *Schools and Staffing Survey, 1999–2000: Overview of the Data for Public, Private, Public Charter, and Bureau of Indian Affairs Elementary and Secondary Schools* (Washington, DC: US Department of Education, Office of Educational Research and Improvement, 2002). The 2005 NCES data (electronic data file) in which the new definition of locale altered the categories for rural schools showed that the number of schools in towns of 2,500 to 25,000 declined from 11,393 in 1999 to 8,982 in 2005, a decrease of 21 percent, and that the number of students in small-town schools dropped from 4.8 million in 1999 to 3.5 million in 2005 (these numbers are derived from the five category locale variable in the electronic data file for school districts).

9. These numbers are from the 1980 and 2000 census, and represent children age five through seventeen in nonurbanized towns that had a total population in 1980 of fewer than twenty-five thousand.

10. As I discuss in chapter 6, empty storefronts are also something that residents considered damaging enough to community spirit that these buildings were razed or town leaders found ways to make them appear occupied. An empty school, however, where children had once played outside, and residents had attended graduation ceremonies and town meetings, held deeper symbolic significance. As one mayor remarked, "They closed the two-story brick schoolhouse

down, and it sat empty for years and years and years. When something sits empty for so long, it just kind of becomes depressing." She said an effort to reopen the building as a city hall was one of the best things that had happened lately.

11. For an extended example of the connection between sports and small-town pride, see Joe Drape, *Our Boys: A Perfect Season on the Plains with the Smith Center Redmen* (New York: Times Books, 2009). Of related interest, see Carlton Stowers, *Where Dreams Die Hard: A Small American Town and Its Six-Man Football Team* (Cambridge, MA: Da Capo Press, 2005.

12. For a rich descriptive discussion of small-town festivals, see Robert H. Lavenda, *Corn Fests and Water Carnivals: Celebrating Community in Minnesota* (Washington, DC: Smithsonian Institution Press, 1997). For a look at small-town rodeos, see Elizabeth Furniss, "Cultural Performance as Strategic Essentialism: Negotiating Indianness in a Western Canadian Rodeo Festival," *Humanities Research* (1998): 23–40; Elizabeth Atwood Lawrence, *Rodeo: An Anthropologist Looks at the Wild and the Tame* (Knoxville: University of Tennessee Press, 1982); Stan Hoig, *Cowtown Wichita and the Wild, Wicked West* (Albuquerque: University of New Mexico Press, 2007), especially 153–68.

13. See, for example, Karen De Bres and James Davis, "Celebrating Group and Place Identity: A Case study of a New Regional Festival," *Tourism Geographies* 3 (2001): 326–37.

14. For a recent example of sociological theory in which the centrality of emotional experience, such as that generated by collective rituals, is emphasized, see Randall Collins, *Interaction Ritual Chains* (Princeton, NJ: Princeton University Press, 2005). For the classic work on this topic, see Emile Durkheim, *Elementary Forms of the Religious Life*, trans. Carol Cosman and ed. Mark S. Cladis (1915; repr., Oxford: Oxford University Press, 2008).

15. For interesting discussions of the ways in which community festivals dramatize changing definitions of membership in the community in other contexts, see the following. On the annual festa and the role it played among immigrants from about 1890 to 1940, see Robert A. Orsi, *The Madonna of 115th Street: Faith and Community in Italian Harlem* (New Haven, CT: Yale University Press, 1985). On how the festa changed with Haitian immigration, see Elizabeth McAlister, "The Madonna of 115th Street Revisited: Vodou and Haitian Catholicism in the Age of Transnationalism," in *Gatherings in Diaspora: Religious Communities and the New Immigration*, ed. R. Stephen Warner and Judith G. Wittner (Philadelphia: Temple University Press, 1998), 123–62; Karen McCarthy Brown, "Staying Grounded in a High-rise Building: Ecological Dissonance and Ritual Accommodation in Haitian Vodou," in *Gods of the City*, ed. Robert A. Orsi (Bloomington: Indiana University Press, 1999), 79–102; Jonathan Rieder, *Canarsie: The Jews and Italians of Brooklyn against Liberalism* (Cambridge, MA: Harvard University Press, 1985); Wesley Monroe Shrum Jr., *Fringe and Fortune: The Role of Critics in High and Popular Art* (Princeton, NJ: Princeton University Press, 1996). For an insightful discussion of the similar role that naturalization ceremonies play, see Sofya Aptekar, "Immigrant Naturalization and Nation-Building in North America" (PhD diss., Princeton University, 2010).

16. For a brief summary of Sampson's research on collective efficacy, see Robert J. Sampson, "Neighborhood and Community: Collective Efficacy and Com-

munity Safety," *New Economy* 11 (2004): 106–13. See also Robert J. Sampson, Stephen W. Raudenbush, and Felton Earls, "Neighborhoods and Violent Crime: A Multilevel Study of Collective Efficacy," *Science* 277 (1997): 918–24; Jeffrey D. Morenoff, Robert J. Sampson, and Stephen W. Raudenbush, "Neighborhood Inequality, Collective Efficacy, and the Spatial Dynamics of Urban Violence," *Population Studies Center Research Report*, Report No. 00-451, March 2001.

17. The data in the figure are from the approximately 2,500 respondents in the national survey of 3,003 adults conducted in July to November 2000 as part of the Social Capital Benchmark Survey, which also solicited information from 26,230 residents in forty-one local communities. I report the results from the national survey because most of the local surveys were conducted in cities. The electronic data file and codebook were obtained from the Roper Center for Public Opinion Research at the University of Connecticut.

18. Terry L. Besser, Nicholas Recker, and Kerry Agnitsch, "The Impact of Economic Shocks on Quality of Life and Social Capital in Small Towns," *Rural Sociology* 73 (2008): 580–604. The study was conducted by a mailed survey among randomly selected residents in ninety-nine towns of under ten thousand population in 1994 and 2004. The results contrast with those of Kai T. Erikson (*Everything in Its Path: Destruction of Community in the Buffalo Creek Flood* [New York: Simon and Schuster, 1977]), who valuably examines the extent to which feelings about community are grounded in the spatial order of a town and are thus negatively affected by a natural disaster. Timothy Philip Schwartz-Barcott (*After the Disaster: Re-creating Community and Well-being at Buffalo Creek since the Notorious Coal-Mining Disaster in 1972* [Amherst, NY: Cambria Press, 2008]), revisits Erikson's argument, and shows how the residents rebuilt their sense of community and the structures undergirding it.

19. For an extensive discussion of warrants, see Kenneth Burke, *A Grammar of Motives* (Berkeley: University of California Press, 1969). Relatedly, for an illuminating essay, see Wendell V. Harris, "The Critics Who Made Us: Kenneth Burke," *Sewanee Review* 96 (1988): 452–63.

20. Jennifer Sherman, "Coping with Rural Poverty: Economic Survival and Moral Capital in Rural America," *Social Forces* 85 (2006): 891–913.

21. For a sharp contrast between sidewalk behavior in small towns and what's been described as "civil inattention," see Erving Goffman, *Behavior in Public Places: Notes on the Social Organization of Gatherings* (New York: Free Press, 1966), 88–99. For a discussion of how the norms of civility also contrast with those in the urban setting, see Mitchell Duneier, *Sidewalk* (New York: Farrar, Straus and Giroux, 2000); Mitchell Duneier and Harvey Molotch, "Talking City Trouble: Interactional Vandalism, Social Inequality, and the 'Urban Interaction Problem,'" *American Journal of Sociology* 104 (1999): 1263–95.

22. For an engaging account of the "finger wave," "highway howdy," and "farmer's salute," see Roger Welsch, *Forty Acres and a Fool: How to Live in the Country and Still Keep Your Sanity* (Osceola, WI: Voyageur Press, 2006), 210–12.

23. Network studies point to the importance of overlapping ties that involve one's friends also being friends with one another. In family research, see especially, for example, Elizabeth Bott, *Family and Social Network* (1957; repr., New York: Routledge, 2003); Joan Aldous and Murray A. Straus, "Social Networks

and Conjugal Roles: A Test of Bott's Hypothesis," *Social Forces* 43 (1966): 471–82; Alexandra Maryanski and Masako Ishii-Kuntz, "A Cross-Species Application of Bott's Hypothesis on Role Segregation and Social Networks," *Sociological Perspectives* 34 (1991): 403–25. Formal studies of network ties rarely emphasize the significance of relationships in which intimate knowledge about third parties is disclosed. For a discussion of this phenomenon in greater detail, see Robert Wuthnow, "Intimate Knowledge as a Concept for Further Research in Studies of Religion," Association of Religion Data Archives at the Pennsylvania State University, 2011, http://www.thearda.com/rrh/papers/guidingpapers.asp. The literature on secrecy and gossip is also suggestive; see, for example, Sissela Bok, *Secrets: On the Ethics of Concealment and Revelation* (New York: Pantheon, 1983); Donna Eder, "Cohesion through Collaborative Narration," *Social Psychology Quarterly* 51 (1988): 225–35; Donna Eder, "The Structure of Gossip: Opportunities and Constraints on Collective Expression among Adolescents," *American Sociological Review* 56 (1991): 494–508; Gary Alan Fine and Lori Holyfield, "Secrecy, Trust, and Dangerous Leisure: Generating Group Cohesion in Voluntary Organizations," *Social Psychology Quarterly* 59 (1996): 22–38; Joshua Gamson, "Normal Sins: Sex Scandal Narratives as Institutional Morality Tales," *Social Problems* 48 (2001): 185–205.

24. *Riffraff* was by far the most common term residents used to describe people who were not doing enough to take care of their own needs. The term also implies a stranger or newcomer who is not sufficiently vetted or known, and thus cannot be trusted. A related term is a *sponger* or someone who sponges off the system, such as abusing charity. A less commonly used term is *packsacker*, referring to someone who is not from the community but who can eventually be accepted over a course of years by showing themselves to be dependable, hardworking, and loyal to the community.

25. Gerald Marwell and Ruth E. Ames, "Experiments on the Provision of Public Goods, I. Resources, Interest Group Size, and the Free-Rider Problem," *American Journal of Sociology* 84 (1979): 1335–60; Oliver Kim and Mark Walker, "The Free Rider Problem: Experimental Evidence," *Public Choice* 43 (1984): 3–24.

26. One of my colleagues has written perceptively about this. See Viviana A. Zelizer, *The Purchase of Intimacy* (Princeton, NJ: Princeton University Press, 2005); Viviana A. Zelizer, *The Social Meaning of Money: Pin Money, Paychecks, Poor Relief, and Other Currencies* (Princeton, NJ: Princeton University Press, 1994).

27. On the taboo against talking about money, see Robert Wuthnow, *Poor Richard's Principle: Recovering the American Dream through the Moral Dimension of Work, Business, and Money* (Princeton, NJ: Princeton University Press, 1996), 138–68.

28. On the closure of social networks, see James S. Coleman, "Social Capital in the Creation of Human Capital," *American Journal of Sociology* 94 (1988): S95–120. Coleman mentions gossip in passing, but mainly suggests that B and C knowing each other can produce a coalition that enforces normative conformity in A. But how this works is complicated in the information provided by small-

town residents. It is the perception that others *might* know as well as whatever possibilities of actual enforcement might exist that people emphasize, and not just any gossip that matters, but hearsay about topics that implies access to intimate, behind-the-scenes information.

29. Ray Oldenburg, *The Great Good Place: Cafes, Coffee Shops, Community Centers, Beauty Parlors, General Stores, Bars, Hangouts, and How They Get You through the Day* (New York: Paragon House, 1989). For a demonstration of the beneficial effects of "third place establishments" and "associations" on community well-being variables for small towns, see Charles M. Tolbert, Michael D. Irwin, Thomas A. Lyson, and Alfred R. Nucci, "Civic Community in Small-Town America: How Civic Welfare Is Influenced by Local Capitalism and Civic Engagement," *Rural Sociology* 67 (2002): 90–113. Other studies that examine the conviviality that occurs in some of these specific settings have generally focused on urban places. See, for example, James P. Spradley and Brenda J. Mann, *The Cocktail Waitress: Women's Work in a Man's World* (1975; repr., New York: Waveland Press, 2008); William H. Whyte, *The Social Life of Small Urban Spaces* (1980; repr., New York: Project for Public Spaces, 2001); Mitchell Duneier, *Slim's Table: Race, Respectability, and Masculinity* (Chicago: University of Chicago Press, 1992); Sean Safford, *Why the Garden Club Couldn't Save Youngstown: The Transformation of the Rust Belt* (Cambridge, MA: Harvard University Press, 2009). On the importance of formal day-care centers in creating informal networks in an urban context, see Mario Luis Small, *Unanticipated Gains: Origins of Network Inequality in Everyday Life* (New York: Oxford University Press, 2009).

30. Susan Fiske ("Envy Up, Scorn Down: How Comparison Divides Us" [paper presented at the fall retreat of Law and Public Affairs, Princeton University, September 2010]) argues that scorn has been relatively neglected in the psychological literature, although in popular culture it generally involves looking down on someone who is regarded as inferior, expressing contempt or derision, wishing they would go away, giving them signals to stay away, and sometimes showing disdain for them by ignoring them or responding to them only with silence. While the person or group scorned may respond by feeling inferior, the more interesting dynamic, and the one I emphasize here, is how the scorned fight back, so to speak, by asserting values and traits they consider to negate the scorn. Historians of American literature note especially the disdain toward small towns and rural areas expressed in the work of Sinclair Lewis and F. Scott Fitzgerald; see, for example, James H. Shideler, "*Flappers and Philosophers*, and Farmers: Rural–Urban Tensions of the Twenties," *Agricultural History* 47 (1973): 283–99. For a related work that examines contrasting imagery in English literature, though one less concerned specifically with small towns, see Raymond Williams, *The Country and the City* (London: Chatto and Windus, 1973). For a broader discussion of popular imagery that marginalizes and denigrates residents of small towns and rural areas, see Gerald W. Creed and Barbara Ching, "Recognizing Rusticity: Identity and the Power of Place," in *Knowing Your Place: Rural Identity and Cultural Hierarchy*, ed. Barbara Ching and Gerald W. Creed (New York: Routledge, 1997), 1–38. For a book that traces the notion of the village idiot or rural idiocy to the Greek root, *idios*, "meaning 'one's own, a private person,' unlearned in the ways

of the *polis*," and thus less civilized or civic spirited than urban residents, see Edward W. Soja, *Postmodern Geographies: The Reassertion of Space in Critical Theory* (London: Verso, 1989), 234–35.

31. Annie Proulx, *That Old Ace in the Hole* (New York: Simon and Schuster, 2002); Timothy Egan, *The Worst Hard Time* (New York: Houghton Mifflin, 2006). For reviews by writers outside the region that praised the book's accuracy, see Candace Smith, "That Old Ace in the Hole," *Booklist*, May 1, 2003, 1213; Gail Caldwell, "Intruder in the Dust," *Boston Globe*, December 15, 2002; Sean Daly, "That Old Ace in the Hole," *People*, December 23, 2002; Stephen Finucan, "Fear and Loathing on the Panhandle," *Toronto Star*, December 8, 2002. Reviewers closer to the region were more critical; see, for example, James Lough, "No Winning Hand," *Denver Post*, December 15, 2002.

32. Although New York City came up from time to time in our interviews as a point of comparison, the distinctive speech patterns that once characterized the city do not appear to signal sophistication, according to an expert who explained, "A New York accent makes you sound ignorant" (quoted in Sam Roberts, "Unlearning to Tawk Like a New Yorker," *New York Times*, November 19, 2010).

33. In the Civic Involvement Survey, 48 percent of respondents in small nonmetropolitan towns said they were very satisfied with the "natural beauty" of their community, compared with 42 percent in small metropolitan towns, 35 percent in suburbs, and 31 percent in central cities.

34. Rebecca Kneale Gould, *At Home in Nature: Modern Homesteading and Spiritual Practice in America* (Berkeley: University of California Press, 2005).

35. William Wordsworth, *The Complete Poetical Works* (London: Macmillan, 1888); written in 1806.

36. LiErin Probasco, "Encountering Difference: Solidarity and Transnational Religious Humanitarian Aid" (PhD diss., Princeton University, 2013). I was involved in Probasco's project as an adviser at the time I was doing the research for this book, and it provided vivid contrasting evidence. Americans who participated in visits to Nicaragua, and Probasco herself, frequently commented on the extended conversations and ritual events that were expected of visitors in Nicaraguan villages, whereas the newcomers I talked with in small towns noted expectations about sidewalk friendliness and brief conversations, but rarely suggested that these encounters took much time or had become burdensome.

5. THE FROG POND: MAKING SENSE OF WORK AND MONEY

1. Among the many works describing the American dream, for a valuable historical discussion, see Cal Jillson, *Pursuing the American Dream: Opportunity and Exclusion over Four Centuries* (Lawrence: University Press of Kansas, 2004). For a work that emphasizes the expectation of leaving home and moving elsewhere, see Robert N. Bellah, Richard Madsen, William M. Sullivan, Ann Swidler, and Steven M. Tipton, *Habits of the Heart: Individualism and Commitment in American Life* (Berkeley: University of California Press, 1985). For books that focus on the freedom of individual choice and expression versus community at-

tachment, see Bellah et al., *Habits of the Heart*; Herbert J. Gans, *Middle American Individualism: Political Participation and Liberal Democracy* (New York: Oxford University Press, 1988); Paul Leinberger and Bruce Tucker, *The New Individualists: The Generation after the Organization Man* (New York: HarperCollins, 1991); Alan Ehrenhalt, *The Lost City: The Forgotten Virtues of Community in America* (New York: Basic Books, 1995). For my own research into popular understandings of the American dream, see Robert Wuthnow, *Poor Richard's Principle: Recovering the American Dream through the Moral Dimension of Work, Business, and Money* (Princeton, NJ: Princeton University Press, 1996); Robert Wuthnow, *American Mythos: Why Our Best Efforts to Be a Better Nation Fall Short* (Princeton, NJ: Princeton University Press, 2006).

2. In my Civic Involvement Survey, 47 percent of residents in small nonmetropolitan towns said that a lack of jobs was a "serious problem" in their community, significantly higher than the proportions giving this response in small towns in metropolitan areas (34 percent) or suburbs (25 percent), though the same as in central cities (47 percent).

3. The data are from the US Census Bureau, incorporated places, 2000, electronic data file. Nonurban towns refer to those classified in the census data as being outside the vicinity of a town of more than fifty thousand. It is true that small towns do not provide opportunities to pursue many kinds of occupations. The CEO of a Fortune 500 corporation may live in a city or suburb, but would be unlikely to live in a small town. With perhaps a few exceptions, that is also the case for most heads of state, Broadway stars, television anchorpersons, and Wall Street traders. Small towns, though, are more diverse than might be supposed. Our interviews included people who ran nuclear power plants, headed major statewide governmental agencies, served in elected and appointed positions in state and federal government, and earned six- and seven-figure incomes from businesses and investments. There were distinguished authors of books, newspaper columnists, college professors, executives of international firms, inventors, engineers, and professional athletes. They were less common than people who worked in offices, taught school, or labored in small businesses. But that is the case in cities as well.

4. Data from the General Social Surveys, electronic data files, conducted between 1998 and 2008, show that among all respondents raised in towns of under fifty thousand, only 16 percent were currently living in a small nonmetropolitan town of under twenty thousand people, 38 percent were living in towns of this size within a metropolitan area, and 47 percent were living in a city or suburb.

5. Seyla Benhabib, "Sexual Difference and Collective Identities: The New Global Constellation," *Signs* 24 (1999): 345.

6. The fact that people in small towns tend on average to earn lower incomes than people do in cities (and work in less prestigious occupations) suggests the relevance of asking whether they are victims of discrimination, exploitation, opportunity hoarding, and related social structural factors that sociologists associate with inequality. See, for example, Douglas Massey, *Categorically Unequal: The American Stratification System* (New York: Russell Sage Foundation, 2007); Erik Olin Wright and Joel Rogers, *American Society: How It Actually Works* (New

York: W. W. Norton, 2010). Standard treatments of inequality generally do not consider differences between small towns and metropolitan areas to be important, presumably because residents voluntarily choose to live there. The exceptions are occasional discussions of new immigrants who work for low wages in small towns as well as manufacturing and agribusiness firms that locate in small towns to take advantage of an inexpensive, nonunionized labor force. See, for example, Donald D. Stull and Michael J. Broadway, *Slaughterhouse Blues: The Meat and Poultry Industry in North America* (San Francisco: Wadsworth, 2004). It is instructive to consider small towns in relation to the theoretical argument put forth by Charles Tilly (*Durable Inequality* [Berkeley: University of California Press, 1998]). Tilly contends that African Americans and women are categorical subordinate groups that employers can easily exploit. The rural/urban distinction might be considered a categorical distinction as well, especially in conjunction with pejorative stereotypes of rustic, ignorant country bumpkins. The difference, however, is that rural Americans were never subject to the same kind of legal definitions that legitimated discrimination against African Americans and women. The part of Tilly's assertion that does apply to small-town residents is that employers engage in opportunity hoarding through structured information networks and emulation, and people who are in subordinate positions often are comfortable with the familiarity and friendships involved in those positions. The evidence I present here from interviews with residents of small towns emphasizes the importance of the local networks through which information about job opportunities flows and the ways in which limited horizons facilitate adaptation to available job opportunities.

7. Mark S. Granovetter, *Getting a Job: A Study of Contacts and Careers* (Cambridge, MA: Harvard University Press, 1974); Mark S. Granovetter, "The Strength of Weak Ties," *American Journal of Sociology* 78 (1973): 1360–80; Mark S. Granovetter, "The Strength of Weak Ties: A Network Theory Revisited," *Sociological Theory* 1 (1983): 201–33.

8. On the concept of cognitive schemata, and discussions of the extent to which they are hardwired or culturally shaped, see William Brewer, "Schemata," in *The MIT Encyclopedia of the Cognitive Sciences*, ed. Robert A. Wilson and Frank C. Keil (Cambridge, MA: MIT Press, 2001), 724–25; Roy D'Andrade, *The Development of Cognitive Anthropology* (Cambridge: Cambridge University Press, 1995); Karen A. Cerulo, "Coming Together: New Taxonomies for the Analysis of Social Relations," *Sociological Inquiry* 68 (1998): 398–425; Paul DiMaggio, "Culture and Cognition," *Annual Review of Sociology* 23 (1997): 263–87; L. A. Hirschfeld and S. A. Gelman, eds., *Mapping the Mind: Domain Specificity in Cognition and Culture* (Cambridge: Cambridge University Press, 1994). My discussion of cognitive schemata in the context of religion is also relevant. See Robert Wuthnow, "Cognition and Religion," *Sociology of Religion* 68 (2007): 341–60.

9. For the most useful discussion of metaphors and vertical metaphors, see George Lakoff and Mark Johnson, *Metaphors We Live By* (Chicago: University of Chicago Press, 1980). For helpful yet brief discussions, see also Samuel Glucksberg, "Metaphor," in *The MIT Encyclopedia of Cognitive Science*, ed. Robert A. Wilson and Frank C. Keil (Cambridge, MA: MIT Press, 2001), 532–34; Tim Rohrer,

"The Cognitive Science of Metaphor from Philosophy to Neuroscience," *Theoria et Historia Scientiarum* 6 (2001): 27–42.

10. For a look at these narratives of trade-off, sacrifice, and gain in the context of immigrants' stories about the American dream, see Wuthnow, *American Mythos*, 79–103.

11. Claudia Strauss, "What Makes Tony Run? Schemas as Motives Reconsidered," in *Human Motives and Cultural Models*, ed. Roy G. D'Andrade and Claudia Strauss (Cambridge: Cambridge University Press, 1992), 197–224; Claudia Strauss, "Who Gets Ahead? Cognitive Responses to Heteroglossia in American Political Culture," *American Ethnologist* 17 (1990): 312–28; Claudia Strauss, "Culture, Discourse, and Cognition: Forms of Belief in Some Rhode Island Working Men's Talk about Success" (PhD diss., Harvard University, 1988).

12. Strauss, "What Makes Tony Run?"

13. I have in mind studies like Kathryn Edin and Laura Lein, *Making Ends Meet: How Single Mothers Survive Welfare and Low-Wage Work* (New York: Russell Sage Foundation, 1997); Katherine S. Newman, *Falling from Grace: Downward Mobility in the Age of Affluence* (Berkeley: University of California Press, 1999); Katherine S. Newman and Victor Tan Chen, *The Missing Class: Portraits of the Near Poor in America* (Boston: Beacon, 2008).

14. Although there was media speculation at the time about the possible impact of the September 11 attacks on residential plans, it seems doubtful that the event prompted many people to flee to small towns. A study of New York City residents, for example, found little impact, but did suggest that fear of terrorism may have encouraged residents who already lived in smaller places to stay put. David Kay, Charles Geisler, and Nelson Bills, "Residential Preferences: What's Terrorism Got to Do with It?" *Rural Sociology* 75 (2010): 426–54.

15. Although national data on precisely this point does not to my knowledge exist, the possibility of patrilocalistic tendencies in small towns is suggested by some of the available evidence. For example, results from the General Social Surveys, electronic data file, for married men and women interviewed between 1998 and 2008 show that among residents of nonmetropolitan communities of less than twenty thousand residents, women are slightly more likely than men (21 versus 18 percent) to have grown up in a city or suburb—meaning that they would not have been raised locally. The largest difference is that 28 percent of men compared with 19 percent of women grew up on farms. The data do not indicate whether people who grew up in small towns are presently living in the same small town or have moved. Because of land transfer patterns and multigenerational farming, the tendency toward patrilocalism may be stronger among farmers. For example, analysis of the 2000 US Census Five Percent Public Use Microsample, electronic data file, for married persons living in nonmetropolitan areas and identifying themselves as farmers, farm managers, or farmworkers, shows that among persons age 18 through 39, 51.1 percent of women were no longer residing in their birth state compared with 36.6 percent of men, and among persons age 40 through 75, 35.4 percent of women were no longer residing in their birth state compared with 24.3 percent of men. On land transfer itself, a small study that provided detail about the decisions of approximately three hundred farmers nearing retirement showed

that 30.4 percent involved legal partnerships with sons, but none involved such partnerships with daughters; 54.1 percent shared management decisions with sons, but only 0.9 percent did so with daughters. Norah C. Keating and Brenda Munro, "Transferring the Family Farm: Process and Implications," *Family Relations* 38 (1989): 215–19. On a larger scale that did not focus on rural communities, Walter D. Koenig ("Sex-Biased Dispersal in the Contemporary United States," *Ethology and Sociobiology* 10 [1989]: 263–78) examined geographic mobility among more than twenty-eight hundred men and women using high school reunion booklets and a survey, and found that dispersal distances were greater among females than among males, but also possible variation attributable to location, education, occupation, and marital status.

16. For a brief discussion of some of these issues, see Ann R. Tickamyer and Debra A. Henderson, "Rural Women: New Roles for the New Century?" in *Challenges for Rural America in the Twenty-First Century*, ed. David L. Brown and Louis E. Swanson (University Park: Pennsylvania State University Press, 2003), 109–17. Analysis of US Census 2000 data for incorporated places shows that in nonurbanized towns of under twenty-five thousand population, 57.3 percent of married women were employed, and in these communities the annual income among females with earnings averaged $17,583 compared with $29,095 among males.

17. A contrasting example that does not involve farming or a woman giving up high career aspirations nevertheless illustrates the adjustments women may make in following husbands to small towns. This instance is a forty-year-old woman who lives in a town of two hundred because her husband wanted to return to his hometown when they started having children. They live in a mobile home next door to his parents and her husband's brother, and besides their own children have custody of a niece whose mother died. The woman has worked at seven different jobs involving one-way commutes of up to forty-five minutes.

18. Although the academic literature has argued that having extended families nearby is generally a good thing, especially among the poor and for raising children (see, for example, Carol B. Stack, *All Our Kin: Strategies for Survival in a Black Community* [New York: Harper and Row, 1975]; for rural communities, see Valarie King and Glen H. Elder Jr., "American Children View Their Grandparents: Linked Lives across Three Rural Generations," *Journal of Marriage and Family* 57 [1995]: 165–78; Valarie King and Glen H. Elder Jr., "The Legacy of Grandparenting: Childhood Experiences with Grandparents and Current Involvement with Grandchildren," *Journal of Marriage and the Family* 59 [1997]: 848–59), the people we talked to were aware of the potential difficulties involved. A telling example was the story that a man who had grown up as an only child told us. When he married, his parents lived in a town an hour and a half away, which he felt was conveniently close and yet not too close. His mother, however, feared becoming an intrusive influence in her son and daughter-in-law's lives, so his parents moved to a new location eight hours away to avoid that happening.

19. David B. Danbom, *Born in the Country: A History of Rural America*, 2nd ed. (Baltimore: Johns Hopkins University Press, 2006).

20. Ashok K. Mishra, James D. Johnson, and Mitchell J. Morehart, "Retirement and Succession Planning of Farm Households: Results from a National Sur-

vey" (paper presented at the National Public Policy Education Committee, Salt Lake City, September 21–23, 2003). For a comparative perspective, see Timothy W. Guinnane, "Intergenerational Transfers, Emigration, and the Rural Irish Household System," *Explorations in Economic History* 29 (1992): 456–76. Recent econometric analyses of wage differentials suggest substantial nonpecuniary benefits from farming. See Nigel Key and Michael J. Roberts, "Nonpecuniary Benefits to Farming: Implications for Supply Response to Decoupled Payments," *American Journal of Agricultural Economics* 91 (2009): 1–18.

21. For a discussion of the ethic of family continuity and land that has been inherited by siblings and cousins being farmed by relatives, see John Hutson, "Fathers and Sons: Family Farms, Family Businesses, and the Farming Industry," *Sociology* 21 (1987): 215–29. For an examination of the factors that influence farm succession, such as operator's education, household wealth, and farm size, see Ashok K. Mishra, Hisham S. El-Osta, and James D. Johnson, "Succession in Family Farm Business: Empirical Evidence from the U.S. Farm Sector" (paper presented at the annual meeting of the Agricultural and Applied Economics Association, Denver, August 1–4, 2004).

22. The data shown in the figure were calculated from information available online from the US Bureau of Economic Analysis and organized as SAS files by John Blodgett at the Missouri Census Data Center. The data were calculated from 674 counties, selected from 1970 county data in which comparisons could be made between the overall value of personal income in the county and the value of agricultural products sold in the county. Those counties include 3,500 nonurban towns with fewer than 25,000 residents in 1980. Mean net farm income per county without adjustments for inflation or number of farmers increased from $6,641,000 in 1969 to $27,079,000 in 2009—the most recent data available at the time the analysis was done. The Consumer Price Index set at 1.0 in 1969 increased to 5.845 in 2009. The net farm income per county adjusted for the change in the Consumer Price Index thus fell from $6,641,000 in 1969 to $4,632,334 in 2009, and when further adjusted by the declining number of farmers, held fairly constant at $6,675 per farmer in 1969 until $6,390 in 2001, and peaked at $14,781 in 1973 and $12,176 in 2008.

23. John A. Schnittker, "The 1972–73 Food Price Spiral," *Brookings Papers on Economic Activity* 4 (1973): 498–507; Shelby W. Herman, "Farm Income in 1973 and Outlook for 1974," *Survey of Current Business* (September 1974): 11–13.

24. These data are for the 667 counties in which the value of agricultural products compared with the overall value of personal income was highest in data from 1970.

25. Ramona Marotz-Baden and Deane Cowan, "Mothers-in-law and Daughters-in-law: The Effects of Proximity on Conflict and Stress," *Family Relations* 36 (1987): 385–90; Ramona Marotz-Baden and Claudia Mattheis, "Daughters-in-law and Stress in Two-Generation Farm Families," *Family Relations* 43 (1994): 132–37; Fiona Gill, "Moving to the 'Big' House: Power and Accommodation in Inter-generational Farming Families," *Rural Society* 18 (2008): 83–94.

26. Rich Allen and Ginger Harris, "What We Know about the Demographics of U.S. Farm Operators," *Agricultural Outlook Forum* (February 25, 2005), http://www.agcensus.usda.gov/Publications/2002/Other_Analysis/.

27. Median age and percentage over age sixty as reported here are from my analysis of data from the US Decennial Census in 1950 and 2000 for males age eighteen and over who listed their occupation as farmer (owner or tenant). The data are from the Public Use One Percent Microsamples, electronic data files, courtesy of Steven Ruggles, Matthew Sobek, Trent Alexander, Catherine A. Fitch, Ronald Goeken, Patricia Kelly Hall, Miriam King, and Chad Ronnander, *Integrated Public Use Microdata Series: Version 4.0* [machine-readable database] (Minneapolis: Minnesota Population Center, 2008). For a discussion of the aging of farm operators, see J. L. Harlin, "The Aging Family Farm: Estate/Succession Planning for Farmers," *Agricultural Finance* 34 (1992): 38–39; Ayal Kimhi and Ramon Lopez, "A Note on Farmers' Retirement and Succession Considerations: Evidence from a Household Survey," *Journal of Agricultural Economics* 50 (1999): 154–62; Keating and Munro, "Transferring the Family Farm." Estimates compiled by the US Department of Agriculture showed that 648,297 of the nation's 2,131,007 farms (30 percent) in 2009 were operated by persons sixty-five years or older; 74 percent of these farms were full-owner operated, 23 percent were part-owner operated, and 3 percent were operated by tenants. See Agricultural Resource Management Survey, US Department of Agriculture, November 2010, http://www.ers.usda.gov.

6. Leadership: Earning Respect, Improving the Community

1. For examples of the formal leadership and community planning literature, see Kristina Ford, James Lopach, and Dennis O'Donnell, *Planning in Small Town America: Observations, Sketches, and a Reform Proposal* (Chicago: American Planning Association, 1990); John Nalbandian, *Professionalism in Local Government* (San Francisco: Jossey-Bass, 1991).

2. Community Involvement Survey, electronic data file. The percentages of people who said they would admire persons involved in these ways were higher in small nonmetropolitan towns than in other communities. Specifically, the percentage of people who said they would admire "a lot" a person who helps the poor was 9 and 5 points higher, respectively, than among respondents in suburbs and central cities; a person who gets things organized was 3 and 13 points higher, respectively; and a person who volunteers was 8 and 11 points higher, respectively.

3. Factors contributing to the decline of membership and participation in community organizations include porous community and institutional boundaries, specialized interest organizations that facilitate short-term and occasional involvement, postponed marriage and child rearing, and declining organizational resources in lower-income urban communities. See Robert D. Putnam, *Bowling Alone: The Collapse and Revival of American Community* (New York: Simon and Schuster, 2000); Robert Wuthnow, *Loose Connections: Joining Together in America's Fragmented Communities* (Cambridge, MA: Harvard University Press, 1998); Robert Wuthnow, "Der Wandel des Sozialkapitals in den USA," in *Gesellschaft und Gemeinsinn: Sozialkapital im internationalen Vergleich*, ed. Robert D. Putnam (Gütersloh, Germany: Verlag Bertelsmann Stiftung, 2001), 655–749.

4. These data were provided by the National Center for Charitable Statistics at the Urban Institute as an electronic data file. The zip code population data are from the 2000 US Census, which corresponded most closely to the zip code designations for associations. The nonprofit associations data underestimate the total number of such organizations because religious organizations are not required to file with the Internal Revenue Service, although those that have done so voluntarily or that have been chartered as 501(c)3 tax-exempt entities are included.

5. The data in the figure are from the Civic Involvement Survey. They are the odds ratios for holding membership in each kind of organization among residents of small nonmetropolitan towns with residents of suburbs as the comparison group, and control for residence in small metropolitan towns or central cities, gender, race, ethnicity, level of education, age, and whether or not the respondent has children living in the household.

6. Mr. Tanka's community is one of ninety-six incorporated towns in the contiguous United States in which 30 percent or more of the population is Native American; the average population of these communities is approximately one thousand.

7. An attorney we interviewed made an important observation about squabbles in small towns. Based on the many civil disputes he had litigated, he thought conflicts between neighbors were often avoided because people knew they had to coexist in a small community for a long time and thus did not voice their grievances unless the problem became acute. He also thought that it was an advantage that small towns have plenty of space between houses and big yards. "A nice wide-open stretch between us [helps] because I'm not stepping on your toes, I'm not looking in your windows, I'm not smelling your funny-smelling food when you cook it. It is a function of just having fewer people per square mile and not having as many people stepping on your toes." This observation squared with the fact that most of the conflicts public officials talked about involved collective goods, such as schools and law enforcement, which could not be so easily resolved.

8. For a discussion of the so-called broken windows theory of social disorder, see Robert J. Sampson and Stephen W. Raudenbush, *Disorder in Urban Neighborhoods: Does It Lead to Crime?* (Washington, DC: US Department of Justice, National Institute of Justice, 2001); Robert J. Sampson and Stephen W. Raudenbush, "Seeing Disorder: Neighborhood Stigma and the Social Construction of 'Broken Windows,'" *Social Psychology Quarterly* 67 (2004): 319–42.

9. In some of the communities we studied, debates about historic preservation had emerged especially in conjunction with passing local ordinances that put the community in conformity with state preservation laws, for example, that required special approvals to modify any building more than fifty years old or that qualified certain buildings for state preservation funds.

10. Not to belabor the point, but the process of historical preservation, which appears from our interviews to be widespread in small towns, is always a matter of nudging aspects of past lived experience into forms that can be consumed easily by visitors and new residents. This process has been perceptively described in other contexts. On Jewish neighborhoods, see Beth S. Wenger, *History Lessons: The Creation of American Jewish Heritage* (Princeton, NJ: Princeton University

Press, 2010). On sections of New York City, see Hasia R. Diner, Jeffrey Shandler, and Beth S. Wenger, eds., *Remembering the Lower East Side: American Jewish Reflections* (Bloomington: Indiana University Press, 2000). For mission parishes in the San Antonia area, see Thomas S. Bremer, *Blessed with Tourists: The Borderlands of Religion and Tourism in San Antonio* (Chapel Hill: University of North Carolina Press, 2003).

11. David Obstfeld, "Social Networks, the *Tertius Iungens* Orientation, and Involvement in Innovation," *Administrative Science Quarterly* 50 (2005): 100–130; Gautam Ahuja, "Collaboration Networks, Structural Holes, and Innovation: A Longitudinal Study," *Administrative Science Quarterly* 45 (2000): 425–55; Simon Rodan and Charles Galunic, "More than Network Structure: How Knowledge Heterogeneity Influences Managerial Performance and Innovativeness," *Strategic Management Journal* 25 (2004): 541–62; Ronald S. Burt, "Structural Holes and Good Ideas," *American Journal of Sociology* 110 (2004): 349–99; David Strang and Sarah A. Soule, "Diffusion in Organizations and Social Movements: From Hybrid Corn to Poison Pills," *Annual Review of Sociology* 24 (1998): 265–90.

12. An attempt to investigate the extent of closed and open networks was included in the 1985 General Social Survey, in which 1,517 nationally representative adults were asked, "Some people have friends who mostly know one another. Other people have friends who don't know one another. Would you say that all of your friends know one another, most of your friends know one another, only a few of your friends know one another, or none of your friends know one another?" Only 12 percent of respondents living in towns of 2,500 to 10,000 people selected the most closed option by indicating that all their friends knew each other, the same percentage as for the whole sample and smaller than the 16 percent of residents of large cities (with populations greater than 250,000) who gave the same response. Combining those who said all or most of their friends knew each other, the proportion (71 percent) was higher in small towns than in large cities (54 percent), but still indicated that most residents of small towns had at least a few friends who did not know each other. Strong and weak ties with people outside the community were abundantly evident in our interviews, in which people talked about relatives and friends who lived elsewhere, acquaintances from having lived elsewhere themselves, business contacts, phone calls, and emails.

13. For a useful review showing mixed results from network studies and the need to consider additional contextual factors, see Alejandro Portes, "Social Capital: Its Origins and Applications in Modern Sociology," *Annual Review of Sociology* 24 (1998): 1–24. On the evident variability of network structure effects in rural villages, although in a different national setting, see Barbara Entwisle, Katherine Faust, Ronald R. Rindfuss, and Toshiko Kaneda, "Networks and Contexts: Variation in the Structure of Social Ties," *American Journal of Sociology* 112 (2007): 1495–533. For a discussion of regional programs that encourage cooperation and the exchange of ideas among communities in US small towns, see Ted K. Bradshaw, "Multicommunity Networks: A Rural Transition," *Annals of the American Academy of Political and Social Science* 529 (1993): 164–75. The farmer quoted was referring to the best-selling book by Thomas L. Friedman, *The World Is Flat: A Brief History of the Twenty-First Century* (New York: Farrar, Straus and Giroux, 2005).

14. An interesting example of innovation via the Internet is the development of eBay markets for used farm machinery. See Florian Diekmann, Brian E. Roe, and Marvin T. Batte, "Tractors on eBay: Differences between Internet and In-Person Auctions," *American Journal of Agricultural Economics* 90 (2008): 306–20.

15. One thing that came through repeatedly in our interviews was the importance of the local newspaper. In towns that had one, residents frequently referred to its role in publicizing local events as well as contributing to the community's identity and sense of community mindedness. In other towns, residents complained that the newspaper had gone out of business or been purchased by a large media chain that no longer did a good job of featuring local events. Several interviewees described successful efforts by local residents to develop blog sites or print community newsletters.

16. The data in the figure are from the 2008 population estimates provided by the US Census Bureau and computed by merging the data for incorporated places with the data for counties. An interesting simulation study of intertown networks (based on commuting in Italy) suggests that large hub towns are likely to be linked to many satellite towns that are disconnected from each other, while smaller towns may have fewer neighboring towns but are still connected to each other. See Andrea DeMontis, Alessandro Chessa, Michele Campagna, Simone Caschili, and Giancarlo Deplano, "Modeling Commuting Systems through a Complex Network Analysis: A Study of the Italian Islands of Sardinia and Sicily," *Journal of Transport and Land Use* 2 (2010): 39–55.

17. The results shown in the figure are from nearest-neighbor analysis in which latitude and longitude are used as the predictor variables, using Euclidean distances and with one iteration to identify the nearest town, and the partition variable selecting for the nearest town that had a population in 1980 of at least twenty-five hundred.

18. Nearest-neighbor analysis was used to compute the predicted value for mean population in 1980 of towns' five geographically closest towns, with algorithm parameters set for Euclidean distances and five iterations.

19. US Department of Health and Human Services, *Results from the 2004 National Survey on Drug Use and Health: National Findings* (Washington, DC: Substance Abuse and Mental Health Services Administration, Office of Applied Studies, 2004). This survey showed that illicit drug use was still lower in nonmetropolitan areas than in metropolitan ones; the proportion of persons age twelve and older who had used illicit drugs in the past month were 4.6 percent in rural nonmetropolitan areas, 5.6 percent in less urbanized nonmetropolitan areas, 8.5 percent in small metropolitan areas, and 8.1 percent in large metropolitan areas (ibid., figure 2.7, 21). National Drug Enforcement Administration figures for methamphetamine seizures showed a steady increase from 198 kilograms in 1987 to 2,161 kilograms in 2005, after which the amount declined to 1,703 kilograms in 2009. The number of seizures in 2009 varied widely among states, from only one or two in Maine and Wisconsin to more than a thousand in Missouri and Indiana.

20. Nick Reding, *Methland: The Death and Life of an American Small Town* (New York: Bloomsbury, 2009).

21. Walter Kirn, "Wasted Land," *New York Times*, July 1, 2009.

22. For annual statistics on crime and law enforcement for Oelwein, and with comparisons for Iowa and the nation, see http://www.city-data.com/crime/crime-Oelwein-Iowa.html.

23. Several of our interviewees blamed local law enforcement officers for lax supervision of drug and alcohol problems, but it was more common for references to law enforcement to mention the difficulties involved in paying for adequate coverage in small towns and rural counties. There was also a wide range of opinion about the merits of law enforcement. At one extreme, residents favored harsher punishment, while at the other end of the spectrum, some residents entertained ideas about legalizing drugs.

24. Robert Wuthnow, *Remaking the Heartland: Middle America since the 1950s* (Princeton, NJ: Princeton University Press, 2011). For a look at colleges that focuses on the distinctive qualities of college towns, but deals more with cities than with small towns, see also Blake Gumprecht, "The American College Town," *Geographical Review* 93 (2003): 51–80. The advantages for small towns of having a college include a higher proportion of well-educated residents, an ability to educate local youths and attract youths who stay in the area, leadership experience gained through college administration, and the cultural events provided by the college. For an examination of the role of county seats in an earlier period, see Glenn V. Fuguitt, "County Seat Status as a Factor in Small Town Growth and Decline," *Social Forces* 44 (1965): 245–51. For an exploration of the effects of highways and highway expansion on population trends in rural areas, see Craig R. Humphrey and Ralph R. Sell, "The Impact of Controlled Access Highways on Population Growth in Nonmetropolitan Communities, 1940–1970," *Rural Sociology* 40 (1975): 332–43; Daniel T. Lichter and Glenn V. Fuguitt, "Demographic Response to Transportation Innovation: The Case of the Interstate Highway," *Social Forces* 59 (1980): 492–512; Guangqing Chi, "The Impacts of Highway Expansion on Population Change: An Integrated Spatial Approach," *Rural Sociology* 75 (2010): 58–89.

25. For similar observations, based on interviews conducted in eighteen rural towns, in which qualities associated with good leadership included an emphasis on community pride, a participatory approach to community decision making, a realistic appraisal of future opportunities, and awareness of competitive positioning, see Milan Wall, "Factors in Rural Community Survival: Review of Insights from Thriving Small Towns," *Great Plains Research* 9 (1999): 115–35. See also Milan Wall, "Clues to Rural Community Survival," Heartland Center for Leadership Development, 2010.

7. Habits of Faith:
The Social Role of Small-Town Congregations

1. These data were collected by InfoGroup, http://www.socialexplorer.com. Another study conducted in 2000 yielded similar results. For example, it identified 3,727 Jewish congregations nationwide, but only 19 were located in counties with populations of fewer than twenty-five thousand people. The same study identified 1,209 mosques nationwide, but only 7 were in counties with populations of

fewer than twenty-five thousand people. See Glenmary Research Center, electronic data file. Congregation leaders reported information voluntarily, which means that some congregations may have been missed. For valuable historical information, see Lee Shai Weissbach, *Jewish Life in Small-Town America: A History* (New Haven, CT: Yale University Press, 2005). Weissbach examines the lives of the minority of the US Jewish population between the 1870s and 1950s who did not live in cities, and argues that accommodation and tolerance between Christians and Jews was often present in these communities. Most of the "small towns" included in the study (such as Fresno, California; Colorado Springs, Colorado; Orlando, Florida; Evanston, Illinois; and Lansing, Michigan) already had populations of more than twenty-five thousand people by 1920. The accommodation and tolerance that Weissbach observes is consistent with studies showing that tolerance, intergroup trust, and lower levels of negative stereotyping toward minority religious and ethnic groups is generally lower in communities where the proportionate representation of those groups is lower, and thus less likely to be regarded by the majority population as a threat. See, for example, Charles Y. Glock, Robert Wuthnow, Jane Allyn Piliavin, and Metta Spencer, *Adolescent Prejudice* (New York: Harper and Row, 1975); Robert D. Putnam, "*E Pluribus Unum*: Diversity and Community in the Twenty-First Century," *Scandinavian Political Studies* 30 (2007): 137–74. The fact that most synagogues and mosques are located in cities does not mean that formal interaction with churches and church members takes place. For a discussion of research on this, see Robert Wuthnow, *America and the Challenges of Religious Diversity* (Princeton, NJ: Princeton University Press, 2005). Among our interviews here, however, residents of large cities notably pointed out the presence of Jews and Muslims in their communities as an aspect of diversity that they appreciated, if only from a distance.

2. Robert Wuthnow and Kevin Christiano, "The Effect of Residential Migration on Church Attendance in the United States," in *The Religious Dimension: New Directions in Quantitative Research*, ed. Robert Wuthnow (New York: Academic Press, 1979), 259–76.

3. Phillip Connor, "Increase or Decrease? The Impact of the International Migratory Event on Immigrant Religious Participation," *Journal for the Scientific Study of Religion* 47 (2008): 243–57; Phillip Connor, "International Migration and Religious Participation: The Mediating Impact of Individual and Contextual Effects," *Sociological Forum* 24 (2009): 779–803.

4. For the soup kitchen study, see Courtney Bender, *Heaven's Kitchen: Living Religion at God's Love We Deliver* (Chicago: University of Chicago Press, 2003). For the church parking lot study, see Penny Long Marler and C. Kirk Hadaway, "Testing the Attendance Gap in a Conservative Church," *Sociology of Religion* 60 (1999): 175–86. For additional discussions, see C. Kirk Hadaway, Penny Long Marler, and Mark Chaves, "What the Polls Don't Show: A Closer Look at U.S. Church Attendance," *American Sociological Review* 58 (1993): 741–52; Paul J. Olson, "Any Given Sunday: Weekly Church Attendance in a Midwestern City," *Journal for the Scientific Study of Religion* 47 (2008): 443–61.

5. Data on churches and church adherence were collected in 2000 by the Glenmary Research Center, electronic data file, http://thearda.com. Those data permitted the tabulation of the number of congregations by population of county. Data

were also collected in 2009 by InfoGroup, electronic data file, http://www.social explorer.com. The population figures provided by each organization are from the 2000 decennial census and 2007 population estimates, respectively. From the Glenmary data, which appears to provide a somewhat more complete count of churches among all denominations, counties with fewer than 5,000 people have a median number of 11 churches, or 1 for every 268 people. That number changes to 1 for every 322 people in counties with populations of 5,000 to 10,000, 1 for every 404 people in counties of 10,000 to 20,000, 1 for every 537 people in counties of 20,000 to 50,000, and 1 for every 895 people in counties of 50,000 or more. The rates shown in the figure are standardized as the number of churches per 1,000 inhabitants. The data are for 3,139 counties.

6. The adherence data were collected in 2000 by the Glenmary Research Center, and the membership data were collected in 2009 by InfoGroup.

7. On the significance of the public expression of religion, including some observations about congregations' visibility in the community, see Robert Wuthnow, *Producing the Sacred: An Essay on Public Religion* (Urbana: University of Illinois Press, 1994). For some information from interviewees about the significance of religious buildings, Robert Wuthnow, *Growing Up Religious: Christians and Jews and Their Journeys of Faith* (Boston: Beacon, 1999), 69–84. Although relatively little attention has been given to the public impact of religious buildings, compared with evidence about church attendance or the political influence of religious groups, in discussions of secularization, this would seem to be a critical topic deserving further investigation, especially as larger proportions of the population live in urban places where the number of churches per capita is lower than in small towns. For some broader observations about the visual impact of religion, see David Morgan and Sally M. Promey, *The Visual Culture of American Religions* (Berkeley: University of California Press, 2001). For a book that explores the theological significance of sacred places, see Robert M. Hamma, *Landscapes of the Soul: A Spirituality of Place* (Notre Dame, IN: Ave Maria Press, 1999).

8. The results summarized in the figure are from a binary logistic regression analysis of cumulative data collected in General Social Surveys between 1972 and 2008 (N = 52,344). The dependent variable is "attend," coded as "1" for respondents who said they attend religious services nearly every week, every week, or more than once a week. Residence in a small town refers to respondents who lived in a nonmetropolitan community of fewer than twenty thousand people. Control variables in the model were year of the survey, respondent's age, respondent's affiliation as an evangelical Protestant, Catholic, Other, or Nonaffiliated (with mainline Protestant as the reference category), respondent's region as the South, Midwest, or West (with the Northeast as the reference category), gender, and race. The education variable was coded from years of education, and consisted of dummy variables for twelve years of primary and secondary education, one to three years of higher education, or four or more years of higher education (with fewer than twelve years as the reference category), and interaction terms for the interaction of small town and high school graduate, small town and some college, and small town and college graduate. In models without the interaction

terms, the effects of all control variables are significant at the .001 level and the effect of small town residence is significant at that level with a modest odds ratio of 1.146. With the interaction terms in the model, the interaction terms account for the binary effect of small town residence, the interaction between small town and high school graduate is not significant, and the interaction terms for small town and some college as well as small town and college graduate are both significant. The figure shows the odds of attending religious services regularly for each level of education among small-town residents and among urban residents compared with the odds of attending religious services regularly among those who have not graduated from high school, taking into account all the control variables and interaction effects. A substantive interpretation of the results is that the odds of small-town residents who have graduated from college attending church weekly are approximately three times greater than the odds among small-town residents who have not graduated from high school, compared with a ratio of approximately two among residents in urban areas.

9. General Social Surveys, electronic data files. These results are from comparisons between residents living in nonmetropolitan towns of fewer than twenty thousand people and all respondents in the nationally representative surveys; surveys conducted from 2000 to 2008. Small towns differ from larger places in terms of demographic factors that affect religious service attendance. For example, small towns are disproportionally located in the South and Midwest, where attendance rates are higher; have larger proportions of elderly residents, who attend more often than younger people; but have a lower proportion of college residents, who attend more frequently than people with less education. These demographic factors largely cancel one another. For instance, the odds ratio of weekly church attendance regressed on a binary variable comparing small and larger towns is 1.235; it is 1.236 when controlling for region (South), education (college graduate), age (sixty-five and older), and gender. There is, of course, a long tradition in the social sciences suggesting that religion is more important in rural places than in urban ones because of closeness of nature, greater exposure to "acts of God," and the like, but there seems to be little reason to think these presumed differences explain much about religion in contemporary small towns. See Kevin D. Breault, "New Evidence on Religious Pluralism, Urbanism, and Religious Participation," *American Sociological Review* 54 (1989): 1048–53; Morgan Luck, "The Miracle of the Religious Divide: An Additional Argument for the Purported Distinction between Rural and Urban Religiosity," in *Where the Crows Fly Backwards: Notions of Rural Identity*, ed. Nancy Blacklow and Troy Whitford (Mount Gravatt, Queensland: Post Pressed, 2010), 59–65. Nor do blanket comparisons of rural and urban areas shed light on local variations resulting from differences in ethnic settlement and denominational practices. See Janel M. Curry, "Community Worldview and Rural Systems: A Study of Five Communities in Iowa," *Annals of the Association of American Geographers* 90 (2000): 693–712.

10. These examples point to what Alejandro Portes ("Social Capital: Its Origins and Applications in Modern Sociology," *Annual Review of Sociology* 24 [1998]: 1–24) terms "enforceable trust." Obligations, Portes writes, "are enforceable, not through recourse to law or violence but through the power of the

community" (ibid., 9). Portes suggests that enforceable trust is present, for example, when a student receives a loan because their coethnic group can be counted on to ensure that the loan is repaid or a banker loans money to a member of the community with the same expectation that the community will bring sanctions to bear if the person does not repay the loan. Similarly, church members in a small town can be trusted by fellow members to attend services, help with cleanup days, and so on, because those fellow members are likely to see that person in the community even if the person considers not participating in church activities.

11. These results are from the Global Issues Survey, a nationally representative survey of active church members, conducted under my direction in 2005. See Robert Wuthnow, *Boundless Faith: The Global Outreach of American Churches* (Berkeley: University of California Press, 2009). In my survey, 411 respondents lived outside a census-defined MSA, and said their church was located in a small town or rural area, while 1,820 respondents lived in an MSA. Respectively, 46 and 17 percent of the small town and metropolitan churchgoers said they attended congregations of fewer than two hundred members, while 8 and 35 percent, respectively, attended congregations larger than a thousand. Nationally, 34 percent of members of congregations of fewer than two hundred said more than ten of their close friends belonged to their congregation, while that figure rose to 40 percent among members of congregations of a thousand or more. A binary logistic regression analysis of the data shows that the odds of having more than ten friends in one's congregation are 1.376 greater among residents who attend congregations in small rural towns than among residents who live in MSAs, controlling for age, gender, marital status, race, education, frequency of attendance, religious tradition, and congregation size.

12. Due to data limitations, there is no ideal way in which to estimate average church attendance by size and location of town, at least not with evidence from surveys with respectable response rates. Thus, the data in the figure were computed as follows: information about frequency of attendance at religious services was drawn from two large nationally representative surveys conducted in 2006 and 2008, which yielded more than sixty thousand respondents when merged (the reported response rate was 47 percent among those initially included in the random sample); because respondents were identified at the county level (which is rare in surveys), it was possible to compute an average weekly church attendance score for each county in the United States by aggregating the responses of the respondents in each county; these scores were then merged with the town-level data, yielding results that indicate the average weekly church attendance rate for the county in which each town is located. For information about the data, see Stephen Ansolabehere, *Cooperative Congressional Election Study, 2006: Common Content*, (Cambridge, MA: Harvard University, 2010); Stephen Ansolabehere, *Cooperative Congressional Election Study, 2008: Common Content* (Cambridge, MA: Harvard University, 2010). For the electronic data files, see http:// projects.iq.harvard.edu/cces.

13. Michael Mayerfeld Bell, *Childerley: Nature and Morality in a Country Village* (Chicago: University of Chicago Press, 1994).

14. As an example of the community-caring activities of small-town churches, focusing on Council Grove, Kansas, with a population of twenty-two hundred,

see Ram A. Cnaan, *The Invisible Caring Hand: American Congregations and the Provision of Welfare* (New York: New York University Press, 2002), 139–55.

15. A longtime member of the Lutheran Church in a town of thirteen hundred, for example, explained that there were good relationships between the Lutherans and Methodists, but said it was different with new evangelical churches in her town and several neighboring communities. "They build a building, and they draw their members from the congregations that have been solid in the communities for years and years. You're seeing this all over with more not-the-traditional religions." Somewhat begrudgingly, she added, "It's OK if that's what they want." But she also felt that church membership and attendance should not be "like rush week for a fraternity or sorority."

16. General Social Surveys, electronic data files; results nationally and for residents living in nonmetropolitan towns of fewer than twenty thousand people; surveys conducted between 1972 and 1978 as well as between 2000 and 2008. Aggregating the surveys yielded an N of 1,367 residents of small towns for the earlier period and 1,796 for the more recent period. Besides the percentages for evangelical and mainline Protestants, Catholics, and historically black denominations, fewer than 1 percent in each period were Jewish, 2 and 5 percent in the respective periods listed other faiths, and 3 and 13 percent, respectively, said they were nonaffiliated.

17. The county-level data collected by InfoGroup in 2009 show that evangelical Protestants make up 37 percent of all church members in counties with fewer than five thousand residents, 45 percent in counties with five to ten thousand residents, 51 percent in counties of ten to twenty-five thousand, 48 percent in counties of twenty-five to fifty thousand, and 32 percent in counties of fifty thousand or more; respectively, mainline Protestants account for 33, 28, 23, 22, and 17 percent; and Catholics account for 20, 14, 12, 16, and 30 percent.

18. Another factor that facilitated the churches' service activities in some of the smaller communities we studied was their location. Unlike churches located in upscale metropolitan suburbs that often are geographically isolated from low-income inner-city neighborhoods, small-town churches were frequently located near the center of the community, and were in close proximity to low-income housing or could operate latchkey programs because of being near the school. Some of the larger communities had difficulty because transportation was lacking, but school buses, van service for the disabled and elderly paid through state programs, and volunteer drivers sometimes solved these problems.

19. Penny Edgell Becker, *Congregations in Conflict: Cultural Models of Local Religious Life* (Cambridge: Cambridge University Press, 1999); Penny Edgell, *Religion and Family in a Changing Society* (Princeton, NJ: Princeton University Press, 2006).

20. Garrison Keillor, *A Prairie Home Companion*, radio program, November 7, 2009.

21. National Congregations Study, designed by Mark Chaves and conducted among 1,234 congregations in 1998, electronic data file. The comparisons refer to the census tract in which the congregation was located. For further information on the study, see Mark Chaves, *Congregations in America* (Cambridge, MA: Harvard University Press, 2004).

22. This was not an isolated event. As denominations discussed policies about gay and lesbian ordination and acceptance into membership, congregations found themselves divided. In a town of nine hundred, the sixty-member United Church of Christ, for example, lost twenty of its members when the majority of the congregation voted to maintain its affiliation with the denomination after the denomination voted to extend ordination and membership to gays and lesbians. The important aspect of the controversy was that nearly everyone thought the conflict could have been avoided, and indeed wished it had been, because they were all friends and neighbors who regularly saw one another in the small town. The pastor recalled, "I really think everybody understood that we were not bound to perform commitment ceremonies or anything unless our congregation decided it wanted to." He also encouraged members to communicate with denominational officials and remains "baffled" that they did not. In retrospect, the people who left were increasingly dissatisfied with what they saw as "liberal" tendencies in the denomination over a period of years.

23. R. Stephen Warner, *A Church of Our Own: Disestablishment and Diversity in American Religion* (New Brunswick, NJ: Rutgers University Press, 2005).

24. These results are from my Global Issues Survey, conducted in 2005. Perspective on the responses given by active churchgoers in small nonmetropolitan areas can be gained by comparing them with the respondents of subjects interviewed in MSAs. The largest differences were in the proportions of respondents who said that at least a few of their fellow congregation members were immigrants (50 and 80 percent, respectively) and that a lot of their fellow congregants were immigrants (3 and 10 percent, respectively). Other items generally showed similarities: the congregation was believed to emphasize international ministry a lot (35 and 38 percent), the congregation had a missions committee (35 and 40 percent), the congregation sent a group abroad on a short-term mission trip (39 and 45 percent), the congregation hosted a guest speaker from another country (40 and 51 percent), the congregation had a hunger relief offering in the past year (74 and 76 percent), and it helped sponsor one or more foreign missionaries (77 and 73 percent). See also Wuthnow, *Boundless Faith*.

25. Although the literature on small town and rural churches is relatively sparse, for several recent volumes of potential interest to clergy and lay leaders, see Lawrence W. Farris, *Dynamics of Small Town Ministry* (Herndon, VA: Alban Institute, 2000); Shannon Jung, ed., *Rural Ministry: The Shape of the Renewal to Come* (Nashville: Abington, 1998); Peter G. Bush and H. Christine O'Reilly, *Where 20 or 30 Are Gathered: Leading Worship in the Small Church* (Herndon, VA: Alban Institute, 2006); papers from the Missouri Rural Churches Project at the Missouri School of Religion (http://www.msr-crm.org).

26. In Father Malone's diocese, more clustering was expected because the average age of priests was sixty-seven and a quarter were scheduled to retire in five years. Meanwhile, the diocese was making greater use of deacons and immigrant priests. On rural Catholic practices, see also Miriam Brown, ed., *Sustaining Heart in the Heartland: Exploring Rural Spirituality* (Mahwah, NJ: Paulist Press, 2005).

27. The data shown in the figure are from the previously cited Glenmary data collected nationally in 2000 and comparable data collected in 1980 (the 2009 InfoGroup data are less comparable), electronic data files courtesy of the Associa-

tion of Religion Data Archives. The data presented here are for nonmetropolitan counties only, of which there were 2,994 with religion data in 1980 and 3,022 with religion data in 2000. During these two decades, 2,001 counties experienced no population loss, and the mean number of adherents increased from 31,082 to 40,242 and the mean number of churches increased from 74.4 to 87.2; 832 counties experienced a total population decline of less than 20 percent, or 1 percent per year, and the mean number of adherents decreased from 24,405 to 21,680 while the number of churches decreased from 61.2 to 60.7; 161 counties experienced a population decline of more than 20 percent, the mean number of adherents declined from 6,314 to 4,847, and the number of churches declined from 25.5 to 23.1. Further analysis comparing smaller and larger counties, using the US Department of Agriculture definition of county population loss, yielded similar results.

28. The results described here are from multiple regression analysis of the 1980 and 2000 religion data with 2,994 nonmetropolitan counties as the unit of analysis. Using the total number of churches per county in 1980 as the dependent variable and with the total county population in 1980 included in the model, the unstandardized regression coefficient for the number of towns with less than twenty-five thousand population each per county is 2.778 and the standardized coefficient is 0.183, significant at or beyond the 0.001 level of probability. Using the total number of churches per county in 2000 as the dependent variable, and with the total county population in 1980 and total number of churches in 1980 included in the model, the unstandardized regression coefficient for the number of towns with less than twenty-five thousand population is −.1.163 and the standardized coefficient is −0.060, significant at or beyond the 0.001 level of probability.

29. Without mentioning the Religious Right specifically, a number of other church members, whose views on social issues ranged from far Left to far Right, said they deplored the divisiveness surrounding moral and political issues. It was the distortion, lies, and hyperbole that especially bothered them along with the seeming inability of people on either side to have calm reasoned discussion.

30. Or as a woman in another small town that included several Jewish and Muslim families observed, "It gets a little creepy sometimes," referring to how closely integrated Christian practices were with school activities.

31. Ronald K. Crandall, *Turnaround Strategies for the Small Church* (Nashville: Abingdon Press, 1995).

32. Ronald K. Crandall, *Turnaround and Beyond: A Hopeful Future for the Small Membership Church* (Nashville: Abingdon Press, 2008). See also Ed Stetzer and Mike Dodson, *Comeback Churches: How 300 Churches Turned Around and Yours Can, Too* (Nashville: B&H Books, 2007).

8. CONTENTIOUS ISSUES:
THE MORAL SENTIMENTS OF COMMUNITY LIFE

1. For one of the most thoughtful discussions of the tensions between progressives and conservatives, see James Davison Hunter, *Culture Wars: The Struggle to Define America* (New York: Basic Books, 1991). See also James Davison Hunter

and Alan Wolfe, *Is There a Culture War? A Dialogue on Values and American Life* (Washington, DC: Brookings Institution Press, 2006).

2. The data in the figure are drawn from the 2006 Common Congressional Election Study in which a nationally representative sample of 36,337 adults age eighteen and over participated, of whom 12,610 said the opinion that best agreed with their view was either that "by law, abortion should never be permitted" or "the law should permit abortion only in case of rape, incest, or when the woman's life is in danger" (and thus did not opt for the statement that read "the law should permit abortion for reasons other than rape, incest, or danger to the woman's life, but only after the need for the abortion has been clearly established" or "by law, a woman should always be able to obtain an abortion as a matter of personal choice"). The odds ratios shown are from logistic regression in which gender, race, living in the South, being age sixty or over or younger than age thirty, and being a college graduate were included, and the median size of towns in the county in which each respondent lived and whether that county was in an MSA or not were introduced, with median population in 2010 of towns between 25,000 and 49,999 as the excluded comparison category.

3. The results shown in the figure are from General Social Surveys, electronic data files, conducted between 1998 and 2008, including approximately 8,850 randomly selected respondents representative of the noninstitutional, English-speaking population of the United States age eighteen and over. The figure shows the odds ratios for respondents living in nonmetropolitan towns of fewer than 20,000 people compared with respondents living in larger metropolitan communities, based on binary logistic regression models in which controls were included for age, sex, race, region, and level of education.

4. This argument is not shared by all historians of witch hunts in colonial America, but was advanced notably by sociologist Kai T. Erikson (*Wayward Puritans: A Study in the Sociology of Deviance* [New York: John Wiley and Sons, 1969]).

5. Joseph Gusfield, *Symbolic Crusade: Status Politics and the American Temperance Movement*, rev. ed. (New York: Greenwood Press); Daniel Okrent, *Last Call: The Rise and Fall of Prohibition* (New York: Scribner, 2010).

6. James Davison Hunter, *Before the Shooting Begins: Searching for Democracy in America's Culture War* (New York: Free Press, 1994).

7. Ziad W. Munson, *The Making of Pro-life Activists: How Social Movement Mobilization Works* (Chicago: University of Chicago Press, 2009).

8. The data in the figure are from the 2008 Common Congressional Election Survey, which was similar to the previously cited 2006 study, and the median size of towns in the county in which each respondent lived was estimated in the same way.

9. In General Social Surveys conducted in 2004, 2006, and 2008, respondents were asked how strongly they agreed or disagreed that "homosexual couples should have the right to marry one another"; 57 percent of respondents in nonmetropolitan areas with fewer than twenty thousand residents said they disagreed or strongly disagreed, compared with 51 percent among respondents in larger metropolitan areas, yet the effect of residence was statistically insignificant in binary logistic regression analysis in which age, gender, race, region, and education were controlled. A question about approval or disapproval of a homosexual being allowed to teach school showed that approval in the small nonmetropoli-

tan towns rose from 49 percent in the 1970s to 75 percent in surveys conducted between 2000 and 2008, which roughly paralleled the rise among all respondents from 51 to 79 percent. Data collected in the American National Election Studies, electronic data files, provide less precise measures, but show that mean "feeling thermometer" scores for feelings toward gays and lesbians rose from 22.4 in 1984 to 41.2 in 2000 in the "rural" population (which comprised approximately a third of the samples, and included persons living on farms, in small towns, and in open-country areas), compared with a rise from 30.5 to 45.9 for suburban residents, and from 35.4 to 47.0 for center-city residents.

10. David Bell, "Cowboy Love," in *Country Boys: Masculinity and Rural Life*, ed. Hugh Campbell, Michael Mayerfield Bell, and Margaret Finney (University Park: Pennsylvania State University Press, 2006), 163–82; Will Fellows, *Farm Boys: Lives of Gay Men from the Rural Midwest* (Madison: University of Wisconsin Press, 2001).

11. These questions were asked in the 2006 Common Congressional Election Survey, and showed that among respondents living in nonmetropolitan counties in which the median population of towns was twenty-five thousand or less, 88 percent said they knew someone who was gay, and among that 88 percent, 20 percent said the person they knew was a family member, 22 percent said the person was a close friend, 14 percent said the person was a coworker, and 4 percent said that they were the person they had in mind.

12. Eleven states, all with sizable rural populations, passed constitutional amendments in 2004 codifying marriage as an exclusively heterosexual institution: Arkansas, Georgia, Kentucky, Michigan, Mississippi, Montana, North Dakota, Ohio, Oklahoma, Oregon, and Utah.

13. *Kitzmiller, et al. v. Dover Area School District*, decided for the plaintiffs on December 20, 2005, complete transcript of testimony, http://www.talkorigins.org. For the remarks of one of the scientists who provided expert testimony in the case, see also Kenneth R. Miller, *Finding Darwin's God: A Scientist's Search for Common Ground between God and Evolution* (New York: Harper Perennial, 2007); Kenneth R. Miller, *Only a Theory: Evolution and the Battle for America's Soul* (New York: Viking Adult, 2008); Harold W. Attridge, ed., *The Religion and Science Debate: Why Does It Continue?* (New Haven, CT: Yale University Press, 2009).

14. General Social Surveys, electronic data files. A question asked in 2004 of 1,304 respondents showed that 6 percent of respondents in nonmetropolitan communities of fewer than twenty thousand residents thought it was definitely true that "human beings developed from earlier species of animal," whereas 52 percent said this was definitely not true and an additional 16 percent said it was probably not true (and among metropolitan respondents, 39 percent said the statement was definitely not true). My qualitative interviews suggest that one of the nuances survey questions often fail to capture is between people who believe generally in evolution within species or some instances across species, and yet reject the idea that humans evolved from other species. An example would be this comment: "I don't think that we started out as one cell, and that we crawled up out of the ocean and grew legs, but by the same token I know there are animals like the walruses, and maybe at one time they had feet they didn't use and so slowly evolved."

15. We talked to devout church members who thought the Ten Commandments should be taught at home or in the church yet not at school because that would necessitate including lessons about other religions at school. This comment from a Southern Baptist is typical: "Personally, I'm not sure that teaching religion in the public schools would be a good idea. As much as I want to see the Ten Commandments taught in schools, in this day and age with our culture what it is, we can't really open the door to teach one religion in our schools without teaching other religions in our schools. I would not want some teacher teaching a different religion to my children. I think the parents need to be teaching these things at home."

16. A seeming exception to the pragmatic approach to school controversies is the view that outsiders are preventing townspeople from having their way, as in this example, "When they say that they can't have a prayer in school, that just burns me. That is a part of our country. A part of our country. It always has been, and then when you try to take it away, I don't like that. I think they need to let prayer stay in school." In other remarks, this woman, who is a local elected official, makes it clear that "they" means forces outside the community, especially the federal government. It makes her mad not to have prayer in schools, but she also is pragmatic in thinking that having prayer would not be a problem in her nearly homogeneous community of fewer than eight hundred people.

17. The six-day creationist elaborated, "As far as what should be taught, we do not live in a theocracy, and I don't want to change anyone. I don't believe in that. I think that evolution should be taught as a theory with evidences pro and con given. I think evolution should be taught. I think intelligent design should be taught as a theory. And I think at least reference should be made to the creation model, which is who that designer is, taking it a step further. Not that that should be debated in a science class, but some type of reference [should be] made to the fact that we see so much intelligence in the design around us. I think it is just wrong that we stifle that conversation."

18. The science teacher felt there "may be some connection" between "the religious belief in creationism and evolution," so he was happy to mention both, but insisted the two should not be confused, and also could easily be separated by presenting evolution as science and intelligent design as something else—possibly religion or faith. The most general term that people who described themselves as open minded used was "theory," by which they meant that evolution was a good scientific account of how things happened, but was an account subject to revision; some, of course, thought it needed more revision than others.

19. Or as one woman says, "They don't want anything shoved down their throats and they certainly don't want you shoving anything down their kids' throats."

9. WASHINGTON IS BROKEN: POLITICS AND THE NEW POPULISM

1. See, for example, Jennifer Bradley and Bruce Katz, "Village Idiocy," *New Republic*, October 8, 2008, 12–13; Ben MacIntyre, "Small Town America Still Dares to Think Big," *Times of London*, September 25, 2008; Mark Greif, "Death

and the Maiden," *Harpers*, November 2008), 18; Andrew M. Langer, "Sarah Palin, Small-Town America," *U.S. News*, September 12, 2008. For one of the best sociological analyses of Palin's rise in popularity, see Jeffrey C. Alexander, *The Performance of Politics: Obama's Victory and the Democratic Struggle for Power* (New York: Oxford University Press, 2010), 193–242.

2. For several works that provide valuable historical overviews and interpretations of late nineteenth-century populism, see Lawrence Goodwyn, *The Populist Moment: A Short History of the Agrarian Revolt in America* (New York: Oxford University Press, 1978); Michael Kazin, *The Populist Persuasion: An American History*, rev. ed. (Ithaca, NY: Cornell University Press, 1998); John Lukacs, *Democracy and Populism: Fear and Hatred* (New Haven, CT: Yale University Press, 2006); Charles Postel, *The Populist Vision* (New York: Oxford University Press, 2007).

3. "Mr. Bush Goes to Washington," Associated Press, January 18, 2001. Among other sources, for a discussion of Truman's small-town roots, see David McCullough, *Truman* (New York: Simon and Schuster, 1992). For a look at Eisenhower's roots in small towns, see Stephen E. Ambrose, *Eisenhower: Soldier and President* (New York: Simon and Schuster, 1990). On Carter's roots, see Erwin C. Hargrove and James Sterling Young, *Jimmy Carter as President: Leadership and the Politics of the Public Good* (Baton Rouge: Louisiana State University Press, 1988). On Reagan's, see Lou Cannon, *President Reagan: The Role of a Lifetime* (New York: Simon and Schuster, 1991). On Clinton's, see Donald T. Phillips, *The Clinton Charisma: A Legacy of Leadership* (New York: Palgrave Macmillan, 2007). On George W. Bush's, see Justin A. Frank, *Bush on the Couch: Inside the Mind of the President* (New York: Harper, 2004).

4. Ron Formisano, "Populist Currents in the 2008 Presidential Campaign," *Journal of Policy History* 22 (2010): 237–55.

5. The results shown in the figure are drawn from General Social Surveys conducted between 1998 and 2008 with the responses for these years aggregated to yield approximately eleven hundred respondents in nonmetropolitan towns of under twenty thousand population and approximately eight thousand for the general public (analysis of responses in the separate surveys conducted biennially during this period showed no significant trends on these questions). The exact percentages indicating that too much is being spent on each topic were, respectively, for small-town respondents and the public generally, 5.8 and 5.4 on education, 7.9 and 7.9 on health, 9.7 and 9.0 on law enforcement, 31.9 and 23.8 on assistance to blacks, 43.1 and 33.6 on assistance to big cities, and 45.2 and 40.2 on welfare (the "y" versions of the questions were used except for welfare). The possibility that differences between residents of small towns and those from larger places on the responses to these items might be because of other demographic factors was examined using binary logistic regression models in which respondents' age, race, gender, region, and education level were controlled. The remaining odds ratios for small-town residence were 1.439 for assistance to cities, 1.383 for assistance to blacks, and 1.238 for welfare—all significant at the 0.001 level, and not significant for education, health, and law enforcement.

6. A similar theme emerged in comments that some interviewees volunteered about the health care reform legislation being debated in Washington, DC, at the

time they were interviewed. Explaining the opposition in her community, the mayor of a town of eighteen hundred remarked, "There's better ways to do it, and we know it and we are thinking, 'OK, common sense, people, common sense.' But we're talking about lawyers [in Washington]. Lawyers and common sense usually don't go together."

7. At the time of the interview, critics of the Obama administration were likening it to the Roosevelt administration, so it is possible that this interviewee was reflecting those criticisms. In predominantly Republican rural communities, however, there were also long-standing perceptions that Roosevelt had been an easterner who did not understand the plight of farmers and residents in small heartland communities. Historians generally credit Roosevelt's policies as being beneficial to agriculture, but also emphasize the controversies surrounding the Agricultural Adjustment Act of 1933, US Supreme Court's ruling against it in 1936, new Agricultural Adjustment Act of 1938, and issues surrounding the exclusion of coverage for agricultural workers in the Social Security Act that Roosevelt signed into law in 1935. See, for example, Adam Cohen, *Nothing to Fear: FDR's Inner Circle and the Hundred Days That Created Modern America* (New York: Penguin, 2009); Kenneth S. Davis, *FDR: The New Deal Years, 1933–1937* (New York: Random House, 1995); Peter Fearon, *Kansas in the Great Depression: Work Relief, the Dole, and Rehabilitation* (Columbia: University of Missouri Press, 2007); Jim Powell, *FDR's Folly: How Roosevelt and His New Deal Prolonged the Great Depression* (New York: Crown Press, 2003); Keith J. Volanto, *Texas, Cotton, and the New Deal* (College Station: Texas A&M University Press, 2004).

8. Although negative sentiments toward welfare recipients are hardly unique to residents of small towns, living in a small town appears to add two distinct dimensions to residents' views: the sense that people in small communities are having to foot the bill for a problem that exists mostly in cities, and the fear that welfare recipients are moving into small towns in increasing numbers to take advantage of cheap housing and local services. Some long-term residents regard these newcomers as particularly violating the community's norms of hard work and self-sufficiency. "Make mom and dad go to work instead of just living off handouts from the government," one man says. He objects even to free or subsidized lunch programs for low-income schoolchildren. "Anybody who is too lazy to get up in the morning and put a bowl of cereal on the table for their kids," he begins, and then trails off. "I don't buy all this social experiment." In another town, a woman who prides herself on being disciplined about the frugal income that she and her husband have, complains about adults who have been coddled so much that they are incapable of functioning as responsible citizens. "Small towns are getting the overflow of these unproductive people," she says, "because of the rundown houses, living on the welfare check, and having the liquor store not too far down the road." She blames the government for creating this "welfare generation" with its "let me do it for you" attitude.

9. "My son has gone four times to Afghanistan to the war," was how one father voiced his sentiments about Washington, DC. "My son is fixing to go back for the fifth time. Last time I was in Washington I said, 'How many more times is

my child going to have to go off and fight this war, congressman?' He couldn't answer that. It was troubling to me." The man went on to describe how people in his community were unhappy with everything in Washington, from questions about taxes and health care to concerns about schools and the environment.

10. The data in the figure are from the national survey conducted in 2000 as part of Robert Putnam's Social Capital Benchmark Survey.

11. A widely used textbook asserts definitively that government in small towns is "likely to be dominated by small cliques" and is "laid-back," decisions are made by a "principle of unanimity," and studies show that political discussions focus "on personalities rather than on issues"; David R. Berman, *State and Local Politics*, 9th ed. (New York: St. Martin's Press, 1999), 233. The only study cited is of one town and was conducted in the 1950s. Another text mentions small towns only once in passing; Kevin B. Smith, *State and Local Government* (Washington, DC: CQ Press, 2007). Yet another does not deal with small towns at all; Ann M. Bowman and Richard C. Kearney, *State and Local Government: The Essentials* (Belmont, CA: Wadsworth, 2008).

12. Some of the details about the community and the damage have been altered to avoid inadvertently disclosing the town's identity.

13. The data summarized in the figure are from General Social Surveys, cumulative electronic data file, conducted from 1972 through 2008, and aggregated by decade to compensate for sampling differences from survey to survey in the representation of small towns, here defined as respondents living in nonmetropolitan communities of 20,000 or fewer population. The total numbers of respondents for each decade equaled 10,652 in the 1970s, 14,241 in the 1980s, 13,223 in the 1990s, and 14, 927 in the 2000s. Party identification was measured by asking respondents if they identified as Republicans, Democrats, or independents. Binary logistic regression models were used to calculate the actual odds ratios for small-town residents relative to people living in larger communities who identified as Republicans or Democrats, and the comparable estimated odds ratios with controls for gender, race, age, year of survey, four regions, and four levels of education.

14. Morris P. Fiorina, Samuel J. Abrams, and Jeremy C. Pope, *Culture War? The Myth of a Polarized America*, 3rd ed. (New York: Longman, 2010).

15. For an interesting discussion of the general tendency in rural communities to avoid disclosing directly how one voted and thus to rely on indirect means of disclosure, see Trudy Peterson, "Rural Life and the Privacy of Political Association," *Agricultural History* 64 (1990): 1–8. This reluctance to disclose how a person voted was evident enough in our pilot interviews that in most of the interviews, we saved asking how the interviewee voted in the last presidential election until near the end of the interview, at which point nearly everyone revealed how they had voted, although some refused even though the interviews were confidential.

16. For a similar, insightfully developed point, see Nina Eliasoph, "Close to Home": The Work of Avoiding Politics," *Theory and Society* 26 (1997): 605–47.

17. Besides online and media sources, the Tea Party's arguments were presented in several books. See, for example, Dick Armey and Matt Kibbe, *Give Us Liberty: A Tea Party Manifesto* (New York: William Morrow, 2010); Joseph Farah, *The Tea Party Manifesto* (New York: WND Books, 2010).

18. The data summarized in the figure are from a poll of 1,008 respondents conducted for CNN by the Opinion Research Corporation, April 9–11, 2010, electronic data file, courtesy of the Roper Center Public Opinion Archives at the University of Connecticut. The usual caution about low response rates applies to these data. The categories were developed by the Opinion Research Corporation, and refer to census definitions of urban, suburban, and rural along with the racial and ethnic composition of respondents' communities.

19. Residents who were opposed to the Tea Party movement more often viewed it as being driven by outside interests, such as the logging, mining, or oil and gas industry.

20. An example of the opposing view was expressed by the city manager of a town in which 70 percent of the population was Hispanic and generally favored Democratic candidates. "I think Sarah Palin and the Tea Party advocates are divisive," he said. "They are not getting us on the table. They are separating us and dividing us." He added, "I may agree with them on some things about taxpayers' rights, but the way they are going about it seems to be very partisan."

21. For a useful summary of this literature through the 1990s, see Rory McVeigh and Christian Smith, "Who Protests in America: An Analysis of Three Political Alternatives—Inaction, Institutionalized Politics, or Protest," *Sociological Forum* 14 (1999): 685–702. For a more recent discussion that emphasizes both local and translocal networks, see Jeffrey Stout, *Blessed Are the Organized: Grassroots Democracy in America* (Princeton, NJ: Princeton University Press, 2010).

22. Markus Prior, *Post-Broadcast Democracy: How Media Choice Increases Inequality in Political Involvement and Polarizes Elections* (New York: Cambridge University Press, 2007); Markus Prior, "News v. Entertainment: How Increasing Media Choice Widens Gaps in Political Knowledge and Turnout," *American Journal of Political Science* 49 (2005): 577–92.

23. Lila K. Khatiwada and Kenneth E. Pigg, "Internet Service Provision in the U.S. Counties: Is Spatial Pattern a Function of Demand?" *American Behavioral Scientist* 53 (2010): 1326–43; Michael J. Stern and Barry Wellman, "Rural and Urban Differences in the Internet Society: Real and Relatively Important," *American Behavioral Scientist* 53 (2010): 1251–56.

24. US Census Bureau, *Census of Governments, 2002: Government Organization* (Washington, DC: Government Printing Office, 2002). This census indicates that the number of general-purpose governmental units totaled 87,525, and the number of special-purpose units was 48,558.

25. We talked to several residents in Rev. Buchanan's community who said they did not share his views, but agreed that people in the area were distrustful of the federal government and thought some of the concern reflected negative attitudes about having an African American president.

10. Keep Your Doors Open: Shaping the Future

1. Whether young people in small rural communities are sufficiently prepared and motivated to go to college is the topic of a long history of debate, of

course, and is not one I address here. The difficulty with statistical generalizations that draw comparisons between rural and urban youths, even when controlling for other variables, such as geographic location and parents' education, is that these generalizations fail to acknowledge the diversity that exists from family to family and town to town, or capture the complex sentiments of parents about the value of higher education and particular difficulties that a young person from a small town may experience. Those are the issues with which I am concerned in this chapter. For the broader debate, see Thomas Espenshade and Alexandria Walton Radford, *No Longer Separate, Not Yet Equal: Race and Class in Elite College Admission and Campus Life* (Princeton, NJ: Princeton University Press, 2009); Elizabeth A. Armstrong and Laura Hamilton, *Exclusion: Class, Gender, and College Culture* (Cambridge, MA: Harvard University Press, 2010); Patrick J. Carr and Maria J. Kefalas, *Hollowing Out the Middle: The Rural Brain Drain and What It Means for America* (Boston: Beacon, 2009). For an interesting example of the sensitivities involved in generalizations about rural residents, especially in conjunction with questions about race, class, and religion, see Ross Douthat, "The Roots of White Anxiety," *New York Times*, July 18, 2010. Douthat drew selectively from the Espenshade and Radford book, and elicited a large number of replies from the newspaper's readers. Espenshade and Radford's study of admission to elite colleges noted, almost in passing, that precollege participation in "career-oriented" extracurricular activities reduced the likelihood of admission, unlike participation in other extracurricular activities that increased it, controlling for a large number of other factors, and offered this additional comment: "These activities include ROTC and co-op work programs. They might also encompass 4-H Clubs, Future Farmers of America, and other activities that suggest that students are somewhat undecided about their academic futures" (Espenshade and Radford, *No Longer Separate*, 126). Douthat's column argued that elite colleges were guilty of a liberal cultural bias that discriminated against students in ROTC, 4-H clubs, and Future Farmers of America, and concluded that the nation would be better off if these colleges "admitted a few more R.O.T.C cadets, and a few more aspiring farmers." Replies from readers ran the gamut from those who agree with Douthat, to those who doubted that farm youths wanted to go to college at all, to those who thought plenty of good colleges and universities existed in states with large rural populations. In *Remaking the Heartland*, I examined data from the Midwest states showing how some of these states did better than others in training and retaining college-educated youths, and how college-educated residents differed from other residents in geographic mobility.

2. The probabilities in the figure are calculated from the Public Use Five Percent Sample from the 2000 census and are for residents currently living in nonmetropolitan areas. Among those living in metropolitan areas, the probability of having left their birth state is 59 percent among thirty-nine-year-olds who have graduated from college and 47 percent among thirty-nine-year-olds who have not graduated from college.

3. Just as in cities and suburbs, rates of college attendance among young people who grow up in small towns and rural areas vary considerably. Data from the 1999 Schools and Staffing Survey conducted for the National Center for Education

Statistics, an electronic data file representing 19,672 high schools (weighted cases) with any twelfth graders during the 1999–2000 academic year shows that in 13 percent of the schools in small towns and rural areas, fewer than 10 percent of seniors were planning to attend a four-year college, between 10 and 29 percent were in 25 percent of the schools, between 30 and 59 percent were in 45 percent of the schools, between 60 and 79 percent were in 14 percent of the schools, and 80 percent or more were in 3 percent of the schools. Compared with schools in central cities and urban-fringe areas, the schools in small towns were clustered more toward the middle range of the distribution—meaning that fewer of these schools were ones in which very low or very high percentages of seniors planned to attend college. Ordinary least squares regression analysis of the data shows that the mean percentage of seniors planning to attend a four-year college is positively influenced by size of high school, negatively influenced by percentage of minority students, and significantly lower controlling for these other factors in the South and West compared to the Northeast and Midwest. Taking these factors into account, location in a small town or rural area has a small positive effect on the mean percentage of seniors planning to attend a four-year college.

4. Public Use One Percent Sample, US Census, 1990, courtesy of Steven Ruggles, J. Trent Alexander, Katie Genadek, Ronald Goeken, Matthew B. Schroeder, and Matthew Sobek, *Integrated Public Use Microdata Series: Version 5.0* [machine-readable database] (Minneapolis: Minnesota Population Center, 2010). Binary logistic regression analysis of the "marst" variable recoded to combine married spouse present, married spouse absent, separated, divorced, or widowed versus never married with the "metro" variable (excluding metro status undefined) recoded as not in metropolitan area versus combined metropolitan in and outside central city and central city undefined, controlling for age, sex, and race recoded as white versus all other categories. The odds ratio for nonmetropolitan versus metropolitan residence was 1.735, significant at or beyond the 0.001 level of probability. See the following note about 1990 versus later definitions of metropolitan and nonmetropolitan.

5. Public Use One Percent Sample, 1960 census, and Public Use One Percent Sample, 1990 census; results for persons age sixteen through twenty-one living in nonmetropolitan areas, separate binary logistic regression models for men and women, with race and age controlled, and currently or ever married versus never married as the independent variable. The adjusted odds ratio for men in 1960 was 0.260, for women in 1960 was 0.128, for men in 1990 was 0.321, and for women in 1990 was 0.236—all significant at or beyond the 0.001 level of probability. In the figure, the columns labeled "baseline" show simply that if there were no differences between those who were married and those who were never married, the odds ratios would be 1.0; the other columns show the odds ratios for each comparison. For example, the column furthest to the right shows that the odds of having at least one year of college among married women are 0.236 as large as the odds among never married women. In these samples, 31 percent in 1960 were classified as living in nonmetropolitan areas and 27.4 percent were in 1990, but that proportion dropped to 8.4 percent in 2000. For a description of the definition of metropolitan areas, see US Census Bureau, *Statistical Abstract of the United*

States: 2010 (Washington, DC: Government Printing Office, 2010), appendix II, 879.

6. The National Center for Education Statistics 1999 Schools and Staffing Survey, electronic data file, showed that graduation rates were higher in small town and rural high schools than in center-city and urban-fringe schools, controlling for differences in size of school, percentage minority students, and region. The effects of state equalization policies were also evident in the fact that student-to-teacher ratios and per pupil expenditures were similar across locations. Schools in small towns and rural areas received 51 percent of their revenue from state funds, as did center-city schools, compared with only 44 percent among urban-fringe schools.

7. David Brooks, "The Odyssey Years," *New York Times*, October 9, 2007. For a sociological discussion of the topic, see Neil J. Smelser, *The Odyssey Experience: Physical, Social, Psychological, and Spiritual Journeys* (Berkeley: University of California Press, 2009).

8. The notion of portable small-town values here is indebted to the wonderful memoir *Portable Prairie: Confessions of an Unsettled Midwesterner* (New York: Thomas Dunne, 2004) by former small-town South Dakota resident M. J. Andersen.

9. Her report of the stories and the exact words that she communicates to her students is an instance of something that was evident in many of the interviews: respondents were not simply making up some hypothetical advice because an interviewer asked them a question; they were repeating advice they had given to their own children, students, young people in congregations, and others they knew. "I was just talking to a young man this morning and told him ....," "I'll tell you what I tell my children." or "The students hear me say this a lot" were the kinds of comments that revealed what in discourse analysis is called quoted speech.

10. For a detailed examination of the more general tendency among Americans to exclude money from their accounts of work, see Robert Wuthnow, *Poor Richard's Principle: Recovering the American Dream through the Moral Dimension of Work, Business, and Money* (Princeton, NJ: Princeton University Press, 1996). I am aware, as I am sure many residents of small towns are, of the correlation in statistical studies between wealth and happiness. See, for example, Derek Bok, *The Politics of Happiness: What Government Can Learn from the New Research on Well-being* (Princeton, NJ: Princeton University Press, 2010). This research also documents a correlation between happiness and feeling integrated into a community.

11. I have been drawn repeatedly to the richness of home as a metaphor for community. For an insightful discussion of this, see Mary Douglas, "The Idea of a Home: A Kind of Space," in *Home: A Place in the World*, ed. Arien Mack (New York: New York University Press, 1993), 253–72. For my own look at homes and dwellings used in religious metaphors, see Robert Wuthnow, *After Heaven: Spirituality in America since the 1950s* (Berkeley: University of California Press, 1998). For an exploration of the idea of permeable boundaries in relation to small towns, see Robert Wuthnow, *Loose Connections: Joining Together in America's Fragmented Communities* (Cambridge, MA: Harvard University Press, 1998).

11. Concluding Reflections: Community in Small Towns

1. Suzanne Keller, *Community: Pursuing the Dream, Living the Reality* (Princeton, NJ: Princeton University Press, 2003). For a brief discussion that mentions many of the same elements of community as Keller's, see Philip Selznick, *The Moral Commonwealth: Social Theory and the Promise of Community* (Berkeley: University of California Press, 1992), 360–65.

2. For an illuminating discussion of the importance of spatial conditions and circumstances in an urban setting, see Mario Luis Small, *Villa Victoria: The Transformation of Social Capital in a Boston Barrio* (Chicago: University of Chicago Press, 2004), 123–44. For a broader survey, see Thomas F. Gieryn, "A Space for Place in Sociology," *Annual Review of Sociology* 26 (2000): 463–96.

3. Ray Oldenburg, *The Great Good Place: Cafes, Coffee Shops, Community Centers, Beauty Parlors, General Stores, Bars, Hangouts, and How They Get You through the Day* (New York: Paragon House, 1989).

4. Sonya Salamon, *Newcomers to Old Towns: Suburbanization of the Heartland* (Chicago: University of Chicago Press, 2003). In her study of six Illinois towns, Salamon argues that these central public spaces symbolize the community's priorities and serve importantly to promote cross-age social relationships.

5. See especially Daniel T. Lichter, Domenico Parisi, Steven Michael Grice, and Michael C. Taquino, "National Estimates of Racial Segregation in Rural and Small-Town America," *Demography* 44 (2007): 563–81. This study, using 1990 and 2000 data, finds that levels of racial segregation are as high in small towns as in metropolitan areas. For another example of contested territory between newcomers and old-timers, see Sonya Salamon and Jane B. Tornatore, "Territory Contested through Property in a Midwestern Post-agricultural Community," *Rural Sociology* 59 (1994): 636–54.

6. Michele Lamont and Virag Molnar, "The Study of Boundaries in the Social Sciences," *Annual Review of Sociology* 28 (2002): 167–95.

7. James W. Loewen, *Sundown Towns: A Hidden Dimension of American Racism* (New York: New Press, 2005); Eileen Diaz McConnell and Faranak Miraftab, "Sundown Town to 'Little Mexico': Old-timers and Newcomers in an American Small Town," *Rural Sociology* 74 (2009): 605–29.

8. For an article based on a detailed analysis of associational ties—in this case, within Bristol and Glasgow—see Delia Baldassarri and Mario Diani, "The Integrative Power of Civic Networks," *American Journal of Sociology* 113 (2007): 735–80.

9. Mircea Eliade, *Myth and Reality* (New York: Harper and Row, 1963).

10. Emile Durkheim, *Elementary Forms of the Religious Life*, trans. Carol Cosman, ed. Mark S. Cladis (1915; repr., Oxford: Oxford University Press, 2008).

11. Randall Collins, *Interaction Ritual Chains* (Princeton, NJ: Princeton University Press, 2005).

12. For an interesting parallel discussion of community definitions being debated at meetings in urban project housing, see Sudhir Alladi Venkatesh, *American Project: The Rise and Fall of a Modern Ghetto* (Cambridge, MA: Harvard University Press, 2000).

13. By neutral public space, I mean venues in which people can interact as if they were equals and are constrained to do so by the presence of bystanders; this usage follows the helpful discussion in Rudolf P. Gaudio, "Coffeetalk: Starbucks and the Commercialization of Casual Conversation," *Language in Society* 32 (2003): 659-91.

14. For an instructive source of insights about the ways in which ritualized interaction in situations otherwise ridden with tense emotions serves in most instances to prevent outbursts or physical violence from occurring, see Randall Collins, *Violence: A Micro-sociological Theory* (Princeton, NJ: Princeton University Press, 2008). I am grateful to Devany Schulz for the example of tension between mothers-in-law and daughters-in-law.

15. For an excellent discussion of the factors, including gender, age, ethnicity, landownership, and farm management styles, that structure social networks in farming communities, see Sonya Salamon, *Prairie Patrimony: Family, Farming, and Community in the Midwest* (Chapel Hill: University of North Carolina Press, 1992).

SELECTED BIBLIOGRAPHY

Ahuja, Gautam. "Collaboration Networks, Structural Holes, and Innovation: A Longitudinal Study." *Administrative Science Quarterly* 45 (2000): 425–55.

Aldous, Joan, and Murray A. Straus. "Social Networks and Conjugal Roles: A Test of Bott's Hypothesis." *Social Forces* 43 (1966): 471–82.

Alexander, Jeffrey C. *The Performance of Politics: Obama's Victory and the Democratic Struggle for Power*. New York: Oxford University Press, 2010.

Allen, Rich, and Ginger Harris. "What We Know about the Demographics of U.S. Farm Operators." *Agricultural Outlook Forum* (February 25, 2005), http://www.agcensus.usda.gov/Publications/2002/Other_Analysis/.

Ambrose, Stephen E. *Eisenhower: Soldier and President*. New York: Simon and Schuster, 1990.

Ammerman, Nancy Tatom. *Bible Believers: Fundamentalists in the Modern World*. New Brunswick, NJ: Rutgers University Press, 1987.

Andersen, M. J. *Portable Prairie: Confessions of an Unsettled Midwesterner*. New York: Thomas Dunne, 2004.

Anderson, Benedict. *Imagined Communities: Reflections on the Origin and Spread of Nationalism*. London: Verso, 1991.

Anderson, Leslie O. *Memoirs of a Country Boy/Newspaper Man*. Elk River, MN: DeForest Press, 2004.

Anderson, Nels. "Review of *Small-Town Stuff*." *American Journal of Sociology* 38 (1932): 294.

Aptekar, Sofya. "Immigrant Naturalization and Nation-Building in North America." PhD diss., Princeton University, 2010.

Armey, Dick, and Matt Kibbe. *Give Us Liberty: A Tea Party Manifesto*. New York: William Morrow, 2010.

Armstrong, Elizabeth A., and Laura Hamilton. *Exclusion: Class, Gender, and College Culture*. Cambridge, MA: Harvard University Press, 2010.

Artz, Georgeanne M., Peter F. Orazem, and Daniel M. Otto. "Meat Packing and Processing Facilities in the Non-metropolitan Midwest: Blessing or Curse?" Paper presented at the annual meeting of the American Agricultural Economics Association, Providence, Rhode Island, July 2005.

———. "Measuring the Impact of Meat Packing and Processing Facilities in Nonmetropolitan Counties: A Difference-in-Differences Approach." *American Journal of Agricultural Economics* 89 (2007): 557–70.

Attridge, Harold W., ed. *The Religion and Science Debate: Why Does It Continue?* New Haven, CT: Yale University Press, 2009.

Baldassarri, Delia, and Mario Diani. "The Integrative Power of Civic Networks." *American Journal of Sociology* 113 (2007): 735–80.

Barabasi, Albert-Laszlo. *Linked: How Everything Is Connected to Everything Else, and What It Means for Business, Science, and Everyday Life*. New York: Penguin, 2003.

Barman, Emily. *Contesting Communities: The Transformation of Workplace Charity*. Stanford, CA: Stanford University Press, 2006.

Barnett, Bob. *Growing Up in the Last Small Town*. Ashland, KY: Jesse Stuart Foundation, 2010.

Becker, Penny Edgell. *Congregations in Conflict: Cultural Models of Local Religious Life*. Cambridge: Cambridge University Press, 1999.

Bell, David. "Cowboy Love." In *Country Boys: Masculinity and Rural Life*, ed. Hugh Campbell, Michael Mayerfield Bell, and Margaret Finney, 163–82. University Park: Pennsylvania State University Press, 2006.

Bell, Michael Mayerfeld. *Childerley: Nature and Morality in a Country Village*. Chicago: University of Chicago Press, 1994.

———. "The Ghosts of Place." *Theory and Society* 26 (1997): 813–36.

Bellah, Robert N., Richard Madsen, William M. Sullivan, Ann Swidler, and Steven M. Tipton. *Habits of the Heart: Individualism and Commitment in American Life*. Berkeley: University of California Press, 1985.

Bender, Courtney. *Heaven's Kitchen: Living Religion at God's Love We Deliver*. Chicago: University of Chicago Press, 2003.

Bender, Thomas. *Community and Social Change in America*. Baltimore: Johns Hopkins University Press, 1978.

Benhabib, Seyla. "Sexual Difference and Collective Identities: The New Global Constellation." *Signs* 24 (1999): 335–61.

Beniger, James R. "Does Television Enhance the Shared Symbolic Environment? Trends in Labeling of Editorial Cartoons, 1948–1980." *American Sociological Review* 48 (1983): 103–11.

Berman, David R. *State and Local Politics*. 9th ed. New York: St. Martin's Press, 1999.

Besser, Terry L., Nicholas Recker, and Kerry Agnitsch. "The Impact of Economic Shocks on Quality of Life and Social Capital in Small Towns." *Rural Sociology* 73 (2008): 580–604.

Blau, Peter Michael. *Inequality and Heterogeneity: A Primitive Theory of Social Structure*. New York: Free Press, 1977.

Bloom, Stephen G. *Postville: A Clash of Cultures in Heartland America*. New York: Mariner Books, 2001.

Blumenthal, Albert. *Small-Town Stuff*. Chicago: University of Chicago Press, 1932.

Bodensteiner, Carol. *Growing Up Country: Memories of an Iowa Farm Girl*. Des Moines, IA: Sun Rising Press, 2008.

Boggs, Carl. "Social Capital and Political Fantasy: Robert Putnam's 'Bowling Alone.'" *Theory and Society* 30 (2001): 281–97.

Bok, Derek. *The Politics of Happiness: What Government Can Learn from the New Research on Well-being*. Princeton, NJ: Princeton University Press, 2010.

Bok, Sissela. *Secrets: On the Ethics of Concealment and Revelation*. New York: Pantheon, 1983.

Boltanski, Luc, and Laurent Thevenot. *On Justification: Economies of Worth*. Princeton, NJ: Princeton University Press, 2006.

Bornstein, Marc H., and Helen G. Bornstein. "The Pace of Life." *Nature* 259 (1976): 557–58.

Bott, Elizabeth. *Family and Social Network*. New York: Routledge, 2003. First published 1957.

Bourdieu, Pierre. *Distinction: A Social Critique of the Judgment of Taste*. Translated by Richard Nice. Cambridge, MA: Harvard University Press, 1984.

Bowman, Ann M., and Richard C. Kearney. *State and Local Government: The Essentials*. Belmont, CA: Wadsworth, 2008.

Boyles, Denis. *Superior, Nebraska: The Common Sense Values of America's Heartland*. New York: Doubleday, 2008.

Bradley, Jennifer, and Bruce Katz. "Village Idiocy." *New Republic*, October 8, 2008, 12–13.

Bradshaw, Ted K. "Multicommunity Networks: A Rural Transition." *Annals of the American Academy of Political and Social Science* 529 (1993): 164–75.

Breault, Kevin D. "New Evidence on Religious Pluralism, Urbanism, and Religious Participation." *American Sociological Review* 54 (1989): 1048–53.

Bremer, Thomas S. *Blessed with Tourists: The Borderlands of Religion and Tourism in San Antonio*. Chapel Hill: University of North Carolina Press, 2003.

Brewer, William. "Schemata." In *The MIT Encyclopedia of the Cognitive Sciences*, ed. Robert A. Wilson and Frank C. Keil, 724–25. Cambridge, MA: MIT Press, 2001.

Brooks, David. "The Odyssey Years." *New York Times*, October 9, 2007.

Brown, David L., and Louis E. Swanson, eds. *Challenges for Rural America in the Twenty-First Century*. University Park: Pennsylvania State University Press, 2003.

Brown, Karen McCarthy. "Staying Grounded in a High-rise Building: Ecological Dissonance and Ritual Accommodation in Haitian Vodou." In *Gods of the City*, ed. Robert A. Orsi, 79–102. Bloomington: Indiana University Press, 1999.

Brown, Miriam, ed. *Sustaining Heart in the Heartland: Exploring Rural Spirituality*. Mahwah, NJ: Paulist Press, 2005.

Brown-Saracino, Japonica. "Social Preservationists and the Quest for Authentic Community." *City and Community* 3 (2004): 135–56.

Brunner, Edmund de Schweinitz. *Rural America and the Extension Service: A History and Critique of the Cooperative Agricultural and Home Economics Extension Service*. New York: Columbia University Press, 1949.

Bryson, Bill. *The Lost Continent: Travels in Small-Town America*. New York: Harper Perennial, 1990.

Burke, Kenneth. *A Grammar of Motives*. Berkeley: University of California Press, 1969.

Burt, Ronald S. "Structural Holes and Good Ideas." *American Journal of Sociology* 110 (2004): 349–99.

Bush, Peter G., and H. Christine O'Reilly. *Where 20 or 30 Are Gathered: Leading Worship in the Small Church*. Herndon, VA: Alban Institute, 2006.

Caldwell, Gail. "Intruder in the Dust." *Boston Globe*, December 15, 2002

Cameron, Catherine M., and John B. Gatewood. "The Authentic Interior: Questing *Gemeinschaft* in Post-industrial Society." *Human Organization* 53 (1994): 21–32.

Campbell, Hugh, Michael Mayerfeld Bell, and Margaret Finney, eds. *Country Boys: Masculinity and Rural Life*. University Park: Pennsylvania State University Press, 2006.

Cannon, Lou. *President Reagan: The Role of a Lifetime*. New York: Simon and Schuster, 1991.

Carr, Patrick J., and Maria J. Kefalas. *Hollowing Out the Middle: The Rural Brain Drain and What It Means for America*. Boston: Beacon, 2009.

Cerulo, Karen A. "Television, Magazine Covers, and the Shared Symbolic Environment: 1948–1970." *American Sociological Review* 49 (1984): 566–70.

———. "Coming Together: New Taxonomies for the Analysis of Social Relations." *Sociological Inquiry* 68 (1998): 398–425.

Charmaz, Kathy. *Constructing Grounded Theory: A Practical Guide through Qualitative Analysis*. London: Sage, 2006.

Chaves, Mark. *Congregations in America*. Cambridge, MA: Harvard University Press, 2004.

Chi, Guangqing. "The Impacts of Highway Expansion on Population Change: An Integrated Spatial Approach." *Rural Sociology* 75 (2010): 58–89.

Ching, Barbara, and Gerald W. Creed, eds. *Knowing Your Place: Rural Identity and Cultural Hierarchy*. New York: Routledge, 1997.

Cnaan, Ram A. *The Invisible Caring Hand: American Congregations and the Provision of Welfare*. New York: New York University Press, 2002.

Cohen, Adam. *Nothing to Fear: FDR's Inner Circle and the Hundred Days That Created Modern America*. New York: Penguin, 2009.

Coleman, James. "Social Capital in the Creation of Human Capital." *American Journal of Sociology* 94 (1988): S95–120.

Collins, Alan F., Martin A. Conway, and Peter E. Morris, eds. *Theories of Memory*. London: Taylor and Francis, 1993.

Collins, Randall. *Interaction Ritual Chains*. Princeton, NJ: Princeton University Press, 2005.

———. *Violence: A Micro-sociological Theory*. Princeton, NJ: Princeton University Press, 2008.

Connerton, Paul. *How Societies Remember*. Cambridge: Cambridge University Press, 1989.

Connor, Phillip. "Increase or Decrease? The Impact of the International Migratory Event on Immigrant Religious Participation." *Journal for the Scientific Study of Religion* 47 (2008): 243–57.

———. "International Migration and Religious Participation: The Mediating Impact of Individual and Contextual Effects." *Sociological Forum* 24 (2009): 779–803.

Corbin, Juliet, and Anselm C. Strauss. *Basics of Qualitative Research: Techniques and Procedures for Developing Grounded Theory*. London: Sage, 2007.

Crandall, Ronald K. *Turnaround Strategies for the Small Church*. Nashville: Abingdon Press, 1995.

————. *Turnaround and Beyond: A Hopeful Future for the Small Membership Church.* Nashville: Abingdon Press, 2008.

Creed, Gerald W., and Barbara Ching. "Recognizing Rusticity: Identity and the Power of Place." In *Knowing Your Place: Rural Identity and Cultural Hierarchy*, ed. Barbara Ching and Gerald W. Creed, 1–38. New York: Routledge, 1997.

Curry, Janel M. "Community Worldview and Rural Systems: A Study of Five Communities in Iowa." *Annals of the Association of American Geographers* 90 (2000): 693–712.

Daly, Sean. "That Old Ace in the Hole." *People*, December 23, 2002.

Danbom, David B. *Born in the Country: A History of Rural America.* 2nd ed. Baltimore: Johns Hopkins University Press, 2006.

D'Andrade, Roy. *The Development of Cognitive Anthropology.* Cambridge: Cambridge University Press, 1995.

Davidman, Lynn. *Tradition in a Rootless World: Women Turn to Orthodox Judaism.* Berkeley: University of California Press, 1991.

Davidson, Osha Gray. *Broken Heartland: The Rise of America's Rural Ghetto.* Iowa City: University of Iowa Press, 1996.

Davies, Richard O. *Main Street Blues: The Decline of Small-Town America.* Columbus: Ohio State University Press, 1998.

Davies, Richard O., Joseph A. Amato, and David R. Pichaske, eds. *A Place Called Home: Writings on the Midwestern Small Town.* Saint Paul: Minnesota Historical Society, 2003.

Davis, Kenneth S. *FDR: The New Deal Years, 1933–1937.* New York: Random House, 1995.

De Bres, Karen, and James Davis. "Celebrating Group and Place Identity: A Case Study of a New Regional Festival." *Tourism Geographies* 3 (2001): 326–37.

DeMontis, Andrea, Alessandro Chessa, Michele Campagna, Simone Caschili, and Giancarlo Deplano. "Modeling Commuting Systems through a Complex Network Analysis: A Study of the Italian Islands of Sardinia and Sicily." *Journal of Transport and Land Use* 2 (2010): 39–55.

Diekmann, Florian, Brian E. Roe, and Marvin T. Batte. "Tractors on eBay: Differences between Internet and In-Person Auctions." *American Journal of Agricultural Economics* 90 (2008): 306–20.

DiMaggio, Paul. "Culture and Cognition." *Annual Review of Sociology* 23 (1997): 263–87.

Diner, Hasia R., Jeffrey Shandler, and Beth S. Wenger, eds. *Remembering the Lower East Side: American Jewish Reflections.* Bloomington: Indiana University Press, 2000.

Douglas, Mary. "The Idea of a Home: A Kind of Space." In *Home: A Place in the World*, ed. Arien Mack, 253–72. New York: New York University Press, 1993.

Douglass, H. Paul. *The Little Town: Especially in Its Rural Relationships.* New York: Macmillan, 1919.

Douthat, Ross. "The Roots of White Anxiety." *New York Times*, July 18, 2010.

Drape, Joe. *Our Boys: A Perfect Season on the Plains with the Smith Center Redmen.* New York: Times Books, 2009.

Dreby, Joanna. "Gender and Transnational Gossip." *Qualitative Sociology* 32 (2009): 33–52.

Duneier, Mitchell. *Slim's Table: Race, Respectability, and Masculinity.* Chicago: University of Chicago Press, 1992.

———. *Sidewalk.* New York: Farrar, Straus and Giroux, 2000.

Duneier, Mitchell, and Harvey Molotch. "Talking City Trouble: Interactional Vandalism, Social Inequality, and the 'Urban Interaction Problem.'" *American Journal of Sociology* 104 (1999): 1263–95.

Durkheim, Emile. *The Division of Labor in Society.* New York: Macmillan, 1933. First published 1893.

———. *Elementary Forms of the Religious Life.* Translated by Carol Cosman. Edited by Mark S. Cladis. Oxford: Oxford University Press, 2008. First published 1915.

Dykstra, Robert R. "Town–Country Conflict: A Hidden Dimension in American Social History." *Agricultural History* 38 (1964): 195–204.

Eckstein, Susan. "Community as Gift-Giving: Collectivistic Roots of Volunteerism." *American Sociological Review* 66 (2001): 829–51.

Eder, Donna. "Cohesion through Collaborative Narration." *Social Psychology Quarterly* 51 (1988): 225–35.

———. "The Structure of Gossip: Opportunities and Constraints on Collective Expression among Adolescents." *American Sociological Review* 56 (1991): 494–508.

Edgell, Penny. *Religion and Family in a Changing Society.* Princeton, NJ: Princeton University Press, 2006.

Edin, Kathryn, and Laura Lein. *Making Ends Meet: How Single Mothers Survive Welfare and Low-Wage Work.* New York: Russell Sage Foundation, 1997.

Egan, Timothy. *The Worst Hard Time.* New York: Houghton Mifflin, 2006.

Ehrenhalt, Alan. *The Lost City: The Forgotten Virtues of Community in America.* New York: Basic Books, 1995.

Eliade, Mircea. *Myth and Reality.* New York: Harper and Row, 1963.

Eliasoph, Nina. "Close to Home": The Work of Avoiding Politics. *Theory and Society* 26 (1997): 605–47.

Entwisle, Barbara, Katherine Faust, Ronald R. Rindfuss, and Toshiko Kaneda. "Networks and Contexts: Variation in the Structure of Social Ties." *American Journal of Sociology* 112 (2007): 1495–533.

Erickson, Rebecca J. "The Importance of Authenticity for Self and Society." *Symbolic Interaction* 18 (1995): 121–44.

Erikson, Kai T. *Wayward Puritans: A Study in the Sociology of Deviance.* New York: John Wiley and Sons, 1969.

———. *Everything in Its Path: Destruction of Community in the Buffalo Creek Flood.* New York: Simon and Schuster, 1977.

Espenshade, Thomas, and Alexandria Walton Radford. *No Longer Separate, Not Yet Equal: Race and Class in Elite College Admission and Campus Life.* Princeton, NJ: Princeton University Press, 2009.

Farah, Joseph. *The Tea Party Manifesto.* New York: WND Books, 2010.

Farris, Lawrence W. *Dynamics of Small Town Ministry.* Herndon, VA: Alban Institute, 2000.

Fearon, Peter. *Kansas in the Great Depression: Work Relief, the Dole, and Reha-bilitation.* Columbia: University of Missouri Press, 2007.

Fellows, Will. *Farm Boys: Lives of Gay Men from the Rural Midwest.* Madison: University of Wisconsin Press, 2001.

Fine, Gary Alan. "The Sociology of the Local: Action and Its Publics." *Sociological Theory* 28 (2010): 355–76.

Fine, Gary Alan, and Lori Holyfield. "Secrecy, Trust, and Dangerous Leisure: Generating Group Cohesion in Voluntary Organizations." *Social Psychology Quarterly* 59 (1996): 22–38.

Finucan, Stephen. "Fear and Loathing on the Panhandle." *Toronto Star*, December 8, 2002.

Fiorina, Morris P., Samuel J. Abrams, and Jeremy C. Pope. *Culture War? The Myth of a Polarized America.* 3rd ed. New York: Longman, 2010.

Fischer, Claude S. *To Dwell among Friends: Personal Networks in Town and City.* Chicago: University of Chicago Press, 1982.

———. *Made in America: A Social History of American Culture and Character.* Chicago: University of Chicago Press, 2010.

———. *Still Connected: Family and Friends in America since 1970.* New York: Russell Sage Foundation Press, 2011.

Fischer, Claude S., and Michael Hout. *Century of Difference: How America Changed in the Last One Hundred Years.* New York: Russell Sage Foundation, 2006.

Fiske, Susan. "Envy Up, Scorn Down: How Comparison Divides Us." Paper presented at the fall retreat of Law and Public Affairs, Princeton University, September 2010.

Ford, Kristina, James Lopach, and Dennis O'Donnell. *Planning in Small Town America: Observations, Sketches, and a Reform Proposal.* Chicago: American Planning Association, 1990.

Formisano, Ron. "Populist Currents in the 2008 Presidential Campaign." *Journal of Policy History* 22 (2010): 237–55.

Fowler, Eric B., and Sheila Delaney. *Small-Town Boy, Small-Town Girl: Growing Up in South Dakota, 1920–1950.* Pierre: South Dakota Historical Society, 2009.

Frank, Justin A. *Bush on the Couch: Inside the Mind of the President.* New York: Harper, 2004.

Friedman, Thomas L. *The World Is Flat: A Brief History of the Twenty-First Century.* New York: Farrar, Straus and Giroux, 2005.

Fuguitt, Glenn V. "County Seat Status as a Factor in Small Town Growth and Decline." *Social Forces* 44 (1965): 245–51.

Fuguitt, Glenn V., David L. Brown, and Calvin L. Beale. *Rural and Small Town America.* New York: Russell Sage Foundation, 1989.

Gamson, Joshua. "Normal Sins: Sex Scandal Narratives as Institutional Morality Tales." *Social Problems* 48 (2001): 185–205.

Gans, Herbert J. *The Levittowners: Ways of Life and Politics in a New Suburban Community.* New York: Pantheon Books, 1967.

———. *Middle American Individualism: Political Participation and Liberal Democracy.* New York: Oxford University Press, 1988.

Gardner, Bruce L. *American Agriculture in the Twentieth Century: How It Flourished and What It Cost.* Cambridge, MA: Harvard University Press, 2002.

Gaudio, Rudolf P. "Coffeetalk: Starbucks and the Commercialization of Casual Conversation." *Language in Society* 32 (2003): 659–91.

Geertz, Clifford. *The Interpretation of Cultures: Selected Essays.* New York: Basic Books, 1973.

———. *Local Knowledge: Further Essays in Interpretive Anthropology.* New York: Basic Books, 1982.

Gieryn, Thomas F. "A Space for Place in Sociology." *Annual Review of Sociology* 26 (2000): 463–96.

Gill, Fiona. "Moving to the 'Big' House: Power and Accommodation in Intergenerational Farming Families." *Rural Society* 18 (2008): 83–94.

Glock, Charles Y., Robert Wuthnow, Jane Allyn Piliavin, and Metta Spencer. *Adolescent Prejudice.* New York: Harper and Row, 1975.

Glucksberg, Samuel. "Metaphor." In *The MIT Encyclopedia of Cognitive Science,* ed. Robert A. Wilson and Frank C. Keil, 532–34. Cambridge, MA: MIT Press, 2001.

Goffman, Erving. *Behavior in Public Places: Notes on the Social Organization of Gatherings.* New York: Free Press, 1966.

Goodman, Robert F., and Aaron Ben-Ze'ev, eds. *Good Gossip.* Lawrence: University Press of Kansas, 2004.

Goodwyn, Lawrence. *The Populist Moment: A Short History of the Agrarian Revolt in America.* New York: Oxford University Press, 1978.

Gould, Rebecca Kneale. *At Home in Nature: Modern Homesteading and Spiritual Practice in America.* Berkeley: University of California Press, 2005.

Granovetter, Mark S. *Getting a Job: A Study of Contacts and Careers.* Cambridge, MA: Harvard University Press, 1974.

———. "The Strength of Weak Ties." *American Journal of Sociology* 78 (1973): 1360–80.

———. "The Strength of Weak Ties: A Network Theory Revisited." *Sociological Theory* 1 (1983): 201–33.

Greif, Mark. "Death and the Maiden." *Harpers,* November 2008, 18.

Grey, Mark, Michele Devlin, and Aaron Goldsmith. *Postville U.S.A.: Surviving Diversity in Small-Town America.* Boston: Gemma Media, 2009.

Guinnane, Timothy W. "Intergenerational Transfers, Emigration, and the Rural Irish Household System." *Explorations in Economic History* 29 (1992): 456–76.

Gumprecht, Blake. "The American College Town." *Geographical Review* 93 (2003): 51–80.

Gusfield, Joseph R. *The Community: A Critical Response.* New York: Harper Colophon, 1975.

———. *Symbolic Crusade: Status Politics and the American Temperance Movement.* Rev. ed. New York: Greenwood Press, 1980.

Hadaway, C. Kirk, Penny Long Marler, and Mark Chaves. "What the Polls Don't Show: A Closer Look at U.S. Church Attendance." *American Sociological Review* 58 (1993): 741–52.

Hamma, Robert M. *Landscapes of the Soul: A Spirituality of Place*. Notre Dame, IN: Ave Maria Press, 1999.

Hanna, Kevin S., Ann Dale, and Chris Ling. "Social Capital and Quality of Place: Reflections on Growth and Change in a Small Town." *Local Environment* 14 (2009): 31–44.

Hargrove, Erwin C., and James Sterling Young. *Jimmy Carter as President: Leadership and the Politics of the Public Good*. Baton Rouge: Louisiana State University Press, 1988.

Harlin, J. L. "The Aging Family Farm: Estate/Succession Planning for Farmers." *Agricultural Finance* 34 (1992): 38–39.

Harris, Wendell V. "The Critics Who Made Us: Kenneth Burke." *Sewanee Review* 96 (1988): 452–63.

Herman, Shelby W. "Farm Income in 1973 and Outlook for 1974." *Survey of Current Business* (September 1974): 11–13.

Hirschfeld, L. A., and S. A. Gelman, eds. *Mapping the Mind: Domain Specificity in Cognition and Culture*. Cambridge: Cambridge University Press, 1994.

Hummon, David M. "Popular Images of the American Small Town." *Landscape* 24 (1980): 3–9.

———. *Commonplaces: Community Ideology and Identity in American Culture*. New York: State University of New York Press, 1990.

Humphrey, Craig R., and Ralph R. Sell. "The Impact of Controlled Access Highways on Population Growth in Nonmetropolitan Communities, 1940–1970." *Rural Sociology* 40 (1975): 332–43.

Hunter, James Davison. *Culture Wars: The Struggle to Define America*. New York: Basic Books, 1991.

———. *Before the Shooting Begins: Searching for Democracy in America's Culture War*. New York: Free Press, 1994.

Hunter, James Davison, and Alan Wolfe. *Is There a Culture War? A Dialogue on Values and American Life*. Washington, DC: Brookings Institution Press, 2006.

Hutson, John. "Fathers and Sons: Family Farms, Family Businesses, and the Farming Industry." *Sociology* 21 (1987): 215–29.

Jillson, Cal. *Pursuing the American Dream: Opportunity and Exclusion over Four Centuries*. Lawrence: University Press of Kansas, 2004.

Jimenez, Tomas R. "Mexican-Immigrant Replenishment and the Continuing Significance of Ethnicity and Race." *American Journal of Sociology* 113 (2008): 1527–67.

———. *Replenished Ethnicity: Mexican Americans, Immigration, and Identity*. Berkeley: University of California Press, 2009.

Jung, Shannon, ed. *Rural Ministry: The Shape of the Renewal to Come*. Nashville: Abington, 1998.

Karr, Mary. *The Liar's Club: A Memoir*. New York: Penguin, 2005.

Kasarda, John D., and Morris Janowitz. "Community Attachment in Mass Society." *American Sociological Review* 39 (1974): 328–39.

Kay, David, Charles Geisler, and Nelson Bills. "Residential Preferences: What's Terrorism Got to Do with It?" *Rural Sociology* 75 (2010): 426–54.

Kazin, Michael. *The Populist Persuasion: An American History*. Rev. ed. Ithaca, NY: Cornell University Press, 1998.

Keating, Norah C., and Brenda Munro. "Transferring the Family Farm: Process and Implications." *Family Relations* 38 (1989): 215–19.

Keillor, Garrison. *A Prairie Home Companion*. Radio program, November 7, 2009.

Keller, Suzanne. *Community: Pursuing the Dream, Living the Reality*. Princeton, NJ: Princeton University Press, 2003.

Key, Nigel, and Michael J. Roberts, "Nonpecuniary Benefits to Farming: Implications for Supply Response to Decoupled Payments." *American Journal of Agricultural Economics* 91 (2009): 1–18.

Khatiwada, Lila K., and Kenneth E. Pigg. "Internet Service Provision in the U.S. Counties: Is Spatial Pattern a Function of Demand?" *American Behavioral Scientist* 53 (2010): 1326–43.

Kim, Oliver, and Mark Walker. "The Free Rider Problem: Experimental Evidence." *Public Choice* 43 (1984): 3–24.

Kimhi, Ayal, and Ramon Lopez. "A Note on Farmers' Retirement and Succession Considerations: Evidence from a Household Survey." *Journal of Agricultural Economics* 50 (1999): 154–62.

King, Valarie, and Glen H. Elder Jr. "American Children View Their Grandparents: Linked Lives across Three Rural Generations." *Journal of Marriage and Family* 57 (1995): 165–78.

———. "The Legacy of Grandparenting: Childhood Experiences with Grandparents and Current Involvement with Grandchildren." *Journal of Marriage and the Family* 59 (1997): 848–59.

Kirn, Walter. "Wasted Land." *New York Times*, July 1, 2009.

Koenig, Walter D. "Sex-Biased Dispersal in the Contemporary United States." *Ethology and Sociobiology* 10 (1989): 263–78.

Kornhauser, William. *The Politics of Mass Society*. Glencoe, IL: Free Press, 1959.

Kvale, Steiner, and Svend Brinkmann. *InterViews: Learning the Craft of Qualitative Research*. London: Sage, 2009.

Lakoff, George, and Mark Johnson. *Metaphors We Live By*. Chicago: University of Chicago Press, 1980.

Lamont, Michele. *Money, Morals, and Manners: The Culture of the French and the American Upper-Middle Class*. Chicago: University of Chicago Press, 1992.

———. *The Dignity of Working Men: Morality and the Boundaries of Race, Class, and Immigration*. Cambridge, MA: Harvard University Press, 2000.

Lamont, Michele, and Marcel Fournier, eds. *Cultivating Differences: Symbolic Boundaries and the Making of Inequality*. Chicago: University of Chicago Press, 1992.

Lamont, Michele, and Virag Molnar. "The Study of Boundaries in the Social Sciences." *Annual Review of Sociology* 28 (2002): 167–95.

Landon, Donald D. *Country Lawyers: The Impact of Context on Professional Practice*. New York: Praeger, 1990.

Langer, Andrew M. "Sarah Palin, Small-Town America." *U.S. News*, September 12, 2008.

Lears, Jackson. *Fables of Abundance: A Cultural History of Advertising in America*. New York: Basic Books, 1995.

Leinberger, Paul, and Bruce Tucker. *The New Individualists: The Generation after the Organization Man*. New York: HarperCollins, 1991.

Lavenda, Robert H. *Corn Fests and Water Carnivals: Celebrating Community in Minnesota*. Washington, DC: Smithsonian Institution Press, 1997.

Levine, Robert V., and Ara Norenzayan. "The Pace of Life in 31 Countries." *Journal of Cross-cultural Psychology* 30 (1999): 178–205.

Levy, Emanuel. *Small-Town America in Film: The Decline and Fall of Community*. New York: Continuum, 1991.

Lichter, Daniel T., and Glenn V. Fuguitt. "Demographic Response to Transportation Innovation: The Case of the Interstate Highway." *Social Forces* 59 (1980): 492–512.

Lichter, Daniel T., Domenico Parisi, Steven Michael Grice, and Michael C. Taquino. "National Estimates of Racial Segregation in Rural and Small-Town America." *Demography* 44 (2007): 563–81.

Lichterman, Paul. "Integrating Diversity: Boundaries, Bonds, and the Greater Community in *The New Golden Rule*." In *Autonomy and Order: A Communitarian Anthology*, ed. Edward Lehman, 125–41. Lanham, MD: Rowman and Littlefield, 2000.

———. *Elusive Togetherness: Church Groups Trying to Bridge America's Divisions*. Princeton, NJ: Princeton University Press, 2005.

———. "Social Capital or Group Style? Rescuing Tocqueville's Insights on Civic Engagement." *Theory and Society* 35 (2006): 529–63.

Lingeman, Richard. *Small Town America: A Narrative History, 1620–the Present*. New York: Putnam, 1980.

Loewen, James W. *Sundown Towns: A Hidden Dimension of American Racism*. New York: New Press, 2005.

Lough, James. "No Winning Hand." *Denver Post*, December 15, 2002.

Lowin, Aaron, Joseph H. Hottes, Bruce E. Sandler, and Marc Bornstein. "The Pace of Life and Sensitivity to Time in Urban and Rural Settings: A Preliminary Study." *Journal of Social Psychology* 83 (1971): 247–53.

Luck, Morgan. "The Miracle of the Religious Divide: An Additional Argument for the Purported Distinction between Rural and Urban Religiosity." In *Where the Crows Fly Backwards: Notions of Rural Identity*, ed. Nancy Blacklow and Troy Whitford, 59–65. Mount Gravatt, Queensland: Post Pressed, 2010.

Lukacs, John. *Democracy and Populism: Fear and Hatred*. New Haven, CT: Yale University Press, 2006.

MacCannell, Dean. "Staged Authenticity: Arrangements of Social Space in Tourist Settings." *American Journal of Sociology* 79 (1973): 589–603.

MacGregor, Lyn C. *Habits of the Heartland: Small-Town Life in Modern America*. Ithaca, NY: Cornell University Press, 2010.

MacIntyre, Ben. "Small Town America Still Dares to Think Big." *Times of London*, September 25, 2008.

Marler, Penny Long, and C. Kirk Hadaway. "Testing the Attendance Gap in a Conservative Church." *Sociology of Religion* 60 (1999): 175–86.

Marotz-Baden, Ramona, and Deane Cowan. "Mothers-in-law and Daughters-in-law: The Effects of Proximity on Conflict and Stress." *Family Relations* 36 (1987): 385–90.

Marotz-Baden, Ramona, and Claudia Mattheis. "Daughters-in-law and Stress in Two-Generation Farm Families." *Family Relations* 43 (1994): 132–37.

Marwell, Gerald, and Ruth E. Ames. "Experiments on the Provision of Public Goods, I. Resources, Interest Group Size, and the Free-Rider Problem." *American Journal of Sociology* 84 (1979): 1335–60.

Maryanski, Alexandra, and Masako Ishii-Kuntz. "A Cross-Species Application of Bott's Hypothesis on Role Segregation and Social Networks." *Sociological Perspectives* 34 (1991): 403–25.

Massengill, Rebekah Peeples. *Wal-Mart Wars: Moral Populism in the Twenty-First Century*. New York: NYU Press, 2013.

Massey, Douglas. *Categorically Unequal: The American Stratification System*. New York: Russell Sage Foundation, 2007.

Mayo, James M. *The American Country Club: Its Origins and Development*. New Brunswick, NJ: Rutgers University Press, 1998.

McAlister, Elizabeth. "The Madonna of 115th Street Revisited: Vodou and Haitian Catholicism in the Age of Transnationalism." In *Gatherings in Diaspora: Religious Communities and the New Immigration*, ed. R. Stephen Warner and Judith G. Wittner, 123–62. Philadelphia: Temple University Press, 1998.

McConnell, Eileen Diaz, and Faranak Miraftab. "Sundown Town to 'Little Mexico': Old-timers and Newcomers in an American Small Town." *Rural Sociology* 74 (2009): 605–29.

McCullough, David. *Truman*. New York: Simon and Schuster, 1992.

McMillan, David W., and David M. Chavis. "Sense of Community: A Definition and Theory." *Journal of Community Psychology* 14 (1986): 6–23.

McNamara, Timothy P., Julia Sluzenski, and Björn Rump. "Human Spatial Memory and Navigation." In *Learning and Memory: A Comprehensive Reference, Volume 2*, ed. Henry L. Roediger III, 157–78. New York: Elsevier, 2008.

McVeigh, Rory, and Christian Smith. "Who Protests in America: An Analysis of Three Political Alternatives—Inaction, Institutionalized Politics, or Protest." *Sociological Forum* 14 (1999): 685–702.

Miller, Carol D. *Niagara Falling: Globalization in a Small Town*. Lanham, MD: Lexington Books, 2007.

Miller, Kenneth R. *Finding Darwin's God: A Scientist's Search for Common Ground between God and Evolution*. New York: Harper Perennial, 2007.

———. *Only a Theory: Evolution and the Battle for America's Soul*. New York: Viking Adult, 2008.

Mills, C. Wright. "Situated Actions and Vocabularies of Motive." *American Sociological Review* 5 (1940): 904–13.

Mishra, Ashok K., James D. Johnson, and Mitchell J. Morehart. "Retirement and Succession Planning of Farm Households: Results from a National Survey." Paper presented at the National Public Policy Education Committee, Salt Lake City, September 21–23, 2003.

Mishra, Ashok K., Hisham S. El-Osta, and James D. Johnson. "Succession in Family Farm Business: Empirical Evidence from the U.S. Farm Sector." Paper presented at the annual meeting of the Agricultural and Applied Economics Association, Denver, August 1–4, 2004.

Morenoff, Jeffrey D., Robert J. Sampson, and Stephen W. Raudenbush. "Neighborhood Inequality, Collective Efficacy, and the Spatial Dynamics of Urban Violence." *Population Studies Center Research Report* Report No. 00-451, March 2001.

Moreton, Bethany. *To Serve God and Walmart: The Making of Christian Free Enterprise*. Cambridge, MA: Harvard University Press, 2009.

Morgan, David, and Sally M. Promey. *The Visual Culture of American Religions*. Berkeley: University of California Press, 2001.

Morin, Richard, and Paul Taylor. "Suburbs Not Most Popular, But Suburbanites Most Content." Pew Research Center Publications, February 26, 2009, http://www.pewresearch.org.

Moss, Richard J. *Golf and the American Country Club*. Urbana: University of Illinois Press, 2001.

Mueller, William. "Do Americans Really Want to Live in Small Towns?" *American Demographics* (January 1987): 34–37, 60.

Munson, Ziad W. *The Making of Pro-life Activists: How Social Movement Mobilization Works*. Chicago: University of Chicago Press, 2009.

Nalbandian, John. *Professionalism in Local Government*. San Francisco: Jossey-Bass, 1991.

National Center for Education Statistics. *Schools and Staffing Survey, 1999–2000: Overview of the Data for Public, Private, Public Charter, and Bureau of Indian Affairs Elementary and Secondary Schools*. Washington, DC: US Department of Education, Office of Educational Research and Improvement, 2002.

Newman, Katherine S. *Falling from Grace: Downward Mobility in the Age of Affluence*. Berkeley: University of California Press, 1999.

Newman, Katherine S., and Victor Tan Chen. *The Missing Class: Portraits of the Near Poor in America*. Boston: Beacon, 2008.

Newman, M.E.J. "Detecting Community Structure in Networks." *European Physical Journal B* 38 (2004): 321–30.

Norton, Anne. *Republic of Signs: Liberal Theory and American Popular Culture*. Chicago: University of Chicago Press, 1993.

Obstfeld, David. "Social Networks, the *Tertius Iungens* Orientation, and Involvement in Innovation." *Administrative Science Quarterly* 50 (2005): 100–130.

Okrent, Daniel. *Last Call: The Rise and Fall of Prohibition*. New York: Scribner, 2010.

Oldenburg, Ray. *The Great Good Place: Cafés, Coffee Shops, Community Centers, Beauty Parlors, General Stores, Bars, Hangouts, and How They Get You through the Day*. New York: Paragon House, 1989.

Olson, Paul J. "Any Given Sunday: Weekly Church Attendance in a Midwestern City." *Journal for the Scientific Study of Religion* 47 (2008): 443–61.

Orbuch, Terri L. "People's Accounts Count: The Sociology of Accounts." *Annual Review of Sociology* 23 (1997): 455–78.

Orsi, Robert A. *The Madonna of 115th Street: Faith and Community in Italian Harlem*. New Haven, CT: Yale University Press, 1985.

Ortner, Sherry. *Anthropology and Social Theory: Culture, Power, and the Acting Subject*. Durham, NC: Duke University Press, 2006.

Payton, Robert L., and Michael P. Moody. *Understanding Philanthropy: Its Meaning and Mission*. Bloomington: Indiana University Press, 2008.

Perrig, Walter, and Walter Kintsch, "Propositional and Situational Representations of Text." *Journal of Memory and Language* 24 (1985): 503–18.

Peterson, Richard A. *Creating Country Music: Fabricating Authenticity*. Chicago: University of Chicago Press, 1999.

Peterson, Trudy. "Rural Life and the Privacy of Political Association." *Agricultural History* 64 (1990): 1–8.

Phillips, Donald T. *The Clinton Charisma: A Legacy of Leadership*. New York: Palgrave Macmillan, 2007.

Portes, Alejandro. "Social Capital: Its Origins and Applications in Modern Sociology." *Annual Review of Sociology* 24 (1998): 1–24.

———. "Migration, Development, and Segmented Assimilation: A Conceptual Review of the Evidence." *Annals of the American Academy of Arts and Sciences* 610 (2007): 73–97.

Portes, Alejandro, and Patricia Fernandez-Kelly. "Segmented Assimilation on the Ground: The New Second Generation in Early Adulthood." *Ethnic and Racial Studies* 28 (2005): 1000–1040.

Portes, Alejandro, and Min Zhou. "The New Second Generation: Segmented Assimilation and Its Variants." *Annals of the American Academy of Political and Social Science* 530 (1993): 74–96.

Postel, Charles. *The Populist Vision*. New York: Oxford University Press, 2007.

Power, Thomas Michael. *The Economic Role of Metal Mining in Minnesota: Past, Present, and Future: A Report Prepared for Minnesota Center for Environmental Advocacy and the Sierra Club*. Missoula: University of Montana, Economics Department, 2007.

Prior, Marcus. *Post-broadcast Democracy: How Media Choice Increases Inequality in Political Involvement and Polarizes Elections*. New York: Cambridge University Press, 2007.

———. "News v. Entertainment: How Increasing Media Choice Widens Gaps in Political Knowledge and Turnout." *American Journal of Political Science* 49 (2005): 577–92.

Probasco, LiErin. "Encountering Difference: Solidarity and Transnational Religious Humanitarian Aid." PhD diss., Princeton University, 2013.

Proulx, Annie. *That Old Ace in the Hole*. New York: Simon and Schuster, 2002.

Putnam, Robert D. *Bowling Alone: The Collapse and Revival of American Community*. New York: Simon and Schuster, 2000.

———. "*E Pluribus Unum*: Diversity and Community in the Twenty-First Century." *Scandinavian Political Studies* 30 (2007): 137–74.

Radicchi, Filippo, Claudio Castellano, Federico Cecconi, Vittorio Loreto, and Domenico Parisi. "Defining and Identifying Communities in Networks." *Proceedings of the National Academy of Sciences* 101 (2004): 2658–63.

Reding, Nick. *Methland: The Death and Life of an American Small Town*. New York: Bloomsbury, 2009.

Rieder, Jonathan. *Canarsie: The Jews and Italians of Brooklyn against Liberalism*. Cambridge, MA: Harvard University Press, 1985.

Riesman, David. *The Lonely Crowd: A Study of Changing American Character.* New Haven, CT: Yale University Press, 1950.

———. "The Suburban Dislocation." *Annals of the American Academy of Political and Social Science* 314 (1957), 123–46.

Rodan, Simon, and Charles Galunic. "More than Network Structure: How Knowledge Heterogeneity Influences Managerial Performance and Innovativeness." *Strategic Management Journal* 25 (2004): 541–62.

Rohrer, Tim. "The Cognitive Science of Metaphor from Philosophy to Neuroscience." *Theoria et Historia Scientiarum* 6 (2001): 27–42.

Ross, E. A. *Changing America: Studies in Contemporary Society.* Chautauqua, NY: Chautauqua Press, 1915.

Rotolo, Thomas. "Town Heterogeneity and Affiliation: A Multilevel Analysis of Voluntary Association Membership." *Sociological Perspectives* 43 (2000): 272–89.

Ruggles, Steven, Matthew Sobek, J. Trent Alexander, Catherine A. Fitch, Ronald Goeken, Patricia Kelly Hall, Miriam King, and Chad Ronnander. *Integrated Public Use Microdata Series: Version 4.0* [machine-readable database]. Minneapolis: Minnesota Population Center, 2008.

Ruggles, Steven, J. Trent Alexander, Katie Genadek, Ronald Goeken, Matthew B. Schroeder, and Matthew Sobek. *Integrated Public Use Microdata Series: Version 5.0* [machine-readable database]. Minneapolis: Minnesota Population Center, 2010.

Safford, Sean. *Why the Garden Club Couldn't Save Youngstown: The Transformation of the Rust Belt.* Cambridge, MA: Harvard University Press, 2009.

Salamon, Sonya. *Prairie Patrimony: Family, Farming, and Community in the Midwest.* Chapel Hill: University of North Carolina Press, 1992.

———. "From Hometown to Nontown: Rural Community Effects of Suburbanization." *Rural Sociology* 68 (2003): 1–24.

———. *Newcomers to Old Towns: Suburbanization of the Heartland.* Chicago: University of Chicago Press, 2003.

Salamon, Sonya, and Jane B. Tornatore. "Territory Contested through Property in a Midwestern Post-agricultural Community." *Rural Sociology* 59 (1994): 636–54.

Sampson, Robert J. "Neighborhood and Community: Collective Efficacy and Community Safety." *New Economy* 11 (2004): 106–13.

Sampson, Robert J., and Stephen W. Raudenbush. *Disorder in Urban Neighborhoods: Does It Lead to Crime?* Washington, DC: US Department of Justice, National Institute of Justice, 2001.

———. "Seeing Disorder: Neighborhood Stigma and the Social Construction of 'Broken Windows.'" *Social Psychology Quarterly* 67 (2004): 319–42.

Sampson, Robert J., Stephen W. Raudenbush, and Felton Earls. "Neighborhoods and Violent Crime: A Multilevel Study of Collective Efficacy." *Science* 277 (1997): 918–24.

Sanders, Irwin T., and Gordon F. Lewis. "Rural Community Studies in the United States: A Decade in Review." *Annual Review of Sociology* 2 (1976): 35–53.

Schnittker, John A. "The 1972–73 Food Price Spiral." *Brookings Papers on Economic Activity* 4 (1973): 498–507.

Schudson, Michael. *Watergate in American Memory: How We Remember, Forget, and Reconstruct the Past*. New York: Basic Books, 1992.

Schwartz, Barry. "The Social Context of Commemoration: A Study in Collective Memory." *Social Forces* 61 (1982): 374–96.

Schwartz-Barcott, Timothy Philip. *After the Disaster: Re-creating Community and Well-being at Buffalo Creek since the Notorious Coal-Mining Disaster in 1972*. Amherst, NY: Cambria Press, 2008.

Schwieder, Dorothy Hubbard. *Growing Up with the Town: Family and Community on the Great Plains*. Iowa City: University of Iowa Press, 2002.

Seidman, Irving. *Interviewing as Qualitative Research: A Guide for Researchers in Education and the Social Sciences*. New York: Teachers College Press, 2006.

Selznick, Philip. *The Moral Commonwealth: Social Theory and the Promise of Community*. Berkeley: University of California Press, 1992.

Sherman, Jennifer. "Coping with Rural Poverty: Economic Survival and Moral Capital in Rural America." *Social Forces* 85 (2006): 891–913.

Shideler, James H. "*Flappers and Philosophers*, and Farmers: Rural–Urban Tensions of the Twenties." *Agricultural History* 47 (1973): 283–99.

Shrum, Wesley Monroe, Jr. *Fringe and Fortune: The Role of Critics in High and Popular Art*. Princeton, NJ: Princeton University Press, 1996.

Simmel, Georg. *On Individuality and Social Forms*. Edited by Donald N. Levine. Chicago: University of Chicago Press, 1971.

Small, Mario Luis. *Villa Victoria: The Transformation of Social Capital in a Boston Barrio*. Chicago: University of Chicago Press, 2004.

———. "'How Many Cases Do I Need?' On Science and the Logic of Case Selection in Field-Based Research." *Ethnography* 10 (2009): 5–38.

———. *Unanticipated Gains: Origins of Network Inequality in Everyday Life*. New York: Oxford University Press, 2009.

Smelser, Neil J. *The Odyssey Experience: Physical, Social, Psychological, and Spiritual Journeys*. Berkeley: University of California Press, 2009.

Smith, Candace. "That Old Ace in the Hole." *Booklist*, May 1, 2003, 1213.

Smith, Christian, and Michael O. Emerson. *Passing the Plate: Why American Christians Don't Give Away More Money*. New York: Oxford University Press, 2008.

Smith, Kevin B. *State and Local Government*. Washington, DC: CQ Press, 2007.

Soja, Edward W. *Postmodern Geographies: The Reassertion of Space in Critical Theory*. London: Verso, 1989.

Spradley, James P., and Brenda J. Mann. *The Cocktail Waitress: Women's Work in a Man's World*. New York: Waveland Press, 2008. First published 1975.

Stack, Carol B. *All Our Kin: Strategies for Survival in a Black Community*. New York: Harper and Row, 1975.

Stern, Michael J., and Barry Wellman. "Rural and Urban Differences in the Internet Society: Real and Relatively Important." *American Behavioral Scientist* 53 (2010): 1251–56.

Stetzer, Ed, and Mike Dodson. *Comeback Churches: How 300 Churches Turned Around and Yours Can, Too*. Nashville: B&H Books, 2007.

Stout, Jeffrey. *Blessed Are the Organized: Grassroots Democracy in America*. Princeton, NJ: Princeton University Press, 2010.

Stowers, Carlton. *Where Dreams Die Hard: A Small American Town and Its Six-Man Football Team*. Cambridge, MA: Da Capo Press, 2005.

Strang, David, and Sarah A. Soule. "Diffusion in Organizations and Social Movements: From Hybrid Corn to Poison Pills." *Annual Review of Sociology* 24 (1998): 265–90.

Strauss, Claudia. "Culture, Discourse, and Cognition: Forms of Belief in Some Rhode Island Working Men's Talk about Success." PhD diss., Harvard University, 1988.

———. "Who Gets Ahead? Cognitive Responses to Heteroglossia in American Political Culture." *American Ethnologist* 17 (1990): 312–28.

———. "What Makes Tony Run? Schemas as Motives Reconsidered." In *Human Motives and Cultural Models*, ed. Roy G. D'Andrade and Claudia Strauss, 197–224. Cambridge: Cambridge University Press, 1992.

Stull, Donald D., and Michael J. Broadway. *Slaughterhouse Blues: The Meat and Poultry Industry in North America*. San Francisco: Wadsworth, 2004.

Swidler, Ann. "Geertz's Ambiguous Legacy." *Contemporary Sociology* 25 (1996): 299–302.

———. *Talk of Love: How Culture Matters*. Chicago: University of Chicago Press, 2001.

———. "Comment on Stephen Vaisey's 'Socrates, Skinner, and Aristotle: Three Ways of Thinking about Culture in Action.'" *Sociological Forum* 23 (2008): 614–18.

Taylor, Charles. *Sources of the Self: The Making of Modern Identity*. Cambridge, MA: Harvard University Press, 1989.

———. *Multiculturalism: Examining the Politics of Recognition*. Princeton, NJ: Princeton University Press, 1994.

Taylor, Clive C., and Alan R. Townsend. "The Local 'Sense of Place' as Evidenced in North-East England." *Urban Studies* 13 (1976): 133–46.

Taylor, Paul, Rich Morin, Kim Parker, D'Vera Cohn, and Wendy Wang. "For Nearly Half of America, Grass Is Greener Somewhere Else." Pew Research Center Social and Demographic Trends Report, January 29, 2009, http://www.pewsocialtrends.org.

Tickamyer, Ann R. "Space Matters! Spatial Inequality in Future Sociology." *Contemporary Sociology* 29 (2000): 805–13.

Tickamyer, Ann R., and Debra A. Henderson. "Rural Women: New Roles for the New Century?" In *Challenges for Rural America in the Twenty-First Century*, ed. David L. Brown and Louis E. Swanson, 109–17. University Park: Pennsylvania State University Press, 2003.

Tilly, Charles. *Durable Inequality*. Berkeley: University of California Press, 1998.

Tolbert, Charles M., Michael D. Irwin, Thomas A. Lyson, and Alfred R. Nucci. "Civic Community in Small-Town America: How Civic Welfare Is Influenced by Local Capitalism and Civic Engagement." *Rural Sociology* 67 (2002): 90–113.

Tönnies, Ferdinand. *Community and Civil Society*. Edited by Jose Harris. Cambridge: Cambridge University Press, 2001. First published 1887.

Trilling, Lionel. *Sincerity and Authenticity*. Cambridge, MA: Harvard University Press, 1972.

US Census Bureau. *Census of Governments, 2002: Government Organization.* Washington, DC: Government Printing Office, 2002.

———. *Historical Statistics of the United States: Colonial Times to 1970.* Washington, DC: Government Printing Office, 1975.

———. *Statistical Abstract of the United States: 1982.* Washington, DC: Government Printing Office, 1982.

———. *Statistical Abstract of the United States: 2008.* Washington, DC: Government Printing Office, 2008.

———. *Statistical Abstract of the United States: 2010.* Washington, DC: Government Printing Office, 2010.

US Department of Health and Human Services. *Results from the 2004 National Survey on Drug Use and Health: National Findings.* Washington, DC: Substance Abuse and Mental Health Services Administration, Office of Applied Studies, 2004.

Vaisey, Stephen. "Motivation and Justification: A Dual-Process Model of Culture in Action." *American Journal of Sociology* 114 (2009): 1675–715.

Valby, Karen. *Welcome to Utopia: Notes from a Small Town.* New York: Spiegel and Grau, 2010.

Van den Ban, Anne W., and H. S. Hawkins. *Agricultural Extension.* Oxford: Blackwell, 1996.

Veblen, Thorstein. *The Theory of the Leisure Class.* New York: Penguin Books, 1967. First published 1899.

Venkatesh, Sudhir Alladi. *American Project: The Rise and Fall of a Modern Ghetto.* Cambridge, MA:: Harvard University Press, 2000.

Vidich, Arthur J., and Joseph Bensman. *Small Town in Mass Society: Class, Power, and Religion in a Rural Community.* New York: Doubleday, 1958.

Volanto, Keith J. *Texas, Cotton, and the New Deal.* College Station: Texas A&M University Press, 2004.

Waldinger, Roger, and Cynthia Feliciano. "Will the New Second Generation Experience 'Downward Assimilation'? Segmented Assimilation Re-assessed." *Ethnic and Racial Studies* 27 (2004): 376–402.

Wall, Milan. "Factors in Rural Community Survival: Review of Insights from Thriving Small Towns." *Great Plains Research* 9 (1999): 115–35.

Warner, R. Stephen. *A Church of Our Own: Disestablishment and Diversity in American Religion.* New Brunswick, NJ: Rutgers University Press, 2005.

Warner, W. Lloyd. *Yankee City.* New Haven, CT: Yale University Press.

Weissbach, Lee Shai. *Jewish Life in Small-Town America: A History.* New Haven, CT: Yale University Press, 2005.

Welsch, Roger. *Forty Acres and a Fool: How to Live in the Country and Still Keep Your Sanity.* Osceola, WI: Voyageur Press, 2006.

Wenger, Beth S. *History Lessons: The Creation of American Jewish Heritage.* Princeton, NJ: Princeton University Press, 2010.

West, James. *Plainville, U.S.A.* New York: Columbia University, 1945.

Whyte, William H. *The Social Life of Small Urban Spaces.* New York: Project for Public Spaces, 2001. First published 1980.

Williams, Raymond. *The Country and the City.* London: Chatto and Windus, 1973.

Wirth, Louis. "Urbanism as a Way of Life." *American Journal of Sociology* 44 (1938): 1–24.

Wordsworth, William. *The Complete Poetical Works*. London: Macmillan, 1888.

Wright, Erik Olin, and Joel Rogers. *American Society: How It Actually Works*. New York: W. W. Norton, 2010.

Wuthnow, Robert. *Acts of Compassion: Caring for Others and Helping Ourselves*. Princeton, NJ: Princeton University Press, 1991.

———. *Producing the Sacred: An Essay on Public Religion*. Urbana: University of Illinois Press, 1994.

———. *Poor Richard's Principle: Recovering the American Dream through the Moral Dimension of Work, Business, and Money*. Princeton, NJ: Princeton University Press, 1996.

———. *After Heaven: Spirituality in America since the 1950s*. Berkeley: University of California Press, 1998.

———. *Loose Connections: Joining Together in America's Fragmented Communities*. Cambridge, MA: Harvard University Press, 1998.

———. *Growing Up Religious: Christians and Jews and Their Journeys of Faith*. Boston: Beacon, 1999.

———. "Der Wandel des Sozialkapitals in den USA." In *Gesellschaft und Gemeinsinn: Sozialkapital im internationalen Vergleich*, ed. Robert D. Putnam, 655–749. Gütersloh, Germany: Verlag Bertelsmann Stiftung, 2001.

———. *America and the Challenges of Religious Diversity*. Princeton, NJ: Princeton University Press, 2005.

———. *American Mythos: Why Our Best Efforts to Be a Better Nation Fall Short*. Princeton, NJ: Princeton University Press, 2006.

———. "Cognition and Religion." *Sociology of Religion* 68 (2007): 341–60.

———. *Boundless Faith: The Global Outreach of American Churches*. Berkeley: University of California Press, 2009.

———. *Remaking the Heartland: Middle America since the 1950s*. Princeton, NJ: Princeton University Press, 2011.

———. "Intimate Knowledge as a Concept for Further Research in Studies of Religion." Association of Religion Data Archives at the Pennsylvania State University, 2011, http://www.thearda.com/rrh/papers/guidingpapers.asp.

Wuthnow, Robert, and Kevin Christiano. "The Effect of Residential Migration on Church Attendance in the United States." In *The Religious Dimension: New Directions in Quantitative Research*, ed. Robert Wuthnow, 259–76. New York: Academic Press, 1979.

Yodanis, Carrie L. "Producing Social Class Representations: Women's Work in a Rural Town." *Gender and Society* 16 (2002): 323–44.

Zelizer, Viviana A. *The Social Meaning of Money: Pin Money, Paychecks, Poor Relief, and Other Currencies*. Princeton, NJ: Princeton University Press, 1994.

———. *The Purchase of Intimacy*. Princeton, NJ: Princeton University Press, 2005.

Zerubavel, Eviatar. "Social Memories: Steps to a Sociology of the Past." *Qualitative Sociology* 19 (1996): 283–99.

Zhou, Min. "Segmented Assimilation: Issues, Controversies, and Recent Research on the New Second Generation." *International Migration Review* 31 (1997): 975–1008.

INDEX

abortion: capital punishment and, 271; incest and, 269, 276, 436n2; morals and, 13, 234–35, 265, 268–82, 287–88, 311–12, 316, 318, 325, 367, 373, 388–89, 436n2; mother's health and, 270; as murder, 273–75; opposition to, 268–78; Planned Parenthood and, 273; politics and, 310–11; polls on, 287; prochoice and, 268, 272, 277, 311–12; prolife and, 268–72, 276–77, 310–11; protecting the unborn and, 268–78; rape and, 269–71, 276–77, 436n2; religion and, 268–78; *Roe v. Wade* and, 276; as sacrifice, 272; safety and, 269–70; sanctity of life and, 274; self–interest and, 278

Abrams, Samuel J., 309

activism: conservatives and, 313, 316, 318; grassroots, 313–18; morals and, 265, 272, 276–78, 282, 285; politics and, 14, 134, 265, 272, 276–78, 282, 285, 292, 313–18; religion and, 252; Tea Party and, 313–14, 317, 441n17, 442n19, 442n20

Addington, Aislinn, xvii

affinity groups, 102, 225–26

After Heaven: Spirituality in America since the 1950s (Wuthnow), 445n11

Agricultural and Applied Economics Association, 423n21

agriculture, xii–xiii, 4–5, 7, 11–12, 256, 266, 272, 363–64, 393n7, 436n9; Agricultural and Applied Economics Association and, 423n21; American Agricultural Economics Association and, 411n52; churches and, 227–28, 230–33, 237, 240–42, 245, 251, 254; civic identity and, 53–59, 62–63, 66, 70, 72, 75, 77–91, 95–98, 344–47, 349, 353, 357, 402n3, 407n32, 408n36, 408n37, 409n44; community spirit and, 115–16, 124–26, 130–35, 138, 415n22; Consumer Price Index categorization and, 165, 423n22; crop reports and, 23; decline in, 80–81, 91, 96, 116, 166–67, 169; Douglass and, 2; drought and, 243; Economic Research Service and, 72, 406n27, 407n32, 408n36; farmers' salute and, 415n22; farm policy and, 297; farm supply stores and, 17, 53, 363; fertilizer and, 17, 31, 33, 240; frog-pond effect and, 142–44, 147–48, 150–51, 157–60, 163–71, 173, 175, 419n6, 421n15, 422n17, 422n20, 423n21, 423n22, 423n24, 424n27; future planning and, 319, 322–23, 326, 329–34, 337; grain production and, 166; Great Depression and, 23; harvest festivals and, 108, 228, 232; housing developments and, xi; immigrants and, 419n6; income fluctuations in, 166–67; Internet and, 427n14; investments and, 131; irrigation and, 23–24, 62–63, 132, 158; John Deere and, 83, 177; leadership and, 177, 180–81, 183–84, 186, 188–90, 193–97, 200, 202, 211, 214, 297; legacy of, 163–71; low US employment rates in, 165; machinery and, xi, 24, 90, 96, 158, 168, 427n14; management styles and, 165, 421n15, 447n15; market fluctuations and, 252; mortgages and, 24, 42; pesticides and, 31, 33, 300; politics and, 291, 297, 300–302, 307, 310, 440n7; ranchers and, 23, 62–63, 195, 207, 300, 324; research methodology and, 365–70, 377, 380–81, 387–88; rural-urban variable and, 394n11; Russia and, 166; small farms and, 22, 29, 37, 39, 42, 83, 90, 138, 167–68; social networks and, 447n15; socioeconomic status and, 17–18, 21–42, 45, 47–48, 401n22; technology and, 33–34, 353; U.S. Department of Agriculture and, 72, 81, 167, 171, 406n27, 407n32, 408n36, 424n27, 434n27; weather and, 225

Ainsley, George, 38–40, 42, 301

homosexuality: flaunting of, 280; gay
marriage and, 278–82, 287–88; masculinity and, 279–80; morals and, 13,
234–35, 265, 278–83, 287–88, 318,
436n9; polls on, 287; religion and, 13,
234–35, 280–81; US Constitution and,
278–79, 281
Hope Springs, 254–56
Hot Dog Day, 108
housing, xi, 254, 256, 353, 361; bloated
markets and, 84; bubble of, 177; cheap,
4, 31–32, 36–37, 40, 74, 89, 95, 98, 144,
152, 156, 165, 206, 210, 229, 246, 274,
319, 351, 409n44, 440n8; civic identity
and, 56, 71, 74, 77–78, 82, 84, 89,
95–96, 98; community spirit and, 109,
114, 121; crop land and, xi; foreclosures
and, 229; frog-pond effect and, 144,
151–52, 155–58, 156, 161, 165, 172–74;
future planning and, 329, 335, 344;
immigrant, 239; Jim Crow laws and,
347; leadership and, 177, 197, 201–2,
206, 209–10; low-income, 95, 433n18;
mansions and, 47, 50, 77–78; mortgages
and, 34, 41, 84; prefabricated, 84;
quality of, 48; religious charity and,
239, 251, 433n18; research methodology and, 366, 380; segregation and,
345–47; socioeconomic status and,
17–18, 23–49, 58; substandard, 151;
suburban developments and, 151–52,
335, 344, 394n11; taxes and, 229; urban
renewal and, 6; valuations of, 409n44;
white flight and, 96
Huckabee, Mike, 318
humility, 136
humor, xii, 119, 127–29, 234, 302
hunting, 118, 134, 170, 317, 335
Hurricane Katrina, 238, 298
hymns, 217, 222, 228, 234, 247

immigrants, xiii, 274; agriculture and,
419n6; American Dream and, 421n10;
civic identity and, 93–100, 410n50;
community spirit and, 111; diversity
and, 11, 92–100, 248–53, 315, 341,
411n52; ethnicity and, 355 (see also
ethnicity); festivals and, 108, 111, 341,
380, 414n15; gossip and, 407n30;
hostility toward, 95, 98, 100, 207, 212,
348, 353, 355, 410n50; illegal, 100, 251;

job stealing and, 95; leadership and,
190, 202, 207, 212; manufacturing and,
419n6; old-timers and, 100; religion and,
218, 239–40, 242, 248–49, 251–52, 273,
284, 434n24, 434n26. See also racial
issues
incest, 269, 276, 436n2
income. See socioeconomic status
inequality, 4, 412n5, 414n16, 419n6
Ingram, Mark, 153–54, 156
inheritances, 21, 24, 26, 40, 180, 375
innovation, 10; creativity and, 202;
enterprise zones and, 201, 347; existing
resources and, 201; industrial, 178;
leadership and, 178, 200–10, 214;
resistance to, 207–10, 214; small businesses and, 200–201; social, 13, 202
institutional framework, 343, 348–49
intelligent design, 283, 287, 438n17,
438n18
Interaction Ritual Chains (Collins), 354,
414n14
Internal Revenue Service (IRS), 182,
425n4
Internet, 352; agriculture and, 427n14;
civic identity and, 73; community spirit
and, 110, 129–30, 132; economic issues
and, 5, 26; education and, 286; email
and, 3, 31–32, 40, 73, 104, 107, 199,
238, 357–58, 363, 382, 426n12; evolution and, 286; frog-pond effect and, 157;
leadership and, 191, 199–200, 212, 214;
politics and, 296, 315; research methodology and, 287, 382; social networks
and, 3
investments: agriculture and, 131; federal
reinvestment programs and, 201;
frog-pond effect and, 419n3; future
planning and, 338; leadership and, 201,
210; socioeconomic status and, 21,
25–26, 28, 37

Janssen, Bud, xiii, 22–23, 26, 44, 49, 170
Jefferson, James, 311
Jews, 5, 217–18, 248, 284, 381, 428n1,
433n16, 435n30
Jim Crow laws, 347
Johansen, Lars, 284–85
John Deere, 83, 177
Johnson, Lyndon Baines, 292, 317
Jones, Yolanda, 156–57

Jorgensen, Izzy, 222–23
Justitia, 148–49

Keillor, Garrison, 71, 234
Keller, Alex, 29–30, 145, 199
Keller, Suzanne, 14, 341–43, 348, 351, 358, 394n10
Kemeny, Janice, 158–59
Kennedy, John F., 292
Kent State shootings, 161
Kief, North Dakota, 18
Kintsch, Walter, 57, 403n7
Kiwanis Club, 26, 49, 127, 186, 355
Knights of Columbus, 186
Korean War, 41, 165
Ku Klux Klan, 88
Kundrats, Sylvia, xvii
Kuttawa, Kentucky, 19

Lakota narratives, xiii, 191
Lamont, Michele, 346–47
Latham, Pete, 154, 156
Laughlin, John, 338–39
Laughlin, Julia, 338–39
lawyers, 10; community spirit and, 122; leadership and, 179–80; morals and, 264; politics and, 439n6; research methodology and, 367; socioeconomic status and, 24, 400n8
leadership: agriculture and, 177, 180–81, 183–84, 186, 188–90, 193–97, 200, 202, 211, 214, 291, 297, 300, 300–302, 307; alcohol and, 210–15, 428n22; amenities and, 196, 210, 214; athletics and, 184, 213; banks and, 177, 180–81, 185, 208, 210; business and, 178, 180–82, 185, 196–97, 199, 201–11, 214; caring and, 184–85, 187, 195; Chamber of Commerce and, 26, 28, 182, 355; charity and, 184, 425n4; children and, 177, 185, 190–93, 196, 199, 201, 207, 210–13, 422n17, 422n18, 424n3, 425n5; city councils and, 123, 178–79, 185, 187, 232, 303, 307; clubs and, 182–86, 190; coffee shops and, 181; college and, 192–95, 199–201, 207–8, 214; community betterment and, 195–200; conservatives and, 208; construction and, 209; cooperation and, 178, 203–4, 426n13; county commissioners and, 31–32, 40, 49, 179, 193, 310, 366;

county seat towns and, 199, 214, 428n24; crime and, 196, 210–15, 428n22; cultural issues and, 13, 181, 188–92, 212, 214, 353; decline and, 178, 182, 186, 206, 211–12, 214; doctors and, 179–82, 188, 193, 199, 205; drug use and, 209–15, 427n19, 428n23; education and, 179–80, 183, 186, 193, 201, 213, 215, 425n5; elections and, 194, 197; employment and, 177–78; envy and, 178, 180; equality and, 187, 355–56; ethnicity and, 183–84, 190, 196, 208, 425n5; family and, 177, 187–88, 210–11; festivals and, 190, 196, 199, 343; gender and, 183, 190, 308, 312, 425n5; golf and, 199; gossip and, 185, 190, 192; government and, 178, 180, 182, 186, 190–91, 194–95, 199–200, 207, 215; health issues and, 194, 199, 202, 210, 215; holding office and, 192–95; housing and, 177, 197, 201–2, 206, 209–10; immigrants and, 190, 202, 207, 212; innovation and, 178, 200–10, 214; Internet and, 191, 199–200, 212, 214; investments and, 201, 210; lawyers and, 179–80; loyalty and, 343; Main Street and, 181, 186, 196, 202, 212, 215; manufacturing and, 194, 200–202, 209, 211, 215; mayors and, 7, 25, 178, 181–82, 185, 192–94, 196, 233, 272, 299, 307, 348, 367, 413n10, 439n6; meth labs and, 210–15; metropolitan areas and, 200, 218, 425n5, 427n19; middle class and, 180; neighbors and, 179–82, 185–90, 194, 196, 202–13; newcomers and, 181, 189, 193, 202, 207–8; newspapers and, 188–89, 191, 193–94, 199, 202, 427n15; nominations and, 180, 185; opportunities and, 24, 177, 181, 189, 193, 199, 208, 212–15, 428n25; outsiders and, 189, 198; parents and, 187, 193–95, 212–13; pensioners and, 210; racial issues and, 183–84; research methodology and, 378–84; respect and, 12, 177–89, 199, 213, 305, 308, 343, 355; retirement and, 188–89, 193, 210; safety and, 207; schools and, 31, 125, 137, 177–78, 181–210, 213, 215, 247, 286, 288, 310, 315, 425n7; self-sufficiency and, 208; slow pace and, 193; small

434n22; frog-pond effect and, 146–56,
163–64, 173, 175; fund-raisers and, 115,
185; future planning and, 319, 329,
335–39; Golden Rule and, 115; gossip
and, 59 (*see also* gossip); knowing
everyone and, 4, 101, 163; leadership
and, 179–82, 185–90, 194, 196, 202–13;
leaving opportunities open and, 338–39;
morals and, 267–68, 274, 276, 288–89;
nearest-neighbor analysis and, 204–6,
427n17, 427n18; newcomers and,
126–28; picnics and, 107, 109, 111,
124–25, 185, 381; politics and, 293–96,
301–2, 305–7, 311–12, 316; privacy
and, 75, 119, 387, 391; religion and,
221, 225, 228–29, 232, 241–42, 245,
255–61, 434n22; research methodology
and, 204–6, 370–71, 376, 388, 427n17,
427n18; respect and, 165 (*see also*
respect); scandals and, 30, 75, 194, 232,
353; school boards and, 137; scorn and,
128–32, 137, 291, 417n30; sending
cards and, 119–20; social networks and,
3–4, 14–15, 50, 148, 191–92, 278, 316,
343, 345, 356–58, 361, 392n5, 416n28,
447n15; socioeconomic status and,
17–18, 22–23, 25, 27–29, 35, 42–43, 47,
49; squabbles with, 425n7; support of,
2, 115, 123, 137, 174, 228, 237–39, 243,
251, 255, 260; tragedies and, 112–18;
trust and, 61, 112–14, 175, 177, 181;
unwritten code of being good, 118–25;
waving and, 60, 119, 137, 348, 415n22
newcomers, 5, 7, 12, 355; challenges of,
120–21, 126–28, 137; civic identity and,
51–53, 56, 62, 76, 94, 98; community
spirit and, 102–3, 107, 111, 117, 119,
126–28, 137, 416n24, 418n36; frog-
pond effect and, 157; future planning
and, 339; leadership and, 181, 189, 193,
202, 207–8; membership criteria and,
342, 346–48; neighbors and, 394n11;
old-timers and, xii, 60, 100, 103, 107,
111, 126–27, 160, 229, 245, 346,
446n5; politics and, 295, 440n8; religion
and, 229, 246, 248, 253, 258–60;
research methodology and, 371; scorn
and, 128–32, 137, 291, 417n30; sense
of belonging and, 346; socioeconomic
status and, 23, 39; volunteers and, 127;
welcome committees and, 127–28

New Deal, 297
newspapers, xii, 284, 347, 391n2, 442n1;
civic identity and, 70–71, 99; community
spirit and, 106–7, 123, 131; frog-pond
effect and, 152, 161, 419n3; leadership
and, 188–89, 191, 193–94, 199, 202,
427n15; politics and, 247, 315; socioeconomic status and, 24, 30–31, 47
New York Times, 211
Nixon, Richard Milhous, 292
nonprofit organizations, 143, 159, 182–83,
425n4
Norenzayan, Ara, 59, 404n13
North Stonington, Connecticut, 197
Norton, Anne, 46, 401n18
nursing homes, 1, 29, 41, 43, 62, 118, 158,
173, 185, 187, 203, 227, 241, 250, 261,
306, 350

Obama, Barack, 309, 314–15, 317–18,
440n7
O'Brien, Margaret, 192–95, 272, 274
Oelwein, Iowa, 210–11
Oglala Sioux, 191
Oktoberfest, 108, 110
old buildings, 40, 142, 195, 198, 256
Old Chuck, 121
Oldenberg, Ray, 125, 345, 417n29
Old Home Week, 108
Old-timers: civic identity and, xii, 60, 100,
103, 107, 111, 126–27, 160, 229, 245,
346, 446n5; community spirit and, 103,
107, 111, 126–27; frog-pond effect and,
160; immigrants and, 100; religion and,
229, 246; slow pace and, 60
open land, xii, 132, 197
opera, 72, 109–10
opportunities, 353, 357, 362–63; American
Dream and, 139–41, 148–51, 418n1,
421n10; balanced life and, 148–51; civic
identity and, 55, 65–67, 73–74, 89, 94,
98; community spirit and, 109, 111,
117, 132, 134–35, 138; denominational
programs and, 238; education and, 1;
employment and, 12–13, 139–40, 142,
145, 147–48, 150, 155–62, 169–71, 175,
419n3, 419n6; farming's legacy and,
163–71; frog-pond effect and, 139–40,
142, 145, 147–48, 150, 155–62, 169–71,
175, 419n3, 419n6; future planning
and, 323–29, 332, 335–39; gender and,